SCIENCE IS...

second edition

Susan V. Bosak

with

Douglas A. Bosak

Brian A. Puppa

THE COMMUNICATION PROJECT

Co-published by

SCHOLASTIC CANADA LTD.
175 Hillmount Road, Markham, Ontario, Canada, L6C 1Z7
(905) 887-7323

THE COMMUNICATION PROJECT
9 Lobraico Lane, Whitchurch-Stouffville, Ontario, Canada, L4A 7X5
(905) 640-8914

Cover Art: Thomas Dannenberg
Cover Design: Andrea Casault

Printed and bound in Canada by Webcom Limited

This book is printed on acid-free, recycled paper containing 20% post consumer waste. All inks used are biodegradable.

This book is bound using Otabind – Webcom's exclusive, durable binding process. The book lays flat and the spine, which is separated from the binding, remains crisp and new.

15 14 13 12 Printed in Canada 1 2 3 4 5/0

Canadian Cataloguing in Publication Data

Bosak, Susan V.
Science is--

Rev. 2nd ed.
Co-published by The Communication Project.
Includes bibliographical references and index.
ISBN 0-590-74070-9

1. Science - Experiments - Juvenile literature.
2. Scientific recreations - Juvenile literature.
3. Science - Juvenile literature. I. Communication Project (Markham, Ont.). II. Title.

Q164.B67 1991 502.8 C91-094432-6

Visit www.bigsciencebook.com

- Sample activities from *Science Is...*
- Updates on related resources
- Activities in *Science Is...* are excellent matches to the National Science Education Standards – get all the details

About the Author

Susan V. Bosak, MA, is a researcher, educator, and bestselling author. Her interest in science began in grade five, with her first science fair project – an electric motor made from a shoebox (the design for that prize-winning motor is found in *Science Is...!*). She entered science fairs throughout elementary and high school, winning numerous prizes including two national gold medals. After graduating from university with degrees in the social sciences, she became interested in sharing her love of science with children. She served on the Board of Directors of the Youth Science Foundation and began running science workshops for both children and adults. This work led to an eight-year research project involving educators, youth leaders, parents, and children throughout Canada and the United States. The result is *Science Is....*

Susan Bosak has written several books, including the intergenerational bestseller *Something to Remember Me By* (visit www.somethingtoremembermeby.org). She is a partner with Brian A. Puppa, MASc, PEng, and Douglas A. Bosak, MA, in The Communication Project. Founded in 1984, The Communication Project is an independent press, and a research and education group.

Her love of science also brought Susan Bosak an unexpected benefit: she first met her husband when they were both entered in a national science fair during high school. She lives in the country near Toronto, Canada.

Acknowledgements

The second edition of *Science Is...* has evolved over more than a decade. Many people have contributed to the book's development and they deserve recognition here.

The activities and information in *Science Is...* have been shaped by the comments and suggestions of hundreds of children, parents, youth leaders, and teachers. In particular, we would like to thank those parents, university professors, and teachers who participated in the interviews and focus groups making up part of the second edition research.

Science Is... began with the support of the Youth Science Foundation (YSF). Although they have now left the YSF for other challenges, we would like to thank Tomer Levy, Anthony Gower, and David Hall. For her work on the early research for *Science Is...*, we would also like to thank Catherine Agnew, former staff member with The Communication Project.

A number of people volunteered their expertise to review the material in *Science Is...* for scientific accuracy. We would like to thank Les Asselstine, Ron Banister, Robert Dick, Gerry Flucke, Marilyn Light, Michael MacConaill, Peter Russell, Uri Schwarz, Edward Thompson, Dennis Wendland, and Roger Woloshyn. We would also like to thank Leo Puppa, Head of Science at Kirkland Lake Collegiate and Vocational Institute, and Jeff Bloom, Assistant Professor, Faculty of Education, Queen's University, for their special assistance with the second edition research/review process.

We would like to thank everyone at Scholastic who was involved in the production of the second edition of *Science Is...*. We would like to particularly thank Fran Buncombe for understanding how very special *Science Is...* is to us.

Finally, we would like to thank our families for their support as we pursue projects like *Science Is...* that we know will make a difference.

Susan Bosak, Douglas Bosak, Brian Puppa

C·O·N·T·E·N·T·S

Major Sections

Sections and Subject Areas

Subject Areas and Topics

In addition to the ten subject areas, activities are organized into forty topics. Topics interrelate activities within and between subject areas. Topics for a given activity are listed at the bottom of an activity's shadowed box – the first topic listed is the one with the strongest tie; more indirectly related topics follow. Use the topic table below together with the index at the end of the book (the index provides an even more detailed breakdown, and references information in Fact and Fun notes as well as activity explanations).

Air	34	339-340	185		89			110-115, 278, 280, 442-446		133, 135, 472-473, 486
Animal Characteristics				205, 208, 213, 220			99-104, 108, 258-268, 416-417, 430-432			
Atmosphere		62, 177		207, 359-361, 363		244		278-280, 439-442, 448	128, 292	
Atoms (and Molecules)	147	44-45, 50-54, 58, 159, 161-162, 164, 173, 180			223					
Birds							104-105, 258-262, 265, 270, 275-276, 422-424			
Brain	25-27		67, 72-73, 78, 193-195, 344-345, 347, 349, 352							136
Chemical Reactions		50, 164, 168-173, 340-341	186	361, 363, 365	225	244, 254, 414				316-317
Classification	23-24		190-191		88, 394-396	92, 242, 246, 250	99, 258-260, 424-425	285, 439		320
Communication	20, 22, 144, 334		77, 196	86		92	99, 103, 105, 107			313, 320
Decision-Making	22, 29-30, 32			83, 354, 382-388					122	
Earth		47-48		359	90, 222, 225-226, 229, 231-237		264		122-126, 290-297, 461	312
Ecosystems				84, 200-211, 213, 355-356, 358-359, 364, 378	240	244, 253	108			
Electricity		50-51, 161-166		367				116		302-305
Energy		45, 58-61, 165, 167, 172-173, 341	182	355, 362, 366-369, 380		244				305-306
Environmental Awareness				80-84, 86, 200, 218, 388-390			432			
Flight	34, 331-332					402	275	113		133, 472-488
Forces	31, 33-37, 42, 144-145, 147, 150, 327-330, 332	46-49, 52-57, 60-61, 160, 167, 338-340	69, 72			249, 407			124	130-132, 307, 311, 472-474, 486
Habitat				80, 85, 210-217, 356-357		253	417, 419, 421-422, 426-430	287-288		
Human Behaviour	41		75, 77-78, 194-195, 198	385-390					120	320

Human Body			66-72, 74-76, 182-191, 348				100-102			310
Insects				85, 212-217		247	106-107, 258, 265-268, 272-274, 425-429			
Light	147	62-64, 174-179	344, 346	369				116	123, 127-128, 295, 297, 470	308
Magnetism		158-160, 165-166			90, 396					302, 312
Mammals							258-260, 268-270, 276, 420-421			
Mapping	152, 333		71, 351	216	90, 232		418	280, 287	300, 461	312-314
Measurement	31, 38, 40, 152, 326	55	70, 78, 182, 185, 198	213, 217, 360, 363, 368	89, 231, 240, 396	95, 245, 248, 252		112, 116, 284, 287-288, 434-438, 442-449	123, 127, 290, 297-298, 455, 460	137, 307, 314
Microorganisms			66, 192	204, 207, 379		413-414	98			
Numbers	40	342	195						127	136-137
Planets									118, 122, 124, 290-292, 456	
Plant Parts				216-217		92-93, 95-96, 242-244, 246-248, 250-252, 254-256, 402-403, 405-406				
Plant Processes				204, 207, 210-211, 358, 364, 370		93-95, 244-245, 247-249, 403-412				
Pollution				202, 357, 359-365, 371, 374-378, 382		94				
Problem-Solving	21, 25, 29-42, 145-154, 327-332	156	193						118	478
Resources				200, 354-355, 358, 362, 366-367, 370-376, 379-384	230, 237-238	250, 412				318
Rock Types					223-230, 392-400				126	
Scientific Method	20-28, 142-144	46, 169	73, 192	364		94, 254, 411, 414			120	310, 317-318
Senses	22, 26, 28	44, 178	73, 78, 186, 344-352	81, 218	88		108			
Snow		156		220, 371	223			279, 284-286, 448		
Soil				212, 216-217, 379	89, 226-228, 237-240	412	416, 430			
Sound	146		71, 184, 347	218		96	103, 105-106	116		134-135
Stars					90				118, 120, 126, 296, 298-300, 454-470	
States of Matter	142	44-46, 56-58, 156-157		370				114, 279, 286		319
Weather Conditions				361, 367				115-116, 278, 280, 287-288, 434-449	296	

SCIENCE IS...

A newborn infant babbles, gurgles, wriggles,
and reaches out to touch the world.
Each day of life commemorates that very first day.
Each day you and I reach out to our
surroundings and wonder.
We are human and we are wonderers.
(Joe Abruscato)

The formulation of a problem is often more essential than its solution, which may be merely a matter of mathematical or experimental skill. To raise new questions, new possibilities, to regard old problems from a new angle, requires creative imagination and marks real advances in science. (Albert Einstein)

People learn nothing unless they proceed from the known to the unknown. (Claude Bernard)

To myself I seem to have been only like a boy playing on the seashore, and diverting myself in now and then finding a smoother pebble or a prettier shell than ordinary, while the great ocean of truth lay all undiscovered before me. (Isaac Newton)

Science is not a list of facts and principles to learn by rote; it is a way of looking at the world and asking questions. (F. James Rutherford)

If science is a topic of general interest and concern -- if both its delights and its social consequences are discussed regularly and competently in the schools, the press, and at the dinner table -- we have greatly improved our prospects for learning how the world really is and for improving both it and us. (Carl Sagan)

Science Is . . . is a comprehensive collection of hands-on activities, experiments, and projects that will help you explore the wonders of the world around you.

There are a lot of science resources out there. Over the last eight years, Douglas Bosak, Brian Puppa, and I have looked through hundreds of them. It can be overwhelming. It can also be intimidating to someone who is hesitant about guiding children in science experiences. Many of the parents and teachers in my science workshops have asked, "Where do I start?" And so *Science Is . . .* was born.

Science Is . . . is intended as a place to start. It is a collection of effective, interesting activities. It synthesizes information and presents it in a readily-accessible form to help parents and teachers answer children's questions. It is also a book designed to prompt questions.

Teachers and parents are always looking for ways to arouse curiosity and guide children as they strive to satisfy that curiosity. When I talk about "curiosity", I mean more than just an anxiousness to touch. I'm talking about a real desire to *understand.* Understanding our world and ourselves is what science is about. Science involves curiosity that turns into the satisfaction of knowledge.

Science is also fun. And that's what we have tried to make *Science Is . . .*. A poem, said Robert Frost, should begin in delight and end in wisdom. What is true of poetry is true of other creative thought -- including authentic science. *Begin in delight.* Science activities that are fun are appealing and addictive. *End in wisdom.* They can also be educational.

Are children developing the scientific literacy essential for life as effective, productive citizens of the twenty-first century?

Science is important to everyone -- young and old; male and female; those who live in cities and those who live in rural areas; white-collar and blue-collar workers. It is science that has brought our world to where it is today. Science has created the comforts we enjoy and the problems with which we must deal. Science used wisely can make the world a better place; science used unwisely can result in global disaster.

Science involves mental discipline. As with so many other things, people must be exposed to that mental discipline when they are young. If children don't learn to think in a scientific, systematic way, they grow up blindly accepting all they are told, confusing science and superstition, and depending on hasty judgement rather than considered opinion.

Science has been given a relatively low priority when compared with the language arts, math, and social studies. In many elementary schools, only a couple of hours per week is spent on science-related learning. Science received more attention in the 1960s and early 1970s, but then the public became disillusioned with science, interest in school science declined, and support for curriculum development decreased significantly. Today, there is hope for a resurgence in the interest in science, prompted by studies bemoaning the lack of science education, the demand for skilled technical people, the increasing pervasiveness of the computer, and serious global environmental problems.

Does "scientific literacy" mean encouraging more children to pursue careers in science? In part. Science and its applications are developing faster than ever before. We need more scientists, technicians, and engineers to run the complex world of the future.

But more importantly, scientific literacy involves recognizing that science isn't something done to us, for us, or at us, by experts; *we* must do it. Knowledge and understanding that exist in isolation in scientific journals, without the understanding and enthusiasm of *people,* is only potential human knowledge, not actual human knowledge. Each individual should be scientifically literate enough to keep abreast of developments throughout their lives. That doesn't mean understanding nuclear physics, but it does mean being able to read *Scientific American.* Scientific literacy also means being able to use basic scientific skills to make intelligent decisions. Life in an advanced technological society is driven by scientific decision-making. Should we build more nuclear power plants? Which diseases should receive research funding? Should the world's population be controlled? And what about "test tube" babies and surrogate mothers?

Scientific literacy can begin with a book of science activities. Science activities can give children a sense of control over a changing, problem-filled world. First of all, the activities provide children with an opportunity to do and learn specific things to make the world a better place. For example, activities on the environment demonstrate actions that children can take immediately. Secondly, science activities allow children to see for themselves what works and what doesn't. For example, children can directly compare water and vinegar for their effect on plant growth. Thirdly, science activities help to replace fear and uncertainty with understanding. For example, going up in an airplane and having your ears "plug" can be scary, until you find out why it's happening and what you can do to relieve the pressure. Fourthly, science activities emphasize that the world is a truly fascinating place. For example, why does it hurt when you cut your finger but not when you cut your fingernail? Finally, science activities encourage active participation and personal responsibility to balance the passive observation fostered in a television-dependent age.

Science is about the miracle of the mundane -- and children can appreciate this best. Every child is a scientist.

Young children want to know *everything about everything.* And if they find someone who knows anything -- usually a parent or teacher -- the questions begin and seemingly never end. It's normal to want to know how things work and why the world is the way it is. At its most basic level, that's what science is all about. Scientists are just professionals doing what children do naturally. A scientist is really a child inside, and children are really just little scientists.

Unfortunately, something happens to children between the time they are full of excitement and curiosity and the time they graduate from high school. Something kills the curiosity. For example, by the time most students reach high school, they're convinced that chemistry and physics are not for them. They've heard that these sciences are tough, nearly incomprehensible. And they believe it. On the other hand, mention chemistry or physics to fifth graders and, without knowing what any of it means, their faces light up. These words represent something special, something exciting for elementary students. *Science Is . . .* has been developed to encourage these children.

USING THIS BOOK

No one is too young -- or "too old" -- for *Science Is . . ..* And an initial lack of scientific training can be an asset.

The activities in *Science Is . . .* tend to be appropriate for children aged 6 to 14 years. But the book itself is a big people/little people book. It is designed so that adults and children work together to discover and explore. I have found that adults can learn just as much as children. I know that I have learned a great deal from the children I've worked with and from researching and writing *Science Is . . ..* Each time I flip through the book, I discover or rediscover something interesting.

Research studies have shown that parents and elementary teachers (as opposed to high school teachers) are most successful in making science exciting for children. Perhaps their own lack of traditional science study, their own wonderment and curiosity, and their freedom to admit their lack of expertise is an advantage in guiding children through science experiences. It may also be related to their greater encouragement of children to share ideas and experiences with others.

Doing science doesn't require a formal lab setting or expensive, exotic materials.

For children, the world is the laboratory. The sidewalk is a great place for a mini nature hike. Conduct water experiments in the classroom sink. Transform windowsills into greenhouses or places to watch weather and test for air pollution. Use a corner of the kitchen to grow molds and yeast.

All the materials in *Science is . . .* are inexpensive and readily-available. Some call for a trip to the hardware or garden store, but most can be found in your home.

One approach to using *Science Is . . .* effectively is to put together a science materials box. With the box and this book in hand, you're ready to do science activities anywhere, at any time. The box should contain the simple materials called for in many of the activities in *Science Is . . .* -- such as plastic bags or containers; magnifying glass; paper; pencil; pencil crayons; scissors; straws; mirror; string; popsicle sticks; elastic bands; balls; coins; drinking glasses; etc.

***Science Is . . .* is organized to reflect the time pressures in your life.**

Time. There's never enough of it and we're all constrained by it. That's why *Science Is . . .* is divided into three main sections that are time-based.

Quickies are short activities. They require few or no materials and many can be done on the spur of the moment. Quickies often introduce basic concepts in a subject area.

Make Time activities require a little planning and some simple materials. They take at least half an hour to complete. Make Time activities often deal with important subject area concepts in depth.

One Leads to Another activities in a particular subject area build on one another. They may emphasize a key theme for the subject area or result in a completed project (e.g. a weather station). They can also be done individually, if you wish. One Leads to Another activities require a little planning and some simple materials.

Science Is . . . has been designed to be interesting and accessible -- to jump off the shelf and scream, "Use me!"

Science Is . . . is meant to be an inviting book you can flip through quickly to get activity ideas. There is a danger in a book like *Science Is . . .*: that children will simply end up jumping from one activity to the next without a sense of the whole, without skills development, and without understanding the scientific concepts behind the activities. On the other hand, many teachers have voiced a concern that other science books and curriculum kits can be too formalized, rigid, and prescriptive.

I have developed *Science Is . . .* to allow parents and teachers maximum flexibility. I have made the book descriptive rather than prescriptive. Use *Science Is . . .* as a foundation for developing science experiences appropriate to *your* situation. Your needs vary, and children are different, with varying needs and interests.

The activities in *Science Is . . .* range from object manipulation, pencil and paper puzzles, and construction projects to games, plays, and physical activities. Some of the activities involve group work; some are competitions; and others are self-challenge activities.

There is one activity per page in *Science Is . . .*. An activity's subject area is shown by a symbol in the lower, outside corner of the page. Activities begin with a two-line introduction. A materials list and detailed description then follow. Background information is provided in the shadowed boxes.

Fact and Fun notes scattered throughout the book contain fascinating facts and fun things to try.

Science Is . . . covers all the basics. The book is broken down into ten subject areas and forty topics.

Science Is . . . reflects the body of knowledge generally deemed appropriate for children aged 6 to 14 years. However, while teachers must be sensitive to the content specified by curriculums, it's important to remember what science is all about. Tossing fact after memorized fact at children just to "cover the curriculum" is to do children a disservice over the long term. Scientific literacy depends not so much on *how much* is covered, but *how* it is covered. *Science Is . . .* encourages a certain perception of science, conceptual understanding, and higher-order thinking skills.

The ten broad subject areas in *Science Is . . .* will help orient you to the book's contents. The first subject area, Discovering Science, introduces the nature of science and the basic elements of the scientific method (e.g. asking questions, hypothesizing, observing). Many of the activities are puzzles and challenges. The One Leads to Another series consists of a science olympics.

The Matter & Energy subject area introduces a number of basic scientific concepts (e.g. atoms, gravity, forces). The subject area touches on the fields of physics and chemistry. The One Leads to Another series consists of a science show which is more entertaining than any magic show -- because you learn the secret behind the "tricks"!

The Humans subject area touches on physiology, psychology, and sociology. The One Leads to Another series looks at the basic human senses of sight, hearing, touch/feeling, smell, and taste.

The Environment subject area is one of the largest in *Science Is . . ..* The subject area begins with simple environmental awareness exercises, moves to the workings of ecosystems, and ends with an extensive One Leads to Another series. The series looks at a number of the environmental problems we face. An important feature of the series is that it includes activities dealing with values, judgements, and decision-making.

The Rocks subject area deals with geology -- the study of the inside and the outside of the Earth. Simple classification activities are included. The One Leads to Another series deals with rock collecting, from gathering specimens to testing and analysing them.

The Plants subject area takes the skill of classification one step further than Rocks, since it is more difficult to work with living things. The One Leads to Another series looks at the growth of green plants, fungi, and yeast.

The Living Creatures subject area explores mammals, birds, insects, fish, reptiles, and amphibians. Activities range from the characteristics and adaptations of particular animals to comparisons of different animals. The One Leads to Another series focuses on watching animals, both by going to their natural habitats and having them come to you (e.g. insect zoo).

The Weather subject area starts with activities on the properties of air and moves to rain, clouds, and microclimates. The One Leads to Another series consists of constructing and using your own homemade weather station.

The Heavens subject area deals with Earth within the larger context of the universe. Activities also cover astronomy versus astrology, the moon, our sun, the stars, and other planets. The One Leads to Another series is an introduction to stargazing.

The final subject area in *Science Is . . .,* Applying Science, looks at technology and some of the ways we put science to work for us. Many of the concepts introduced earlier in the book are "put into action". The One Leads to Another series focuses on flight and includes several paper airplane and kite designs.

If you're concentrating on a particular subject area, look through all the activities in that subject area. If you're just looking for information and facts for a particular subject area, flip from page to page and read the shadowed boxes. In general, each page builds on ideas presented on earlier pages.

In addition to the subject areas, *Science Is . . .* is broken down into forty topics. The topics provide a broad interrelation of activities within and between subject areas; the index provides a much more detailed breakdown of very specific concepts, and references all information related to a given concept (including information contained in Fact and Fun notes). Topics for a given activity are listed at the bottom of an activity's shadowed box. The first topic listed is the one with the strongest tie. More indirectly related topics are then listed. A contents table at the beginning of this book will help you find activities by topic.

The subject areas in *Science Is . . .* can help teachers fit activities into their curriculum requirements. But the subject areas are deemphasized by the fact that the major divisions in the book are based on time (i.e. Quickies, Make Time, and One Leads to Another). Further, the real world isn't compartmentalized into subject areas -- and children's interests may not progress neatly from one activity in a subject area to the next. The topics -- together with the detailed index at the end of the book -- might be more important than the subject areas because they encourage a true spirit of scientific exploration. A given activity may prompt questions that are outside the subject area but are related to the activity nonetheless. Use the topics to find your own path through *Science Is . . ..* Sometimes, the same

activity approached through different paths can, even if repeated two or more times, help children learn completely different things. The topics will also help you to interrelate activities. When activities are interrelated, children increase their understanding, insight, and motivation, as well as develop a more positive attitude toward science in general.

Children will get the most from *Science Is . . .* if activities and information are presented in a way that's appropriate for their level of cognitive development.

The more we know about children and how they learn, the more successful we can be in helping them learn. Research over the last forty years or so has dealt in depth with the development of children: their physical capabilities, social-emotional development, intellectual development, and the range and extent of their individual differences.

Although there are many researchers who provide insights into children's cognitive development, the work of Swiss psychologist Jean Piaget is often used as a starting point. For over fifty years, Piaget did research into how the minds of children develop. He explored the nature of children's spontaneous ideas about the physical world and their mental processes. He found, among other things, that children think quite differently from adults. He also argued that children do not learn so much from doing, but from *thinking about what they are doing.*

Piaget describes four major stages in children's intellectual/cognitive development:

Sensory-Motor (0-2 years): At the beginning of this stage, children have neither a sense of objects as distinct from themselves nor a sense of self as distinct from objects. In other words, when an object disappears from sight, it is not only out of sight, but out of mind. In the second year of life, a sense of objects develops -- a sense of their permanence and a limited interaction with them (including memory and labelling).

Preoperational (2-7 years): In this stage, children view the world from a very self-centred perspective. They acquire language. They discover and practice symbolic play. This stage is "preoperational" because children are unable to reverse the order of events in thought; operational thinking involves being able to reverse events and return to the beginning point.

Concrete Operational (7-11 years): During this stage, children develop an ability to reason in a systematic, logical way. They are able to create and follow rules. They begin to *think about things* and recognize relationships between things.

Formal Operational (12-15 years): At this stage, children move from a dependence on the perception of objects for intellectual stimulation to independent, abstract thinking. Children begin to *think about thinking* and to trace step-by-step procedures for solving a problem.

This is not the place to go into an extensive discussion about cognitive development. My mention of Piaget is intended only as a reminder that activities must be appropriate for where children "are at". This means that *Science Is . . .* presents parents and teachers with a bit of a challenge in adapting activities as required. I have not identified particular activities as appropriate for certain ages. I think parents and teachers can best adapt activities by listening to children. It can be helpful to begin a science experience by asking children, "What would you like to know about . . .?" Then, present an activity in keeping with the answer(s). I also think that a given activity can be repeated by a child at several ages and each time he or she will take away something valuable from the experience.

One of the most important ideas that comes from Piaget's work is the idea that children need concrete, hands-on experiences. This is why *Science Is . . .* is activity-based. Children also need to be able to share their experiences with

others and to consider other viewpoints so that they can move beyond themselves. Finally, children must be encouraged to move to successively higher levels of thinking -- from thinking about things to thinking about thinking.

Children often have too much practice with the lower-order mental tasks of remembering and recalling -- tasks that require single, "right" answers and depend on the storage and retrieval of information. In *Teaching for Thinking: Theory, Strategies and Activities for the Classroom,* Louis Raths identifies thirteen higher-order "thinking functions":

1. *Comparing:* Looking for similarities and differences.
2. *Observing:* Making visual, auditory, and tactile observations.
3. *Classifying:* Examining an assortment of items, sorting them, and categorizing them to some purpose.
4. *Imagining and Creating:* Inventing new ideas, new techniques, and new apparatus; tapping the inner resources of inventiveness.
5. *Hypothesizing:* Coming up with a variety of appropriate explanations for a particular question, problem, or dilemma.
6. *Evaluating and Criticizing:* Making judgements and offering opinions based on formulated criteria.
7. *Identifying Assumptions:* Differentiating between what is observably true and what is taken for granted.
8. *Collecting and Organizing Data:* Locating information, locating sources, examining and culling relevant data, and developing procedures for assembling the data.
9. *Summarizing:* Condensing the essential meanings from a body of data.
10. *Coding:* Using a shorthand system to identify certain patterns of thinking.
11. *Interpreting:* Explaining the meanings of an experience; reading into the data and extracting supportable conclusions from them.
12. *Designing Problems and Investigations:* Identifying problems, hypothesizing, collecting and organizing data, testing hypotheses, and evaluating results.
13. *Decision-making:* Examining the beliefs, attitudes, and feelings that lie behind the choices we make and examining the consequences of personally-made choices.

The activities in *Science Is . . .* have been developed to encourage higher-level thinking, particularly through the kinds of questions included as part of the "Doing It" section of each activity. Most of the activities are open-ended and allow for many different results that are appropriate and acceptable.

You can't just talk about science, you have to do it. Children thrive in an active, hands-on environment.

Research has shown that the use of hands-on activities can result in substantial improvements in science process and creativity; increased performance on tests of perception, logic, language development, science content, and math; and improved attitudes toward science and science class. It is also interesting to note that children who are disadvantaged -- academically, economically, or both -- can benefit significantly from activity-based science.

Sometimes, it is possible for children to work directly with "the thing" being discussed. For example, they can experiment directly with light and making shadows. Other times (e.g. dinosaurs, other planets), direct experience is impossible. When this is the case, I have kept the underlying goal in mind: to get children actively involved. So, instead of direct experience, I have substituted activities such as games, stories, and plays.

There are challenges in activity-based science. You have to deal with some dread and anxiety (yours) and/or possible boredom and misbehaviour (the children's). I have had the opportunity to discuss these issues with many parents and, in particular, teachers. Here are some tips helpful for a classroom situation:

- Start from a point of order. Make it clear that everyone must be seated, quiet, and ready to listen to the instructions.
- Introduce activities. Put an activity into context, perhaps asking children to draw on their own experiences.
- Pair children, perhaps a fast-learner with a slower learner.
- Establish work stations. Everyone should have their own space.
- Handing out a sheet describing the activity can help children follow the steps and understand the whole. Many teachers have children work directly with pages from *Science Is . . .*, while other teachers write up their own activity description.
- Repeat instructions several times. Give clear, one-step directions. Some longer, more detailed activities can be overwhelming.
- The materials in *Science Is . . .* are inexpensive, so it should be possible for each child or group of children to have their own materials -- and therefore be able to work at their own pace.
- Control materials. Distribute only what is needed when it is needed. Too many materials invites attention being drawn away too quickly and scattered unproductively.
- Keep everyone busy. If a child thinks he or she has "finished", ask questions to encourage further exploration.
- When discussing findings with children, it's important to make children wait before they answer any questions you ask. Start with, "Listen carefully to the question and take time to think before answering." Then repeat the question twice and wait several seconds before inviting responses.
- Conclude activities. Children need a sense of closure. A formal summary also helps children remember what they have learned and reinforces key concepts.

A good general approach for doing science activities is the three-step "Learning Cycle".

The Learning Cycle is a powerful -- yet simple -- approach to science experiences. The Learning Cycle was developed as part of the Science Curriculum Improvement Study (SCIS), sponsored by the American National Science Foundation and started in the 1960s. It has been effective as a teaching strategy that directly involves children in active, investigative science experiences.

Under the Learning Cycle, children engage in an activity before being introduced to new terms or concepts. The idea is to begin with and continuously build on direct, personal experience. Children start by exploring, by *doing* an activity in a structured yet flexible way. The next step is *discussing* the activity. The final step involves *repeating* the activity or some form of the activity to apply concepts.

The first step in the Learning Cycle -- the initial exposure to an activity -- allows children to explore new ideas and materials. When children first "play" with an activity, they get the experience upon which scientific concepts are built. Play is the basis for acquiring information, and concept development is built through direct, hands-on experience. Children are able to make observations, collect data, infer, interpret, and experiment. A teacher or parent fills the role of observer and facilitator, posing questions and assisting children when required. Refrain from telling children what to do or giving "the answers". There should be no pressure to do the activity "correctly"; the emphasis is simply on doing.

After the initial exposure to an activity, the process moves into discussion. This helps children extract meaning from the experience. Also, once children have observed something and formulated an idea, they have a natural desire to communicate about it, to put it in some external form. Look at *Science Is . . .* as a catalyst for communication. It is discussion which will bring activities in the book to life.

You can use the background information in *Science Is . . .* to introduce basic concepts and vocabulary during the discussion. The information in *Science Is . . .* can be enhanced with other resources such as textbooks, a dictionary, encyclopedias, and audio-visual aids. Some of the background explanations in this book may need to be adapted for younger children. However, if the language is too easy, it isn't challenging to decode and children don't concentrate on the concepts behind the words.

The discussion should take place in a supportive, nonjudgemental atmosphere. Your communication skills are important for making the discussion dynamic and effective:

- Develop active listening skills. Paraphrase children's statements to show children you are listening and understand.
- Ask open-ended questions such as "What do you think about . . .?"; "What happened to . . .?"; "What would happen if . . .?"; "How can we find out . . .?"; "How could you be sure that . . .?"; "How many ways can we . . .?".
- As children ask questions, turn the questions back to the questioners. Ask for more information and examples; encourage description; and encourage a number of alternative answers rather than focusing on one "correct" answer.
- Ask children to evaluate what they say. The group can make a list of the strengths and weaknesses.

Of course, all this takes practice on the part of the teacher or parent and must be adapted to the level of the children involved.

Once you've had a good discussion about an activity, children can do the activity again. This gives them an opportunity to apply concepts. Each time they do an activity, they will explore in greater depth, discover something new, and concepts will be reinforced. The final stage of the Learning Cycle can also serve as a start to a new application of the cycle; children can engage in a new activity which requires them to extend concepts.

As an example of using *Science Is . . .* under the Learning Cycle, say you are interested in the Plants subject area. You might go to the One Leads to Another section. The first step in the cycle could consist of a seed activity -- displaying different seeds and having children use a magnifying glass to examine and compare the seeds. For the second step, you would discuss children's observations and list the physical properties of the seeds they viewed. Then children might read a book about seeds. For the final step, you could have children go on a seed search, cut open different kinds of fruits to compare seeds, or even move to an activity in which they soak lima beans overnight and dissect them.

Structure science activities with the "scientific method". Using the scientific method is like being a detective investigating a mystery.

The basics of the scientific method are introduced in the Discovering Science subject area, Make Time section.

Use the scientific method as a guide for structuring activities in *Science Is . . .*. The scientific method is a plan for organizing an investigation. It's not really a set of procedures as much as a way of asking questions and exploring answers.

Here's a ten-step primer on the scientific method:

1. Decide on a *question*. What exactly do you want to know? While it's all right to initially generate several, related questions, narrow them down to one specific question that can be explored at the elementary level. You can't do a test with a real rocket, but you can use a balloon to explore the principles on which rockets operate.

2. Gather *information* about the question. This is the research part. Research prompts intuition, which is critical in science. Intuition is based on the mind working unconsciously on the information it has accumulated. Intuition can come at odd moments and in odd circumstances. Sometimes intuition is right, often it is wrong. It must be proved or disproved through experiment.

3. Move to making a *guess* about the answer to the question. This is the "hypothesis".

4. Determine the *variables,* the things that can be changed or manipulated. This is often the hardest part of the scientific method. It requires a close look at the hypothesis. There will be at least one variable you will change from one trial to the next. Then there are the variables that you must keep the same to isolate whether the variable you're changing is the one that's important. For example, say you are exploring the effect of watering plants with salt water. You have two plants. Each plant is treated in exactly the same way -- the same type of seed, same soil, same amount of light, same temperature, etc. These are the controlled variables. The only thing that's different between the two plants is that you water one with tap water and the other with salt water. This is the manipulated variable.

5. Decide how to answer the question. Write out, in detail, each of the *steps* you're going to take. Don't make assumptions or omit things that seem "obvious".

6. Gather together the *equipment and materials.*

7. Do the experiment and *collect the data.* Remember to measure and record data accurately. It can be useful to repeat an experiment to check data.

8. Compare the *findings* with the hypothesis. Do the data agree or disagree with your original guess? Hypotheses are never right or wrong, they are simply supported or not supported. In either case, you learn something.

9. Make your *conclusions.* At this point, there are usually more questions to answer. What were the results? What do they mean? Are they useful? How? What did you learn? What do you need to investigate further?

10. *Tell others* about what you found. Scientists discuss their findings so that ideas can build on ideas. In swapping wisdom, scientists have created impressive, world-wide networks to communicate with one another. Newton said that if he saw farther, it was because he stood on the shoulders of giants. Most of us are familiar with this quote, and yet we haven't asked how those shoulders came to be available or why their owners allowed them to be used. We take this behaviour for granted, but it is very special and important behaviour.

Whenever you use the scientific method, keep in mind that it's only a general plan. The rules are flexible. How scientists actually do science and how we describe the scientific process often don't match. The description often lacks the wrong turns, the hunches that didn't work out, and the mistakes. What's usually missing is the challenging, frustrating, exciting, human adventure of scientific discovery.

Activities in *Science Is . . .* have been tested. But if something doesn't work as planned the first time, be scientific. Don't be afraid to say, "I don't know."

Sometimes, teachers and parents are apprehensive about getting into science. They may not have had much formal training in science. They may worry about doing activities and experiments "correctly". The activities in *Science Is . . .* have been tested and are solid learning experiences for children. But activities may not always work out as planned. That's okay.

There's usually more than one way to do a given activity, and there's more than one possible result. The world isn't black and white, and the activities aren't about right and wrong. Keep in mind that science involves much more than dispensing scientific "fact". In fact, very little in this world is "fact", particularly in science! The more we learn, the more "fact" changes to reflect our new knowledge and perspective on reality.

I've found that some of the best learning experiences can come from activities that don't "work" initially. The real challenge in that situation is saying, "I don't know, but let's see if we can find out." Then you get into authentic science -- the trial-and-error, the guessing, the tentative ideas. Admitting errors and lack of knowledge humanizes science. Children learn that it's okay not to know, and they learn what to do when they don't know something. You can't teach children *what* to think. If you tried to teach them what to think, it would literally take forever -- and by the time you finished, all the facts and information would be obsolete. But you can teach children *how* to think -- how to explore scientifically.

Old men in white lab coats experimenting with test tubes, beakers, and rats. These are the stereotypes. *Science Is . . .* is a "no rat" book.

As I was working on the second edition of *Science Is . . .*, some teachers and parents I spoke with commented on a serious flaw of otherwise strong science resources: their perpetuation of the stereotypes. Lighthearted science activity books often caricature the mad scientist. The books picture rats and all the other paraphernalia associated with science. I consciously avoided these stereotypes in *Science Is . . .*. For example, the cartoon characters are pictured in natural settings rather than laboratories. And although the book is filled with cartoon animals -- bears, birds, rabbits -- there's not a rat among them.

When you ask children to describe or draw a picture of a scientist, you almost always get the stereotypes: white males with glasses in white lab coats experimenting with beakers, test tubes, and rats. Most children tend to rely on fictional images of scientists because they have little contact with real scientists. When asked to name a scientist, children often start with popular children's figures such as Dr. Zed and Mr. Wizard, or they will mention Albert Einstein. Other scientists that receive less frequent mention include Thomas Edison, Louis Pasteur, Benjamin Franklin, Jacques Cousteau, Isaac Newton, Marie Curie, Alexander Graham Bell, and Carl Sagan. In terms of the fields children think of when you mention science, inventing, biology, chemistry, and medicine top the list. Some children do picture and describe themselves as scientists, which is encouraging. But there is still too much of a sense of "otherness" to science. Children spend more time learning facts and techniques than understanding what real people do in the real world.

It is unsettling to discover that adults' perceptions of scientists are not much different than children's. Dozens of studies have demonstrated that, for several reasons, the general public has a number of misconceptions about science. When asked how they perceive science, typical answers from adults include "very dry and difficult", "I think of another world", "men working on rats to find a cure for cancer or AIDS", "nothing, really, except working in a lab", "it's all Greek to me", "astronomy and astrology". The public is also often distrustful of science.

So the challenge becomes overcoming your own stereotypes as you guide children in science experiences so that the stereotypes are not perpetuated. Be conscious of the stereotypes, and when they do surface, discuss them. Also, try to expose children to scientific examples which counteract the stereotypes (e.g. a botanist studying plants in a field rather than a lab).

Sugar and spice and . . . science. Encouraging girls in science is particularly important.

Every science fair project I did, starting with my first one in grade five, was in the field of physics. I remember one teacher suggesting that perhaps the thermoelectricity project I was working on wasn't "appropriate" -- for a girl, that is. But I was determined (my mother might use other adjectives!) and decided to do exactly the opposite of what was expected.

Too many children -- and adults -- still think that science isn't for females. The subtle messages a society sends can have a powerful effect. Women represent less than 10% of the scientific and engineering work force in North America. In Saudi Arabia, where the society overtly limits the number of acceptable career choices for women, only 5% of women pursue science-related careers. On the other hand, in Poland, where societal views differ, 60% of women go into science.

If we are to improve science education for girls and young women, we must start early -- with the age of children toward which *Science Is* . . . is targeted. Research studies indicate that differences between boys' and girls' achievement, attitudes, and interest in science begin in the middle elementary school years. After the fourth grade, girls are less likely than boys to have an interest in science, to elect to take a science class, and to experience success in science activities.

The masculine stereotype of science should be counteracted by example. Female role models for girls -- from chemist and physicist Marie Curie to astronaut Roberta Bondar -- should be brought forward as background information for science activities. A female science teacher, or a mother who shows a personal interest in science, can also serve as a powerful role model. My mother is a thinking woman who is constantly reading and learning. She would always ask questions about my science projects and her questions would prompt me to investigate further, to dig deeper. She helped me discover my brain.

At times, girls seem to be almost unconsciously drawn toward "feminine" areas of science, such as plants and environmental studies. Encourage girls in "masculine" activities, like those involving electricity and magnetism. Girls should be given more time and attention as they become familiar with traditionally "male" equipment (e.g. batteries, electric circuits, or compasses). They shouldn't be forced into areas such as physics, but they should be given an opportunity to explore these areas so that they can make a conscious, informed choice.

The skills stressed in the teaching of the "masculine" and "feminine" sciences also seem to differ. Studies indicate that a problem-solving approach is favoured in physics and chemistry, with more of a lecture and directed lab approach preferred in biology. Girls often feel intimidated by the more open-ended, process approach, and so fall away from problem-solving. They may be intimidated not because of their lack of ability, but because of a general lack of confidence. This does, of course, become more prevalent in the high school grades.

Many educators feel that the ability to mentally manipulate or rotate an object in space and the ability to construct three-dimensional models are necessary skills in science. Researchers disagree about the extent and nature of the differences in spatial abilities between boys and girls. The majority of research indicates that spatial abilities differences do not appear until age 14 or 15. These differences may be due more to socialization and education than some predetermined genetic inclination. Encourage girls to work on activities that promote spatial abilities (e.g. constructing 3-D geometric shapes from paper).

Every activity in *Science Is* . . . is for every child -- male or female. As a general rule, when you guide children through the activities in *Science Is* . . ., consciously encourage girls to *actively* participate. Research has shown that girls tend to fall into the passive role of observer or note taker, while boys take the lead. One way to deal with this problem in the classroom is to have children do science in single-sex groups.

Great science projects begin here. *Science Is . . .* will prompt ideas and help you to follow through on those ideas.

Each time I do a science workshop with children, and they discover I am a former science fair winner, I am assaulted with questions. They all want to know "the secret". The secret lies in *Science Is . . . .*

Science Is . . . is full of things to wonder about, and that's where science projects begin. Too many children -- and parents and teachers -- believe that a science project is about making something, like a radio or a volcano. But science projects are about *doing* something -- science. Begin with a question, and follow through on the question with the scientific method (as discussed earlier).

Flipping through *Science Is . . .* can help children think of questions. Or they can think about what they think about. Don't worry about whether or not it's "science". Almost anything can be explored in a scientific way, and almost anything can be a science project.

My award-winning, grade five motor received recognition not because I made a motor and plopped it down for display. I asked questions about that motor, and experimented to find the answers. I tried different batteries to see how fast I could make the motor turn. I made several electromagnets for the motor from different metals and made a list of which worked and which didn't. I tried different numbers of turns of wire on the electromagnet to see how I could make it stronger. And I wrote down everything I did, what happened, and what I thought about it so I could explain it in detail to the judges. So there it is -- the secret is out.

A special note to parents: Quality, fun time with children can include science.

Some of the fondest memories I have of childhood involve working on my science fair projects with my father in our basement. It would be late at night and I would beg to try "just one more thing". My father -- no matter how tired he was or whether or not he had to go to work in the morning -- would oblige. He made me feel that what I was doing was worthwhile. When something didn't work, he encouraged me and made suggestions. He helped me make a motor from a shoebox and radios from scavenged parts. He taught me how to solder. He taught me how to organize my display board. And on judging day, he would stand off in the corner of the exhibit area smiling at me as I nervously explained my project to the judges.

Nobel Prize-winning physicist Richard Feynman felt the involvement of his parents contributed to his love of science. Among his other scientific accomplishments, Feynman discovered that the O-rings in the space shuttle Challenger failed because of cold weather and caused the tragic explosion. He also composed music and picked top-secret government safes at Los Alamos (for fun and challenge only, of course!). Feynman tells this story in one of his books:

> We had the *Encyclopedia Britannica* at home. When I was a small boy [my father] used to sit me on his lap and read to me from the *Britannica*. We would be reading, say, about dinosaurs. It would say something like, "This dinosaur is 25 feet high and its head is 6 feet across." My father would stop reading and say, "Now, let's see what that means. That would mean that if he stood in our front yard, he would be tall enough to put his head through our window up here." (We were on the second floor.) "But his head would be too wide to fit in the window." Everything he read to me he would translate as best he could into some reality. . . . I learned from my father to translate: everything I read I try to figure out what it really means. . . . That's the way I was educated by my father, with those kinds of examples and discussions: no pressure -- just lovely, interesting discussions. It motivated me for the rest of my life, and it makes me interested in *all* the sciences.

Parental influence can be a vital force in scientific literacy. We cannot depend solely on schools to teach our children science. We are asking our schools to do more and more with less and less. Japanese students have the highest math and science test scores in the world. Research has indicated that one reason may be that parents play a key role in education. Most Japanese children learn to read and write at home, before they even enter school.

Children's questions don't stop when they leave the classroom. When parents help children explore their questions, children realize that science is something important and something they can do. Families who do science activities together, at home, demystify science and make it a part of everyday life. Both parents and children benefit: children gain enthusiasm for learning and parents gain satisfaction as participants in their children's education. I hope that *Science Is . . .* helps you to get started.

QUICKIES

Quickies are short activities. They require few or no materials and many can be done on the spur of the moment. Each page in this section contains a separate Quickies activity.

There are ten subject areas. An activity's subject area is shown by a symbol in the lower, outside corner of the page. Quickies activities often introduce basic concepts in a subject area.

Activities begin with a two-line introduction. A materials list and detailed description follow. All the materials are readily available and inexpensive. Background information is provided in the shadowed boxes.

If you're looking for information and facts for a particular subject area, flip from page to page and read the shadowed boxes. In general, each page builds on ideas presented on earlier pages. Topics listed for each activity will help you combine activities to suit your interests and needs.

QUICKIES

DISCOVERING SCIENCE

There is a famous ancient Greek myth that asks, "What goes on four legs in the morning, two at noon, and on three when evening comes?"

Answer: Human beings, who crawl as babies, then walk as adults, then use a cane in old age

Science is a way of thinking. It's sometimes called "organized common sense", but that isn't quite right. Many times a new scientific idea seems to contradict common sense. After all, what's a more common-sense notion than the idea that the Earth is flat? It's obvious -- just look around you! But we now know the Earth is a sphere. Science is actually a form of organized curiosity.

Pi is an interesting number. Most books give its value as about 3.14, or perhaps 3.1416. But, in reality, pi seems to go on forever. In 1983, two computer workers in Japan divided pi out to 8,388,608 decimal places. It hasn't shown a repeating pattern yet.

Draw a square on a piece of paper. Pretend the square is one surface of a cube. How many edges (not surfaces) of the cube are hidden?

Answer: Eight

Bet you can't fold a sheet of paper -- any paper -- in half more than nine times! The way the layers of paper included in a fold increases is called a "geometrical progression". On the first fold, you have two layers of paper; on the second, four. The third fold creates eight layers. By the time you get to the seventh fold, you already have 128 layers. It's like trying to fold a book!

Fill a plastic bag 2/3 full with water. Hold the bag tightly closed at the top. Stick a sharp pencil straight through the bag and leave it there.

Not a single drop of water will leak out! Why? The polyethylene film molecules pull together to form a seal around whatever is puncturing the film.

QUESTIONS, QUESTIONS

Scientists ask a lot of questions. This game involves asking a lot of questions to guess the identity of a mystery object from among a group of very similar objects.

MATERIALS: None.

DOING IT:

1. Choose a particular object from the nearby surroundings -- a specific tree, a chair, a mark on the wall. The idea is to choose something of which there are many, so people are forced to carefully distinguish between similar objects.

2. Tell everyone that you're thinking of an object. You may or may not want to give a clue. Invite people to ask questions in order to figure out the mystery object. But, you can answer *only* "yes" or "no".

3. As people narrow down the possibilities, let them know that they'll have to ask precise questions to get the exact object. If everyone is stumped, give a general clue.

4. The first person to run and touch the object, or pick it up, wins the game.

Developing observational and questioning skills is important in science. Scientists are people who are curious. They want to know about the things around them. They are always asking questions and trying to answer them. Science is what scientists use to answer questions. Sometimes finding a good question is hard -- a weak question can point you to a wrong answer. This activity encourages asking strong questions that will quickly zero in on a mystery object.

What kinds of questions do you wonder about? Things close to you -- like why you yawn when someone else yawns? Things about long ago -- like what happened to the dinosaurs? Things about far away -- like whether there is life on other planets? Or do you wonder about questions themselves -- and whether scientists have all the answers?

Topics: Scientific Method; Communication.

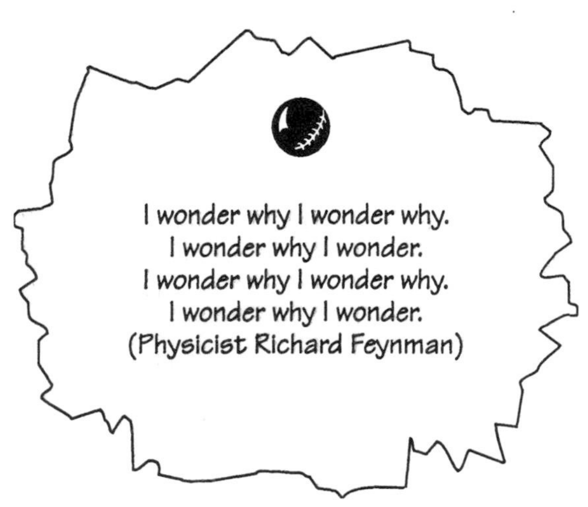

RIDDLE ME

Science is about answering puzzling questions. These riddles are quick to read, but may take some time to figure out.

QUICKIES

MATERIALS: None.

DOING IT:

1. *A Change in Direction Riddle:* The man was almost out of breath. But home was in sight. Then he spotted a masked figure. The figure came toward him. The running man stopped and quickly turned around. He ran all the way back to where he started. Why?

2. *A Real Killer of a Riddle:* John, Laura and Toby shared a house. One day, Belinda came to live with them. John and Laura went out to a party that evening. When they arrived home, Toby was hovering over Belinda's dead body. Toby wasn't arrested. He wasn't even questioned for any crime. Why?

3. *A Travelling Riddle:* A girl with a fox, a goose, and a bag of corn wanted to cross a river. She could take only one animal or object at a time. The fox would eat the goose if they were left alone together; but if the girl took the fox first, the goose would eat the corn. How did the girl get all three safely across?

4. *An Old Riddle:* In medieval England, a king's jester was imprisoned (the king didn't like the jester's jokes). The jester was locked in a room at the top of a high tower. The room had only one tiny window. The jester found a piece of rope. It wasn't long enough to reach the ground. So, he divided it in half and tied the two halves together. This made the rope long enough and he escaped. How?

5. *A Rainy Day Riddle:* A man out jogging felt the first few raindrops fall. He didn't have an umbrella or a raincoat or a hat. He started jogging a little faster. It started to pour. The rain seeped through his clothing. His running shoes got wet. The rain rolled off the end of his nose. But his hair didn't get wet. Why?

6. *A Really Sweet Riddle:* A woman had a sweet tooth. She put one spoonful of sugar into her coffee. She put in another. Then she put two more spoonfuls into her cup. But the sugar didn't get wet. Why?

Answers: 1) It was a baseball game and the masked man was the catcher; the player ran back to third base. 2) Toby was a cat and Belinda was a bird. 3) The girl first crossed with the goose and then returned. She then took the corn over and brought back the goose. The fox was next across the river. Finally, the girl went back and got the goose. 4) The clever jester didn't cut the rope in half -- he untwisted the two full strands of which the rope was made. When he tied the two strands together, the rope was twice as long. 5) The man was bald. 6) The coffee was instant, and the water hadn't been added yet.

You think about many things when you try to answer a question or solve a puzzle. You try to remember things you know that might help you. You look for new information about the question. Sometimes you try to guess how someone else would answer the question. Other times you might pick an answer because of what you would *like* the answer to be. These things may help you find a correct answer. Or, they may lead you to a wrong answer. When you're trying to answer a question, it's often important to ask yourself some other questions: What do you know about the situation? What more do you need to know? What assumptions are you making?

Topics: Scientific Method; Problem-Solving.

COMMUNICATION CHALLENGE

Science is about asking and answering questions. So, you have to be able to communicate well. Try giving precise drawing instructions to a blindfolded partner.

QUICKIES

MATERIALS: Two different coloured pencils; paper. Optional -- blindfold.

DOING IT:

1. Your partner should close his or her eyes, or put on a blindfold.

2. Draw a path on a sheet of paper with one colour of pencil. Don't lift the pencil until the path is complete. The path can go in any direction, be easy or complicated, take up the whole sheet or only a corner, cross itself, or form geometric shapes. Put an arrow at the start and an X at the end.

3. Give your blindfolded partner a pencil of a different colour and position it at the arrow. The blindfolded person has to trace over the path -- following only the verbal instructions you provide. You can give any verbal instructions you wish, but you can't touch the pencil or the blindfolded person's hand.

4. How difficult is this communication challenge? Why? What can you do to make your instructions clearer?

5. Switch roles and try the activity again.

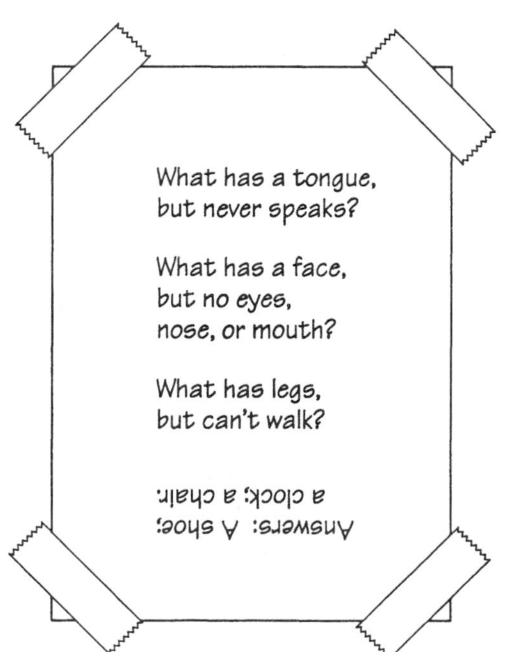

We often take communication for granted. But sometimes it's not so easy to get someone to understand something. Communication is important in science because the more complex our world gets, the more we have to understand in order to make responsible decisions. This activity challenges people to develop communication strategies, as well as demonstrates that people think differently. What means one thing to one person may not mean the same thing to another. Meanings aren't in words; they are in people.

Topics: Scientific Method; Communication; Decision-Making; Senses.

A CLOSE LOOK

Take a look around you. What do you see? Science involves exploring and examining the world. Try a game that tests your observation skills.

QUICKIES

MATERIALS: A group of small objects (there must be similar objects in the immediate surroundings); a covering for the objects (e.g. cloth, jacket); paper; pencils.

DOING IT:

1. Gather together five to fifteen small objects. There should be other examples of the objects in the immediate surroundings. For example, if you're outside, include one leaf from a tree full of leaves. If you're inside, take one piece of chalk from a shelf with several pieces of chalk, or take one pencil from a container full of pencils.

2. Don't let anyone see the objects you've collected. Place them on a flat surface and cover them with a cloth or jacket.

3. People should stand in a circle around the objects. Pull the covering away for about 30 seconds (for younger observers, you may want to allow a longer period of time). Everyone should take a good look at each object.

4. When the time is up, cover all the objects. People now work individually to hunt for objects "exactly" like all the ones they just looked at. Each person makes a secret list of the objects he or she remembers, and notes a place in the immediate surroundings where an "identical" object can be found.

5. When the hunting time is up, everyone gathers to compare secret lists. Take the cover off the initial collection of objects. How many people remembered all the objects? What "identical" objects did people find? Was it possible to find objects "exactly" the same? For example, there may be a piece of chalk in the initial collection of objects and a piece of chalk on a shelf, but are the two pieces the same length? Do they have the same markings on them? Observe all the differences between apparently "identical" objects.

If you look closely enough, you'll realize that even the most "ordinary" things around you are fascinating. Observation is a cornerstone of science. Observation prompts people to ask questions, and it helps to answer questions. Observation involves closely inspecting things. It involves seeing and sensing through careful analytic attention. It's all about coming to know and understand something by putting together all the information that you can collect through direct experience.

Topics: Scientific Method; Classification.

YOU NAME IT

Observation is involved in all aspects of science. Use your observation skills to make up your own names for living and nonliving things.

MATERIALS: Paper; pencils.

DOING IT:

1. Choose a large area, either outdoors or indoors.

2. Set a time limit, perhaps 10 minutes. Each person must find a certain number of objects (five to fifteen) and write down a name for them. All the objects may be living; all may be nonliving; or some objects can be living while others are nonliving. Make up names based on appearance, location, needs, or function. For example, a purple plant with tall, pointed leaves might look like a church steeple at sunset; why not name it the Purple Steeple plant? No real names can be used, even if people know them.

3. When the time is up, everyone shares their list of names. Visit each living or nonliving thing. What really looks like the name(s) people have given it? What was given the most names?

4. *Variation:* Select objects in the immediate surroundings and name them, one name per folded slip of paper. Mix up the slips of paper and have each person choose a slip. Can people find the objects based on the clues in the new names?

A name is just a name. But making up your *own* name for a living or nonliving thing puts everything in a whole new light. Naming is fun. It also encourages people to think about the thing they're looking at and to notice details. Once people notice details, it's easy to go back to an identification guide to find a real name for a plant, for example. Names are often based on observing the characteristics of things, and it's the characteristics that are most important. If you don't know what poison ivy looks like, it doesn't help you to know its name.

Topics: Scientific Method; Classification.

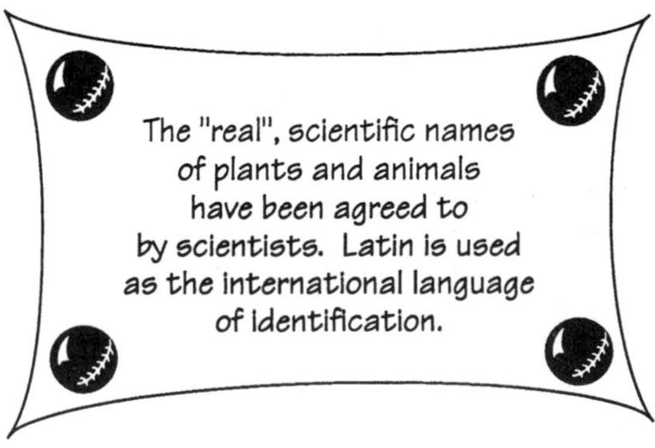

Alphabet Patterns

Science involves understanding patterns. Play with the basic patterns in the alphabet to make a new alphabet.

MATERIALS: Paper; pencil.

DOING IT:

1. Redesign the capital letters of the alphabet so that no redundancy occurs. Take away as much as possible from each letter, but not so much that the letter becomes unrecognizable. How many letters are you able to change? Are there any letters which stay the same? If redundancy is inefficient, how inefficient is our alphabet? How are redundant features useful, even if they are inefficient?

2. *Extension:* Write a message using the new version of the alphabet. Make it at least twelve words long. Can someone else read your message correctly?

> The whole of science is nothing more than a refinement of everyday thinking.
> (Albert Einstein)

> There are things around us and right at our very feet that we have never seen, because we have never really looked.
> (Alexander Graham Bell)

DEAR MOM...

Looking for patterns involves looking for relationships between things. The human brain is good at detecting patterns. Many patterns contain "redundant" features. A redundant feature is one that repeats information given by other features. Redundant features can give unnecessary information, and therefore redundancy can be inefficient. There are certain patterns in the English language, such as the visual appearance of the alphabet. For example, think about the capital letters of the alphabet. This letter, Λ, is clearly recognizable although a part of it is missing. The cross bar is redundant. Being able to identify and work with patterns, and focus on central features, is an important scientific skill.

Topics: Scientific Method; Problem-Solving; Brain.

IT'S AN ILLUSION

Science involves recognizing that there's often more than one way to look at things. What do you see?

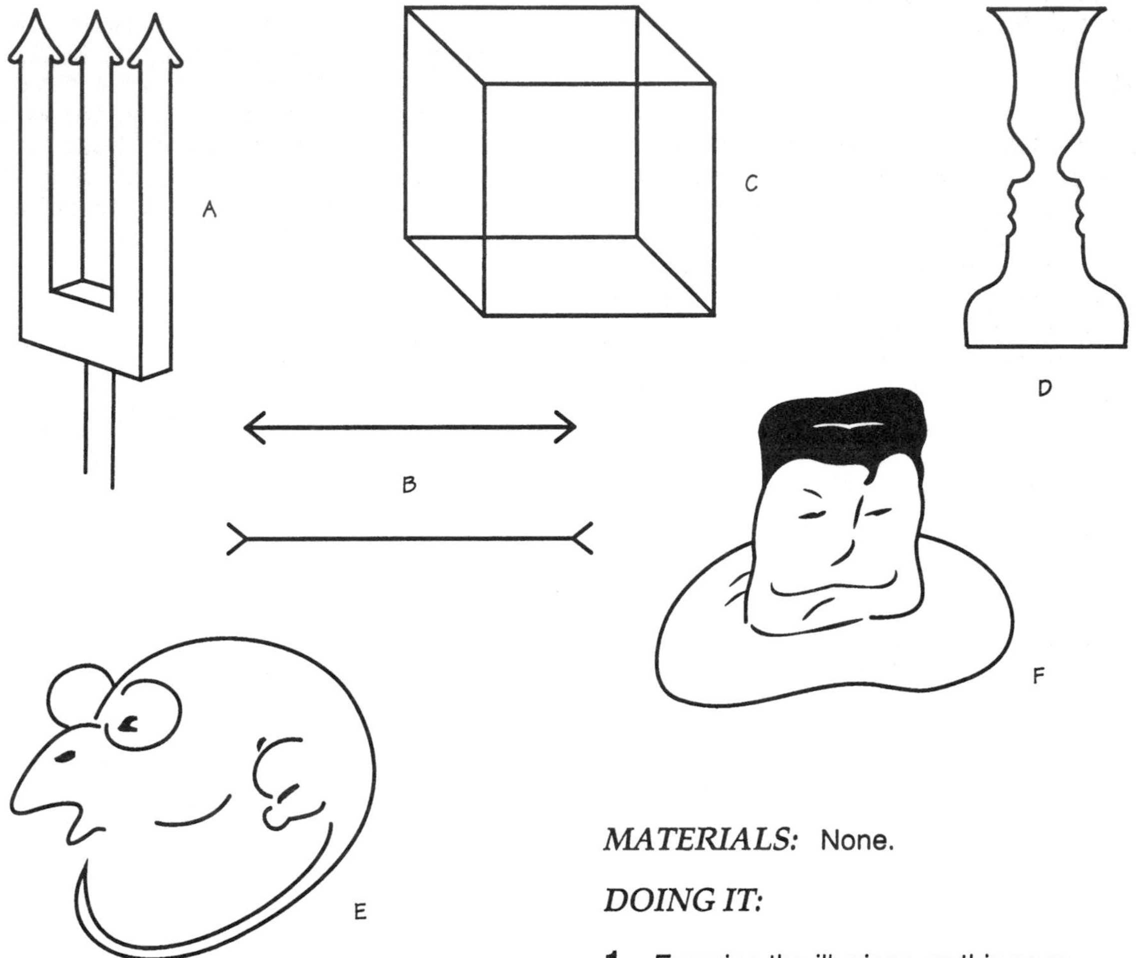

QUICKIES

MATERIALS: None.

DOING IT:

1. Examine the illusions on this page.

2. Interpreting the Illusions: A) Cover the top of the pitchfork and you see two prongs; cover the bottom and you see three prongs. You can draw the pitchfork, but it's impossible to actually construct. B) Both lines are the same length; outward arrows make the line look shorter and inward arrows make the line look longer. C) The box does a flip -- it can slant downward to the right or it can slant upward to the left. D) Do you see a candlestick holder or two faces? Your eyes can focus on the background or the foreground of the picture. E) Is this a man or a mouse? Your brain can't accept both pictures at once. F) Do you see the cowboy hat and the man at the barber's? Do you also see the man wearing a turban?

> There are two general types of optical illusions. "Cognitive" illusions involve experience and assumptions -- based on your past experiences, you assume something is as it appears and you don't really think about it. "Physiological" illusions are created by problems in your eye seeing and your brain interpreting what's in front of you. Many artists, such as Salvador Dali, Rene Magritte, and M.C. Escher, have made use of optical illusions.
>
> **Topics:** Scientific Method; Senses; Brain.

WHAT YOU SEE ISN'T WHAT YOU GET

Sometimes science involves realizing that what you see isn't what you think you see and that what seems impossible has an explanation.

MATERIALS: Paper plate; scissors; four table knives; five drinking glasses.

DOING IT:

1. *Plate Pieces:* Cut a paper plate in half; trim off the rim; cut the piece of rim in half (see illustration A). Hold the two new pieces together and trim them to make them *exactly* the same size. Now put both pieces flat on a table, one piece above the other (illustration B). Do the pieces look to be the same size? Put the pieces into various positions. When do the pieces look the same size (illustration C)?

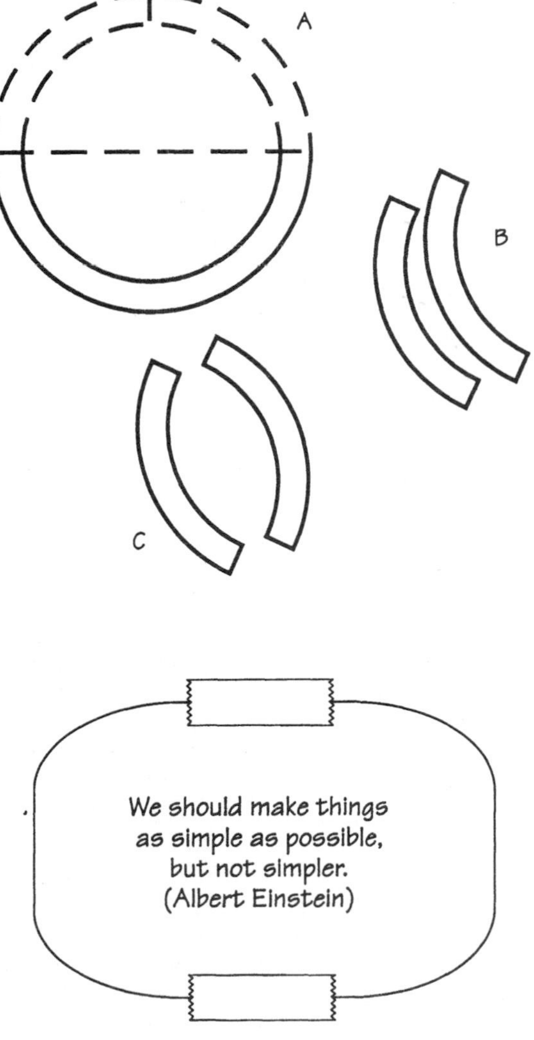

2. *Floating Glass:* Arrange four glasses in a square. Put a fifth glass in the centre. Rest four knives on the glasses, overlapping the tips of the knives. As you slip the fourth knife into position, raise the other three a bit. The tips of all four knives will then be interlocked above the centre glass. You can slip out the centre glass and balance it on top of the centre of the knives. The glass will look like it's floating in air.

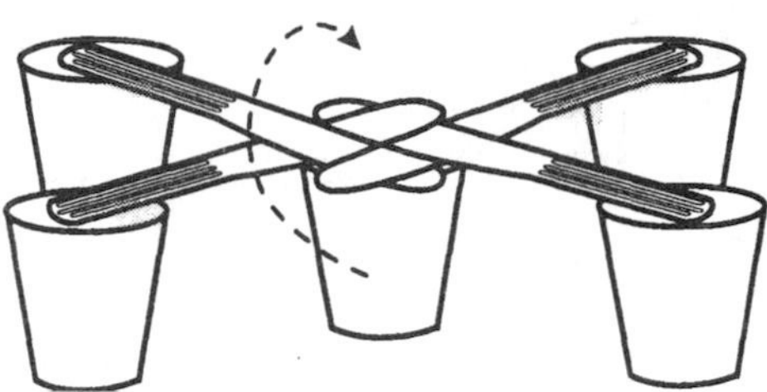

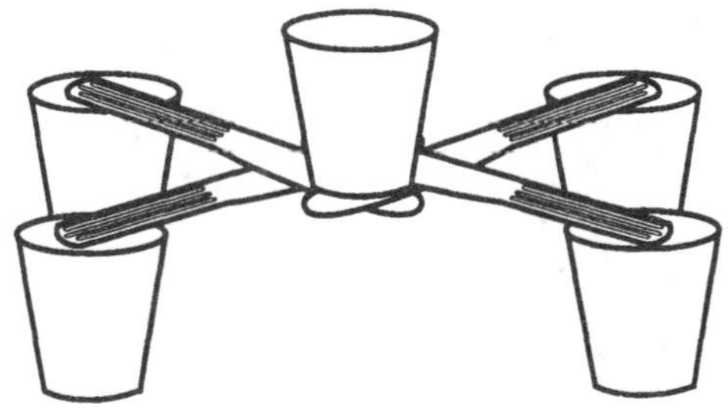

In *Plate Pieces,* your eye-brain system compares the shorter upper arc of one piece of plate rim to the longer bottom arc of the second piece. The bottom piece always looks shorter. The only way you can get around the optical illusion is to turn the top piece upside down. The shorter arcs then face each other and you see the pieces as the same length. In *Floating Glass,* the final set-up looks impossible unless you know what came before. If you arrange the knives properly, so that they interlock, you construct a rigid frame and the knives can then be used as a support system.

Topics: Scientific Method; Brain.

IMAGINE THAT!

Scientific discoveries require creativity. Try to imagine some commonplace tastes, smells, sounds, and sensations. It isn't as easy as you might think!

MATERIALS: None.

DOING IT:

1. Imagine the things listed below. If you wish, you can use ratings: easy, hard, can't do at all.

2. *Starters:* The taste (and smell) of peanuts. The smell of gasoline. The sound of a car starting. The sensation of swinging high on a swing. The taste (and smell) of a banana. The smell of toothpaste. The sound of a dropped book hitting the floor. The sensation of biting into an apple.

3. *More Complicated Things to Imagine:* The taste (and smell) of rich, chocolate ice cream changing into the taste (and smell) of a piece of orange. The sensation of hopping on one foot changing into the sensation of skipping. The smell of bread toasting changing into the smell of peanut butter. The sound of a friend laughing changing into the sound of a baseball bat hitting the ball.

4. *Real Challenges:* Travel down the vent of a volcano. Become a rock and follow your path as you're tossed along a river bed. Become an ocean wave crashing onto the beach. Become a raindrop in a thunderstorm. Grow and bloom like a flower. Follow the path of a sound wave.

5. Can you come up with something to imagine that stumps everyone else?

What do scientists do? They do the same kinds of things you do: read, observe, think, try to find answers to questions, write things down. But scientists do everything they do with a creative twist. A good imagination is a real asset for a scientist. Mental gymnastics like the ones in this activity are great for keeping the old brain in shape!

Topics: Scientific Method; Senses.

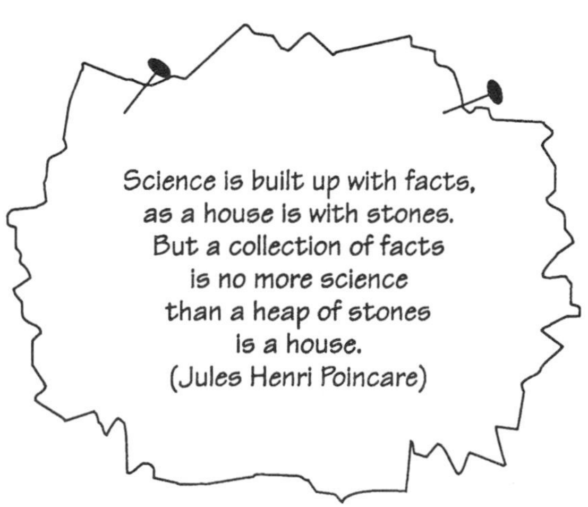

A Classic: The Dot Problem

Science involves problem-solving. Can you join these nine dots without lifting pencil from paper?

QUICKIES

MATERIALS: Paper; pencil.

DOING IT:

1. Draw nine dots as follows:

O O O

O O O

O O O

2. The challenge is to connect the dots without lifting pencil from paper. How many lines do you have to use? How would you use five lines? How would four lines work? Can you use only three lines?

Suppose you have a plastic bag filled with half a cupful of salt mixed with a teaspoon of pepper. How can you get the pepper out? There's no right answer, but the question does require some scientific problem-solving. For example, you could pick the pepper out grain by grain (but that would be slow and tedious). You could dissolve the salt in hot water and then strain the solution through a cloth. How many approaches can you come up with?

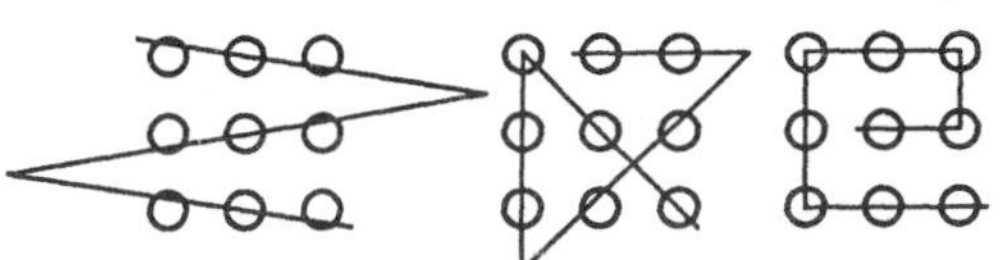

Possible Solutions:

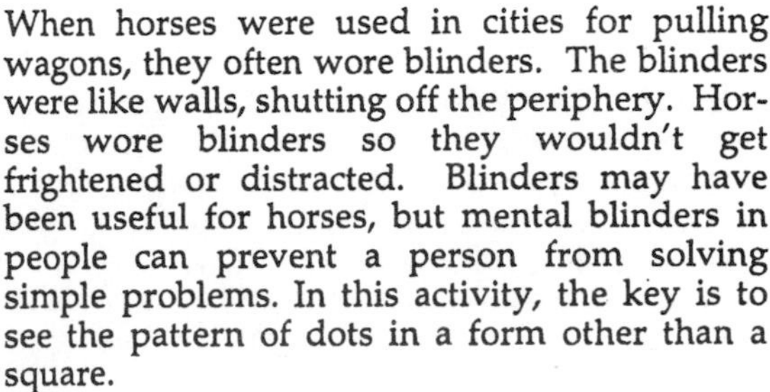

When horses were used in cities for pulling wagons, they often wore blinders. The blinders were like walls, shutting off the periphery. Horses wore blinders so they wouldn't get frightened or distracted. Blinders may have been useful for horses, but mental blinders in people can prevent a person from solving simple problems. In this activity, the key is to see the pattern of dots in a form other than a square.

Topics: Problem-Solving; Decision-Making.

THE GLASS PUZZLE

One way to solve a problem is to see it differently. Can you rearrange these glasses in a certain way in only one move?

MATERIALS: Six drinking glasses; water.

DOING IT:

1. Arrange six glasses, three empty and three full, as shown.

2. The challenge is to arrange the glasses so that they stand alternately, one full, one empty, one full, one empty, one full, one empty. You can only move or touch *one* glass.

Suppose you have a drawer holding eight white socks and eight black socks. The socks are all the same size and are mixed up in the drawer. If you close your eyes and reach into the drawer, how many socks do you need to pick out to be sure you have at least one matching pair?

Answer: Three. After you've picked out two socks, the next one has to be either black or white.

Scientific discoveries often occur because someone has been able to see an obvious solution to a problem -- a solution which, to many others, may not have been quite so obvious. In this activity, people often put unnecessary restrictions on their options -- like thinking that it isn't "legal" to pour the water from one glass to another.

Topics: Problem-Solving; Decision-Making.

A Solution: Lift the fourth glass and pour its contents into the first glass. Return the fourth glass to its original position, and the problem is solved.

HEAVY FINGER

"What happens if I . . .?" Solving problems can involve guessing what will happen if you do a certain thing. Sometimes you're surprised by what actually happens.

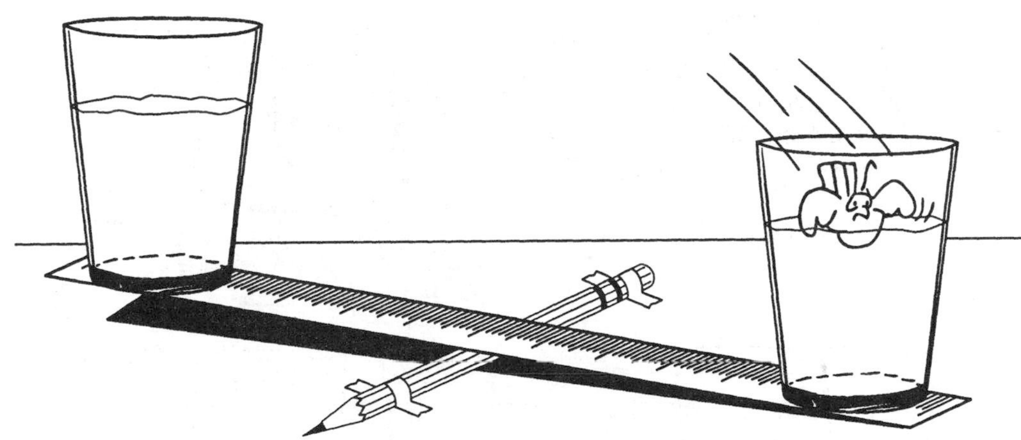

QUICKIES

MATERIALS: Two lightweight drinking glasses; water; pencil (don't use a perfectly round pencil; one with several flat surfaces is best); stiff, wooden ruler; masking tape.

DOING IT:

1. With one of the flat surfaces on the pencil facing upward, tape a pencil to a level table top.

2. Balance a ruler across the pencil.

3. Fill two glasses about 2/3 full of water.

4. Balance the two glasses on opposite ends of the ruler so that the ruler isn't touching the table.

5. Guess what will happen if you dip your finger into the water in one of the glasses.

6. Put part of your finger into one glass of water (don't touch the glass itself!). Remove your finger from the water and put it into the other glass of water. Are you surprised by what happens? Why does it happen?

A ruler and pencil are like a little see-saw. Try balancing objects on the see-saw (e.g. coins). What happens if there is equal weight on both ends? What happens if there is unequal weight? When the weight is unequal (e.g. stack of three coins on one end and stack of six coins on other end), try moving one or both weights toward the centre of the ruler. Can you balance the weights? Then try putting the unequal weights at the ends of the ruler again, but move the ruler's position over the pencil (i.e. pencil closer to one end of ruler).

When you make a guess, sometimes things don't happen the way you thought they would. Then the challenge is figuring out *why* they didn't happen as you anticipated. When you just dip your finger into the water, why does a glass of water get heavier? Your finger "displaces" (pushes aside) some water. The water level in the glass rises as your finger takes the place of some of the water. The water your finger replaces is still in the glass; your finger increases the volume in the glass. It's as if you added extra water to the glass. This increases the mass of the glass of water.

Topics: Problem-Solving; Forces; Measurement.

CHANGE IN DIRECTION

You can solve problems by approaching them from different directions. Can you move coins in the triangle to change the direction it's pointing?

QUICKIES

MATERIALS: Ten coins or bits of paper.

DOING IT:

1. Arrange the objects in the shape of a triangle, as shown.

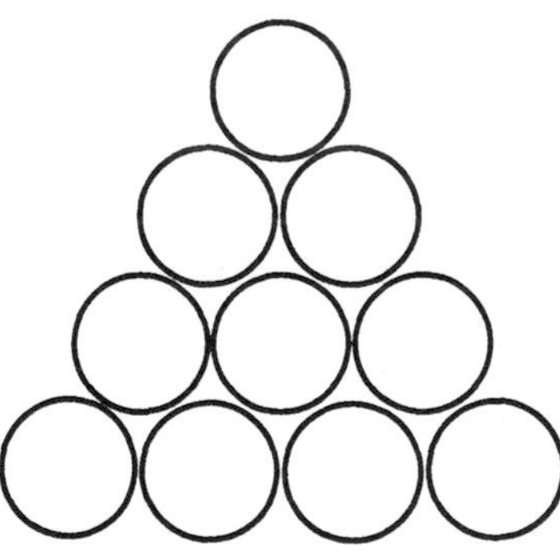

One way to solve a problem is simply to jump in and start trying things. This is called trial and error. The approach isn't bad, if you get a solution before you get frustrated. A better strategy for solving the coin problem is to think about where you want to end up -- and work backwards from there.

Topics: Problem-Solving; Decision-Making.

2. The challenge is to make the triangle point in the opposite direction. You can move only *three* of the objects.

The following letters are in a logical sequence: O, T, T, F, F, S. Can you figure out the pattern? What are the next four letters?

Answer: The missing letters are S, E, N, T. The sequence is one, two, three, four, five, six, seven, eight, nine, ten.

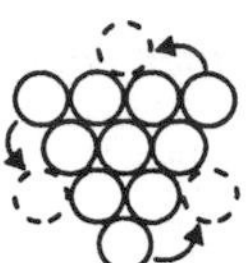

A Possible Solution:

DOLLAR BRIDGE

Solving problems often involves understanding the way things work. Can you figure out a way to support a glass on a bridge made out of a dollar bill?

QUICKIES

MATERIALS: A lightweight glass or cup; a fresh bill (any denomination) or a piece of paper; two glasses or books to act as supports for the bridge.

DOING IT:

1. The only materials available are the bridge supports, the glass, and the bill. The challenge is to lay the bill across the two supports so that the bill will bear the weight of the glass.

Another dollar trick: Hold the corner of a dollar bill in your left hand, using your thumb and index finger. Have someone put their thumb and index finger around the middle of the bill, poised to grasp it. Tell the person to grab the bill as it falls, but don't tell him or her when you're going to let the bill drop. Gravity accelerates falling objects. The dollar bill whips through the person's fingers in about 1/8 second, and no one can catch the bill that fast (unless they cheat!).

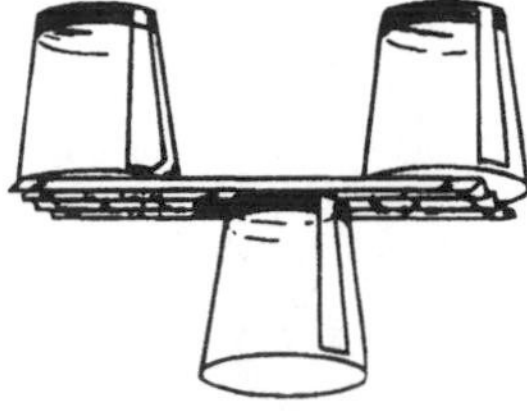

A solution is to pleat the bill lengthwise:

The key to this problem-solving activity lies in understanding the physical properties of bridges. Folding the dollar bill lengthwise makes it more rigid and the downward force of the glass is distributed along the length of the bill.

Real bridge builders have to do a lot of problem-solving. Concrete arch bridges are built by pouring concrete around reinforcing rods; the concrete is held by temporary wooden forms until it hardens. The concrete is poured section by section. Steel arches are constructed by riveting or welding beams in place one at a time. The ends of the bridge are constructed first. The ends are built up until they meet in the middle. The bridge won't support itself until the arch is complete; so, during construction, it must be held up by temporary supports. In some places, it's possible to build a scaffolding under the bridge. Where this is impossible, the temporary supports are provided by heavy steel cables that run from the unfinished front ends of the arch to temporary towers behind the back ends. Making a bridge from a dollar bill is easy in comparison to building a real bridge!

Topics: Problem-Solving; Forces.

Aerodynamic Drag Race

If you understand aerodynamic principles, it's no problem at all to meet the challenge of making a slip of paper and a coin hit the ground at the same time.

QUICKIES

MATERIALS: Quarter; paper.

DOING IT:

1. Cut or tear a slip of paper so that it's slightly smaller than a quarter (when placed on top of the coin, no corners of the paper should stick out).

2. The challenge is to drop the coin and the slip of paper from the same height, at the same time, and have the paper and coin reach the ground at the same instant. Can anyone do it?

3. The trick: Put the paper on top of the coin (make sure that there aren't any corners of the paper sticking out over the edge of the coin). Press the paper down on the coin, so that there is as much contact between the two surfaces as possible. The idea is to keep air from moving under the paper and lifting it from the coin. Drop the coin and paper together, ensuring that the coin remains horizontal as it falls.

4. *Variation:* Putting the paper under the coin should also work because the coin presses down on the paper as both fall to the ground. The paper-under-coin approach is a little harder to set up. You must quickly remove your finger from the paper, and drop the paper and coin without shifting the paper's position under the coin.

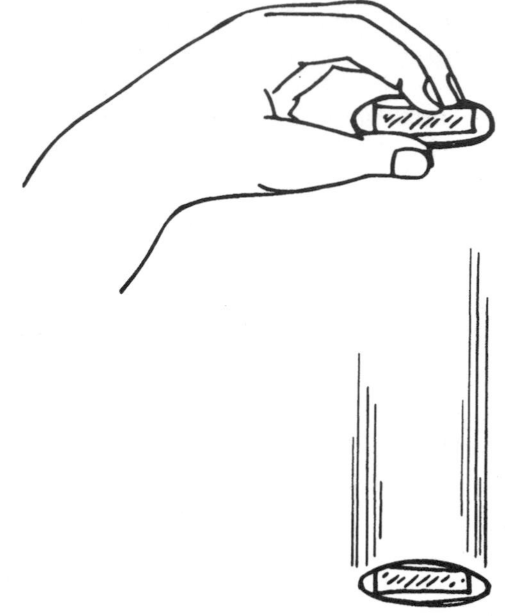

Air exerts friction on objects moving through it. The amount of this air resistance, or drag, depends on the shape of an object and its speed. Streamlining and smoothing surfaces reduces drag. A slip of paper flutters to the ground slowly because drag acts against the force of gravity. Drag also affects a falling coin, but the coin's weight counteracts the drag. If the slip of paper is placed properly on top of the coin, the coin shields the paper from the effects of motion through the air. The paper and coin then reach the ground at the same time. If there were no air (e.g. as on the moon), all objects dropped from the same height would reach the ground at the same time.

Topics: Problem-Solving; Flight; Air; Forces.

Drop a playing card, thin edge downward. Can you make it fall perfectly straight? Now try holding the card flat and dropping it. In the first case, the thin edge slices through the air and is easily pushed off course by slight differences in the air resistance met by the two sides of the card. In the second case, air strikes the bottom face of the card, but not the top face. The fall is slower, more balanced, and therefore straighter.

STRAW STRENGTH

Stick a straw through a raw potato? Lift a pop bottle with only a straw? If you know the secret of straw strength, meeting these challenges isn't a problem.

The problem: to prevent an ice cube from melting. Use materials such as cardboard, cloth, paper, aluminum foil, and plastic to make an "insulating" container for the ice cube. An insulator is a poor conductor of heat. It keeps cold air near the ice cube and warmer room air away. What's the best insulator?

MATERIALS: Plastic straws; potatoes (older potatoes don't work well because they are drier); pop bottle.

DOING IT:

1. *Straw and Potato:* Can you stick a straw through a raw potato? Hold a potato over the edge of a table. Hold the top of the straw between your thumb and index finger. With as much force as you can, plunge the straw straight into the top of the potato. It may take some time and a few straws, but you should be able to get the right combination of force and angle.

2. *Straw and Pop Bottle:* Can you pick up a pop bottle with a straw without touching the outside of the bottle? The trick is to bend up a part of the straw and then stick the bent straw into the bottle. The bent part should wedge against the side of the bottle and up goes the bottle!

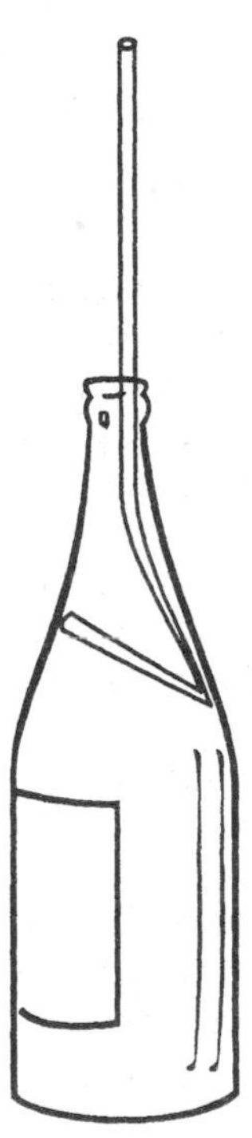

A straw has more strength than you might think. Although it's weak if you bend it in half across its width, it's strong if a push or pull is applied along its length. The trick to getting a straw through a potato is plunging it with a lot of force and at a right angle to the surface of the potato. The plastic straw is relatively sharp and moves so rapidly that it cuts through the potato before it bends. You can also use a straw to pick up a pop bottle. A bend in the straw means that the pull you apply on the long, straight part can go down the length of the straw and work as a push against the bottle by the short, bent part.

Topics: Problem-Solving; Forces.

COME-BACK BALL

Solving a problem usually means trying a number of strategies before you find one that works. How can you make a ball spin along the table so that it returns to you?

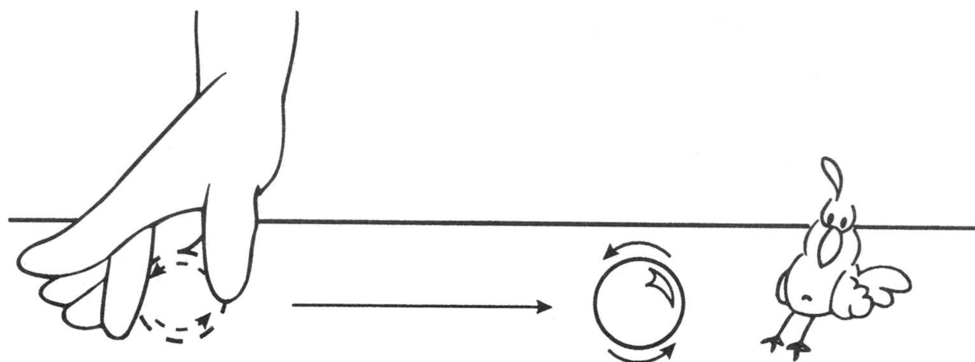

MATERIALS: Any type of small ball (e.g. golf ball or ping-pong ball); a smooth surface. Optional -- other balls such as a superball, football, volleyball, basketball.

DOING IT:

1. The challenge is to spin a ball along a smooth surface like a table top so that the ball returns to you.

2. A good way to start is to roll the ball easily back and forth, from your right hand to your left hand. Get a feel for the ball.

3. Once you have a feel for the ball, try rolling it, sliding it, and spinning it. What ideas do you have for solving the problem?

4. The trick: Hold the ball in your right hand, thumb on top of the ball, second finger below, and with the knuckle of your finger close to the smooth surface. Give your hand a slight jerk toward the left and, at the same time, snap your thumb and fingers in opposite directions.

5. How long does it take to become an expert ball snapper? Try different sizes and masses of balls. Can any ball be made to return to its sender? Does the same method work for all the balls?

The trick here is to send the ball forward with a jerk, while snapping your fingers so that the ball also spins backward. The ball appears to roll forward, but it actually slides. Once that motion is counteracted by the spin, the ball rolls in the opposite direction. The forward slide and backspin motion is like a car tire coming out of a skid and starting off in another direction as the treads take hold. You need to use different techniques with balls of different sizes/masses, and sideways or angled spins are also possible.

Topics: Problem-Solving; Forces.

How can you tell a hard-boiled egg from a raw egg -- without breaking the shell? Start an egg spinning on its side. Then briefly stop it with your finger and quickly pull your finger away. A cooked egg will sit still, but a raw egg will begin to turn again. When you temporarily stop the raw egg, the fluid inside is still swirling around and causes the egg to start spinning again. This has to do with part of Newton's First Law (Inertia): Moving objects tend to stay in motion unless they're acted upon by some outside force.

RIP OFF

Sometimes problem-solving involves recognizing limitations. Ripping apart a sheet of paper into three equal pieces isn't as easy as you might think!

MATERIALS: Sheets of paper. Optional -- scissors; various types of paper.

DOING IT:

1. Tear or cut a sheet of paper (or a small piece of paper) into three sections, as shown.

2. The challenge is to hold the outside, top corners of the paper and rip the paper apart so that the centre piece falls out. Can anyone do it?

3. If someone insists the paper has initially been ripped or cut in some special way, let them rip their own paper. No matter who initially rips the paper, the task is impossible.

4. *Extension:* Each type of paper is made for a different purpose. Try this challenge with different kinds of paper (e.g. paper towel, typewriter paper, grocery bag). Is it easier to rip apart certain types of paper?

How can you throw a raw egg without breaking it? Get two volunteers to each hold two corners of a twin-sized bed sheet (one corner above their head, the other at waist level). Now throw eggs as hard as you can at the sheet. No matter how hard you throw, the eggs won't break unless they slip out the sides of the sheet. Why? The longer it takes to slow something down, the less force is required (e.g. a padded dashboard takes longer to bring your head to a stop in an accident than a hard steering wheel).

When you list all the things you have to control to rip apart a sheet of paper into three equal pieces, you realize why it's next to impossible. The initial two tears partially separating the three pieces would have to be exactly the same; the three pieces would have to be exactly the same size; the paper would have to be perfectly uniform; and you'd have to pull with identical force and equal speed on each end of the paper. Paper, like all other materials, gives in to force at its weakest point. The two initial tears in the paper are the weakest points. When you pull on the ends of the sheet of paper, the weaker tear begins to give way first. This makes the weaker tear even weaker, so any more force just serves to rip apart the paper at that spot.

Topics: Problem-Solving; Forces.

PAPER PROBLEMS

How can you get a large coin through a small hole in a sheet of paper? How can you make a big hole -- big enough for a person to walk through -- in a sheet of paper?

MATERIALS: Quarter; nickel; dime; pencil; sheets of letter-size paper; scissors.

DOING IT:

1. *Little Hole:* Trace the outline of a dime in the centre of a sheet of paper. Cut out the circle to make a hole. The challenge is to get a nickel through the hole without tearing the paper. The trick is to loosely bend the sheet of paper in half along its length. Lay the nickel inside the fold, at the hole. Hold the paper at the bottom, on either side of the hole. Bend the two doubled corners up and toward each other. The coin should slip through the hole. Once you've mastered getting a nickel through the hole, try a quarter.

2. *Big Hole:* The challenge is to make a hole -- big enough to step through -- in a letter-size sheet of paper. Start by folding the paper in half. Make cuts in the paper from alternating sides, as shown. Your first and last cuts must be made from the folded side. Each cut should end approximately 1.5 cm before the edge of the paper. It doesn't matter how many cuts you make, as long as the total is an odd number and the pattern is as shown. The more cuts you make, the larger the final hole and the thinner the paper border that makes up the hole. When you're finished making cuts, snip along the fold, between the top cut and the bottom cut. Carefully unfold the paper and gently pull at the top and bottom of the sheet to get a large paper loop. How small a sheet of paper can you start with and still make a hole large enough to step through?

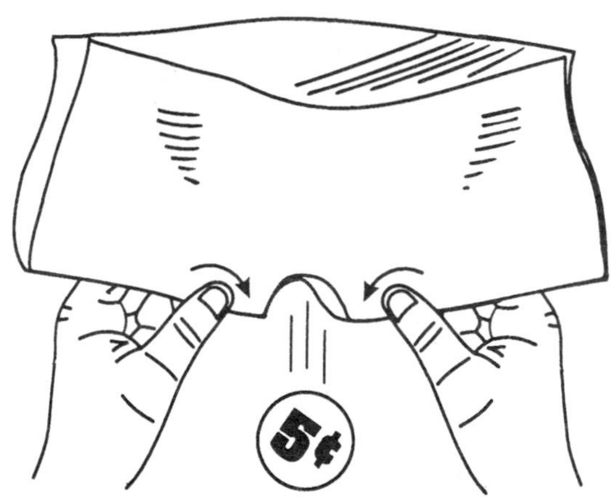

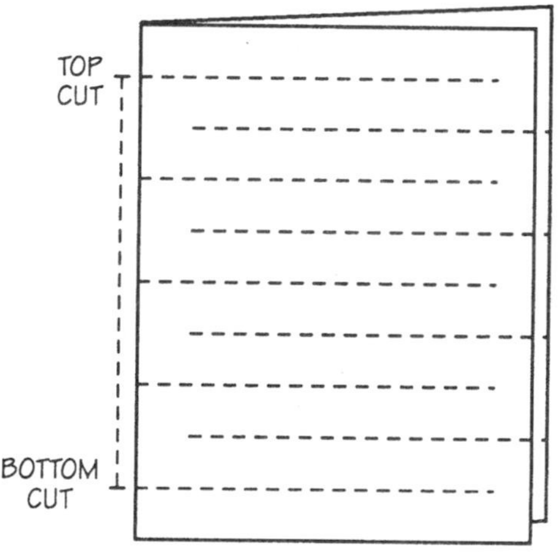

A sheet of paper can be a wonderful thing. It can be torn, folded, cut, or crumpled. To solve these paper puzzles, you need to be able to think about all the things you can do to a sheet of paper. You have to look at the paper in different ways and be able to visualize what will happen if you fold or cut it in certain ways.

Topics: Problem-Solving; Measurement.

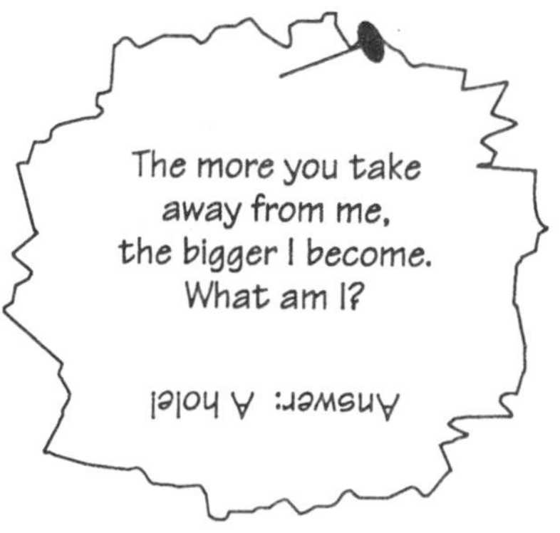

REVERSE TIC-TAC-TOE

To win this game you have to lose! You have to think of the strategies you'd normally use -- and then do exactly the opposite.

MATERIALS: Paper; pencils.

DOING IT:

1. Draw a regular tic-tac-toe game board. Play the game using Xs and Os.

2. To win, try to force your opponent to make three marks in a row. In regular tic-tac-toe, the player getting the three marks in a row shown below would be the winner. In reverse tic-tac-toe, the same player is the loser.

A game can sometimes be reversed so that the goal becomes forcing the other player to win. Reverse tic-tac-toe is more complicated than the regular game. In reverse tic-tac-toe, the second player has a strong advantage and, if he or she plays correctly, can always force the other player to win. One exception to this fact occurs when the first player starts in the centre square. In that case, if the first player always takes a square directly opposite his or her opponent's last move (so that three marks are in a line) the game will end in a draw. The best strategy to follow in playing against a first player who starts in the centre square is to play each time so that you leave your opponent a maximum number of ways to win the game.

Topics: Problem-Solving.

Volcanic Islands

The problem: Some castaways are stranded on a volcanic island. How do you get them to safety using only the available materials?

MATERIALS: Some way of marking each of the "islands" (e.g. pencil and paper, three rocks); three sticks or strips of paper.

DOING IT:

1. Arrange the "islands" in the form of an isosceles triangle (i.e. two sides equal in length). The distance between islands A and B should be approximately 15 cm, and between B and C approximately 30 cm.

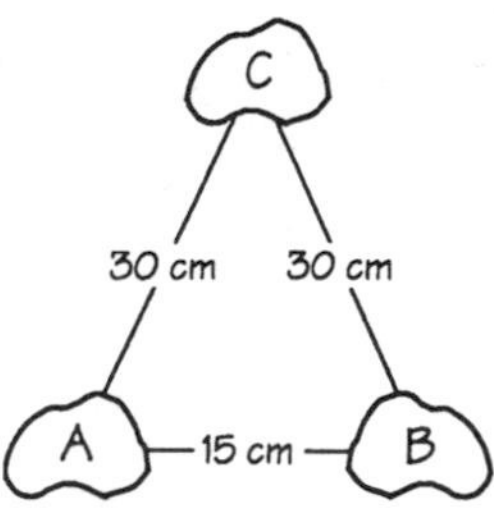

2. There are three stick "bridges". One bridge is slightly less than the distance between A and B (approximately 13 cm). The second bridge is slightly less than the distance between B and C (approximately 28 cm). The last bridge is approximately 20 cm long.

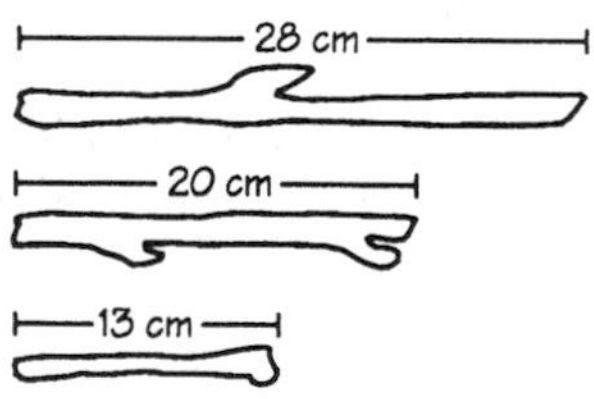

3. There's been a shipwreck and the castaways are stranded on island A. A volcano is erupting on the island. Island B is a little safer than island A, but B's volcano is rumbling. Island C is the safest. The challenge is to figure out a way -- using *only* the given bridges -- to get to island C.

There's a popular old guessing game in which you estimate how many small things are in a jar. Whoever comes closest wins a prize. What's a scientific way of attacking this problem? Let's say you want to find out how many dried peas are in a package. Weigh the package on a scale. Then weigh a small cup. Fill the cup with peas and weigh it again. Subtract the mass of the cup to find the mass of the peas. Count the peas in the cup. Divide the total mass of the package of peas by the mass of the sample. Multiply your answer by the number of peas in the sample to find the total number of peas in the package. You win the prize!

This "volcanic islands" problem involves some basic geometric concepts. People may be able to find the solution by using their knowledge of geometry, or just by using old-fashioned trial and error.

Topics: Problem-Solving; Measurement; Numbers.

A Possible Solution:

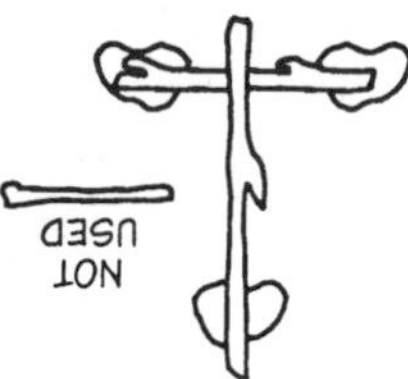

Pin The Tail On The Tree

Some problems require that people work together for a solution. The challenge is to get a ribbon as high as possible on a tree.

QUICKIES

MATERIALS: Sturdy tree or pole, or a wall; a ribbon or slip of paper; tape. Optional -- measuring tape.

DOING IT:

1. People work in groups (5 to 10 people per group; the older the people, the smaller the group). The goal is to place a ribbon as high as possible on a tree.

2. Basic Rules: Each person's body must be in contact with at least one other person's body. People cannot climb the tree. Only the materials listed above may be used. The task must be accomplished in a set time.

3. Safety: Everyone should understand that they are responsible not only for completing the task, but also for ensuring the safety of others. A couple of people should act as spotters. Each time someone does any climbing, jumping, or lifting, spotters should be asked if they're ready. If someone falls, the spotters' job isn't to catch the person, but to cushion the fall using their hands.

4. The activity is over when the ribbon is successfully placed on the tree or when the time is up. Use a piece of tape to secure the ribbon.

5. Use a measuring tape to determine the ribbon's height -- or invent your own measure (e.g. height in shoe lengths).

6. After trying the activity once, people are often eager to beat their own record or another group's record.

In this activity, people must cooperate with one another to come up with a good strategy given certain limitations (e.g. a person's arm only reaches so high!). There's no one right method. Some possible approaches: people can stand on each other's shoulders, lie on top of each other, or form a pyramid.

Topics: Problem-Solving; Human Behaviour.

Alligator Pit

The problem: Alligators are swimming around a small island. How does everyone balance on the island until the alligators are gone?

MATERIALS: Large rock, box, or cushion (size will depend on weight and number of people), or any other large object which can be an "island".

DOING IT:

1. Safety: The "island" shouldn't have any sharp edges or protruding objects, and should be a stable structure. The "water" should be a soft surface, such as a carpet, mat, or grass. A couple of people should act as spotters to cushion people who fall.

2. Set the scene: The waters around the island are infested with alligators. And the alligators are *really* hungry! The group of people can save themselves only by staying on the island until the alligators are gone.

3. The challenge: Everyone has to fit onto the island at once and stay there for a set period of time until the alligators are gone. What are the different strategies for solving this problem?

4. 10 seconds is a challenging goal for balancing on the island. Set the goal time before people start. When the first goal time is reached, try a longer time.

This "alligator pit" activity combines problem-solving, physical agility and balance, and a consideration of individual differences in size and strength. There isn't a single, "right" approach. One good approach involves people balancing each other as opposite pairs within a large circle. With their feet as a base on the box or rock, and arms outstretched, people can counterbalance each other and stay on the island.

Topics: Problem-Solving; Forces.

MATTER & ENERGY

QUICKIES

Everything in the world
can be organized around two concepts:
matter and energy.
If something isn't matter,
it's energy.

Matter is made up of tiny particles called "atoms". There are more than 1,000,000,000,000,000,000,000 -- that's one sextillion -- atoms in a single drop of water!

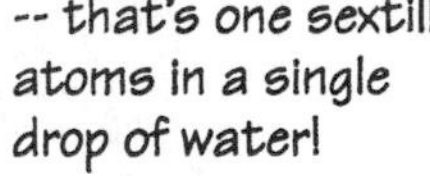

One of the most famous formulas in the world is $E = mc^2$, where E is energy, m is mass, and c is the speed of light. Albert Einstein derived this formula, which simply says that matter can be transformed into energy, and energy can be transformed into matter.

Can you remove the shell from a hard-boiled egg without cracking it?
Of course you can -- with some vinegar and a jar.
Put the egg in a jar filled with vinegar and leave it overnight.
The next day the shell will be gone and you'll have a pickled egg!
Eggshells contain calcium. Vinegar is an acid which dissolves
the calcium in the shell, but leaves the egg.

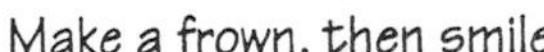

Make a frown, then smile.

Which takes more energy?

Instead of building blocks, try peas. Soak some dried peas overnight. Using toothpicks as the pieces of a structure and peas as the joints, you can build almost anything -- a house, a bridge, molecules, geometric designs. When you're finished creating, give the peas a couple of days to dry out. They'll shrink and hold the toothpicks firmly in place.

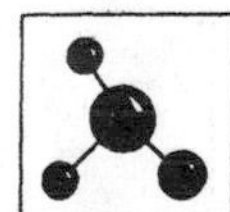

SEARCH FOR MATTER

What's matter and what's not? Find some matter and then challenge a partner to guess the object by feeling it -- without looking.

MATERIALS: None.

DOING IT:

1. Don't explain what "matter" is. Just give the instructions: "Find some matter, but don't show anyone." People can look around the nearby surroundings to find a small piece of matter -- a pencil, a book, a shoe, a strand of hair, an apple.

2. With eyes closed, each person tries to guess a partner's object by feeling it.

3. After each person has guessed his or her partner's object, examine all the objects. Was anything found that isn't matter? Explain what matter is and that it's everywhere.

4. *Variation:* Run a race. Everyone has a set amount of time (e.g. 3 minutes) to find matter with certain characteristics (e.g. hard and rough; hard and smooth; too large to hold in one hand; small enough to balance on one finger). Then the guessing game can begin.

A rock, a jelly doughnut, your finger, and an airplane all have something in common. They are all matter -- something which occupies space and has mass. If something isn't matter, then it's energy.

Everything alive, dead, and never living is made up of atoms. Atoms are microscopically minuscule units of matter. Pretend you could take anything you wanted -- the rock, the jelly doughnut, your finger, or an airplane -- and divide it up. Pretend you could divide it up, smaller and smaller, until you couldn't even see the pieces any more. You would eventually get down to the atom. The universe is a collection of atoms and the space between them. The same atoms have been here since the day the universe began and they will be here until the day it ends. When anything new appears in the world, it's only the old atoms arranging themselves in a new way. Matter cannot be created and it cannot be destroyed.

Topics: States of Matter; Atoms; Senses.

Energy makes things happen. It has many forms. Some of these are more obvious than others because you use them to sense the world around you. Light, which you use to see, is one energy form. Sound, which you hear, is another. You can also feel energy with your skin, like when you stand in front of a fire and feel the heat. Movement and electricity are two other forms of energy that you use every day.

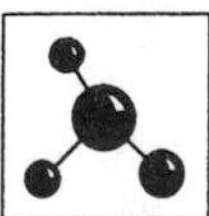

WATER IN A JAR

Solid, liquid, and gas -- the three basic states of matter. Make a people model of matter that shows how energy affects these three states.

MATERIALS: Masking tape.

DOING IT:

1. Mark off a large square on the ground with masking tape; leave one side open. The marked area represents an open jar. People will pretend that they're water in the jar. Individuals will be atoms as a solid (ice) changes to a liquid (water) and then a gas (steam). Note: This is a simplified model. Water is actually made up of groups of atoms (i.e. a water molecule is made up of two hydrogen atoms combined with one oxygen atom).

2. Everyone begins by standing close together at the bottom of the "jar" (end opposite the opening): "You're atoms in ice. You're frozen solid. But, look -- the sun is coming out! You're beginning to get a little warmer."

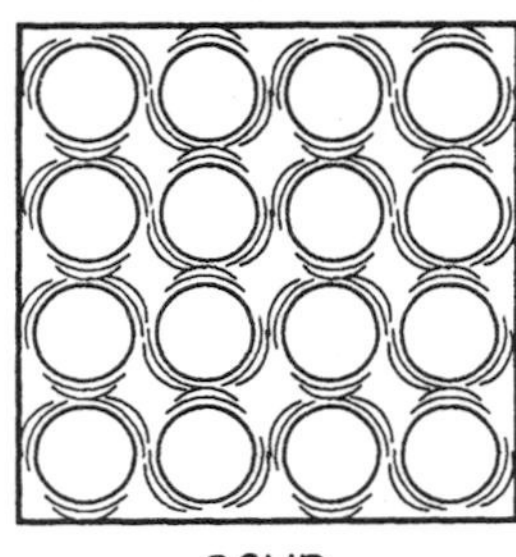

SOLID

3. Everyone sways a little from side to side to represent atoms vibrating: "You can feel the heat. You start to sway back and forth. You sway a little more. You're melting. You're becoming a liquid."

4. Everyone continues to sway, but also starts to move around slowly: "You're a liquid now. You rock back and forth as you walk around. You walk *slowly* around in the bottom part of the jar. Stay in the lines. You're water in a jar."

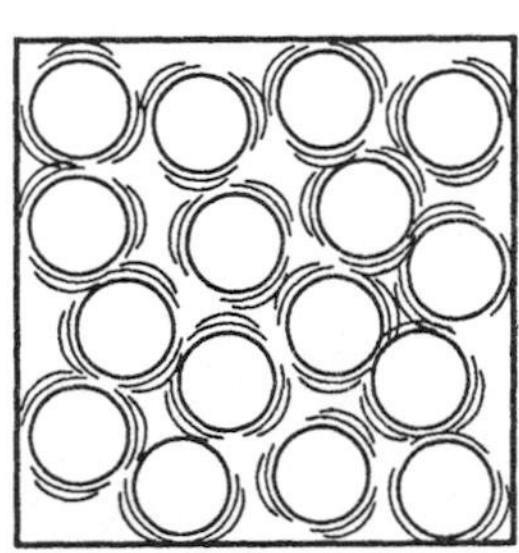

LIQUID

5. A few "atoms" near the "mouth" of the "jar" break away: "It's getting warmer. Someone is holding the jar over a stove. You rock back and forth more. A few of you evaporate from the top of the jar. You move around quickly outside the jar."

6. Everyone sways more (bends far to one side and then far to the other) and continues to *walk* until they leave the "jar": "Hey, it's really hot. You're boiling. You're rising up out of the jar into the air."

7. People now move quickly outside the "jar": "You're a gas now. You move quickly all over the place. You move in a straight line until you hit something. Then you bounce off and move in a straight line in a new direction."

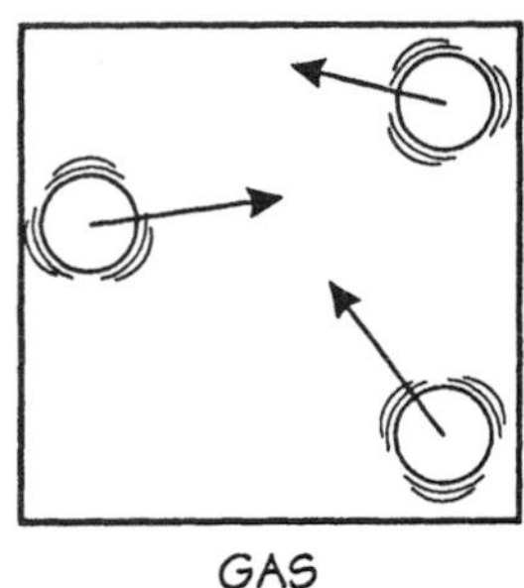

GAS

8. Repeat the process, going from liquid in a jar to a solid.

Heat energy can cause one state of matter to change into another state. The particular state of a type of matter depends both on the matter itself and the temperature.

A "solid" is something that maintains its shape. The atoms (or molecules) of a solid vibrate in a fixed place. When heat is applied, the atoms begin to vibrate more. At a temperature called the "melting point", the atoms vibrate enough so that they break out of their fixed positions and the solid becomes a liquid. A "liquid" maintains its volume (the amount of space it takes up), but takes the shape of its container. The atoms of a liquid still vibrate, but they also move around slowly. When heat is applied, some atoms near the surface begin to vibrate enough to break away from the liquid (evaporate). At a temperature called the "boiling point", atoms throughout the liquid vibrate more and gas bubbles rise to the surface. The liquid then changes completely to a gas. A "gas" has no fixed volume, but takes up the volume of its container. The atoms of a gas move around quickly and are spaced far apart. When heat is applied to a gas, the atoms move faster.

Topics: States of Matter; Atoms; Energy.

Marble Race

And they're off! Drop marbles into different liquids to see which liquid allows a marble to fall the fastest.

MATERIALS: Four marbles of the same size; four drinking glasses or test tubes; water; cooking oil; honey; thick, clear shampoo.

DOING IT:

1. Fill each of four glasses or test tubes with one of four liquids -- water, cooking oil, honey, shampoo.

2. Four people should each hold a marble over each of the glasses or test tubes.

3. On the count of "Three, two, one, go!", the marbles are released into their liquids. Which marble goes through the liquid the fastest and wins the race?

All liquids are not created equal. Different liquids have different "viscosities".

Some liquids pour quickly and others pour slowly. The viscosity of a liquid causes it to resist flowing (or pouring). Liquids with a high viscosity pour slowly and are usually fairly thick, while liquids with a low viscosity pour quickly and are usually fairly thin. The speed at which a marble falls through a liquid is related to the liquid's viscosity: the greater the viscosity, the more slowly a marble falls. Viscosity is caused by the internal friction of a liquid's molecules moving against each other. The more strongly a liquid's molecules interact, the more viscous the liquid.

Topics: States of Matter; Forces; Scientific Method.

The Leaning Tower of Pisa has been leaning for 800 years. The ground it's built on is soft, and the architect didn't make the foundation deep enough to reach firm ground or broad enough to spread the tower's weight. The tower's centre of gravity is still over its base, but the building is slipping by as much as 1.5 mm/year. Many engineers have tried to work out a way to keep the tower up, but have met with no success. If anyone does come up with a practical plan, the people of Pisa will make that person an honourary citizen of the city.

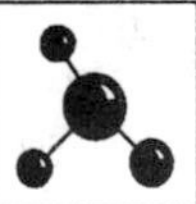

BALANCING THE "IMPOSSIBLE"

Matter is governed by the laws of gravity. These balancing stunts seem to defy the laws of gravity.

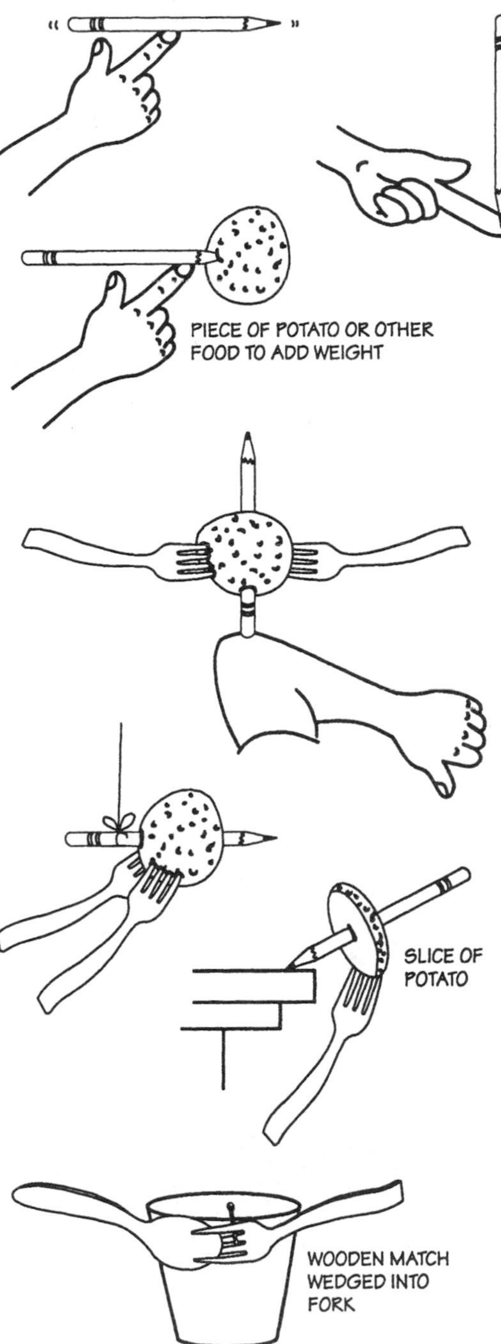

MATERIALS: Pencil; forks; spoon; drinking glass; wooden match; string; potato.

DOING IT:

1. Get the feel for balancing objects by balancing a pencil or fork on your finger. The centre of gravity is above the point at which the pencil or fork rests in a level position.

2. Try the other balancing stunts illustrated on this page.

The story goes that while Sir Isaac Newton was in his garden, an apple fell on his head from a tree. The great scientist immediately began to wonder what caused the apple to fall while the sun, moon, and other stars remained overhead and (fortunately) showed no sign of following the apple. The answer lies in the force of gravity. Matter is governed by Earth's gravity. An object's "weight" involves both its "mass" (quantity of matter) and the strength of the surrounding gravitational pull. On the moon, an object will have the same mass it has on Earth, but it will weigh less because the moon's gravitational pull is not as great as the Earth's. Gravity is involved in the phenomenon of balance.

If everything were weightless, balance would be no problem. In order to balance, objects must be in danger of falling; in order to fall, there must be gravity around to give objects weight (i.e. pull them to the ground). The steadiness of an object depends on how its weight is distributed. Every object has a point around which all its weight seems to be centred. The "centre of gravity" is the balance point of an object. An object is balanced when its centre of gravity is directly on, below, or above its point of support. For example, in a set-up using a fork, a spoon, a wooden match, and a glass, the centre of gravity of the fork and spoon is somewhere between the handles of the two. The fork and spoon balance on the match when their centre of gravity lies directly below this point of support (the spot where the match rests on the glass).

Topics: Forces; Earth.

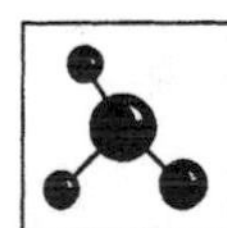

IMPOSSIBLE TO STRAIGHTEN CORD

No matter how hard you pull and tug and strain at the ends of this cord, you just can't straighten it.

QUICKIES

MATERIALS: Heavy book or large plastic jug, with handle and cap, filled with water; 2 to 4 m length of strong cord.

DOING IT:

1. Tie the middle of the cord around the book or jug handle.

2. One person takes one end of the cord and another person takes the other end. The challenge is to pull at the ends of the cord so that the cord becomes perfectly straight.

3. The cord will always sag slightly in the middle. Any ideas for "cheating" and getting the cord straight? (Hint: The book or jug no longer hangs in midair)

You can use energy to create forces which will act against the pull of gravity. In this case, the weight of a book initially causes the cord to sag a great deal. When you first begin pulling on the cord, you exert both a horizontal and a vertical force on the book. The vertical force pulls the book upward. However, as the book rises, the rope becomes more horizontal. The vertical force you can create by pulling on the rope decreases until the book can't be raised any higher. Thus, neither you nor gravity wins in controlling the situation.

Topics: Forces; Earth.

Fill a clear container halfway with water. Tilt the container to any angle and the surface of the water will always be horizontal. Water (and everything else on Earth) is pulled toward the centre of the Earth by an invisible force called gravity. In some places, the water gets no further than the surface -- and forms rivers, lakes, and oceans -- because rock prevents it from draining through. In other places, different types of rock let the water soak through. All water on Earth eventually settles at the lowest level it can possibly reach.

REVOLVING BUCKET

Swing a pail around so that the paper inside doesn't fall out. If you're really brave, try the same trick using water instead of paper!

MATERIALS: Pail or plastic bucket; rope; sheets of letter-size paper. Optional -- water.

DOING IT:

1. Crumple several sheets of paper into tight balls. Put the paper balls into a pail.

2. Swing the pail vertically (keep your arm straight and swing from the shoulder), over your head. The goal is to swing the pail completely around without any of the paper balls falling out.

3. Try different speeds of rotation. What happens when you swing the pail slowly? What's the slowest you can swing the pail without any of the paper balls falling out?

4. Try attaching a rope to the pail. How fast do you have to swing to keep the paper in the pail? Repeat the swing with ropes of different lengths.

5. *Variation:* Use water instead of paper balls. Swing the pail when it's half full; then try swinging the pail when it's almost completely full. What changes have to be made to the speed of rotation to compensate for different amounts of water?

Get a wide-mouthed jar and a ping-pong ball. Put the jar upside down over the ball on a table and start to move the jar with a circular motion. The ball should move around the edge of the jar and start climbing inside as it swirls around. Keep swirling and lift the jar off the table. The ball will stay inside! Why? The ball's inertia -- it wants to go in a straight line -- is countered by the inward force (centripetal force) exerted by the jar. That force makes the ball go in a circle.

Objects in motion want to continue moving in a straight line. This is called "inertia". An object moving in a circle is being *pulled* inward (if no force pulled the object inward, it would move in a straight line). The inward force is called "centripetal force". You feel centripetal force when you're in a car that turns a corner at a high speed. Your body wants to keep going in a straight line; but as you sway toward the car door, it exerts centripetal force and pushes you around the corner with the car (if the door wasn't there, you would fly out of the car!). Centripetal force keeps the paper or water in a swinging pail. As you start swinging the pail, the paper/water wants to fly away from you in a straight line. The centripetal force exerted by the pail counteracts the paper/water's inertia and forces it to keep rotating in a circle. The higher the pail's speed of rotation, the greater the centripetal force.

Topics: Forces.

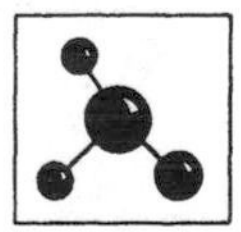

ELECTRIC LEMON

What can you do with a lemon besides eat it? With a little know-how and some wire, you can generate electricity!

MATERIALS: Fresh lemon; clean, short piece of bare copper wire (a test for copper: it isn't attracted by a magnet); clean, steel paper clip. Optional -- galvanometer (detects electric current); potato; onion; apple; orange; fruit juices.

DOING IT:

1. Straighten a paper clip and stick one end into a lemon, through the rind into the pulp.

2. Take a piece of copper wire about as long as the paper clip and poke it into the lemon (through the rind, into the pulp) about 2 cm away from the paper clip.

3. Bend the free end of the wire close to the free end of the paper clip. Touch both ends to your tongue several times. Can you feel a slight tingle?

4. *Variation:* Attach the wire and paper clip to a galvanometer.

5. *Extension:* Try a potato, onion, apple, and orange. Compare galvanometer readings. Also try sticking the paper clip and wire into a glass of fruit juice.

Basically, all matter is electrical. The atoms of all matter are made up of small particles called "electrons" (which carry negative charges) and "protons" (which carry positive charges). The electricity we use to light lamps and power computers involves a flow of electrons. All matter contains electrons, so it's not necessary (or possible) to "make" electricity; all you need is something to push the electrons along. When you put two wires in a lemon, the lemon juice prompts a flow of electrons between the two wires. Your wet tongue completes the path for the flow of electrons. Current runs across your tongue -- and you feel the current as a tingle.

Topics: Electricity; Atoms; Chemical Reactions.

In 1753, an American scientist, Benjamin Franklin, invented the lightning conductor. He flew kites into thunderstorms in order to collect an electric charge along the kite lines. Electricity flowed down the wet line of a kite. When it reached a metal key on the line, a spark was produced. Franklin was lucky not to have been killed doing this experiment because it's very dangerous.

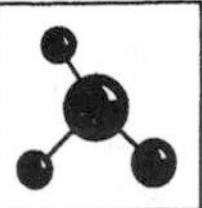

ELECTRONS ON THE GO

You can't actually see an electron, so it can be hard to understand how electricity is generated. Make a people model of an electric circuit.

MATERIALS: 50-60 paper sheets crumpled into balls; two large boxes; marker.

DOING IT:

1. Label two boxes "BATTERY", but put a "+" on one box and a "-" on the other. Put all the paper balls into the "-" box.

2. Six to eight people stand in a circle and each receives a paper ball: "Each person is one atom in a wire. Atoms each have electrons. Electrons are too small to see, but we'll pretend these paper balls are electrons. Each of you gets a paper ball to represent your electrons. Now we want to get the electrons flowing."

3. Hold up the "BATTERY" boxes: "A battery is one way to generate electricity. Inside a battery are atoms with billions of electrons. Batteries have two ends, or terminals. The negative end has a lot of extra electrons and has a negative charge. If you attach a wire to the negative end of a battery, the extra electrons flow into the wire."

4. Make the "BATTERY" boxes a part of the circle. The person nearest the "negative terminal" begins passing "electrons" through the "wire": "Pass the electrons to the person beside you. There's a push and a pull going on here. A negative electron pushes another negative electron, just like the two north poles on a magnet repel each other. The battery's electrons are pushing your electrons along. But the positive end of the battery is also pulling electrons toward it. Positive charges attract negative charges."

5. When all the balls have been transferred to the "positive terminal" of the "battery": "All the extra electrons are gone from the negative terminal of the battery. There's no more voltage left. Voltage was the push and pull caused by the battery's extra electrons at the negative terminal."

6. Make a "new battery" by putting all the "electrons" back in the "negative terminal": "Now we have a new battery. This time, imagine the battery has a higher voltage. The higher voltage increases the electric current. The current is the number of electrons that move through a wire at one time. Electric current is measured in amperes, which are usually just called amps."

7. People pass two "electrons" along as quickly as possible: "To increase the current, we're going to pass along two electrons at a time. Take two electrons as quick as you can, pass them along, and take the next two. . . . Keep going! Faster!"

8. When all the "electrons" are again at the "battery's" "positive terminal": "When the current was increased, did you feel yourself getting warmer? When current increases, a real wire heats up too. That's the way that some appliances like toasters and hair dryers work."

9. *Extension:* Running a wire from the negative to the positive terminal of a battery is a "short circuit"; all the electrons simply rush through. A real circuit would include, for example, a switch (which turns the flow of electrons on/off) and a light bulb (which would make use of the electricity and provide a resistance to limit the flow of electrons). Model a complete circuit.

Electricity involves a flow of electrons. A battery, for example, helps electrons escape from their paths around an atom's nucleus and flow through a wire. The movement of electrons through a wire is called "electric current". The number of electrons that move through the wire at one time is measured in "amperes" (amps). The force that moves the electrons through the wire is measured in "volts". Electricity travels in a continuous path, a "circuit". When you throw a switch, you complete a circuit -- you put a bridge in place for electrons. When you snap the switch off, you lift the bridge out of the circuit and the electrons can no longer flow.

Topics: Electricity; Atoms.

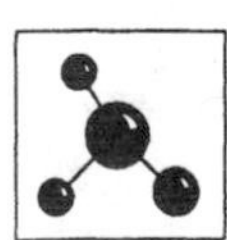

Sticky Water

Water isn't sticky -- is it? Use two sheets of ordinary paper to see whether water can act like glue.

QUICKIES

MATERIALS: Two sheets of paper; water. Optional -- two sheets of paper towel; two pieces of construction paper; two pieces of cardboard; two pieces of newsprint.

DOING IT:

1. Hold two sheets of paper together. Do the sheets stick to each other?

2. Completely wet each sheet of paper with water. Hold the two sheets together. Do they stick to each other? How easy is it to peel the sheets apart? How easy is it to slide them apart?

3. Place the stuck sheets of paper in a warm place to dry. When the sheets dry, do they stick together?

4. *Extension:* Try the same test with paper towels, construction paper, cardboard, and newsprint.

Matter is made up of atoms, and atoms join together to form "molecules". A water molecule is made of two hydrogen atoms and one oxygen atom (H_2O).

The combination of hydrogen and oxygen atoms in water makes water molecules "polar". A polar molecule has two ends; one end has a positive charge and the other has a negative charge (just like a magnet has a north pole and a south pole). The positive end of water molecules attracts the negative end of other water molecules. That's why two wet sheets of paper stick together. It's more difficult to slide two sheets of wet paper apart than to peel them apart because sliding involves breaking the attraction of many more water molecules. Water molecules are also attracted to paper; paper contains molecules that have polar parts.

Topics: Atoms; Forces.

"Stickiness" involves two forces of attraction. When two different substances are attracted, the force is "adhesion". For example, water adheres to grains of sand on a beach. When a substance is attracted to itself, the force is "cohesion". Water coheres to itself. The combination of adhesion and cohesion is what makes it possible to build sand castles. Dry sand won't stick together, but add a little water and you can form the sand into all sorts of shapes.

"FULL" GLASS

Even if a glass of water looks "full", you'll be surprised at what you can add to it: one paper clip, two paper clips, three paper clips, . . .

Dew and rain stand in round drops on a leaf rather than spreading out.
The water molecules pull in toward the centre of the drop.
The waxy surface of a leaf also repels the water.

MATERIALS: Glass of water; paper clips; dishwashing liquid. Optional -- milk, vinegar, oil, pop.

DOING IT:

1. Fill a glass to the rim with water.

2. Slowly drop paper clips into the water, one at a time. Be careful not to drop the paper clips from high above the water.

3. How many paper clips can you get into the "full" glass before the water spills? Five? Ten? Twenty? Thirty?

4. What happens if you add a few drops of dishwashing liquid to the water? Can you get more or less paper clips into the glass?

5. *Extension:* Try liquids other than water (e.g. milk, vinegar, oil, pop). The more paper clips you can get into the glass, the stronger the surface tension.

Make three small holes close together near the bottom of a can. Fill the can with water. If you pinch the three water streams together with your fingers, and then take your fingers away, the streams will stay together. The water is held together by surface tension.

The force that attracts molecules of the same substance to each other is called "cohesion". Water molecules have a cohesive force -- they are strongly attracted to one another. Water molecules that are surrounded by other water molecules are attracted in all directions. However, water molecules at the surface of a glass of water have no water molecules above them. They are all pulled strongly in the same direction -- downward to the water molecules underneath them. The attraction between molecules on a liquid's surface is called "surface tension". The surface of the water acts as if it has a thin skin over it. The surface tension is strong enough to prevent a "full" glass of water from spilling as paper clips are added. As more and more paper clips are added, the surface of the water begins to look curved -- like a lens -- until the water finally spills over the rim of the glass.

Topics: Atoms; Forces.

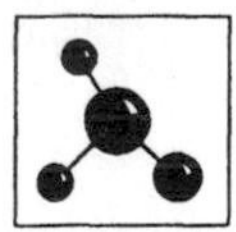

MATCH BOAT

A drop of dishwashing liquid on the split end of a match makes the match whip around in the water like a speedboat.

MATERIALS: Cardboard or wooden matches (wooden matches float longer), or little pieces of cardboard cut into the shape of boats; dishwashing liquid; knife or scissors; bowl of water or sink. Optional -- pepper; paper.

DOING IT:

1. Split open the back end of a match.

2. Carefully put a drop of dishwashing liquid in the split end of the match. Float the match on the water. The match should zip forward.

3. Try making the notch in the back end of the match (the "boat's" stern) closer to the right side or to the left side. The "boat" will curve around instead of moving directly forward.

4. *Variation:* Make a paper spiral and lay it on the water. Put a drop of dishwashing liquid in the open centre of the spiral. The spiral will spin as the surface tension of the water is broken along the inner areas of the spiral.

5. *Extension:* Sprinkle pepper over the surface of cold, clean water. Put a drop of dishwashing liquid into the centre of the pepper. What happens?

Surface tension is caused by an attraction between molecules on the surface of a liquid. The attraction of water molecules to each other can be weakened by adding soap (or detergent). Soap has a lower surface tension than water. Soap molecules are interesting because they are both polar and nonpolar. A soap molecule is long; one end is polar, the other end is nonpolar. The polar part of soap mixes with the polar water molecules and lowers the surface tension of water. So, when you put a drop of dishwashing liquid at the back end of a match "speedboat", the surface tension is greater at the front of the "boat" than at the rear and the "boat" is pulled forward.

Topics: Atoms; Forces.

Why does dishwashing liquid clean greasy dishes so well? Water on its own is repelled by grease. Oil molecules are nonpolar (they don't have any charges), and nonpolar molecules don't mix with polar molecules like water. When dishwashing liquid is added to the greasy dishes, the nonpolar end of the dishwashing liquid molecule mixes with the nonpolar oil. The polar end of the dishwashing liquid mixes with the polar water.

POPPING PING-PONG BALLS

Ping-pong balls insist on floating on water. You push them down and they pop back up. What do you have to do to make them stay down?

In ancient Greece, King Hiero had a beautiful gold crown. But he was suspicious that the goldsmith who made the crown had mixed in some silver instead of using all gold. The king summoned Archimedes, a very knowledgeable man -- a philosopher, mathematician, physicist, and inventor. Archimedes knew silver was not as heavy as gold. Therefore, a crown made of the two metals would be larger than one made from an equal mass of gold. But how could he tell if the new crown was the right size? The story goes that while Archimedes was pondering this problem, he took a bath. He happened to notice that some water spilled out as he stepped into the full tub. Archimedes' body took up space and displaced (pushed aside) some water. It occurred to Archimedes that the volume of this water must be the same as his body's volume. "Eureka!" he shouted (which is Greek for "I've found it!"). Archimedes got a bar of gold and a bar of silver, each exactly the same mass as the crown. Using the water test, he found that the crown displaced less water than the silver bar, but more than the gold bar. The crown was not pure gold.

QUICKIES

MATERIALS: Ping-pong ball; drinking glass; water; tape; dimes. Optional -- golf ball; super-ball.

DOING IT:

1. Fill a glass about 2/3 full of water. Mark the water level with a piece of tape.

2. Put a ping-pong ball in the glass. The ball floats. Push on the ball. What do you feel?

3. Push about 1/4 of the ball into the water. Push the ball halfway into the water. Now push the ball almost completely into the water. What happens to the water level each time?

4. Push the ping-pong ball into the water and then let it go. How high can you make the ping-pong ball pop up?

5. Tape a dime to the ball. Does the ball sink? How many coins do you have to tape to the ball before it sinks?

6. When the ping-pong ball is at the bottom of the glass of water, look at the water level of the glass. Why is it higher than before?

7. *Extension:* Experiment with a golf ball and a superball. Compare them to the ping-pong ball.

Two things cannot occupy the same space at the same time. If you drop an object into a glass partially filled with water, the object "displaces" (pushes aside) some water and makes the water level rise. The volume of water displaced equals the volume of the object below the surface of the water. If the mass of the water displaced by the object equals the mass of the object itself, then the object floats. If the object's mass is greater than the mass of the water it displaces, the object sinks. A ping-pong ball floats because it displaces a volume of water that has mass exactly equal to the mass of the ball.

"Buoyancy", the upward force of water that works against an object's mass, depends on the object's volume. The buoyant force is equal to the mass of the water displaced by an object. The greater the volume of an object, the greater the displacement of water, and therefore the greater the buoyancy. A kilogram of lead sinks, but a kilogram of wood floats because the kilogram of wood has a much bigger volume. To sink a ping-pong ball in a glass of water, you can't change its volume, but you can add to its mass. If you push the ping-pong ball under water, the upward force of buoyancy is greatly increased. More water is displaced than if the ball was just floating on the water's surface. When you release the ping-pong ball, the force of buoyancy causes the ball to pop up.

Topics: Forces; Measurement.

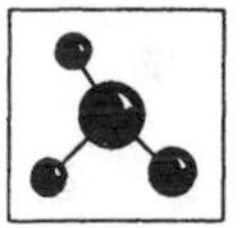

AN EGG FLOAT

Why is it easier to float in salt water than in fresh water? Do this eggs-periment to find out!

MATERIALS: *Fresh* egg; large drinking glass; water; salt; teaspoon. Optional -- small piece of carrot; large piece of carrot.

DOING IT:

1. Fill a large glass halfway with water.

2. Carefully put an egg into the water. It should sink.

3. Stir salt into the water, one teaspoon at a time. How much salt do you have to add before the egg floats up to the surface of the water?

When a warm ocean current meets a cold ocean current, the two don't mix -- the warm water flows above the cold water. Warm water is less dense than cold water, so warm water floats on top of cold water.

4. Once the egg is floating, add more water to the glass until the glass is almost full. Add the water slowly, dribbling it along the side of the glass with a *clean* spoon, so that the salt water and fresh water don't mix. The egg should end up floating between a layer of salt water (at the bottom of the glass) and a layer of fresh water (at the top of the glass).

5. *Extension:* Repeat the steps with a small piece of carrot. Can you make the carrot float like the egg? What happens if you use a larger piece of carrot? A large piece of carrot has the same density as a small piece of carrot; density depends on the type of substance, not the amount of substance.

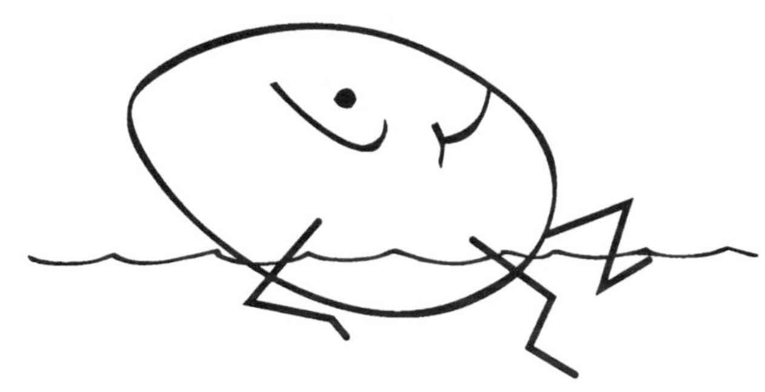

"Density" is the term used to compare the mass of the same volume of different substances. The same volume of two different substances can have a different mass. A glassful of water has a greater mass than the same glassful of oil. Water is denser than oil. Ice floats on water because ice is less dense than water. Wood, cork, and styrofoam float on water because they are less dense than water. Stone, iron, lead, and an egg are denser than water, so they sink. An egg floats in salt water because the mass of the salt water displaced is equal to the mass of the egg. The egg's density is less than the density of the salt water. The egg floats between a layer of salt water and a layer of fresh water because it falls through the fresh water but is supported by the denser salt water.

Topics: States of Matter; Forces.

Two identical, sealed, one-litre jars sink in a pond. One contains a kilogram of jam; the other, five kilograms of lead. On which jar is the force of buoyancy greater?

Answer: Neither. Both jars displace the same volume of water, so the force of buoyancy on each is equal.

LIQUID LAYERS

Once you know about density, you can get creative and produce some interesting pieces of "liquid art".

MATERIALS: Five glasses; spoon; hot water; cold water; salt; four different colours of food colouring (e.g. blue, green, red, yellow). Optional -- corn syrup; cooking oil.

DOING IT:

1. Get four glasses. Put cold salt water in one, cold fresh water in the second, hot salt water in the third, and hot fresh water in the fourth.

2. Add drops of a different colour of food colouring to each glass and stir. The food colouring makes it easier to tell the liquids apart; it doesn't affect their density.

3. Take a glass and carefully pour in a layer of each liquid, going from the most dense to the least dense: cold salt water on the bottom; cold fresh water next; then hot salt water; finally, hot fresh water. Be careful not to mix the layers as you pour into the glass. Tilt the glass slightly and run a new liquid along the side of the glass as you add a layer.

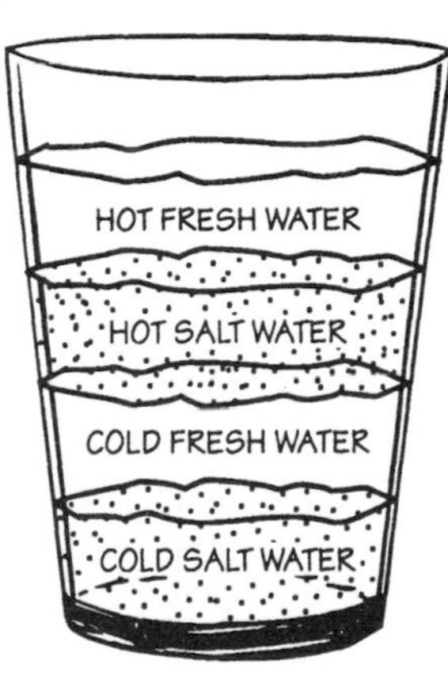

4. Experiment with different temperatures of water and different amounts of salt.

5. *Extension:* Put different colours of food colouring (avoid yellow) in a glass of water and a glass of corn syrup. Make a liquid layers creation with oil on the top, water in the middle, and corn syrup on the bottom. Try adding the three liquids in different orders. Does changing the order change the final positions of the liquids in the glass?

How can huge cruise ships and supertankers float? After all, they're all made of heavy metal. However, the mass of these large ships is spread out over a large volume. Most of that volume is air space -- air space in the cabins and passageways, air space in the engine room, air space within the steel hull itself. The density of the ships is less than the density of the water they displace.

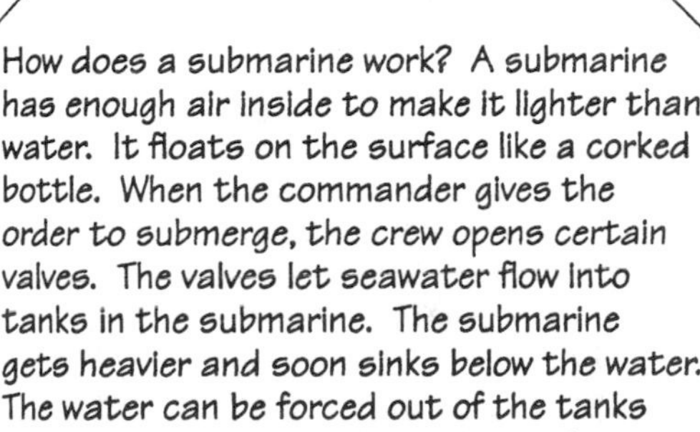

How does a submarine work? A submarine has enough air inside to make it lighter than water. It floats on the surface like a corked bottle. When the commander gives the order to submerge, the crew opens certain valves. The valves let seawater flow into tanks in the submarine. The submarine gets heavier and soon sinks below the water. The water can be forced out of the tanks whenever the commander wishes to bring the submarine up.

The same volume of two liquids may have different masses. The heavier the liquid, the greater the density. A liquid that is less dense than water will float on the water; a liquid that is more dense will sink. In general (depending on variables such as temperature of water and amount of salt added), if you compare hot and cold fresh water to hot and cold salt water, the order of density from most dense to least dense is: cold salt water, cold fresh water, hot salt water, hot fresh water. Corn syrup has a greater density than water, but oil is less dense than water.

Topics: States of Matter; Forces.

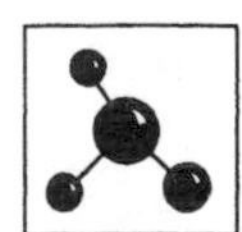

SPLITTING AN "ATOM"

Oil and water don't mix. Use that scientific fact to have some fun splitting an oil-drop "atom".

MATERIALS: Glass; water; rubbing alcohol; cooking oil; spoon; table knife; paper towel.

DOING IT:

1. Fill a glass about half full with rubbing alcohol (about 100 ml). Add enough water (about 50 ml) to fill the glass 2/3 full. Stir the alcohol-water mixture.

2. Dry the spoon off and fill it with cooking oil. *Carefully* bring the spoon to the surface of the alcohol-water mixture and *gently* tip the spoon over. If you do this just right, a single, large blob of oil -- a model "atom" -- will slide into the glass. The drop will be perfectly spherical.

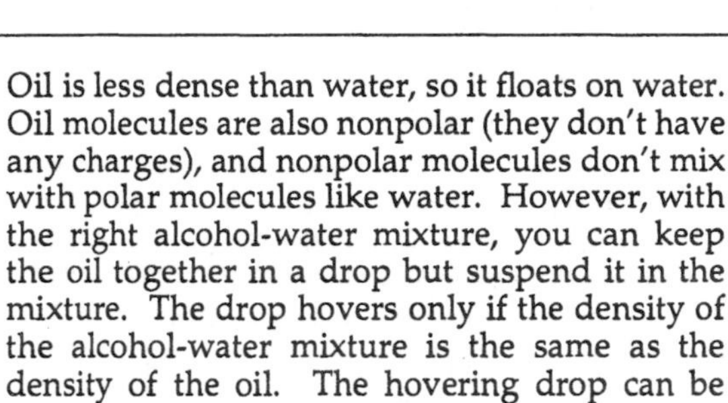

Oil is less dense than water, so it floats on water. Oil molecules are also nonpolar (they don't have any charges), and nonpolar molecules don't mix with polar molecules like water. However, with the right alcohol-water mixture, you can keep the oil together in a drop but suspend it in the mixture. The drop hovers only if the density of the alcohol-water mixture is the same as the density of the oil. The hovering drop can be used as a model atom.

All matter is composed of atoms. No one has ever seen an atom, even with the most powerful microscope. But scientists have made some guesses about the properties of atoms. Nuclear energy is based on the properties of atoms. Nuclear "fusion" involves making larger atoms from smaller ones. In the sun, hydrogen is turned into helium and this gives out vast amounts of energy. Nuclear "fission" involves splitting large atoms into smaller ones. Many scientists have suggested that a splitting atom behaves something like a drop of liquid when it breaks up into droplets. In nuclear reactors, atoms of uranium are smashed apart, letting out the energy that was inside them. The heat from this process can be used in the production of electricity. The process also results in very dangerous waste. The waste is "radioactive"; it can kill living things.

Topics: Atoms; Energy; States of Matter.

3. If the blob floats on the surface, add a bit more alcohol to the mixture; if the blob sinks to the bottom of the glass, add a bit more water. The idea is to create an oil drop that hovers in the middle of the glass.

4. Use a knife to *gently* prod the drop apart. At first, the drop will bulge. Then, it will break apart into two perfectly round oil drops. The oil-drop "atom" will have split into two smaller "atoms". Can you make two identically sized atoms? Can you split the two new "atoms" to make more atoms?

5. When you're finished, pour the alcohol-water mixture down the drain. Do not drink it; it is poison.

Unfortunately, scientific discoveries aren't always put to peaceful uses. Nuclear energy made nuclear war possible. On August 6th, 1945, an atomic bomb was dropped on the city of Hiroshima, Japan. It destroyed the city and killed 80,000 people. Many more were to die later from radiation sickness.

ELASTIC BAND ENERGY

Heat is one form of energy. You can stretch an elastic band over and over, and each time you'll produce a little heat.

MATERIALS: Large, flat elastic band.

DOING IT:

1. To get an idea of the temperature of the elastic band, touch it to your forehead (your forehead is very sensitive to temperature). The elastic band should feel cool.

2. Pinch a piece of the elastic band between the thumb and index finger on your left hand.

3. With the thumb and index finger of your right hand, pinch the elastic band at a point *right next to* your left hand. Your two thumbs should be touching. You're only going to stretch a little bit of the elastic band.

4. Quickly pull your hands so that the elastic band stretches. While the elastic band is stretched, touch it to your forehead. Does the elastic band feel warmer?

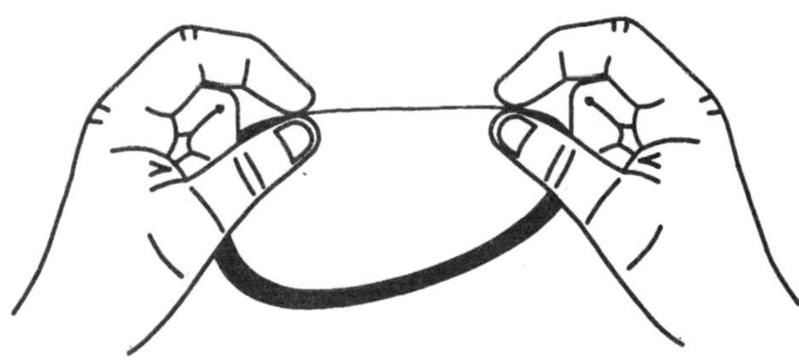

5. Let the elastic band go back to its regular size. Touch it to your forehead again. Does the elastic band go back to the original, cooler temperature?

6. You can stretch the elastic band again and again, and each time it will get warm.

Rub your hands together hard and fast. What do you feel? Heat. The heat is created from the friction caused by rubbing.

Heat has only three ways to travel. In "conduction", heat flows from a hot object to a cold one. Wrap your hands around a warm mug of hot chocolate and the heat is conducted from the hot chocolate, to the cup, to your hands. In "radiation", heat flows out from a very hot object. Hold your hands in front of a fireplace and you can feel the heat. In "convection", heat rises through the air. An electric heater warms the air around it; you can stand by the heater and immediately feel the heat. As the hot air rises up from the heater and air moves around the room, the whole room is gradually warmed.

You can change one form of energy into another. You exert work energy as you stretch an elastic band, and that energy is converted to heat. An elastic band is made of coiled molecules. When you stretch an elastic, the coiled molecules are temporarily straightened. When you stop exerting energy, the molecules return to their coiled shapes.

Topics: Energy.

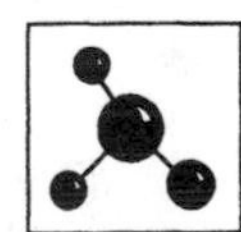

SCIENCE FRICTION

This tricky little ball slides easily up and down a string until you tighten the string to put on the "brakes".

MATERIALS: 65 cm of aluminum foil; 1 m of string; pencil; scissors. Optional -- tweezers.

DOING IT:

1. Crumple a sheet of aluminum foil into a tight ball.

2. Use a pencil to make a shallow, V-shaped tunnel in the ball, first poking through one side of the ball and then poking through the other.

3. Push the string through the tunnel in the foil ball. You may want to use tweezers to pull the string through the tunnel.

4. If you leave the string relaxed, the foil ball should slide easily up and down the string. When you pull hard on the ends to tighten the string, the ball will stop until you relax the string again. (Note: If the foil ball doesn't stop when you pull on the string, your tunnel doesn't have enough of a V shape.)

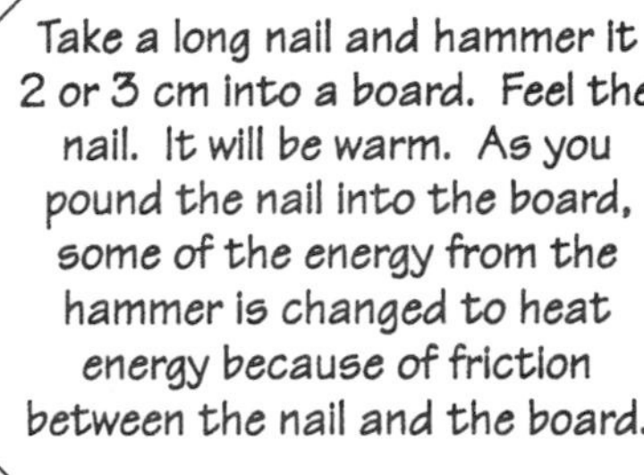

Take a long nail and hammer it 2 or 3 cm into a board. Feel the nail. It will be warm. As you pound the nail into the board, some of the energy from the hammer is changed to heat energy because of friction between the nail and the board.

Friction is the force that resists the motion of one surface over another. If two surfaces are very smooth, there's little friction and they slide easily over each other. If the surfaces are rough, like sandpaper, the friction is much greater and they are hard to slide over each other.

The aluminum foil ball stops when you pull the string tight because the string rubs against the V-shaped tunnel. The ball and string work a little like bicycle brakes. The brake pads and the rim of the bicycle wheel rub against each other to slow the bicycle down. The more you squeeze the brakes, the greater the friction and the faster the wheel slows down.

Topics: Forces; Energy.

When a rocket returns from its orbit, it heats up because of friction between the rocket body and the air as the rocket plunges through the Earth's atmosphere.

PENNY POWER

Bump the back end of a row of pennies -- or any other coins -- and watch the first penny shoot forward.

QUICKIES

MATERIALS: Ten pennies (or any other coins); smooth surface. Optional -- quarter, dime.

DOING IT:

1. Place nine pennies in a row on a smooth surface so that each penny is touching the one next to it.

2. Put another (tenth) penny about 12 cm from the back end of the row. Give the tenth penny a quick push so that it slides into the back end of the row. What happens?

3. Try pushing the tenth penny harder, and then more gently. What happens to the first penny?

4. Place eight pennies in a row so that each penny is touching the one next to it. Put the remaining two pennies about 12 cm from the back end of the row. Give the two pennies a quick push so that they both slide into the back end of the row. What happens?

5. *Extension:* Place ten pennies in a row. Use a quarter (heavier than the pennies) as the knocking coin. Is more than one penny moved? Do you have to push the quarter with more or less energy than a penny to move a coin in the row? Use a dime (lighter than either the quarter or the pennies) as the knocking coin and see what happens.

How can you make a ball bounce higher? By moving your hand down fast before you let go of the ball. The fast movement of your hand before you let go gives energy to the ball. The extra energy adds more force to the bounce of the ball. The ball pushes off the ground with more force, and the ball bounces higher than when it's just dropped.

When you ride a bicycle, you give, or transfer, some of your energy to the bicycle. Energy from food you've eaten is changed into the energy of motion. If, as you're riding along, you hit a rock, the rock moves and you slow down. Some of the bicycle's energy has been transferred to the rock. These examples demonstrate an important aspect of energy: energy can be passed from one object to another. In this activity, you give the last penny energy by pushing it. The energy passes through all the pennies until it reaches the first penny in the row. There's no penny in front of the first penny to prevent it from moving, so it shoots forward with about the same energy you gave the last penny.

Topics: Energy; Forces.

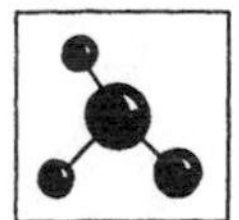

Broken Pencil

Bears are more scientific than you think. They are able to sweep fish out of the water even though the fish aren't where they appear to be. What do bears know?

QUICKIES

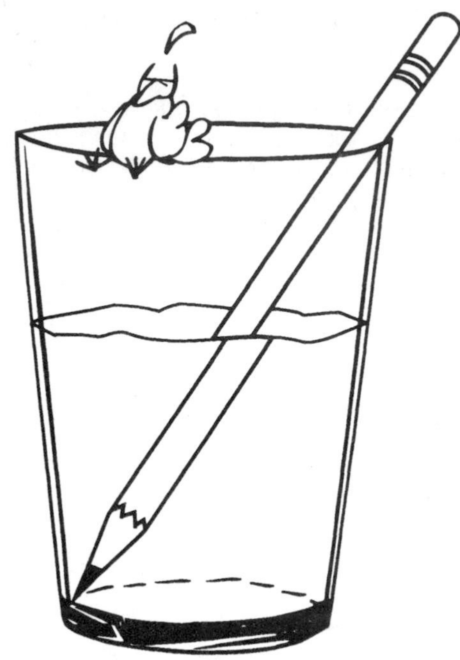

MATERIALS: Drinking glass; water; pencil.

DOING IT:

1. Fill a drinking glass about 2/3 full with water.

2. Put a pencil in the glass (at a slant, not straight up and down).

3. Look at the pencil at, above, and below the water line. What do you see? Why?

Mirages occur because of refraction. A mirage appears when there's a clear sky and little wind. As the sun heats up the ground, the air closest to the ground is warmer than the air above it. Light passing through the boundary between the warmer and colder air is bent and you see things that aren't really there -- like a pool of water on a highway that's actually an image of the sky.

Light travels through the air in what appears to be a straight line. But light bends when it moves from one medium to another, like from air into water.

Even though water is clear, looking through it changes the way you see things. Light travels more slowly through water than through air. The bending of light is called "refraction".

When you put a pencil in a glass of water, the pencil appears to bend at the water line. You see the pencil in the first place because light bounces off it to your eyes. The light from the end of the pencil in the air goes to your eyes from a different direction than the light from the end of the pencil that's underwater. Light bends (refracts) as it leaves the water and enters the air. So, the pencil underwater isn't really bent; the pencil isn't where it appears to be. The bent light fools your eyes and creates an optical illusion. Note that the pencil also looks bigger underwater. The curved surface of the glass and the water in it act as a convex lens.

Topics: Light; Atmosphere.

You see the sun several minutes before it actually rises above the horizon in the morning. You also see the sun for a few minutes after it has gone below the horizon in the evening. This is because the Earth's atmosphere refracts light, making objects like the sun appear higher in the sky.

INVISIBLE GLASS

You look into a container filled with liquid and there's nothing inside. But when you stick your hand into the liquid, you pull out a drinking glass!

MATERIALS: Large glass container or jar; small drinking glass; water; cooking oil; paper towels.

DOING IT:

1. Put the drinking glass inside the larger glass container. Fill the container with water. Look at the container from different angles. Do you see the drinking glass?

2. Spill out the water and wipe out the drinking glass and container.

3. Put the drinking glass inside the larger glass container. Fill the container with cooking oil. Look at the container from different angles. Do you see the drinking glass?

QUICKIES

Some fish have built-in bifocal lenses in their eyes. The top part of their eye is for seeing in air, the bottom half is for seeing underwater. People can't see well underwater because our eyes are made for seeing in air.

As light passes from one medium to another (e.g. water to air, glass to air), the light is bent (refracted) at the boundary between the two mediums. This happens because light travels through different mediums at different speeds. Light moves through petroleum products (including cooking oil) at about the same speed as it does through glass. Therefore, as light passes between glass and oil it doesn't bend at the boundaries, leaving the boundaries invisible.

Topics: Light.

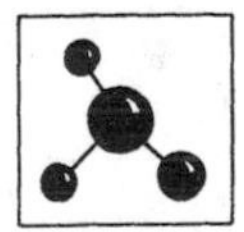

CATCH A SHADOW

Boxers often improve their reflexes by boxing with their shadows. Improve your reflexes -- and have some fun! -- by playing shadow tag on a sunny day.

QUICKIES

MATERIALS: Sunshine.

DOING IT:

1. One person is chosen as "It".

2. The object of the game is for "It" to try to step on someone else's shadow. If "It" succeeds in stepping on someone's shadow, then that person becomes "It".

3. The key to the game lies in looking at the sun's position and angling your body so that your shadow will be made larger, or smaller, or thinner, or disappear -- whatever is necessary to prevent "It" from stepping on the shadow. A useful tip: In general, you should run away from the sun. Your shadow will fall in front of you, making it hard to spot.

4. *Variation:* Try playing shadow tag at different times of the day. Shadows are longer in late evening and early morning, because the sun is lower in the sky.

Light is a form of energy. We do know that much. The big question is whether light is made up of particles or waves. There are two theories about light -- and both seem right. The particle theory of light explains reflection, for example, as light particles bouncing off a mirror like a ball bouncing off the ground. The wave theory sees light waves as being reversed at the surface of the mirror. Whatever light is, it has certain properties. When light cannot pass through an object, a shadow is formed. Light spills around the object and creates an outline of the object's shape. Shadows can be manipulated in a number of interesting ways. By realizing that an object's position with respect to a light source affects the nature of the shadow formed (e.g. whether it's small or large, fat or thin, etc.), you can control the shadow.

Topics: Light.

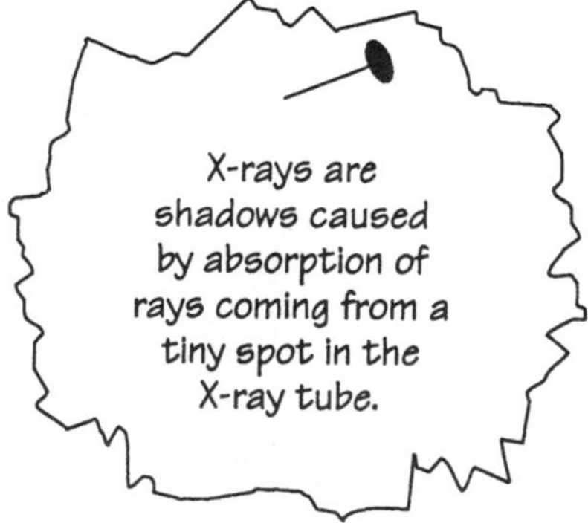

HUMANS

Humans are amazing creatures. Our potential is incredible, especially when you realize that, on average, less than 10% of human mental capacity and less than 30% of physical capacity is developed. The excuse "I'm only human" just doesn't wash. We can do a lot more than we think we can.

In the last forty years, the number of people in the world has doubled, from 2.5 billion people in 1950 to over 5 billion people now. Scientists estimate that by the year 2100 the world's population could climb to over 10 billion people. There are a lot of us out there!

Try to kiss your elbow -- the very tip of your elbow. Can you do it? Your body just isn't made to do it.

One thing that makes humans rather unique is our opposable thumb; that is, a thumb that faces the other fingers on the hand. Tape your thumbs down securely across your palms. Leave the other fingers free. Try a variety of activities -- writing, eating, getting dressed, throwing a ball -- and see what a difference your thumb makes.

The average life expectancy of women in North America is 78 years, while for men it's only 70 years. Women may have longer lifespans because they live healthier lives or because of something in their bodies -- scientists don't know for sure.

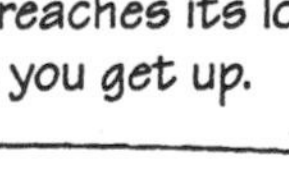

Normal body temperature is 37 degrees Celsius. Body temperature may vary normally during the course of each day by as much as a degree. It peaks in late afternoon and reaches its low point an hour or two before you get up.

Measure your exact height right when you get up in the morning and again late in the day. Does your height change? Your backbone is made up of separate bones called "vertebrae" joined together by elastic cartilage discs. The discs act as shock absorbers to cushion the vertebrae when you jump, bend, or twist. As you stand upright during the day, gravity pulls the bones down and squeezes out liquid in the discs. When you lie down at night, the liquid has a chance to gather again, making you temporarily taller. Astronauts actually grow a few centimetres taller while they are in space, because there is no gravity pulling the bones of their spines tightly together.

Invasion Of An Unknown World

This short story provides a fascinating introduction to the world you carry around with you every day -- your body.

QUICKIES

MATERIALS: None.

DOING IT:

1. Read the following story:

WARNING: The story you are about to read will shock and surprise you. It is a true account of the invasion of a strange yet vaguely familiar world.

The surface had barely begun to dry when the first of the invaders arrived. Alone, and in groups, they drifted in on gusts of wind. They carried no weapons, despite the fact that their simple bodies were almost defenceless against the hostile new environment. To colonize this world they would have to rely on luck and the size and variety of their invasion force.

Millions of invaders were doomed immediately: they landed in dry, barren areas that could hardly support any life at all. Yet, miraculously, a few of them did survive on the crusty, slab-like surface, only to face continual hazards. From time to time, the surface heaved, causing some of the slabs to break loose. Any aliens unlucky enough to be on loosened slabs were carried off by raging winds as the slabs were whirled away.

But the surface of the new world wasn't totally hostile. Some areas offered shelter from the terrible winds. These rough, irregular landscapes were full of strange towering growths that rose like leafless, scaly tree trunks out of deep pits. Many of the invaders who settled in these sheltered pits thrived. Sausage-shaped aliens grew to almost impossible lengths before splitting in two, and clusters of spherical aliens became swollen as their numbers grew. Other invaders, who found the atmosphere poisonous, wriggled to the very bottom of the pits. Here they discovered a type of air lock, where poisonous gases couldn't reach them. And so, they too survived.

Some aliens landed close to the opening of a huge cave. The wind here was overpowering, gusting from ever-changing directions. First it seemed to come from the mouth of the cave itself, then suddenly it reversed and sucked everything in its path, including hundreds of aliens, into the warm, moist interior of the cave.

Inside, the invaders came face to face with the cave's inhabitants. Some were strange, corkscrew-shaped creatures, others lashed around with whip-like tentacles. But they took no notice of the invaders, as if to say there's room for all.

Being inside the cave was much better than being on the surface. But as on the surface, there were unseen hazards. Gases constantly rushed back and forth through the opening of the cave. At times, the floor of the cave convulsed and darkness descended. And there were sudden floods, bringing fork-shaped invaders into the cave and sweeping them down into a dark, gaping tunnel at its rear. The invaders who were swept down the tunnel, however, turned out to be the luckiest of all. They found themselves in a labyrinth of connecting tunnels and chambers where the heat and wetness suited them perfectly. They wedged themselves into cracks and folds in the tunnels' walls. And there they thrived, silently growing and splitting until the innermost tunnels were stuffed with them.

The invasion was a success. The new world was colonized and the invaders would be at home there forever.

2. Where is the strange world? Who are the invaders? How do you explain the different parts of the story?

The desert at the beginning of the story is the baby's arms and legs. The crusty slabs are dead skin cells which get blown away as the baby moves. The scaly, tree-like growths are hairs. The deep pits are pores in the baby's scalp where the hairs are rooted. The cave is, of course, the baby's mouth (the floor being the tongue). As milk enters the baby's mouth, it carries bacteria down the throat to the stomach and then to the baby's intestines.

The unknown world in the story is the body of a newborn human being. The invaders are bacteria -- tiny organisms which can't be seen by the human eye. Millions of bacteria begin growing on and in a human being at the minute of birth and remain until a person's death -- and even after that! The bacteria are actually quite harmless and, in fact, can work to keep other, more harmful bacteria away. Different types of bacteria live in each area of the human body.

Topics: Microorganisms; Human Body.

LEFTY OR RIGHTY?

The brain is your body's control centre. It has two sides, and each side controls different things. Which side of your brain is most in control?

MATERIALS: Paper; pencil; ball.

DOING IT:

1. Are you left- or right-handed? Try writing with the hand you don't normally use. Why is it difficult? What does this tell you about the side of your brain that's dominant for the task of writing?

2. Are you left- or right-footed? Kick a ball around. Which foot do you use? If you're right-handed, chances are you're right-footed too.

3. Quickly clasp your hands together. Which thumb is on top? The thumb on top indicates whether you're right- or left-thumbed. Clasp your hands the opposite way. How does it feel? Is anyone you know right-handed, but left-thumbed?

4. When you fold your arms, one arm is on top and one is tucked under. Guess which one will be on top, and then try it. The arm on top is the dominant one.

5. With your right eye shut, sight along your thumb to a distant object. Open your right eye. If your thumb seems to jump to the left, the right eye is dominant. If not, the left eye dominates.

6. People also have a dominant ear and a dominant side of the face and tongue. How could you test for these?

By the time you're 10 years old, one side of your brain is usually dominant (more in control) for certain functions. The left side of the brain controls the right side of the body, and the right side of the brain controls the left side of the body. This reversal is due to the fact that nerve fibres cross over on their way in and out of the brain.

The left side of the brain seems to specialize toward tasks that require logic and language (e.g. writing, numerical skills, scientific skills, reasoning). The right side is involved in music and art appreciation, the use of symbols, pattern recognition, and creativity. The two halves of the brain work together for complex tasks. For example, within a couple of days, your left brain can learn where the letters of the alphabet are on a computer keyboard. But that doesn't seem to help you learn to type. Your right brain, which not only recognizes patterns but oversees how your hands and eyes work together to use the patterns, must then teach your fingers what to do. In the same way, your right brain may be able to memorize melodies, but the left brain is needed to read the musical notes. For direct physical acts like writing, one side of the brain is usually in charge; if you're right-handed, the left side of the brain is in control. Some people are "ambidextrous" -- they can use either hand to do a task. Other people are "mixed-handed" -- they do different tasks with different hands.

Topics: Brain; Human Body.

BEND-ABILITY

Your body is of most use to you when it's healthy and physically fit. Flexibility is one of the basic elements of physical fitness. How flexible are you?

MATERIALS: None.

DOING IT:

1. Try the flexibility exercises on this page and compare the flexibility of various parts of your body. **Don't do more than feels comfortable.**

PULL YOUR HEEL UP AS FAR AS POSSIBLE ALONG YOUR LEG.

LIFT YOUR LEG AND POINT YOUR TOE. HOW STRAIGHT CAN YOU MAKE THE TOP OF YOUR LEG?

TRY TO JOIN YOUR HANDS BEHIND YOUR BACK.

CAN YOU TOUCH YOUR HEAD TO YOUR TOES?

LIFT YOUR LEG, PULL YOUR TOE BACK AND PUSH YOUR HEEL FORWARD.

LEAN BACK AS FAR AS POSSIBLE, KEEPING YOUR BODY STRAIGHT.

HOW FAR DOWN CAN YOU BEND, WHILE YOUR HEELS STAY ON THE GROUND?

SIT ON THE GROUND WITH YOUR LEGS IN FRONT. TRY TO TOUCH THE GROUND WITH YOUR TOES BY TURNING THEM OUTWARD.

PULL ONE LEG TOWARD YOUR NOSE. THEN STRETCH THE LEG OUT TO THE SIDE.

There are four basic elements of physical fitness: cardiovascular endurance, muscular strength, muscular endurance, and flexibility. Perhaps the most important of these four elements is cardiovascular endurance -- the sustained ability of the heart, blood vessels, and blood to carry oxygen to the cells, the ability of the cells to process oxygen, and the ability of the blood, once again, to carry away waste products. Exercises that promote cardiovascular endurance don't necessarily promote the other three elements of fitness.

Flexibility is an indicator of what kind of shape your muscles are in. Younger people tend to be more flexible than older people, and females (because of their bone and joint structure) tend to be more flexible than males.

Topics: Human Body.

BODY BALANCING

When you think about it, keeping your body balanced as you walk upright, on those two sticks called legs, is pretty amazing. Try these balancing challenges.

> Your ears and eyes help you balance. Canals inside your ears are filled with fluid that detects any tilting of the head and feeds the information to your brain. As for your eyes -- well, try balancing on one leg with your eyes closed. Now see how many seconds you can balance on one leg with your eyes open. Any conclusions?

MATERIALS: Chair; coin; wall.

DOING IT:

1. *Hopper:* Put your feet together, bend over, and grab hold of your toes with both hands. Can you hop forward? In order to hop, you have to lean forward to shift your centre of gravity ahead of your feet -- but you can't do this because you're hanging onto your toes.

2. *Stand Up:* Sit in a chair with your back straight, feet flat on the ground, and arms straight at your sides. Now try to stand up, using no hands and without leaning forward. It's not possible. Your centre of gravity is over the chair; to shift your centre of gravity over your feet -- which you need to do to get up -- you have to lean forward.

3. *Coin Sniff:* Kneel on the floor with your knees together. Put your arms on the floor in front of you, with your elbows against your knees. Put a coin on the floor at your outstretched fingertips. Kneel upright. While holding your hands behind your back, try to touch the coin with your nose. If you have a low centre of gravity, it should be easier for you to touch the coin.

4. *Leg Up:* Put your right arm and foot against a wall. Try to lift up your left leg. You won't be able to do it. To balance on your right foot, you have to shift your centre of gravity directly over that foot, which means leaning in that direction. Since you can't lean through the wall, you need your left foot on the ground to keep your balance.

5. *Extension:* Can you lift a chair by the bottom of one leg, while the chair is upright? Why is it so difficult?

> Your centre of gravity is the point around which your body weight is centred. All objects have a centre of gravity. For example, a pencil's centre of gravity is above the point at which you can balance the pencil perfectly on your finger. To stay balanced as you walk, you generally have to keep your centre of gravity over your feet (your body's support). Adult women's centre of gravity is usually in the hip area; their hips tend to be wider than men's. Adult men's centre of gravity is usually in the upper torso.
>
> **Topics:** Human Body; Forces.

FOOT = FIST

There's a reason that your foot is the size that it is. Your body parts are related to each other. Measure different parts to compare them.

QUICKIES

MATERIALS: Measuring tape.

DOING IT:

1. *Whole Body:* Outstretch your arms on either side of your body. Measure the distance from longest fingertip to longest fingertip. Now measure your height. The two measurements should be about the same. Your height should also equal about 6 to 7.5 times the length of your head (chin to top of head).

2. *Half Body:* Find the top of your thigh bone by bending over and putting your hands just below your hips. Sway from side to side and you should feel the top of the thigh bone stick out. Now measure from a point level with the top of your head to the top of your thigh bone. Measure from the top of the thigh bone to the bottom of your foot. The two measurements should be about the same.

3. *Foot:* Measure the distance around your closed fist. Measure the distance between your wrist and elbow. Measure the length of the inside of your foot, from the very end of your heel to the end of your big toe. All three measurements should be about the same.

4. *Elbow:* Measure the distance between your shoulder and your elbow and your elbow and your wrist. The two measurements should be about the same. When your arm is straight down at your side, your elbow should be at the same level as your navel.

Bones and muscles that you can see or feel are called "landmarks". Can you feel your jaw bone around your chin? Feel the tip of your elbow. Relax your leg and you can push around your knee cap. Stand on your toes and you can feel the muscles in the lower part of your legs. The tricep/bicep muscle team in your upper arm allows you to raise and lower your forearm. Pull in your "gluteus maximus" (your bottom) and you'll feel the very strong muscles that straighten the hip joint and hold you upright.

The sizes and locations of adult human body parts (children's body parts may vary more) are based on certain measurements and relationships. For example, your eyebrows are on the same level as the tops of your ears; the bottom of your ears line up with the base of your nose. Your eyes fall in the middle of your head -- between the tip of your head and the tip of your chin. Artists use body proportions to help them draw the human body so that it looks right.

Topics: Human Body; Measurement.

PERCUSSING

What can differences in sound tell you about the parts of your body? Try thumping in different spots to find out what's underneath.

MATERIALS: None.

DOING IT:

1. Place one hand flat, palm down, on a spot on your body. Strike the *tip* of the third finger of the hand with the third finger of your other hand. Practice until you get a good sound.

2. Try mapping your whole body according to sounds to get an idea of what's underneath. A *dull* sound indicates solid muscles (like on the thighs). A *hollow* sound indicates airy parts (like the stomach). A "resonate" or *ringing* sound indicates air and mass (like the ribs).

Ask someone to point to their stomach, and they'll often show off their intestines -- and their poor knowledge of anatomy. The stomach is actually between the ribs, above the waist.

The vibration of "vocal cords" in your throat enables you to make sounds. Long, thick cords make low sounds and short, thin cords make high sounds. Men's vocal cords are generally longer and thicker than women's, so men tend to have deeper, lower voices.

Percussing is the kind of thumping a doctor uses to examine a person's chest. It's rather like thumping a watermelon. If the watermelon is solid and juicy inside, you get a clear, ringing thump. If the melon is dried up, the thump sounds fuzzy. You can tell a great deal from a simple thump.

Topics: Human Body; Sound; Mapping.

OUT-OF-ORDER HANDS

You can make body parts do certain things because of a complex interrelationship between your muscles, nervous system, and brain. Fool your hands with these tricks.

QUICKIES

MATERIALS: None.

DOING IT:

1. *Mixed Up:* Have someone cross their wrists and arms and interlock their fingers as shown. Point to one of their fingers -- but make sure you don't touch the finger. The person won't be able to move the correct finger. What happens when you touch the finger instead of just pointing to it?

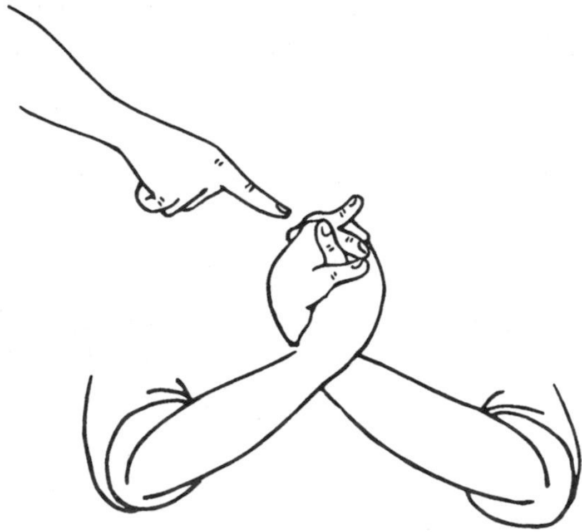

2. *Pressing Problem:* Ask someone to stretch both arms out straight in front of their body. Have the person put one fist on top of the other and press both fists together as hard as possible. Announce that you can separate the person's fists using only your fingertips. Quickly push sideways on the back of each fist. The person's hands will fly apart.

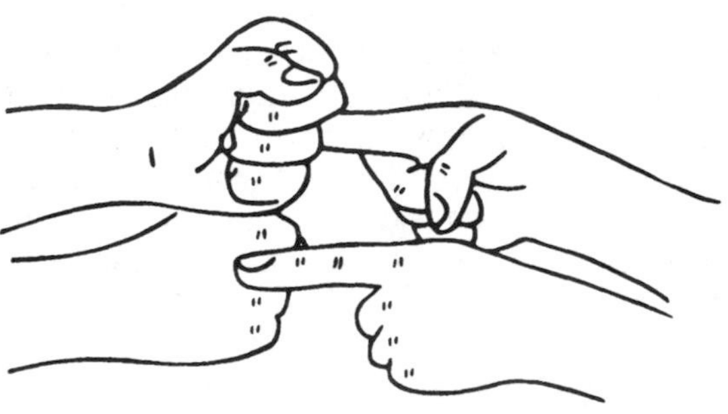

3. *Glued Finger:* Press the palm of your hand on a flat surface. Spread your fingers a bit. Pull your middle finger under your hand so that the first two joints are pressed against the surface. While all the other fingers are pressed against the surface, try lifting up one finger at a time. Why is your ring finger stuck?

In *Mixed Up,* when the wrists and arms are crossed, the normal relationship between fingers is changed. The brain gets confused by the information it receives from the eyes. When someone touches a finger, the brain receives a sensation from that finger and the finger can be lifted more readily. In *Pressing Problem,* a person has to concentrate all their force in an up-and-down direction to push their fists together. They also can't exert as much force sideways because there's nothing to push against. Therefore, the sides of the fists are most vulnerable to a surprise outside force. In *Glued Finger,* you can't lift up your ring finger because of the position of the middle finger. The bone and tissue structure of the ring and middle fingers are interrelated so that if the middle finger is immobilized, the ring finger is immobilized too.

Topics: Human Body; Brain; Forces.

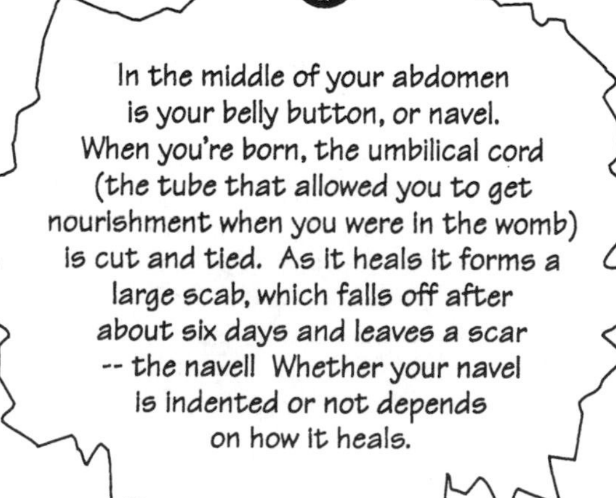

DUCK!

It takes time for information to get from one part of your body to another. You see a ball coming straight toward you. How quickly can you duck? Test your reaction time.

MATERIALS: Ruler; coin.

DOING IT:

1. *Ruler Drop:* Hold a ruler just above a partner's open thumb and index finger, with the lowest number on the ruler at the bottom. Drop the ruler without warning. At what number on the ruler does your partner catch the ruler? This number is a measure of reaction time. Who has the fastest reaction time (smallest number)? Does reaction time change when the cue is sound rather than sight? Have your partner close his or her eyes and wait for a sound you make (e.g. tongue click) just as you let the ruler go. How does reaction time change when the cue is touch? Have your partner close his or her eyes again. This time, touch his or her arm lightly with your finger just as you let go of the ruler. Does practice improve reaction time? Does the hand which is used make a difference? Make sure you always do the test in the same way: hold the ruler at the same distance above the fingers before you let it go; the fingers should always be the same distance apart (use the ruler's width to separate the fingers the same amount each time; then turn the ruler so that the flat part will be pinched)

2. *Coin Grab:* Hold one arm straight in front of you, palm down. Put a coin in the centre of the back of your hand. Slowly tilt your hand so the coin starts to slide off. Then quickly flip your hand around to catch the coin as it falls. How many times can you catch the coin in five attempts? Do you get better with practice? How does the reaction time of your left hand compare to your right hand?

3. *Slapper:* Start with one-hand slapper. Hold your right hand out (palm up) while your partner lightly rests his or her left hand (palm down) on your hand. The idea is for you to turn over your hand and slap the back of your partner's hand before he or she can remove his or her hand. After you've tested your right hand, try your left hand. When you've mastered one-hand slapper, try two-hand slapper (hold both hands palms up, while your partner covers them with his or her hands palms down). When you're doing either slapper test, *take off any rings or bracelets and don't slap too hard.*

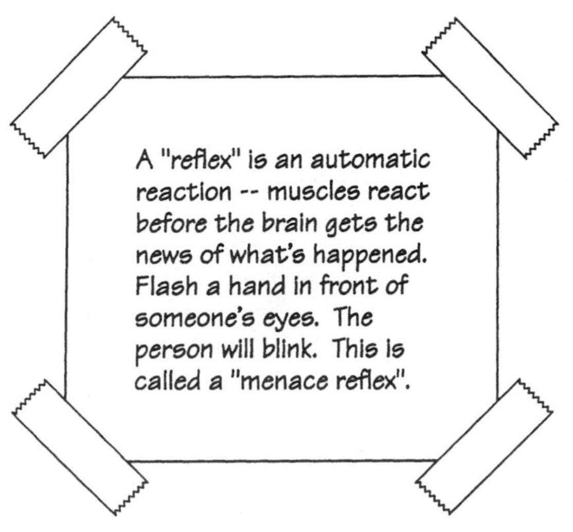

A "reflex" is an automatic reaction -- muscles react before the brain gets the news of what's happened. Flash a hand in front of someone's eyes. The person will blink. This is called a "menace reflex".

The time between when your body senses something (e.g. your eyes see a ball coming toward you and send the information to your brain) and when you actually act (e.g. your brain tells your body to bend and duck) is called "reaction time". Different people have different reaction times and, in general, young people have faster reaction times than older people. The sense signal to which people react also makes a difference to their reaction time. Most people can speed up their reaction time with practice.

Topics: Senses; Brain; Scientific Method.

TIRED MUSCLES

You've been running for a while and your legs just don't want to move any more. The muscles are tired. Try this simple fatigue test with your arm.

QUICKIES

MATERIALS: Watch which indicates seconds or stopwatch; table.

DOING IT:

1. Lay one arm on a table with the palm of your hand facing upward.

2. How many times can you make a fist in 30 seconds? Your hand must open *completely* and then form a *tight* fist each time.

3. Do the fatigue test three or four more times. Can you make the same number of fists each time? When does your arm begin to feel tired? Which muscles are fatigued?

The human body contains about 650 muscles. Some of them enable us to make conscious movements; others act automatically. "Fatigue" occurs when a muscle becomes tired. The muscle may feel strained, or it may not respond when you want it to. If a muscle gets fatigued very quickly, it may mean that it's not getting enough exercise. This activity tests the forearm muscles. Forearm muscles operate the fingers through "tendons" -- tough cords of dense connective tissue that attach muscle to bone.

Topics: Human Body.

How long a person sleeps is more a matter of body temperature and bedtime habits than how tired they are.

Hiccoughs are caused when your diaphragm -- a large muscle across your chest -- starts contracting in jerks, instead of moving smoothly up and down. To stop hiccoughs, you have to shock the diaphragm back to its normal movements. There's no sure-fire cure for hiccoughs, but some things that can work include a good scare, swallowing water while someone plugs your ears, eating a spoonful of crushed ice, sucking on a lemon, and holding your breath.

THE SPONGE

When you're stressed, your muscles are pulled tight. Stress can put a lot of wear and tear on the human body, so it's a good idea to learn how to relax.

QUICKIES

MATERIALS: None.

DOING IT:

1. Lie on your back on a flat surface. Close your eyes. Picture yourself as a sponge lying in a puddle on a hot, sunny day. Breathe slowly and deeply.

2. Start by thinking about your right foot. Curl the toes. Tighten the muscles. Point the right foot out, then up, then let it go loose.

3. Do the same thing with your left foot. Curl the toes. Tighten the muscles. Point your left foot out, up, and let it go loose.

4. Feel the muscles in your right leg. Tighten your right calf. Tighten your right thigh. Pull up your knee. Can you bring your knee to your chest? Let your leg go down straight again. Relax your whole right leg.

5. Feel the muscles in your left leg. Tighten your left calf. Tighten your left thigh. Pull up your knee. Can you bring your knee to your chest? Let your leg go down straight again. Relax your whole left leg.

6. Feel the lower part of your body going limp. Now turn your mind to the trunk of your body. Tighten your bottom, hold, and let go. Pull your stomach in as far as you can, hold, and let go. Arch your spine, pushing your chest out, and let go. Shrug your shoulders, then relax.

7. Now get in touch with your hands and arms beginning with your right side. Stretch out the fingers on your right hand. Make a fist. Let your right hand go. Tighten the muscles in your right forearm. Then let them go.

8. Do the same with your left side. Stretch out the fingers on your left hand. Make a fist. Let your left hand go. Tighten the muscles in your left forearm. Then let them go.

9. Now feel the muscles of your face. Smile. Purse your lips (as if you were going to kiss someone). Frown. Squeeze your eyes tightly shut and move your eyeballs in two complete circles. Then relax them. Yawn slowly.

10. Your whole body should feel relaxed. Let yourself float like a sponge that has soaked up water. Breathe in and out slowly four times. Feel your heart beat.

11. Take a deep breath and hold it as you raise your arms slowly over your head. Stretch like a cat. Breathe out. Shake loose. Stand up slowly.

> Stress is a major part of our lives and is caused by both pleasant and unpleasant events. The big key to relaxing is to concentrate on the insides, not the outsides. To get uptight muscles un-tight, you have to get better acquainted with your muscles. This exercise is based on the scientific fact that after you tighten up a muscle by squeezing it hard, it's easier to relax the muscle (to let it go completely limp). As the muscles relax one by one, your whole body feels less tense.
>
> **Topics:** Human Body; Human Behaviour.

FACIAL FUN

Did you know that it takes 34 muscles to frown (*really* frown) and only 13 to smile? Exercise your facial muscles with these expressions.

PULL YOUR SCALP BACK.

PULL YOUR SCALP DOWN.

OPEN YOUR MOUTH WIDE.

PULL YOUR EARS BACK.

PULL YOUR TOP LIP DOWN.

LIFT YOUR EARS.

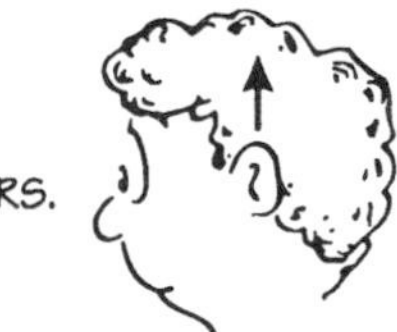

MAKE A BIG FROWN, THEN A BIG SMILE.

OPEN YOUR NOSTRILS.

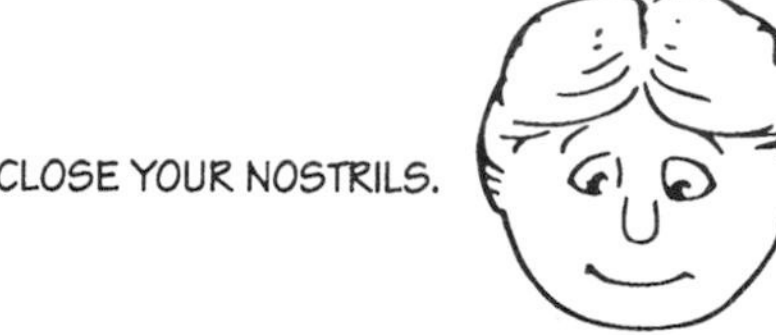

MATERIALS: None.

DOING IT:

1. Examine the facial muscle patterns and then try the exercises on this page. Which muscles do you use in each exercise?

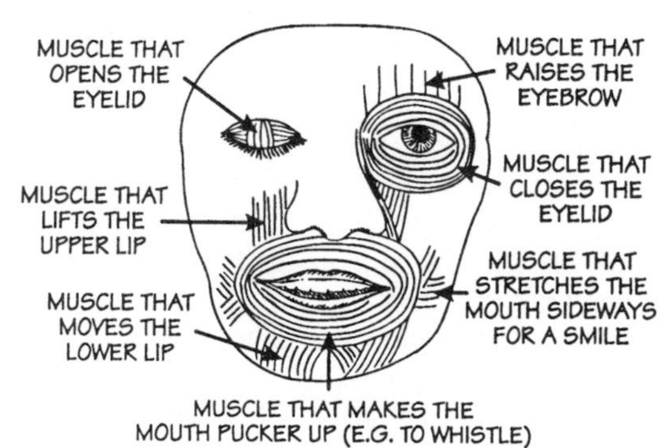

Human beings are capable of more changes of expression than any other animal on Earth. Anger, disappointment, grief, happiness are only a few of the emotions that our facial muscles help us to display. The human face is laced with dozens of small muscles. All muscles are made up of thousands of long, slender units called "muscle fibres". Groups of fibres are wrapped in bundles by thin connective tissue, and are well-supplied with blood vessels and nerves. If you don't exercise certain muscles, they become useless (e.g. most people have lost the ability to use their ear-wiggling muscles).

Topics: Human Body.

Guess The Emotion

They say a picture is worth a thousand words. Well, sometimes one expression is worth a thousand words! No words allowed in this emotion guessing game.

MATERIALS: Paper; pencil.

DOING IT:

1. Write down a number of emotions, one emotion per slip of paper. Examples of emotions: angry, happy, surprised, sad, disgusted, afraid, bored, in love, confused, embarrassed, impatient, nervous, stubborn, amazed, attentive. Include some similar emotions, like happy and ecstatic or bored and inattentive.

2. Talk about the kinds of feelings the words represent. Give examples. An example for the word "surprised" might be: "I can't believe I got a D on this test. I studied so hard." An example for the word "disgusted" might be: "Uck! There's mold growing on this bread."

3. Fold the slips of paper in half and in half again. Scramble them in a pile.

4. Each person chooses a slip of paper. One at a time, people must communicate their emotion to the rest of the group. They can use facial expressions, body movements, and sounds, but *no words.*

5. The group must guess the emotion being demonstrated. How long does it take before someone guesses the exact emotion? How different are people's perceptions of the emotion? What are the most difficult emotions to demonstrate? The easiest? Why?

As they age, women tend to get more wrinkles than men. That's because most men have a thicker "dermis" (the layer of skin just under the surface), which may stay elastic longer than a woman's.

Humans are capable of feeling and displaying a wide spectrum of emotions. Some emotions are so similar that it's amazing we actually look at them as separate emotions (what's the difference between being "pleased" and "happy"?). The ways in which we display emotions are as numerous as the emotions we feel. One of the most common ways of expressing emotions is through facial expressions. In addition to the types of and ways of expressing emotions, there are dozens of subjective responses to emotions. All people don't perceive the same emotion when they observe a person expressing an emotion. Also, different people have different ideas of what is meant by "pleased" or "stubborn" or the other labels we give emotions.

Topics: Human Behaviour; Communication.

JUST A MINUTE

As you interact with the world, you're aware of things that you can't see and touch, but are still real -- like emotions or time. How is your body aware of time?

QUICKIES

MATERIALS: Stopwatch or watch which indicates seconds; dictionary; storybook.

DOING IT:

1. *Second:* How long is one second? Try clapping your hands once. Wink quickly. Say "second" out loud. Take a deep breath. Each of these things takes about a second. What else takes one second?

2. *Minute:* How long is one minute? Put on your jacket and fasten it. Clap 60 times. Do 30 jumping jacks (one jumping jack is starting with your arms and legs out, bringing them in, and then taking them out again). Each of these things takes about a minute. What else takes one minute?

3. *Estimating:* Guess how long it will take to do certain things. How long does it take to say the words "how are you?" How long does it take to touch the ground and stand up ten times? How long does it take to write your full name? One person can look at a watch while the other person does a task.

4. *Guessing Time:* While someone looks at a watch, guess how long it takes for 30 seconds to pass. Try it several times. After each try, find out how long the actual length of time was. Do you get better at guessing the time? Come up with strategies for marking time (e.g. counting one lollipop . . . two lollipops . . . three lollipops . . . etc.).

5. *Relativity:* Read to someone from a dictionary -- a relatively boring pastime. Have them estimate when one minute is up. Then read from an interesting storybook. Have them estimate when one minute is up. Being bored seems to make time pass much more slowly. Being interested in something makes the time seem to pass much faster.

The perception of time is a function of the human mind. It's your brain that tells time, not the clock.

Your awareness of time involves a combination of several basic senses as well as what you've learned. Your senses of sight and smell can help you estimate how long a cake has been in the oven. Watching something happen can help you estimate how long it will take the next time.

Time is also related to the biological functioning of your body. "Circadian rhythms" are the daily cycles of living creatures. Your body has a daily pattern -- your heart beats slower at night, your body temperature falls when you sleep, blood pressure is lower in the morning than at night, and you can even catch a cold more easily at night because your immunity to infection is at its lowest. It's interesting to note that based on experiments that confined people to artificially-lighted rooms without clocks, the human internal day lasts 25 hours rather than 24. That's why it's easier for us to lengthen our days than to shorten them.

Topics: Senses; Measurement; Human Behaviour; Brain.

THE ENVIRONMENT

Environment to each must be
All that is
That isn't me.
Universe in turn must be
All that isn't me
And me.
(Buckminster Fuller)

Have you thanked a green plant today? Plants, animals and people all need each other. Green plants are the foundation of life. Only plants can make living organic matter from inorganic materials like water and minerals. Plants make the oxygen that people and animals breathe; people and animals exhale the carbon dioxide that plants need to live.

"Ecology" comes from a Greek word meaning "home". The "home" ecologists study is our big home -- Earth. Ecology involves looking at how living things interact with each other and with the physical environment.

Hide a variety of "unnatural" items (e.g. sock, coin, broom, pine cone in a maple tree) in a natural area like a neighbourhood park. People can then walk along the "unnature" trail to try to find all the items.

Our environment is changing. If you could travel back to the prairies 500 years ago, you would find them covered with many kinds of grasses, some shrubs, and few trees. There would also be a number of animals -- buffalo, coyotes, rabbits, prairie dogs, field mice, snakes, hawks and other birds, and loads of insects. Today, in the same area, you're likely to come upon acres of corn or wheat. Stretching as far as the eye can see, there's just one kind of plant. There are also far fewer animals.

Take one minute to look over a given area, like a field. Then, turn around and make a list of all the colours you remember seeing. When you've written down everything you can remember, re-examine the area to find at least two colours you don't have on your list (remember, there are many shades of green!).

QUICKIES

A Home Of Many Homes

Each living creature has its own home in some part of the world. Think about your home and how it fits into the larger environment of other homes.

QUICKIES

MATERIALS: Paper; pencils; small, natural objects (e.g. pine cone, snail shell, feather).

DOING IT:

1. *Your Home:* Where do you live? Draw a picture of your house, showing all the rooms. Now draw a picture of all the things around your house -- the other houses and buildings, the sidewalks, the roads, the trees, etc. Finally, draw a picture showing all the places you go in one week, like school, the shopping mall, the grocery store, the park, the sports field, etc. Use all three pictures together to describe where you live.

2. *Another Home:* Choose a wild creature that might live near you, like a bird, a worm, a squirrel, or a deer. Draw a picture of what that animal's home might look like. Use your imagination. Where would the home be located? What would the home be made of? What would it look like? What kind of food might the animal have in its home? Compare your home with the animal's home. What do you both need in or around your home? What parts of the environment do you share?

3. *Environment:* Everyone sits in a circle. Place a natural object in the middle of the circle. What would ordinarily "fill in" the spaces around the object? What would be right next to it? Right underneath it? Directly above it? Further away, but still around it? Describe living and nonliving surroundings (e.g. tree, air, city). Everyone takes a turn at describing one aspect of the surroundings, but each person's contribution must be something new. The idea is to build layers, or circles, from the focal point. Do the same thing with a second object; discuss the layers that overlap or are in common with the first object.

The environment is what's around you: human-built structures like houses and other buildings, but also plants, animals and their homes, the air you breathe, the water you drink, the land you walk on. How you describe your environment depends on how you want to look at things. For example, you can say that you live at 224 Maple Street; you can say you live in Canada; or you can say that you live on planet Earth. Being "environmentally aware" means really looking at, thinking about, and caring for the big environment, the world around you, rather than taking it for granted.

Topics: Environmental Awareness; Habitat.

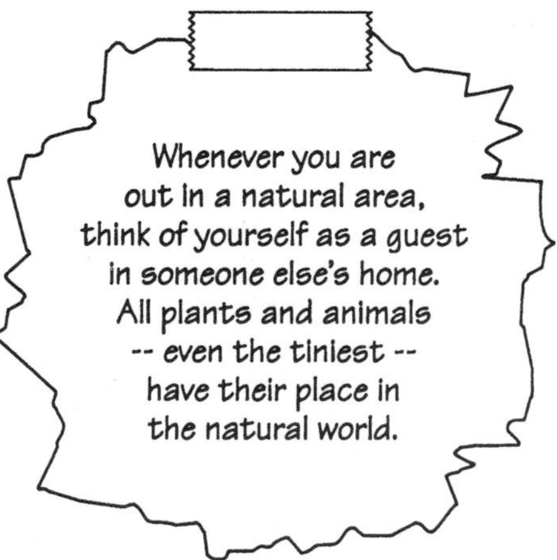

TAKE A WALK

Aside from being good exercise and guaranteed fun, these mini-walks are a great way to really look at and appreciate parts of the environment around you.

A QUESTION WALK

QUICKIES

MATERIALS: Optional -- paper and pencils.

DOING IT:

1. *Shape Walk:* Look for *natural* shapes. Find two of each of the following: circle, square, rectangle, triangle, ellipse, diamond.

2. *Colour Walk:* List as many colours as you can spot. Or, choose one colour and find objects of that colour. Distinguish between lighter and darker shades.

3. *Change Walk:* Make a list of all the changing things around you (e.g. bird landing, plant bending in breeze, twig breaking as you pass). Which changes aren't reversible?

4. *Question Walk:* Ask questions and don't worry about answers. The only "answer" allowed is another question. Questions must be about things on the walk. How many questions can people pose? What's the longest question chain (i.e. a question that leads to a related question) you can make? Example of a question chain: Do you see any living things on that stump? Does rotten wood hold water like a sponge? How many colours can you see on the stump? What animal does the stump look like? (If you want, you can talk about answers after the walk!)

5. *Stop, Look, and Listen Walk:* Walk for a certain number of steps. Stop for 30 seconds. Record all objects heard and seen. Repeat.

6. *Coin-Flip Walk:* To start the walk, flip a coin: heads go right, tails go left. Look for unusual or interesting objects. Stop to look at them closely. At each stopping point, flip the coin to determine a new direction.

7. *Tree Walk:* Pick up a leaf and show it to everyone. People must search for trees that have the same type of leaf.

8. *Centimetre Walk:* Identify things that are one centimetre long, wide, high, or around.

9. *Silent Walk:* Walk quietly, without speaking. Listen carefully. Make as little noise as possible to discover how many sounds you can hear.

10. *Up, Down, Around Walk:* While walking, look for objects from one field of view -- looking up or down, for example. On the next walk, change your view.

11. *ABC Walk:* Find living and nonliving things that begin with each letter of the alphabet. If certain letters are posing serious problems, people can use an adjective beginning with the required letter to describe an object.

12. *Backward Walk:* Turn around and walk while facing where you've been.

Do you know the ABCs of the environment? The environment has "abiotic" (A), "biotic" (B), and "cultural" (C) parts. Parts of the environment that are alive or were once alive are called biotic (from the Greek word for "life"). Some parts of the environment are not alive and have never been alive (e.g. sunlight, water, minerals). They are abiotic (the prefix "a" comes from the Greek word meaning "not"). Parts of the environment that are made by human beings or which have been changed from their original forms are cultural (a word that refers to everything humans think, do, say, or make).

Topics: Environmental Awareness; Senses.

PIECES OF THE PICTURE

The environment is made up of many parts that work together. Use these tricks to "zoom" in on certain parts of your environment.

MATERIALS: None. Optional -- binoculars.

DOING IT:

1. *Frame It:* Make a frame around certain parts of the environment. Bring together your slightly closed fists to make a tube, something like a telescope. Look through your hands with one eye. Look at *one* leaf or *one* flower petal or *one* rock. How do objects look different than they did before? Make a square frame using the index finger and thumb of each hand. Find objects that fill the square frame: a section of ground, a stump, or a tree trunk. Now hold the frame close to your eyes and sweep your hands across the landscape. If you were a painter or photographer, what views would you choose to paint or photograph?

There are times when you look around you and see the environment as one sweeping landscape. Other times, you look at only certain parts of the environment, like a flower or a tree or the shapes made by the clouds above you. Parts of the environment can be just as interesting -- sometimes even more interesting -- than all of the environment. Exploring the pieces also helps you to understand how they work together to make up the bigger picture.

Topics: Environmental Awareness.

2. *Zoom In and Out:* Start by looking at objects close by and then increase your view slowly. Close one eye and focus on the tip of your nose. Open your eye and shift your vision to something about 0.5 m in front of you. Now focus on an object 1 m away; then 10 m away; then 30 m away; and then 60 m away. Finally, focus on the horizon. Let your eyes wander all over the landscape. Sweep back and forth over the entire scene without stopping. Take your time. Then bring your eyes back, following the same steps as before, to the tip of your nose. You may want to try this using binoculars.

3. *Group It:* Look for ways to group objects. Find a comfortable place with a good view. Be aware of the amount of light around you. Look for shadows, textures, and colours. Which objects seem to go together? Can you see a square or circle or other shape if you look at how objects are located near each other? Based on common characteristics, name certain groups of objects. How many different ways can you group objects?

Try some environmental poetry. Find at least ten different colours and five different sounds in your immediate surroundings. Describe where you see the colours or hear the sounds in relation to yourself. The final poem can have any number of lines, as long as each line describes one colour or sound and tells the location in relation to the writer (e.g. green and blue water stretches in front of me; a few white clouds up high in the sky; the chirping of a bird in a tree near me).

IT DEPENDS HOW YOU LOOK AT IT

The world is one large environment, with smaller environments within it. Try these tricks to get a different perspective on natural environments.

MATERIALS: Small, natural objects (e.g. pine cone, snail shell, feather); small mirrors.

DOING IT:

1. What is the smallest environment you can think of? The largest? The darkest? The highest? The noisiest? The wettest? Can one environment be seen in many ways?

2. *Seeing It Differently:* Pass around a natural object. As each person receives the object, he or she must describe it in one or two sentences. Each person must describe the object *differently* from the people before him or her. Some people might look at the object from different angles. Others might talk about its colour, shape, smell, texture, or sound. Yet others might describe the object's role in the world or how it might feel if it had feelings.

3. *Perspectives:* Each person stands, sits, or lies in a different position or at a different angle to some natural object (e.g. stump, tree, large rock). People must then describe what the object looks like from their vantage point. How does the object look from different sides? From ground level? From a higher perspective? From far away? From very close up? People should rotate positions to get as many perspectives as possible.

Have you heard the story of the blind men and the elephant? One man felt the elephant's leg and pictured the elephant as a giant tree supported by a massive trunk. The blind man who felt the elephant's tail pictured the elephant as a small snake, while the man who felt the trunk pictured a long serpent. What each of the men "saw" depended on their perspective.

4. *Mirror Images:* Hold a mirror at waist level and walk around to examine the environment. What do you see in the mirror? How much of the environment can you see at one time? Do things seem different than normal? Why and how?

5. *Ant's-Eye View:* Lie down, face up, in tall grass or anywhere that the ground vegetation surrounds your body. Shut your eyes. Imagine that your fingers are an ant crawling across the ground. Feel along the ground with your fingers. Stretch out your arms and probe with your hands. Now open your eyes. Look up at people looking down at *you*. Turn your head to the side and peer out through the vegetation at ground level. How is an ant's environment different from yours?

An environment is anything that surrounds something else. A drop of pond water is a very small environment in the larger environment of the world. Other examples of environments include a flower pot, a tree, a city block, a campground, a river, and a country. The way you define an environment at any given time depends on your perspective, attitude, interests, and needs. Different people perceiving environments differently is one cause of pollution. For example, polluters might not worry about contaminating a stream because they don't get their drinking water from the stream; they don't see the stream as a part of their environment. Perhaps one solution to our environmental problems is to encourage people to see as many perspectives as possible.

Topics: Environmental Awareness; Decision-Making.

QUICKIES

MICRO-TRAIL

A full-scale nature trail is fun because of the interesting things to look at along the way. Make your own micro-trail to explore a small part of the environment.

QUICKIES

MATERIALS: Pieces of string 1-2 m long. Optional -- magnifying glasses.

DOING IT:

1. Everyone gets a piece of string. If possible, have several magnifying glasses available. Magnifying glasses enhance a micro-trail because they make things look larger and more impressive.

2. Each person has about ten minutes to create their own micro-trail, using the string to mark the trail. What living things can you find along the trail? How do you know they are living? Do you see any plants? Any worms? Any insects? How many do you see? What nonliving things can you find along the trail? How do you know they aren't alive? Can you find an interesting rock or clump of soil? Trails can be marked based on a certain theme (e.g. colours of flowers, different textures, insect homes).

3. When the time is up, each person takes a turn leading the others along his or her trail and pointing out interesting features.

Small living -- and nonliving -- things may be more important than you think. There are so many different life forms that no one knows for sure what each does -- or how important it may be. All life is connected in delicate balances called "ecosystems". The interaction of biotic (living) and abiotic (nonliving) components creates an ecosystem. The interacting components within an ecosystem are so tightly knit that even if only one relationship is broken, the entire ecosystem may be threatened. All life exists within a thin shell of air, water, and soil called the "biosphere". The biosphere is Earth's life-support system, or the parent ecosystem.

Topics: Environmental Awareness; Ecosystems.

Wood Buffalo National Park in the Northwest Territories, Canada, is the world's largest national park at 44,804 sq. km. Some of the world's highest tides occur at Fundy National Park in New Brunswick, Canada. Mount Everest in Nepal/China is the world's highest mountain at 8,848 m. The Nile River in Africa is the world's longest river at 6,671 km. And the biggest island in the world is Greenland at 2,175,600 sq. km.

SMALL PLACES

Some creatures are so small that the only environment they know is what falls in the few centimetres around them. Explore some small environments.

QUICKIES

MATERIALS: None.

DOING IT:

1. *Life Under a Rock:* Find a rock -- large or small -- and carefully flip it over. Do any animals scurry out as you lift up the rock? Where do they go? What other animals do you find on or in the ground? What types of plants live under the rock? Are there plants rooted under the rock, but growing around it? What is the soil like under a rock? What does the underside of the rock look like? Why? Is there any life on the rock's surface? Put the rock back, *exactly as it was*, when you've finished looking underneath.

2. *Life in a Rotting Log:* Find a rotting log and look it over carefully. Look on the outside of the log for fungi and mosses; you may also find small seedlings of trees and wild flowers growing in decaying spots. Are there any animals inside? You may find a few insects on the outside of the log, but most live inside. Look for evidence of animal activity such as insect holes, woodpecker holes, or animal tracks. Pull away a strip of loose bark. Use a small stick to dig into the rotting wood. You'll probably find passageways and tunnels of all kinds. Examine the different degrees of rotting along the log. Some parts of the log may crumble away at a touch, while other parts will still be firm. Look underneath the log for parts that are already changing to soil. Can you dig to find earthworms? When you've finished your exploration, *return the log to its original condition.*

What makes
something good or bad,
happy or sad?
Find a happy object,
like a brightly-coloured flower.
Find a sad object,
like a dying plant.
Think of ways to make
a sad thing happy.
For example, you could make
a dying, thirsty plant happy
by watering it.

There can be all sorts of things going on under a rock. And a rotting log is far from dead. The kinds of living things you find under a rock or in a rotting log depend on location and time of year; living things in a rotting log also depend on what kind of tree it was and how long the log has been decaying. In general, small animals found under rocks and in rotting logs include ants, millipedes, centipedes, slugs, caterpillars, spiders, beetles of all kinds, and sow bugs (they can roll into a pill-like ball, so look carefully). Larger animals found in rotting logs include mice, chipmunks, rabbits, or perhaps a snake. Small mammals often make homes inside logs.

Topics: Habitat; Insects.

NATURE CHARADES

What is it like to be a tree? How does a baby animal feel? Get an understanding of different parts of the environment by pretending that you *are* those parts.

MATERIALS: None.

DOING IT:

1. *Natural Objects:* Choose a plant, rock, or other natural object and pretend you are that object. Move like the object and show what kind of feelings it might have. Try simple things first (e.g. leaf, tree). Then graduate to more difficult things (e.g. avalanche, waterfall). Can people guess what you are?

2. *Baby Animals:* Act out the story of a baby animal (e.g. squirrel, bird, raccoon), using no words. Pretend the baby animal is discovering the world for the first time through the use of its senses. After a period of time, other people try to guess which animal you are portraying.

3. *Present Event:* Mimic an event occurring in the environment around you, at that moment (e.g. a tree blowing in the wind, a bird building a nest, an insect crawling on a flower). Act out the event, using no words. People must not only guess the event, but must find the real event in the environment.

The age-old game of guessing what another person is acting out has the benefit of involving everyone. The actor must have an awareness of the environment in order to play the role, while spectators must notice details and patterns in order to guess the charade.

Topics: Environmental Awareness; Communication.

Some living creatures take up more room than others. People are a lot larger than ants. Some living creatures use more resources than others. One person needs much more food than one ant does. And one person produces a lot more waste than one ant does. Populations that are the wrong size for their environments are often the result -- and the cause -- of environmental problems.

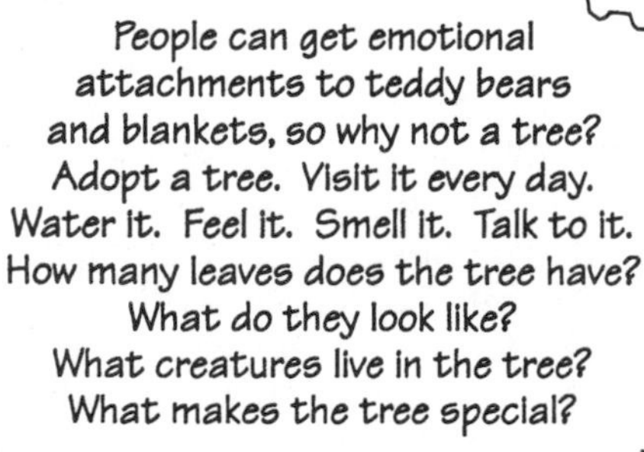

ROCKS

About 6 m below the surface of the Earth the seasons are reversed. For example, underground in the northern hemisphere it's coldest in June and warmest in January. That's because the underground rock is slow to change temperature. The cold of winter doesn't add up until early summer, and the effect of hot weather doesn't show until the air is cold again.

Some sand grains are magnetic, particularly black grains. Hold a magnet close to the sand on a beach and see how many magnetic grains you can find. These grains may be "micrometeorites" (tiny, dust-like particles of matter) from space. Billions of micrometeorites have fallen to Earth. They are most often particles of iron and nickel.

When you look at the ground around you, the most common thing you see is soil. It's easy to forget that Earth is made of rock which is relatively solid. The soil is only a thin blanket covering the "bedrock". Places where the bedrock is visible through the soil are called "outcrops".

Throughout history rocks have been used as tools, as weapons, and as materials for building shelter and monuments. Rocks were first used as tools over one million years ago. The Stone Age is divided into the "Palaeolithic", or Old Stone Age, and the "Neolithic", or New Stone Age. During the Old Stone Age, crude, fist-sized tools were formed when a person split one stone with another. Very basic spears, chipping tools, gougers, and cutters were also made. With the New Stone Age came polished stone implements; polishing was achieved by "percussion" -- striking one object with another -- or abrasion with sand.

Quartz and feldspar together make up about 90% of the Earth's crust (outer layer of the Earth).

Everyone knows you can make paperweights with rocks. Put your imagination to work for other rock creations. How about a "rock group"? You need a large stone (lead singer) and lots of small pebbles (back-up singers). Paint the stones, glue on little eyes, and/or add hair. Glue the small stones to the sides of the large one and then name your band. For a more functional work of art, decorate a stone -- or use several stones to create a ladybug, owl, butterfly, or other animal -- and glue a small magnet on the back. Use the decorated magnet to stick notes onto the refrigerator.

THE BIG C

What makes a rock a rock? What makes one rock different from another rock? This challenging classification game illustrates how small details can make a big difference.

MATERIALS: Dozens of rocks (a variety of different sizes, shapes, and types); several rock-sized objects, some of which are similar to rocks (e.g. pottery shards, pieces of cement, bits of brick, bits of sponge, paper clips, seeds); container of water; bag.

DOING IT:

1. Put together a pile of objects; most of the objects should be rocks, but a few nonrocks should be included in the pile. What is a "rock"? Which objects in the pile are rocks? Why are they rocks? How is a rock different from a seed or a paper clip or a piece of brick?

2. Choose a rock from the pile. Get to know your rock. How does it feel? How many sides does it have? What colour is it? Does it have any marks on it? How does it smell? What happens to it when it gets wet? Is it heavy or light? Will it float?

3. Everyone puts their rock into a bag. Mix up all the rocks. Each person must then find his or her rock. How easy is it to find a particular rock? What clues can be used? How is one rock different from another rock? Are some differences more important than others?

4. Organize all the rocks into different groups based on certain characteristics. For example, begin by classifying rocks by size. Then divide each group of similar-sized rocks into subgroups of different colours. Try classifying the rocks again, but this time start by dividing them by colour and then by size. Are the groups different than they were after the first classification process? Classify the rocks in other ways (e.g. by shape or smoothness).

To "classify" objects is to arrange them into groups. Classification involves comparison, description, and development of subsets. It helps people order and therefore better understand the world around them. Can you imagine what a library would be like if the books were just scattered all over, rather than being classified into categories on the shelves? Classifying objects like rocks is a stepping stone to classifying living things, like plants and animals (which are often quite difficult to classify). By grouping things which are similar, and then comparing groups and noting differences, we can better understand the relationships between objects, between living organisms, and between living and nonliving things.

Topics: Classification; Senses.

SPACES

A gravel road might look like a solid layer of rocks, but rocks don't fit together perfectly and there's usually plenty of space between them. Estimate the space between rocks.

QUICKIES

MATERIALS: Clear glass or plastic jar; cup; water; rocks; sand; paper; pencil. Optional -- different sizes and shapes of rocks; tape.

DOING IT:

1. Take a clean, empty jar and fill it with water, one cupful at a time. How many cupfuls of water fit into the jar? Write this number down.

2. Fill a jar to the brim with clean, dry pebbles. Is the jar "full"? Estimate the amount of space, in all, between the pebbles. Is there half a jarful of space? A third? A tenth?

3. Check the accuracy of your guess. Pour water into the jar a cupful at a time. The water will fill the spaces between the pebbles. How many cupfuls of water fit into the jar (shake out any trapped air bubbles)? Compare this number to the number of cupfuls of water that fit into the empty jar. The amount of space between pebbles can be expressed as a fraction, such as 3/10 (there are 3 cups of space between pebbles in a jar that holds 10 cups when empty). How close was your estimate?

4. Now fill the jar with sand. Is the jar "full"? How many cupfuls of water fit into the jar? Do rocks or sand leave more space?

5. *Variation:* Try different sizes of rocks, rocks that have sharp edges, and rocks that are more rounded. What shape and size of rocks leave the most space?

6. *Variation:* Another way to measure the space in a jar is to hold the pebbles tightly in the jar, turn the jar over, and lower it straight down into some water. Let the pebbles fall out gradually, so that all the air between them stays in the jar. Mark the volume of this air with a strip of tape at the exact water level (stick the tape down while holding the jar so that the water level is the same inside as out). Then lift the jar out and fill it with water up to the mark. The water has the same volume as the air that stayed in the jar when the pebbles fell out. It shows how much space there was between the dry pebbles.

If you look closely at gravel or sand, you can see the spaces between the individual stones or grains. Sometimes sand and gravel appear solid. Minerals cement together the individual pieces; sand hardens into "sandstone" and gravel forms a "conglomerate". But even the sandstone and the conglomerate have spaces within them. These spaces are very important. Water from rain and snow soaks into the spaces. Deep within the ground, the spaces are usually completely filled with huge amounts of water. Countless wells get their water from water-saturated sand or gravel. In some places, the spaces hold natural gas and petroleum.

Topics: Measurement; Soil; Air.

ONE BIG MAGNET

The Earth acts like a giant magnet. Use a model Earth and a compass to explore the biggest magnet of them all.

MATERIALS: Grapefruit or large orange; bar magnet; toothpicks; compass.

DOING IT:

1. Stick a bar magnet through a grapefruit or orange. The ends of the magnet should be visible. The fruit represents Earth, and the bar magnet represents the magnetic north and south poles. Toothpicks near the magnetic poles can represent geographic north and south.

2. Bring a compass near the "Earth". The compass will point to the north and south "poles".

3. When you take a compass outdoors, the compass will point to the real magnetic north and south poles.

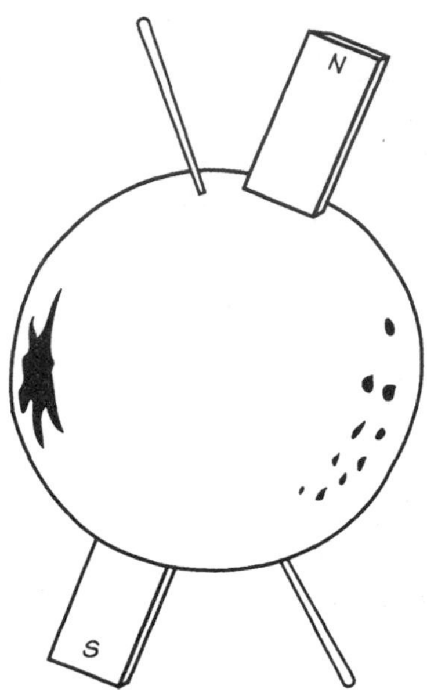

The Earth has a north pole and a south pole, just as a magnet has a north pole and a south pole. The Earth's magnetic field exerts an influence on all compasses, causing them to line up in the direction of the field -- in a generally north-south direction. What's the source of the Earth's magnetism? The current theory is that the Earth's core is made up of a giant iron-nickel sphere. The outer part of the core is like a thick pudding. The flow of this thick liquid around the inner, solid part of the core generates an electric current. The electric current generates a magnetic field.

The north and south magnetic poles shouldn't be confused with the north and south geographic poles. The geographic poles fall on the axis on which the Earth turns. The geographic and magnetic poles are about 1600 km apart in the north and about 2400 km apart in the south. When a compass points north it doesn't point to geographic north, toward the North Star. Charts must be made for navigators that show the angular variation between geographic (true) north and magnetic north (the direction toward which a compass points). These charts must be periodically changed, as the magnetic poles are slowly but continually shifting.

Topics: Magnetism; Earth; Mapping; Stars.

Northern (aurora borealis) and southern (aurora australis) lights consist of beautiful bands of colour high in the sky. Scientists believe auroras are caused by solar particles hitting the Earth's atmosphere. The particles are attracted to the north and south by the pull of the Earth's magnetic poles. Low-energy solar particles come to about 240 km above the Earth's surface; when they hit oxygen atoms a red light is produced. High-energy particles can come as low as 80 km; they strike oxygen atoms much harder and a pale green light is given off. From the Earth, the auroras look like rippling arcs and sheets of light; satellites have taken photos from above the Earth that show each of the planet's magnetic poles crowned with a halo of light.

PLANTS

Plants have many functions. They produce oxygen, absorb carbon dioxide, increase underground water resources, filter out dust, act as windbreaks, moderate temperature, reduce noise, cover and protect soil, provide shade, provide food and shelter for wildlife, provide food for humans, provide wood and paper, provide fibres for clothes and other products, and create natural beauty.

Just the slightest touch will make the mimosa plant play dead by drooping all its leaves.

Make puzzles out of branches that have fallen from trees naturally or during pruning. Saw a branch into four or five pieces. In order to realign the pieces, you must use both bark and ring formations as clues. You can also make mini-puzzles using twigs.

The trees, flowers, bushes, and grass around you are constantly growing. "Adopt" a plant to watch for a couple of minutes each day. Focus on something that will grow and change fairly obviously (e.g. flower, young bud). Write down how the plant looks on the first day. Look at its physical characteristics (e.g. size, leaf shape, colour). Count the number of leaves, branches, shoots, etc. Each day, add a little more information to the plant's description. Measure any growth that occurs. How does the plant change?

Most people are amazed when they realize all the wild plants they can eat. The very young leaves of dandelions are great as salad greens or as cooked greens. The new, leafy stems and young shoots of milkweed are good as cooked vegetables. But before you get into edible plants, learn which plants and plant parts are poisonous. For example, the petiole on the rhubarb is edible, but the leaf is poisonous.

Act out how a plant might look and feel in a gentle breeze, in a violent windstorm, in a gentle rain, in a hard rainstorm with thunder and lightning, in a snowstorm, in a forest fire, when a person is planting it, and when a person is harvesting it. How would a small flower's reactions and feelings be different from a large tree's? How do you think a tree might feel when a squirrel is running up its trunk, a bird is nesting in its branches, a person is climbing it, or a person is carving on the tree's bark?

DANDELION SEED IN A VIOLENT WINDSTORM

QUICKIES

DESCRIBE-A-PLANT

Plants have certain parts and characteristics that make them plants. The object of this game is to provide written clues so that others can find a specific plant.

QUICKIES

It's an unlucky fly that lands on an open leaf of a Venus flytrap. If three fine hairs in the centre of the trap are touched, the trap snaps shut. The plant squeezes the fly to death, secretes digestive juices, and digests the fly.

MATERIALS: Paper; pencils. Optional -- plant identification guide.

DOING IT:

1. While everyone else keeps their eyes closed or completes a certain task, one person chooses a "secret" plant and writes a description. The group must then find the *specific* plant using only the written clue. Or, people can work with partners; partners exchange plant clues and try to find each other's secret plant.

2. For each secret plant, closely examine the plant for a couple of minutes before writing a description. What makes the plant unique? For example, does it have a very colourful flower or a leaf with strange markings? Write as detailed a description as possible. Always include a hint on where the specific plant grows to help people find the plant's general location.

3. For the first few secret plants, describe the plants in terms of one part only (e.g. the stem, or the leaves). How easy is it to find a specific plant when only one of its characteristics has been described? How many plants fit the description?

4. As the game progresses, describe more parts and characteristics of the secret plants. Is it easier to find a plant when more parts are described?

5. How do different parts of plants differ? For example, how can you tell a flower from a leaf? How are parts of different plants similar? For example, even though the leaves might be a different shape, how do you know the leaves on two different plants *are* leaves?

How can you tell that a plant is a plant? It has certain parts and characteristics unique to plants. How can you tell one plant from another? You can look at how plant parts vary from plant to plant. Most plants are green. They have roots, a stem (or stalk or trunk), leaves, and many have flowers and seeds. The stem and roots can be seen as the key parts of a plant; leaves and flowers can be thought of as stem growths or shoots, with special jobs to do.

Topics: Classification; Plant Parts; Communication.

How's your plant anatomy? Do you know from what part of the plant we get certain foods? Spinach, lettuce, and cabbage are leaves. Broccoli and cauliflower are flowers. Asparagus is a stem. Potatoes are underground stems. Carrots, radishes, turnips, and beets are roots. Apples, corn, cucumbers, green peppers, and pineapples are fruits. Peanuts, walnuts, popcorn, peas, wheat, and rice are seeds. Onion and garlic are bulbs (underground stem and leaves).

Natural Elastic

You may think of trees when you think about sap, but sap is a fluid -- mainly water -- found in most green plants. Make an elastic band using sap.

MATERIALS: Sap.

DOING IT:

1. Never collect sap from trees because you may damage the trees. Suitable sap can be collected from milkweed plants and dandelions. If you break the stems or leaves of these plants, you should be able to squeeze out a fair bit of sap. You'll need just a few millilitres of sap.

2. Coat the end of your finger with sap, to just above the first knuckle.

3. Let the sap dry for several minutes until it is colourless.

4. Gently roll the rubbery substance off your finger, like rolling off a sock. Once you roll off the sap, you'll have a tiny elastic band. Stretch the band and it will act like any other elastic band -- but don't stretch too much or it will break.

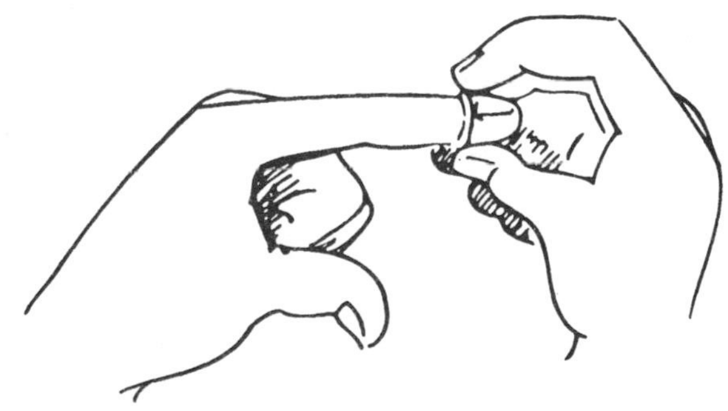

5. *Extension:* Compare elastic bands made from the sap of different plants. Which plants work and which ones don't? Why?

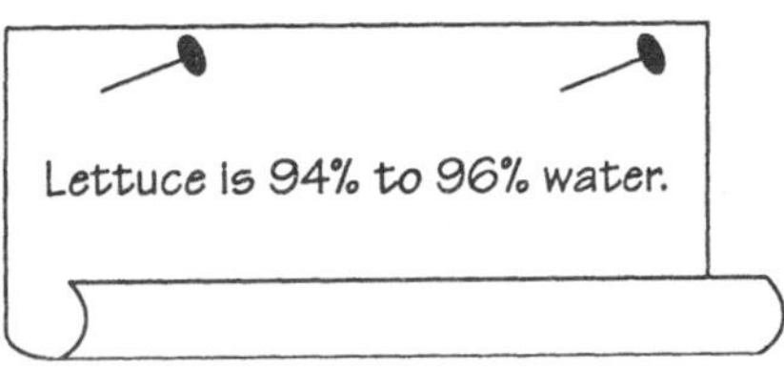

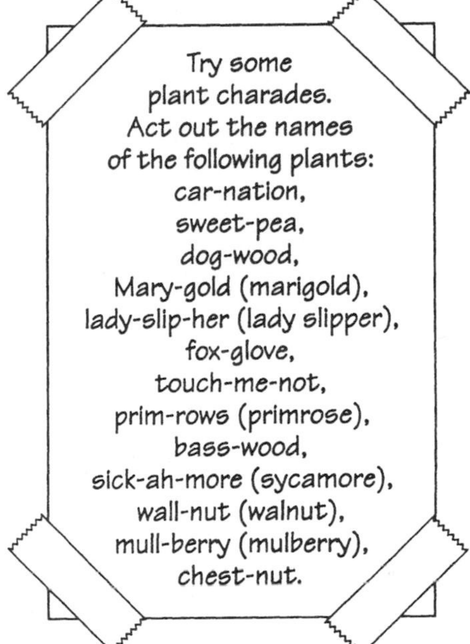

During the spring and summer months, trees take up water and nutrients from the soil through their roots. The water and nutrients are transported through the plant to the leaves. In the leaves, photosynthesis takes place and a sugary food is produced. The sugar manufactured in the leaves is then dissolved in water. Sap flows through the tree, nourishing the tree just as blood running through the human body feeds the body's cells. In autumn, the sugary sap moves from the leaves (where it would be lost once the leaves drop off) and is stored in the roots and trunk (where it becomes starchy). The tree is dormant during the winter, but in early spring the starch becomes sugar again and resumes its travels in the sap to aid in opening buds and producing new leaves. This is the time when, if the tree is a sugar maple, the trunk can be tapped and the sap collected and boiled to produce maple syrup and sugar. In this activity, sap seems to "turn into" a rubber-like material. Actually, the rubbery substance is present all the time; it's in tiny pieces, which are suspended in the watery sap. As the water evaporates, the tiny pieces come together in long strands.

Topics: Plant Parts; Plant Processes.

WHODUNIT?

Taking a scientific approach to answering a question often involves acting like a detective in a mystery story. Next time you spot a dead plant, find its "killer".

QUICKIES

MATERIALS: Magnifying glass.

DOING IT:

1. Find a dead or dying plant. For example, an old tree may still be standing, but may not have any leaves or other signs of life. The top of a tree's trunk may be dead. Perhaps there are dead limbs near the base of a group of trees.

2. Make a guess about why the plant died or is sick. Possible causes of death and sickness include old age, lack of water, strong winds, insects, wildlife, disease, and human activity. For example, certain weeds in a large patch of plants may be dry and brown because they have been overgrown by larger plants or because weed killer has recently been sprayed in the area. Plants near a nature trail may be yellow and bent because humans have trampled them or because they are not getting enough water to maintain their green colour.

3. Find some evidence to support your guess. If you think a tree died of old age, look for dried bark or count the rings on its stump or the stumps of similar trees nearby. If you think humans are trampling plants, observe the area for a while to spot people stepping on the plants. Use a magnifying glass to make close examinations for insects and insect holes.

4. First guesses may be incorrect. A healthy, mature tree may not be dying, but may simply be losing its bottom, shaded branches by natural pruning. Is there more than one possible cause of death or sickness for a given plant?

"Whodunit", mystery shows generally take a very scientific approach to solving the mystery. The show usually starts with a problem: A person is dead. Then the hero, a detective, looks the situation over and makes a guess -- formulates a hypothesis -- to explain the situation: What was the cause of death? Murder! How was the murder committed -- gun shot? poisoning? strangulation? The rest of the show follows the detective as he or she gathers evidence to support the hypothesis. The detective looks for motive, opportunity, and means such as a murder weapon. Finally, the investigation concludes by finding the murderer. Follow the same series of steps to find the killers of dead or dying plants.

Topics: Scientific Method; Plant Processes; Pollution.

Look for a damaged tree. How does the tree heal itself? What causes sap to run from a cut in the bark or, in the case of a pine tree, globs of pitch to form? How does the healing process compare to the scab that forms when you cut your finger?

STUMPED

A tree stump can tell you about a tree's insides, the past climate, and the tree's age when it was cut. Estimate a tree's age by counting the rings in the stump.

MATERIALS: Tree stump; pins.

DOING IT:

1. Examine a tree stump and count the dark rings. Mark every tenth ring with a pin to make counting easier.

2. If one ring was formed each summer, how old was the tree when it was cut? If you know when the tree was cut down, you can figure out when it began to grow. How old was the tree when you were born? How big was it when it was as old as you are now?

3. Was the tree's growth the same each year? If not, in which years did the tree make good growth? In which years did it make poor growth? What causes differences in the thickness of the layers? Was the tree growing evenly in all directions? If not, why do you think it grew more on one side than the other?

4. *Extension:* From the stump, can you tell in which direction the tree fell when it was cut?

5. *Extension:* If possible, count the number of layers in several sections of a cut-up tree trunk and branches. Why is the number of layers so different from place to place?

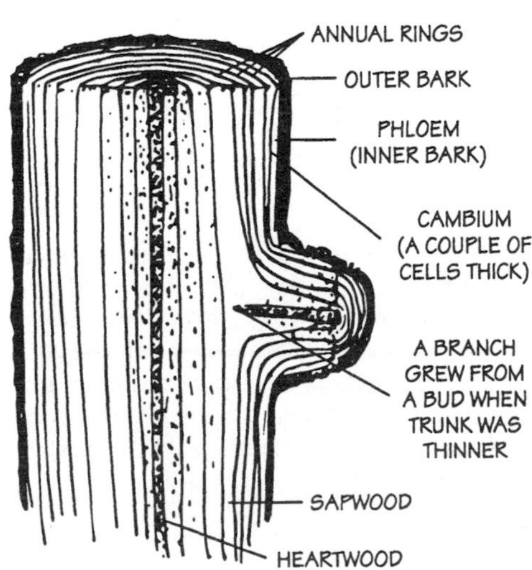

Some trees (e.g. oak, yew) live to 500 or 600 years. The oldest living things on Earth -- 4,500 years old -- are bristlecone pines in the American west.

The rings in tree stumps and logs are really the edges of layers of wood. A new layer forms each year, surrounding all that came before it. For each year of a tree's life, there's one light and one dark band, together called an "annual ring". In the spring, a tree grows quickly and produces the light-coloured wood. During the summer, when the tree grows more slowly, the wood is darker. Counting the concentric circles in a stump provides only an estimate of a tree's age. A more accurate name for the annual ring is growth ring, because it's possible for more than one ring to form in a year. This may happen when a very cold spell occurs during the summer. In tropical countries where conditions are favourable for growth all year round, there are no growth rings at all. Tree rings can also provide a lot of information about past climate. Their width, density and other features tell how the climate changed from year to year. For example, a year of low temperatures or rainfall causes a narrow ring.

The part of a tree's trunk and branches you can see from the outside is the "outer bark". It is a tough, protective covering for the tree. The "phloem", or inner bark, carries sap from the tree's leaves to the branches, trunk, and roots. If this bark is stripped away, the tree can die. Beneath the phloem is the "cambium" layer, about two cells thick. Each year, the cambium grows new phloem to the outside, new cambium itself, and "sapwood" to the inside. The sapwood, whitish in colour, carries nutrients and water up from the roots to the rest of the tree. Some parts of the sapwood can move stored water and nutrients horizontally to other parts of the tree. The central, darker part of a tree, the "heartwood", is the oldest part. It is dead sapwood; it can no longer transport water and nutrients up from the roots. The heartwood mainly provides support for the tree.

Topics: Plant Parts; Plant Processes; Measurement.

Grass Whistle

Grasses are hardy plants able to withstand the challenges of weather and wildlife. Whistle a happy tune while examining different kinds of grasses.

QUICKIES

Look at plants that have spiral patterns (e.g. leaves arranged in a spiral up a plant stem, petals on flowers like the rose, bracts on pine cones). Follow a spiral around until you have counted the leaves, petals, or bracts in one complete loop. Continue to the next loop (be careful, because some plants have loops that go in opposite directions) and then the next until you've looked at all the loops. You'll usually get a series something like: 1, 1, 2, 3, 5, 8, 13, 21, ... What's the next number in the series? Each of the numbers, beginning with the number 2, is the sum of the preceding two numbers. No one knows yet why this pattern occurs.

Many of the plants people commonly refer to as "grasses" may be sedges or rushes. Generally, grasses prefer dry areas while rushes and sedges prefer wet areas. Grasses have jointed stems. Pluck a blade and it will break at the joint. Grasses have a thick mat of roots. In most plants, the growing goes on at the tip of the plant's shoots. When the top of such a plant is eaten or cut off, it takes a long time for the plant to recover. In grass plants, however, the growing goes on at the base. When the top is cut off, the plant keeps right on growing. Most members of the grass family (e.g. wheat, rice, corn, oats, barley, rye) produce grains that are a vital food source.

"Sedges" have triangular stems near the base. Most species of sedges grow in wetlands. "Rushes" have round, hollow stems. Flowers appear near the tip of the stem. Rushes grow in wetter sections of marshes. And then there's the word "reed". Reed is a common name that generally refers to thick, tall grasses. One of the most typical reeds is reed grass, which grows in coastal and freshwater wetlands around urban areas.

Topics: Plant Parts; Sound.

MATERIALS: Grass. Optional -- measuring tape.

DOING IT:

1. One of the best ways to appreciate grass is to *do* something with it. Since mowing the lawn isn't most people's idea of fun, look for different kinds of grass to make grass whistles. Choose a blade of grass about 15 cm long.

2. Hold the blade of grass between your thumbs, as shown. The edge of the blade should face you.

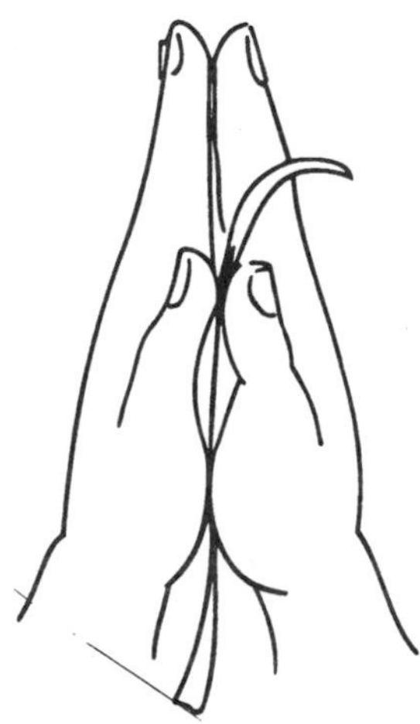

Your hands should come together in two key places: at the top of the thumbs and at the ball of the hand below each thumb. Make sure the blade of grass is locked in at these two points; keep the blade as rigid as possible. It doesn't matter how you hold the rest of your fingers.

3. Now blow steadily through your thumbs -- not too strong, not too weak. Practice until you get a smooth, confident sound. Adjust the tension on the blade of grass to get slightly different sounds. Do certain grasses make better whistles? How many different grasses can you find?

4. *Extension:* As you hunt for grasses, measure their height. What's the tallest grass you can find? Where does it grow?

LIVING CREATURES

An "animal" is any living organism -- including mammals, birds, insects, fish, reptiles, and amphibians -- other than a plant. "Wildlife" refers to animals that are not tamed or domesticated; the animals live in natural habitats and find their own food and shelter.

Some birds, like turkeys and chickens, swallow small stones. They have an organ called a "gizzard" which acts as a second stomach, holding the stones. The rocks in the gizzard help grind up food so that it can be digested. The African crocodile eats rocks too -- but for a completely different reason. Since the crocodile spends so much time in the water, it swallows stones as a way of keeping its balance when swimming.

Insects outnumber all other living creatures on Earth combined. They make up more than 80% of Earth's animals.

The tallest land mammal is the giraffe, which may stand 6 m high. The giraffe's long neck helps it reach leaves and other food high in treetops.

The blue whale is the largest animal in the world. It may grow to a length of 30 m and weigh more than 135 tonnes. The largest land animal is the African elephant, which may stand more than 3.2 m tall at the shoulder and weigh more than 6 tonnes.

Some people think owls look wise because of their wide-open eyes. But for a bird its size, the owl has a tiny brain. On the bird intelligence scale, the owl would likely fall somewhere in the middle. Laboratory experiments have found that geese, crows, and ravens are "smarter" than owls.

The strange-looking swellings you often see on plants are called "galls". Many common galls are caused by insects. A female insect lays her eggs in a plant. When an egg hatches, the "larva" (young insect) that comes out secretes a special chemical that causes the plant part to grow in an unnatural way. The gall provides food, shelter, and water for the growing larva. Galls come in all shapes, sizes, and colours, from pink, round, and woolly to flat and spiny. Look for galls on oak, willow, hickory, cottonwood, poplar, and cherry trees; other gall-forming plants are blackberry, rose, and goldenrod.

AMOEBA RACE

Cells are the basic units that make up all living things. It takes several people to make this simple, one-celled organism called an amoeba.

All living organisms -- large and small, plant and animal -- are made up of "cells". All cells are quite similar to each other, having many structural features in common. It's one of the marvels of nature that the endless variety of living organisms on Earth are constructed of or depend on such similar units. It's easiest to understand what a cell is if you compare a living organism to a building. The rooms of a building are like the cells of an organism. Both rooms and cells have boundaries with exits and entrances -- rooms have walls, floors, ceilings, doors, and windows, whereas cells have walls and/or "membranes" with pores of various sizes. Both rooms and cells come in a variety of shapes and sizes, with various contents. Each kind of room and each kind of cell has its own particular use, function, or specialty. A building may consist of only one room or many rooms; organisms may be composed of many cells or only one cell.

An "amoeba" is a one-celled, microscopic organism, one of the tiniest and simplest on Earth. It's found in fresh and salt water. The amoeba consists of a naked mass of "protoplasm" (a jelly-like substance) which constantly changes shape as the amoeba moves and engulfs food. The amoeba's protoplasm -- like the protoplasm of other cells -- has two key parts: a "nucleus" (a large, spherical structure which acts as the cell's control centre) and "cytoplasm" (everything in the cell other than the nucleus).

Topics: Microorganisms.

MATERIALS: None.

DOING IT:

1. To make an amoeba, you need a lot of protoplasm, a cell membrane (amoebae, and the cells of animals, have only a cell membrane; plant cells also have a cell wall), and a nucleus. Protoplasmic people should be those who don't mind being close. People who like to contain themselves (and others) make a good cell membrane; they should surround the protoplasm, facing outward, and link elbows. A person with good eyesight and the ability to keep on top of things should be the nucleus, seated on one of the protoplasm's shoulders.

2. Try a trip down a field or around the block. People must move as a group and shouldn't push or shove, or a part of the amoeba might get hurt! A rhythmic chant might be helpful for coordinating movements (what sort of sound does a one-celled organism make?).

3. *Extension:* Try a little cell division. The amoeba should pull itself into two new amoebae (don't forget to hoist up a new nucleus in the needy amoeba). Which amoeba gets to a finish line first? Whether both amoebae make it or not, they're sure to develop an appreciation for single-mindedness.

WHAT ANIMAL AM I?

What makes an elephant an elephant or a goldfish a goldfish? One-word answers to specific questions are the only clues people have in this animal guessing game.

MATERIALS: None.

DOING IT:

1. One person is chosen as "it". "It" moves away for a minute while a leader whispers the name of an animal to the group.

2. "It" returns and must ask questions to determine the animal he or she has "become". For example: Does the animal have fur? Can it fly? Does it eat meat? Does it live in the water? Does it make a growling sound? The group can only respond yes, no, or maybe. How long does "it" take to guess his or her animal?

3. *Variation:* Add charades to the game to make things a little more challenging, or to enable a person to guess a specific animal after narrowing it down. For example, a group member might stand and shiver to represent an Arctic fox.

4. *Variation:* Pin the name of an animal on everyone's back. The group begins to mingle. People must guess the animal they've "become" by walking from person to person and asking each person *one* question about the animal. How long does it take before everyone in the group has guessed their animal?

A famous photograph shows a bird feeding fish. The bird is a cardinal. The fish are goldfish. The place is the edge of a pond. The bird apparently mistook the open mouths of the goldfish for the gaping beaks of its chicks.

Cut out about forty pictures of different animals from magazines. How many ways can you group the animals? Try classifying the animals by colour, how big they are, what they have covering their body (e.g. feathers, hair, scales), how they move, where they live, what they eat, and which make good pets.

Small birds can recognize a hawk just from its silhouette or general shape. To prove this, scientists passed cardboard shapes resembling a hawk's silhouette over some birds, and they scurried away. The small birds didn't react to silhouettes of birds that don't hunt them.

This activity combines questioning skills, knowledge of animal names, and awareness of details. It can be simple or sophisticated. For example, the mystery creature might be a "deer", or the more specific "white-tailed deer".

Topics: Classification; Communication; Animal Characteristics.

ANIMAL YOGA

Can you stretch like a cat? Can you sit like a frog? Let the animals give you a lesson in relaxation and body awareness.

QUICKIES

MATERIALS: Soft surface.

DOING IT:

1. Try the animal yoga positions on the following page. As you go through the positions, move slowly and smoothly. **Never stretch muscles until they hurt.** Hold each position for a slow count of 3 to 10 (depending on what feels right). Breathe in through your nose and out through your mouth while holding a position.

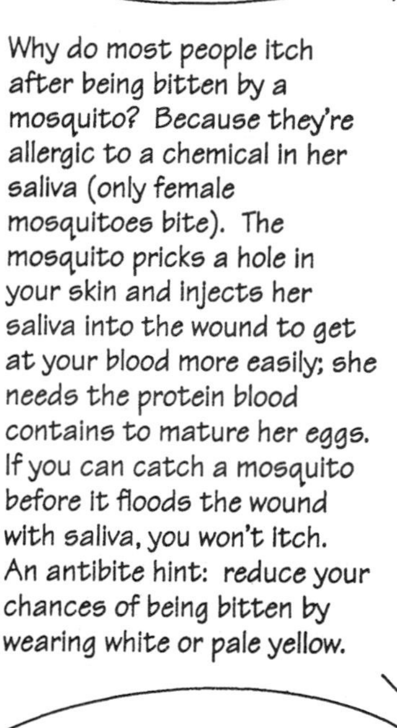

Why do most people itch after being bitten by a mosquito? Because they're allergic to a chemical in her saliva (only female mosquitoes bite). The mosquito pricks a hole in your skin and injects her saliva into the wound to get at your blood more easily; she needs the protein blood contains to mature her eggs. If you can catch a mosquito before it floods the wound with saliva, you won't itch. An antibite hint: reduce your chances of being bitten by wearing white or pale yellow.

Everyone knows that a group of cattle is called a herd. But did you know a bunch of toads is called a knot? Here are some other names for groups of animals: a labour of moles; a trip of goats; a gaggle of geese; a pride of lions; a murder of crows; a sloth of bears; a leap of leopards; and a parliament of owls.

Snakes move by "snaking" -- by wiggling forward and pushing against stones or bumps in the ground for leverage. In desert sand, snakes cannot get enough of a grip for snaking, so some species, such as the rattlesnake, move in a series of loops known as "sidewinding". The snake lifts its head up, moves sideways, puts its head on the ground again, and then draws up its tail and lays it beside its head. Only two parts of the snake's body touch the ground at one time, and the snake moves along sideways.

Becoming more aware of and mimicking animal movements can help people better understand animals and the similarities and differences between animals and humans. Human beings may have more brain power, but that doesn't mean we can't learn a few things from other living creatures.

Topics: Animal Characteristics; Human Body.

Animal Yoga Positions

Fly Like A Bird: Hang your arms loosely at your sides. Lean forward and slowly lift your arms up behind you as high as possible. Hold, then relax in a standing position.

Relax Like A Jellyfish: Lie on your back. Shut your eyes, and relax all the muscles in your body. Pretend your body is made of jelly. Breathe slowly and deeply for several minutes.

Yawn Like A Lion: Sit on your feet. Put your hands on your knees. Lean forward while opening your eyes and mouth wide. Stick out your tongue as far as possible. Let out a loud roar! Sit back and relax.

Kneel Like A Camel: Kneel on the ground with your right hand resting on your right heel and left hand on your left heel. Raise your chest up, bend your head back, push your chest toward the sky, and hold. Return to a kneeling position and take your hands off your heels. Bend back slightly. Move one arm up over your head and hold it straight. Then try your other arm. Relax in a kneeling position.

Walk Like A Monkey: Stand very straight. Bend forward until your hands touch the ground while your legs remain straight. Walk around on all fours, keeping your legs as straight as possible (don't let your knees touch the ground!). Stop. While you keep your legs straight, slowly push yourself upright, lift your hands off the ground, and return to a standing position.

Balance Like A Stork: Stand up straight with your arms at your sides. Slowly lift up one leg and balance on the other leg. Slightly bend the leg you're balancing on; bring your index fingers from both hands to your nose. Then lift up your bent arms. Hold. Return to a standing position and reverse legs.

Stretch Like A Cat: Stand on all fours, with your back straight. Slowly raise your back up high and hold. Lower your back. Stretch out one leg until it's straight and hold. Then stretch the other leg. Relax on all fours again.

Pose Like A Cobra: Lie on your stomach. Move your hands under your shoulders. Push up on your hands and lift your head up and back. Push up until your arms are straight. Hold, then relax.

Sit Like A Frog: Sit with knees bent out and the soles of your feet touching each other. Use your hands to gently pull your feet in toward your body. Keep your back straight and flex your knees downward. Relax and sit comfortably.

ANIMAL ABILITIES

There can be a lot of similarities between certain animals. But each animal also has its own, special characteristics. Compare your abilities to those of certain animals.

QUICKIES

In proportion to their size, insects are the strongest animals on Earth. In one experiment, a bumblebee hauled a toy car more than 300 times its own weight. Beetles have been shown to carry 850 times their weight. An elephant can only pull twice its own weight.

MATERIALS: Chalk; measuring tape; wall; stopwatch or watch which indicates seconds.

DOING IT:

1. *Hold Your Breath:* How long can you hold your breath? **Don't hold it any longer than is comfortable!** A sperm whale can hold its breath for over an hour. The whale needs this ability because it must dive way down to the sea floor to get food.

How do humans compare to certain animals? How are certain animals different from certain other animals? Some animals can have many common characteristics. For example, mammals are all warm-blooded, most give birth to live young, and all nurse their young with milk. Human beings are mammals. The tiny, insect-eating shrew is also a mammal. So you and a shrew have something in common. Both humans and shrews are also omnivores (i.e. eat both plants and meat). But there are things which make a shrew special and different from you. A shrew weighs less than a penny; you might weigh around 30-35 kg. A shrew has a very high metabolic rate (its heart rate, breathing rate, and other body functions are very fast compared to a human's) and can starve to death in about 6 hours; humans can go as long as a month without food. A shrew has a lifespan of about a year; you'll probably live 70 or more years. Comparing yourself to animals can help you learn more about all living creatures.

Topics: Animal Characteristics; Human Body.

2. *High Jump:* Make a chalk mark about 1 m up on a wall. Can you jump so that your feet are even with the mark? Make a standing, not running jump. A red kangaroo can jump more than 3 m high -- and can jump a distance of more than 12 m. This jumping ability helps kangaroos bound away from predators.

3. *Broad Jump:* How far can you jump from a standing-still position? A cougar can jump a distance of 9 m -- and can jump more than 5 m high. This leaping ability helps cougars catch prey.

4. *20 m Dash:* How long does it take you to run 20 m? A cheetah could run this race in less than a second. The cheetah is the fastest land mammal over a short distance. It may run at speeds of over 100 km/hour for 180-270 m. This helps the cheetah catch prey. The cheetah can't achieve this speed from a standing-still position though. To make your comparison more realistic, you might want to run a 40 m dash and time only the last half of the race.

5. *90 m Dash:* How long does it take you to run 90 m? A pronghorn could run this race in about 3.5 seconds. The pronghorn is the fastest land mammal over a long distance. It can easily run 55-70 km/hour for 6 km and can reach speeds of 90 km/hour for shorter distances. This helps the pronghorn outrun predators. The pronghorn needs some time to build up these speeds though. To make your comparison more realistic, you might want to run a 110 m dash and time only the last 90 m of the race.

Creature Symphony

If you were a cow, what noise would you make? What about if you were an elephant? Animals can be identified by the distinctive noises they make.

MATERIALS: None.

DOING IT:

1. A leader whispers the name of a different animal in each person's ear (e.g. mouse, cat, dog, donkey, cow, owl, elephant, pig).

2. Each person can take a few seconds to practice the noise that his or her animal makes. Then, everyone makes animal noises at once.

3. People must arrange themselves in a line according to animal size -- from smallest animal to largest -- using only the noises of the animals.

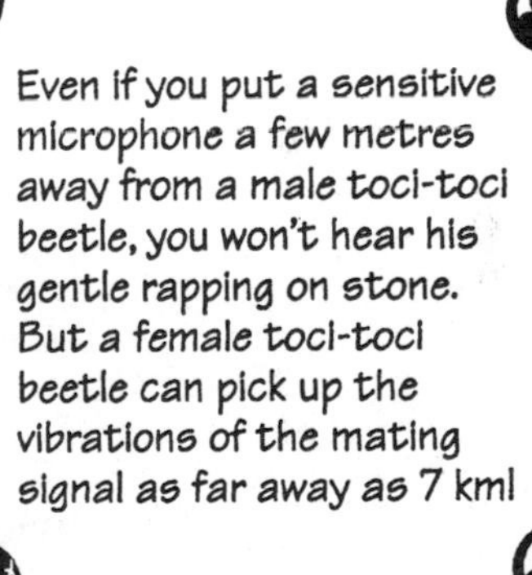

Animals (birds, in particular) make unique noises which can be used to find and identify them. Some animals make distinctive sounds or a pattern of sounds when it's the mating season. This activity requires that people not only recognize sounds, but also that they visualize the animal to which a certain sound belongs and compare animals to one another.

Topics: Animal Characteristics; Communication; Sound.

THE GREAT SPECIES MIGRATION

Everyone knows that many birds head south in the fall. But other animals migrate too. Run this migration race -- where speed is only one factor.

QUICKIES

More than one third of the world's bird species migrate with the seasons. For example, Canada geese, with their distinctive honking, fly across the sky in huge V's. The birds rotate the job of leader at the point of the V. Scientists believe that the V formation lowers the air resistance so that birds behind the leader have easier flying. Snow geese fly in loose U-shaped waves and make a beagle-like yelp. And you can tell swallows are getting ready to migrate when they line up in the thousands on telephone wires. Some birds migrate only short distances, but most fly thousands of kilometres each year. The long-distance champion migrator is the Arctic tern, which raises its family close to the North Pole and then flies over 20,000 km toward the South Pole to winter feeding grounds off Australia.

Most birds migrate from the north in the fall. Cold winters pose them problems because food isn't as available, days become shorter which means less time to hunt for food, and the amount of energy birds need to keep warm increases. Land birds that migrate by day use their eyes to guide them, recognizing such check points as river valleys, coastlines, and ridges. Birds may also use the position of the sun and stars, the Earth's gravitational pull, and changes in atmospheric temperature and pressure to navigate. Migration is very risky and millions of birds never reach their destinations. Strong winds can carry them so far off course that they are unable or too weak to find their way. Fog can confuse their sense of direction; on misty nights, light attracts birds and they often crash into lighthouses or tall, lighted buildings.

Many animals other than birds fly, hop, swim and even slither to their winter homes. Frogs hop the equivalent of less than one city block from their winter home to their spring breeding ground (but this short hop can take several hours!). The most orderly migrators are lobsters, which march single file along the seabed (each lobster keeping in feeler contact with the lobster ahead). The most determined migrators are garter snakes. Even a town on the snakes' migration route won't stop them. Twice a year, the residents of Inwood, Manitoba, Canada have to step aside while the snakes slither through.

Topics: Birds; Animal Characteristics.

MATERIALS: Measuring tape.

DOING IT:

1. Establish a race track at least 50 m long. People migrate from their northern/summer home (start) to their southern/winter home (finish).

2. Everyone lines up at the starting line. A leader calls out the name of an animal. Everyone must race to the finish line like the animal called. For example, if the chosen animal is a duck, everyone waddles to the finish line. The first "duck" to reach the winter home is the Great Duck.

3. You can start with birds, since they are the most common migrators, and then move to other animals (e.g. snake, worm, fish, wild dog, kangaroo, turtle, hare, lobster).

4. *Variation:* Mix different animals in the same race.

5. *Extension:* Show the dangers involved in migration and that many animals do not survive. Mark the racing course and set boundaries at the sides. Three-quarters of the people can run the race; the rest act as obstacles. The "obstacle" people stand in the race course. While keeping their left foot planted in one spot, they try to tag the migrators. If tagged, a migrator "dies" by stopping in place or falling to the ground.

CALLING ALL BIRDS

Have you ever wanted to talk with animals? You may not be able to talk with them, but you can call them. All you need is your mouth for this bird call.

MATERIALS: None. Optional -- bird identification guide.

DOING IT:

1. The best time to call birds is when you see or hear them. Stand, sit, or kneel absolutely still among shrubs or trees so that you are partially hidden, and birds have some place to perch.

2. The bird call is made up of a series of "pssh" sounds, repeated rhythmically. Different birds respond to different rhythms. Here are three simple rhythms you can try first:

pssh . . . pssh . . . pssh . . .

pssh-pssh . . . psssssssh . . .

pssh . . . pssh . . . pssh-pssh . . .

Each series of "pssh" sounds should last approximately 3 seconds. Repeat a series two to four times. You will have to experiment to come up with rhythms for attracting different types of birds.

3. If birds are attracted by your call, they will come fairly quickly. Some birds will approach you slowly and cautiously; others will fly to a perch high in the trees to see what's happening.

4. Once you have a bird's attention, keep it close by with an occasional series of rhythms.

Of all the animals on Earth, only certain birds can imitate the human voice. These birds can also copy other sounds. The best bird mimics are so good that people often can't tell the real sound from its imitation. Jackdaws, magpies, and some other crows are among the best mimics. The most famous of all talking birds are some members of the parrot family. The world champion talking bird was an African gray parrot that spoke almost 1000 words.

The ostrich is the world's largest living bird. It is nearly 3 m tall, weighing an average 160 kg. It cannot fly and is found only in Africa. Ostriches lay the biggest eggs in the world (about 17 cm long and weighing close to 1.5 kg) and these are often laid in one nest shared by several females.

After insects, birds are the creatures we see most often. "Birders" (bird watchers) discovered long ago that birds are beautiful, graceful animals that are fascinating to watch. The bird call described here attracts many smaller bird species: jays, wrens, sparrows, warblers, chickadees, nuthatches, hummingbirds, and orioles. Some naturalists say the reason the call works is that the "pssh" sound is similar to the scolding call of many birds. Others say it sounds like a mother bird calling her young for a feeding. Yet others think the sound simply makes birds curious. The sounds birds make are also used as territorial songs, warnings, and mating calls.

Topics: Birds; Communication; Sound.

BUGGING INSECTS

Instead of insects bugging you, why don't you "bug" an insect? Listen to insects using a simple chamber that amplifies the sounds they make.

MATERIALS: Paper cup or foam cup; waxed paper; elastic band.

QUICKIES

DOING IT:

1. Use a cup to capture the insect to which you want to listen.

2. Stretch a piece of waxed paper over the top of the cup and secure the paper in place with an elastic band. The waxed paper should be pulled tight across the cup.

3. Hold the cup next to your ear and listen to the beat of the insect's wings. Can you hum along to the beat? When you have finished listening to the insect, *carefully release it.*

4. Do different insects sound different? In what ways do they sound different? Can you imitate the sounds you hear?

The insect amplifier increases the volume of the sound of an insect's wings beating. The beating wings cause the air in the amplifier chamber to vibrate; in turn, the air moves the waxed paper covering the cup. An insect which works especially well in the chamber -- and is easy to catch -- is the mosquito. A mosquito's wings flap 300 times/sec. A honeybee's wings flap about 250 times/sec and a fly's flap 190 times/sec.

Topics: Insects; Sound.

Most people don't like insects. Perhaps that's because, of all the animals on Earth, insects look the least like humans. Insects also spread diseases, bite and sting, destroy crops, and can ruin stored food such as flour and rice. But there are a lot of good things about insects: they are important plant pollinators; some provide useful things like honey, wax, and silk; certain insects help control other pests (e.g. dragonflies eat mosquitoes); they provide food for many other animals; some can be used to treat diseases in people; and they are good indicators of water pollution.

BEE DANCE

Some animals communicate using sound. Others use smell. Bees communicate by "dancing". Try to do their dance.

MATERIALS: None.

DOING IT:

1. Practice the two basic bee dances: the round and the waggle. The patterns are related to each other, as is illustrated between the dances. Try dancing from the round into the waggle, and then back again.

2. Try the dances in a small space, then over a large area. Is it more difficult to repeat the smaller or the larger patterns?

3. *Variation:* Try group dances. Everyone forms a human chain and goes through the dance patterns together.

4. *Extension:* Each person finds a partner. One partner chooses a spot as the location of some imaginary food. Then, the object is to communicate to the other person, through a bee dance, the food's location. If food is up to 10 m away, bees do the round dance. If food is more than 100 m away, bees do the waggle. Between 10 and 100 m, bees dance a combination of the two dances -- the actual combination depending on the distance to the food.

A cockroach can live 9 days without its head.

Honeybees live in hives and share their work. A hive is headed by one queen bee. She spends all her time laying eggs. She lives for 3 to 5 years and is then replaced by a new queen. It takes 21 to 24 days for an egg to develop into an adult bee.

A strong bee colony can have tens of thousands of bees at the peak of the season. Of these, only a few hundred are drones. Drones are the only males in the hive and live only to fertilize the queen. They have no stinger and depend completely on the females for food and protection. The female worker bees run the hive, gather nectar, and possess the stingers. Honeybees' stingers are barbed so that, once pushed into a victim, they cannot be pulled out. The whole stinger mechanism pulls out of a bee's body when she tries to pull away, so she dies shortly after stinging. Bees (and wasps) only sting when bothered or frightened.

Bees perform the important function of pollination as they travel from flower to flower in search of nectar. Bees must make thousands of trips to flowers to make just one teaspoon of honey. Bee "dances" are a complex form of communication through which bees tell each other about the type and location of nectar supplies. Bees also use the sun as a compass to indicate directions; they see the sun even on hazy days.

Topics: Insects; Communication.

PREDATORS AND THEIR PREY

Living creatures that hunt other animals and living creatures that are hunted each have special adaptations. Play these predator/prey games.

MATERIALS: Blindfolds; breakfast cereal; sheets of paper.

DOING IT:

1. *Fox and Mouse:* Two people stand in the centre of a circle formed by a group of people. One of the two people is a fox and the other is a mouse; both are blindfolded. Using their sense of hearing only, the fox tries to tag the mouse and the mouse tries to stay away from the fox. How important is the sense of hearing for the survival of some animals? What other senses are important? What kinds of strategies can prey use to stay alive? What kinds of strategies can predators use to catch food?

2. *Deer:* Everyone kneels down in front of a sheet of paper piled with breakfast cereal. They pretend that they are deer, grazing in an open field. They put their heads down and eat. One person walks slowly among the group and acts as a lookout. When a leader gives a certain *subtle* signal (e.g. smiles) the lookout stands still and raises his or her hand. The feeding deer must stop eating and run to a designated safety area. How long does it take for everyone to get to the safety area? Is it difficult to eat and be alert for danger at the same time? What special adaptations might be useful to the deer? How would a good sense of smell or hearing, or the ability to run quickly, be helpful? What strategies can deer use to stay alive?

Predators must adapt successfully for catching their food or they will starve. For example, bears must be able to judge the location of fish as they scoop the fish out of the water. Birds have keen eyesight to help them spot small insects and worms. Owls and lions have eyes in the front of their head so that they can keep track of the small animals they pursue. Animals that are hunted must also have special adaptations. For example, keen senses, particularly hearing and sight, help prey get early warnings of approaching predators. Mice, squirrels, and deer have eyes on the sides of their head so that they can detect an enemy that might sneak up from any direction.

Topics: Animal Characteristics; Senses; Ecosystems.

Owls aren't picky eaters. They swallow their prey as nearly whole as possible. Owls can't digest fur and bones though, and these can't pass through an owl's digestive system. So, about 12 hours after consuming a meal, the owl coughs up a "pellet". The pellet contains the fur and bones (which can be put together like a puzzle) of one or more small animals. Owl pellets are uniformly dark gray, 4 to 8 cm long, and 2 to 2.5 cm in diameter. Look for the pellets on the floor of abandoned buildings, beneath a grove of tall trees, or under other structures that offer owls shelter from daylight.

WEATHER

"Onion's skin very thin, mild winter coming in; Onion's skin thick and tough, coming winter cold and rough." This old gardener's rhyme has some truth in it. Onions grow differently depending on the summer's average air and soil temperature, which can be related to the upcoming winter. Scientific studies have confirmed that other plants can also provide weather clues.

There are more than 7,000 weather observation stations around the world. In addition, crews of thousands of transport ships and aircrafts regularly collect weather data.

There's a lot of folklore in which animals are said to be able to forecast the weather. Scientific studies have shown most of this folklore to be inaccurate. For example, some say that certain animals grow an extra-thick coat if the winter ahead is going to be particularly cold. This isn't true. Mule deer, for one, have often failed to grow an extra-thick coat when they needed it and many have died as a result.

The units "kilopascal" and "degrees Celsius" get their names from two European scientists who were pioneers in the study of weather phenomena: Anders Celsius (1701 to 1744), a Swedish astronomer; and Blaise Pascal (1623 to 1662), a French scientist and philosopher.

What if scientists learned to control the weather? What would it mean? Would humans playing with the weather affect the balance of nature? How would we decide when and where it was going to rain or be sunny? Could controlling the weather have any military or political significance? What if the knowledge got into the hands of an incompetent person? In the long run, would controlling the weather be useful or harmful?

Count the number of chirps a male snowy tree cricket (found in leafy bushes and small trees 2 m or higher; chirps during the day and early evening) makes in eight seconds. Add four. The resulting number is temperature, in degrees Celsius. The result will be accurate within one degree Celsius, nine times out of ten. The frequency of the cricket's chirps increases as the air temperature climbs higher.

POURING AIR

The properties of air play a major role in weather phenomena. Air takes up space, has weight, and has pressure. Try to "pour" air underwater.

MATERIALS: Two clear drinking glasses; a large container or sink full of water.

DOING IT:

1. Hold a drinking glass upside down and, keeping it straight, push it completely under the water. Does the glass stay full of air?

2. With your other hand, put a second glass into the water. This time, put the glass into the water on its side so that it fills up with water.

3. Move the two glasses together and tilt the first glass so that air bubbles rise into the second glass. What happens to the first glass? What happens to the second glass?

4. Can you transfer all of the air from the first glass into the second? How much air escapes? What makes it difficult to "pour" air?

To prove that air exists, wave a plastic bag around and then twist the bag's mouth shut. There's obviously something in the bag -- air! In this activity, you can actually "see" and manipulate air. When the first glass is initially submerged underwater, it's filled with air and water doesn't spill into it. By holding the glass at a slant, air bubbles are free to escape and thus water can take the air's place. The air bubbles rise in the water -- hopefully into a second glass -- because air is much lighter than water. The water in the second glass is driven out by the air bubbles.

Topics: Air.

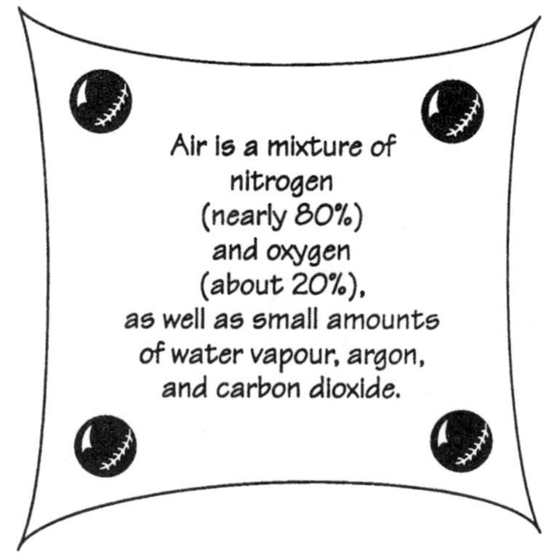

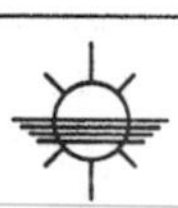

Air Takes Up Space

Air occupies space that looks empty. Put a piece of paper or a towel underwater -- without getting it wet!

QUICKIES

"Radar" is an acronym used since World War II to describe the technique and equipment used for the "radio detection and ranging" of objects in the atmosphere. Just as a beam of light from a flashlight picks out an object in the dark, radar detects objects -- but it does so both in daylight and darkness, through thick clouds, and at greater distances than can a light beam. Weather radar is used to detect, locate, and measure the amount of precipitation in clouds. A microwave beam transmitted by weather radar passes through cloud and fog, but when it strikes precipitation particles -- such as raindrops, snowflakes, or hail -- some of the energy is back-scattered as an "echo" to the radar antenna.

MATERIALS: A clear drinking glass; paper (e.g. kleenex, tissue paper, writing paper); large container or sink full of water. Optional -- pail; small stick a bit longer than the diameter of the pail; towel; bathtub, pool, or large sink full of water.

DOING IT:

1. Crumple up a piece of paper and jam it into the bottom of a drinking glass.

2. Hold the glass upside down and, keeping it straight, push it completely under the water. Does the paper get wet? Why not? What happens if you put the glass into the water mouth up?

3. *Variation:* Can you do the same trick with a towel wedged into a pail with a stick?

Air occupies space, which means that nothing else can occupy the space at the same time. Many weather phenomena occur because two masses of air -- with different temperatures, pressures, and humidities -- are vying for the same space in the atmosphere. In this activity, air takes up space in the glass and acts as an invisible "wall" between the water and the paper.

Topics: Air.

AIR HAS WEIGHT

Does a balloon filled with air weigh the same as a balloon which has been punctured? It may seem like there's nothing to air, but it does have weight.

MATERIALS: Two identical balloons; metre stick; tape; string; sharp object.

DOING IT:

1. Blow up two balloons so that they're the same size.

2. Tape one balloon to one end of a metre stick and the other balloon to the other end of the stick.

3. Tie one end of a piece of string around the metre stick, between the two balloons. Hold the other end of the string (or tie or tape it to a bar or doorway) so that the stick hangs horizontally and the balloons are balanced.

4. What will happen if one of the balloons is punctured? Will the balloons remain balanced? Why or why not?

5. Puncture one of the balloons. The end of the stick with the punctured balloon on it will rise. The full balloon has air in it, which makes it heavier than the punctured balloon.

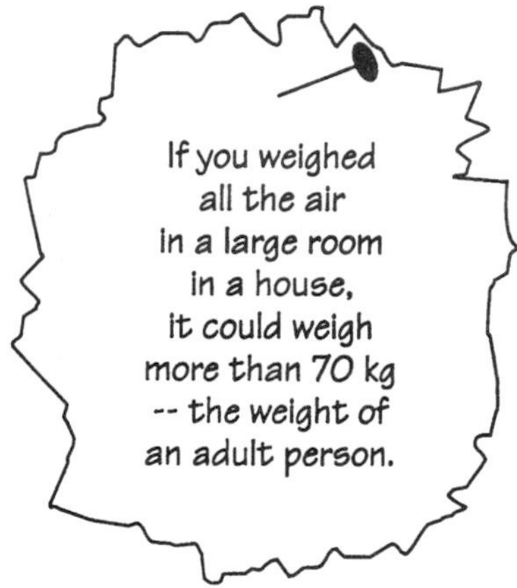

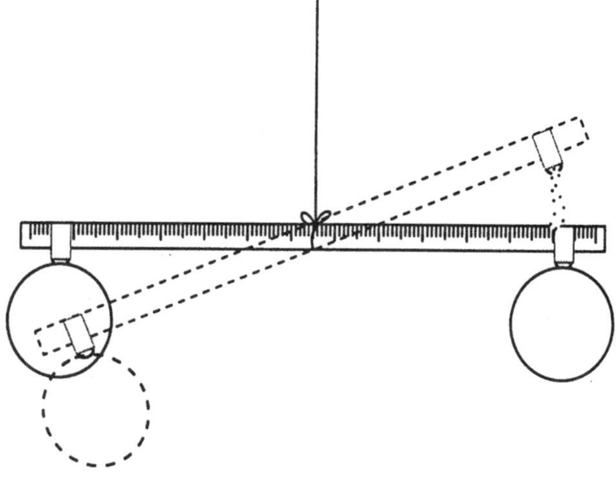

The weight of air depends in large part on its temperature. The warmer the air, the greater the space between molecules, and thus the less the weight. Many weather phenomena are caused by warm, lighter air rising, or cool, denser air falling. The former often causes the formation of clouds, while the latter usually causes or assists the breakdown of clouds.

Topics: Air; Measurement.

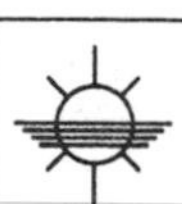

Air Has Pressure

Explore air pressure with paper strips that move inward instead of outward, cups that "stick" to a balloon, and water that doesn't spill out of an upside-down glass.

MATERIALS: Paper; scissors; balloon; paper, plastic, or foam cups; drinking glass; piece of cardboard or stiff paper (about 15 cm x 15 cm); water.

DOING IT:

1. *Paper Strips:* Cut two strips of paper about 22 cm x 3 cm. Take a strip in each hand and hold them *facing* each other, about 12 cm apart, in front of your mouth. Blow steadily between the two strips. What happens? Why?

2. *Balloon and Cups:* Blow up a balloon about 1/3 of full size. Hold two paper, plastic, or foam cups against the sides of the balloon, and finish blowing up the balloon. How many cups can you attach to a single balloon?

3. *Upside-Down Glass:* Fill a drinking glass about 3/4 full of water. Wet the rim of the glass. Put a piece of cardboard on top of the glass. While holding the cardboard tightly against the mouth of the glass (no air bubbles should be allowed to enter between the cardboard and the glass), turn the glass upside down. Gently let go of the cardboard. How many tries does it take before you get the water to stay in the glass? What happens if you turn the glass sideways?

Air pressure plays an important role in weather. Slight, temporary changes in air pressure occur frequently. For example, when the temperature in an area drops, air molecules come closer together, thus raising the local air pressure. When the atmosphere warms, the molecules spread out, and the air pressure is lowered again. These kinds of slight changes don't usually result in major changes in the weather. Larger pressure changes, due to movements of huge low- and high-pressure areas, are the ones which can turn a sunny, clear day into a rainy one.

In *Paper Strips,* blowing between two strips of paper reduces the air pressure between the strips (flowing air exerts less pressure than stationary air). The greater pressure of the surrounding air forces the strips together. In *Balloon and Cups,* the pressure of the outside air is greater than the air pressure in the cups, so the cups are "pushed" onto the balloon and "stick" to it. In *Upside-Down Glass,* the water stays in the glass because the pressure of the outside air against the cardboard is greater than the pressure of the water against the cardboard.

Topics: Air; Flight.

AIR ON THE MOVE

Warm air rises. Air also moves from areas of high pressure to areas of low pressure. Air in motion is wind. Use air in motion to expand a balloon. Then test for air currents.

MATERIALS: Plastic bottle; balloon; pail or sink; hot water; different thicknesses of paper; scissors; thread.

DOING IT:

1. *Expanding Balloon:* Put a plastic bottle in the refrigerator for a while to cool it down. Loosen up a balloon by blowing it up and then letting out the air. Stretch the end of the balloon over the mouth of the bottle. Put the bottle and balloon into a pail or sink of hot water. What happens to the balloon? Why? Then put the bottle and balloon into the refrigerator. What happens? Why?

2. *Air Spiral:* Cut out a circle of paper 10-15 cm in diameter. Make a small hole in the centre. Cut the circle into a spiral, as shown. Hang the spiral from a knotted piece of thread. Use the air spiral to find rising currents of warm air. If you're viewing the spiral from above, when it turns clockwise it indicates an updraft. Hold the spiral in place for about 30 seconds to take a reading. Where can you find an updraft? Try holding the spiral over a lamp that has been on for a while. Can you find a downdraft (when the spiral turns counterclockwise it indicates a downdraft)? Compare the way the spiral turns near the ground in a certain area to how it turns when you hold it as high as possible. Experiment with different thicknesses of paper and different numbers of spirals to find the best air spiral design.

When air molecules are heated, they move faster and faster and the air expands (takes up more space). In *Expanding Balloon,* the hot water heats the air inside the bottle. The air expands, rises into the balloon, and makes the balloon expand. When you then cool the air in the bottle, the balloon contracts. As air expands in a *closed* container, the air pressure increases (air in the *open* atmosphere is not restricted and when it expands, its molecules move farther and farther apart, resulting in lower air pressure). Air moves from areas of high pressure to areas of low pressure. For example, air rushes out of a balloon because the pressure inside the balloon is greater than the pressure outside. Air in motion is wind. The greater the pressure difference between two areas, the stronger the wind.

Warm air rises and cool air falls. When heated air (e.g. air warmed by contact with the warm Earth) rises, it creates an updraft. When cool air (e.g. air cooled at cold, upper levels of the atmosphere) falls, it creates a downdraft. The *Air Spiral* enables you to test air currents around you. The movement of large air masses of different temperatures across regions of land plays a major role in the weather. On a local scale, air currents vary in different areas and at different times of the day.

Topics: Air; States of Matter.

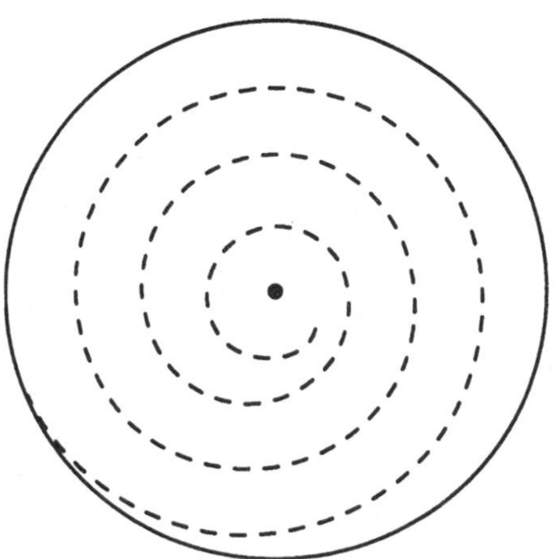

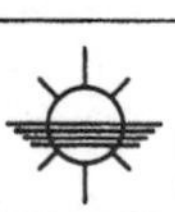

Wind Spinner

You may not be able to see wind itself, but you can see what it does. This spinning paper plate helps make wind "visible" and is great fun to chase.

MATERIALS: Paper plates; ruler; scissors. Optional -- glue or tape.

DOING IT:

1. Cut a paper plate from the middle to make eight equal, triangular flaps, as shown.

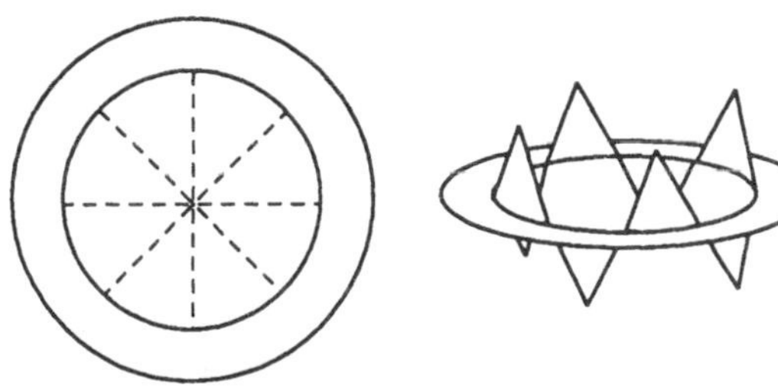

2. Fold the flaps outward, alternating between each side of the plate as you go around.

3. The spinner works best on a windy day. Roll it on a flat piece of ground. Quickly determine the wind direction by wetting your finger and holding it in the air. The part of your finger that feels cool is affected by quick evaporation from air movement, and indicates the direction from which the wind is blowing. For example, if the part of your finger facing west feels cool, the wind is a west wind (i.e. a wind that comes from the west and blows toward the east). Send the spinner with the wind and then against the wind. In which direction does the spinner go fastest? How easy is it to chase the spinner? Can you send the spinner spinning directly toward someone?

4. *Variation:* Glue or tape two paper plates together, bottom to bottom (*not* one inside the other). Then, follow the steps above. Which wind spinner design works best? Why?

The wind spinner works well because the flaps increase the surface area of the paper plate that is perpendicular to the wind. The larger exposed surface area gives the wind more to push against.

Wind brings with it changes in weather. The nature of the changes depends on the direction from which the wind is blowing, and so wind direction is one of the most important factors in weather prediction. Winds are named after the direction *from* which they blow; for example, a wind blowing from the north, toward the south, is called a north wind. There are six belts of "prevailing winds" that blow around the Earth in a regular pattern. For example, the "trade winds" (which are near the equator) blow toward the equator; weather in the area of the trade winds moves from east to west. The "westerlies" (which, in the northern hemisphere, blow across much of Canada and the United States) move away from the equator; weather in the area of the westerlies moves from west to east. Regular wind patterns are created and driven by two key factors. First, there is the rotation of the Earth itself, which "drags" a mass of air with it. Secondly, there is the constant interchange between the warm air of the tropics and the cold air of the polar ice-caps.

Topics: Air; Weather Conditions.

FLASH, CRASH!

You can figure out the distance of a thunderstorm from your location by using the time between a lightning flash and a thunder crash.

MATERIALS: None.

DOING IT:

1. As soon as you see a lightning flash, start counting off the seconds (e.g. one lollipop, . . . two lollipops, . . . three lollipops, . . .) until you hear the thunder crash.

2. Every 3 seconds means that the core of the storm is about 1 km away (if sound travels at 340 m/sec, then a sound takes about 3 seconds to travel a kilometre). To determine the nearness of the storm, take the total time between the lightning flash and thunder crash and divide by 3 (e.g. 6 seconds divided by 3 equals 2, which means the storm is 2 km away).

3. To determine whether a storm is approaching or moving away, estimate the storm's distance for a number of successive lightning flashes and thunder crashes. If the distance continually increases, you know that the storm is moving away.

Lightning is caused by static electricity. Sparks jump between two areas in which opposite electrical charges have built up (e.g. from one area of a cloud to another, or from a cloud to the ground); these sparks are like those which occur when you rub your feet along a carpet and then touch a metal doorknob. First, a "leader" lashes out (e.g. a bolt from a cloud toward the ground), followed by the main "return stroke" along the same path (e.g. a bolt upward from the ground). There can be several back and forth strokes, but it all looks like one lightning flash and takes place in less than a second. Leaders can travel at up to 2600 km/sec, while return strokes can travel at 140,000 km/sec. The core of most lightning bolts is only about the thickness of a finger. But, a single lightning bolt can have a temperature of up to 30,000 degrees C, can be 30 km long, and can contain enough energy to power a home for several months.

A bolt of lightning heats the air along its path. It causes the air to expand quickly. This expansion causes vibrations which are heard as thunder. The faster the air expands, the louder the thunder. Thunder and lightning both originate from the core of a storm; but you see lightening before you hear thunder because light travels faster to your eyes than sound travels to your ears. Light travels at a speed of 300,000 km/sec, and sound travels at only about 340 m/sec (depending on the air temperature). On average, 44,000 thunderstorms occur every day throughout the world.

Topics: Weather Conditions; Electricity; Light; Sound; Measurement.

Lightning can strike twice -- or more! Roy Sullivan, an American Park Ranger, has been struck by lightning seven times. Amazingly, he has survived. The world's tallest free-standing structure, the CN Tower in Toronto, Ontario, Canada, is struck by lightning about 60 times a year.

THE HEAVENS

"Universe" comes from the Latin *universum*, meaning "the whole" or "everything together." The universe includes all space and everything contained in the space -- all the stars, planets, satellites, galaxies, nebulas, comets, and other interstellar matter and energy that exists. The universe is so vast that we can't really imagine it.

Most scientists believe that the universe began about 15 billion years ago. According to the "Big Bang" theory, all the matter and energy in the universe were concentrated into a very small volume that exploded and has been expanding ever since. The strongest support for this theory comes from weak radiation -- the remains of the explosion -- that can be detected as radio waves coming from all parts of the universe.

There are more stars in the universe than there are grains of sand on all the beaches in the world.

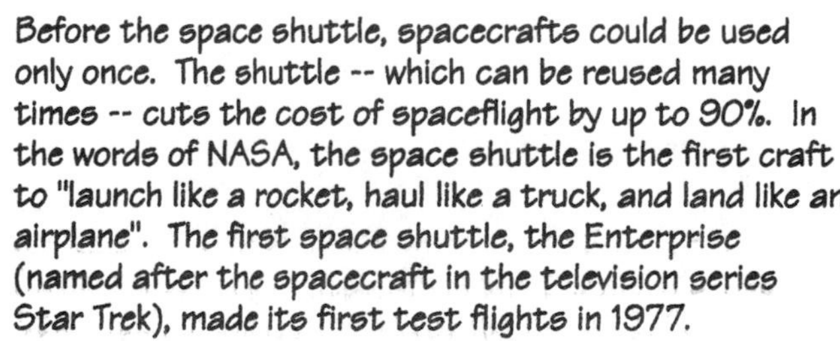

Before the space shuttle, spacecrafts could be used only once. The shuttle -- which can be reused many times -- cuts the cost of spaceflight by up to 90%. In the words of NASA, the space shuttle is the first craft to "launch like a rocket, haul like a truck, and land like an airplane". The first space shuttle, the Enterprise (named after the spacecraft in the television series Star Trek), made its first test flights in 1977.

The first human being in space was Yuri Gagarin in the USSR's Vostok 1 rocket on April 12, 1961. Alan Shepard, in the American Freedom 7 spacecraft, made the next trip into space on May 5, 1961.

"Man's best friend" in outer space may be a goat. A goat's key asset is its versatile stomach -- a chamber inhabited by microorganisms that break down all kinds of waste. Research has shown that astronauts could feed goats sludge (the woody parts of plants and other materials that people don't eat), which would mean that a much smaller waste treatment unit would be needed on a spacecraft. The goats would also provide astronauts with abundant food and milk.

Alphabet Soup

How many words that relate to the heavens do you know? When you unscramble these 64 letters, they spell several astronomy-related words.

MATERIALS: Paper; pencil.

DOING IT:

1. Here are 64 letters: M, A, N, N, T, S, Y, O, O, L, M, E, A, D, L, G, Y, T, S, U, P, L, R, A, N, R, T, S, M, A, N, M, E, O, R, O, O, E, X, A, A, C, O, N, E, T, N, O, O, C, S, T, L, A, T, E, R, T, I, O, I, S, E, T.

2. The challenge is to unscramble the letters to make ten astronomy-related words (hint: the first word is in these instructions!). You can unscramble the letters using a single sheet of paper and a pencil, but it may be easier if you write each of the letters on a separate slip of paper and then arrange the slips of paper.

3. Some of the words are easy; others are a little harder. Aside from the first word, all the words are natural objects in space (heavenly bodies). You must use up all the letters.

In an age of space shuttles and science fiction movies with breathtaking visual effects, a lot of astronomy-related words are thrown around. People are often surprised at how many "space" words they know -- and are even more surprised to find out exactly what the words mean!

Topics: Problem-Solving; Stars; Planets.

4. Can you find all ten words? Do you know what each word means? Read the following page to learn more about each of the heavenly bodies.

Science fiction isn't always scientifically accurate, but it's usually thought-provoking. Writing science fiction involves combining known facts in new ways. Try it! Combine two separate ideas into a third, new idea that somehow connects the original ideas. Think of a substitute for an object or idea and then use the original and the substitute. If the two existed at the same time, how would they affect each other? Think of something that's impossible -- then dream up a way to make it "possible". Finally, you can use the opposite of an idea. For example, everyone knows that an elephant is bigger than a mouse. But what if a mouse were bigger than an elephant?

STUDYING HEAVENLY BODIES

ASTRONOMY: The scientific study of heavenly bodies. It takes in everything from the amateur star-watcher with a pair of binoculars to the highly-trained scientist analysing radio waves given off by distant stars. "Astronomy" comes from a Greek word meaning "arrangement of the stars." The following are the different types of heavenly bodies.

STAR: A huge, glowing globe of gas. It shines by its own light, rather than reflecting light (like planets) or glowing from heat friction (like meteors). Seen from Earth, stars look like points of light. A normal star's size and temperature can be judged from its colour and brightness:

- A *red* star is the coolest type of star (about 2,600-3,000 degrees C). The red colour is produced by the relatively cool gases near the surface of very large stars or by the cooling surface of dying stars.
- A *yellow* star is hotter than a red star (about 5,000-11,000 degrees C).
- A *blue* star is a very hot, very bright star (about 19,000-30,000 degrees C). Often a new star.

All stars are born in huge clouds of gas and dust. The gases and dust swirl around and form into clumps which then contract, becoming very hot and dense. Eventually, nuclear reactions begin inside the clumps and the clumps start to shine. Stars eventually run out of fuel and become unstable. Some stars shrink into white dwarfs (small, very dense stars) while others explode through supernova or turn into black holes. No one has ever seen a black hole. It cannot be seen because nothing can escape a black hole, not even light. Anything that comes close to a black hole is pulled in and disappears.

These are some special stages in the life of a star:

- A *white dwarf* is a dying star that has collapsed to planet size. It burns very brightly for its tiny size and old age.
- A *giant* is a star that has expanded to many times the size of our sun, that burns with all the brightness of at least one hundred suns.
- A *super giant* is a star billions of kilometres in diameter that burns thousands of times brighter than our sun.
- A *pulsating star* is a star which expands and shrinks periodically.
- A *nova* is a star whose surface layers explode. The star survives and may nova repeatedly.
- A *supernova* is a huge explosion, a star's last explosion. A supernova might release as much energy in 24 hours as our sun would in a billion years and can outshine hundreds of billions of stars.

SUN: Our local star. As stars go, it's a rather ordinary, middle-aged, medium-sized yellow star.

PLANET: A body that orbits a star.

MOON: A smaller body orbiting a planet.

CONSTELLATION: A group of bright stars which make a pattern in the sky. Constellations have been named after mythological characters and events.

GALAXY: A large group of stars and planets isolated in space from other such groups. Our galaxy is the Milky Way (named because it looks like drops of milk spilling across the sky). It contains over 100 billion stars.

METEOR: A meteor is also called a "shooting star". It's produced when a particle, drifting through space, collides with the Earth's atmosphere. The friction between the particle and the air causes the air to glow. We see this as a brief streak of light in the sky. Before the particle hits the Earth's atmosphere, it's called a "meteoroid". After it has fallen to the ground, the particle is called a "meteorite".

COMET: A cosmic wanderer. A mass of frozen gases and dust that may take several million years to orbit the sun. It produces a tail of glowing gas as it approaches the sun. "Comet" comes from the Greek *aster kometes*, meaning "long-haired star".

ASTEROID: Rocks, smaller than a planet, which orbit the sun. It's believed that asteroids are made from materials left over from the formation of the solar system. There is a large asteroid belt, a band of orbiting chunks, between Mars and Jupiter. Diameters of asteroids range from a few kilometres to several hundred kilometres.

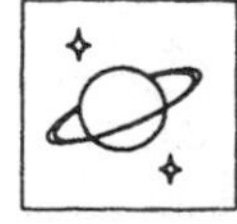

Astronomy Versus Astrology

Many people confuse astronomy and astrology, but it's easy to show how the two are different.

MATERIALS: Following page.

DOING IT:

1. Announce that you're going to "prove that astrology is a science -- that predictions can be made about a person's personality and life using the stars" (of course, astrology isn't a science at all, but don't let on yet).

The sun appears to follow a yearly path among the stars. The zone of the sky in which the path lies is called the "zodiac". The paths of the moon and the planets lie in this narrow zodiac too. People divide the zodiac into twelve sections. Each section has the name of the constellation (group of stars) that was closest to the section when the names were given about 2000 years ago. Constellations represent only an arbitrary relationship between stars; no real, astronomical relationship exists. Some people believe the sign of the zodiac in which the sun, moon, and planets appeared on the day you were born influenced your personality. This belief is called "astrology". Astrology doesn't have much scientific support. Astronomy and astrology are both concerned with the study of heavenly bodies and with pinpointing the locations of planets and stars. But, astrology involves personal viewpoints; predictions are not based on tested facts. Astronomy involves explanations based on observation and testing. Astronomy meets the definition of a science, whereas astrology does not.

Topics: Scientific Method; Human Behaviour; Stars.

2. Who knows their sign? Most people do. Do people think it's an important and useful bit of information? We tend to have a lot of things in our head that we don't understand, and therefore misuse.

3. Describe the activity as follows: "Science is based on direct observations. So we're going to make direct observations and collect facts to support the idea that astrology is a science. I have the horoscopes from the day before yesterday's paper (that means they're the horoscopes for yesterday). Tell me your birth date and we'll look at your sign and read your horoscope. I want everyone to give me one example of something that happened to them yesterday that shows their horoscope was right."

4. People should think about each phrase -- and even each word -- in their horoscope. Almost everyone will come up with even the smallest example to show their horoscope had some truth.

5. Disclose that the horoscopes weren't for yesterday. What was unscientific about the study? How did subjective feelings distort the findings? What does this say about astrology being a "science"? It's interesting to note that many serious astrologers don't accept newspaper horoscopes. Does this leave any possibility for astrology as a "science"? What's the difference between astrology and astronomy?

Space exploration has given us numerous by-products, useful in seemingly unrelated areas. For example, the miniaturization of space equipment led to the development of automatic devices which would otherwise have been too bulky for practical purposes. So now you know how your camera and your radio got to be so small.

"YOUR HOROSCOPE FOR YESTERDAY"

THE RAM

ARIES (MARCH 21 - APRIL 19): What seemed like a lost cause comes through -- in your favour. You break past habits. You have an opportunity to get rid of a problem that wasn't supposed to be yours in the first place.

THE BULL

TAURUS (APRIL 20 - MAY 20): If you don't know what to do, do nothing! Focus on patience, ability to play the waiting game. You're willing to finish unfinished chores.

THE TWINS

GEMINI (MAY 21 - JUNE 20): You'll be more popular and there will be additional demands on your time. There may be a family reunion or a new friend which will make you more secure and happy.

THE CRAB

CANCER (JUNE 21 - JULY 22): A request will be granted. You'll be more aware of your physical appearance, body image. Your intellectual curiosity is going to be high.

THE LION

LEO (JULY 23 - AUGUST 22): Be ready to change your ideas. Keep your mind open to fresh opportunities. You'll be around lively people. Something exciting may happen which will brighten your whole day.

THE VIRGIN

VIRGO (AUGUST 23 - SEPTEMBER 22): What has been lost you will now find. You have a new sense of confidence. You may take a short trip or get a break from daily routines. If you ask in the right way, you will get what you want.

THE SCALES

LIBRA (SEPTEMBER 23 - OCTOBER 22): You'll be at the right place at the right time. You may get an unusual gift or token. You'll need to get exact instructions when someone asks you to do something for them.

THE SCORPION

SCORPIO (OCTOBER 23 - NOVEMBER 21): It's a quiet day for you. You don't have a lot of energy. But you're still busy and something unexpected happens. You have more responsibility.

THE ARCHER

SAGITTARIUS (NOVEMBER 22 - DECEMBER 21): This can be a day full of energy and excitement for you! Things will be happening all day. You meet someone new. The day goes quickly. Someone gives you a valuable hint.

THE GOAT

CAPRICORN (DECEMBER 22 - JANUARY 19): Throw away any ideas you have about something you "can't" do. Think positively and you'll do something you really want to do -- and you'll do it exceptionally well!

THE WATER CARRIER

AQUARIUS (JANUARY 20 - FEBRUARY 18): Your original approach to a problem or challenge brings results for you. You display courage and stick to your feelings. People will look to you for help with something important.

THE FISH

PISCES (FEBRUARY 19 - MARCH 20): Follow through on a hunch. Spotlight on creativity and added popularity. Something unexpected happens, with pleasant results. You start out unhappy, but the day brightens.

HOME, SWEET, HOME

The Earth is the fifth largest planet and the third planet from the sun. This decision-making problem shows some things that make Earth a unique home.

MATERIALS: Paper; pencil.

DOING IT:

1. You have the following sixteen items: matches; food concentrate; 50 m of nylon rope; parachute silk; mosquito repellent; two .45 calibre pistols; dehydrated milk; two tanks of oxygen; stellar map; blanket; magnetic compass; bottles of water; signal flares; first-aid kit with injection needles; solar-powered FM receiver/transmitter; pressure suit.

2. Scene One: Your plane crashes in an isolated area in the summer. It's 300 km to civilization. Assume that no one knows you have crashed. Survival depends on reaching civilization. Sixteen items are left intact after the crash. You can take only some of them with you on your 300 km trip. Which are most important?

3. Scene Two: You are in a spacecraft traveling to rendezvous with your mother ship on the lighted side of the moon. You crash-land 300 km from the rendezvous point. Assume that no one knows you have crashed. Survival depends on reaching the mother ship. Sixteen items are left intact after the crash. You can take only some of them with you on your 300 km trip. Which are most important?

4. List the sixteen items on a sheet of paper. Number the items in order of importance for scene one, and then for scene two. How are the orderings different? Why are they different? How are they the same? Possible orderings are listed below. Are your orderings different from those suggested? How and why?

The Earth is a ball (about 13,000 km in diameter) of stone and metal covered with water, rocks, and dirt. Scientists believe the Earth is about 4.6 billion years old, and it's home for over 5 billion people.

Earth is unique in a number of ways. It has a fluid core, which is thought to be mostly iron. Iron, in fact, is the most abundant element on our planet, followed by oxygen, silicon, aluminum, calcium, and magnesium. Eighty-six other elements exist naturally on Earth, in relatively tiny quantities. 70% of Earth is covered by water, which means it has more water in liquid form than any other planet. The final unique thing about Earth is its life-sustaining atmosphere (about 80% nitrogen and 20% oxygen, with small amounts of argon, carbon dioxide, water vapour, and other gases). Earth's atmosphere acts as a blanket keeping the Earth warm. It also acts like a shield by preventing the sun's deadly ultraviolet rays from getting through.

Topics: Earth; Decision-Making; Planets.

Possible orderings:

Scene One: 1. bottles of water (key to survival); 2. magnetic compass (find direction); 3. food concentrate (food); 4. matches (warmth and cooking); 5. solar-powered FM receiver/transmitter (distress signal); 6. first-aid kit with injection needles (any first-aid kit is useful); 7. mosquito repellent (body protection); 8. 50 m of nylon rope (climbing); 9. blanket (warmth); 10. signal flares (distress call); 11. dehydrated milk (have other food); 12. two .45 calibre pistols (protection); 13. pressure suit (possible body covering); 14. parachute silk (little use); 15. stellar map (little use); 16. two tanks of oxygen (no use).

Scene Two: 1. pressure suit (critical with moon's gravity and atmosphere); 2. two tanks of oxygen (no oxygen on moon, therefore essential); 3. bottles of water (important to survival); 4. stellar map (key way of finding direction); 5. food concentrate (food); 6. solar-powered FM receiver/transmitter (distress signal, contact mother ship); 7. 50 m of nylon rope (climbing); 8. first-aid kit with injection needles (oral or injection needed when no gravity); 9. parachute silk (shelter against sun's rays); 10. two .45 calibre pistols (self-propulsion devices); 11. dehydrated milk (have other food source); 12. blanket (have space suit); 13. matches (little or no use); 14. signal flares (no oxygen in atmosphere, so little or no use); 15. magnetic compass (no magnetized poles, so no use); 16. mosquito repellent (no use).

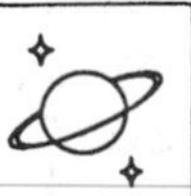

ON THE MOVE

The Earth is constantly on the move. A simple, quick observation can make a powerful point about Earth's rotation relative to the sun.

MATERIALS: Sunshine; long stick; clear, sunny patch of ground; rocks or other markers; watch. Optional -- masking tape; pencil; compass.

DOING IT:

1. Never look directly at the sun. It can damage your eyes permanently.

2. Push a long stick into level ground so that it stands upright, perpendicular to the ground. Mark the tip of the stick's shadow with a rock or other marker.

3. Where will the tip of the shadow be in 10 minutes? Predict the position and mark it.

4. When the 10 minutes is up, check your prediction. Are you surprised at how the shadow moved or how quickly? Given its diameter (13,000 km), the Earth has to move fairly quickly to make a complete rotation in 24 hours.

5. *Extension:* Mark the position of the shadow's tip at different times of the day (use masking tape to label the time on each marker). What general pattern of movement does the shadow follow each day? Can you use the shadow with the markers to tell time? When is the shadow shortest? When is it longest? Why does the length of the shadow change (think about the position of the sun in the sky)? Use a compass to find out what direction the shadow is pointing when it is different lengths. Watch the shadow pattern over several weeks. How does it change?

Stand up and slowly turn around from west to east. In which direction do the surroundings appear to be moving? The same idea applies to the Earth's rotation: the Earth spins from west to east, making the sky appear to move from east to west.

During one orbit around the sun (one year), the Earth actually rotates 365 times *plus* an extra 1/4 of a turn. Every four years -- in a leap year -- we add an extra day to the year to make up for the extra 1/4 turn (4 x 1/4 = 1 day). Leap years are years that can be divided exactly by 4 (e.g. 1992 divided by 4 = 498).

The Earth spins around an axis that passes through the centre of the globe. One complete rotation, which takes about 24 hours, marks the passing of an entire day and night. Contrary to what it looks like, the sun doesn't really move across the sky. The Earth does the moving. It's actually incorrect to talk about the sun "setting and rising". But, talking about sunrises and sunsets is practical because we look at the sun from the perspective of Earth. Before people had clocks, one way they told time was by watching shadows on sunny days. Shadow lengths change during the day; the shortest shadow is always found in the middle of the day (which may not be exactly at noon). At the same time that the Earth spins on its axis, it also orbits around the sun. 365 days and nights (or 365 Earth rotations) make one calendar year, the approximate time it takes Earth to make a complete orbit around the sun.

Topics: Earth; Light; Measurement.

THE PULL OF GRAVITY

What keeps a satellite up? This toy is easy to make, fun to use, and demonstrates an important concept.

QUICKIES

"Weight" is the force of gravity acting on an object's mass (quantity of matter). On the moon, an object has the same mass as on Earth, but it weighs less because the moon's gravitational pull is not as great as Earth's. If we're going to travel in space, one of the problems we'll have to deal with is low or zero gravity. Many tasks are difficult to perform in zero gravity (e.g. it can be difficult to eat while you and the food are floating aimlessly!). Muscles also weaken rapidly and, over long periods, may deteriorate irreversibly.

"Gravity" is the force that pulls an object downward, toward the centre of the Earth. Gravity pulls all objects downward at the same rate, regardless of the size or mass of the object. Other heavenly bodies (e.g. other planets, the moon) also exert gravitational force; the pull of the gravitational force depends on the mass of the heavenly body. Gravity helps to keep human-built satellites as well as natural satellites (e.g. moon around the Earth, Earth around the sun) in their orbits.

A human-built satellite is essentially a self-contained unit that has sensors; a central data processor to manage the collection, storage, and transmission of information; transmitters and receivers; and a power supply made up of solar panels and batteries. As a human-built satellite circles the Earth, Earth's gravity keeps the satellite from flying off into space. An initial push from a rocket gets the satellite into space. The satellite's orbital speed keeps it in space. At the same time, gravity constantly pulls at the satellite and keeps it going in a circle. There is an optimum orbital speed a satellite must maintain; otherwise, it's pulled closer and closer to Earth. The farther away from Earth a satellite is traveling, the weaker the Earth's gravitational pull. Because the pull of gravity is less, the satellite can then orbit at a slower speed without being pulled back to Earth.

Topics: Forces; Earth; Planets.

MATERIALS: Book; pencil; narrow, rigid tube (e.g. straw, ballpoint pen barrel); string; small balls, erasers, or nuts from bolts (or anything that can act as a weight). Optional -- tape; chair.

DOING IT:

1. Drop a book. What happens? Gravity pulls it down. Hold a book in one hand and a pencil in the other; drop both at the same time. Which one hits the ground first? Try this from a height (e.g. stand on a chair).

2. Run a length of string (about 1 m) through a tube and tie a weight to each end. Make sure the string is securely fastened to the weights; use tape if necessary. The objects could be dangerous if they fly off.

3. The upper object is the satellite and the lower object represents gravity. Spin the satellite around. Does the lower object rise? Can you spin the satellite so that the lower object remains level (i.e. does not move up or down as the satellite spins)? It takes practice. To maintain an "orbit", the outward pull caused by the rotation of the satellite must be balanced by the pull of gravity (the lower object).

4. Change the radius of the "orbit" (e.g. spin the satellite in a larger circle). Does the satellite have to go faster or slower for the lower object to remain level?

5. What happens if you have a greater mass for the upper and/or lower object (e.g. tie two objects to the string for the satellite, or two for the force of gravity)? With what mass combination do you have to spin the satellite fastest to keep it in a steady "orbit"?

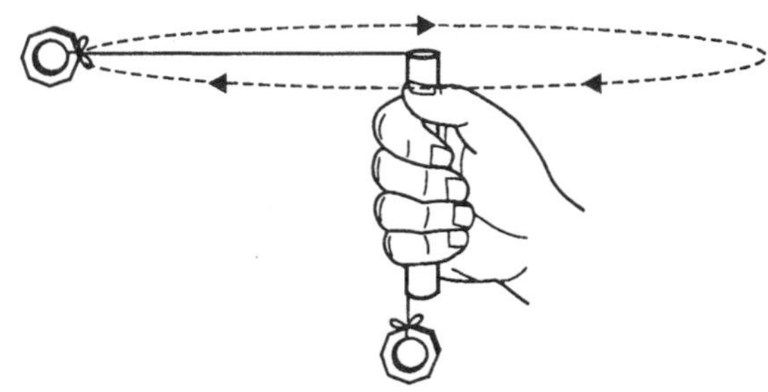

OUR MOON

The moon is a satellite of Earth; it completes an orbit, or path, around the Earth approximately once a month. Try "landing on the moon".

MATERIALS: Large area; measuring tape; rocks or other markers.

DOING IT:

1. In a large, clear area, measure about 50 m for the diameter of a big circle. Mark the circle -- which represents the moon's orbital path -- by putting down rocks or other markers at certain points.

2. Measure about 4 m for the diameter of a smaller circle, Earth, in the centre of the larger circle. Mark the smaller circle.

3. Mark a gradual spiral swirling out from the small circle and eventually hitting the larger circle. The point at which the spiral meets the large circle is the "landing point".

4. One person acts as the moon. He or she begins jogging around the large circle at a steady pace, while looking at the ground so that he or she can't see the "spacecraft".

5. Another person acts as the spacecraft. The "spacecraft" begins jogging steadily around the inner circle. The "spacecraft" decides when to break away from "Earth" and begin jogging along the spiral in order to meet the moon at "landing point". Once the "spacecraft" breaks away, he or she must look at the ground and maintain a steady pace (no cheating!). It will take practice before someone is able to start on the spiral at exactly the right time so that the "moon" and "spacecraft" meet at the "landing point".

6. Change the spiral so that the position of the landing point changes (e.g. make spiral tighter or looser).

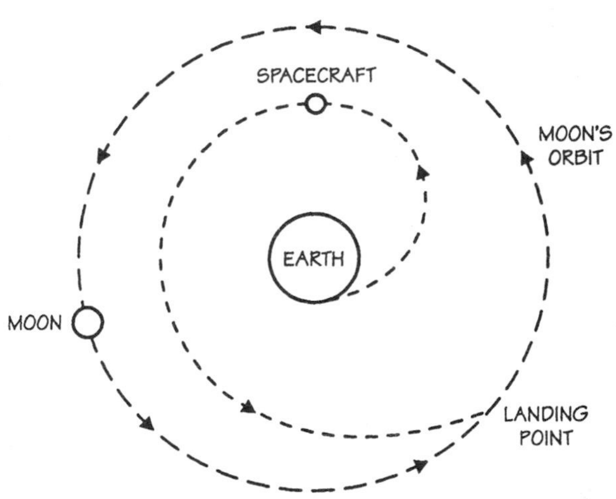

Saturn's rings are caused by billions of pieces of ice trapped in orbit around the planet. The rings may also contain rock fragments left over from moons which have broken apart.

Earth's moon is our nearest neighbour, about 385,000 km away. It's relatively small; it could easily fit into Canada. Although it looks round, it's actually egg-shaped; the pointed end, which has a thinner crust, faces Earth. Some scientists think that the Earth's strong gravitational pull may have sucked the moon into its shape. Because the moon has almost no atmosphere, the temperature on its surface swings much more wildly than the temperature on Earth. The moon's surface temperature can reach the boiling point of water (100 degrees C) and drop as low as -150 degrees C. The moon may have formed when a planet about the size of Mars smashed into Earth and caused a large amount of rock to blast into space around our planet. Over time, this material collected into a body one-quarter the size of the Earth's diameter. Earth's moon is not the only moon in the solar system -- Pluto has 1 moon; Mars has 2; Neptune has 8; Uranus has 15; Jupiter has 16; and Saturn has 18.

The moon and Earth are constantly on the move. This means that there are timing challenges involved in landing on the moon. Exact calculations must be made so that a spacecraft escapes the Earth's force of gravity at that precise instant which gives the spacecraft the correct direction to travel toward and meet the moon.

Topics: Earth.

METEOR SHOWER

Create your own "meteor shower" and learn firsthand about the shape, size, and features of craters on Earth and on the moon.

MATERIALS: Area with sand or soft, loose soil; rocks of various sizes. Optional -- water.

A "meteoroid" is a chunk of rock, ice, and metal drifting in space. The same chunk, when it collides with Earth's atmosphere and causes the air to glow in a bright, fiery trail, is called a "meteor" (or shooting star). Once the chunk hits the ground, it's called a "meteorite". Most boulder-sized meteors never reach Earth's surface; they burn up before they hit the ground. However, billions of "micrometeorites" (tiny particles of matter) reach Earth's surface. Micrometeorites add about 400 tonnes of matter to Earth each day. Large meteorites may strike the Earth every few years. Every 10,000 years, there's a good chance that Earth will be struck by something more the size of a mountain. When it does happen that a large meteorite reaches Earth, there's only about a 1 in 4 chance that it will strike land. Most meteorites fall into the sea. Once large meteorites strike the Earth (or the moon), they leave a large crater. There's a crater about 3 km wide in Quebec, Canada that geologists believe was caused by a meteorite.

Topics: Rock Types; Stars; Earth.

DOING IT:

1. The idea is to throw rocks into the sand or soil and leave "craters" behind. Stand a couple of metres away from a small area (e.g. 0.5 sq. m) and throw "meteors". Some will hit the area (meteorites); others will miss (meteoroids).

2. Carefully pick the "meteorites" out of the soil or sand. Are different craters caused by different rocks? In what ways are craters different? How does a meteorite's angle of impact affect a crater? How many different ways can you make a deep crater? How can you distinguish between older and newer craters?

3. *Variation:* How does the nature of the craters change if you throw meteors into wet sand or soil rather than dry sand or soil?

Meteorites are made mainly of iron and nickel. Both of these elements are magnetic. If you drag a magnet over the ground it will pick up some particles. About 20% of the particles will be dust from outer space.

At The Speed Of Light

How long does it take light to reach the Earth from the sun? Do a few simple light-year calculations and then time it for yourself.

MATERIALS: Paper; pencil; kitchen timer. Optional -- calculator.

DOING IT:

1. Light travels at a speed of about 300,000 kilometres in one second. Calculate the distance light travels in one minute: 300,000 km x 60 (there are 60 seconds in one minute) = A km.

2. Calculate the distance light travels in one hour: A km (answer from above) x 60 (there are 60 minutes in one hour) = B km.

3. Calculate the distance light travels in one day: B km (answer from above) x 24 (there are 24 hours in one day) = C km.

4. Calculate the distance light travels in one year: C km (answer from above) x 365 (there are 365 days in one year) = D km. The answer, D km, is one light-year.

5. Now calculate the time it takes for light to reach Earth from the sun. The sun is approximately 150,000,000 km away from the Earth. 150,000,000 km divided by 300,000 km/sec gives you the time in seconds. Divide the time in seconds by 60 to get the number of minutes it takes light to travel from the sun to the Earth.

6. Time light as it travels from the sun to the Earth. Count down: "Three . . . two . . . one . . . some light is on its way!" As you end the count, set a kitchen timer to the correct number of minutes (calculated above). When the timer goes off, you'll know the light has reached the Earth.

If you sent a message into space, how would you know someone was listening? How would you recognize a reply? Astronomers are aiming radio telescopes at all parts of the universe. So far, they believe they have picked up radio waves from natural sources only. Radio waves travel at the speed of light (300,000 km/sec). Even at that speed, it would take years for a message to travel the distance between Earth and its closest stars. Can you imagine saying "hello" -- and then waiting 100 years for an answer?

Our atmosphere is largely heated from below, by the Earth itself. The sun's radiant energy is first absorbed by Earth's water, rocks, and soil, and changed into heat. These warmed substances then heat the layer of air closest to Earth's surface through "infrared radiation" (radiant heat). The temperature of the atmosphere is warmer closer to Earth than farther away because of this heating process. Also, air closer to Earth -- which is denser, dustier, and moister than air in upper layers -- is able to absorb more of the sun's radiation, as well as more of the infrared radiation from the Earth.

Distances in space are so large that they are measured in "light-years". One light-year is the distance light travels through space in one year. How far is that? Light travels at almost 300,000 km/sec. That's about 9.5 trillion km in a year. It takes light only 8 minutes and 20 seconds to travel the millions of kilometres between the Earth and the sun.

Topics: Light; Numbers; Measurement.

QUICKIES

SKY BLUE

Why does the sky look blue from Earth? In photographs taken from the moon, why does space look black? Use milk and water to find out.

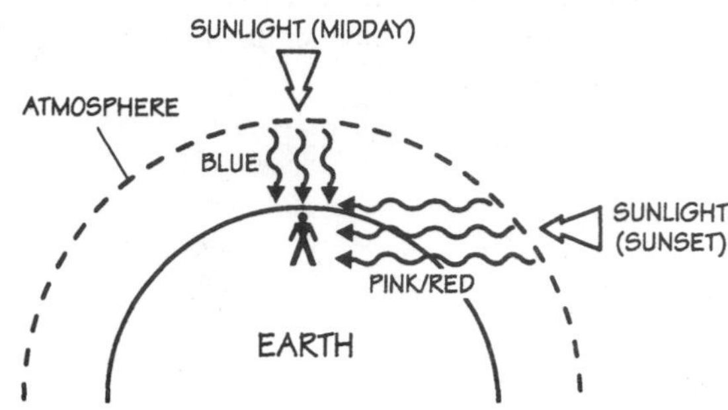

The Earth's atmosphere is filled with all sorts of microscopic particles (e.g. gas molecules, dust, soot, pollen, bits of rock, salt from the oceans, as well as particles added by humans through car exhaust and smoke from factories). When sunlight hits these particles, the light is scattered. Visible, white light from the sun is made up of all the colours of the rainbow. As the light hits and bounces off particles, different colours become visible. Colours with short wavelengths (i.e. blue/violet) are scattered differently than colours with longer wavelengths (i.e. red). When the sun is directly overhead (i.e. midday), blue light is scattered most and so the sky looks blue. When the sun is lower on the horizon (i.e. sunrise, sunset), the sky is tinted pink/red. The angled light must travel through more of the atmosphere and blue light is scattered so much that it doesn't reach your eye; only red light is left to reach the Earth. The moon doesn't have an atmosphere. There are no floating particles and light isn't scattered. If you looked into space from the surface of the moon, you would have a clear view of the blackness of never-ending space. Different atmospheres make a sky look different. For example, if you looked up from Mars, the atmosphere would make the Martian sky look pink.

In this activity, the clear water represents the way space looks from the moon. When you stir milk into the water, you create an "atmosphere". The light is scattered and you can see faint colours. The more milk you add, the "thicker" the atmosphere, representing angled light having to travel through more of Earth's atmosphere. The colours you see move from one end of the colour spectrum (the blues) to the other end of the spectrum (pinks/reds).

Topics: Light; Atmosphere.

MATERIALS: Large, clear drinking glass or jar; water; milk; spoon; black construction paper; large, bright flashlight.

DOING IT:

1. Do this activity in a dark area (e.g. a closet).

2. Fill a glass or jar 3/4 full with water. Prop up a sheet of black paper behind the glass.

3. Shine a flashlight down into the water or through the side of the glass. Does the water look clear? Can you see the black paper easily through the water? This is like looking into space from the surface of the moon.

4. While you're shining the flashlight into the water, stir milk into the water a small spoonful at a time. Do you see a faint blue in the glass? Can you still see the black paper? Does the blue eventually change to pink/red? Move the flashlight around and shine light through the glass from all angles. How is this like Earth's sky?

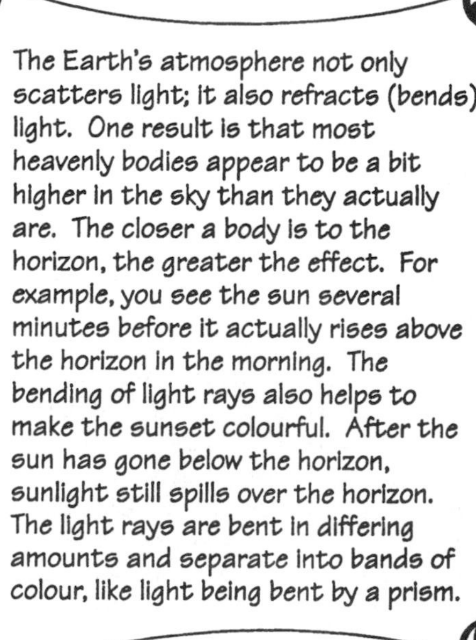
The Earth's atmosphere not only scatters light; it also refracts (bends) light. One result is that most heavenly bodies appear to be a bit higher in the sky than they actually are. The closer a body is to the horizon, the greater the effect. For example, you see the sun several minutes before it actually rises above the horizon in the morning. The bending of light rays also helps to make the sunset colourful. After the sun has gone below the horizon, sunlight still spills over the horizon. The light rays are bent in differing amounts and separate into bands of colour, like light being bent by a prism.

APPLYING SCIENCE

In *The Seven Follies of Science*, written in 1906, John Phin listed seven things that scientists, mathematicians, inventors, and dreamers had been attempting to do for thousands of years. Even today, no one has done them. The seven things are found on this page.

Perpetual Motion Machine: This machine could operate forever without any outside source of energy. It wouldn't require a battery or need to be plugged in; it wouldn't burn gasoline; and it wouldn't need even an occasional push or pull.

Trisecting an Angle: The challenge is to take any angle and divide it into three equal parts without using a protractor.

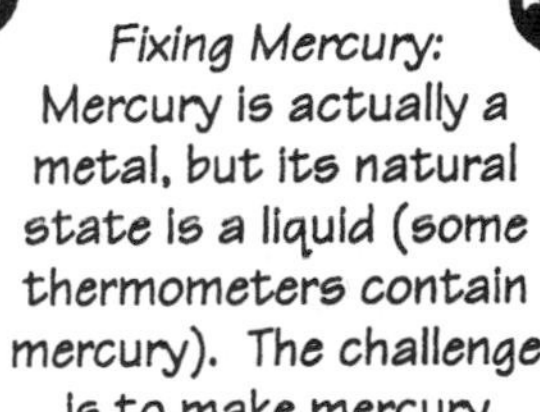

Fixing Mercury: Mercury is actually a metal, but its natural state is a liquid (some thermometers contain mercury). The challenge is to make mercury solid, like steel. (Note: Never experiment with mercury because it is dangerous!)

Squaring a Circle: The challenge is to take the area (i.e. the surface covered) of any given circle and find a square with precisely the same area.

Doubling a Cube: This cubic challenge involves finding a way to make a second cube with exactly twice the volume (i.e. space inside) of an initial cube without using a ruler.

Lead into Gold: The challenge is to change any one metal into another. Some might argue that this has been accomplished -- lead has been changed into gold in an atomic particle accelerator. But people want to change lead into gold to become rich, and the accelerator method is so expensive that it just isn't worth it.

The Elixir of Youth: There's nothing to keep you eternally young and, despite what beauty product ads proclaim, nothing to keep you looking young throughout your entire life.

TO LOOK ETERNALLY YOUNG PUT CUCUMBER SLICES ON YOUR EYES AND MUD ON YOUR FACE . . . THEY'VE GOT TO BE KIDDING!!

SAVED BY TECHNOLOGY!

A little technological know-how can make your life a lot easier. Use technology to easily pull two sticks together while two people are trying to hold the sticks apart.

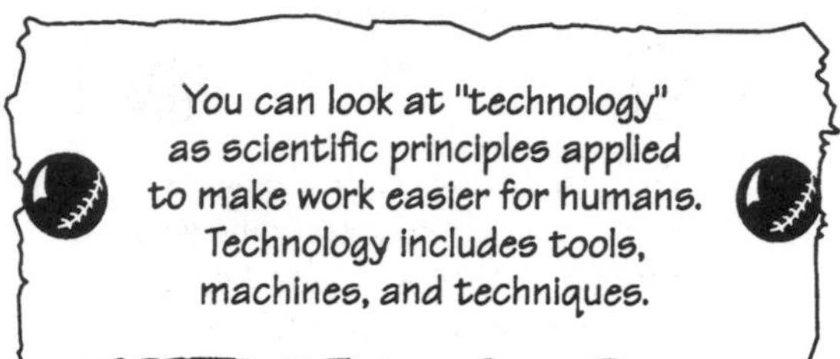

MATERIALS: Two brooms, hockey sticks, or other type of rods; long piece of rope.

DOING IT:

1. Two people hold two sticks about 30 cm apart. The challenge is for a third person to try to pull the sticks together using only a length of rope. The two people holding the sticks must try their hardest to keep the sticks apart.

2. The secret to success is to tie one end of the rope around one end of one of the sticks. Then loop the rope around the two sticks, as shown. As you pull on the rope, the sticks will be forced toward each other.

Something so simple -- and useful -- and yet it wasn't around until 1940. That's when Canadian Norman Breakey invented the paint roller.

This activity is based on the simple "block and tackle", which consists of a system of pulleys and ropes designed to increase human strength (e.g. used to lower pianos from buildings, used on construction sites to lift heavy objects). For every one loop of the rope around the sticks, your pulling power increases significantly. In theory, the pulling power doubles; but in practice there are some losses due to friction. How much pulling power is lost depends on the materials you use (e.g. a round-handled broom results in less friction with a rope than a square-handled hockey stick). The one catch in this activity is that every time you increase your pulling power, the distance you have to pull the rope doubles.

Topics: Forces.

In 1938, Canadian Thomas Carroll built the first experimental model of the self-propelled combine in a Massey-Harris factory in Toronto. The machine revolutionized wheat farming and saved time, money, and back-breaking work.

SUPER STRENGTH

Need to break a piece of string? Technology to the rescue once again! Here's a simple way to break string with your bare hands.

MATERIALS: Long piece of string.

DOING IT:

1. Caution: If the string is too strong, it will cut into your hand. Do this activity carefully.

2. Wrap one end of the string around your left index finger.

3. Loop the string around your hand, as shown.

4. With your other hand, grasp the free end of the string 30 to 60 cm below your hand. Wrap the string several times around your right hand.

5. Make a fist with each hand. Hold the fists close together; then quickly pull your right fist down and your left fist up. The string should break inside your left fist at the point marked X.

Technology has made life much easier, but it has also resulted in serious problems. Technologies have been put to use without considering the possible harmful side effects. For example, people thought cars would be more convenient and less smelly than horses -- and therefore an improvement. But, as more people drove more cars, noise and air pollution became new problems we must now solve.

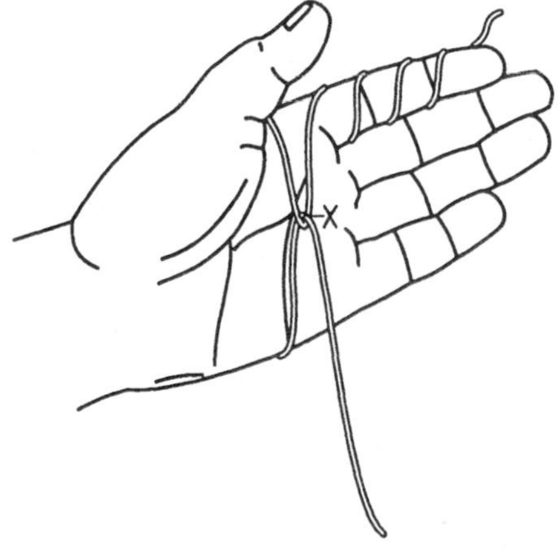

As you pump up a tire, it fills with air. The more you pump, the more air is forced into the tire. The air inside the tire is squeezed into a very small space and is called "compressed air". Compressed air can support heavy objects like cars.

The first zipper was patented in 1891, the same year as the flashlight. The paper clip wasn't invented until 1900.

This feat demonstrates that pressure is the force divided by the area on which the force operates. Obviously, one part of the string is as strong as another part. The trick is to make one part of the string work against another part. By looping the string as shown, the force when you pull on the string is concentrated on the tiny area where the string intersects itself. This increases the pressure so that the string acts like a dull knife blade and actually cuts through itself.

Topics: Forces.

FLIP THAT SPOON

A lever is a simple machine. You can use a spoon as a lever to flip another spoon into a drinking glass.

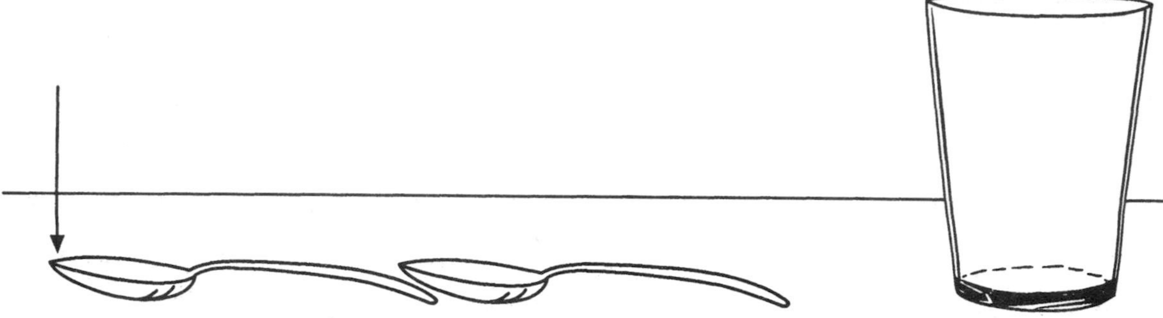

MATERIALS: Drinking glass; two spoons.

"Machines" are arrangements of fixed and moving parts designed to perform useful work or a specialized task. Machines enable people to use a small amount of force to move a very large load. There are six simple machines that play a key role in technology: the *inclined plane* (a sloping surface, which makes it easier to slide a load upward than lift it directly); the *screw* (which is actually a tiny inclined plane wrapped in a spiral around a shaft); the *wheel and axle* (used to transport heavy goods by rolling rather than sliding); the *pulley* (a wheel over which runs a rope or cable); the *wedge* (a gently tapering triangle; when struck with a hammer, it exerts force sideways to, for example, split a log); and the *lever*. Complicated machines are really just combinations of these six simple machines. Machines used to change other forms of energy (e.g. heat) into mechanical energy are called "engines" (e.g. steam engine). The first machines were built as weapons for war (e.g. catapult). The first manufacturing machines, powered by steam engines, appeared in the 1700s and started the industrial revolution.

The lever is one of the earliest and simplest machines. It consists of a rigid bar supported at a fixed point (the fulcrum) along its length, and which can be acted on by a force. A crowbar is an example of a lever. In this activity, the bottom of a spoon's bowl serves as the fulcrum. You apply force to the tip of the bowl. The end of the handle does the work for you.

Topics: Forces.

DOING IT:

1. Set up two metal spoons and a drinking glass as shown.

2. Make a fist and bring your fist down to hit the tip of the spoon farthest from the glass. If you hit the spoon just right and the spoons are lined up correctly, the second spoon should flip into the glass.

What's the easiest way to break a tree branch over your knee? (Hint: Your knee acts like a lever. The force exerted against the centre of the branch depends on the forces exerted by your hands holding the ends of the branch and their distance from the support point.)

In 1908, Canadian Peter Robertson invented a square-holed screw and a matching screwdriver. The screw/screwdriver set provides greater torque turning power, can't slip, and requires only one hand.

Half A Ball

Science is important in sports. For example, balls for certain sports are made in specific ways. Explore ball characteristics by playing a game of base-half-ball.

MATERIALS: Baseballs or rubber balls; saw; baseball bat. Optional -- piece of garden hose; tape.

DOING IT:

1. An adult should saw a ball in half. You may need to wrap tape around the half-ball to keep it together.

2. Try batting around the half-ball. How does it compare to a whole ball? Can the half-ball travel the same distance as the whole ball? What's the relationship between how far the half-ball travels and the side of the half-ball that contacts the bat? When you hit a half-ball, is it deformed more or less than a whole ball?

The first bicycles, built in the late 1700s, had no pedals; riders simply pushed their feet against the ground. Later bicycles had pedals, but consisted of huge front wheels and small rear wheels; riders were perched 1.5 m above the ground and often toppled off. It wasn't until the 1880s that safer, more comfortable bicycles began to appear.

3. *Extension:* Try hitting an 8 cm long piece of garden hose. Is it easier or harder to hit the "hoseball" than the half-ball? Can you hit a "hoseball" as far as a half-ball? Why or why not?

A ball's round shape lessens the air resistance and helps the ball slice through the air. The air curves around the sides of the ball rather than being blocked. If a half-ball's rounded surface is facing forward, it doesn't do too bad a job of cutting air resistance. However, if the flatter, open side of the half-ball is facing forward, air hits the ball straight on and slows it down. Sawing a ball in half limits both the distance it can travel and the damage it can do when it hits something.

Balls for different sports are designed based on various physical characteristics -- mass, size, type of material, surface texture, and shape. A *baseball* consists of wool wrapped around a solid, cork and rubber core. Two pieces of leather are stitched tightly onto the ball. The uneven surface caused by the stitches makes the ball spin through the air in unusual ways. A knowledgeable pitcher can make the ball curve so that it is difficult for a batter to hit. A *tennis ball* is about the same size as a baseball, but it is lighter and bounces easily. It consists of hollow rubber covered with wool and nylon. The ball's fuzzy texture increases air resistance, as well as friction when it hits your racket or the court. A *ping-pong ball* is very light and fairly small. It consists of a smooth plastic shell filled with air. An ideal combination of surface texture and weight ensure that this ball travels fast, but not so fast that the game becomes impossible. A *bowling ball* is very heavy for its size and is solid except for the finger holes. It is made of hardened rubber. The ball's smooth surface enables it to roll easily down a bowling lane. The ball's mass allows it to have enough force to knock down bowling pins. A *football* is a rather odd ball because it is oval-shaped. If you don't throw the ball with a spin, it wobbles through the air and is difficult to catch. The ball's rough leather surface helps players grab it.

Topics: Air; Flight.

Roaring Cup

Science is important in music. This toy is based on the same scientific principles used in the construction of musical instruments.

QUICKIES

Tie one end of a 17 cm long piece of string around a metal spoon. Hold the other end of the string tightly against your ear. The spoon should hang down freely. Tap the spoon with the handle of a metal knife. What do you hear? The sound travels up the string and resonates in your ear. Try tying other objects to the string.

MATERIALS: A paper or foam cup; scissors; string.

DOING IT:

1. Tie a large knot at one end of a string about 35 cm long.

2. Make a tiny hole in the middle of the bottom of a paper cup.

3. Run the unknotted end of the string through the inside of the cup and poke it through the hole; the knot should prevent the string from going completely through the hole.

4. Rub your thumbnail down the string, while squeezing and pulling the string tightly. You should hear a roaring sound. Why?

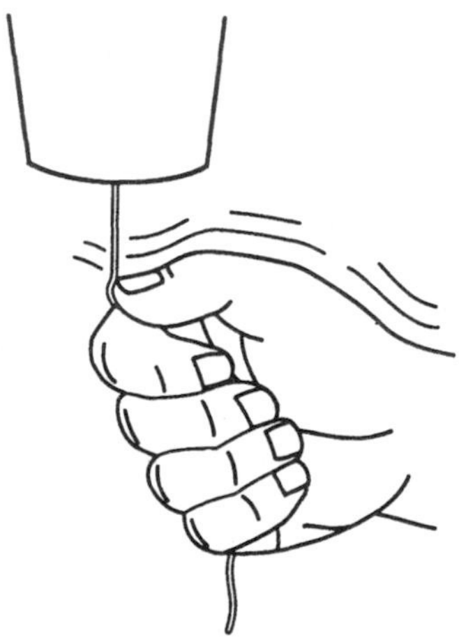

5. Try rubbing the string without the cup. Do you get the same effect? Why not?

The roaring cup is a popular toy found in Spain and other parts of Europe. The cup acts as a cavity which increases sound. A cavity helps to amplify and prolong sound because sound waves inside the cavity hit the walls, bounce back, and reinforce each other. This is called "resonance". Musical instruments such as bells have cavities; others, such as the violin, have sound boxes. In a musical instrument, the walls of the cavity or sound box vibrate at the same frequency as the source of the sound (e.g. the violin strings). If this were not so, the sound wave would cause an echo when it bounced back instead of reinforcing the original sound.

Topics: Sound.

Sandford Fleming was a Canadian railroad engineer who invented standard time for the world. On November 17, 1883 (the day before the world went on standard time), the clocks of every city were set according to the sun's position there. For example, two cities only 600 km apart could have a time difference of as much as half an hour. These differences within small areas meant that, in an era of steam trains, trying to keep a master train schedule was chaos. So Fleming divided the world into 24 time zones, each 15 degrees of longitude wide. Now, for every location within a time zone, the time is exactly the same.

AEOLIAN SOUNDS

If the wind is blowing right, telephone and electric wires sometimes start to whistle and sing very loudly. Make elastic bands sing.

MATERIALS: Four elastic bands (each about 8 cm long); six paper clips.

DOING IT:

1. Loop four elastic bands together to form a chain.

2. Hook six paper clips on one end of the chain.

3. Hold the other end of the elastic-band chain in your hand, and spin the chain around as fast as you can. **Don't spin the chain near your face or other people; if it breaks, it can be dangerous.** You should begin to hear a shrill whistle.

4. Twirl the chain faster and then slower. Can you produce different sounds?

5. Does it make a difference how many paper clips you attach to the chain?

QUICKIES

Until the mid 1940s, there were only two ways to get orange juice: by squeezing oranges yourself or from a can. But canned orange juice just didn't taste fresh. So, scientists developed juice concentrate. Most of the water from orange juice is evaporated in a vacuum chamber so that a syrupy liquid remains. A little fresh juice is added to the liquid for appearance and taste, and then the mixture is frozen.

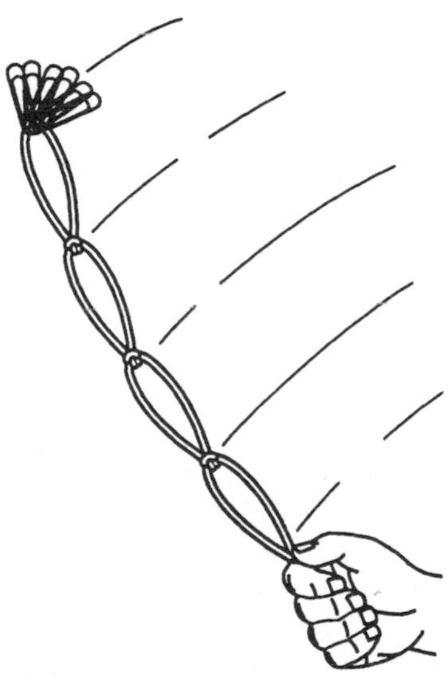

The world's most famous baby cereal, Pablum, was developed at The Hospital for Sick Children in Toronto, Canada. In 1930, Drs. Brown, Drake and Tisdall were concerned about the fact that many of the babies they saw weren't eating well. So, they developed a formula for a nutritious cereal that you just mix with warm water and serve.

Any tightly-stretched wire, string, or elastic band will vibrate when wind blows over it. When you spin an elastic-band chain, the weight of the paper clips makes the elastic bands stretch. "Wind" is created by the spinning motion of the chain (the air itself is still, but it's moving across the chain). How does this motion create sound? The spinning chain produces eddy currents of air behind it, much like a boat leaves a swirl of water behind as it travels. The small, irregular swirls of air make the elastic-band chain vibrate back and forth as it moves through the air. As the chain spins through the air faster, it vibrates more rapidly. Finally, the vibrations result in sound waves which you can hear. Wind-borne or "aeolian" (from a Latin word meaning "god of the winds") sounds were once quite common, as people hung aeolian harps outdoors or in screened porches; every time the wind blew, the harps made "music".

Topics: Sound; Air.

LIGHTNING CALCULATIONS

Numbers are interesting because they behave in predictable ways. Amaze people as you demonstrate your ability to be as fast as a calculator.

MATERIALS: Paper; pencil.

DOING IT:

1. No calculators allowed!

2. Offer to multiply any 3-digit number by 143 -- and to do it quickly in your head. Someone else can use paper and pencil to figure out the answer the long way and show that you're correct.

3. For the lightning multiplication of any number by 143, follow the same steps. Say you want to multiply 825 by 143. Take the number 825 and picture it in your head as 825825. Then divide it by 7. Dividing the number this way isn't hard, with a little practice. Your answer to the multiplication of 825 by 143 is 117,975.

4. Here's a more detailed example: Multiply 307 by 143. Picture 307 in your head as 307307 and mentally divide by 7. 7 goes into 30 four times and 2 left over; 7 goes into 27 three times and 6 left over; 7 goes into 63 exactly nine times; finally, 7 times 0 is zero and 7 into 7 is one. So, the answer is 43,901. If you have to, write down the digits in the answer one by one as you do the division.

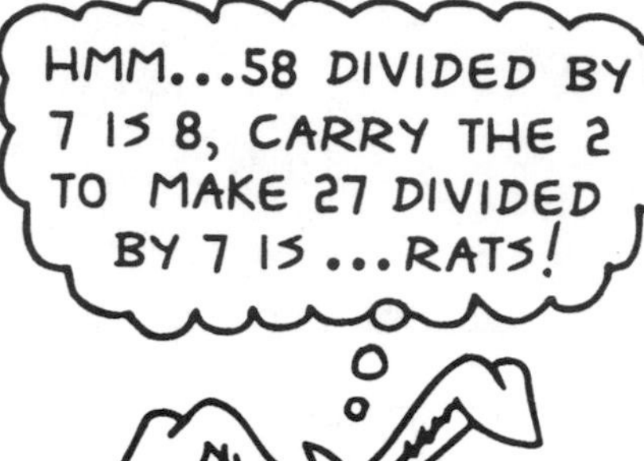

There are a number of tricks you can do with numbers. Some numbers have special properties, and if you know these properties you can use them to your advantage. For example, the number 142,857 is a special number because when it's multiplied by any number between 1 and 6, it will always give a product with the numbers 1, 4, 2, 8, 5, 7 in a cyclical order (e.g. 2 x 142,857 = 285,714, and 3 x 142,857 = 428,571). In this activity, the special number is 143. Multiply 143 by any number and, while someone sits and multiplies out the answer the long way, you can quickly come up with the answer in your head.

Topics: Numbers; Brain.

On November 7, 1885, the last spike of the Canadian Pacific Railroad was driven in at 9:22 am in the village of Craigellachie, near Revelstoke, B.C. That last spike -- an ordinary iron spike -- represents an extraordinary achievement. Thousands of kilometres of railroad track, twisting and turning through rock and muskeg and bush, link Canada from end to end.

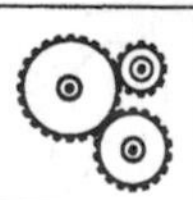

GUESSTIMATIONS

Using numbers precisely and accurately is a whole science in itself. Test your estimation skills while treating your taste buds and then move on to dot counting.

MATERIALS: Chocolate chip cookies; paper; pencil.

DOING IT:

1. Start thinking in numerical terms. Can you estimate the number of: slices of bread in a loaf; raisins in a box of Raisin Bran; blades of grass in a field; leaves on one tree; or stars in the sky?

2. Chocolate chips are one of the more tasty things to count. Several people should each get five cookies. First, estimate the number of chocolate chips per cookie. Then, break apart each cookie to count and record the actual number of chocolate chips per cookie. After counting, you can eat the evidence!

3. How close were the estimates? How do different people's counts compare? What's the fewest number of chips per cookie? The greatest? Is there a big difference between the fewest and the greatest, or do most cookies have about the same number of chocolate chips? What's the average number of chips per cookie (i.e. add all the totals and divide by the number of cookies)? What factors control the maximum number of chips per cookie (e.g. flow properties of batter, cost)?

4. Move on to dots. Each person should draw dots randomly on his or her own sheet of paper. People should secretly count their dots as they draw them (an easy way to do this: for every ten dots you draw, make a mark on the back of the paper). Then, the challenge is to try to guess the number of dots on someone else's paper.

5. What strategies can be used for estimation? One strategy is to subdivide whatever is being estimated into manageable components. For example, mentally divide a sheet of dots into quarters or eighths; estimate the number of dots in one of the divisions and then multiply the estimate by the number of divisions to get the overall total.

6. *Extension:* After the first round of dot guessing is over, make new dotted sheets. This time, people should arrange dots so that they are more difficult to count (e.g. clustering dots here and there, rather than spreading dots evenly across the page). How many different strategies can people develop to make dot guessing more difficult? What counter-strategies can people develop to make their "guesstimations"?

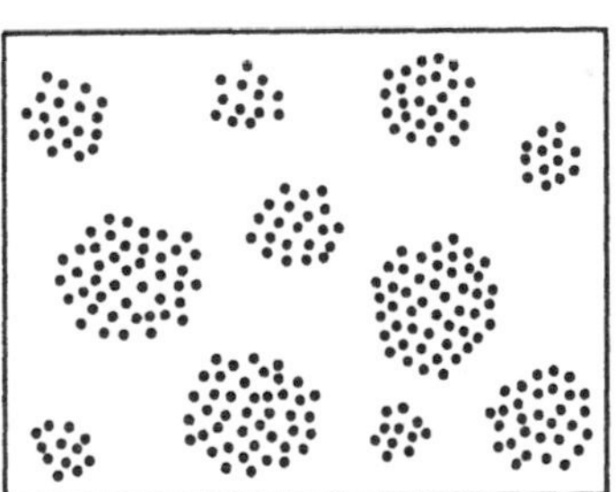

Putting a number to something can be very important because it often emphasizes the complexity and wonder of the world around us, allows for easy comparison, and puts things into a bigger context. For example: During an average lifetime, a person's heart beats almost 3 billion times. A sneeze can produce wind speeds almost as great as those in a tornado (150 m/sec). Blonde people can have as many as 150,000 hairs on their head. On the vast scale of the solar system, the 13,000 km diameter of Earth makes it a very, very tiny object.

Topics: Numbers; Measurement.

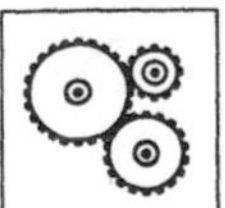

Make Time activities require a little planning and some readily-available, inexpensive materials. They take at least half an hour to complete. Each page in this section contains a separate Make Time activity.

There are ten subject areas. An activity's subject area is shown by a symbol in the lower, outside corner of the page. Make Time activities often deal with key subject area concepts in depth.

MAKE TIME

Activities begin with a two-line introduction. A materials list and detailed description follow. Background information is provided in the shadowed boxes.

If you're looking for information and facts for a particular subject area, flip from page to page and read the shadowed boxes. In general, each page builds on ideas presented on earlier pages. Topics listed for each activity will help you combine activities to suit your interests and needs.

Make Time

DISCOVERING SCIENCE

Open up a double page from a large-format newspaper. Hold a corner of the page in your right hand (or left, if you're left-handed). Using only that hand, crumple the sheet into a tight ball. Not as easy as you might think, is it?

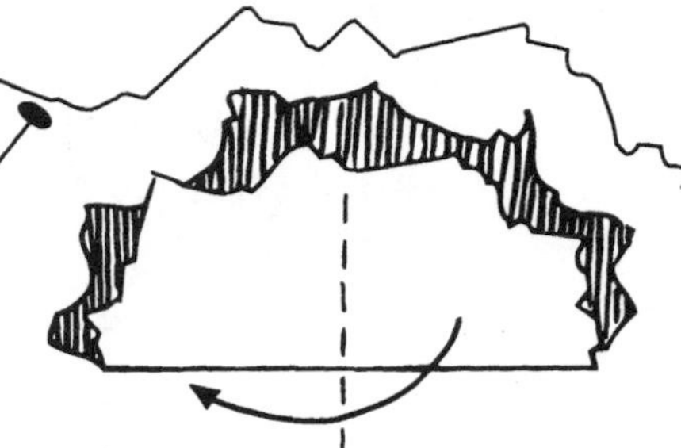

How can you make a perfect right angle using only a scrap of torn paper? The trick is to fold the paper roughly in half, then in half again using the straight base line as a guide.

Examine the following series of letters:
XYYXZXYZXYYYXZXY
What should the next three letters be?

Answer: The next three letters are Z, X, and Y. The pattern is that there is an X followed by two Ys and another X. Then there is a Z followed by X Y Z. The pattern repeats.

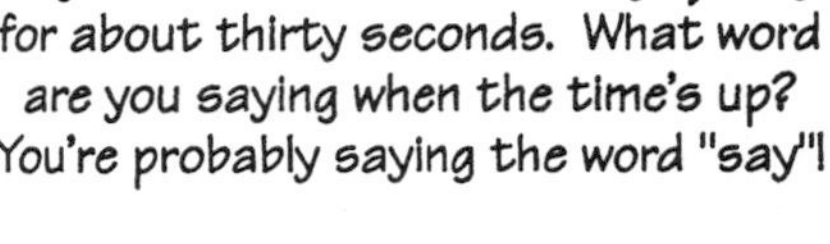

Say the word "ace" aloud very quickly for about thirty seconds. What word are you saying when the time's up? You're probably saying the word "say"!

Instead of talking to someone, try writing a message with your finger on the person's back. That's a real challenge in communication!

Try rolling spheres, discs, and hoops down a slope. All spheres will beat all discs which will beat all hoops -- every time. It doesn't matter how heavy or how big objects are. Rolling speed is directly related to the distribution of mass around an object's centre of gravity. A sphere has its weight most closely distributed around its centre, so it rolls fastest.

The most incomprehensible thing about the world is that it is comprehensible.
(Albert Einstein)

Soak It Up

Science involves answering questions in an organized way. Use the scientific method to investigate what happens as a sponge dries out.

MATERIALS: Large sponge; water; small drinking glass; metre stick; string; tape; paper and pencil.

DOING IT:

1. Start by asking a question: What happens to a sponge as it dries out?

2. Now you want to gather information about the question. Get to know your sponge. Use your powers of observation. Pick it up when it's dry. How heavy is it? What does it look like? What does it feel like? Slowly add water to the sponge using a drinking glass. How much water does the sponge hold? When the sponge is soaked with water, how heavy is it? How does it compare to a dry sponge?

3. Using what you've learned, make a guess about what happens to a sponge as it dries out. Write down your hypothesis.

4. The next step is to test your hypothesis. Soak the sponge with water and then wring it out as much as you can. No matter how hard you squeeze, the sponge will still be damp. Tie the damp sponge to one end of a metre stick. Tie and tape a string around the metre stick to suspend the metre stick so that it balances with the sponge on one end. Write down the time and draw a picture of how the set-up looks. Every 5 minutes for half an hour, record the time and draw a picture of how the metre stick looks. (Note: Depending on the sponge and the air temperature/humidity, observations may have to be done at shorter or longer intervals.)

5. Was your hypothesis right? What happens to the sponge and metre stick over the half hour? What's the answer to the original question? As the water in the sponge evaporates, the sponge becomes lighter. The final part of the scientific method involves explaining to other people what you found out. Use your pictures to help you explain what happened.

Science is a way of looking at the world. Science is like a game for understanding the world, and the game is played by special rules called the "scientific method". There are five basic steps involved in the scientific method: 1) Ask a question; 2) Gather information about the question; 3) Form a hypothesis (take a guess about the answer); 4) Test the hypothesis; 5) Tell others what you found.

Topics: Scientific Method; States of Matter.

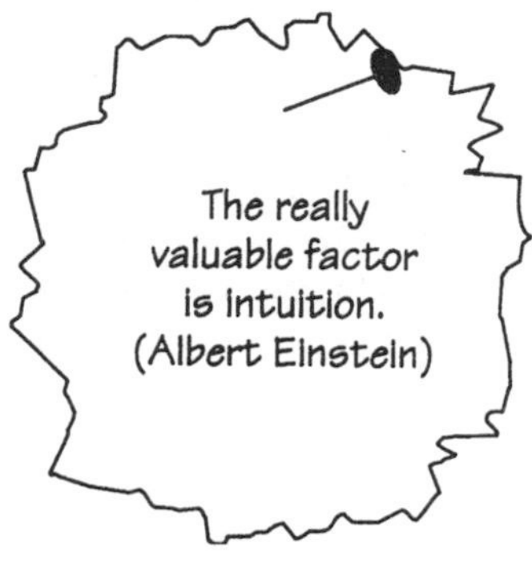

STUCK ON YOU

How sticky is sticky? How strong is strong? Use the scientific method to experiment with the stickiness and strength of different types of tape.

MATERIALS: Paper; pencil; different kinds of tape (e.g. clear, magic, masking, electrical, carpet, double-sided); coins or other small, heavy objects; piece of fuzzy fabric; ruler.

DOING IT:

1. Start by asking the key questions: Which tape is the strongest? Which is the stickiest?

2. Gather information about the questions using your observation skills. How do different types of tape look different? How do different tapes feel? Do some tapes feel stickier than others? What do you do with the different types of tape? Why does tape stop being sticky after it's used for a while?

3. Using what you've learned, make a guess about which tape is stickiest and which is strongest. Why do you think a certain tape is stickiest or strongest? Write down your hypothesis. Now test your hypothesis.

4. *Sticky Test:* Hang the *same length* of each type of tape from the bottom (not the side) of a table. There should be a short length of tape attached to the bottom of the table, and a longer length hanging down. Stick the same small objects to each piece of tape until the tape is pulled off the table. Count the number of objects each tape holds before it falls and write down your findings.

5. *Another Sticky Test:* Test each type of tape by attaching and removing the same piece to some fabric. Count how many times each kind of tape sticks to the fabric before it loses its stickiness. Write down your findings.

6. *Strength Test:* Cut the same length of each type of tape. Two people, one at each end, should pull at the tape as hard as they can. Which tapes break and which don't? For tapes that don't break, how far do they stretch? Write down your findings.

7. Was your hypothesis right? Which tape is stickiest? Which tape is strongest? The final part of the scientific method involves explaining to other people what you found out. Use your notes to help you explain what happened.

For thousands of years, people got thread from living things -- wool from sheep, linen from flax plants, silk from silkworms. Then one day a scientist had an accident. In 1878, the French chemist Hilaire de Chardonnet was about to take a photograph. While preparing the wet glass plate in the darkroom, he spilled a chemical. He didn't wipe it up right away. By the time he did, the liquid had turned sticky. As he mopped it up, it formed threads. De Chardonnet noticed that the threads looked like silk. His accidental discovery led to the thread we now call rayon.

Anytime you're comparing different things in an experiment, you must make sure that the test is fair. Each type of tape in this activity should have an equal chance to be the best. For example, all the pieces of tape should be the same size and the same kind of object (e.g. quarter) should be attached to each piece to test for stickiness. This is called "controlling the variables". The "variables" are the things you can change in an experiment.

Whenever you use the scientific method, keep in mind that it's only a general plan. The rules are flexible. How scientists actually do science and how we describe the scientific process often don't match. The description often lacks the wrong turns, the hunches that didn't work out, and the mistakes. What's usually missing is the challenging, frustrating, exciting adventure of scientific discovery!

Topics: Scientific Method.

SINK OR FLOAT

After experimenting with objects that float and objects that sink, try a Coke float -- not the kind you make with ice cream, but the kind you make using the whole can!

MATERIALS: Pail of water; objects that will float and objects that will sink (e.g. rock, stick, keys, cork, nails, paper clips -- include objects that are similar in appearance but different in mass such as ping-pong ball and golf ball or plastic spoon and metal spoon or plastic button and metal button); several cans of Coke Classic; several cans of Caffeine-free Diet Coke.

Being scientific involves more than just following the scientific method. It means being creative. It also means thinking things through -- like what you mean by the words you use. For example, does a plastic button sink or float? If you push the button down into the water, it may sink to the bottom of the container. If you carefully lay the button on the water's surface, it may float there. Whether a button sinks or floats depends on what you mean by "sink" and "float". You have to define your terms. And just because a word means one thing to you doesn't mean it means the same thing to someone else. Terms are defined through observation and communication. For example, after several people try floating and sinking an object, they may agree on a definition: if you push the object all the way to the bottom of a container filled with water, and the object stays at the bottom, it's a sinker. Then this definition is used for the rest of an experiment, with each person trying to sink each object in exactly the same way.

Topics: Scientific Method; Communication; Forces.

DOING IT:

1. *Basic Testing:* Sort objects into two groups: those you think will float and those you think will sink. Using a pail of water, test your predictions.

2. *Defining Meanings:* What does "sink" mean? What does "float" mean? Explore some ambiguous situations, like a cup that will float unless you push it underwater to make it sink.

3. *The Real Thing:* Put a can of Coke Classic and a can of Caffeine-free Diet Coke into a pail of water. Often, the Coke Classic sinks and the Caffeine-free Diet Coke floats. Try several cans of each drink. Why does the Coke Classic sink and the Caffeine-free Diet Coke float? Perhaps one can contains more pop than the other. One can may have a greater mass than the other. Maybe the caffeine makes a difference. It might have something to do with the carbonation. It could also be that sugar and artificial sweetener don't weigh the same.

4. *Extension:* Following the scientific method, test your hypotheses about the sinking and floating cans of Coke. Remember that the scientific method is only a guide. Be creative. If you find something that doesn't make sense at first -- like some cans of Coke Classic that sink and others that float -- ask more questions.

DROP IT!

A scientific approach and a little practice will enable you to meet this four-fold, flick-and-balance challenge involving a coin and a marble.

MATERIALS: Drinking glasses; playing cards, index cards, or pieces of stiff cardboard; coins; marble; strip of paper; cotton, sand, or tissue; loop (3 cm x 15 cm) made of heavyweight paper; pencil.

DOING IT:

1. *Flick Challenge 1:* Place a card across the top of a glass. Put a coin in the middle of the card. Get the coin to drop into the glass by giving the card a quick flick in a horizontal direction with your index finger.

2. *Flick Challenge 2:* Put some cotton, sand, or tissue at the bottom of a glass. Place a card across the top of the glass. Put a marble in the middle of the card. Get the marble to drop into the glass by giving the card a quick flick with your index finger.

3. *Balance Challenge 1:* Lay a strip of paper over the lip of a glass. Put a coin on the paper strip so that the coin is balanced on the lip of the glass. Grasp the end of the paper strip. Give the strip a quick karate chop so that the strip zips out from under the coin, but the *coin remains balanced.*

4. *Balance Challenge 2:* Make a loop of heavyweight paper. Put the loop upright in a glass. Balance a coin at the top of the loop. Hit the inside of the loop with a pencil so that the coin falls into the glass.

5. How many trials does it take before succeeding at a given challenge? Which challenge is most difficult? Why?

This activity is based on a common characteristic of all objects -- inertia. Newton's First Law of Motion states that objects in motion tend to stay in motion and objects at rest tend to stay at rest unless they're acted upon by some outside force. If the outside force acts quickly enough, the inertia of an object keeps it from moving -- just like in the old magician's trick of pulling a tablecloth out from under dishes. For example, a coin lies inert (at rest) on a playing card or index card, on a glass. By flicking the card, you produce enough momentum (the force with which a body moves) to knock the card off the glass. The inertia of the coin keeps the coin from moving sideways, and when the coin loses its support, gravity causes it to fall into the glass. The more sudden the movement of the card, the more easily you'll be able to do the trick. If the card is pulled away slowly, the coin will move with it. The larger the mass of an object, the greater its inertia.

Topics: Problem-Solving; Forces.

Homemade Music

Experiment with an instrument made from eight bottles filled with water. As your musical skills get really "sharp", you'll be giving concerts in no time "flat"!

To change the pitch (how high or low the sound is) of this homemade instrument, you vary the level of water in a bottle. The pitch can also be affected by the shape of the bottle and by the material from which the bottle is made (bottles made of plain glass make clearer, purer sounds then those made of rippled glass). In general, as mass increases, pitch lowers. With less mass, the pitch gets higher.

When you hit the bottles with a pencil to make sounds, the instrument is rather like a xylophone. A xylophone is made up of a row of different-sized blocks of wood. You make sounds by striking the blocks with two special sticks. Instead of pieces of wood, the homemade instrument uses bottles of water. As you tap a bottle, the water vibrates and produces a sound.

If you blow across the mouth of a bottle, you'll get a different sound. The water isn't what's vibrating now. The unfilled portion of the bottle is called the "resonating chamber". It's filled with air. The air vibrates when you blow across the bottle, making sound waves. If the resonating chamber is large (only a little water in the bottle), the vibrations are slow and the pitch is low. If the resonating chamber is small (bottle is almost full with water), the vibrations are fast and the pitch is high.

Topics: Sound; Problem-Solving.

MATERIALS: Eight glass bottles of the same type and size (you should wash the bottles with detergent and hot water before you use them); water; pencil. Optional -- simple sheet music.

DOING IT:

1. Fill three bottles with different levels of water (i.e. a little water, halfway, almost full). Tap on each bottle with a pencil. Try tapping in different spots. How do the bottles sound? Put the bottles in order from lowest sound to highest sound. How much water is there in the bottle with the lowest pitch? How much water is there in the bottle with the highest pitch?

2. Now blow across the mouth of each bottle. How do the bottles sound? Are they still in order from lowest to highest sound?

3. You'll play your eight-bottle instrument by blowing across the mouth of each bottle. To tune the instrument, begin by filling the first bottle almost completely full of water. The water depth in the second bottle should be a little lower than the first bottle to produce the next note on the musical scale. Continue lowering the level of the water in each successive bottle (as shown) until the entire musical scale is reproduced. Each bottle should have a note higher than itself on one side, and a lower note on the other side.

4. Try to play some simple songs. Try this Canadian folk song: G F E E F G F E G C (low) G F E E F G F E G. Can you write a song so that someone else can play it correctly?

SOAP BUBBLE DERBY

Soap bubbles are great for scientific experimentation and for just plain fun. How large a bubble can you blow? How many bubble tricks can you do?

Here's a bubble trick for winter: *Go outside when it's very cold and there's no wind. Use a round bubble blower made from a piece of wire to gently blow a large bubble. Don't let the bubble blow away and hold it very still. If it's cold enough, the thin bubble should begin to freeze as you watch. You should begin to see tiny crystals forming over the surface of the bubble until it freezes completely. Then you'll have a very thin ice crystal ball.*

MATERIALS: Clear dishwashing liquid (Joy works best); water; large bowl; wire; stick (about 15 cm high); shallow pans (e.g. cake tins); straws; thin string or thread; sharp pencil. Optional -- glycerine (available at a drugstore).

DOING IT:

1. Begin by mixing a good bubble-making solution. Half the fun here is experimenting! In general, 2 parts (e.g. glassfuls) dishwashing liquid to 6 parts of water works well. If you use glycerine (glycerine makes stronger bubbles), then use 2 parts dishwashing liquid, 6 parts water, and 1 to 4 parts glycerine.

2. Practice basic bubble-blowing techniques. Blow bubbles using simple bubble loops made of wire. Bubble loops can be made by forming a circle out of a piece of wire, while leaving one end of the wire longer than the other, and then twisting the wire around itself to form a handle. Experiment with different sizes and shapes of bubbles.

3. Once you've got the basics down, try the bubble tricks on the following pages. Can you come up with other tricks?

4. *Variation:* Run a Soap Bubble Derby with groups of people moving from one bubble-trick station to another. Timing visits to each station (e.g. 3 minutes to complete a trick) makes the derby really exciting.

Sir Thomas Dewar made a bubble that lasted 108 days. Physicist Eiffel Plasterer blew a bubble that lasted for 340 days!

Bubbles are held together through surface tension. Water molecules at the surface of water are more attracted to each other than to the air; it's as if they stick together. If the molecules want to stick together too much, bubbles won't form very easily. Soap "breaks" the surface tension of water. Soap can decrease the surface tension of water to about 1/3 of what it usually is -- ideal for making bubbles.

Water tends to evaporate quickly. When the water evaporates, a bubble's wall is broken and the bubble bursts. Something has to be added to the bubble solution to keep the water from evaporating. Substances that have water-holding properties are called "hygroscopic". Glycerin is a hygroscopic liquid. Glycerin forms a weak chemical bond with water that delays evaporation.

While a bubble is whole, it makes a very pretty sight. When light passes through a soap film, it's reflected from the top and bottom layers of the film. A film can contain as many as 150 different layers. We see a scrambled combination of colours because these layers are uneven. The thickest parts bounce back red light, the thinnest parts bounce violet, and in between is a rainbow of colours.

Topics: Problem-Solving; Atoms; Forces; Light.

BUBBLE TRICKS

BASIC BUBBLES: Make small and big round hoops out of wire and blow some bubbles. How large a bubble can you blow? How small a bubble can you blow? How long can you make a bubble last? How high can you make a bubble float? Try bending wire into different geometric shapes, like a diamond or a figure eight. What happens to the bubbles?

HEMISPHERE: Wet the surface of a shallow pan with some bubble solution. Wet one end of a straw in the bubble solution. Hold the end of the straw slightly above the pan's surface and blow gently. After you've blown a bubble about the size of half a tennis ball, gently withdraw the straw. Try touching the bubble first with a wet finger and then with a dry finger. What happens in each case?

CATERPILLAR:

Put together several hemispheres. Try to start small and end small.

FISSION: Fission involves splitting large atoms into smaller atoms.

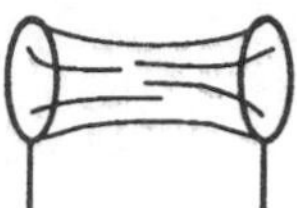

This bubble trick is a model of fission. Split one bubble into two.

FUSION: Fusion involves making larger atoms from smaller atoms.

This bubble trick is a model of fusion. Combine two bubbles into one.

LITTLE-BUBBLE HEMISPHERES IN BIGGER-BUBBLE HEMISPHERES:

Follow the same approach as in the hemisphere trick, but instead of taking the straw out when you've blown the first bubble, push the straw down to the soap solution and start again. How many inner bubbles can you make?

LITTLE BUBBLE IN BIGGER BUBBLE: Put a stick about 15 cm high into the ground. Wind one end of a piece of wire around the stick. The other end of the wire should have a loop, about 10 cm in diameter. Dip the loop in the bubble solution. Blow a large bubble on the loop. Wet a straw in the bubble solution, and then carefully place the straw through the large bubble. Blow a smaller bubble in the larger one.

Bubble Tricks

Bubble Frame: To make a bubble frame, cut a long straw into two shorter straws. Run about 0.5 m of thin string or thread through the two straws. Knot the string and pull the knot inside one of the straws. Place the frame in the bubble solution, then lift it out carefully so that there is a soap-film window stretched across the rectangle (if you can't get the bubble solution to stay on the frame, try thicker or thinner string). Hold the rectangle to the light. Can you see rainbow colours? Twist the frame around to see what interesting shapes you can create. Experiment with different frame sizes.

Double Trouble:
What shapes can you make using two bubble frames?

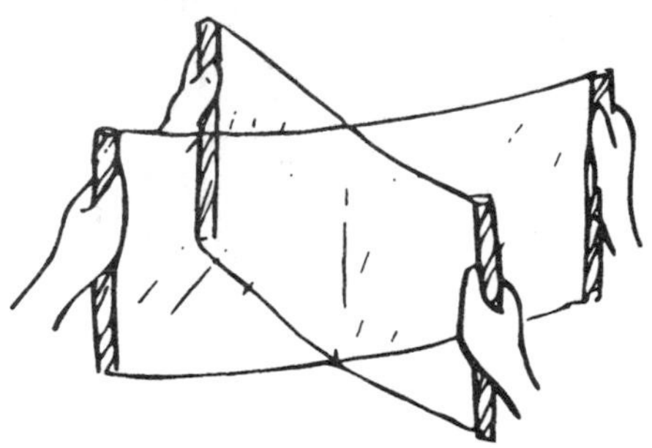

Touch two bubble films together and then move them slowly apart. Pass one frame through the other.

Hand Through Bubble Window: Have someone hold the bubble frame while you put your hand through the bubble film. It can be done, all the way up to your elbow, if the conditions are right. Experiment to find the "right" conditions.
Hint: Wetting your hand and arm may help.

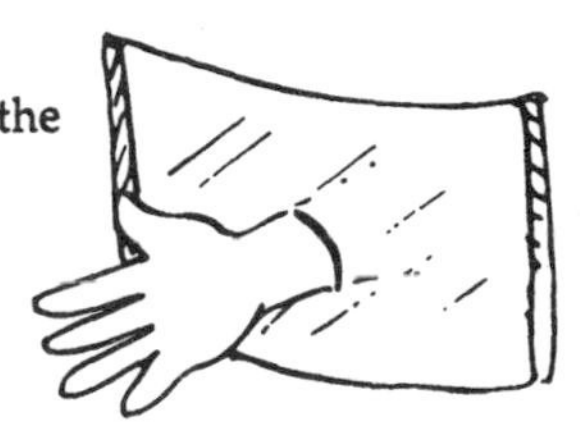

Bubble Circle:
How can you make a perfect bubble circle? Make a loop on one end of a piece of thin string or thread. Tie the string or thread to the bubble frame, as shown. Dip the frame into the bubble solution, and then lift it out. Pop the film inside the string loop with a pencil point to see a perfect circle form. The molecules of the bubble film around the string are all pulling on the string equally.

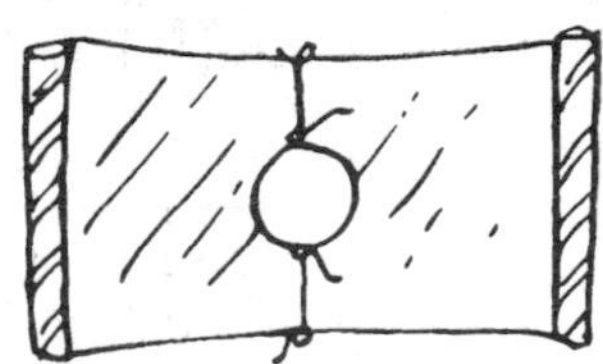

Bubble Frame Super Bubble:
Make a super bubble by holding the bubble frame at arm's length just below your waist. Pull the frame upward, toward you, but don't go too quickly. As you move the frame, a bubble will start to form. To close it off and make it float, gently bring the two straws together until they touch as you swing the frame up. This technique takes practice!
Note: Stand back when the bubble breaks because it pops with a powerful force and bubble solution may get into your eyes.

CARD TOWER

How high can you build a card tower? How stable is your high-rise structure? All you need is a deck of playing cards for this construction competition.

MATERIALS: One or more full decks of playing cards.

DOING IT:

1. This activity works well with several people. People may work individually or in teams. The challenge is to construct a card tower, using an entire deck of cards, within 20 minutes. No other materials except the playing cards may be used.

2. If a tower collapses, the person or team working on it may start over again (but the clock keeps ticking).

3. At the end of the 20 minute time limit, towers can be judged for height and creativity. In the first category, the tallest tower standing long enough for a judge to measure it is the winner. In the second category, everyone votes to determine the most creatively designed tower.

Building card towers is an entertaining game -- and it can be quite scientific. Tower construction involves considering the shape and mass of cards in order to balance them. It also involves planning and building a foundation which will support the tower you wish to build.

Topics: Problem-Solving; Forces.

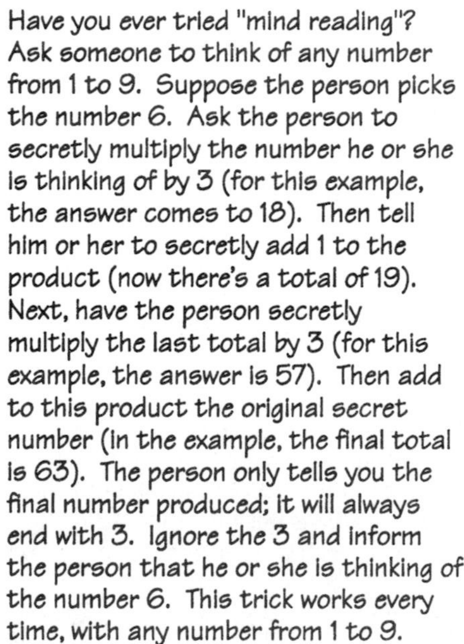

Have you ever tried "mind reading"? Ask someone to think of any number from 1 to 9. Suppose the person picks the number 6. Ask the person to secretly multiply the number he or she is thinking of by 3 (for this example, the answer comes to 18). Then tell him or her to secretly add 1 to the product (now there's a total of 19). Next, have the person secretly multiply the last total by 3 (for this example, the answer is 57). Then add to this product the original secret number (in the example, the final total is 63). The person only tells you the final number produced; it will always end with 3. Ignore the 3 and inform the person that he or she is thinking of the number 6. This trick works every time, with any number from 1 to 9.

3-D STRUCTURES

Experiment with different ways to take a drawing on a flat surface and make it into a 3-D structure.

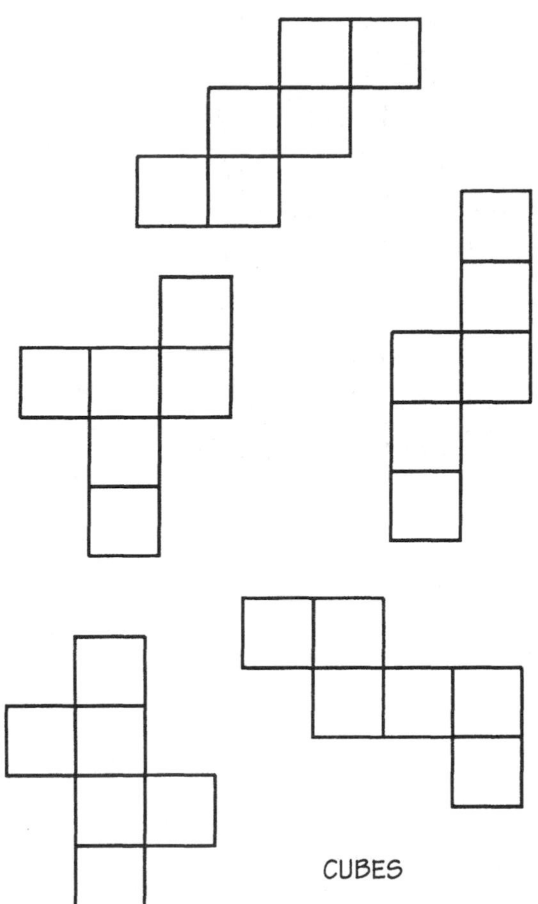

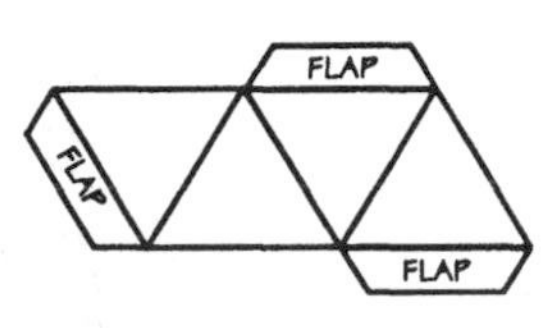

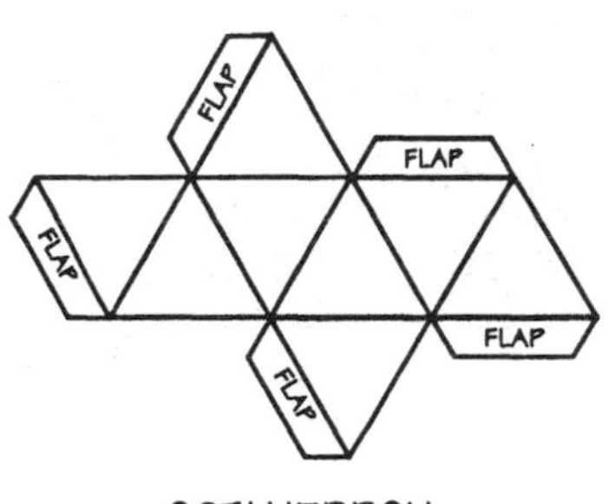

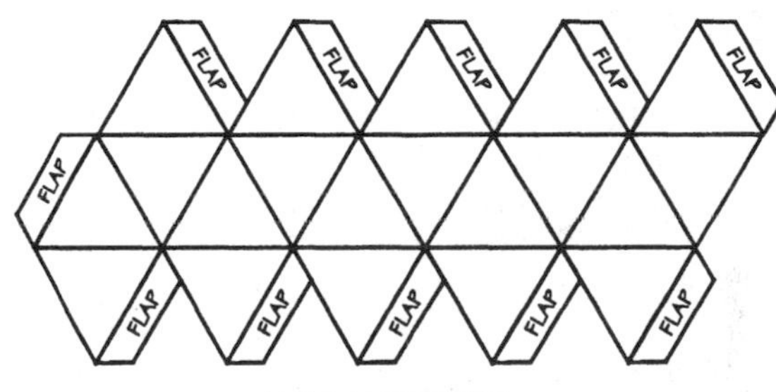

MATERIALS: Paper; pencil; scissors; glue; tape.

DOING IT:

1. Following the patterns on this page, construct some 3-dimensional structures: cubes; a tetrahedron; an octahedron; and an icosahedron.

2. *Extension:* Can you develop patterns for and construct other 3-dimensional structures?

The world around us is in three dimensions -- objects have height, width, and depth. A plane or a surface -- like a sheet of paper -- is in two dimensions (it has height or length, and width). The line you draw on a sheet of paper is one-dimensional; it has only length. A "hedron" is a three-dimensional geometrical shape. Hedrons can have different numbers of surfaces. For example, a tetrahedron has four surfaces ("tetra" means "four"). An octahedron has eight surfaces. An icosahedron has twenty surfaces. The Greeks used hedrons to represent the four elements that they believed made up the world: cube for earth; tetrahedron for fire; octahedron for air; and icosahedron for water.

Topics: Problem-Solving.

MAKE TIME

ORIENTEERING

How do you get from here to there? A Science Fun Course can have participants follow an orienteering route and do science activities at stations along the way.

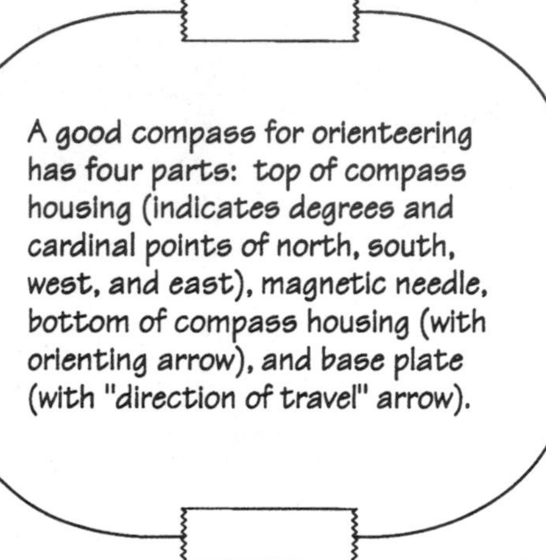

A good compass for orienteering has four parts: top of compass housing (indicates degrees and cardinal points of north, south, west, and east), magnetic needle, bottom of compass housing (with orienting arrow), and base plate (with "direction of travel" arrow).

MATERIALS: Markers (wooden or cardboard signs); compasses; orienteering maps or sets of instructions; paper; pencils; materials for science activities (as required).

Basically, orienteering is finding your way through an area as quickly as possible, and arriving at a predetermined destination. It involves interpreting a set of instructions or reading a map, using a compass to find direction, and measuring distance.

Orienteering can be very challenging. For beginners, orienteering is easiest if it involves using a set of instructions for following a specific course through a small, familiar area. There is a certain order in which stations along the course are to be found, and the emphasis is on interpreting instructions and determining direction and distance. A more advanced approach to orienteering is one in which participants navigate through an area (often unfamiliar) based on a series of circles on a map. Participants choose their own route between circles (stations) using information from the map. The emphasis is on route choice and planning.

Topics: Mapping; Measurement; Problem-Solving.

DOING IT:

1. Decide on a general orienteering area -- an outdoor, wooded area or a number of rooms in a building. The boundaries of the area should be clear, based either on natural features or boundary indicators of some sort.

2. Choose between five and fifteen "stations" (depending on the skill of participants and the time available). Stations consist of markers indicating the station number and telling participants what to do at the station. It can be fun to have participants complete a scientific activity at each station (use Quickies activities from *Science Is . . .!*). Participants can write down the information they gather at each station.

3. Once you've selected the stations, decide whether participants will be provided with a set of instructions or a map. In either case, clearly indicate the starting point and the destination. For beginners, tips (e.g. "do you see the flag pole?") should be included to let participants know whether or not they're on the right track.

4. *If you provide a set of instructions,* first determine the sequence in which stations are to be found. Measure the distances between the stations. Pacing out the distances between stations is easier than measuring distances (a pace is a normal walking stride, measured from heel to heel). Then, develop the instructions.

Try some "compass warm-up" activities:
1) Face 360 degrees and walk 30 paces; turn to 90 degrees and walk 30 paces; turn to 180 degrees and walk 30 paces; turn to 270 degrees and walk 30 paces. What geometric shape have you made?
2) Turn to 120 degrees and walk 30 paces; turn to 240 degrees and walk 30 paces; turn to 360 degrees and walk 30 paces. What shape have you made now?

5. There are a variety of different methods you can use for the instructions: "Go N 20 paces, go W 15 paces"; "Go NW 15 m"; "Go N 10 m, turn 30 degrees E and go 12 m"; "Go N 15 m and find note on oak tree. At oak tree turn 30 degrees E, go 25 m and find note under granite rock"; or "Go N 20 m and find note on tree. If it's an oak tree, turn 30 degrees E and go to the parking lot. If it's a maple tree, turn 75 degrees E and go to the boulder".

6. *If you provide a map*, the map should clearly indicate each station (with a circle), direction (N, S, W, E), and important features such as trees, buildings, rivers, etc. Participants must plan their own route from station to station. There is a general procedure for using an orienteering map: Place the edge of the base plate of a compass along the desired route (joining your present location to your next destination), with the "direction of travel" arrow pointed in the direction you want to go. While holding the base plate firmly on the map and disregarding the needle, turn the compass housing until the orienting arrow on the bottom of the housing is parallel with the north-south lines of the map. The compass is now set. Finally, hold the compass level in front of you with the "direction of travel" arrow pointed straight ahead. Turn your entire body until the north part of the compass needle covers the orienting arrow on the bottom of the compass housing. The "direction of travel" arrow should point toward your destination.

7. Participants may run the orienteering course in teams or individually. At the starting line, everyone receives a compass, paper, pencil, and a set of instructions or a map pre-marked with the stations. Participants can start the course from the same place at a set time interval, or from different stations.

8. Record the amount of time participants take to complete the course. The highest possible score is 100 points. The participant who finds all the stations, completes all the tasks correctly, and has the fastest time, receives 100. Other participants are penalized a set number of points for each minute more than the winning time, each station missed, and each task completed incorrectly.

Try to walk a straight line on a level surface while you're blindfolded. Repeat the task several times and have someone tell you the direction in which you tend to deviate. Most people have a consistent natural deviation either to the right or to the left (and a person wearing a backpack tends to be thrown off even more by the pack's weight). That's why people who are lost often walk in a circle when they think they're going in a straight line.

DROP RACING

Experimenting with simple things can be exciting. Water can slide around and waxed paper is slippery. Put the two together and you have a challenge of skill and speed.

MATERIALS: Water; sheets of waxed paper (30 cm x 36 cm); hole punch (or sharp pencil); blunt pencil, pen, or other rounded object (to scratch lines on the waxed paper).

DOING IT:

1. Try some warm-up exercises first. Smooth a sheet of waxed paper down flat and carefully put a drop of water on it. Pick up the paper, holding it at both ends. Tip the paper back and forth and watch the drop race around. How quickly can you make the drop go? Can you control the drop well enough so that it doesn't fly off the paper's edge?

2. Make a path on the waxed paper for the drop to follow. The path can be made by scratching lines on the paper with a blunt pencil or a pen, or other similar object. The lines should be about 4 cm apart. Cut or punch a small, round hole in the middle of the paper, large enough for the drop to splash through.

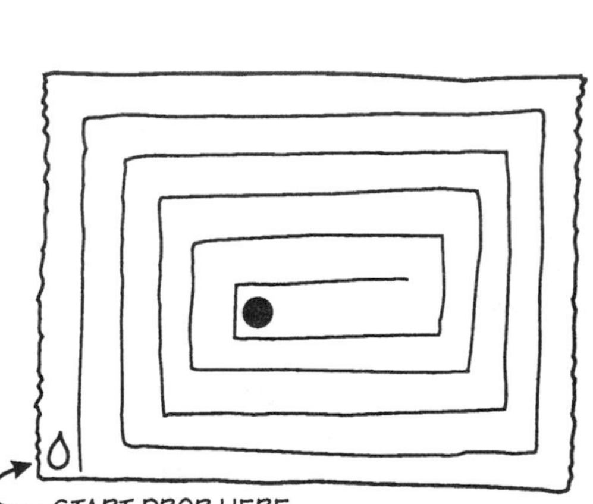

3. Move a drop of water along the path as quickly as possible, keeping the drop within the lines. Finish the race by making the drop go through the end hole.

4. *Extension:* For a more challenging drop race, cut hole traps alongside the path to make the journey trickier.

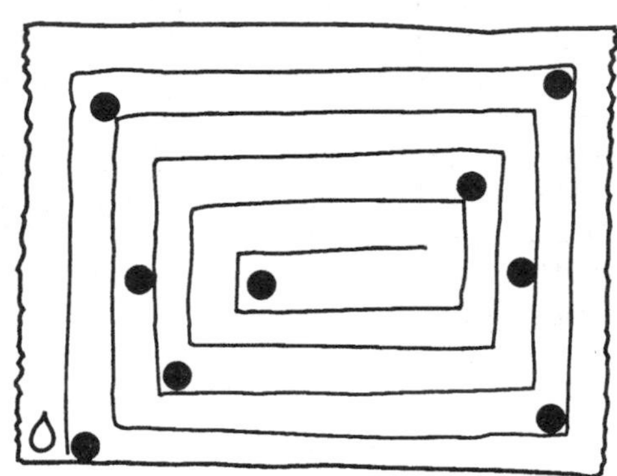

Waxed paper isn't something most people get excited about. But waxed paper can be used for a game which rivals the excitement and challenge of any modern video game. The game takes advantage of waxed paper's special waterproof property and the ease with which waxed paper allows water drops to slide around.

Topics: Problem-Solving.

Examine the following numbers:
21 24 22 25 23 26 24.
What should the next three numbers be?

The next three numbers are 27, 25, 28. Simply put, the pattern is up 3, down 2. Add 3 to the first number to get the second number. Subtract 2 from the second number to get the third number. The pattern repeats.

MAKE TIME

MATTER & ENERGY

Drop a raisin -- or two or three! -- into a glass of fresh, carbonated drink (e.g. Sprite, 7UP). The drink contains carbon dioxide gas, which collects as bubbles that rise to the surface. Gas bubbles rise because the buoyant force of the water is greater than the weight of the bubbles. The rough surface of a raisin provides many points of attachment for bubbles. The bubbles lift the raisin to the surface. At the surface, some of the bubbles burst and the raisin sinks. The raisin may then pick up more bubbles and bob to the surface again.

YUM! YUM! CREAM SODA MY FAVOURITE!

How can you tell if water is hot or cold without touching it? Put in a drop of food colouring. The colouring mixes more rapidly in the hot water because the molecules in the hot water are vibrating more.

"Beam me up, Scotty!" is one of the most famous lines from the television and film series, Star Trek. But, in reality, moving a person through obstacles and across great distances seems quite impossible. Transmitting matter means exactly duplicating every single atom being moved. And there's so much information in even one of a human being's cells that this would be an incredibly complex task.

MAKE TIME

Heat energy always goes from warmer things to cooler things. Heat goes from a hot fire to your cold hands. Heat also goes from your warm hands to a cold snowball.

The most beautiful thing we can experience is the mysterious. It is the source of all true art and science. (Albert Einstein)

If you skip a stone across hard-packed, wet sand, the marks in the sand provide a record of the stone's flight. The first bounce is usually short (several centimetres), the next long (a metre), and this sequence repeats itself until the stone stops. Can you change this pattern?

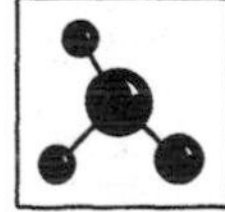

ICE IS NICE

How quickly can you melt a pile of ice cubes? What kind of "bait" do you use to "catch" an ice cube?

MATERIALS: Ice cubes; plates; dark cloth; dark paper; string; salt; paper towels.

DOING IT:

1. *Ice Race:* Each person receives paper towels and a certain number of ice cubes on a plate. Who can completely melt their ice cubes first? People can heat their ice by any means except smashing the cubes, placing cubes in their mouths, or applying heat from an outside source such as a match. Dark paper and a piece of dark cloth should be made available. When the race is over, describe the steps in the melting process.

2. *Ice Fishing:* Put an ice cube on a plate. Lay a piece of string over the ice cube. Sprinkle a little bit of salt on the string. Wait a few seconds and then lift up the string. What happens? Why?

There are three states of matter: solid, liquid, and gas. Water freezes (turns from a liquid into a solid) at a temperature of 0 degrees Celsius. To melt ice, you have to use heat energy. You could just leave an ice cube to melt in a warm room. To speed up the melting process, you could hold the ice cube in your hand. To make your hand warmer before holding the ice cube, you could rub your hands together. You could generate heat from friction by rubbing the ice cube on a cloth. Or, you could place the ice cube on dark cloth or paper in sunlight (dark colours absorb heat).

Salt is another way to get ice to melt. Salt lowers the freezing point of water. When you put a piece of string over an ice cube and sprinkle the string with salt, the ice melts a little and then refreezes around the string as the water dilutes the salt.

The particular state of any type of matter depends both on the matter itself and the temperature. For example, while ice melts at 0 degrees Celsius, tin won't melt until the temperature reaches 232 degrees Celsius.

Topics: States of Matter; Snow; Problem-Solving.

Put a plastic cup of water and a plastic cup of salt water (mix four teaspoons of salt with water) into the freezer overnight. In the morning, are both cups completely frozen? Water freezes at 0 degrees Celsius. Different liquids have different freezing points. The freezing point of salt water is lower than water.

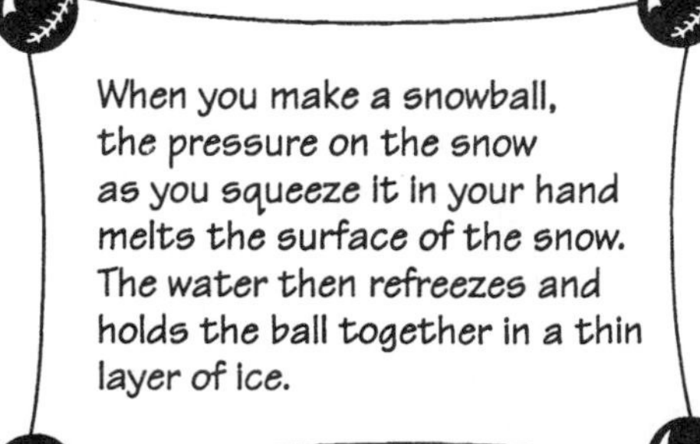

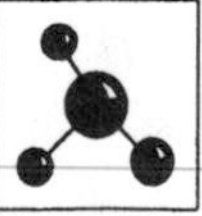

MAKING GOO

Is it a solid? No, not really. Is it a liquid? Well, sort of. The only thing for sure is that it isn't a gas!

MATERIALS: Cornstarch; water; large, shallow bowl; measuring cup; spoon.

DOING IT:

1. Pour 200 ml of water into a bowl.

2. Stir in 300 to 350 ml of cornstarch, a bit at a time. As you stir, occasionally test the mixture's thickness by tapping the surface with the spoon.

3. When the mixture is "just right", you will be able to stir it but it will be difficult. The mixture won't splatter when you hit it with the spoon.

4. Try to scoop up some of the mixture. Can you shape some of the mixture into a ball? Let the mixture dribble off your fingers. Show other people the bowl and tell them it's full of cream. Then slap your hand down onto the mixture hard and fast. How do people react? Why? Is the mixture a liquid or a solid?

5. Important Note: Don't pour the mixture down the drain; it will clog the pipes. When you're done, put the mixture into a plastic bag or jar and throw it into the trash.

MAKE TIME

Here on Earth, the three basic states of matter -- solid, liquid, and gas -- make sense, even though there are exceptions. At certain temperatures and pressures there isn't a dividing line between a liquid and its gas. Solids can flow (e.g. tar) and liquids can act as solids for short periods of time (e.g. silly putty flows and also bounces). But when you're not on Earth, the three states of matter become less relevant. 99% of the material in the entire universe isn't a solid, a liquid, or a gas. The dominant form is called "plasma". Our sun consists of plasma, as do most other stars.

In a liquid, the molecules move around a little. In a solid, the molecules stay in a fixed position. Some substances have the properties of both a liquid and a solid. In the mixture of water and cornstarch, long chains of molecules coil together like a pile of spaghetti. The molecules don't flow easily under high pressure or force. When you squeeze the water and cornstarch mixture, it feels like a solid; when you stop squeezing, it goes back to a liquid.

Topics: States of Matter.

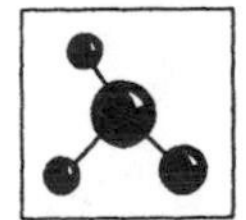

MAGNETIC ATTRACTION

A magnet is an object that can pick up some things. Can a magnet pick up a dime? A marble? A paper clip at the bottom of a glass of water?

Can a magnet do work? Work is defined as moving something (force acting through a distance). Put a magnet on a table. Put a steel ball on the table about 2-3 cm away from the end of the magnet. What happens when you let go of the steel ball?

Natural magnets are a kind of iron called "magnetite". They are usually irregular in shape; they look like ordinary stones you might pick up anywhere. It's believed that magnetite became magnetized by the Earth's magnetic field during the slow hardening of the rock when the Earth's crust cooled down from its molten state.

MATERIALS: At least one magnet; paper clips; paper; string; tape; glass of water; a number of metallic and nonmetallic objects (e.g. glass marble, penny, dime, nickel, needle, thumbtack, plastic, cork, wood, cloth, rubber eraser, pencil lead). Optional -- large container of sand.

DOING IT:

1. *Pick Up:* Sort a group of objects into two piles: objects you think a magnet will pick up and objects you think it won't. Test your predictions with a magnet.

2. *Attractive Power:* Drop a paper clip into a glass of water. Will a magnet attract the clip through the water? Put one bar magnet in the palm of your hand. Hold another strong magnet at the back of your hand. Slowly raise your hand vertically. Does the magnetic force keep the two magnets in place?

3. *Super Strength:* Count the number of paper clips a magnet will pick up at once. How many paper clips can the magnet pick up through a piece of paper? How many pieces of paper can you put between the magnet and a paper clip before the magnet won't pick up the paper clip? Compare the strengths of two different magnets.

4. *Amazing Paper Clip:* Put a paper clip in the palm of your hand. Hold a strong magnet against the back of your hand. The magnet will attract and move the paper clip. Now take the paper clip and tie it to one end of a piece of string. Tape the other end of the string to a table top. Bring the magnet close enough to the clip to make the clip dance in the air.

5. *Extension:* Hide 20 to 30 paper clips in a container of sand. Use a magnet to find the paper clips.

In general, nonmetallic objects aren't attracted to magnets (a magnetic field can go through nonmetallic materials though -- such as paper and plastic -- without any apparent loss of power). That doesn't mean that all metallic objects *are* attracted; in fact, only iron, nickel, and cobalt are attracted. Some combinations of metals (alloys), such as steel and alnico, are also magnetic. Common magnets (e.g. bar magnets, horseshoe magnets) are usually made of steel.

Topics: Magnetism.

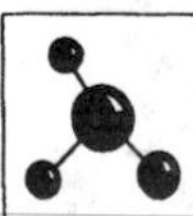

MAKING MAGNETS

Use the force exerted by a permanent magnet to temporarily change an ordinary nail into a magnet.

MATERIALS: Strong permanent magnet; iron nail; paper clips.

DOING IT:

1. Drop an iron nail on the ground to make sure it hasn't accidentally been magnetized. Will the nail pick up a paper clip?

2. Hold a magnet near one end of the nail. Will the other end of the nail attract a paper clip? This is "magnetizing by induction". Take the magnet away from the nail. What happens?

3. Stroke the entire length of the nail in one direction with one pole of a magnet. Lift the magnet clear at the end of each stroke before beginning another (just rubbing the nail back and forth won't magnetize it).

4. How many strokes do you need to magnetize the nail? The magnetic power of the nail should increase with the number of strokes you give the nail.

5. Experiment with the new nail magnet. How many paper clips will it pick up? Does it pick up everything that the original magnet picks up? How long does the nail magnet last?

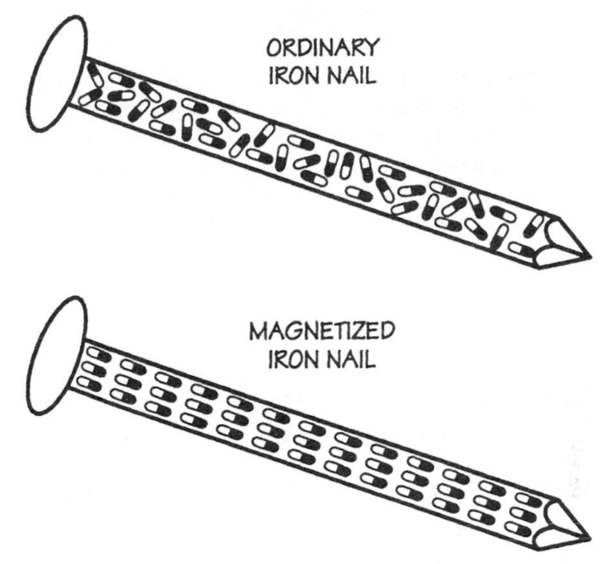

If you break a magnet in half, each half becomes a perfect magnet with new poles at the break. If you continue breaking these halves into quarters and so on, each piece becomes a new magnet. The theory is that each atom of a magnetic substance is a tiny magnet itself -- an atom magnet.

In an ordinary nail, atoms are arranged like a group of people standing in no particular order and facing all directions. In a magnetized nail, atoms are arranged like people seated in straight rows. In the unmagnetized nail, the atom magnets neutralize each other; in the magnetized nail, the atom magnets add to each other to make the whole nail a magnet.

You can magnetize an iron nail by rubbing it with a permanent magnet or by "induction" (bringing a magnet near the nail without touching it). Magnetizing a piece of soft iron doesn't require much energy; but once magnetized, the iron atoms can be readily disarranged. Steel is more difficult to magnetize, but once the magnetic atoms are aligned they resist being disarranged. If you heat or frequently drop any magnet, it can lose its magnetism. The atoms become unaligned. If kept properly, permanent magnets retain their magnetism for a long time. To increase the life of bar magnets, they should be stored in pairs, side by side, north pole next to south pole. Horseshoe magnets should have a "keeper" -- a piece of iron placed across their ends.

Topics: Magnetism; Atoms.

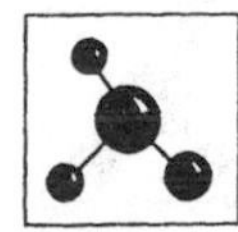

MAGNETIC PATTERNS

An invisible magnetic field exists around a magnet. Explore this field by making magnetic patterns with iron filings.

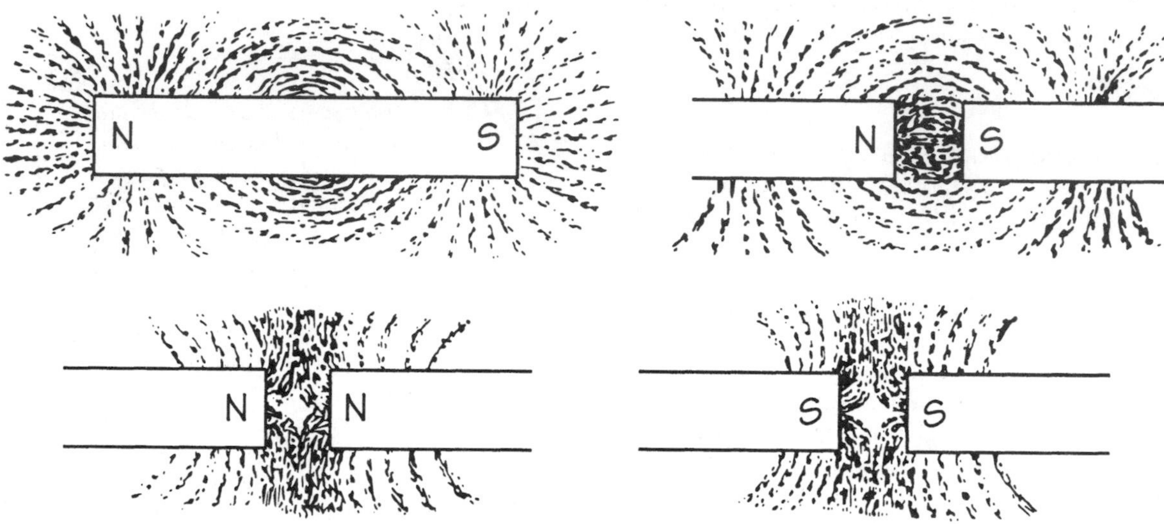

MATERIALS: Bar magnets; sheet of glass or stiff acetate film (i.e. clear plastic covering on some folders or plastic used for overhead projectors); iron filings or steel wool cut into little bits. Optional -- paper clips.

DOING IT:

1. Put a sheet of glass or a piece of acetate film over a bar magnet.

2. Sprinkle iron filings over the magnet. **Handle the filings carefully! Do not get them in your eyes.** What pattern do the filings form?

3. Try sprinkling filings over two magnets with like poles facing and then with unlike poles facing.

4. *Extension:* How can you tell where a magnet is strongest? See how many paper clips are attracted at various places on a magnet.

The space around a magnet is called the "magnetic field". It's the area where the force of a magnet acts or can be felt. Iron filings can be used to reveal a magnetic field and also to show the repulsion between similar magnetic poles and the attraction between opposite poles. Each bit of iron becomes a tiny temporary magnet and takes a position following the "lines of force" that extend from the magnet. Together, the filings form a map of the field.

Topics: Magnetism; Forces.

Clasp your hands together to show attraction. Separate your hands to show repulsion. Hang a bar magnet from a piece of string. Bring the south pole of another magnet close to the north pole of the hanging magnet. Now bring the north pole of the second magnet close to the north pole of the hanging magnet. Unlike poles attract and like poles repel. This is the "law of magnets".

Balloon Play

When you rub your feet along a carpet and then touch a doorknob, you feel a small charge -- static electricity. Balloons are great for exploring static electricity.

MATERIALS: Balloons; cloth (wool sweater, nylon, or polyester); cotton thread; scissors; tape.

DOING IT:

1. Blow up two or three balloons. To charge a balloon with static electricity, rub it quickly back and forth on a piece of cloth, like the sleeve of a wool sweater.

2. *Push and Pull:* Tie a piece of thread to the end of an uncharged balloon. Tie another thread to the end of another uncharged balloon. Hold the two balloons up by their threads so that they hang about 5 cm apart. Does anything happen? Charge one of the balloons and hold it near the uncharged balloon. What happens? Charge both balloons and hold them near each other. What happens?

3. *Hanging Balloon:* Place a charged balloon on the wall. How well does it stay? How long will it stay on the wall?

4. *Pet Balloon:* Tie a piece of thread about 35 cm long to the end of a charged balloon. Tape the balloon to the edge of a table (so that the balloon hangs freely). Hold your open hand near the balloon. Is the balloon attracted to your hand? Will it follow your hand as you move?

5. *Dancing Thread:* Tape one end of a 15 cm long piece of thread to a table top. Now move a charged balloon over the thread. Can you make the thread stand straight up? Can you make it dance?

The atoms of all matter are made up of small particles called electrons, protons, and neutrons. "Protons" (which carry positive charges) and "neutrons" (which carry no charge) are confined to the centre of the atom, in the "nucleus". "Electrons", which carry negative charges, whirl around the nucleus and have the ability to move from one atom to another. There are an equal number of electrons and protons in each atom. As a result, atoms are ordinarily electrically neutral.

When you rub a balloon on a cloth, some electrons are transferred from the cloth to the balloon. The balloon becomes negatively charged (it has more electrons than protons). If you bring two charged balloons together, they push each other away. Like magnets, negative charges repel negative charges. If you bring a charged balloon near an uncharged balloon, the balloons attract each other. If a balloon comes in contact with a neutral wall, it pushes away electrons from that section of the wall, which results in a positive charge on that part of the wall. Since opposites attract, the balloon sticks to the wall -- for a while. After a bit, the negative electrons pass from the balloon to the wall and also into the air. Then the balloon falls. Note that it's easier to generate static electricity on cold, dry winter days than on warm, humid days. Moisture can pick up charges; moist air will quickly discharge a negatively charged balloon.

Topics: Electricity; Atoms.

ELECTRIC WAND

Rub a plastic comb with a piece of cloth. The comb becomes charged with static electricity and can be used for several amazing tricks.

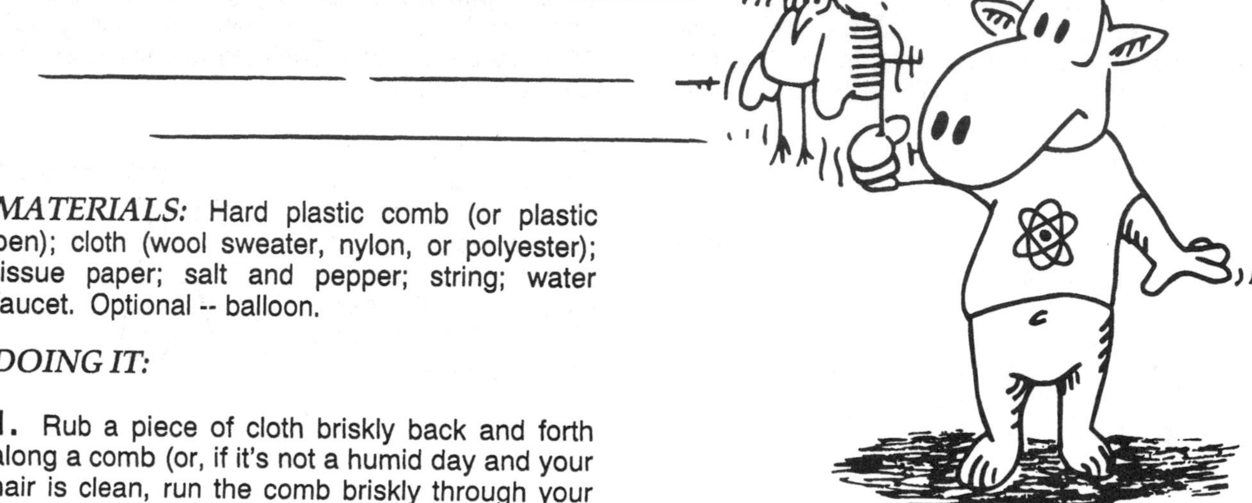

MATERIALS: Hard plastic comb (or plastic pen); cloth (wool sweater, nylon, or polyester); tissue paper; salt and pepper; string; water faucet. Optional -- balloon.

DOING IT:

1. Rub a piece of cloth briskly back and forth along a comb (or, if it's not a humid day and your hair is clean, run the comb briskly through your hair). Your "electric wand" is charged.

MAKE TIME

When you rub a comb with a cloth, electrons from the cloth are transferred to the comb, giving the comb a negative charge. The comb then attracts or repels other objects, depending on their charge. For example, the positive and negative charges on bits of tissue paper are evenly distributed, so the paper is electrically neutral. As the negatively charged comb approaches, the electrons on the paper are pushed away. As the electrons retreat, they leave the edge of the paper positively charged. The comb and the paper then attract each another. If you continue to hold the comb by the paper, the comb will transfer electrons to the paper and the paper will be pushed away. Then the process repeats itself. When you bring the comb near a thin stream of water, the water is attracted. A water molecule is made of two hydrogen atoms and one oxygen atom (H_2O). The combination of hydrogen and oxygen atoms in water makes water molecules "polar". A polar molecule has two ends; one end has a positive charge and the other has a negative charge (just like a magnet has a north pole and a south pole). The plastic comb is negatively charged and attracts the positive end of the water molecule.

Topics: Electricity; Atoms.

2. *Bouncing Bits:* Put several tiny bits of tissue paper into a pile. Hold the "wand" close to the pile for 3 or 4 minutes. What happens?

3. *Salt and Pepper:* Mix some salt and pepper together in a pile. Hold the "wand" close to the pile for 3 or 4 minutes. What happens? Watch carefully to see the *same* grains attracted and then repelled (they don't fall off; they are thrown off), over and over. How can you separate the pepper from the salt?

4. *Paper Ball:* Crumple a small piece of tissue paper into a ball and hang it on a string. What happens when you hold the "wand" near the ball?

5. *Crooked Water:* Turn on a faucet so that a very thin stream of water is flowing from it. Make the water bend by holding the "wand" near the stream. With some practice, you can pull the water dramatically off course.

6. *Extension:* What happens if you bring the charged "wand" near an uncharged balloon? What happens when you charge the balloon?

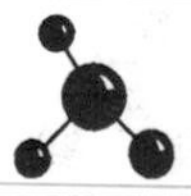

ELECTROSCOPE

How can you tell if the balloon you've rubbed with a piece of cloth is really charged with static electricity? Use an electroscope -- a device that detects static charges.

MATERIALS: Clear, glass bottle with cork or rubber stopper; copper wire; lightweight aluminum foil (a foil gum wrapper works well); lightweight or regular aluminum foil; nail; scissors; balloon or hard plastic comb; cloth (wool sweater, nylon, or polyester). Optional -- ruler; newspaper.

DOING IT:

1. Cut a 20 cm long piece of copper wire. Remove all the insulation from both ends of the wire.

2. Use the nail to make a hole through the middle of a cork or rubber stopper. The hole should be just big enough to slide the wire through.

3. After you've pushed the wire through the cork or stopper, bend (make a flat hook) the end of the wire that will be inside the bottle.

4. Cut a strip of foil about 0.5 cm x 3 cm.

5. Fold the foil strip in half and let it hang over the end of the wire. There should be no insulation between the foil and the wire.

6. Put the cork or stopper snugly into the bottle, ensuring that the foil stays on the wire. The bottle should be completely dry inside; otherwise, the electroscope will not work.

7. Make a foil ball and press it around the top of the wire. Charges leak quickly from sharp objects; the round ball will keep charges inside the bottle so that they can be detected.

8. Charge a balloon or comb and test the electroscope. What happens when you touch the foil ball with a charged object? What happens when you bring a charged object near the glass? What happens if you touch the foil ball when the leaves are apart?

9. *Variation:* Try a long, thin strip of newspaper folded over a ruler; it works like the leaves of an electroscope. Rub the paper with a cloth to see if the leaves spread apart.

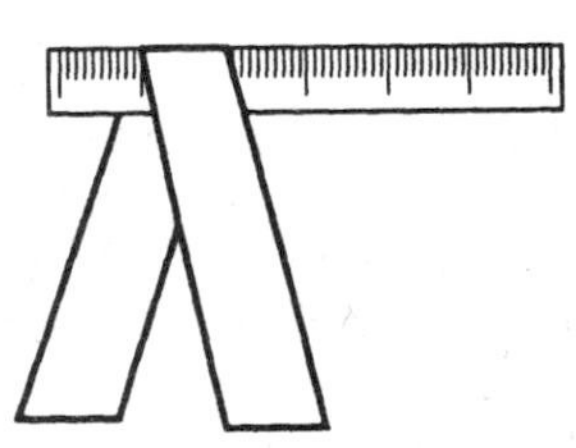

MAKE TIME

The earliest known reference to static electricity goes back at least 2600 years. The Greeks discovered that, when rubbed, amber (the hardened resin from a tree -- a sort of natural plastic) would attract bits of lint, dust, and paper. The word "electricity" comes from the Greek word "elektron", which means amber.

You can use an electroscope to detect the presence of a static charge on a comb, a balloon, or any other charged object. As you bring a charged object near the foil ball at the top of the wire, the wire, being a conductor, carries the charge to the foil. Since both leaves of the foil strip receive the same charge, they are repelled and move apart from each other. The leaves collapse when the charge is neutralized (e.g. when you touch your finger to the foil ball).

Topics: Electricity.

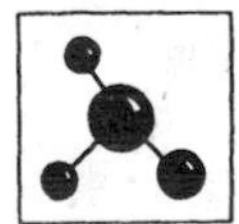

ELECTRICITY VOLTA'S WAY

The chemical way of generating electricity in cells and batteries is the older of two key methods. Put together a homemade battery.

MATERIALS: Drinking glass or plastic container; strip of copper; strip of zinc; water; vinegar; knife; insulated wire; steel wool; paper clips; L.E.D. (light emitting diode, which uses a very small amount of electric current; you can purchase one in a hobby or electronics store) or galvanometer (which detects electric current and its direction).

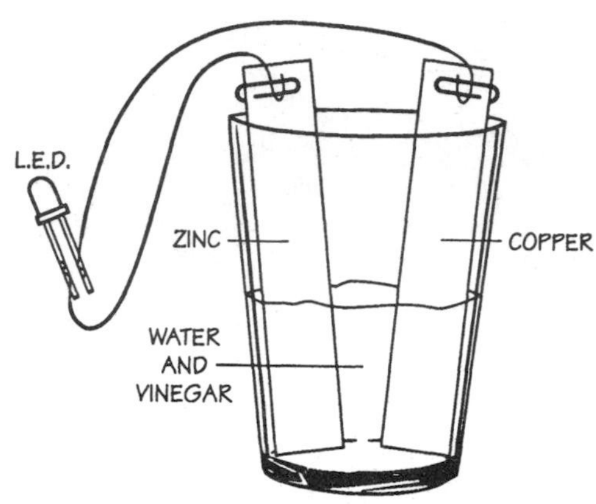

DOING IT:

1. Clean the metal strips with steel wool.

The electrical measurement "volt" is named after Alessandro Volta, an Italian scientist, because of his experiments with electricity. About 200 years ago, Volta discovered that a chemical reaction could produce a continuous flow of electricity. He found that when he placed a strip of copper and a strip of zinc in a sulphuric acid solution, and then connected the dry end of each of these metals with a wire, electricity began to flow in the wire. Atoms in both pieces of metal contain negatively charged electrons and positively charged nuclei (protons and neutrons). A chemical reaction in the acid solution dissolves some of the zinc, leaving the zinc with a lot of electrons and a negative charge. Positive charges from the zinc flow through the acid solution toward the copper, where they attract some of the copper's electrons. The copper becomes positively charged. The difference in charge between the two metal strips causes electrons to flow from the negatively charged zinc, through the wire, to the positively charged copper.

Volta's experiment consisted of a "wet cell". The common "dry" cells used in flashlights and for portable radios aren't really dry. If you compare the dry cell with Volta's cell, there are a lot of similarities. Zinc is still one of the metals used; in the dry cell it also serves as the container. Instead of copper, a carbon rod is used; it stands vertically in the centre of the cell. Instead of sulphuric acid in water, a moist chemical paste of ammonium chloride fills most of the cell. As in the wet cell, chemical action produces a flow of electricity.

Topics: Electricity; Chemical Reactions; Atoms.

MAKE TIME

2. Put the metal strips on opposite sides of a drinking glass or other container.

3. Scrape about 3 cm of insulation off the ends of two lengths of insulated wire. Attach one end of the wires to the metal strips (paper clips are handy for attaching the wires). Attach the other end of the wires to an L.E.D. or a galvanometer.

4. Pour a little water into the glass to cover the bottom third of the metal strips. If you're using a galvanometer, the meter should register a small amount of electricity.

5. Add vinegar to the water. If you're using a galvanometer, the meter should go off the scale. If you're using an L.E.D., it should light up.

Wires are used in electric circuits because electricity flows readily along metal. Most metals are good "conductors" of electricity. Most nonmetals are poor conductors of electricity; they are called "insulators". Rubber is one of the best insulators. Cloth, leather, glass, porcelain, and many plastics are also good insulators. Insulators are used to keep electricity from going where it's not wanted. For example, electricians wear rubber gloves so that they won't be shocked.

ELECTRICITY FARADAY'S WAY

The chemical way of generating electricity was used for more than 100 years. Then Faraday came along. Recreate Faraday's discovery.

MATERIALS: Bar magnet; several metres of insulated wire; toilet paper roll; knife; galvanometer (which detects electric current and its direction).

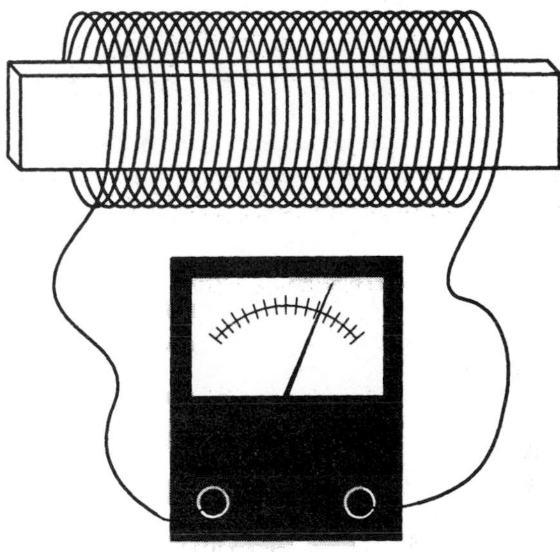

DOING IT:

1. Scrape approximately 3 cm of insulation off the ends of a length of wire.

2. Wind the wire twenty to thirty times around a toilet paper roll to form a coil. You can leave the wire on the toilet paper roll (which may make it easier to use) or you can slip the coiled wire off the roll.

3. Connect the wire to a galvanometer.

4. Pull a bar magnet in and out of the wire coil. What happens on the galvanometer?

5. Put the magnet on a table and move the coil back and forth over the magnet. What happens on the galvanometer?

6. *Extension:* Experiment with different numbers of loops in the coil. Do more loops result in more electricity?

The electron flow in a circuit using a dry-cell battery is always in one direction. This kind of current is called "direct current". A generator can produce this kind of current, but most generators produce "alternating current". In alternating current, electrons flow in one direction, come to a complete halt, and then go in the opposite direction. This change of direction occurs very rapidly, usually 120 times every second.

In his 50 years of research, Michael Faraday performed more than 16,000 experiments. In one of these experiments, he found that under certain conditions magnetism could produce electricity. When Faraday thrust a magnet into a coil of wire, electricity flowed one way through the wire. When the magnet stopped moving, the electricity stopped. When he pulled the magnet out, electricity again flowed in the wire, but in the opposite direction. When he kept moving the magnet in and out, a regular, but pulsating, current was produced. Faraday also found that moving the coil back and forth over the magnet had the same effect as moving the magnet in the coil. Faraday's discovery has been put to many uses. Some bicycles use "dynamos" instead of batteries to power the headlight. Inside a dynamo there's a magnet, bent so both poles face inward. Between the poles is a coil of wire. When the bicycle wheel turns, the wire coil moves and electricity is generated. Power stations make use of "generators", which are like large dynamos. In hydroelectric stations, the rush of falling water is used to provide the motion needed to turn huge coils of wire near huge magnets. Other types of stations use steam engines fuelled by oil, coal, gas, or nuclear power.

Topics: Electricity; Magnetism; Energy.

MAKE TIME

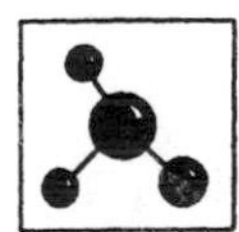

ELECTROMAGNET

Electricity is very closely related to magnetism. An electric current can, in fact, produce magnetism. Try it for yourself!

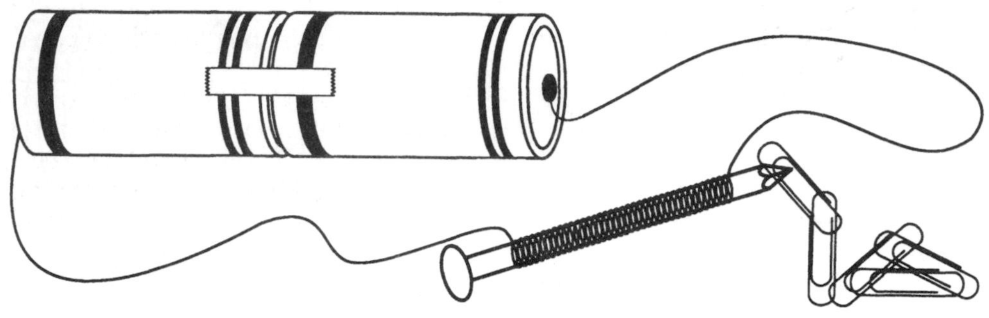

MATERIALS: 7-8 cm long iron nail; about 2 m of insulated copper wire; two D flashlight batteries; knife; paper clips; tape.

DOING IT:

1. Scrape approximately 3 cm of insulation off the ends of a length of wire.

2. Wind the wire around a nail, leaving about 20 cm of wire at each end.

3. Stack two batteries (negative end touching positive end) and tape them together.

4. Tape one end of the wire to the bottom of the battery stack. Hold or tape the other end of the wire to the top of the battery stack.

5. Test the nail. Is it a magnet? How many paper clips will it pick up? What happens if you disconnect the battery?

6. *Extension:* Try various lengths of wire wrapped around the nail. What happens to the strength of the electromagnet?

Wherever there's electricity -- overhead power lines, home appliances, computers -- there are "electromagnetic" fields. Electricity has a magnetic influence; a wire carrying electricity has a magnetic field around it. When you wind wire around a nail and connect the wire to a battery, the electric current creates a magnetic field around the nail. The nail becomes an electromagnet.

Electromagnets have two key advantages over permanent magnets. First, they can be made very strong -- by increasing the number of turns of wire or by increasing the amount of current that goes through the wire. Secondly, electromagnets can be turned on and off; when the current is on, they are a magnet and when the current is turned off, they aren't. Very strong electromagnets are attached to cranes in junkyards to pick up loads of scrap iron. Electromagnets are also used in loudspeakers, clocks, telephones, doorbells, and generators.

Topics: Magnetism; Electricity.

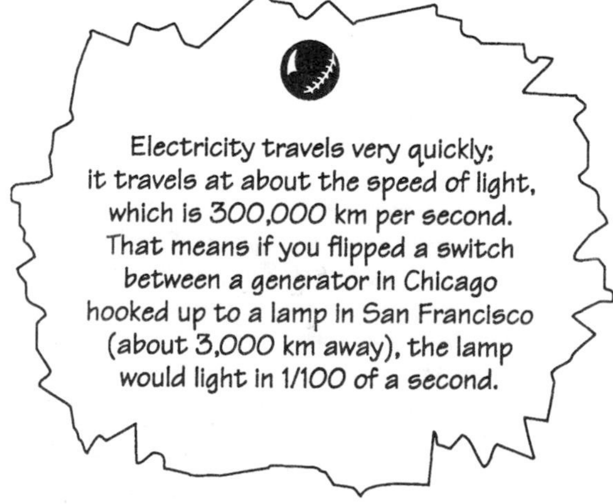

No-Motor Rotor

The rotor blade on the end of a notched stick seems to turn by itself. Frictional energy is the "fuel" for this toy.

MATERIALS: Small-diameter dowel; second, smaller-diameter dowel; wood file; straight pin with a head; paper; scissors; ruler.

DOING IT:

1. Use a file to make several notches in a small-diameter dowel, as shown.

2. Make a rotor out of paper. Make sure the rotor is symmetrical. Make a *round* hole, about 3-4 mm in diameter, in the centre of the rotor.

3. Jam a straight pin into the centre of the notched end of the dowel. Slip the rotor onto the straight pin.

4. Grasp the end of the notched shaft in one hand; tilt the shaft so that the rotor doesn't fall off the straight pin. Use a second dowel as a stroking stick. Hold the stroking stick in your other hand, as shown. Run the stroking stick back and forth over the notches. Vary the way you stroke the shaft (e.g. more/less pressure, speed, position of hand on stroking stick) until the rotor turns in one direction.

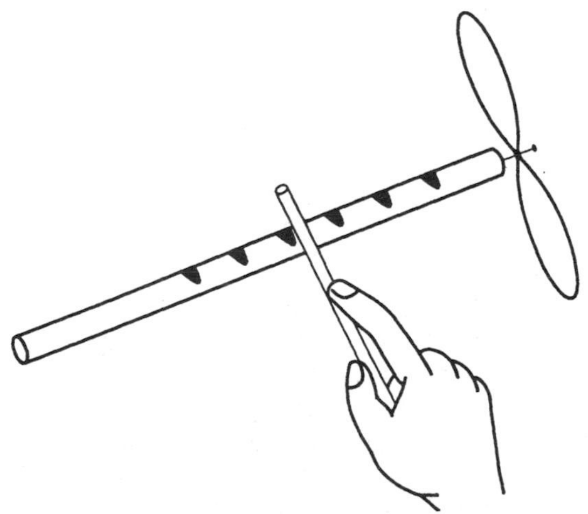

5. To turn the rotor in the opposite direction, use a finger or a thumb from the hand doing the stroking. As you run the stroking stick back and forth, the finger or thumb should also rub against the side of the notched shaft. Try different stroking speeds.

6. *Variation:* Experiment with different rotor shapes (e.g. thicker/thinner, shorter/longer).

7. *Extension:* Try different designs. All four rotors will turn in the same direction in the four-rotor design. If you mount two rotors one behind the other, both rotors can go in the same direction -- or one rotor can go in one direction and the other in the opposite direction!

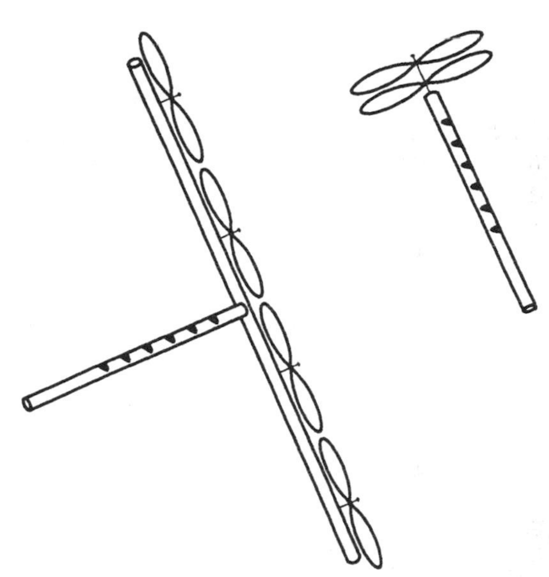

The notches in the shaft of the toy are the key to the "no-motor" secret. When you apply energy by rubbing the shaft with a stick, you make the shaft vibrate. The shaft vibrates because of friction between the stick and the notches (friction is the force that resists the motion of one surface over another). The horizontal and vertical vibrations aren't the same in frequency or amplitude. This is because the shaft's width is different from its length and because of the way you put pressure on the shaft. The resulting vibrational motion of the shaft, and the pin on the end, is elliptical. The friction between the pin and the rotor makes the rotor spin. If you put pressure on the shaft with your finger or thumb, the elliptical oscillations (and the movement of the rotor) can be made to go in the opposite direction.

Topics: Energy; Forces.

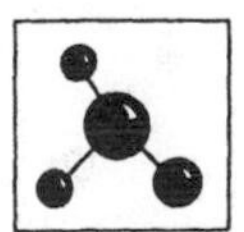

Colour Clues

Matter can interact with matter to produce chemical changes. Red cabbage juice is a great indicator for determining acids and bases.

MAKE TIME

MATERIALS: Pour the juice off a can of cooked red cabbage or make your own cabbage juice using shredded red cabbage leaves (raw red cabbage is dark purple in colour), water, a pot, and a stove or other heat source; tablespoon; teaspoon; glass; acid and base test substances (e.g. baking soda, vinegar, pop, egg whites, lemon juice, lemonade, soap, aspirin, fruit juices, saliva, tomato juice, milk, cottage cheese). Optional -- white paper towels; grape juice; cherry juice; onions; beets; apple skins; tea.

Chemicals are grouped together because of common properties. "Acids" are a group of sour chemicals; they contain hydrogen. When a food tastes sour, like lemon juice or vinegar, it usually contains an acid. "Bases" are the opposite of acids; they contain a chemical unit called a "hydroxide ion", and feel slippery or soapy. Bases in food have no strong taste (like baking soda dissolved in water). Acids can neutralize bases. Bases can react with acids to form "salts" (still another group of chemicals). Acids and bases will each turn an indicator such as litmus paper or cabbage juice a different colour. Cabbage juice turns a wide range of colours, from yellow-green for strong bases to bright red for strong acids.

Topics: Chemical Reactions.

DOING IT:

1. *Making Cabbage Juice:* Boil the shredded leaves from a cabbage and 3 to 4 litres of water in a covered pot for a few minutes. Once the mixture has cooled, squeeze any remaining juice in the leaves into the water. Pour the purple juice into a jar. If you're not going to use it right away, store the juice in the refrigerator.

2. *Juice Testing:* In a glass, mix 3 tablespoons of the cabbage juice with a little of a test substance. Start by testing a quarter of a teaspoon of baking soda. The colour will change to green, showing the solution is a base. Add half a teaspoon of vinegar and the solution will turn to red, showing it's now an acid. Test other substances.

3. *Variation:* Make cabbage juice paper. Cut strips about 2 cm wide and several centimetres long from a white paper towel. Thoroughly wet the strips with cabbage juice and set them aside to dry. The dry strips can be used like litmus paper: put drops of a test substance on a strip and watch for a colour change. (Note: You can put a base on the strip and watch for a colour change; then put an acid on the same spot and it will change back to the original colour.)

4. *Extension:* Use grape or cherry juice or the juice from boiled onions, beets, apple skins, or tea to make indicators.

TAKE A POWDER

If you've seen one white powder, you've seen them all -- right? Powders may look the same, but if you do a little detective work you'll find they can have big differences.

MATERIALS: Magnifying glass; black construction paper; water; measuring cup; aluminum foil (to mix on); toothpicks and spoon (for mixing); glass; diluted tincture of iodine (28 g per 500 ml water); vinegar; baking soda; red cabbage juice or litmus paper; dry baker's yeast; *small* plastic zip bags; test powders (e.g. baking powder, baking soda, crushed antacid tablets, artificial sweetener, sugar, cake flour, white cake mix, chalk dust, cleansers, cornstarch, dishwashing and laundry detergents, instant mashed potatoes, powdered milk, garlic or onion powder, unflavoured gelatin, instant pudding, instant tapioca, salt, white sand, talcum powder, yeast).

DOING IT:

1. All the powders to be tested should be labelled. For each powder, complete all the tests. Make a chart describing how specific powders react to each test. Which powders have what properties? Can you organize powders into groups (e.g. acid, base, sugar, starch)?

2. *Observation:* Take a good look at a powder. Put a bit of the powder on black construction paper for easy visibility and use a magnifying glass. Sometimes a quick sniff can help to identify a powder. Rub the powder between your fingers -- are the grains large or small? **Powders should never be tasted.**

3. *Water Test:* A drop or two of water on a small amount of a test powder provides a lot of information. Does the water soak right in or does it bead and roll off? Are gas bubbles produced? If so, the powder may contain an acid and base that react with each other in the presence of water. A little water in a glass can be used to see whether a powder floats or sinks when dropped on the water and whether it dissolves.

4. *Iodine Test:* A drop or two of diluted tincture of iodine indicates the presence of starch. Iodine changes to purple or black immediately when it's added to a little flour or cornstarch.

5. *Vinegar Test:* Mix a couple of drops of vinegar with a small amount of a test powder. If the powder is baking soda, it will start to fizz as carbon dioxide gas bubbles are produced. Do any other powders react with vinegar (an acid)?

6. *Baking Soda Test:* Dissolve a spoonful of baking soda in 500 ml of water. Put a drop or two of the baking soda solution on a test powder. If it's acidic, it will start to fizz as carbon dioxide gas bubbles are produced.

7. *Acid/Base Test:* Use red cabbage juice (see previous page) or litmus paper to test whether a powder is an acid or a base.

8. *Sugar Test:* Put a test powder in a plastic zip bag with a little dry baker's yeast and warm water. Make sure you get all the air out of the bag before you seal it. Place the bag in a pan of warm water for about 15 minutes. If the powder contains a simple or complex sugar, the yeast consumes it and releases carbon dioxide gas. The gas collects in the plastic bag and is proportional to the amount of sugar in the sample. If you test the same mass of different powders, you can compare the volume of gas produced, which tells you the relative amount of sugar in each powder. Compare the results for sugar and an artificial sweetener, in particular.

9. *Extension:* Once people are familiar with the tests and how different powders react to each test, put together a collection of unmarked powders. The challenge is to use various tests to identify as many powders as possible.

Chemistry is the study of the physical and chemical characteristics of materials. It doesn't take a lot of fancy equipment and difficult-to-pronounce chemicals to be a chemist. In fact, most people are chemists and don't know it. We depend on known chemical reactions and the physical characteristics of a variety of materials to cook and clean.

Topics: Chemical Reactions; Scientific Method.

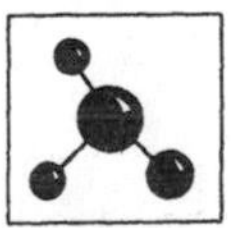

STICKY BUSINESS

"Little Miss Muffet sat on her tuffet, eating her curds and whey". Use Miss Muffet's curds and whey and a little chemistry to make glue.

MATERIALS: Skim milk; measuring cup; glass or enamelled pan; stove or other heat source; strainer; vinegar; baking soda; tablespoon; jar or other container; paper.

DOING IT:

1. Put 470 ml of skim milk and six tablespoons of vinegar into a pan. Heat slowly, stirring constantly.

2. As soon as the milk begins to curdle (form into tiny blobs), remove the pan from the heat. Continue stirring until the curdling stops.

3. You have artificially soured the milk. Let the soured milk cool. The curdled part will settle to the bottom; the liquid above the curds is the whey.

4. Pour the curds and whey into a strainer and let all the whey drain out. The curds should then sit until they are completely dry.

5. Put the curds into a container. Stir in 60 ml of water and a level tablespoon of baking soda. The baking soda reacts with the vinegar that remains in the curds.

6. You now have glue. Test the glue by pasting together two sheets of paper. Once the glue is dry, how easy is it to separate the sheets of paper?

Glue made from skim milk is called "casein" glue; casein is another name for the curd. Casein glue is similar to the white glue you buy in stores, but commercial white glue is more refined and has greater holding power than the homemade casein glue. In order for glue to stick two materials together, the materials must be very close to each other. The glue spreads out between the materials and flows into all the tiny, microscopic spaces in the surfaces of the materials. The ability of liquid glue to spread out depends on its surface tension -- the attraction between molecules on the surface of the liquid. A good glue has a low surface tension -- it spreads out quickly and easily to thoroughly wet all the parts being stuck together.

Glues have been around for a long time. The Egyptians used a paste made of flour and water over 4,000 years ago. Other early glues were made with honey, tree resins, tar, and egg white. Then, glue was made by boiling the bones and skin from animals. But there came a time when stronger glues were needed -- to hold airplanes together. Early airplanes were made of wood; screws and nails popped out when the planes vibrated during flight. So, glue was used to hold the airplanes together. The search for a better glue for airplanes led to the very strong glues we have today. Modern glues are made by mixing together various chemicals and are so strong they can even replace the rivets in metal airplanes.

Topics: Chemical Reactions.

A CHEMICAL HELPER

Have you ever tried to burn sugar cubes? They don't burn very well at all. But you can make them burn better if you add a "secret" ingredient.

MAKE TIME

MATERIALS: Sugar cubes; matches; plate; small amount of cigarette ashes.

DOING IT:

1. Use extreme caution with fire. This activity should be done with adult supervision.

2. Put a sugar cube on a plate. Try to set the cube on fire. The cube will sizzle and melt, but it won't burn.

3. Rub cigarette ashes all over the surface of a fresh sugar cube. Put this sugar cube on the plate. Hold a lit match next to the cube until the cube starts to burn. The cube's surface should burn for a short time with a strong blue flame. Why?

Make sparks in your mouth! Get some Lifesavers (wintergreen work well) that contain sugar and put them in the freezer for a while. When the Lifesavers are cold, go into a dark closet with a mirror. Give your eyes a minute to adjust to the darkness. Then pop a Lifesaver into your mouth. Look into the mirror as you crunch down on the Lifesaver. You should see blue-white sparks. When you crunch on the candy, the sugar crystals are broken. This causes gas molecules inside the crystals to obtain extra energy. The extra energy is quickly given off as light.

The cigarette ashes in this activity act as a "catalyst". Many chemical reactions proceed very slowly, but they can be speeded up if you add another substance. A catalyst is something that helps along a chemical reaction. The catalyst isn't involved in the reaction though; it isn't changed in any way. Catalysts are important in many chemical industries and are widely used in oil refining. A large number of catalysts, called "enzymes", are found in living tissue. Digestive system enzymes are found in saliva and in gastric juices. These enzymes hasten the breakdown of large molecules, such as starch and protein, into simpler molecules that can be used by the body. It isn't easy to find a catalyst for a given chemical reaction. It usually requires many, many tests to find just the right substance to catalyse a certain reaction.

Topics: Chemical Reactions.

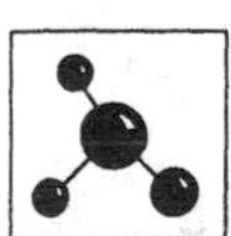

SECRET MESSAGES

It looks like an ordinary sheet of paper. But if you hold it over a light bulb, a message suddenly appears! Use a special ink to write secret messages.

MATERIALS: Freshly-squeezed lemon juice (you must use *real* lemon juice), white vinegar, or *whole* milk; small containers; toothpicks or cotton swabs; paper; heat source (e.g. light bulb, candle).

DOING IT:

1. Lemon juice, vinegar, or milk is the ink. A toothpick or cotton swab is the pen. Write a secret message on paper. If you're using a toothpick as the pen, write with the round end so that the paper doesn't tear, and press lightly.

2. Allow the paper to dry thoroughly.

3. Heat the paper by holding it over a light bulb or other heat source. **Don't hold the paper too close to the heat source or the paper may burn.** Move the paper around so that all the invisible writing is warmed. The secret message should slowly become visible.

4. Is it possible to make the visible writing become invisible again? Why or why not?

5. *Extension:* Try different liquids as the secret ink. Which liquids work well? What types of liquids don't work?

"India" or "China" ink is the oldest known ink, and is still used with brushes in the Orient. Plant dyes and other fluids have been used as ink. Most inks today evaporate from the surface of the paper, leaving the pigment (colouring) behind. Newsprint ink is absorbed into the paper.

Energy can cause changes in matter. For example, heat energy can change ice into water and water into steam. In this case, heat causes a chemical change in lemon juice, vinegar, or milk. The heat causes the formation of molecules which absorb light, giving the liquid a dark colour. Chemical changes can rarely be reversed. In contrast, when matter undergoes a physical change (e.g. liquid to solid), the change is usually relatively easy to reverse.

Topics: Chemical Reactions; Energy.

When you rub an eraser across paper, the friction between the eraser and the paper actually rubs away the top layer of the paper -- which means any pencil marks are taken off too.

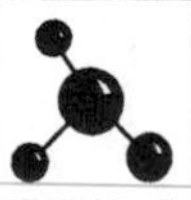

NO MATCHES ALLOWED!

What if you need fire, but don't have a match? Making fire without a match takes patience and know-how, but it isn't difficult. Construct a fire bow and give it a try.

MATERIALS: Fire bow (arm-long, stiff branch with a strong, rough cord, such as a boot lace, tied between the ends); fireboard (soft wood such as poplar or white pine); spindle (hard wood); bearing (wood, rock, or shell with small depression in it); tinder (dry grass, or shredded cedar bark); fire extinguisher or bucket of water/sand.

DOING IT:

1. Use extreme caution with fire. This activity should be done with adult supervision. Take all possible safety precautions -- avoid dry grass and bush, and have a fire extinguisher or a bucket of water/sand close by.

2. Construct a bearing, spindle, fireboard, and fire bow as shown. The wood must be *very* dry -- use an oven to dry it, if necessary.

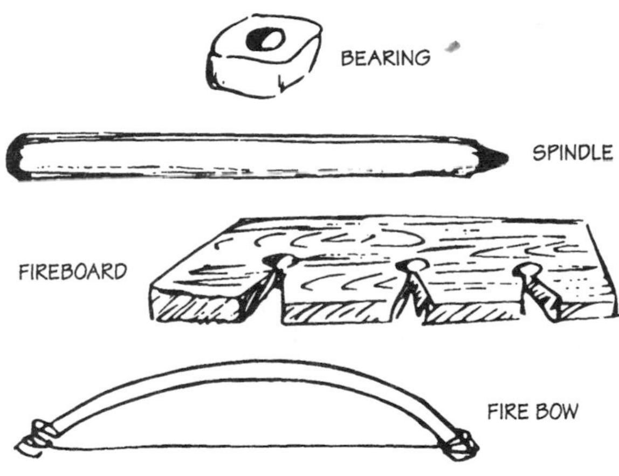

3. Place some tinder on the ground. Put the fireboard on top of the tinder. Kneel on one knee, and place your other foot on the fireboard. Twist the cord of the fire bow once tightly around the spindle. Hold the spindle upright with the bearing (to prevent injury to your hand).

4. Spin the spindle with long strokes of the bow. At the same time, increase the downward pressure on the spindle. When smoke begins to rise, knock the embers formed in the notch in the fireboard into the tinder. Supply the embers with oxygen by blowing on them steadily until the fire starts.

5. It can take a little time before smoke appears. Novice firemakers should work in pairs. Partners can alternate between moving the bow and blowing on the embers.

6. Fire has been made in 6.4 seconds. Can you start a fire any faster?

MAKE TIME

Fire is nothing more than oxygen atoms combining with atoms in the substance being burned, like a piece of wood. Atoms have to get excited before they'll burn. The initial excitement is provided by heat from an external source, such as a match. The atoms on the surface of the wood then start to vibrate as they heat up. They vibrate more and more until they start to move apart. The atoms of oxygen, carbon, and hydrogen in the wood begin flying apart in all directions. As this happens, oxygen in the air combines with the loose atoms and molecules. The wood is on fire. As the wood burns, many new forms of matter result -- water, carbon dioxide, methane, pentane, hexane, and octane -- plus heat, light, and sound. A piece of burning wood is like a chemical factory. You can make a fire using a fire bow because of a series of steps involving matter and energy. You start by putting energy into moving the bow. The mechanical energy is then converted to heat energy through friction. A chemical reaction is started by the heat, and the result is a fire.

Topics: Chemical Reactions; Energy; Atoms.

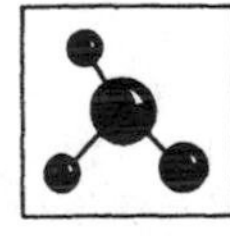

SHADOWS

Use shadows to experiment with the properties of light. You can also use shadows to create a lot of creepy creatures!

MATERIALS: Light source (e.g. 100 to 300 watt light bulb without a shade, slide projector, flashlight); screen (e.g. bed linens, sheets of white paper taped to a wall).

DOING IT:

1. Try the hand positions shown on the following page.

2. Where is the darkest part of a shadow? How does moving your hand closer to or further from the light source affect the size of the shadow? What's the largest shadow you can make? The smallest? The most distinct? How does the shadow formed when your hand is parallel to the light source compare to one made when your hand is held at right angles to the light source? What is the longest or widest shadow you can make?

3. What new shadow creatures can you create?

4. *Variation:* What am I? One person makes a shadow, while others guess what the shadow represents.

Light is a form of energy that travels at very high speeds. It can pass through air, water, glass, and many other materials. Some materials do not permit light to pass through. Light hitting an object made from such a material is blocked, while light that even slightly misses the object continues on. A shadow is formed in the shape of the object blocking the light. Shadows have many interesting properties. For example, the closer an object is to a light source, the larger and less distinct is its shadow. The larger a light source, the less distinct the shadow.

Topics: Light.

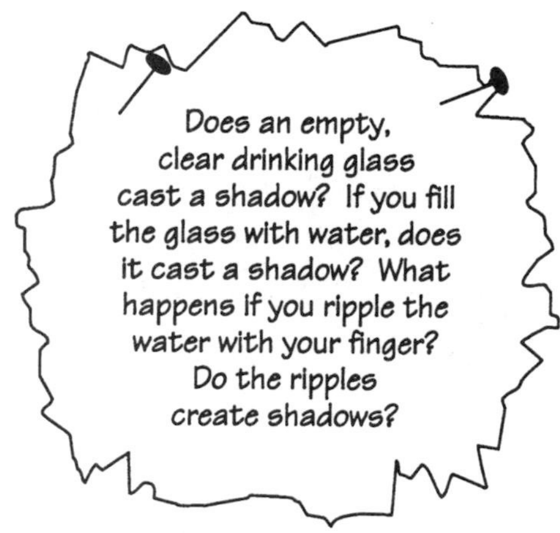

SHADOW CREATURES

GIRAFFE

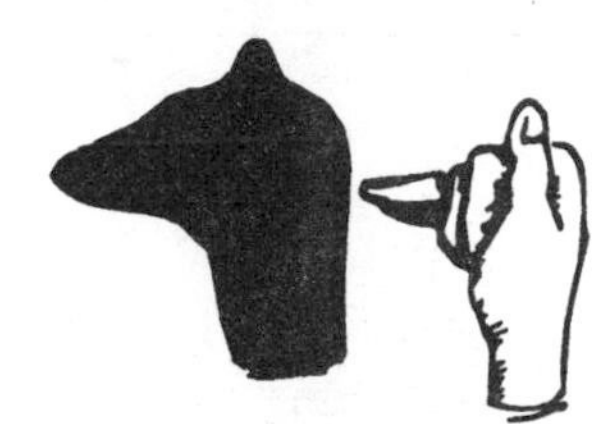

HOUND

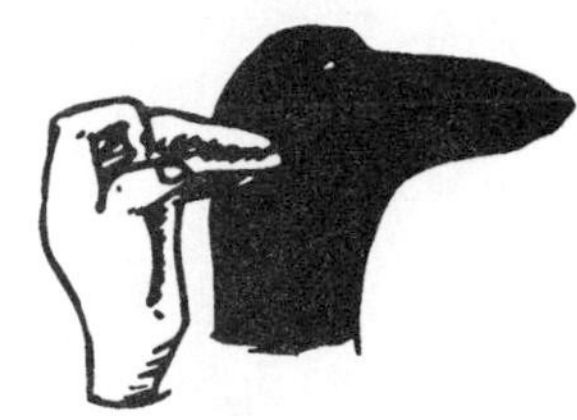

CAMEL

RABBIT

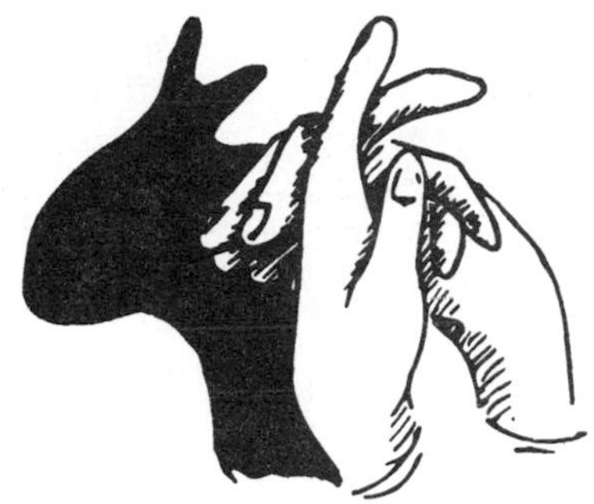

ANOTHER RABBIT!

GOAT

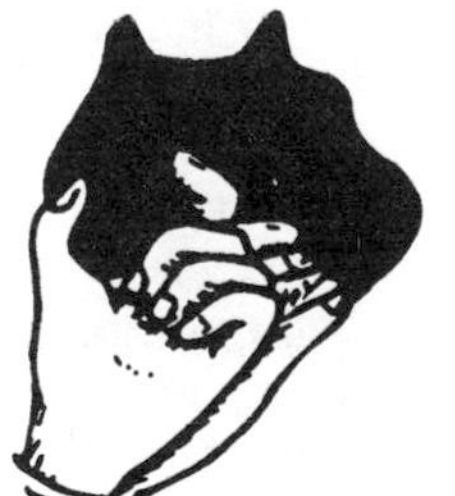

BEAR

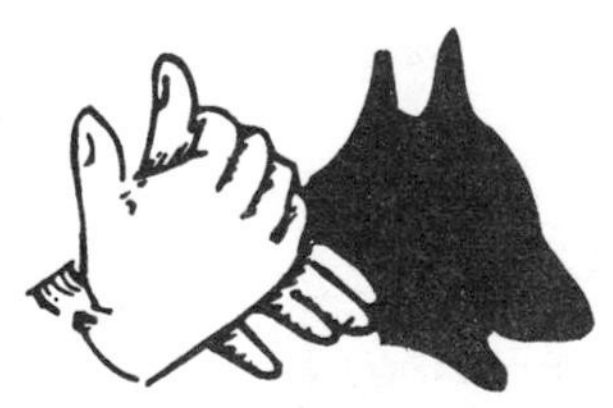

DOG

WOLF

ELEPHANT

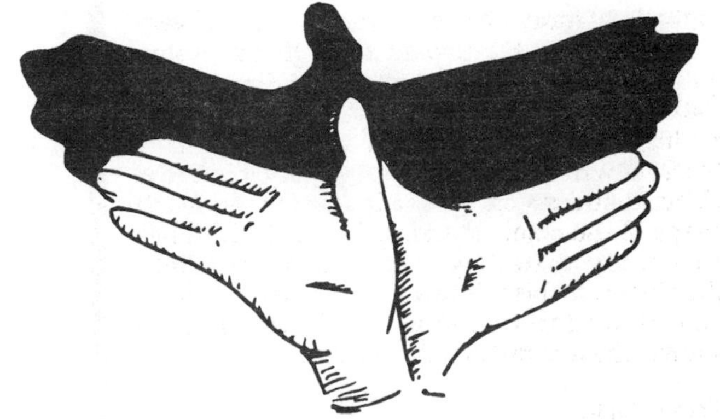

BIRD

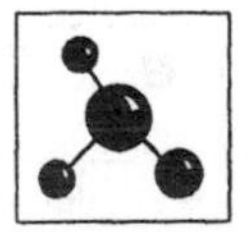

Mirror, Mirror On The Wall

Reflection occurs when a surface returns light that hits it. Mirrors are good reflectors. Explore mirrors and how they reflect light.

MATERIALS: Window; sheets of white paper; sheet of black paper; tape; two small mirrors; pen; penny; metre stick; metal tablespoon.

DOING IT:

1. *Window Reflection:* Face a window with sunshine or bright light behind you. Can you see yourself in the window? Is it easier to see your image when the background behind the window is light (white paper taped behind glass) or dark (black paper)?

Mirrors are made of glass with a special reflective silver film on the back. To understand mirrors, it's useful to look at ordinary glass. Not all light that strikes a transparent window goes through it; a tiny bit is reflected back. When light strikes a white sheet of paper behind the window, much of it is reflected in all directions back through the glass. This interferes with the small amount of light that reflects your image. Black paper absorbs more of the light entering the window. This allows the small amount of light that reflects off the window to visibly produce your image.

Mirrors aren't a real picture of the world, only a reflection of it. Light rays travel in straight lines. To see an image of an object in a mirror, you have to turn the object away from you, toward the mirror. The light rays are reflected straight off the mirror's surface, to your eyes, and you see a *reversed* image. When you use two mirrors at a right angle to see the real you, each mirror reflects half of the image onto the adjoining mirror. So, the image is reversed once and then reversed again (which makes it normal) before the light hits your eyes. When light strikes a mirror at an angle, it is reflected at the same angle in a different direction. That's why if you can see someone in a mirror, they can see you. It also explains why a full-length mirror needs to be only half as long as you are tall. When light hits a curved, or "concave" mirror, light rays cross each other as they are reflected outward. This produces an upside-down image.

Topics: Light.

2. *Reversed:* Examine a partner's face. Stand behind your partner as you both look into a mirror. How do you look different to each other?

3. *Word Flip:* How does a page of text look when you hold it in front of a mirror? Write your name and the alphabet on a sheet of paper. How do the letters as you wrote them compare to their image in the mirror? Why do some letters look the same? Make words that look the same in a mirror and on paper.

4. *The Real You:* Look in a mirror. Think of the image as another person facing you. Wink your left eye, then your right. Which eye does the image wink? Fit two mirrors together like two walls joined to make a corner. Move the mirrors slightly so you see half of your face in one mirror and half in the other. Wink each eye. Touch your left ear. What happens each time?

5. *Multiplying Penny:* Fit two mirrors together like two walls joined to make a corner. Put a penny between the mirrors. How many pennies do you see? Change the angle of the mirrors. Move the penny. What's the largest number of pennies you can make? The smallest?

6. *I See You:* Tape a mirror *flat* against the wall at eye level. One partner stands to the right of the mirror while the other stands to the left. Move around slowly until you can see your partner's eyes. Can your partner see your eyes?

7. *I See Me:* Tape a mirror *flat* against the wall at eye level. Hold a second mirror flat against the wall underneath the first mirror. A partner stands in front of the mirrors. Move the bottom mirror down until your partner can see his or her feet. Tape the bottom mirror to the wall. How does the distance between the top of one mirror to the bottom of the other mirror compare to your partner's height? Does moving farther back from the mirrors change the distance needed between mirrors? Does the distance between mirrors depend on a person's height?

8. *Upside-Down:* Look at your face in a mirror. Now look at your face on the inside of a spoon. How are the two images different?

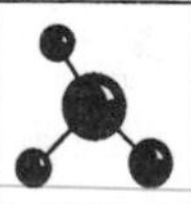

Colours Of The Rainbow

The light around you is made up of many colours. Use a prism to break the light into a mini-rainbow, and then make your own prism.

MATERIALS: Prism; flashlight or slide projector; white wall or white sheet of paper; mirror; pan of water; sunlight.

DOING IT:

1. Shine a beam of light on a white surface.

2. Put a prism in the path of the beam of light. What do you see? Which colour seems to bend the most as light passes through the prism? Which colour bends the least?

3. Place a pan of water in direct sunlight.

4. Place a mirror in the pan. Most of the mirror should be underwater. **Never look at the sun or its reflection in a mirror because you can permanently damage your eyes.** Tilt the mirror so that reflected sunlight falls on a white surface. The water should be still. What do you see on the white surface?

"Photons" are particles of energy that make up light. Visible, white light is made up of the colours of the rainbow: red, orange, yellow, green, blue, indigo, and violet (an easy way to remember these: ROY G. BIV). Each colour of light is made up of photons that carry a particular quantity of energy. For example, red-light photons each carry less energy than photons of blue light. Each colour also has its own wavelength. Violet has the shortest wavelength and red has the longest. A "prism" breaks visible, white light into a "spectrum", an arrangement of light separated according to wavelength, frequency, and energy. Light is bent (refracted) as it passes through the glass that makes up the prism. The prism bends different wavelengths of light to a different degree; violet is bent the most and red the least, with the rest of the colours in between. In a homemade prism, light rays are bent as they pass through the water. When conditions are right, water droplets in the air can act as a prism to separate the colours in sunlight -- that's when you get a rainbow. Sometimes you can see rainbows in fine sprays of water, like from a lawn sprinkler.

Topics: Light; Atmosphere.

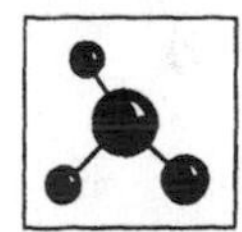

COLOUR DISC

How do you change a black-and-white disc into a coloured disc? All you have to do is give it a little spin!

MATERIALS: Photocopy of disc illustrated (or draw a disc using a compass and black marker); glue; stiff cardboard; scissors; paper clip.

DOING IT:

1. Glue a photocopy of the disc illustrated on a piece of cardboard. Cut away the excess cardboard around the disc.

2. Make a small hole in the centre of the disc.

3. Bend up the outside end of a paper clip (so that you have a long, straight piece above the rest of the paper clip).

4. Hold the paper clip between your thumb and index finger so that the straight part sticks up. Slip the disc onto the straight part; the disc should rest on your thumb and index finger.

5. Spin the disc. What colours do you see? What happens to the colours when you spin the disc in the opposite direction?

Colour depends on light. Colour isn't part of an object the way, for example, shape is. In a dark closet, an apple is still round, but it isn't red. It has no colour. If, while in the closet, you shine a bright blue light on the apple, it looks black. If you hold the apple in daylight, then it looks red.

How you see colour depends on two things: what's actually in front of you, and what your eyes perceive to be in front of you. Colour results from the ability of your eyes to distinguish between the different wavelengths or frequencies of light. The apparent colour of an object depends on the wavelength of light that it reflects. In white light, an opaque object that reflects all wavelengths looks white; an opaque object that absorbs all wavelengths looks black. When your eye receives repeated flashes of white light, your brain interprets the flashes as colour. That's why the black-and-white disc looks like it has coloured circles on it when the disc spins.

Topics: Light; Senses.

The colour red attracts attention. That's why red is used for stop signs, danger signals, and brake lights. Its stimulating effect makes it a favourite colour for advertising and displays. Some scientific studies have shown that red in bedrooms can cause restlessness and insomnia.

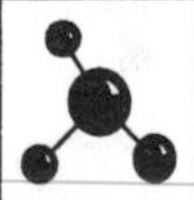

Mixing Colours

Two plus two equals four, but did you know that red plus yellow equals orange? See how many new colours you can make from just three primary colours.

MATERIALS: Red, yellow, and blue tissue paper; sheets of white paper; glue; water; paint brush. Note: You can also do this activity by mixing together different colours of paint.

DOING IT:

1. Cut red, yellow, and blue tissue paper into 5 cm squares.

2. Place one red and one yellow piece of tissue paper on a sheet of white paper, overlapping the colours in the middle.

3. Carefully brush watered-down glue onto the tissue paper until the tissue paper is thoroughly wet. The two primary colours should change to orange, a secondary colour.

4. Repeat the steps using different combinations of the three primary colours. How many different colours can you make?

5. *Extension:* Use paint to mix different proportions of the three primary colours together. For example, what do you get when you mix 1/3 yellow with 2/3 blue? See how many other colours you can make.

You see objects because light is reflected to your eye. The *colour* of an object depends on the portion of visible, white light that is reflected. White light is made up of the colours of the rainbow. A red wagon looks red because all the colours in the white light hitting the wagon are absorbed, except for the red which is reflected to your eye. You can make different colours by using three "primary" colours: red, yellow, and blue. Any three primary colours can be combined in various proportions to produce other, "secondary" colours. For example, equal amounts of red and yellow make orange. Equal amounts of red and blue make purple. Equal amounts of yellow and blue make green. Equal amounts of red, blue, and yellow make a grayish-black.

Topics: Light.

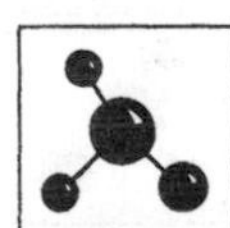

FELT PEN SECRETS

The inks in marking pens are often combinations of several basic coloured dyes. Here's a method for testing whether your felts contain a rainbow of other colours.

MATERIALS: Drinking glasses, plastic cups, or any other small, clear containers; water; absorbent paper such as coffee filters or paper towels; a variety of *watercolour* ink markers (some colours and markers may not work because of the way they are made).

DOING IT:

1. Cut one 10 cm diameter disc from absorbent paper for each marker to be tested.

2. Make two cuts, approximately 1 cm apart, from the edge of each disc toward the centre. This portion is folded back so that it hangs down into a glass.

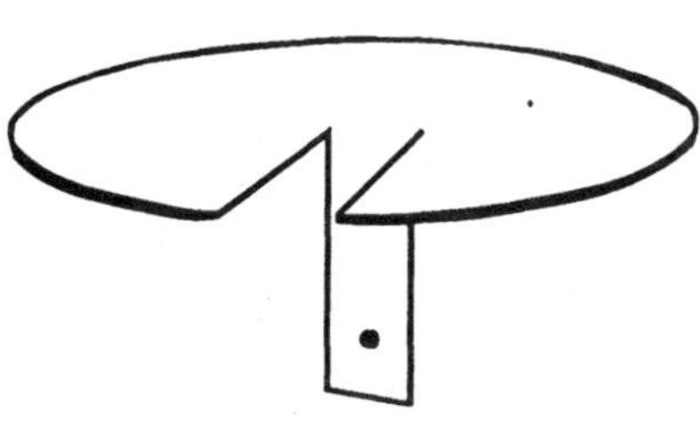

Different types of matter can be combined; colours can be mixed to get new colours. Inks and dyes consist of molecules of colouring substances that are dissolved in a liquid base. When you write, the liquid part dries and leaves just the colour behind. In this activity, when the water creeps up the test strip, it contacts the dried colour. The colouring molecules in the ink are loosened (dissolved) and carried up the strip. Different colours get carried along faster and farther than others, because some colour molecules are bigger and heavier than others. This colour separation process is called "chromatography". Chromatography means "colour writing". Chemists use the process to test a liquid mixture, such as a drug or dye, to find out what substances are in the mixture. Chromatography was invented in 1903 by Russian botanist M.S. Tswett. He was studying the colouring materials that occur in plant life.

Topics: Atoms.

3. Each marker gets its own disc. Make a large, heavy marker dot approximately 2 cm up from the bottom of the folded piece of the disc.

4. Fill a glass with water so that the water doesn't quite reach the marker dot when the disc is resting on the rim of the glass. The marker is water soluble, so if the dot is immersed in the water, the ink will dissolve into the water.

5. The separation process takes about 15 minutes. Based on your knowledge of which colours need to be mixed together to get other colours, guess what new colours might be formed from each marker.

6. What colour of marker contains the most other colours? Which colours or types of markers refuse to separate? Which colours move highest on the test strips?

7. *Variation:* Change the temperature of the water. How does temperature affect the separation process?

HUMANS

"Psychology" is the scientific study of human behaviour. It involves understanding people and the many things that influence the way we act and think.

"Sociology" is the scientific study of human interaction. It involves understanding our relationships with other people. We like to believe that we think for ourselves, but much of what we think and how we act depends on the people around us and the society in which we are raised. That's why people from one culture may have different customs and attitudes than people from another culture.

Breathe through your nose. Now swallow. Can you swallow and breathe through your nose at the same time? No one can. The nose and throat are connected by a small tube which makes it impossible to breathe and swallow at once.

Swallow some water while you're standing up. It goes down your throat and into your stomach. Now put some water in your mouth and bend over so that your mouth is lower than your stomach. Swallow the water. Is gravity needed for swallowing or is it only helpful?

Every human being has 206 bones in his or her body. The thigh bone is the longest; the 3 tiny bones deep inside the ear are the smallest. Your brain is protected by a helmet of seven bones that fit together like a jigsaw puzzle.

The mass of the human body is made up of 65% to 70% water.

In one year, the average North American eats about: 13 kg of ice cream, 11 kg of apples, 50 kg of potatoes, 12 kg of eggs, 7 kg of fish, 90 kg of milk, and 40 kg of sugar.

PERSON POWER

Do a little physical work and a little mental work to figure out how many watts the human body can generate.

MATERIALS: Stairs or a hill; tape measure. Optional -- scale; watch which indicates seconds.

DOING IT:

1. Measure the vertical height, in metres, of a flight of stairs, a hill, or a portion of a hill. The vertical height is the vertical distance between the bottom and top of the stairs or hill, not the length of the slope.

2. Estimate your body mass, in kilograms, or use a scale.

3. Time the number of seconds it takes to run up the stairs or hill. Use a watch, or count "1001, 1002, 1003, . . .".

4. Use the following formula to calculate watts:

(mass x 9.81 x vertical height) / time = watts

Mass is in kilograms; 9.81 is the gravity factor; the vertical height is in metres; and time is in seconds. If a 54 kg person runs up a 3 m hill in 5 seconds:

(54 x 9.81 x 3) / 5 = 318 watts

How much power can you generate?

5. *Extension:* Who can generate the most power? Do tall people generate more power than shorter ones? Does a person's power decrease after several runs?

Most people associate power with muscles -- the more muscles, the more powerful a person. This is true -- sort of. "Work" is the amount of force (or effort) required to move an object, multiplied by the distance the object moves. "Power" is the rate at which work is done, or how long it takes. The watt, named after James Watt (developer of the steam engine), is the standard measure of power. A car engine can have a power of 200,000 watts. A washing machine may have 375 watts.

Topics: Human Body; Energy; Measurement.

Feel your teeth with your tongue. How many different kinds of teeth do you feel? Try eating some crackers, a carrot, and an apple. Front "incisors" bite while back "molars" chew.

MAKE TIME

MODEL ARM

Muscles and bones give your body shape and help you move around. Make a bone-and-muscle model of an arm and a finger.

MATERIALS: Cardboard; brass paper fasteners; elastic bands; string; tape; scissors.

DOING IT:

1. Cut out two pieces of cardboard, each about 16 cm x 5 cm. Round the corners.

2. Punch two holes in each piece of cardboard, close to the long edges and 8 cm from the ends. Arrange the pieces as shown, using a paper fastener to make the "joint".

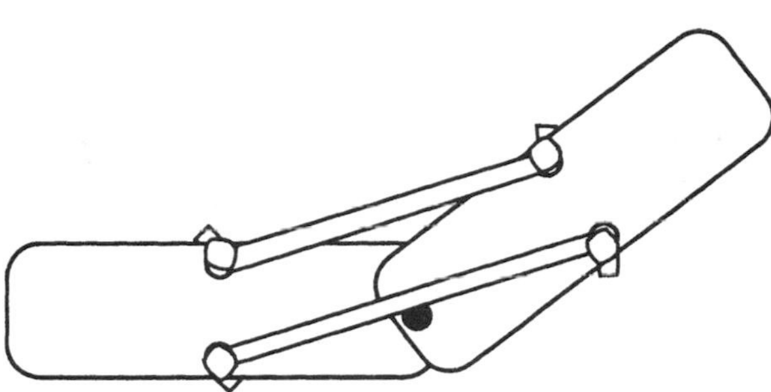

3. Cut elastic bands to make two strips about 15 cm long. Thread the elastic strips through the holes; each strip should go from a hole in one cardboard piece to the corresponding hole in the other piece. Tie knots in the ends of the elastic strips or tape them to the cardboard to keep the strips from slipping through the holes.

4. The cardboard pieces are the bones, and the elastic strips are the muscles. The model arm has only two muscles; a real arm has many. To pull the "bones" and make the "arm" bend, give a slight push. Give a push in the opposite direction to make the arm straighten. For real muscles, the "push" is supplied by the brain.

5. Change the model from an arm into a finger by using string to replace about half of each elastic strip. The string and elastic strip then work together, with the elastic strip doing the pulling and the string carrying the pull to the "finger". If you place your left-hand fingers on the lower part of your right arm, and wiggle the right-hand fingers, you can feel the movements of the arm muscles. These muscles are attached to string-like tendons, which carry the pull to all parts of your fingers. Because of this arrangement, people have fingers that are both powerful and slender. If the muscles were actually in your fingers, the fingers would be huge!

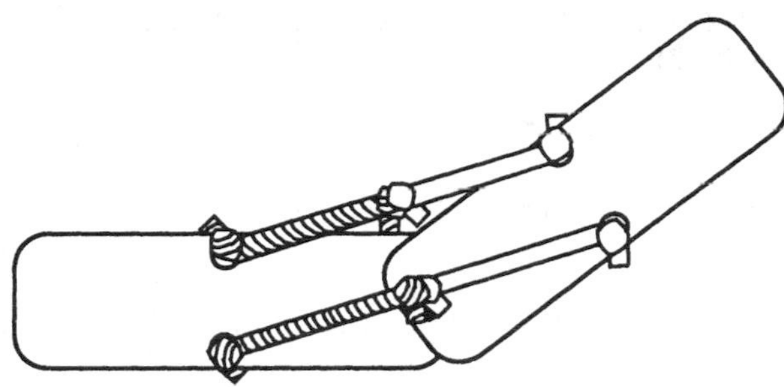

Humans have over 600 muscle groups and more than 200 bones. Muscles and bones work together. Every moving bone has at least two muscles attached to it. This is because muscles can only move in one direction; they only contract (pull). One muscle contracts and pulls a bone to get you into a certain position. Then its partner must contract to pull the bone back and get you out of the position. Muscle partners also help coordinate movements, because one acts as a brake while the other is moving. When a muscle isn't contracting, it's relaxing. Muscles have different strengths and lengths, and provide different amounts of pull. In some muscle pairs, one muscle may be much stronger than the other. Scientists have spent years studying exactly how muscles work. They do know that a muscle receives an electric command from the brain through the nerves. The command triggers a lightning-quick change of chemical fuel which causes the muscle to contract.

Topics: Human Body.

HAVE A HEART

Your heart is a muscular organ that pumps blood around your body more than 1000 times a day; each trip takes less than one minute. Explore your pulse points.

MATERIALS: Paper; watch which indicates seconds; thumbtack or small ball of Plasticine; match or toothpick.

DOING IT:

1. The first stethoscope, a hollow tube, was invented by a doctor in 1819. Roll a sheet of paper into a tube and listen to someone's heart, or use the old ear-on-chest method. There are two sounds during every heartbeat. The pattern is something like: lub-DUB . . . lub-DUB . . . lub-DUB . . .

The heart starts beating six months before you're born. During an average lifetime, it will beat almost 3 billion times. Your heart is about the same size as your fist. The right side of the heart takes blood from the veins and pumps it into the lungs; the left side takes blood from the lungs and pumps it around the body.

The rhythmic contraction of the heart is the "heartbeat". You can't hear a heartbeat, but you can hear the heart valves opening and slapping shut. The heart is in the middle of your chest. The bottom tip actually touches your chest wall; where it touches -- to the left of centre -- is where you can hear or feel the heart best. When the heart contracts (pumps), it forces blood out into the "arteries" (tubes that carry blood from your heart to all parts of your body). The walls of the arteries stretch. As the heart relaxes, the artery walls contract elastically to push the blood along. Each time the heart beats, the artery walls expand and contract once to produce one "pulse beat".

You can tell how fast your heart pumps by counting your pulse beats. A healthy, fit heart can do the same amount of pumping work with fewer beats than a weak heart. A person's resting pulse rate decreases with age (e.g. newborn baby, 130-150 beats/minute; 11 year old, 70-100 beats/minute; adult, 60-80 beats/minute).

Topics: Human Body; Sound.

2. Some arteries are too deep in the body to feel. Others are nearer the surface and can be felt by gently pushing on the skin above them. Try it! The inside of your left wrist, between the bone and tendon on the thumb side, is a good pulse point. Also try on each side of your throat, just under your chin. The correct way to take a pulse is to place three fingers on the spot. Never use your thumb because there's a large artery in the thumb; if you're trying to feel someone else's pulse, you might only feel your own.

3. Find at least one pulse point at each of these places: face, armpit, elbow, abdomen, hip joint, knee, ankle.

4. While you're sitting still, count the number of pulse beats in 15 seconds. Multiply this number by four to get resting pulse/minute. Try it twice. Do you get the same results each time? Do different people have different pulse rates?

5. How do different activities affect your pulse rate (make sure you rest after each activity so your rate returns to normal)? Take your pulse while sitting, standing, and lying down. Hop 25 times and take your pulse. Hop 100 times and take your pulse. Run on the spot or skip for two minutes and take your pulse. Can you change your pulse rate by imagining a time when you felt a strong emotion (e.g. excitement, fear)?

6. Make a pulse meter. Stick a match or toothpick into a thumbtack or ball of Plasticine. Place the device on your wrist. Move it around until you locate the spot with the strongest beat. The head of the match or toothpick will vibrate back and forth slightly with each pulse beat.

TAKE A BREATHER

Your lungs are elastic organs on either side of your heart. Check your breathing rate and measure your lung capacity.

MATERIALS: Large (e.g. 4 litre), clean bottle or jar transparent enough to see the water level inside and preferably with a cap; measuring cup; marking pen or masking tape; 0.5 m of rubber tubing; sink or large bowl; water; rubbing alcohol and sterile cotton balls.

DOING IT:

1. Sit and count the number of times you breathe out in one minute. How does your breaths/minute compare to other people's? Bend and touch your toes 50 times; then count your breaths for one minute. How does exercise affect breathing?

2. Calibrate a large bottle or jar. Use a measuring cup to add 400 ml of water to the bottle at a time. Mark the water level after each addition with a marker or masking tape.

3. Fill the bottle *completely* with water. Put the cap on or put your hand over the opening. Invert the bottle into a sink or bowl three-quarters full of water. *Make sure that no water gets out of the bottle.*

4. Take the cap off the bottle. Insert a length of tubing into the bottle, underwater. If any air gets into the jar, work the tubing into the air cavity and suck on the free end of the tubing to draw the air out. Stop sucking the instant that water starts entering the tubing in the jar; pinch the tubing to stop any further water flow.

5. Take a regular breath. Then blow out the air through the tube. Blowing into the tubing forces water out of the jar. When you've run out of air, pinch the tubing.

6. Your lung capacity is the amount of air in the jar. Read the volume from the marks on the side of the jar.

7. Try measuring a regular breath again. (Each time you do a test, refill the bottle with water; clean the end of the tubing with water and disinfect it with a cotton ball soaked with rubbing alcohol.) How do your two tests compare? How do your tests compare to other people's?

8. Do the test with a deep, deep breath. This should give you your maximum lung capacity. How does your maximum capacity compare to a regular breath?

Human beings need oxygen to survive. Oxygen comes from the air around us. Our breathing system allows us to take in air, remove oxygen from it, and exhale a body waste product called carbon dioxide. On average, a person goes through about 16 kg of air every day, which is about six times more than the total amount of food and water you take in. Different people have different breathing rates; what's natural for one person may not be for another.

When you inhale as deeply as you can, you fill your lungs full with air. You can determine the maximum volume, or "capacity", of your lungs by blowing all the air out through a tube, catching the exhaled air in a jar, and measuring it. One indicator of a healthy body is a large lung capacity. By the way, it's a well-documented fact that continuous exposure to polluted air over a long period of time damages the lungs. One of the results of this damage is that the lungs slowly lose their ability to absorb oxygen from the air and throw off carbon dioxide.

Topics: Human Body; Measurement; Air.

BURGER TO GO, PLEASE

Digestion is such a complex process that you need more than one organ to take care of it. What happens to a hamburger when you eat it? This play reveals all.

MATERIALS: Script on following pages; any sort of props and costumes you wish.

DOING IT:

1. Use real people or puppets to put on the following play. You may have to add or take out characters depending on the size of your group. As written, the characters are: Harriet Hamburger; 2 to 32 Teeth, including no more than 11 molars, 8 premolars, 4 canines, and 7 incisors (special teeth are Iggie Incisor and Mike Molar); Phantom Plaque; Tiffany Tongue; Sally Salivary Gland and her 5 sister Glands; Eunice Uvula; Erin Esophagus; Stephanie Stomach; Peyton Pancreas; Louie Liver; David Duodenum; Greasy Gloria Gallbladder; Silas Small Intestine and the Villi (as many as possible); Larry Large Intestine.

MAKE TIME

The food you eat must be "digested" -- changed in form -- so that your body can get exactly the nutrients it needs. All the body parts involved in digestion make up the digestive system. Everything you eat travels through the digestive system for a distance equivalent to two large cars parked end to end! Whatever isn't needed in the body is simply eliminated. Most meals consist of some combination of seven main food components: carbohydrates (sugars, plant fibres or cellulose, starch), fats, protein, vitamins, minerals, fibre (essential for bulk), and water. A hamburger has all these components; but, it has too little of some of the components your body really needs, and too many of some other components which, in large quantities, aren't good for you. That's why a continuous hamburger diet isn't very healthy.

One plain hamburger on a bun has about 350 calories. A "calorie" is a measure of how much energy is stored in food. You burn food in your body to get the energy you need to live. If the number of calories you take in is equal to the number of calories you burn up, your weight will stay the same. Most people who count calories to lose weight pay attention only to incoming calories. But outgoing calories used in activity count too. To work off one plain hamburger, you need about a 40-minute jog, a 60-minute bike ride, or 270 minutes of just sitting around.

Topics: Human Body; Chemical Reactions; Senses.

Put some ice cubes in a glass of cold water. Close your eyes as you drink the water. As you swallow, you should feel the coldness travel down your "esophagus", a tube to your stomach.

Chew on a sugarless soda cracker. How does the taste change as you chew? A soda cracker is made up mostly of starch. The saliva in your mouth starts changing the starch into sugar (it's changed the rest of the way in your small intestine). Changing starch into sugar helps the body use food.

The Incredible Journey Of Harriet Hamburger

(Scene: Table and chairs, centre left. Two chairs stage right. HARRIET HAMBURGER centre stage.)

HARRIET HAMBURGER: Good day everyone! I'm Harriet Hamburger. Why, I bet just last week you were sitting in a restaurant holding one of my relatives in your hand. Don't I look snazzy, all dressed up in my lettuce and tomato and ketchup? Wait until you see what happens to me when you eat me for lunch. Come along with me on my incredible journey through your body.

(IGGIE INCISOR, with scissors, walks on stage with up to 31 teeth including MIKE MOLAR. Teeth do deep knee bends in unison.)

IGGIE INCISOR: Hi! I'm Iggie Incisor, doorkeeper of the mouth. I'm the first thing people see when they open their mouths.

HARRIET: Oh, you're what people see when they smile.

IGGIE: Yeah, that's right. There are eight of us incisors.

(Seven of the TEETH join IGGIE. They are linked into two groups, one of three and the other of four, with aluminum foil-covered string.)

Some people think we're just here for smiles, but we do a lot more than that.

HARRIET: Like what?

IGGIE: Why, without us, people would never get corn off the cob. We're known as the scissors of the mouth *(snaps scissors)*. Come on in, but watch your step.

(HARRIET steps forward as IGGIE and the other TEETH do scissor kicks.)

HARRIET: What are these silver wires here?

IGGIE: Braces. My brothers and I are getting straightened out. Oh, look at my next-door neighbours Cathy Canine and Peggy Premolar.

(CATHY and PEGGY bend up and down at the waist.)

HARRIET: Have you always lived next door to each other?

IGGIE: Well, Cathy's baby sister lived here before, but we had a falling out about three years ago.

HARRIET: What kind of neighbour is Cathy?

IGGIE: Well, frankly, she's been known to tear things to pieces. But if you want to meet someone really tough, you ought to get acquainted with Mike Molar. Hey, Mike, here's someone who wants to meet you.

(MIKE MOLAR swaggers forward.)

MIKE MOLAR: Yeah, what ya' want?

HARRIET: I just came here to be digested. How can you help?

MIKE: Well, I'm just one big grind *(makes grinding motion with hands.)*

HARRIET: You mean you're going to break up with me?

MIKE: Not up, down. I'm going to break you down. Me and my next door neighbour Bruce Bicuspid'll manage to get the job done.

(MIKE and another TOOTH put their arms around HARRIET.)

HARRIET: Oooooh, you must be the strongest things around. Aren't you afraid of anything?

MIKE: Hardly anything. Only sugary treats and . . . Watch out, Iggie! It's Phantom Plaque!

(PHANTOM PLAQUE sneaks up behind IGGIE and taps him on the shoulder. Then he chases IGGIE and MIKE and the rest of the TEETH around and sticks black spots on them.)

PHANTOM PLAQUE: Hi, hi, hi! I'm a tricky, sticky guy. Hey, hey, hey! All the way with tooth decay. Don't brush your teeth. Eat lots of sweets. Hee, hee, hee! I'll help you make a cavity.

(PHANTOM chases IGGIE and MIKE and the rest of the TEETH offstage.)

HARRIET: Oooooh! Is there another way out of here?

(TIFFANY TONGUE enters, wearing spots.)

HARRIET: What a weird spotted rug!

TIFFANY TONGUE: Don't call me a rug, you old burger! I'll lick you! *(She tries to lick HARRIET.)*

HARRIET: Stop it! Why do you have those silly spots all over you?

TIFFANY: *(Continues to lick HARRIET.)* What a dumb question! These aren't spots; they're taste buds. *(Points to spots.)* Why, back here I can taste bitter things like coffee. Over here on the side are the taste buds that make people pucker up when they suck lemons.

HARRIET: But I'm salty tasting.

TIFFANY: Here's the place I taste you *(pointing to her front)*. Right up here I taste goodies like popcorn and pretzels.

HARRIET: But why aren't there spots on your middle?

TIFFANY: Oh, that's because I have no taste buds there. You don't expect me to taste food everywhere, do you?

HARRIET: You seem to have a lot of muscles. Have you been working out at the health spa?

(TIFFANY does a short exercise routine.)

TIFFANY: Well, I do always try to get a really good workout, but some days I just feel licked *(flops back in a chair)*.

HARRIET: Don't you ever do anything but lick and taste?

TIFFANY: *(Licking HARRIET.)* Yes. Without me, you'd go around sounding like this.

(TIFFANY holds her tongue and tries unsuccessfully to talk. Then, gets up and shoves HARRIET.)

HARRIET: Hey! Stop pushing me around!

TIFFANY: That's my job, too. I have to be rough and tough. Do you know Sally Salivary Gland? Hey, Sally! Harriet needs a treatment. Come on over and get to work.

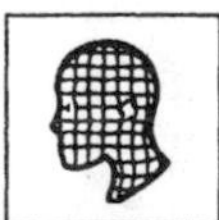

Harriet Hamburger (cont.)

(TIFFANY dances offstage as SALLY SALIVARY GLAND and her five sister GLANDS enter, twirling.)

SALLY SALIVARY GLAND: We six are here to give you a bath.

HARRIET: But I only take showers.

SALLY: Tough luck!

(GLANDS go at HARRIET making motions of washing with soap, water, and scrub brushes.) A bath will help you change your starch to sugar. Take me with you, and I'll smooth your journey.

(To audience.)

Shut your eyes everyone. Imagine your favourite food in the whole world. Is your mouth beginning to water? Well, that's me, Sally Salivary Gland, going to work.

HARRIET: Hey, this bath is all right. Where do I go from here, Sally?

SALLY: On a dangerous ride through a long, dark tube.

HARRIET: That sounds scary.

SALLY: Never fear. My friend Eunice Uvula will guide you through. Hey, Eunice, come here and meet Harriet.

(SALLY exits and EUNICE UVULA enters carrying a large stop sign.)

EUNICE UVULA: Glad to meet you, Harriet *(shakes hands with HARRIET)*. I hear you're about to embark on a journey. I'm here to guide you. My real name is Eunice Uvula, but my friends call me "One Way" for short.

HARRIET: What a strange nickname. How'd you get it?

EUNICE: Well, I make sure food takes the right road on its journey.

(To audience.)

Have you ever looked down your throat and seen that little flap of skin hanging down from the top? Well, that's me, Eunice Uvula.

HARRIET: I still don't understand why they call you "One Way".

EUNICE: Well, when you swallow, I just flip up and close the passage to your nose. That way, I make sure you follow the right path.

HARRIET: Now I understand.

EUNICE: If you think my name is weird, you should meet my neighbour. Her name is Elizabeth Epiglottis, but we call her "Trapdoor". She's a traffic director, just like me.

HARRIET: Epiglottis. Trapdoor. Those are strange names. Is her job important?

EUNICE: Absolutely. One wrong signal from her, and you'll end up in the windpipe *(coughs and motions HARRIET forward)*. Watch your step.

(HARRIET twists and twirls as though falling down a tube.)

HARRIET: Ohhhhhhh! I'm falling!

ERIN ESOPHAGUS: *(Enters dancing.)* Hi, Harriet! I'm Erin Esophagus. Oh, yeah! I'm totally awesome. Why I squeeze you down and out of the throat just like this *(pulls out a large tube of toothpaste and squeezes it)*. Why, I can get you from here to there in only seven seconds *(quickly moves HARRIET to other side of stage)*.

HARRIET: Ouch, you're hurting me.

ERIN: Sorry.

(To audience.)

Go ahead and swallow while standing on your head. I even work upside down. *(Does headstand.)*

(Loud growl is heard offstage.)

HARRIET: What's that? It sounds like a hungry lion.

ERIN: Not quite. But it means it's time for you to meet Stephanie Stomach.

(STEPHANIE STOMACH enters and stands centre stage with plastic spray bottle. ERIN pushes HARRIET toward STEPHANIE.)

STEPHANIE STOMACH: *(Growls.)* I'm Stephanie Stomach . . . and I'm hungry!

HARRIET: *(To audience.)* I don't think I like the looks of this stomach.

STEPHANIE: Stop complaining. Be brave and let me digest you. You might as well be quiet while I break you down. After four hours with me, you won't recognize yourself. *(Walks around HARRIET gently squeezing her.)*

HARRIET: Four hours! You mean I have to stay in here that long? *(STEPHANIE squirts HARRIET.)*

HARRIET: Ouch! What are you doing?

STEPHANIE: Oh, those are just my acid gastric juices.

HARRIET: *(Slips and falls down.)* Why is it so slippery in here?

STEPHANIE: That's just a slippery coating I put on myself. If I didn't have it, why I'd start digesting myself! Then I'd have what some people call an ulcer. I'd call it pain! Well, I'm about done with you. You'll feel completely new when you go through this valve.

(HARRIET twirls as if she is going down further.)

(DAVID DUODENUM strolls on reading a large map.)

HARRIET: Hey, this doesn't look too bad. Who are you?

DAVID DUODENUM: I'm David Duodenum, the beginning of the small intestine.

HARRIET: *(Looks both ways.)* I see there are two passageways leading from here. Where do they go?

DAVID: Let's go left first, and I'll introduce you to my friend Peyton Pancreas.

(PEYTON PANCREAS wanders onstage and stops. He is carrying a plastic spray bottle.)

DAVID: Oh, hi, Peyton. I'd like you to meet Harriet.

HARRIET HAMBURGER (CONT.)

PEYTON PANCREAS: *(Shyly.)* Hi, Harriet.

HARRIET: Gee, Peyton. I've never heard of you until this very minute.

PEYTON: *(Mysteriously.)* Most people don't know my name. I go about my work very quietly.

DAVID: Some people think Peyton is unimportant, but I couldn't do my job without him. Peyton, explain to Harriet exactly what you do.

PEYTON: Well, Harriet, when you come to visit David, I go to work. I give David squirts of these special juices to help him digest you *(squirts DAVID)*.

HARRIET: You mean like orange juice? That's my favourite.

PEYTON: No, no. These special juices are made of enzymes that help break down food.

DAVID: Come on, Harriet. I think it's about time you met my other two friends. But, I want to warn you ahead of time that they're a couple of really loony characters.

(PEYTON exits, as LOUIE LIVER and GREASY GLORIA GALLBLADDER walk onstage, holding hands. LOUIE has bottle filled with brown liquid. GLORIA has a jar of stones, which she places on the ground.)

LOUIE LIVER: Hi! My name is Louie Liver, and this is my girlfriend, Greasy Gloria Gallbladder.

HARRIET: Hi, Gloria. What are you going to do to me, Louie?

LOUIE: I am a man of many talents. Why, I'm the largest gland in the body. People couldn't live without me. Sometimes I weigh almost a kilogram and a half. *(Makes like Superman.)* I am the guardian of people's blood! If I see poison about to sneak into people's blood, I try to neutralize it.

DAVID: Louie, tell Harriet about the amazing tricks you do for digestion.

LOUIE: Well, I mix up this wonderful stuff called bile. *(Shakes bottle of brown liquid.)* Then I send it on over to Greasy Gloria Gallbladder. Hey, Gloria, are you ready for another shot?

(GLORIA dances around LOUIE, DAVID, and HARRIET. LOUIE exits.)

DAVID: *(To audience.)* Gloria looks like a dizzy blonde, but you french-fry lovers couldn't do without her. Gloria, tell everyone what you do.

GREASY GLORIA GALLBLADDER: Well, life's pretty easy for me.

(To audience.)

If you kids want to get me rocking, eat a lot of greasy goodies like hamburgers and french fries. Then I really go to town. *(Dances frantically.)* I shoot bile into old David Duodenum here *(squirts David)* to help him break down that yucky old fat.

HARRIET: Oh, I get it.

GLORIA: Once in a while, I do get bored and create some action of my own.

HARRIET: Like what?

GLORIA: Do you know that I can actually make stones -- real stones. *(Picks up jar of stones and shakes it.)* Sometimes they get stuck on the road to David! What a pain!

DAVID: That's enough, Gloria. *(GLORIA dances offstage. DAVID turns to HARRIET.)* How do you like roller coaster rides?

HARRIET: They make me sick to my stomach.

DAVID: Too bad, kiddo. You're about to take one!

(DAVID shoves HARRIET offstage. SILAS SMALL INTESTINE and VILLI enter, and HARRIET returns. SILAS has long rope.)

SILAS SMALL INTESTINE: Welcome to the amusement park. Are you Harriet? David Duodenum said you'd be coming. I'm Silas Small Intestine, and these are my Villi. Are you ready for your ride?

HARRIET: Oh, please, I'm afraid of roller coasters.

(SILAS and the VILLI push HARRIET into a chair and strap her in.)

A VILLUS: Relax and enjoy yourself. You're now in the small intestine, the most important part of the digestive system.

SILAS: Let's show Harriet how long her ride will be.

(SILAS unrolls six metres of rope.)

A VILLUS: And did you know you could be in here for as long as 24 hours?

HARRIET: I'm not sure I can stand a 24-hour roller coaster ride.

SILAS: My villi will help you along the ride. They feel like velvet.

HARRIET: *(Touches SILAS and a VILLUS.)* Oh, you do feel soft.

SILAS: Our walls are very thin. When we get finished with you, we can push you right through our walls and into the bloodstream.

A VILLUS: Come on. Let's get to work.

(The VILLI and SILAS push HARRIET three times around the stage and then off. HARRIET's voice trails off . . . Bye! Bye! Bye!)

(LARRY LARGE INTESTINE enters dragging a stuffed trash bag.)

LARRY LARGE INTESTINE: *(To audience.)* I take all the stuff that's left over after a person has digested some food and carry it to the dump. Before I do that, I remove the water and give it back to the body of the person who ate the food. It's a dirty job, but someone has to do it. *(Pauses.)* Now the body is full of the nutrients it needs to survive. That's the end of the incredible journey of Harriet Hamburger.

(Cast enters and takes a bow.)

Skin Prints

No two people have the same fingerprints, not even identical twins. That's why fingerprints are used to identify people. Make fingerprints to explore your skin.

ARCH

LOOP

WHORL

Human skin comes in a variety of colours. Skin colour depends on pigments (or colouring matter), skin thickness, and blood supply to the skin. The key pigment is "melanin", which ranges in colour from yellow to black. The cells that produce melanin are between the outer and inner layers of the skin. The "dermis" (inner layer) is alive and contains blood vessels, glands, nerve cells, and hair roots. The "epidermis" (outer layer) is made up of dead skin cells.

The dermis and epidermis are "locked" together by little cone-like bumps called "papillae" that go upward from the dermis and fit into hollow spaces in the epidermis. Skin may be as thick as 5 mm on the soles of your feet and as thin as 0.05 mm over your eyes. Papillae are arranged in parallel rows, "friction ridges", that make swirling patterns. These are the lines that you see in a fingerprint.

"Dermatoglyphics" is the study of skin patterns present in the friction ridges of the fingers, toes, palms, and soles. All skin prints can be divided into three general ridge patterns: arches (5% of population), loops (60%-65%), and whorls (30%-35%). In the arch pattern, ridges extend across the bulb of the finger and rise slightly at the centre. The loop pattern has one or more ridges curving into a hairpin turn. Ridges in the whorl pattern create a spiral or circle in the finger.

Topics: Human Body; Classification.

MATERIALS: Magnifying glass; paper; soft lead pencil and clear tape, or ink pad.

DOING IT:

1. Use a magnifying glass to examine your fingers. Can you see the ridge pattern? The pattern will be clearer when you take a fingerprint.

2. *Pencil Smudge Method:* Rub a pencil over and over the same spot on a sheet of paper. Cover a large area and make the blob as black as possible. Rub your finger back and forth in the pencil blob to get a dark black smudge on your finger. Press a piece of tape over the black part of your finger. The tape will pick up your fingerprint. Stick the tape on a clean, white sheet of paper to examine the fingerprint.

3. *Ink Pad Method:* Roll your finger on an ink pad. Put the outside edge of your finger (the side furthest from your body) on a piece of paper. Roll your finger in toward your body to get a print of a large part of the finger. Roll the finger gently and evenly, in just one direction. Don't press too hard.

4. What kind of ridge pattern do you have? Make a print of each finger and your thumbs. Are all the patterns the same? How do your fingerprints compare to other people's?

5. *Extension:* Can you make skin prints from other parts of your body?

UNIQUE YOU

Human beings are all similar, but no two people are exactly alike. Check the things that make you unique and how your traits come from your parents.

MATERIALS: Paper; pencil.

DOING IT:

1. Make a list of the traits you have from the following group (a "D" indicates a dominant trait, while "R" is a recessive trait):

- Hair -- dark (D) vs. light (R)
- Eyes -- dark or hazel, green (D) vs. blue or gray (R)
- Eye Lashes -- long, 9 mm or more (D) vs. short (R)
- Nose -- turned-up (D) vs. turned-down (R)
- Dimples -- yes (D) vs. no (R)
- Ear Lobes -- free (D) vs. attached (R)
- Hair on Middle Joints of Fingers -- yes (D) vs. no (R)
- Freckles -- yes (D) vs. no (R)

2. Put an "F" beside a trait you share with your father and an "M" beside a trait you share with your mother. Do you get more traits from your mother or your father? Which traits are shared by both parents?

3. Compare your list to other people's. How many people have each trait? Which traits are most common? Are recessive traits less frequent than dominant traits?

4. *Some Special Traits:* Can you roll your tongue into a lengthwise tube? (One study found that people who can roll their tongue are more likely to study science!) Can you bend the tip of your tongue back sharply without touching your teeth? Can you spread your toes and wiggle your little toe sideways without moving any of the other toes? Can you bend the top joint of one of your fingers without bending the other joint? Can you bend your thumb as far backward as you can forward? Can you form your two middle fingers into a "V" shape?

How you look is determined by instructions in your body provided from your mother and father. These instructions are carried on "genes". Thousands of genes are needed to produce the intricate recipe resulting in a single person. All human beings are similar, but there are also many variations in the basic human plan. Some variations are internal, like blood type. Others are as plain as the nose on your face or the colour of your eyes. A person inherits one gene for a certain trait from his or her mother, and another gene for the trait from his or her father. Some traits are "dominant" while others are "recessive". For example, if a person inherits a gene for attached ear lobes from one parent and a gene for free ear lobes from the other, chances are he or she will have free ear lobes because free ear lobes are dominant. It's not always possible to determine whether a person carries two dominant genes for a particular trait or one dominant and one recessive gene (in either case, the person would exhibit the dominant characteristic). This is why it's helpful to look at parents and grandparents to trace back dominant and recessive traits.

Topics: Human Body; Classification.

WASH YOUR HANDS

Microorganisms are everywhere -- inside your body and around you. Try an experiment to discover why things you can't see can affect your body.

When a doctor gives you a shot for measles, he or she is actually giving you a very mild infection. Usually, this infection is so weak you don't notice it -- but your body does. Your body immediately begins to manufacture disease-fighters called "antibodies". Once in your body, the antibodies are like guards, ready to fight off a real attack of measles if it ever comes along.

MAKE TIME

"Microorganisms" or "microbes" are living organisms of different shapes and sizes that are so small your eye can't see them. There are both beneficial and harmful microbes. Simple health practices -- like washing your hands -- control the spread of disease microbes. If you have a cold and sneeze on your hand, even though you can't see the germs on your hand they can be transferred to another person and make them sick. You pick up microbes anytime you touch things, particularly objects handled by many other people, like money.

There can be as many as 5,000 microbes in one millilitre of pasteurized milk. In the experiment, microbes in the control jar grow and reproduce. They change the pH of the milk and cause it to separate into two layers -- curds (thick layer) and whey (watery layer). When soil is in the milk, the layers appear more quickly because the soil contains millions of microbes. The curd may also start to deteriorate: the liquid turns brown and smells very foul. An acid in the milk changes the pH without the action of microbes; the milk separates into layers, but doesn't smell foul. An open jar of plain milk separates more quickly than the control but not as fast as with soil; microbes fall into the jar from the air. The jar in the refrigerator should be the least affected of the five jars. The cold keeps the microbes from growing rapidly.

Topics: Microorganisms; Scientific Method.

MATERIALS: Five small, clean jars with lids; 250 ml of pasteurized milk; pinch of soil (not sterilized); teaspoon of lemon juice or vinegar; refrigerator. Optional -- potato; pot of water and stove; plastic zip bags.

DOING IT:

1. Label the jars one through five. Divide about 250 ml of milk evenly among the jars.

2. One jar is the "control". Put the lid on and keep the jar at room temperature.

3. Put a pinch of soil in the second jar. Put the lid on and keep the jar at room temperature.

4. Add a teaspoon of lemon juice or vinegar to the third jar. Put the lid on and keep the jar at room temperature.

5. Don't put anything into the fourth jar. Leave the lid off and keep the jar at room temperature.

6. Don't put anything into the fifth jar. Put the lid on and keep the jar in the refrigerator.

7. Watch the jars over a week or so. What happens in each jar? What does the liquid in each jar look like? How does the liquid smell? **Don't drink any of the liquid; discard the jars and contents when you are finished the experiment.**

8. *Extension:* Why is washing your hands important? Slice a raw potato and blanch it for one minute in boiling water. When the potato slices have cooled, rub your fingers on a slice after you've been outside touching a lot of things. Then wash your hands and rub your fingers on another potato slice. Put each slice in a separate plastic zip bag; seal the bags; leave them for a few days. How do the two potato slices compare?

BETTER THAN A COMPUTER

Your brain translates electrical and chemical body signals into perceptions, thoughts, and movements. This puzzle shows how your brain is even better than a computer.

MATERIALS: Copies or drawings of puzzle; three pencils of different colours.

DOING IT:

1. Use three different colours of pencil to colour the parts of the puzzle. *The same colour can't touch itself!* For example, you can't have a purple part right beside another purple part.

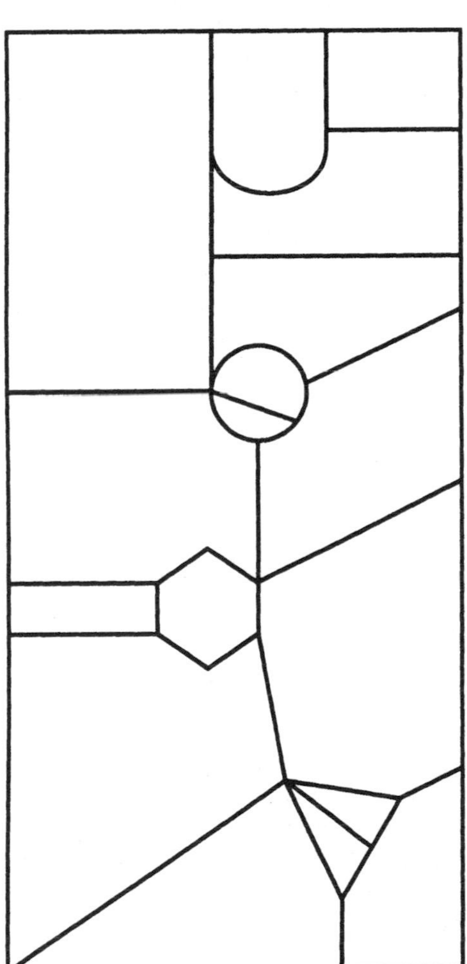

What happened to the brain of Albert Einstein? It's in a jar of formaldehyde, in a cardboard box, in the office of a medical supervisor in Kansas. Most of the brain was sectioned and given to various scientists for study. It doesn't seem that they've uncovered much. The key to special intelligence does not appear to reside in dead tissue; the physical brains of a genius and a moron have proven to be virtually indistinguishable.

The brain looks like a large, wrinkled walnut. It's made up of between 15 and 100 billion nerve cells (neurons) and is one of the heaviest parts of the human body. The brain is the "computer" of your body. It receives 100 million signals every second from all parts of your body. For example, your knee itches. The itchy sensation is picked up and sent flashing along nerve fibres to your brain. Your brain interprets what the impulses mean and decides what to do about the itch. New impulses are flashed out from your brain. The muscles of your eyes, fingers, arms, back, and legs are all given instructions to help you scratch.

Humans are fascinated by the challenge of making a computer that can match the abilities of the brain -- but we still have a long way to go. A computer just can't think. It needs humans to do the thinking for it, to program it. A computer works by using "algorithms". An algorithm is a method for solving a problem. If you know how to multiply two numbers together, you know an algorithm. Algorithms always work and don't require any guessing. You can do the puzzle fairly easily by thinking; that is, by guessing and using your intuition. Once you solve the puzzle, you could try to come up with an algorithm for a computer. You could also program a computer to solve the puzzle using only trial and error -- but there are *millions* of possible ways to colour the picture!

Topics: Brain; Problem-Solving.

Do Your Homework

Your brain needs exercise just as much as your muscles do. The more you use your brain, the better and faster you'll be at using it. Try this experiment to prove it.

MATERIALS: Paper; pencil; small mirror; clay; book; stopwatch or watch which indicates seconds; ruler.

DOING IT:

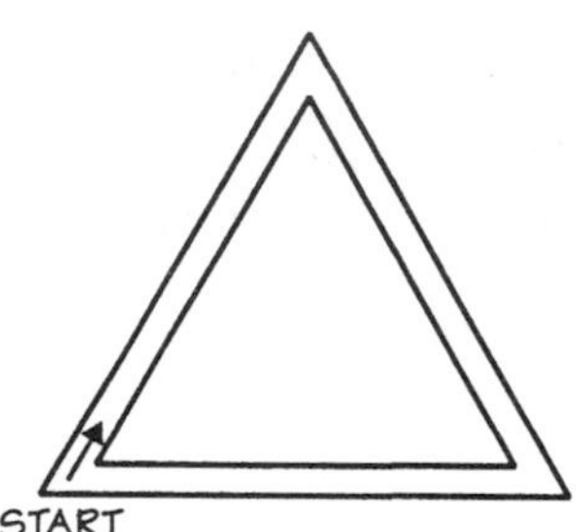

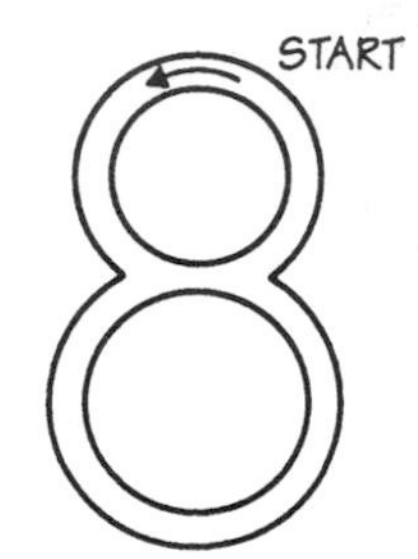

1. Trace the triangle onto a sheet of paper. Make the triangle the same size shown.

2. Arrange the sheet of paper as shown, with a mirror stuck into bits of clay. Hold a book up in front of the triangle. Sit so that you can see the triangle in the mirror.

3. Put your pencil at the point marked start. Time yourself to see how long it takes you to draw a line around the whole triangle, between the two border lines. Use the mirror to see what you are doing -- *don't look directly at the triangle on the paper.* If you go over the inside or outside border, lift up your pencil and start drawing again from where you left the border.

4. Write down how long it takes you to finish drawing.

5. Repeat the process five to ten times. Does practice improve the time you need to draw around the triangle? How do your drawing times compare to those of other people? Do some people learn more quickly than others?

6. *Extension:* Do the same experiment with the figure eight.

"Learning" is a change in behaviour and ability based on experience and practice. The more you do something, the better you get at it. Your brain is a very complex circuit that runs on electrical impulses. The more interconnections between the brain's cells, the better the circuit works. Research has indicated that by practising a task over and over again you help your brain create new connections for that task. When you first try a new task -- a task for which there are no existing connections -- an impulse must wind its way through all the connections to help you complete the task. Once you establish new connections for the task, the impulse can travel a short, specific path and you can complete the task more easily and quickly.

Sometimes, earlier learning can interfere with later learning. Your mind gets used to doing something in a particular way; impulses get used to following a certain path through your brain. To change the way you do a task, you not only have to create a new path but you have to "pull" the impulse away from the old path. That's why learning to draw backward is such a challenge.

Topics: Brain; Human Behaviour.

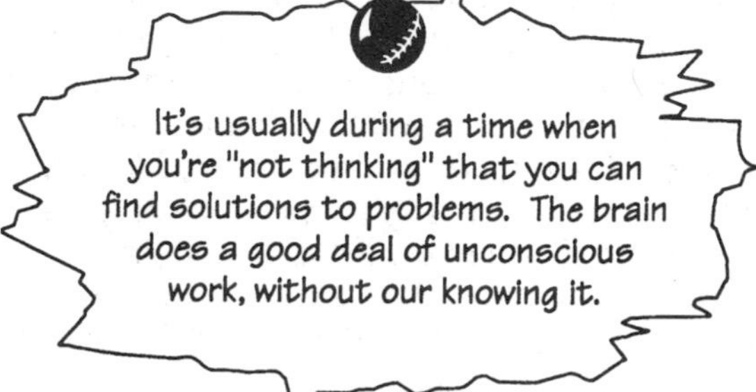

DON'T FORGET

You have to know how to use your brain. Everyone forgets things. But you can learn a trick to use your brain better and remember all sorts of amazing things.

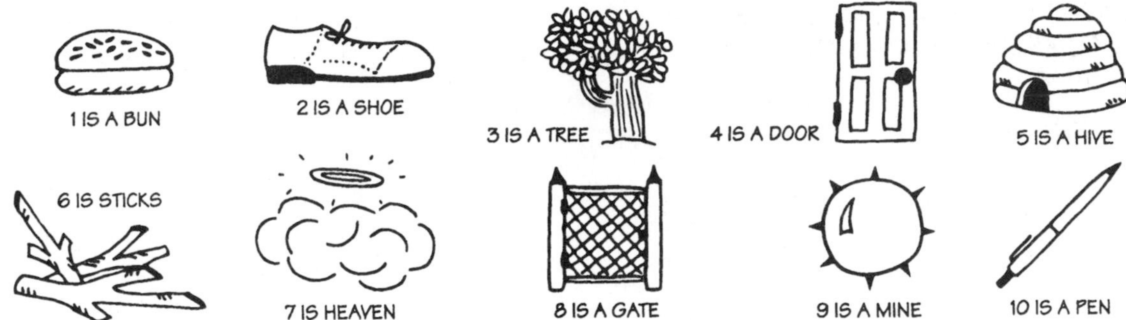

MATERIALS: None.

DOING IT:

1. Learn the numbers and pictures on this page. Read the rhyming number list aloud. Examine the pictures. Practice going from one to ten until you know the list backward and forward.

2. The next time you need to remember something, associate it with the One-is-a-Bun list. For example, pretend you have to memorize the following shopping list: baseball cards, gum, pop, comic book, eraser, shirt, birthday present, potato chips, yo-yo, ball. Start by making up a silly picture in your head connecting baseball cards and a bun: baseball cards stuffed into a hamburger bun or a baseball card showing a player hitting a bun. Once you have the first picture, think of a picture of gum and a shoe together. Gum stuck to the bottom of a shoe is easy. But what about a shoe made out of gum so that the shoe sticks to your foot? The sillier the picture, the better; your brain remembers silly things more easily.

3. It should take you about 30 seconds to connect each word in your list to the One-is-a-Bun list. Once you go through One-is-a-Bun, you will remember your list easily. You can go through it frontward and backward, and even remember a certain item, like item seven. You can remember any kind of list, from a shopping list to a list of items for a test. And, you can use only part of the One-is-a-Bun list or, if the items you have to remember total more than ten, you can associate two or more items to one number in One-is-a-Bun.

Humans today are no smarter than they were 10,000 years ago; but we do have a greater storehouse of knowledge to draw on, to remember. There are two basic types of memory: "short-term" and "long-term". Short-term memory helps you retain information that you gather in the present but don't need to store for future use. For example, it helps you to remember a telephone number you've looked up in the directory just long enough to dial the number. In long-term memory, the brain "locks in" information for long periods of time. If you dial a telephone number often -- like the number of a close friend -- it enters into your long-term memory. In many cases, long-term memory stores information for life. Unfortunately, although scientists believe that your long-term memory is packed with information, you often can't get at it when you need it; you "forget".

There are three "Rs" to remembering: registration (you receive the information); retention (you file the information); and retrieval (you can find the information when you need it). "Mnemonics" are tricks to help with retention and retrieval. They are based on the way the brain works. For example, you tend to remember things that have meaning for you. It's easier to remember the pair CAT-SKY than JQT-ZNR because the words "cat" and "sky" mean something to you. The "One-is-a-Bun" mnemonic helps your brain remember things in a group (your brain likes groups) with "pegs" (rhymes and visualization).

Topics: Brain; Human Behaviour; Numbers.

Talking Without Your Mouth

You communicate every day by speaking and writing words. Learn a new way to communicate -- sign language.

Most animals communicate by simple motions or odours. Some apes have been taught a simple sign language. But humans are the only creatures that can engage in complex communication, using everything from motions to symbols. Isn't it amazing that you and another person can both look at the word "rose" and not only think of a flower but see the same kind of flower in your mind? A word is a powerful thing. Learning different ways to communicate helps you understand how important communication is to being human and how complex it is. Many blind people use their fingertips to read. Your fingertips are very sensitive -- containing about 100 "touch receptors" each. "Braille" consists of patterns of raised dots that stand for different letters of the alphabet. For example, one raised dot is an "A"; four raised dots in the shape of a square are a "G". Many deaf people use sign language to communicate. They use hand signals in two ways. The first way is "finger spelling", where each letter of the alphabet has its own hand sign. People can "talk" by spelling out all the words they want to communicate. The second way is called "signing". A sign is made with one or both hands to communicate a word or idea; words aren't spelled out letter-by-letter.

Topics: Communication.

MATERIALS: None.

DOING IT:

1. Learn the letters and signs used by deaf people. How long does it take you to feel comfortable using them? Can you teach them to someone else?

2. *Variation:* Write short messages on slips of paper. Fold the pieces of paper in half and in half again. Scramble them in a pile. Each person chooses a slip of paper. Finger spell and/or sign the message for others to guess (it might be easiest if everyone writes down each letter or sign a person makes, and then puts the letters and signs together to figure out the sentence). Here are some sample messages: I said hello on the telephone. I love you. Ants are small. The ghost was funny. Snow is cold. He is weird. Help!

Sign Language

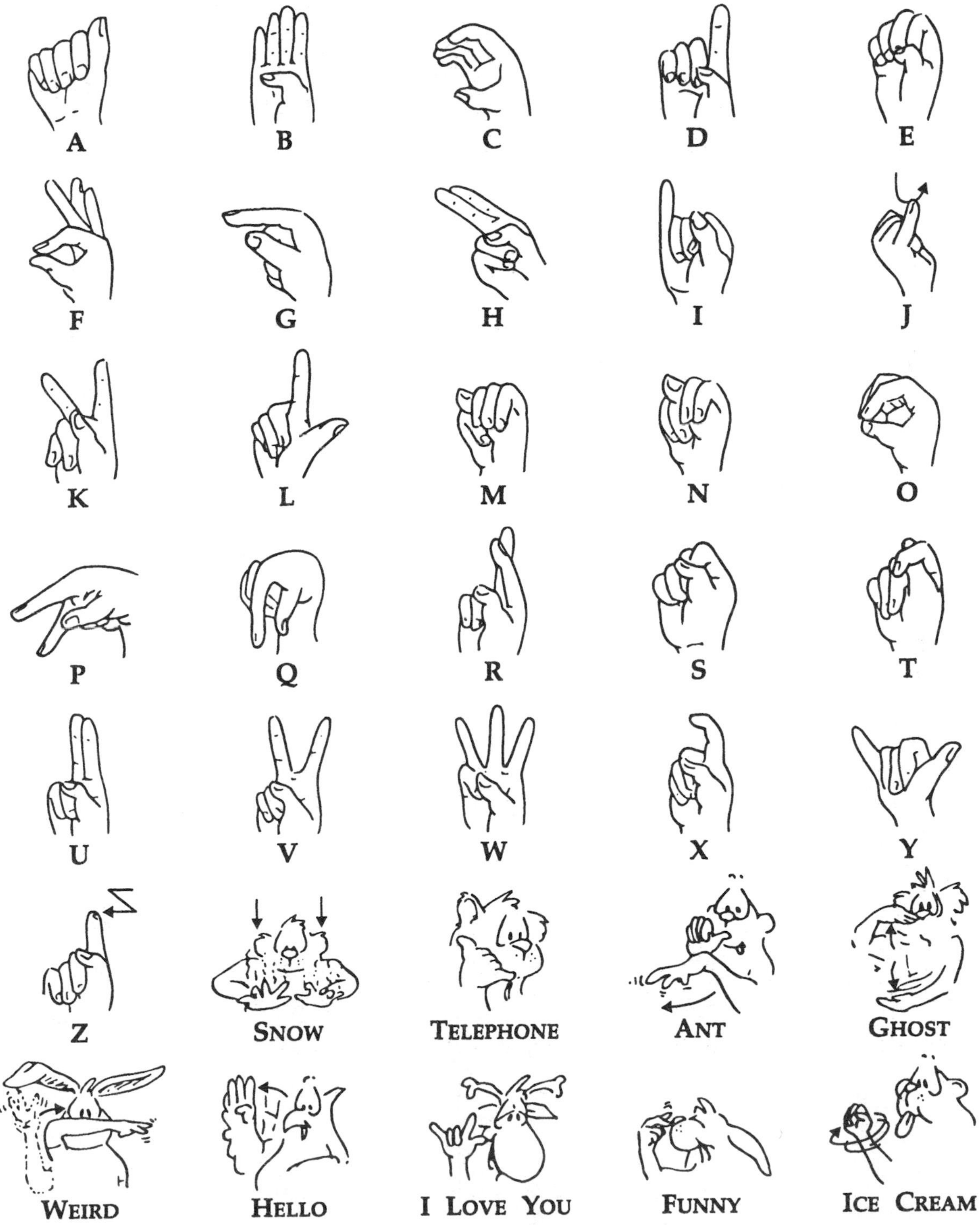

A B C D E

F G H I J

K L M N O

P Q R S T

U V W X Y

Z Snow Telephone Ant Ghost

Weird Hello I Love You Funny Ice Cream

A DAY IN THE LIFE OF YOU!

Different people spend their time differently, but there are similarities (we all need sleep!). You might find some surprises when you look at your typical day.

MATERIALS: Paper; pencil; ruler; coloured pencils.

DOING IT:

1. Make a large rectangle on a sheet of paper. Divide the rectangle's length into 24 equal strips. The rectangle represents one day. Each strip in the rectangle equals one hour.

2. Choose a colour or pattern for each kind of major activity you do during the day.

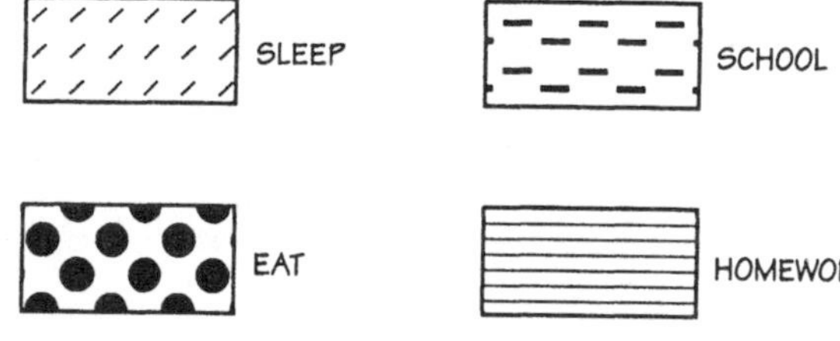

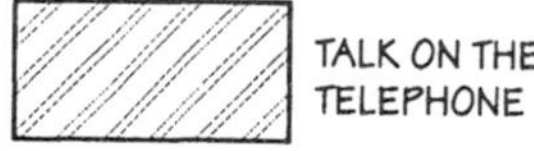

3. Colour in the amount of time you spend doing each activity on a typical day. For example, you might spend eight hours sleeping; colour in eight side-by-side strips in the rectangle. If you do two things at once, colour part of the strip one colour and the other part the other colour.

4. Are you surprised by how you spend your day? Did you think you spent so much time sleeping? What activity takes the least time? Do you ever do two things at once -- like watching television and doing homework? How does your typical day compare to someone else's?

5. *Variation:* Colour in a rectangle to show how you would *like* to spend a typical day. How does the "I wish" day differ from a real day? Is the "I wish" day possible (e.g. it's not practical to think you could go without sleep)? What changes are possible and how could you make them?

6. *Variation:* Colour in rectangles to show how familiar animals spend their day. How does your cat or dog spend its day? How does the monkey at the zoo spend its day? How do the animal days differ from your day?

7. *Extension:* Colour in rectangles for every day for two weeks. How does one day compare to the next? Are weekends different than weekdays? Is the first week different from the second week?

Most animals operate on instinct -- they do what they do naturally and without conscious thought. Their daily activities revolve around survival. While human beings have to do basic things like eat and sleep, we're rather unique because that's not all we do. Humans spend time in all sorts of activities -- activities which challenge our minds and which make us a part of society. How you spend your day is a combination of personal choice (playing ball, watching television), biological needs (eating, sleeping), and social requirements (going to school or work).

Topics: Human Behaviour; Measurement.

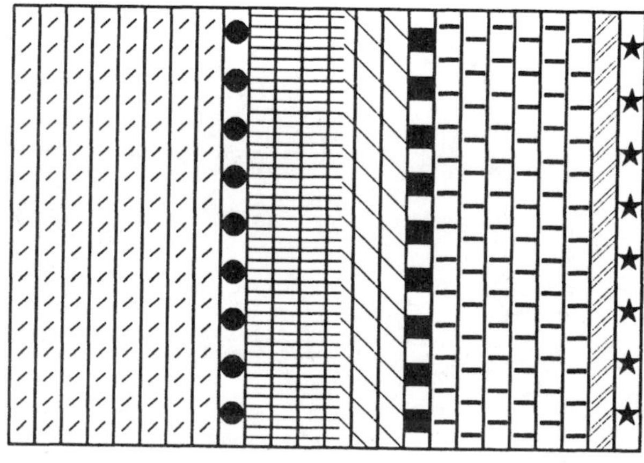

THE ENVIRONMENT

We travel together as passengers on a little spaceship -- spaceship Earth --, dependent on its vulnerable reserves of air and soil; all committed for our safety to its security and peace; preserved from annihilation only by the care, the work, and the love we give our fragile craft.
(Adlai Stevenson)

Plants can be indicators of air pollution. If exposed to high levels of certain oxidants, plants like tobacco, petunias, and spinach get small dark dots or larger white spots. The bottom surface of the leaves may also become shiny. The leaves of alfalfa, tomatoes, lettuce, and carrots turn yellow with long-term exposure to sulphur dioxide pollution. If exposed to sudden high levels of sulphur dioxide, the leaves collapse and become water-soaked.

If we go on as we are,
we will destroy in the next century
everything that poets have been singing about
for the past two thousand years.
(Fred Bodsworth)

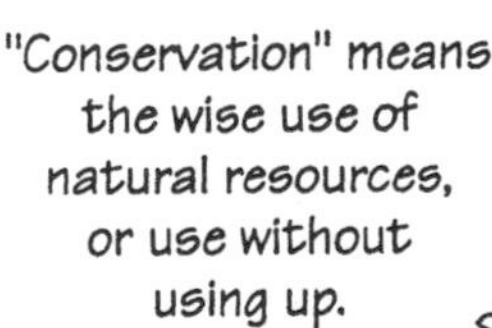

"Conservation" means the wise use of natural resources, or use without using up.

The "World Conservation Strategy" says that our way of life can only be sustained by conserving the living resources -- the plants and animals -- on which our lives depend, and by balancing development with conservation.

Instead of pesticides, why not "pests"? To protect their crops, farmers often use pesticides (poisons that kill insects that eat crops) and herbicides (poisons that kill weeds). But pesticides and herbicides may also harm other living things, directly or indirectly, and get into our water supply. An alternative method of control is to find a natural predator and invite it to dinner. This type of idea was applied to prickly pear cacti in Australia; the huge number of the cacti once made them a problem. The cacti were brought under control by the deliberate introduction of a moth whose larvae feeds on them.

MAKE TIME

KEEPERS OF THE EARTH

Human beings are keepers of an Earth in which everything is connected. This Native American story explores relationships in the environment.

MATERIALS: Yellow ball or other symbol of the sun; index cards representing parts of the Earth, with a picture on one side and description on the other:

- *Plants* -- use sunlight and make food and oxygen for other living things.
- *Soil, Rocks* -- feed the plants to make them grow.
- *Air* -- gives the breath of life to living things.
- *Water* -- quenches thirst and brings life to all plants and animals.
- *Seasons* -- bring change each year: heat and cold, wet and dry, sleep and wakefulness, new life and old.
- *Animals* -- feed people and each other, help to pollinate flowers and sow plant seeds, and bring movement and sounds to the Earth.
- *Stars and Moon* -- light the night sky, guide the way, and (moon) bring the tides.
- *People* -- care for the Earth and hold all parts of the Earth in our hands.
- *Stories* -- bring the world to life in your imagination.
- *Life and Death* -- life brings living things where there were none before and death makes room for new life.
- *Circles* -- keep the life on Earth going and keep everything in good balance.

MAKE TIME

American Indian cultures generally involve a great respect for the environment. The story brings together the parts of the Earth. The parts of the sacred pipe represent the animals, the plants, and the breath that carries prayers to the Creator. The White Buffalo Calf Woman shows the people how to offer the sacred pipe to the Earth and Sky and the Four Sacred Directions. The sacred pipe touches the heart of contemporary wisdom in ecology and environmental conservation. Our world is beautiful and giving, yet finite and fragile. The "web of life" binds all together so that one part of the environment cannot be altered without affecting the others. The sacred pipe and the circle represent the unity of all things and the balance of the cycles that perpetuate life: cycles of life and death, nutrients, tides, stars, moons and seasons, water, gases, and of giving and receiving. The lesson of the White Buffalo Calf Woman is one of respect -- to live in ways that honour the interconnectedness of all things and keep the Earth for those whose song is yet to be sung.

Topics: Ecosystems; Resources; Environmental Awareness

DOING IT:

1. Read the story on the following page.

2. People should sit in a circle. Begin by discussing the story. What do the parts of the White Buffalo Calf Woman's sacred pipe stand for? She shows the people how to offer the Pipe to six places: the Sky, Earth, and Four Sacred Directions. What are these places? Why are they important? What does she mean when she tells the people to take the right direction of the Good Red Road? What does it mean for the people to live by remembering that all things around them are connected, like the parts of the pipe? How can we affect plants, animals, people and the rest of the Earth by the things we do?

3. Each person should have one index card. If there are more people than cards, more than one person can have the same card. Begin by putting the sun in the centre of the circle; the sun gives light, heat and energy to make plants grow. Then, one at a time, people go to the centre of the circle, describe what their part of the Earth does, and place their index card beside the sun.

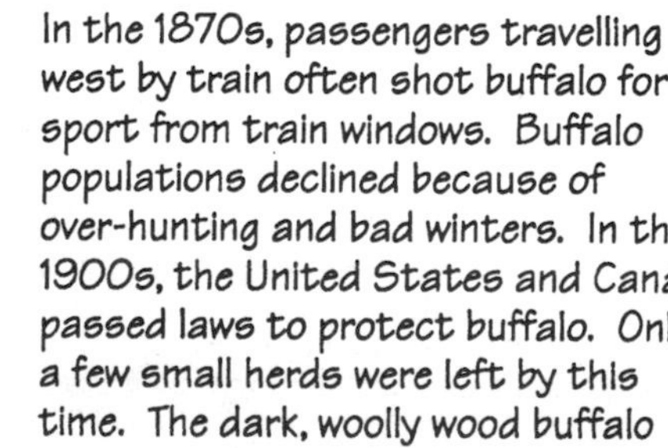

THE WHITE BUFFALO CALF WOMAN & THE SACRED PIPE

(LAKOTA [SIOUX] -- GREAT PLAINS)

It was a time when there was little food left in the camp and the people were hungry. Two young men were sent out to scout for game. They went on foot, for this was a time long before the horses, the great Spirit Dogs, were given to the people. The two young men hunted a long time but had no luck. Finally they climbed to the top of a hill and looked to the west.

"What is that?" said one of the young men.

"I cannot tell, but it is coming toward us," said the other.

And so it was. At first they thought that it was an animal, but as the shape drew closer they saw it was a woman. She was dressed in white buffalo skin and carried something in her hands. She walked so lightly that it seemed as if she was not walking at all, but floating with her feet barely touching the Earth.

Then the first young man realized that she must be a Holy Person and his mind filled with good thoughts. But the second young man did not see her that way. He saw her only as a beautiful young woman and his mind filled with bad thoughts. She was now very close and he reached out to grab her. As soon as he did so, though, there was a sound of lightning and the young man was covered by a cloud. When it cleared away there was nothing left of the second young man but a skeleton.

Then the White Buffalo Calf Woman spoke. "Go to your people," she said, holding up the bundle in her hands so that the first young man could see it. "Tell your people that it is a good thing I am bringing. I am bringing a holy thing to your nation, a message from the Buffalo People. Put up a medicine lodge for me and make it ready. I will come there after four days have passed."

The first young man did as he was told. He went back to his people and gave them the message. Then the crier went through the camp and told all the people that something sacred was coming and that all things should be made ready. They built the medicine lodge and made an earth altar which faced the west.

Four days passed and then the people saw something coming toward them. When it came closer, they saw it was the White Buffalo Calf Woman. In her hands she carried the bundle and a bunch of sacred sage. The people welcomed her into the medicine lodge and gave her the seat of honour. Then she unwrapped the bundle to show them what was inside. It was the Sacred Pipe. As she held it out to them she told them what it meant.

"The bowl of the Pipe," she said, "is made of the red stone. It represents the flesh and blood of the Buffalo People and all other Peoples. The wooden stem of the Pipe represents all the trees and plants, all the things green and growing on this Earth. The smoke that passes through the Pipe represents the sacred wind, the breath that carries prayers up to Wakan Tanka, the Creator."

When she finished showing them the Pipe, she told the people how to hold it and how to offer it to Earth and Sky and the Four Sacred Directions. She told them many things to remember.

"The Sacred Pipe," said the White Buffalo Calf Woman, "will show you the Good Red Road. Follow it and it will take you in the right direction. Now," she said, "I am going to leave, but you will see me again."

Then she began to walk toward the setting sun. The people watched her as she went, and they saw her stop and roll once on the Earth. When she stood up she was a black buffalo. Then she went farther and rolled again on the Earth. This time when she stood up she was a brown buffalo. She went farther and rolled a third time and stood up. Now the people saw that she was a red buffalo. Again she walked farther and for a fourth and final time she rolled upon the Earth. This time she became a white buffalo calf and continued to walk until she disappeared over the horizon.

As soon as the White Buffalo Calf Woman was gone, herds of buffalo were seen all around the camp. The people were able to hunt them and they gave thanks with the Sacred Pipe for the blessings they had been given. As long as they followed the Good Red Road of the Sacred Pipe and remembered, as the White Buffalo Calf Woman taught them, that all things were as connected as parts of the Pipe, they lived happily and well.

CHAIN REACTION

You can never do "just one thing". Parts of the environment are related to each other. Here's a puzzle in which finding one word leads to finding the next word.

MATERIALS: Copy of the puzzle on the following page; pencil.

DOING IT:

1. The word search puzzle is a chain reaction. The first letter of every word is the same as the last letter of the word before it. Find the first word and then the following words will connect to each other. Put a line through the letters as you find the words.

2. Once you've found all the words, the letters that are left over make a poem. Take the spare letters in the *exact* order they are written and fill in the blanks at the bottom of the page. When the poem is finished, all the spare letters will be used up.

3. What do you think about the poem's environmental message?

Solving environmental problems is difficult because the environment is complex, with parts that are interrelated directly and indirectly. Driving a car seems straightforward enough. You get in, turn the key, and go where you want to go. But the chain reaction that converts gasoline into the mechanical energy that makes a car move also releases pollutants. These pollutants start another chain reaction in the atmosphere, and the result is acid rain, among other things.

Topics: Ecosystems; Pollution.

One day, someone realized that if you push some seeds into the soil, plants grow. With this discovery, people no longer had to depend on wild wheat; they could plant seeds where they wanted wheat to grow. A few people now could produce enough food for many others. People settled in one place. Where before people hadn't remained in one place long enough to pollute it, now they began to have an effect on their environment. To produce food for many people, farmers had to overcome many obstacles -- bad weather, insects, loss of soil. In overcoming these obstacles, agriculture has created environmental problems of its own, like pollution from pesticides.

ENVIRONMENTAL WORD SEARCH

T	H	E	T	R	A	S	H	R	E	S	L	E
B	I	R	T	T	E	E	R	L	A	L	S	L
U	I	L	O	V	A	E	A	A	R	I	A	E
D	N	D	S	T	M	R	O	W	O	G	I	C
N	T	H	R	E	U	A	L	N	I	R	I	T
T	W	E	I	T	L	I	I	L	G	E	T	R
E	E	V	A	D	T	E	O	N	W	O	R	I
S	U	N	U	T	E	S	S	D	U	O	L	C
E	I	M	E	F	W	E	E	D	O	N	T	S
T	P	R	E	U	S	E	W	A	R	T	T	O
C	A	O	R	E	W	E	A	O	M	U	S	T
R	E	C	L	Y	C	L	E	R	L	O	U	R
R	E	W	O	L	F	A	E	L	S	L	G	A
R	I	B	A	E	U	G	E	L	A	T	E	N
M	D	V	A	L	C	T	L	E	E	A	E	Y
R	A	R	E	O	N	U	E	M	G	R	I	M
A	T	N	P	R	O	U	G	S	A	R	G	E
H	R	O	M	U	N	D	O	R	B	S	A	T
N	D	R	E	A	P	L	M	A	E	C	E	A
U	N	N	E	E	D	D	S	E	G	E	D	L
L	S	E	D	O	R	E	N	E	A	O	N	S
U	P	D	N	O	E	I	I	S	B	E	S	W
W	I	I	T	D	U	S	T	H	R	O	Q	E
U	L	I	E	T	E	R	S	O	A	U	R	E
N	L	I	T	T	E	R	B	U	G	D	S	P

BUD
DIRT
TRASH
HEAT
TREES
SUN
NATURAL
LAWN
NOISE
ELECTRIC
CLOUDS
SOIL
LITTER
REUSE
EARS
STEM
MY
YELLOW
WEED
DUMP
POLLUTES
SMELL
LEAF
FLOWER
RIVER
ROLE
EARTH
HARM
MANMADE
ERODES
SPILL
LITTERBUG
GARBAGE BAG
GRIM
METALS
SWEEP
PROBES
SEED
DUST
TINS
SMOG
GREEN

MAKE TIME

_ _ _ _ _'_ _

_ _ _ _ _ _ _ _, _ _ _ _ _ _ _ _ _ _ _ _ _

_ _ _ _ _ _ _ _ _ _ _ _'_ _ _ _ _ _ _ _ _ _ _ _ _.

_ _

_ _ _ _ _ _ _ _ _ _ _ _ _ _ _ _ _, _ _ _ _ _ _ _ _ _ _

_ _

_ _ _ _ _ _.

ECOSYSTEM JOBS

Living things do specific kinds of "jobs". These "jobs" are related to each other. Try a fast-paced game of tag to demonstrate the interrelation of living things.

MATERIALS: Objects which can be tossed around (e.g. balls, frisbees, crumpled paper); name tags or coloured shirts; chalk. Optional -- large boxes.

DOING IT:

1. People form three groups: decomposers, consumers (about twice the number of decomposers), and producers (about twice the number of consumers). Each group should be easily identifiable (e.g. name tags).

2. Set a boundary for a large playing area; players must remain in the area. Use objects such as balls to represent abiotic components. The number of objects equals the number of producers. Place objects in two or more piles within the playing area; you may want to keep the objects together by putting them in boxes.

3. The game involves the basic chain of abiotic components to producer, producer "eaten" by consumer, and consumer "broken down" by decomposer to return abiotic components to the environment. The overall idea is to maintain the ecosystem, while each group fulfills its goal.

All life is connected in delicate balances called "ecosystems". Living things do one of three different "jobs" to maintain ecosystems -- they are either producers, consumers, or decomposers. "Producers" are green plants. They use the sun's energy to manufacture their own food from abiotic (nonliving) elements; this process is called "photosynthesis". Green plants provide food and oxygen for other living things. "Consumers" are living things that eat other living things. Some consumers eat producers; they are "herbivores", which means "plant eaters". Some consumers eat other consumers; they are "carnivores", which means "meat eaters". "Decomposers" break down dead plant and animal materials into abiotic elements. Decomposers are recyclers; the abiotic elements return to the soil, water, and air for use again. Decomposers include bacteria, fungi, earthworms, and snails. It's important to note that decomposers can also be consumers (e.g. snails also eat plants).

Topics: Ecosystems; Plant Processes; Microorganisms.

4. Producers are the only players who can take objects from the piles. A safety zone (marked in chalk) around a pile protects a producer from being tagged while he or she is picking up an object. The goal of the producers is to get all the objects (or as many as possible) out of the safety zones and hold onto the objects.

5. Consumers get objects by making a two-handed tag on a producer holding an object. The goal of consumers is to get as many objects as possible from producers and keep the objects.

6. Decomposers can only get objects by making a two-handed tag on a consumer holding an object. When decomposers get an object, they return it to the safety zone. The goal of decomposers is to get all the objects (or as many as possible) back to the safety zones.

7. Players can hold only one object at a time. When players are tagged, they must give up the object they are holding. Players can toss and pass objects to members of their own group.

8. Producers begin the game by running to collect objects. Consumers are allowed into the playing area a few moments after producers. Decomposers enter the area last. Play continues as long as you wish (producers keep taking balls, decomposers keep returning them). Adjust the number of objects used in the game or players in each group if play is not progressing smoothly.

9. How are all the groups dependent on one another? How does each group contribute to the continuous functioning of the ecosystem (i.e. abiotic components recycled and all groups have food)? Can the ecosystem continue to function if, for example, decomposers are removed?

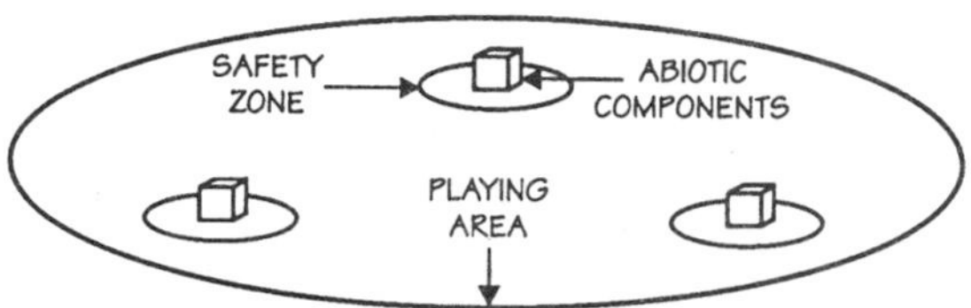

WHO'S EATING WHOM?

Animals depend on plants and each other for food. Make a food chain mobile to explore who's eating what -- and whom.

MATERIALS: Coloured construction paper; coloured yarn; crayons or felt pens; scissors; tape or glue.

DOING IT:

1. Prepare a list of plants or plant parts, herbivores, carnivores that eat herbivores, and carnivores that eat carnivores. You should be able to make several food chains using the list.

2. Discuss the list. Which animals eat plants? Which animals eat other animals? What food chains can be made?

3. Cut sheets of construction paper in half. Fold these pieces in half again.

4. Write the names of the plants, herbivores, and carnivores on both sides of the folded pieces of construction paper, one name per piece of paper. If you wish, draw pictures.

5. Arrange the pieces of paper into food chains. There should be a plant at the bottom of each chain; the final carnivore is at the top.

6. Cut equal-length pieces of yarn. Lay a piece of yarn between each part of the food chains. Lay a piece of yarn at the top of each food chain.

7. Tape or glue together the two sides of the folded pieces of construction paper, making sure that the ends of two pieces of yarn (one from above and one from below) are in between.

8. Hang up the food chain mobiles. What would happen to the other animals if one of the animals in the chain disappeared?

Human beings, grizzly bears, chimpanzees, hedgehogs, and raccoons are "omnivores"; they eat both plants and animals. Vultures and condors are "scavengers"; they eat dead, decaying animals.

A "food chain" consists of a series of animals that eat plants and other animals. A plant is eaten by an animal, which in turn is eaten by another animal, which in turn is eaten by yet another animal, and so on. Animals are classified based on where they fall on food chains (i.e. what they eat). Herbivores (plant eaters) are near the bottom of food chains. They can be very small or very large animals. Most people think of the grass-eating cow as a prime example of a herbivore, but plant-sucking and plant-chewing insects consume the most plants. Some carnivores (meat eaters) feed on herbivores. Examples of these carnivores are lady bugs eating aphids, coyotes eating mice, insect/worm-eating birds, and lions feeding on antelope. Some carnivores eat other carnivores. They tend to be larger, more fierce, and fewer in number (within each species) than the carnivores that eat herbivores.

A particular food chain might begin with a leaf-eating beetle. The beetle then walks into a trap and becomes a spider's supper. The spider is then gobbled up by a small bird. Then that bird is caught by a cat. The cat is the final link in the chain. Examples of other food chains: nectar from plants ➛ butterfly; clover ➛ rabbit ➛ fox; clover ➛ grasshopper ➛ frog ➛ snake ➛ hawk; tree ➛ aphid ➛ lady bug ➛ small bird ➛ flying squirrel ➛ snake. Many food chains have only three or four links; rarely are there more than five or six links (largely because a great deal of food energy is lost in going from one link to another).

Topics: Ecosystems; Animal Characteristics.

MAKE TIME

WEB OF LIFE

Food chains usually have many branches and combine to form a food web. It's easy to get all tied up -- literally! -- in this webbing exercise.

MATERIALS: Big ball of string; blue, green, and red name tags; tape or pins (to attach name tags); scissors.

DOING IT:

1. Write the ecosystem LAWS on blue tags, one per tag: light, air, water, soil. Write the name of plant parts on green tags, one per tag: seed, bud, leaf, twig, bark, nut, flower, berry. Write the name of consumers on red tags, one per tag: insect, hummingbird, robin, mouse, deer, squirrel, chipmunk, rabbit, raccoon, weasel, hawk, owl, coyote, woodpecker, fox, wolf.

2. Each person pins on one name tag. If there are more people than tags, there can be duplicate tags. Everyone sits in a circle, with colours of tags mixed up.

> Most animals have several sources of food. Therefore, food chains aren't really distinct, but interconnect to form a "food web". The larger web of life incorporates the limiting LAWS in ecosystems: Light (from the sun), Air, Water, and Soil. Decomposers complete the cycle in the web of life. The web of life represents the fragile ties that underlie an ecosystem. No matter how distant the relationship may seem, all things are connected.
>
> **Topics:** Ecosystems.

3. Begin by using pieces of string to connect the LAWS to plant parts.

4. Connect plant eaters to plant parts. Then connect plant eaters to the LAWS they use directly. For example, the rabbit is first connected to a leaf and is then connected to water.

5. Which meat eaters eat which plant eaters? Don't forget to connect meat eaters to the LAWS they need. For example, the fox is connected to the rabbit and is also connected to air.

6. Make as many other connections as you can. People will be holding several pieces of string each. Discuss what each connection means. Also, discuss interdependence.

7. What would happen if a fire destroyed all the plants (plants drop their strings)? The plant eaters would starve, which would cause the meat eaters to starve. The web would be destroyed. What would happen if the water became badly polluted?

8. Which component in the web seems least important? Remove it. Continue to remove components that seem "unnecessary" and components which cannot survive because other components have been removed. What happens as the web becomes less complex? Are changes more dramatic as the web has fewer components?

STRIP TEASE

Some things, like a story, begin and end. Other things, like the seasons, don't really end, but change and return. Explore natural cycles with a Moebius strip.

MATERIALS: Scissors; letter-size sheets of paper; tape; pencil.

DOING IT:

1. Cut two strips about 2.5 cm wide from the long edge of a sheet of paper. Tape the two strips together to make one long strip. Make four long strips.

2. For each of four natural cycles, write side A phrases on one side of a long paper strip and side B phrases on the other side. Side B phrases must start at the same end that side A phrases start, but are written upside down to side A. Phrases fill a side and are spaced equally from one another. The beginning of the first phrase on a side and the end of the last phrase should be slightly in from the ends of the strip.

- *Water Cycle:* A -- lakes and rivers; heated by sun; water evaporates. B -- water condenses; clouds develop; water falls as rain.
- *Air Cycle:* A -- plants take in carbon dioxide; plants return oxygen to air. B -- humans and animals inhale oxygen; humans and animals exhale carbon dioxide.
- *Carbon Cycle:* A -- living thing dies; decomposers release carbon into atmosphere. B -- carbon dioxide taken in by plants; plants form carbohydrates; plants eaten by living creature.
- *Nitrogen Cycle:* A -- bacteria take nitrogen from atmosphere; nitrogen added to soil; soil nitrogen used by plants. B -- plants eaten by living creatures; nitrogen returned to soil through wastes and remains; nitrogen returned to atmosphere by bacteria.

3. To make a Moebius strip, give a half turn to a strip of paper, as shown, and tape A to B.

4. Find the cycle's starting phrase and mark it with an X. Draw arrows from phrase to phrase until you complete the cycle. The Moebius strip has no beginning and no end, just as natural cycles involve a constantly repeating series of steps.

5. *A Moebius Trick:* Cut the Moebius strip down the centre to create one very large loop. Each cycle in nature is part of the bigger world ecosystem.

6. *Another Moebius Trick:* Instead of making a half-twisted loop, give the strip one full turn before sticking the ends together. Then cut down the middle. The result is two interlinked loops. Each cycle in nature is related to other natural cycles. You can cut each of the two loops in half to make four interlinked loops. Try different twist and cut combinations.

In 1858 a German mathematician named August Ferdinand Moebius came upon a loop of paper with a truly astonishing property: it has only one side. The Moebius strip can be used to demonstrate how abiotic (nonliving) components are recycled, or used again and again in nature.

Water Cycle: Water in lakes and rivers is heated by the sun and evaporates into the air; the vapour condenses and forms tiny droplets around microscopic particles in the air; clouds begin to form; when the droplets grow to a certain size they fall back to the ground as rain.

Air Cycle: Plants take in carbon dioxide and return oxygen to the air; humans and animals inhale oxygen and exhale carbon dioxide.

Carbon Cycle: When a living thing dies, carbon compounds remain in its body; decomposers release the carbon into the atmosphere as carbon dioxide; the carbon dioxide is taken in by plants; the plants form carbohydrates; a form of carbon returns to living creatures as they eat the plants.

Nitrogen Cycle: Nitrogen-fixing bacteria take nitrogen from the atmosphere and add it to the soil; soil nitrogen is used by plants; plants are eaten by living creatures; nitrogen is returned to the soil through organic wastes and remains; nitrogen is returned to the atmosphere by bacteria.

Topics: Ecosystems; Atmosphere; Plant Processes; Microorganisms.

SURVIVAL

In this large-scale game, which can last an hour or more, people play the role of animals meeting nature's challenges and trying to survive.

MATERIALS: Approximately 10,000 sq. m (2 to 3 acres) of natural area with well-defined boundaries; cardboard "life" tags (8/small herbivore, 4/large herbivore, 3/omnivore, 2/carnivore); strong string (so that players can carry life tags like a necklace); at least ten food and ten water boards (placed throughout game area, 0.3 m to 1 m above ground), each with a different colour of felt marker; food card and water card for each player; disease cards (at least as many as the number of players); sets of headbands, shirts, or brightly coloured tags to allow different animals to be easily identified.

DOING IT:

1. Choose the playing area carefully. Avoid areas with poisonous plants, sharp rocks, fast-flowing streams, and other potential dangers.

A wild animal's survival depends on a number of factors: finding enough water and food, avoiding predators, avoiding humans, avoiding natural disasters, and staying healthy. Each player in this game has certain goals as he or she tries to survive. *Herbivores* must not become food for carnivores or omnivores, or die at the hands of disease, humans, or fire. They must also find as many food and water stations as possible. *Carnivores* must not die at the hands of disease, humans, or fire. They visit only the water stations they come across, and "eat" herbivores and omnivores by tagging them and taking a "life" card. *Omnivores* must not become food for carnivores, or die at the hands of disease, humans, or fire. Omnivores visit as many food and water stations as they find, and "eat" herbivores by tagging them and taking a "life" tag. *Disease carriers* give a disease card to all animals they touch. *Humans* can play a helpful or a harmful role in the game. They may take away a disease card and give a "life" tag (a bonus tag). Or, humans can simply point a finger like a gun and "shoot" an animal, taking as many lives as they wish. Animals never know exactly what humans will do. *Fire* destroys all that it touches.

Topics: Ecosystems; Animal Characteristics.

2. Each person is assigned a role: small herbivore (rabbit, mouse, squirrel), large herbivore (deer, moose), omnivore (weasel, raccoon), or carnivore (wolf, fox). The pyramid illustration indicates the number of each animal for a group of 35 players. In general, there should be more omnivores than carnivores, and significantly more herbivores than either omnivores or carnivores. One person plays the role of a human, one person is fire, and one person is a disease carrier.

3. Each player receives a means of identification, as well as the appropriate number of life tags, a water card, and a food card. Tags and cards each have the player's animal name and real name written on them. Carnivores do not receive food cards.

4. The object of the game is for each player to survive. Animals must hunt for food and water, as well as avoid predators, humans, disease, and fire. Before the actual game begins, players should have some time to discuss their roles and develop strategies (e.g. carnivores might hang around food and water stations).

5. It's helpful if people sit in the pyramid formation so that they can visualize the predator-prey relationships. Players may only kill animals below them in the pyramid; they may not kill animals above them or at the same level. There is one important exception: weasels, raccoons, and foxes may not kill deer and moose. Although they are herbivores, deer and moose have fewer predators than most.

6. Killing an animal is simulated by tagging it and taking one life tag. The tag is added to the predator's set. Predators may not catch the same player consecutively (i.e. they must catch another animal in between). Predators may cooperate on a kill, but only one may obtain the life card. A second predator happening upon a recent kill must give the prey a reasonable chance to escape, but may attack the first predator immediately.

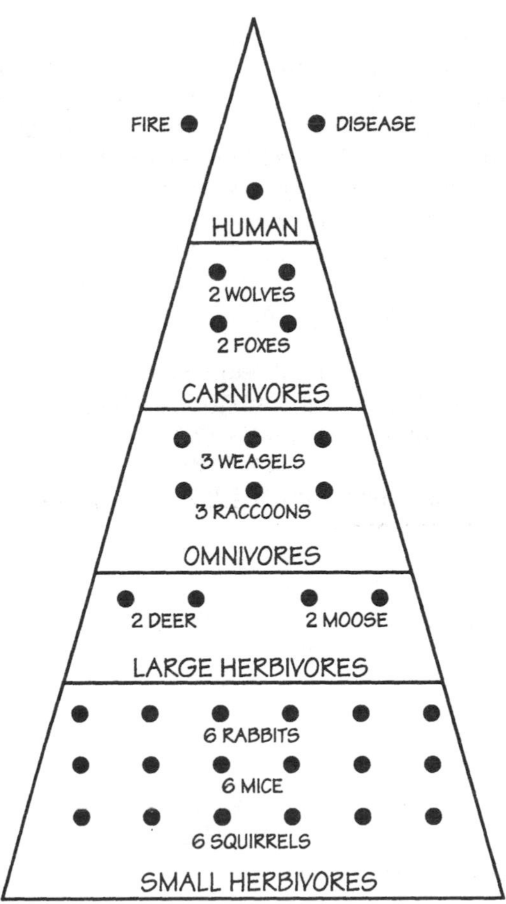

7. When an animal loses all its life tags, it leaves the game. Predators may only survive on their own life tags; they may not use those of their prey.

8. When players find a food or water station, they mark their food or water card (each station is coded with a different colour marker). They may visit a given station only once.

9. The disease carrier gives a disease card to everything he or she touches. A diseased animal passes its disease card to its predator. An animal can also get rid of a disease card when cured by a human. An animal does not survive if it finishes the game with a disease card.

10. Play begins as small and large herbivores scatter throughout the playing area. At 5 minute intervals, send off omnivores, and then carnivores. The game continues for an indefinite length of time. The disease carrier enters the game 5 minutes before the human. A human should never enter the playing area before the last 10 minutes of the game. He or she should be clearly identifiable and come equipped with life tags. When only a few minutes are left in the game, the fire player enters. The player runs through the forest yelling "fire" and takes all the life tags away from any animals he or she touches.

11. The most important part of the game is the follow-up discussion. Who survived? By how many life tags? How many animals were killed by natural predators? By disease? By humans? How many food and water stations did animals find? Where did animals get caught most often (e.g. in a field, hunting, at food or water stations, in a hiding spot)? What strategy did players use most often (e.g. hiding, hunting, an equal portion of hiding and hunting)? What frustrated herbivores? Carnivores? What happened when the human entered the game? What happened when fire entered? How did players feel during the game? What did people learn about being an animal?

12. *Variation:* Pretend that it is mating season. Animals are paired and exchange life tags with each other. The males (with female tags) start in one part of the playing area and the females (with male tags) start in another. Before the animals begin searching for food, they must relocate their mate and obtain their own tags. A mating call (no words or whistles) which is made up beforehand is the only sound that may be used. If an animal is unable to locate its mate or is captured before finding its mate, then it must return to the starting area, wait for its mate, and then restart the game with only half its normal number of life tags. This represents a realistic reduction in population if an animal is killed before finding a mate.

MINI AQUATIC ECOSYSTEM

Are you fascinated by aquariums, but not too thrilled about keeping them clean and feeding the fish? Set up a closed aquatic ecosystem in a jar.

MATERIALS: Large, very clean jar (at least 3 or 4 litres, and ideally 15 to 27 litres) with lid; aquatic plants (elodea) and animals (snails and 3 or 4 small mollies); 6-8 cm of bottom sediments (e.g. sand, gravel); water in large containers. (Note: Materials can be purchased from a tropical fish store.) Optional -- paraffin wax.

DOING IT:

1. Allow several large containers of tap water to stand for a few days so that the water is aerated.

2. Place bottom sediments in a large jar.

3. Place some aquatic plants into the jar (if necessary, secure plants in the bottom sediment by tying them to a weight such as a stone).

4. Add snails to the jar and then fill it 3/4 full with the aerated water.

5. Make sure the lid is securely on the jar. Place the jar near a window (avoid direct sunlight or the water temperature will become too high). The ecosystem (in particular the plants) must have adequate light.

6. Wait for several weeks until the ecosystem becomes adapted to the light source. Put the fish in a sealed plastic bag. Put the bag and contents into the ecosystem so that the temperature of the water in the bag gradually becomes the same as the water in the ecosystem. After several hours, release the fish into the jar.

7. After a few weeks, when the ecosystem is functioning and appears to be balanced, seal the jar by melting some paraffin wax and applying it around the lid so that no air can enter or escape.

A jar ecosystem is inexpensive to set up and, once established, requires little maintenance. It has the added benefit of actually being a miniature picture of an aquatic ecosystem.

There are certain keys to set-up that will allow the jar's contents to function as an ecosystem. Balancing the ecosystem can be tricky, especially with a smaller jar. Filling the jar only three-quarters full of water leaves the remaining quarter for air. The amount of oxygen in the air and water is constantly replenished by green plants, which give off oxygen during the day when they manufacture food for themselves (photosynthesis). Although algae may work in a closed aquatic ecosystem, they aren't ideal because they reproduce rapidly and use up a lot of oxygen. Elodea are a better plant choice. The plants provide animals in the ecosystem with food and oxygen. The fish must be plant-eaters (herbivores or omnivores), tolerant of salinity, and able to survive in low-oxygen conditions. Snails in a closed aquatic ecosystem act as consumers as well as decomposers. If the ecosystem is a balanced one, the animals should never go hungry. If their population becomes too large for the food supply, the weaker members will die off until their numbers are in proportion to the food available.

Topics: Ecosystems; Habitat; Plant Processes.

MAKE TIME

MINI LAND ECOSYSTEM

How would you like a forest in your room? Explore a real forest or field and then construct a closed terrarium that simulates the ecosystem.

MATERIALS: Glass aquarium; pebbles; horticultural charcoal; potting soil (not sterilized); vermiculite; peat moss; aquarium sand; water; measuring cup; ruler; nylon stockings; scissors; plastic wrap; trowel; small containers for mixing soil and for gathering plant specimens. (Note: Materials can be purchased from a gardening shop and a tropical fish store.) Optional -- bone meal.

DOING IT:

1. Collect plant specimens for a terrarium by visiting a real forest or field. Choose a variety of small specimens. *Disturb natural areas as little as possible. Take only what you need and only plants of which there are many.* An ideal site for collecting plants is a construction or logging site, because the plants will be cleared away anyway. When taking a specimen, dig out the entire small plant -- including root system and surrounding soil -- with a trowel. You might also want to collect small rocks, insects, and other natural ground litter.

2. Set up the terrarium in a large glass aquarium. Start by washing some pebbles and charcoal. Cover the bottom of the aquarium with a 2.5 cm layer of pebbles. Cover the pebbles with about a 0.5 cm layer of charcoal. The pebbles and charcoal serve as the terrarium's "drainage bed"; the charcoal filters water running over the pebbles.

3. Cut up some nylon stockings. Use the material to make a thin layer covering the drainage bed. This keeps soil from getting into the drainage bed.

4. Mix together 6 parts potting soil, 2 parts vermiculite, 2 parts peat moss, 1 part aquarium sand, and 1 part charcoal. If you have it, add 1/3 part bone meal.

5. Cover the drainage bed with about a 4 cm layer of your soil mixture.

6. Landscape your terrarium. Make small holes in the soil for each of the specimens you are planting. There should be plenty of growing space between plants. Put a little water in the holes. Knock as much soil as possible off plant roots; then, put one specimen into each hole and cover all the roots with soil. Sprinkle some water over the soil. Add other natural items.

7. Cover your terrarium securely with plastic wrap. There should be a good seal between the lip of the terrarium and the plastic.

8. Keep the terrarium near a window, *but not in direct sunlight.* Rotate the terrarium regularly so that plants don't grow in one direction. You should always be able to see some water droplets on the plastic. If there are no water droplets, add some water to the terrarium. If there seems to be too much water in the terrarium, take the plastic off for a few hours. How is the terrarium like a real forest or field?

9. *Extension:* Experiment with the terrarium by altering conditions (e.g. removing plants, putting in too much or too little water, limiting the light, changing soil ingredients, adding salt to the soil). What happens to the terrarium? What would happen in a real forest or field?

A forest terrarium can be made up of small flowering plants, tiny tree seedlings, ferns, mosses, a piece of rotting log, rocks, and small animals such as insects and snails. A terrarium based on a field ecosystem can contain native grasses, mosses, insects, dead grass stems, and leaves. By covering the terrarium with plastic, you create a closed system (you don't have to water the plants!) that takes advantage of the process of "transpiration". Transpiration occurs when the roots of plants absorb moisture from the soil. The water passes through a plant's stem or trunk, through the branches to the leaves, and then evaporates into the air from the surface of the leaves. In the terrarium, the water vapour condenses on the plastic sheet (it's cool because of the cooler air outside the terrarium) and water droplets "rain" down on the plants.

Topics: Ecosystems; Habitat; Plant Processes.

MICRO-HABITAT

Commonly studied habitats include oceans, streams, ponds, lakes, marshes, deserts, tundras, grasslands, and forests. Start small and work your way up.

MATERIALS: String; metre stick or measuring tape; magnifying glass; trowel or stick; paper; pencil.

DOING IT:

1. Find a small area of ground to investigate. Use string to mark out a 1 m x 1 m square.

2. Use a magnifying glass to closely examine the plot of ground. Write down *everything* you see (e.g. grasses, loose dirt, decaying leaves, weeds, pebbles, insects).

3. What is the dominant kind of plant (e.g. dandelions, grass)? Approximately how many of that type of plant are in the plot? How much of the area does the plant cover (e.g. a quarter, half, more than half, almost all)?

4. List all other plants in the plot. How many types of plants are there? How much of the area do they cover?

5. What animals (in particular insects) are present? How many of each?

6. Dig -- very carefully -- into the soil with a trowel or stick. Notice the layers in the soil. How would you describe the soil: wet, dry, sandy, rocky, and/or clay-like? Make a list of everything you find in the soil, from earthworms to rocks. *After examining the soil, return it to its original place.*

7. Is there some evidence of humans in the plot (e.g. garbage)?

8. Repeat the micro-habitat investigation in a totally different area and compare your findings.

9. *Extension:* Create your own micro-habitat. Make a pile of leaf litter on the soil in a damp, shady corner. Get some air bricks (bricks with several holes drilled through them) and put them in long grass or under bushes. Or, put a large, clear plastic container upside down in a corner of a garden or lawn. If you make a few small holes in the container, they will allow air and small animals to get in. Water the soil and the container from time to time. Visit your habitat over several weeks and you should see some animals settle in and some plants (e.g. moss, algae) begin to grow.

A "habitat" is where living things live. It's more than a home; it's more like a neighbourhood. For an animal, a habitat includes all the land the animal needs to hunt, gather food, find a mate, and raise a family. Different combinations of ecosystem LAWS (light, air, water, and soil), together with variations in climate and topography, create different habitats. A shady area supports different species of trees and shrubs than an area in bright sunlight. Pure air helps growth, but polluted air retards or stops it. Less water creates a desert, while more water creates a marsh. Poor soil supports only certain plants, and rich soil produces greater growth.

Most plants and animals are very specialized and able to survive in only a very specific habitat, where conditions are suited to them. For example, earthworms -- which live in the moist soil -- often have delicate, moist skin. Organisms found in drier habitats have thick, hard, outer shells (e.g. beetles) to prevent them from drying out. No two species in a habitat can occupy the same ecological niche for long. For example, if two types of birds in the same area feed on the same kind of berries, one or the other will be squeezed out or will have to adapt itself to a new source of food.

Topics: Habitat; Insects; Soil.

WATERY WORLDS

How is a pond different from a stream different from a lake? Choose an aquatic habitat to explore.

MATERIALS: Paper; pencil; thermometer; magnifying glass; floating marker (e.g. orange, grapefruit); stopwatch or watch which indicates seconds; measuring tape; plastic cup; rubber boots; water scope, nets, hand screen, pail dredge, depth gauge, and Secchi disc. (Instructions for equipment on following page.) Optional -- field guides.

DOING IT:

1. *General Appearance:* How still does the body of water, or parts of the body of water, look? Stagnant areas of fresh water often become covered with a layer of algae known as "pond scum". On the surface of some ponds, a green sheet is formed by masses of tiny plants known as "duckweed" (its name comes from the fact that ducks like to feast on it). A shiny film on the water can mean there's oil in the water. Do you see any other signs of pollution?

2. *Smell:* How does the area smell? A rotten egg smell can mean that sewage is leaking into the water.

3. *Water Colour/Clarity:* What colour is the water? Is it light brown, dark brown, or clear? Use a Secchi disc to test the water's clarity. The nature of the water, the chemicals dissolved in it, the quantity of microscopic plants and animals, and the amount of suspended particles such as silt and soil affect the penetration of light. A heavy rainfall will stir up small particles and cloud a body of water, often for several days. What is the difference in the depth at which you can see the Secchi disc before and after a rain?

4. *Regions:* A body of water can usually be divided into a number of regions. How many can you find? Regions vary in physical conditions, amount of light falling on them, and depth of the water.

5. *Depth:* You can guess at water depth by looking at water patterns on a calm day: swirls of water often indicate deep water, while ripples suggest shallow water. Use a depth gauge for a more accurate measure of depth.

6. *Layers:* Get a feel for different water layers. Use a water scope for a visual inspection. Take temperature readings at different depths, in both sunlight and shade. Take a reading close to the water's surface, halfway down, and at the bottom. Hold the thermometer in place for a few minutes to ensure an accurate reading.

7. *Water Velocity:* A key factor determining the plant and animal life in a stream is the oxygen content, which is affected by the stream's water velocity. Estimate water velocity by positioning two people 50 m apart along the shore. The person upstream drops a floating marker into the water and the second person records the time it takes for the marker to reach him or her. A good current marker must ride low in the water to avoid being affected by wind. Divide the distance the marker travels (50 m) by the time it takes (in seconds); this gives the current's velocity in m/second.

One of the first things to look for when you're exploring a pond is its stage of development. "Succession" is the gradual process by which one habitat is replaced by another. As soon as a pond forms, it begins to disappear. Plants grow along the shore, die and settle to the bottom. Soil washes in and begins to fill the pond. Dead animals add their bodies to the fill. The pond becomes more and more shallow. The plants grow in more and more toward the centre. The pond is filled in and becomes a swamp, then a bog, and finally a grassy field or a forest.

"Wetlands" are swamps, bogs, and marshes. They are an important part of ecosystems. They are habitats for many plants and animals. Coastal wetlands are needed by different types of birds, fish, and shrimp for laying eggs and raising young. Wetlands provide a buffer against floods. They remove some kinds of pollution from the water. Rice is a wetland crop and billions of people rely on rice for food. Unfortunately, many of the world's wetlands are being drained and used for farmland or housing, or become reservoirs for power dams.

Topics: Habitat; Ecosystems; Measurement; Insects; Animal Characteristics.

8. *Rocks:* Find a boulder partially submerged in the water. Does the portion of the boulder below the water's surface appear different than the portion above? Boulders often become rounded below the surface from water wear. Where there are different rocks and stones, do some animals live on one type of rock and others on another type? For example, if a stream has some very smooth stones and some very rough ones, animals such as water mites will usually be found on the rough and not on the smooth stones. More animals will be found on stones covered with moss, algae, and other plant material. Some animals may be found on the upper surface and others on the under-surface of stones.

9. *Plants In and Around the Water:* Look closely at plants in and around the aquatic habitat. Identify and group the plants you find. On dry land close to the water you'll find shrubs and trees. In the water, but close to the shore, you'll find plants rooted in the bottom mud and emerging from the surface. Look for cattails; measure their stems to see how tall they must grow to keep their heads above water. Further into the water you'll find submerged plants that are rooted in the bottom, but do not grow above the surface. Finally, you'll find a group of floating plants that have no roots down at the bottom. There is yet another group of plants, but these are too small to be seen without a microscope.

10. *Tiny Animals In the Water:* Scoop up a little surface water and examine it for life. Many aquatic worms and larvae are clear or have a very light colouring, so look carefully. It may take your eyes a few minutes to see anything move.

11. *Animals in the Water:* How many different animals can you find in and around the water? If you find fish or lots of bugs in the water, it's a good sign; it means there's lots of oxygen. Animals usually visible in a pond include tadpoles, fish, turtles, frogs, crayfish, snakes, birds, and many insects. Use a hand-dip net, a flat-bottomed net, and a hand screen to explore animal (and plant) life at various depths in the aquatic habitat. Do animals from near the surface of a body of water differ from those in the middle?

12. *Animals at the Surface and at the Bottom:* Do animals near the surface of a body of water differ from those at the bottom? How do animals found on the surface of the water move? What do their legs look like? Do they make particular noises? What colour are they? Why do you think some of the animals are at the water's surface? Have they come up to catch their food? Have they come up to breathe? Water beetles take a supply of air with them under their wing covers; look carefully to see an air bubble at the tip of the beetle's abdomen. Do animals at the surface stay at the surface if disturbed? Do any animals burrow into the mud at the bottom when they are disturbed? Water beetles and tadpoles often burrow when frightened. Look for snails and planaria (flatworms) in the water and at the bottom under rocks and leaves.

13. *Plants and Animals at the Bottom:* Use a pail dredge to scoop up some of the materials at the bottom of the body of water. Use a hand screen to sift through the materials. The type of bottom has a big effect on plant and animal life. Bedrock provides little food and protection. A rubble or gravel bottom is usually associated with a high water velocity and carries an ample supply of food and oxygen. In a sandy soil bottom, there is no solid rooting material for higher plants and no smooth surfaces on which plants can attach themselves. There is abundant rooting material in muddy or silt-bottomed soil.

14. *Plant and Animal Relationships:* Are some animals always found on or near certain plants? In the case of plants with large leaves, do animals vary from leaf to leaf? Turn over the leaves of plants such as water lilies and floating pondweed. You may find leeches, hydra, snails, or even snail eggs.

15. *Plant and Animal Adaptations:* What adaptations do plants and animals have which help them live in the water? For example, some animals are adapted to swiftly flowing water. The water blackfly larva holds onto stones with hooks on its abdomen and on its legs.

EQUIPMENT FOR EXPLORING AQUATIC HABITATS

HAND-DIP NETS: Hand-dip nets are useful for collecting insects and other small aquatic life on the surface of the water, among plants, and under stones and logs along the shore. Straighten the hook on a coat hanger. Bend the rest of the hanger into a circle. Sew or staple some sturdy cloth, a nylon stocking, or nylon netting onto the wire loop so that it forms a bag about 12 cm deep around the wire. Bind the straight end of the hanger onto a piece of broom or hockey stick handle.

FLAT-BOTTOMED NET: Use a flat-bottomed net to collect larger aquatic organisms from different depths in a pond or stream. The differences between a hand-dip net and flat-bottomed net are that the flat-bottomed net is constructed using a coat hanger bent into a D-shaped frame about 35 cm in diameter, the bag is about 60 cm deep, and the bag is attached to a long pole up to 2 m long.

PAIL DREDGE: Use a pail dredge to collect sediment from the bottom of a body of water. Take a hammer and nail and punch holes close together on the bottom of a pail. Attach a brick to the inside of the pail by winding wire around the brick and through a few holes punched close together, in the middle of one side of the pail. Attach a length of rope to the pail's handle. Lower the dredge into the water and pull it along the bottom to collect samples.

HAND SCREEN: Use a hand screen to examine samples of mud dug up from a pond or stream bottom. Make the hand screen with at least a 1 mm wire screening. Attach the wire screening to a square frame made with 30 cm long pieces of wood. Place mud on the screen and pour water over it. Finer particles will wash through; remove large stones by hand.

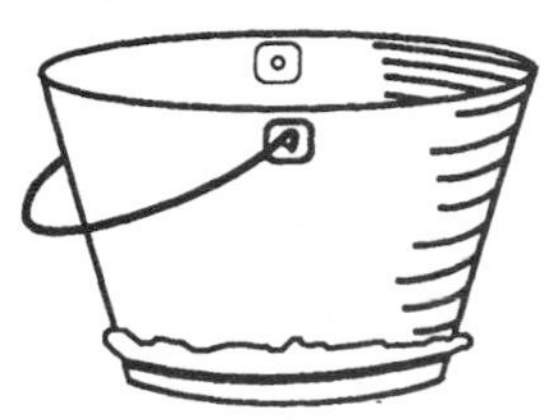

WATER SCOPE: Use a water scope to look at animals and plants on a pond or stream bottom. Cut the top and bottom from a can or the bottom from a pail. Painting the inside of a water scope with flat black paint reduces reflection. Secure plastic wrap or heavy, clear plastic on one end of the scope with elastic bands. You need to submerge the water scope only a few centimetres to see into the water. The pressure of the water causes the plastic to become a convex lens, so plants and animals are magnified. Your success in viewing through the water scope will depend on the brightness of the overhead sunlight and the clearness of the water.

DEPTH GAUGE: A depth gauge can be a useful piece of equipment. Attach a weight securely to a length of cord. Put knots in the cord at regular intervals (e.g. every 0.5 m). Find the water depth at various locations by slowly lowering the weight into the water as you count the number of knots which become submerged. Attach a thermometer to the weight (bend some wire screen around the thermometer to prevent it from breaking) to measure the temperature at different depths. Leave the thermometer underwater for several minutes to ensure an accurate reading.

SECCHI DISC: Light penetration is fairly easy to measure with a Secchi disc. Use light metal for the disc (e.g. soup or paint can lid). The disc's diameter should be 15 to 20 cm. Drill or punch a hole in the centre. Divide the disc into four quarters. Paint two opposite quarters white and the other two quarters black (as shown). Use two nuts to attach an eyebolt to the disc. If the disc tends to float, attach some weights to its underside. Fasten a length of cord to the eyebolt. Place knots in the cord at regular intervals (e.g. every 0.5 m). To determine the clarity (clearness) of an area of water, slowly lower the Secchi disc into the water. Keep track of the number of knots that become submerged. Shade the water area to prevent reflections or interference in seeing the disc clearly. Your eyes should be about 1 m away from the surface of the water. The depth at which you can no longer see the Secchi disc indicates the approximate depth to which light is penetrating the water. Light is essential to green plants wherever they live. The depth to which light penetrates bodies of water determines the level below which photosynthesis cannot occur. If you can see the Secchi disc in only the top 2 m of a pond, then you know that all the food production is taking place in that 2 m.

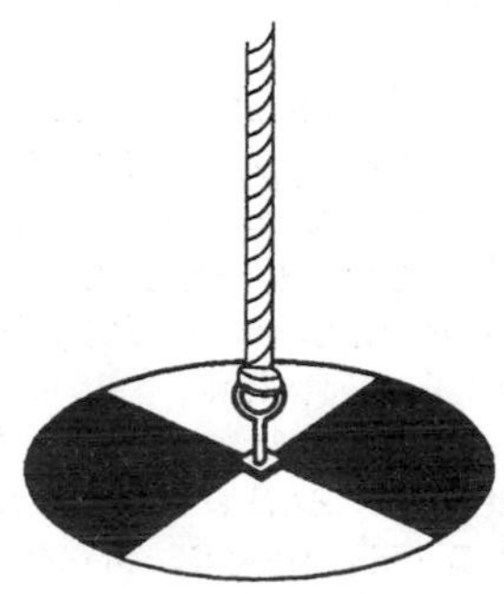

A FIELD TRIP

A weedy, overgrown field may not look full of life; the only animals around may seem to be a butterfly or two, or perhaps a bird. But walk into the field and look closely . . .

MATERIALS: Paper; pencil; collection net (make one using netting or cheesecloth, a coat hanger, and a broom handle); magnifying glass; trowel; measuring tape; several stakes; string. Optional -- field guides.

DOING IT:

1. A simple approach to exploring a large area is to mark the area into quadrants (squares). The quadrants can be any size. Measure out the quadrants using a measuring tape. Mark the quadrants with stakes and string. Compare information collected from different quadrants.

2. Begin a field exploration by making a rough sketch of the field. Include noticeable trees or rocks. If the field isn't too large, pace off the edges so that you can get an idea of its size; you may want to draw a map of the field to scale.

3. Try a colour hunt. Find five different shades of green. Find at least one shade of red, pink, orange, brown, yellow, white, and purple.

4. Look for different kinds of plants and grasses. Find plants as high as your waist, as high as your knee, and as high as your ankle. Larger and more showy kinds of plants include milkweed, ragweed, dandelion, and goldenrod. Find plant leaves with smooth edges, edges with tiny teeth, and deeply-cut edges. **Watch out for poison ivy, a shiny, three-leaved vine; don't touch it or even go near it!**

Fields can contain a wide diversity of plant and animal life. But the edges of habitat zones often contain even more of a variety of life since organisms from all adjoining zones may be present. Forest-edge habitats are usually where a forest and an adjacent field meet. They always consist of partial or full shade (in contrast to the closed shade of a forest or the open sunshine of a field) and a mixture of vegetation types (e.g. trees, shrubs, broad-leaf plants, and grasses).

Topics: Habitat; Mapping; Plant Parts; Insects; Soil.

5. If the field has been around for a while, it should be filled with wild flowers. If any plants are in flower, examine them with a magnifying glass. Look for developing seeds. Often, field flowers are subjected to dry conditions and large daily fluctuations in temperature. Examine the plants for adaptations to their environment. For example, some plants have a thick, waxy coating on their leaves or stem to reduce water loss. Hairs on the leaves and stem (such as those found on milkweed) may also reduce water loss by creating dead air space or insulating layers.

6. Look for signs of animals such as holes in leaves, eggs on the underside of leaves, holes in the ground, animal tracks, or a path made by animals. Larger animals found in fields include mice, rabbits, woodchucks, snakes, and birds.

7. Use a collection net to sweep through lighter grasses. How many insects can you sweep up?

8. Examine ten different plants and note the animal life on each. Look for insects living inside a leaf or stem, or an insect gathering pollen from a flower. Look for spiders -- and their webs.

9. Dig up some soil to discover a whole new list of animals. Earthworms are common soil animals. You may find animal tunnels or burrows. The soil should also contain a jungle of plant roots. *After examining the soil, return it to its original place.*

10. Compare different sections of the field in terms of plants and animals. What are the differences? The similarities? Which factors might account for differences or similarities (e.g. moisture, sunlight, trees)?

Forest Foray

Look way, way up. Look down at the ground. Look in between. There's plenty of life at all levels in a forest. Walk into a forest and look closely . . .

MATERIALS: Paper; pencil; trowel; magnifying glass; thermometer; measuring tape. Optional -- field guides.

DOING IT:

1. When you first walk into the forest, what are the major types of trees you see? Do "conifers" (e.g. pine, spruce) or "deciduous" trees (e.g. oak, beech, maple) dominate?

2. Look down. There are more living things on the forest floor than at any other level. Most plant and animal life begins and all life ends on the forest floor. **Watch out for poison ivy, a shiny, three-leaved vine; don't go near it!**

3. Can you find any decaying matter on the forest floor? Dig deep into the soil. Spread out a handful of soil and examine it for living creatures. Use a magnifying glass. Look for millipedes, centipedes, earthworms, beetles, and spiders. *Return the soil to its original place.*

4. The forest floor is a nursery for young trees. Look for seeds, seedlings, and young trees. How did the young trees get there? How do they compare in size? Are the seedlings in direct sunlight larger than those in the shade?

5. Are temperature and light conditions the same in all parts of the forest? How do the amounts of sunlight at the top level compare to amounts at lower levels? Are parts of the forest floor in deep shade, even when the sun is shining? Are some parts wet and some parts dry? How does this affect the plant and animal life?

6. Examine tree trunks. What colour is the bark? What does it feel like? *Never peel the bark from trees.* Look for bare patches and insects. Are all the trunks the same? Are different sides of a given trunk different? On what side do you find lichens, algae, moss, or fungi? Why?

7. Examine the physical condition of several trees. Are there any tree roots exposed above the soil? What's the height of the lowest branches from the ground? What's the percentage of dead branches on each tree?

8. Closely examine lower-level branches. Do any leaves have insect spots? Are leaves covered in soot? How many animals can you find? Look for willow galls, oak balls, tent caterpillars, bag worms, leaf rollers, and carpenter ants. How do the insects found on leaves differ from those found on the bark?

9. Estimate the height of trees. Have someone whose height is known stand next to a tree. He or she becomes the "standard" unit of measurement. Walk about twenty paces away from the tree. At arm's length, hold up a straight stick or pencil. Sight the top of the stick with the top of the person's head. Move your thumb down along the stick until your thumb appears even with the person's feet. Now move the stick upward one "standard" unit at a time. Multiply the person's height by the number of "standards" to get the approximate height of the tree. What's the height of the tallest tree you can find?

10. Look way, way up to find living things in the tops of trees. You may see birds, squirrels, and flying insects. Do these creatures also come down to the ground, or do they spend most of their time up high? How are these animals affected by the life lower down? How many of each species of animal can you find? Can you spot a bird's nest? *Never disturb birds and their nests during the nesting season.*

11. Are there any dead trees in the forest? How do you know a tree is dead? How is a dead tree similar to a live tree? Are there different animals in the dead tree than in trees which are alive? What value might dead trees have in a forest?

"Forestry" is the management of forests for wood, water, wildlife, and recreation. Wood is very important economically, and so forestry has traditionally focused on timber management, including reforestation, maintenance, and fire control.

Topics: Habitat; Plant Parts; Soil; Insects; Measurement.

DON'T BE AFRAID OF THE DARK

The changes that come with the night can transform a familiar place into an entirely new world. Take a night hike to get a new perspective on the environment.

MATERIALS: Flashlight; red cellophane or red sock. Optional -- several metres of rope.

DOING IT:

1. A night hike requires some careful planning. Choose a route during the daytime to make sure the hike is safe. Try to select a route through a natural area. Plan a pace suitable for the terrain (e.g. if trail is rocky and steep, keep pace slow). Remove any sharp, dead branches at eye level.

2. Talk about fears before starting on the night hike. What makes night different than day? Are you afraid of "the dark"? Most people aren't really afraid of the dark itself. People can see that it's dark. They're scared of what they can't see; they're scared of what they imagine to be hidden in the dark.

Obvious differences between night and day include changes in temperature, humidity, smells, sounds, and animal life. An example of a more subtle change is the size of tree trunks. Scientists have noticed that a tree's trunk gets fatter at night and thinner by day because of differences in the amount of water movement inside the tree.

Topics: Environmental Awareness; Senses; Sound.

3. It takes human eyes about 20 minutes to become fully adapted to the dark. Leave enough time for this adaptation process to take place. Avoid using a flashlight during the hike, but take one along for emergencies. If you need to look at a map, cover the flashlight with a red sock or red cellophane (red light doesn't affect your eyes' adaptation to the dark).

4. As you begin the hike, one way to reduce anxiety is to lead people in single file by a rope with knots at 3 m intervals to maintain both distance and reassurance.

Some animals -- like meadow voles and wolverines -- are active day and night. Other animals have more restricted activity periods. Guess which of the following animals are chiefly diurnal (active by day) and which are nocturnal (active by night): 1) woodchuck or groundhog; 2) red squirrel; 3) mountain goat; 4) black bear; 5) least chipmunk; 6) meadow jumping mouse; 7) snowshoe hare; 8) mink; 9) Arctic ground squirrel; 10) lynx.

Answers: 1) diurnal; 2) diurnal; 3) diurnal; 4) nocturnal; 5) diurnal; 6) nocturnal; 7) nocturnal; 8) nocturnal; 9) diurnal; 10) nocturnal.

5. Identify as many light sources and reflectors as possible. The night is never completely dark. Light comes from the stars, moon (especially a full moon), certain fungi, animals, and synthetic sources. It's reflected from clouds, water, animal eyes, and substances such as glass and metal.

6. Vision has limited usefulness in the dark. Your eyes are a little more helpful if you don't focus directly on objects. Look to the side of objects (e.g. stars), so that you use your rods (the part of the retina designed for dim-light conditions) most effectively. One interesting vision challenge is to look at tree silhouettes in the distance against the night sky. Can you distinguish one type of tree from another by shape alone?

7. Use senses other than vision to their fullest. Walk in silence so that you can hear and appreciate the sounds of the night. Can you identify the sounds? Stop and listen to sounds. Cup both hands behind your ears to increase the sound-gathering surface. Where are sounds coming from?

8. Echoes provide a great sound experience. On still nights, echoes can often be heard very clearly. Shout or clap sharply and loudly. Try facing different directions. Try a group shout or clap. If a sound bounces from many reflecting surfaces, you'll hear the original sound more than once. Sound waves travel about 1 km in 3 seconds. Estimate the distance of reflecting surfaces (e.g. for echo heard 6 seconds after making noise, reflecting surface is 2 km away).

9. Smell is a useful sense at night. Sniff the air. How does the smell differ from the daytime?

10. Touch is a sense that works well in light or darkness. Use your hands to feel trees. Do larger tree trunks retain more warmth from the sun than smaller ones?

11. As you walk from one area to another, can you detect any general temperature changes. Which areas are coolest? Why?

12. When the night hike is over, sit in a comfortable spot outside, in the dark. Talk about the hiking experience. What makes day different from night? Complete unfinished sentences like "The night makes me feel . . ." or "I felt scared when . . .". What's the prettiest thing about the night? What are the real dangers of night in the woods? Are human beings nocturnal (night) or diurnal (day) creatures?

Test your night vision: Place large white boards or poles in a relatively straight line, at 3 m intervals. After being in a well-lit area for a while, stand in a designated spot outside, in the dark, and count the number of poles you can see. Repeat the test after being outside in the dark for half an hour. Can you see farther? Why?

"Bioluminescent" plants and animals make their own light. A firefly has certain chemicals in its body that produce light when mixed together. Nothing burns to produce the glow so, unlike most light sources, there is no heat. The firefly doesn't use the light to see, but to attract mates or prey. Look for the glowing larvae and eggs of fireflies on the ground. Luminescent mushrooms and other fungi (e.g. foxfire), as well as photobacteria can be found glowing on rotting logs in some moist areas (you may need to break up the decaying wood to see the luminescence clearly). Look in shallow water, especially near the ocean, to see light-emitting marine animals.

A Blanket Of Snow

How does winter affect the natural environment? How does snow affect plant and animal life? Make a model forest and simulate a snowfall.

Winter snows in the mountains determine the water supply for irrigation and power use. The snow melts in the spring and fills lakes and rivers. If spring comes late, the melting happens faster and can cause floods.

A blanket of snow *really is* a blanket. It holds in the warmth of the Earth and protects against the frost of winter air. Where there is no snow, the soil freezes to a much greater depth. Snow brings down nutrients from the air and spreads them on the ground like fertilizer. The amount of snow that falls over a certain area affects the area over the next summer season; the more snow that falls, the more water that will melt into the ground. Although snow and winter are synonymous in northern parts of the world, most of the changes that come with winter are more subtle. Winter is the dormant season. It is the period when birds migrate south from northern climates. It is the time of lower temperatures.

Life for many animals is the same in winter as it is in summer. The meadow vole carries on as usual in an elaborate system of runways beneath the snow cover. Although there are periods when skunks, raccoons, foxes, and squirrels remain secluded in their shelters waiting out a severe storm, most often you can see their tracks on the surface of the snow. Many animals adapt to the change in season. Some birds change their diet back and forth from insects to seeds with the seasons. To survive in cold temperatures, the birds depend on trapped air spaces between their feathers to insulate them and they must eat enough food to provide caloric heat. The most unique adaptation in mammals is "hibernation": the heartbeat slows dramatically, body temperature drops, and respiration slows to a few sporadic breaths. Some hidden internal clock wakes the animals in spring. These animals have a special temperature regulation system in their brains and they have the ability to put on large quantities of fat weight in the fall.

Topics: Snow; Animal Characteristics.

MAKE TIME

MATERIALS: 1 sq. m piece of cardboard or wood; toothpicks; bits of paper, tissue, or sponge; glue; white, powdered laundry detergent.

DOING IT:

1. Create a simulated forest on a piece of wood or cardboard. Make tiny trees using, for example, bits of sponge glued to one end of toothpicks. Glue the "trees" to the "forest floor". Use pieces of sponge, for example, to simulate low shrubs. Place some trees close together; leave other areas quite open, with only low shrubs.

2. Sprinkle laundry detergent over the "forest" to simulate a snowfall. The detergent should have an average depth of about 1 cm.

3. Where is the "snow" cover the deepest? How do tall trees affect the amount of snow reaching the ground? How does snow affect tall trees? How does it affect low shrubs? How would the snowfall affect animal movement?

ROCKS

"Geology" isn't just about collecting rocks. It started out that way though. For many years, geologists examined the stones, but not the mountains. Then, they began to look at the bigger picture. Geology is the study of the Earth and all changes taking place on and in the Earth.

What's the difference between a "rock" and a "mineral"? A mineral is a chemical element or compound (a combination of elements) found naturally in or on the Earth. Iron ore, ruby, gold, and quartz are minerals. More than 2,000 minerals are known. Of these minerals, less than a dozen are common to most rocks. Rocks are made up of minerals, but rocks themselves are not minerals. Rocks are mixtures of minerals.

In the mountains of western Australia, geologists have found some mineral grains that are 4.1 to 4.2 billion years old. These are by far the oldest grains ever found on Earth. The grains are zircon, which isn't too surprising. Zircon is a mineral that is so stable it can stay the same through billions of years of volcanic activity.

The Canadian Shield is the core of the North American continent. The Shield underlies about half the total area of Canada. It contains some of the oldest rocks in the world and is one of the most productive mining areas in the world. The Shield is especially rich in such base metals as copper, nickel, iron, lead, and zinc.

Water is "hard" or "soft" depending on the amount and kinds of minerals it has dissolved in it. Fill a jar with about 500 ml of water. Add liquid soap or detergent a tiny drop at a time, covering and shaking the jar after adding each drop. The harder the water (the more minerals dissolved in it), the more drops it will take before a lot of suds begin to form. Test water samples from different sources.

Can you find any gullies in the making? Some of the moisture that falls to Earth is absorbed in the soil; the rest gathers in thin streams of water moving from higher to lower elevations. The water picks up soil and rock particles and begins to carve a channel in the land. At first, "rills" a few centimetres wide and deep form. Over many years (in some exceptional cases, days) rills turn into deep gullies. Eventually, great valleys are created.

MAKE TIME

Planet Apple

Geology is the study of what's on and in the Earth. You can see what's on the Earth, but what's inside? Cut into an apple to get an idea of the Earth's insides.

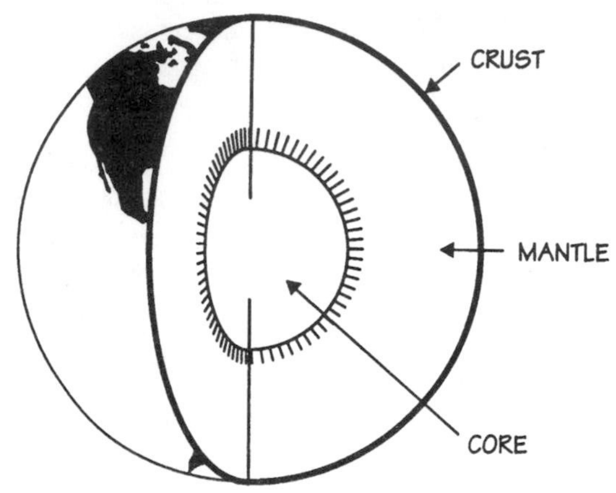

MATERIALS: Apple; knife.

DOING IT:

1. What do you think is inside the Earth? Is the Earth solid or hollow?

2. Cut an apple in half vertically. Cut the apple in half again, this time horizontally.

3. Examine the apple. Apples and the Earth have a lot in common. They are both round and solid. They are both surrounded by a very thin skin or crust; look how thin the apple's skin is relative to the whole apple. Both an apple and the Earth have a core. And they both have a thick layer between the skin or crust and the core.

4. Look closely at the apple's core. You should see the seeds surrounded by a hollow space which is surrounded by a harder shell. This is something like the Earth's inner and outer core; the Earth's inner core is solid and its outer core is a thick liquid.

The Earth is like a big, round ball floating in space. We live on a small section of the Earth and we can't see all of it, so it looks flat. Satellite pictures of the Earth show its roundness.

The outer layer of the Earth is called the "crust". The crust is the part of the Earth we live on, dig into, and when we crawl into a cave, it's the part we explore. It's very thin relative to the size of the entire Earth. From the top of its mountains to the floor of its oceans, the crust is at most 70 km thick. The crust is made up of three major layers: topsoil, subsoil, and bedrock. No one has ever dug beneath the Earth's crust (the deepest hole so far took 20 years to drill and goes down only 12 km). But scientists have some clues about the "mantle" that lies below. Volcanic lava is from the mantle, and scientists can study the lava. Also, because vibrations travel at different speeds through different kinds of rock, scientists have studied vibrations caused by earthquakes for other clues. Beneath the mantle, at the very centre of the Earth, is the "core". The core seems to have two parts: the inner core, which is a solid iron-nickel ball, and the outer core, which is a thick, pudding-like mixture. The deeper into the Earth you go, the hotter it gets; scientists believe the temperature in the core is about 6000 degrees Celsius.

Topics: Earth.

No one knows for sure how the Earth came to exist. One scientific explanation is that the Earth formed over billions of years from a whirling cloud of gas and dust. The cloud circled the sun, which, at the time, was a new star. The effects of static electricity and then of gravity could have caused the dust particles to lump together, gradually forming a larger and larger body.

CRYSTAL CLEAR

Rocks are mixtures of minerals, and minerals form crystals. Every mineral has its own unique crystal form. Grow crystals using sugar and salt.

MATERIALS: Boiling water; sugar; salt; food colouring; vinegar; small pieces of charcoal briquette; drinking glasses; shallow glass container; measuring cup; tablespoon; *clean* string or thread; *clean* paper clips; pencils, sticks, or straws; paper towel; magnifying glass.

DOING IT:

1. *Rock Candy:* Fill a drinking glass about a third full with boiling water. Stir sugar into the water until no more dissolves. You can dissolve *a lot* of sugar in a little water; the ratio is about two parts sugar to one part water. You should end up with a thick syrup; you may see a few sugar grains floating in the solution. Tie one end of a piece of string to the middle of a pencil and the other end to a clean paper clip. Wet the string and paper clip and brush them through dry sugar so that grains of sugar stick to them. Place the pencil across the rim of the glass so that the paper clip is suspended midway in the solution. Put the glass where it won't be disturbed; cover it loosely with a paper towel to keep out dust. After several days, crystals will form around the paper clip and string. If the water evaporates slowly, the crystals will be quite large. Use a magnifying glass to examine them. What shape are the crystals? Compare the shape of the crystals to the shape of some grains of sugar. How did the sugar crystals form? Taste the crystals. Why do you think they're called "rock candy"?

2. *Salty Crystals:* Make salt crystals. Follow the same procedure used for sugar crystals; the only difference is you use less salt (less than one part salt to one part water). How do salt crystals look different from sugar crystals?

3. *Crystal Garden:* Scatter several small pieces of charcoal briquette in a glass container. Fill a measuring cup with 250 ml of boiling water. Stir salt into the water until no more dissolves. Add two tablespoons of vinegar to the salt solution. Pour the mixture over the charcoal briquette pieces; the charcoal should still stick up out of the mixture. Put several drops of food colouring over the briquette pieces. Put the container where it won't be disturbed. In a few weeks, you'll have a colourful crystal garden. The crystals are fragile, so don't move the container. **Don't taste these crystals.**

Pretend the molecules of a certain material are like bananas. No matter how hard you try, you can't fit them together exactly. Now suppose the molecules are like wooden building blocks. They will pack together nicely, no matter how many cubes you add. When the molecules of a material are all the same shape, they can fit together in a solid, clear, many-sided package with flat, smooth surfaces. This package is called a "crystal". Each type of crystal has its own characteristic shape. For example, table salt crystals -- which are cube-shaped -- are different than quartz crystals. Some crystals -- such as diamonds, emeralds, sapphires, and rubies -- are called "gems" because they are so beautiful when cut and polished.

Hundreds of different kinds of crystals are formed in nature. A snowflake is a crystal. So are most of the minerals in the Earth. Billions of years ago the materials making up the Earth were so hot they melted. When this rock solution cooled, the minerals crystallized. You can use the same process to make salt or sugar crystals. When sugar dissolves in water, the water molecules cause the "sucrose" (sugar) molecules to break away from each other. Much more sugar dissolves in hot water than cold water; the solution is "saturated" with sugar. As the water cools, the large number of sucrose molecules are attracted to each other again. They pack close together in a specific pattern. Grains of sugar on a string act as "seed crystals", as a starting place for the sugar crystals to grow. It's possible to grow sugar crystals without seed crystals, but it takes longer. A crystal garden using pieces of charcoal briquette makes use of the many tiny empty spaces inside the briquette. When a salt solution is poured over the briquette pieces, water is drawn into the spaces. Water also evaporates from the surface of the solution. As the water disappears, the salt that's left behind forms tiny crystals on any nearby solid surface (like a piece of briquette). Crystals grow on crystals to make the crystal garden.

Topics: Rock Types; Atoms; Snow.

A Rock Is Born

Rocks are classified according to the way they were formed. This board game for two to six players shows that all types of rocks are related to each other.

MATERIALS: Large version of the rock cycle game board shown; markers; die.

DOING IT:

1. All players start as igneous rock. The object of the game is to go around the game board in a counterclockwise direction and finish as igneous rock.

2. Each throw of the die tells a player how many spaces to move. When you land on or pass a circle with an arrow leading from it (e.g. sediments, metamorphic rock), you must make a special throw of the die. If a 1 or 2 appears, you follow the arrow back to the space indicated at the end of the arrow. If numbers other than 1 or 2 appear, you don't follow the arrow backward; wait until your next turn to continue moving forward. Note: No special throw is required when players are first leaving the igneous circle, but a throw is required when players finish on the circle.

3. To end the game, players must reach the igneous circle by exact count (i.e. if you're one space away from landing on igneous, you must roll a 1 on the die).

4. The winner is the player who reaches the igneous circle, makes the final special throw, and does not obtain either a 1 or a 2. If a 1 or a 2 appears, the player must follow the arrow from the igneous circle and begin play again from the space at the end of the arrow.

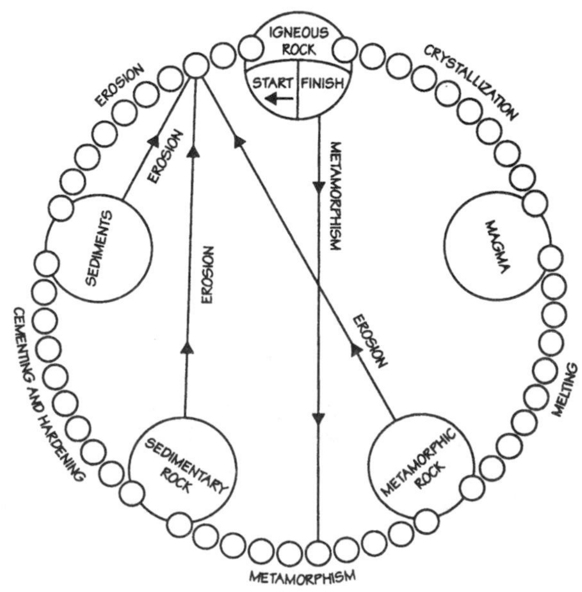

There are three basic types of rocks. Any one type of rock can become another type -- given time and the proper conditions. *Igneous* or "volcano, fire-formed" rocks are formed from cooled and hardened "magma" (an extremely hot, liquid-like mixture of rock material deep within the Earth). Cooled lava, basalt, and granite are examples of igneous rocks. *Sedimentary* or "water-deposited" rocks result from the "erosion" (breaking into smaller bits) of any type of rock material (even other sedimentary rock). Small rock fragments called "sediments" roll downward from high places such as hills and are carried along by streams and rivers until they reach oceans or low-lying places on land. As more and more sediments are deposited over the years, the layers of loose material become hard, compact, and turn into rock. For example, sandstone consists of sand grains that have cemented together. *Metamorphic* or "changed" rocks are also made from other rocks. With sufficient heat or pressure, rocks can be folded, squeezed, and hardened into new rocks. For example, marble is metamorphosed limestone (a sedimentary rock).

In summary, igneous rocks can be seen as the first or parent rocks of the Earth's crust. When igneous or other types of rocks erode, they break into fragments which are deposited and form sedimentary rocks. Sedimentary rocks -- as well as igneous rocks -- may be changed into metamorphic rocks. Sometimes, high temperatures beneath the Earth remelt rocks and form new igneous rocks.

Topics: Rock Types.

ERUPTION!

Volcanoes give us clues about the Earth's insides and are involved in the formation of igneous rocks. Make a model volcano.

MATERIALS: Clean, clear bottle, preferably with a longer neck (e.g. salad dressing bottle); baking soda; vinegar; dishwashing liquid; red food colouring; tablespoon; large pan (or you can do this activity in a sink).

DOING IT:

1. Place a bottle in a large pan. How is the bottle like a volcano? The inside of the bottle is the magma chamber; the neck is the pipe; and the opening at the top of the bottle is the crater.

2. Put about 4 tablespoons of baking soda into the bottle (so that there is at least a 1 cm layer at the bottom of the bottle). Add several squirts of dishwashing liquid, as well as several drops of food colouring.

3. What happens when a volcano erupts? Pour vinegar into the bottle to equal the amount of baking soda in the bottle. The mixture of ingredients sets off a chemical reaction; the baking soda and vinegar react to produce carbon dioxide gas. Pressure builds up inside the "volcano". The gas in the "magma chamber" expands and moves up and out of the "volcano", forcing "magma" (suds) out as well. "Lava" then flows from the top of the "volcano" down the sides.

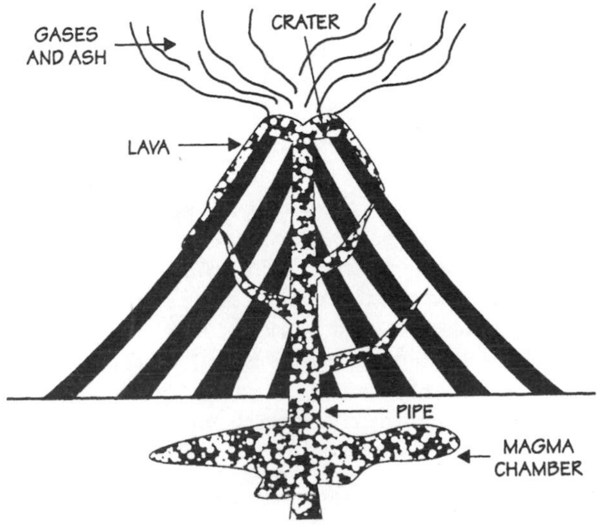

4. What happens to lava as it cools on the sides of a volcano? Why do volcanoes look the way they do (i.e. cone-shaped)?

A "volcano" is an opening -- like a safety valve -- in the Earth through which magma, gases, solid rock fragments, poisonous fumes, and ash can be discharged. There are about 500 active volcanoes in the world today; almost all are found close to mountain chains in areas where there are weaknesses in the Earth's crust. Underneath volcanoes, in the Earth's mantle, there are pockets of magma -- a hot, liquid-like mixture of rock material -- and gases. As heat and pressure build up in these magma chambers, the gases expand. The increasing internal pressure finally causes an eruption. The magma is forced up the volcano's pipe and out the crater, the opening at the top of the volcano. The eruption ends when all the pressure has been relieved. When the magma reaches the surface of the Earth, it's called "lava". Lava can flow as quickly as 80 km/hour, but speeds of less than 16 km/hour are more usual. As the lava cools, it solidifies into rock.

Igneous rocks such as obsidian, pumice, and basalt result from cooled lava. Obsidian, sometimes called volcanic glass, occurs when surface lava cools quickly; it's a dark, glassy rock. Pumice is often light enough to float in water because it's full of holes formed by escaping gas at the time of its origin. Basalt is a dark-coloured, heavy, dull rock. Sometimes, magma doesn't reach the surface of the Earth's crust. Instead, it forces its way into or beneath areas of rock. Here, the magma solidifies into coarse, granular rocks like granite. Granite is the most common of all igneous rocks in the continental crust of the Earth. Granite is often found exposed because the overlying rocks have been slowly worn away. Granite has a speckled appearance. The speckling is caused by different minerals in the rock. These minerals can include quartz (a glass-like mineral), mica (a sparkling mineral), and feldspar (which exists in many colours).

Topics: Rock Types; Earth; Chemical Reactions.

Boulders To Bits

Over millions of years, erosion has changed the Earth. Erosion levels mountains and helps form sedimentary rock. Use water to erode your own "mountain".

Big rocks into pebbles,
pebbles into sand.
I really hold a million million
rocks here in my hand.
(F. Parry Heide)

MATERIALS: Sand; large, shallow pan; book; water; watering can; fallen leaves; drinking straw; popsicle sticks; ruler; different colours of crayons.

DOING IT:

1. Start with a pile of dry sand. Blow onto the pile with a straw to create "wind". What happens to the sand? Can you make holes in the pile of sand? This is a model of wind erosion.

2. Divide both sides of several popsicle sticks into 1 cm thick bands. Use crayons to colour each band a different colour; all bands at the same level should be the same colour (e.g. all top bands are red).

3. Pack down damp -- not wet -- sand to build a "mountain" on one side of a large pan. Put a book under the pan to tilt it so that water will flow away from the "mountain". Stick the popsicle sticks into the "mountain" -- on different sides and at different elevations. Only the top band (1 cm) of the sticks should be visible (break sticks as required).

4. Sprinkle the "mountain" gently and steadily with a watering can so that "rain" falls straight down. This is a model of water erosion. How do the popsicle sticks show the erosion? Where is erosion most rapid? Where do the eroded particles go? Look for miniature streams, lakes, canyons, and landslides. The erosion of a pile of sand is based on the same principles as the erosion of exposed soil on hills and mountains.

"Erosion" is the wearing away and movement of rocks and soil by natural forces. When rocks erode, they break apart and become smaller and jagged; eventually they become smooth. When small bits of rock are pressed together for many, many years, they can form a layer of sedimentary rock. "Weathering" -- exposure to air, wind, water, and temperature shifts -- is a major cause of erosion. For example, sand particles blown by the wind against solid rock can act in the same way as sandpaper rubbing against wood. Windstorms can swirl away huge amounts of dry soil in a matter of minutes. Glaciers -- moving ice fields whose huge masses of ice can survive even the hottest summer -- cause considerable erosion as they scrape rocks along the ground for long distances. Water can cause erosion when it trickles into cracks in rocks, freezes (expands), and then refreezes (contracts and trickles deeper into cracks), thus forcing the cracks to open wider. Water in motion is one of the most powerful causes of erosion. Rivers are formed by running water; river banks are eroded away by running water; gullies are formed in fields when heavy rains wash away soil; and water in motion can even cause landslides and detach solid blocks of rock.

Topics: Rock Types; Soil; Earth.

Fill a can or thick-walled glass jar one-third full with water. Drop in several small, sharp chunks of brick. Secure the container's lid. Ten people should each give the container a hundred vigorous shakes. Open the container and look at the fragments, the water, and also scrape the inside of the container with your fingernail. You should see the effects of erosion. It takes a lot of work to break down the chunks of brick even a little bit. It took thousands of years to produce the rock particles in present-day soil.

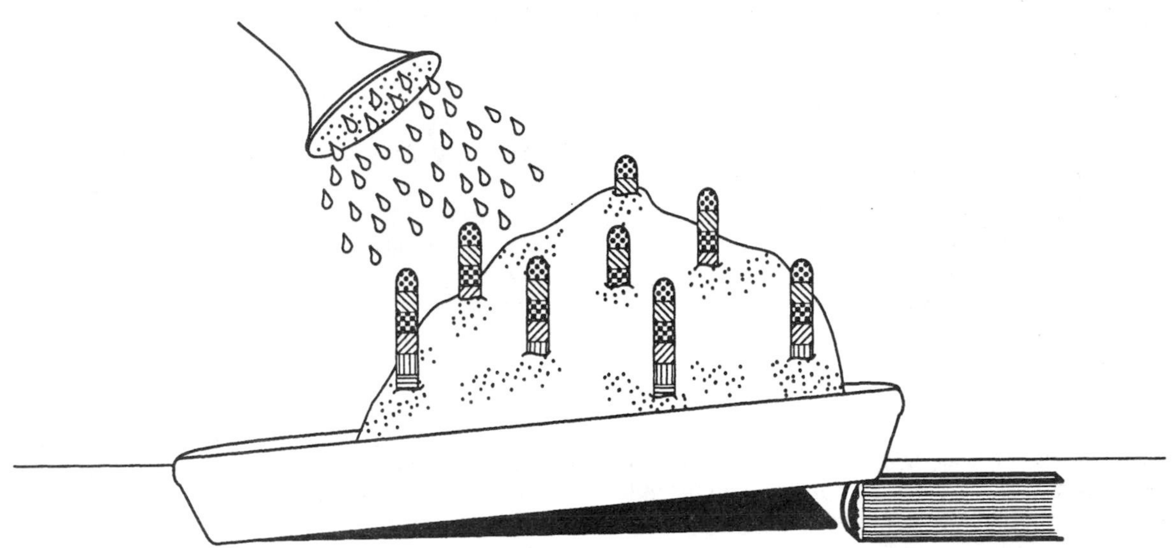

5. Rebuild the "mountain". Make the "rain" fall quickly and then more slowly. Hold the watering can high above the mountain. Then hold the can close to the mountain. How does the nature of the erosion change? When do eroded particles splash the most? When water falls on bare soil, small soil particles are dislodged and splash erosion occurs. You can see splashed soil on walls and garden vegetables after a heavy rain.

6. Rebuild the "mountain" again. Lay fallen leaves over the sides. Pour "rain" on the mountain. What happens? The erosion should be less pronounced. How does stripping vegetation from large areas of land cause problems?

7. *Variation:* Make a large "mountain" outdoors using soil. Put marked popsicle sticks into the "mountain". Observe the "mountain" over several days to see what natural forces do to it.

Visit an area before a rainstorm and try to predict where puddles will form. During or after the rain, take a look at how accurate you were. Puddles are usually found where the ground is very hard, or where there is a low spot. Which puddles continue to fill after the rain has stopped? Look for mini-streams flowing into puddles. Follow a stream of water away from a puddle. Where does the stream originate? Predict which puddles will dry first. How is the area different once the puddles dry?

MAKE TIME

The Grand Canyon in the United States was created through erosion. For millions of years, the Colorado River tore its way through the countryside and -- aided by wind and frost -- carved a number of canyons. The greatest of these canyons is the Grand Canyon. Some 350 km long and varying from 6 to 30 km in width, the Grand Canyon is well over 1.5 km deep. Geologists can "read" the exposed, multicoloured layers of rocks on the sides of the gorge to learn about the Earth.

Sand Sculpting

A great deal of sand has been created through erosion. Making sand sculptures is fun -- and useful for understanding how sand packs together to form sedimentary rock.

MATERIALS: Sand; water; containers for water; digging and molding tools (e.g. stick, small shovel, paper cup, pail). Optional -- cornstarch.

DOING IT:

1. Start by testing your sand to make sure it's the right consistency -- not too dry and powdery, and not too wet. Take some sand in your hands. Form it into a small ball. Does the shape hold?

2. The possibilities for sand sculptures are endless (e.g. dinosaur, beetle, alligator, camel, dog, frog, hippo, mermaid, seahorse, shark, snail, turtle, whale, flowers, pyramid, castle or other building, canal, highway system, relief map). Make sculptures large enough so that you can put in a lot of details.

3. Here's a good general approach for sand sculpting: lay out the sculpture's length; make the outline; mound the general shape or make it in relief; pat it smooth and firm; add features; undercut around the base to "separate" the sculpture from the sand. To "mound" a sculpture means to pile sand up into the design; to make a sculpture in "relief" is to cut the sand away.

There are three basic kinds of small rock particles: sand, silt, and clay. Each of these terms has an everyday and a technical meaning. People usually call anything they find at a beach, "sand"; technically speaking, sand particles range from 0.05 mm to 2.0 mm in diameter. "Silt" is what you find at a river's mouth; technically speaking, silt particles are from 0.002 mm to 0.05 mm in diameter. "Clay" is generally thought of as a sticky, slippery, gray mass; clay particles are defined as anything smaller than 0.002 mm in diameter -- some are so small that even an ordinary microscope won't show them. Particles larger than 2.0 mm are called "gravel" or stones.

Topics: Rock Types; Soil.

4. As you work, completed areas may dry out, especially if you're making something large. Sprinkle on water now and then to keep the sand damp (don't pour the water on because this might destroy the sculpture).

5. A small amount of wet sand added around certain features (e.g. bulging eyes of a frog) will "glue" them in place.

6. "Pressing" is a helpful technique, especially for castle walls. The sand should be wet, but not as wet as for gluing. Mold the sand with your hands. To make narrow, high ridges, gently press the sand between your hands, first on one side, then on the other.

7. "Dripping" is a technique in which the sand builds drip upon drip. You need plenty of water. Lift up a handful of water-soaked sand (consistency of molasses). Hold your hand over the site; then dribble the sand through open fingers while raising and lowering your arm. Raising forms high, narrow peaks; lowering forms low, thick peaks.

8. What factors determine how big or high you can make sand sculptures? Do fine sand grains stick together better than large grains? Does more or less water help the sand to stick?

9. *Extension:* Small sand figurines make great gifts. Mix two parts sand with one part water and one part cornstarch. Heat and stir the mixture until it's thick. Let the mixture cool, then use your hands to mold it into a figurine. Let the figurine dry and harden.

SANDWICH GEOLOGY

In some construction sites, you can see a cross-section of the layers of rock underground. Build a sandwich and explore how natural forces create rock layers.

MATERIALS: Slices of white, dark rye, and brown bread (cut off all the crusts); jam; chunky peanut butter; raisins; plate; knife; spoons.

DOING IT:

1. An empty plate represents igneous bedrock.

2. Pretend there's a river flowing over the bedrock. White sand -- from rocks eroded by the river -- is being carried along in the water. Where the water flows more slowly, the sand is deposited on the river bottom. Over many years, the sand is pressed and cemented together to form white sandstone. Put down a slice of white bread for the sandstone.

3. One year, there's a major flood. Tonnes of mud and rocks are swept over the sandstone. Spread chunky peanut butter over the white bread to represent the mud and rocks. Throw on several raisins for big boulders that have been caught up by the rushing water. This mud, rock, and boulder mixture becomes a sedimentary rock layer called a conglomerate.

4. As time passes, the flow of the water slows. The water now carries small bits of rock called silt. The silt accumulates and forms another layer. Over many years, the silt turns into shale rock. A slice of brown bread is the shale.

5. Around this time, the Ice Age ends. Glaciers start melting. The oceans rise and cover the existing layers of rock. As time goes on, living creatures in the salt water die and their shells and skeletons line the ocean floor. Over many years, this calcium-rich layer becomes limestone. Spread a thick layer of jam on the brown bread to represent the limestone.

6. Finally, pretend there's a bad drought. Strong winds pick up particles of eroded rock. The particles swirl against a mountainside and you get a layer of brown sand. Over many years, this layer becomes brown sandstone. Finish your sandwich with a slice of dark rye bread to represent the brown sandstone.

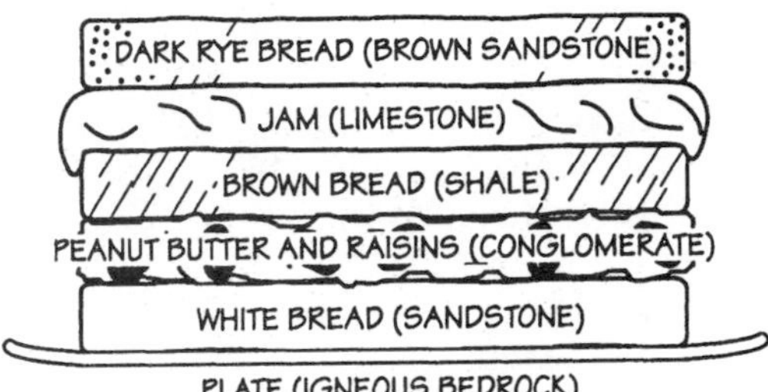

7. Review what each part of the sandwich represents (keep the white bread on the bottom). What's the oldest part of the sandwich? Why? Is the middle part of the sandwich younger or older than the oldest part? Why? How do geologists tell the age of rocks?

8. Geologists studying rocks rarely find level layers. Rock layers are often bent or broken. Bend the sandwich to form a mountain, and then a valley. Watch how the layers bend.

9. Munch away at your geological creation!

MAKE TIME

Over many, many years, sediments compact together to form layers of sedimentary rock. The "law of superposition" says that, in general, before the topmost layer (stratum) of rock can be formed, the layer beneath it must already be formed. Thus, in any sequence of layered rock in the Earth's crust, a given layer will be older than the layer above it and younger than the layer below. For example, lava may cover an area around a volcano, cool to form igneous rock, and later be covered by a layer of sedimentary rock. The sedimentary rock would be younger than the igneous rock. However, there are exceptions to this guide. Magma may not come up through a volcano; instead, it may squeeze in between layers of existing rock in the Earth's crust. The igneous rock formed as the magma cools would then be younger than the layer of rock above it. One way to tell this is by looking for evidence of heat effects on the layers above and below the igneous rock; igneous rock from volcanic lava would create a heat effect only on the layer beneath it (because the layer above it doesn't exist yet).

Topics: Rock Types; Earth.

FAKING FOSSILS

By studying what fossils are found in which rock layers, scientists have learned about life on Earth millions of years ago. Make your own fossils.

MATERIALS: Mud *or* plaster of Paris and sand; water; cake pan or shallow container; container for mixing; spoon; objects to be "fossilized" (e.g. shells, leaves, bones, bits of rock); petroleum jelly (e.g. Vaseline).

"Fossils" are traces of animal or plant life, from a previous geological age, found in the Earth's crust (usually in sedimentary rocks like limestone, shale, and sandstone). There are three general forms of fossils: actual plant or animal remains; a petrified (turned to rock) specimen; or an imprint. The *remains* of whole plants and animals are rarely preserved; frequently, only pieces which do not decompose readily, such as bones, teeth, or a shell, fossilize. A key factor in remains being preserved is that they are covered quickly by some sort of protective material. For example, marine animals are often preserved because they fall to the ocean floor shortly after death and are buried by soft mud and sand. A *petrified* specimen is one in which the organic material has been partly or completely replaced by minerals from the Earth. Most fossils are mineralized. For example, no dinosaur bones are original "bone"; they are all mineralized fossils. An *imprint* is really another type of mineralized fossil. It occurs when a dead plant or animal leaves a mold of its shape in mud and the mold hardens. If the mold fills up with a mineral, then it forms a fossil. Fossils take thousands of years to develop.

Fossils help us reconstruct life in the past. By studying successive rock layers, scientists believe that life began with tiny, simple forms that gave rise to larger and more complex plants and animals. Fossils can show a time relationship between rocks in different places (e.g. the same animal may be fossilized in different areas). Fossils reveal ancient land and water areas and how these areas have changed. For example, fossils of giant tree ferns found in Greenland reveal that the climate there was once quite warm. Marine fossils at the top of Mount Everest (the world's tallest mountain) indicate that it was once under the ocean! Finally, fossils are sources of natural resources such as coal, oil, lime, and building stones.

Topics: Rock Types; Resources.

DOING IT:

1. *Option One:* Collect enough mud (perhaps from a dried-up puddle) to fill a large pan. Stir in some water. Coat any objects to be "fossilized" with petroleum jelly. Carefully stir the objects into the mud (keep leaves flat). Press the mud down firmly. Put the pan in a warm, dry place (e.g. in the sun). When the mud is hard, carefully break it apart to discover the "fossils" in it. Look for leftover impressions. How many forms of "fossils" can a single object create?

2. *Option Two:* Put a layer of sand, about 2 cm thick, at the bottom of a pan. Coat any objects to be "fossilized" with petroleum jelly. Lay the objects on the sand. Mix equal amounts of sand and plaster of Paris. Add enough water so the paste is moist and just thin enough to pour. Spread the paste evenly over the sand to a depth of about 4 cm. Put the pan in a warm, dry place. When the mixture is hard, flip the pan over and carefully clean the sand away to observe the "fossils".

3. *Extension:* Examine mud puddles or a sandy shoreline to spot possible "fossils" in the making. How much of a chance do dead fish, insects, leaves, or the footprints of birds have of becoming fossilized? Instead, what almost always happens to them?

TIME WALK

Scientists have put together a theory of the history of Earth based on information from rock layers, fossils, and other dating techniques. Walk a geological time line.

MATERIALS: Measuring tape; pen; string and stakes (or other marking system); index cards.

DOING IT:

1. Measure a distance of 46 m to represent the estimated age of the Earth -- 4.6 billion years.

One technique geologists use for determining the age of rocks is "radioactive dating". Many rocks have radioactive elements (e.g. uranium) in them that change in a certain way over time. By looking at how far along the changes are, scientists know the age of the rock. It works like this: Suppose a cookie jar starts out with ten chocolate cookies. Each day, one chocolate cookie turns into a vanilla cookie. If you look in the jar one day and see four vanilla cookies, you know the jar has been around for four days.

Try some garbage-can geology. Get a large, empty garbage can. Over a week, people deposit crumpled paper. Some pieces can be blank, others may have notes, and some should have the date. Every so often, put in a special note or drawing just for fun. You may have to stomp the paper down during the week. At excavation time, people go through the trash, layer by layer. Use a tape measure to record the depth at which papers are found. Where are the newest layers? The oldest? How are paper layers like layers of rock in the Earth? If an undated paper is found near a dated one, can you guess the age of the undated paper? Why might different dates be near one another? What forces might have scrambled papers (e.g. stomping, spilling, stirring)?

2. Divide the 46 m to represent Earth's history. Use string and stakes, with index cards at key points listing the date, distance, and event. Some key events, distances, and dates (approximate numbers of years ago) are as follows:

- 4.6 billion (46 m) -- Earth forms.
- 3.9 billion (39 m) -- Oldest rocks found today formed.
- 3.4 billion (34 m) -- Life on Earth begins.
- 500 million (5 m) -- Animals with hard parts (e.g. shell, skeleton) appear.
- 350 million (3.5 m) -- Insects appear.
- 300 million (3 m) -- Coal begins to form.
- 200 million (2 m) -- Dinosaurs appear.
- 190 million (1.9 m) -- Huge, single land mass begins to break into continents.
- 130 million (1.3 m) -- Flowering plants appear.
- 65 million (65 cm) -- Dinosaurs extinct; North American Rockies begin to form.
- 60 million (60 cm) -- Modern plants and birds appear.
- 300,000 (3 mm) -- Humans (Homo sapiens) appear.
- 40,000 (0.4 mm) -- Modern humans (Cro-Magnon) appear.
- 6,000 (0.06 mm) -- Recorded history begins (i.e. ancient Egypt).
- 2,000 (0.02 mm) -- Modern Christian calendar begins.
- 100 years (0.001 mm) -- Industrial Revolution begins; humans begin to drastically change the environment.

3. Walk the time line. Stop at each marker to read the index card. How do you feel walking through Earth's history? Do you think about certain events differently after walking the time line?

By examining the composition and order of rock layers, geologists theorize that the Earth is about 4.6 billion years old. It's hard to imagine that amount of time. Pretend that the Earth was born twelve hours ago. Most of the events that have contributed to the world as we know it today have taken place in the last 400 million years, or what would work out to be the last hour. Modern human beings have existed on the Earth for about 40,000 years, or the last half second. The 4.6 billion year geological time scale is divided into five major "eras": azoic, precambrian (earliest life), palaeozoic, mesozoic, and cenozoic (most recent). This time scale is then divided into "periods" and "epochs".

Topics: Earth; Measurement.

CONTINENTAL DRIFT

Rock formations and fossils indicate that the continents were once joined in a single land mass. Put together a motion booklet showing how the continents came to exist.

Look at a map of the world. Do you see how the bulge of Africa fits the shape of the Caribbean Sea? In the early 1900s, Alfred Wegener, a German meteorologist, developed a theory around the fact that all the continents seem to fit together like pieces of a jigsaw puzzle. He theorized that the continents were once joined in a single land mass -- Pangaea, a Greek word meaning "all lands". There is much scientific evidence to support this idea. Rocks in Newfoundland, Canada are of the same kind and age as those found in Scotland and Scandinavia. Fossils of similar plants and animals have been found in Africa and South America. At some point, Pangaea started to break up, and the pieces began to "drift" away from each other. Over millions of years, the six main land masses we know today were formed.

During the 1960s, scientists -- key among them Canadian geophysicist Tuzo Wilson -- developed the theory of "plate tectonics" to explain continental drift. The theory says that the entire surface of the Earth is broken up into giant plates of rock about 70 km thick and thousands of km wide and long. Scientists differ on the exact number of plates; six large plates have been discovered, along with several smaller ones. The places where the rock reaches up high are the continents; the places where the rock forms huge basins are the oceans. The giant plates are like closely packed rafts floating on the Earth's mantle. Up until about 200 million years ago, the plates seem to have been pushed together so that there was one supercontinent where the Atlantic Ocean is today. The plates are always moving, sliding over and under each other and even bumping into one another. They move slowly, over very small distances (2.5 cm to 5 cm a year). When two plates move away from each other, they leave a gap between them. Magma from the Earth's mantle oozes out through the gap; huge chains of volcanoes form in this way. Sometimes, two plates scrape together and one gets caught on the other. Pressure builds up until it is finally released and felt as an earthquake. Plates can also push up against each other, folding the land upward into mountains. This is usually a slow process; the Himalayan mountains started to develop 25 million years ago.

Topics: Earth; Mapping.

MATERIALS: Three copies of each of the following three pages; stapler.

DOING IT:

1. One motion booklet is made up of three copies of each frame on the following pages; you need multiple copies so that you have enough pages to flip and so that your eyes can catch the image of each picture.

2. Cut out each frame. Put the frames in order in a pile, with the most recent dates at the bottom of the pile. Place identical copies of a frame next to each other. Staple the pile of frames together along the left side to make the booklet.

3. What do you see as you flip the pages quickly and look at the pictures? It may take some practice, but you should see one large land mass break into several continents. How did the continents come to exist? Flip through the booklet and focus on one land mass at a time. For example, watch India move upward from beside Antarctica.

4. *Extension:* Use an extra set of the pictures. Cut out each frame and black out the date. Mix up the frames. Can you put the frames in the right order to demonstrate the formation of the present-day continents?

MAKE TIME

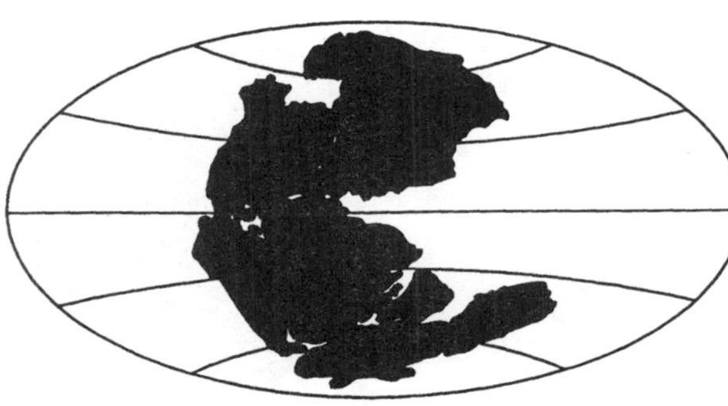

225 MILLION YEARS AGO

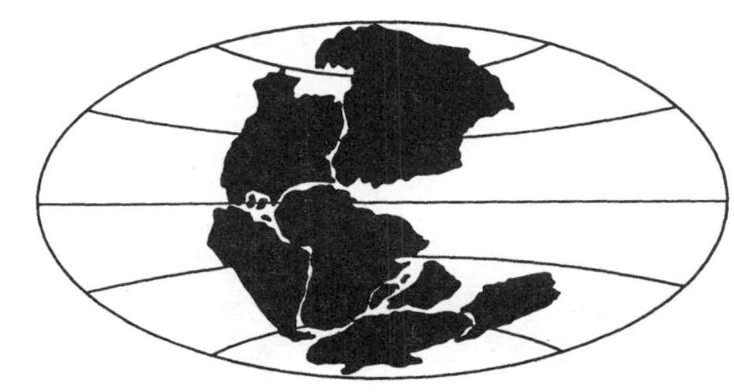

200 MILLION YEARS AGO

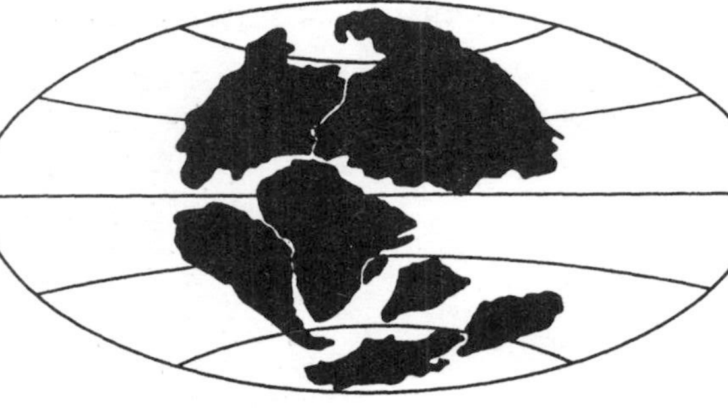

180 MILLION YEARS AGO

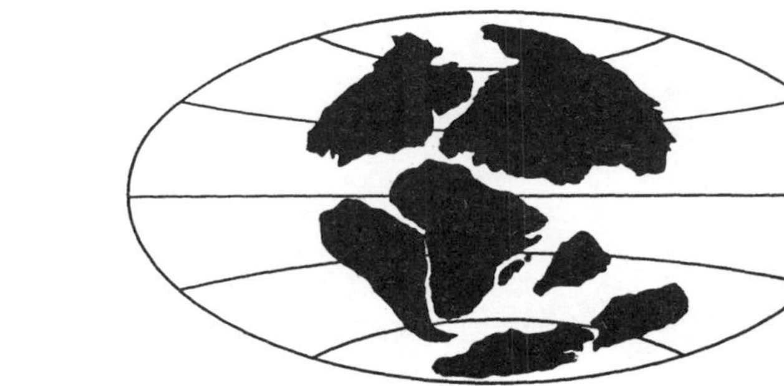

160 MILLION YEARS AGO

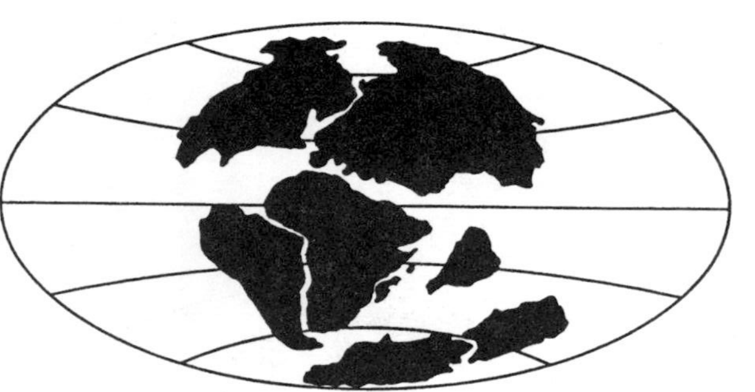

135 Million Years Ago

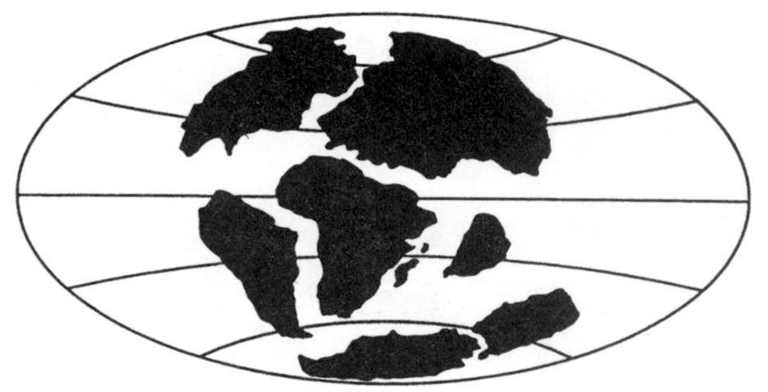

110 Million Years Ago

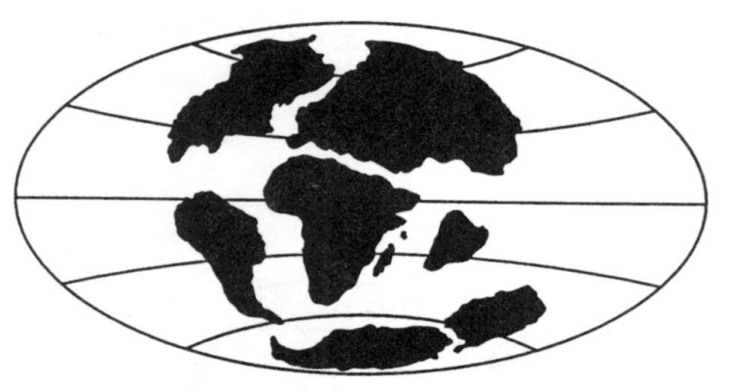

85 Million Years Ago

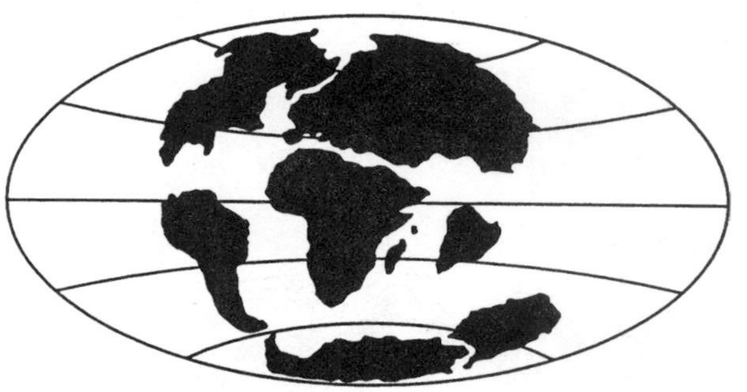

65 Million Years Ago

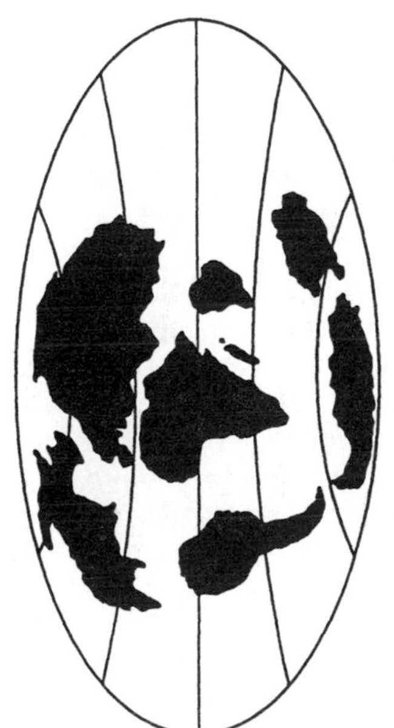

50 Million Years Ago

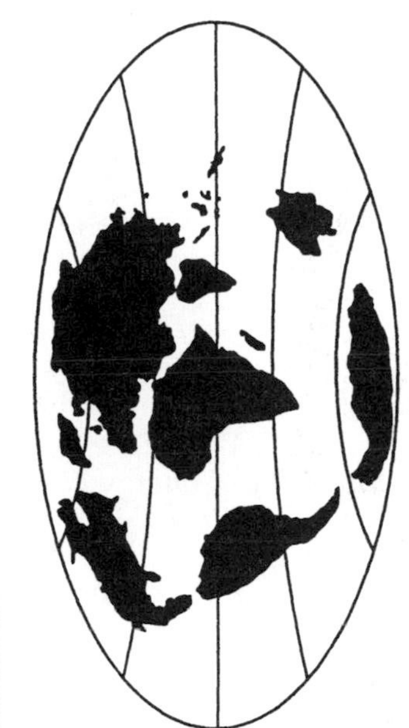

35 Million Years Ago

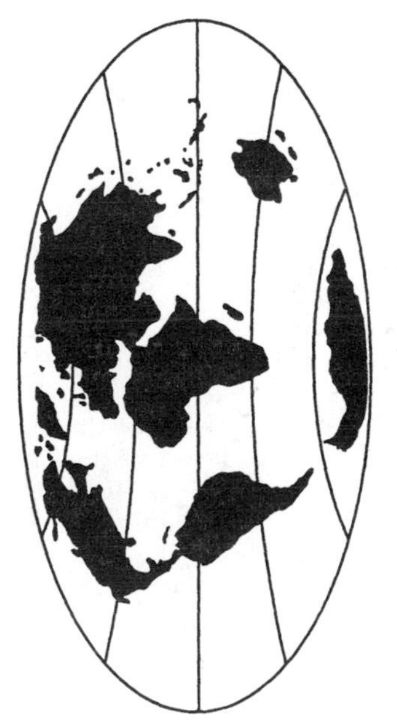

20 Million Years Ago

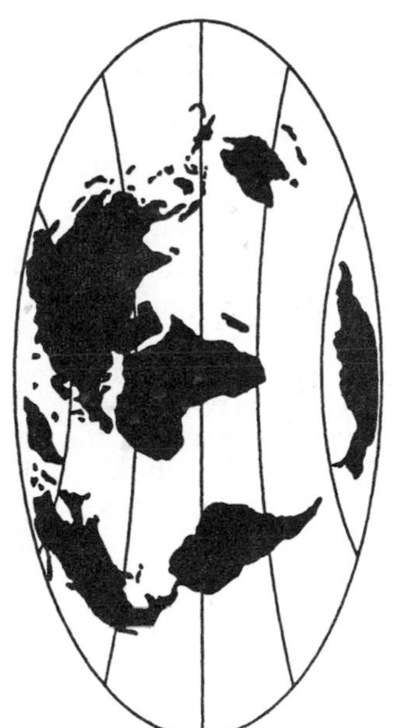

Present

QUAKE AND SHAKE

When pressure on the Earth's crust builds up, the result can be an earthquake. Explore the vibrations involved in earthquakes.

An "earthquake" is a shaking movement of the Earth's surface. Big earthquakes usually begin with slight tremors, rapidly increase to one or more violent shocks, and are followed by several less severe aftershocks. Earthquakes occur along "faults" -- cracks in the Earth's crust. The crust is broken up into giant plates of rock. Sometimes, two plates scrape together and one gets caught on the other. Pressure builds up until the plates snap to a new position. The release of pressure causes vibrations that we feel as an earthquake. An earthquake's origin deep in the Earth is called the "focus"; the point on the Earth's surface directly above the focus is the "epicentre". There are two types of earthquake vibrations, or "seismic waves". "Surface waves" travel *along* the Earth's surface, usually have the strongest vibrations, and cause most of the damage near the epicentre. Faster moving "body waves" travel *through* the Earth from the focus of an earthquake to distant points on the Earth's surface. Primary (compressional) body waves reach the Earth's surface first. They can travel through all layers of the Earth; their speed varies through different rock layers, and particles of rock move back and forth in the same direction as the waves. Secondary (shear) body waves travel about half as fast as primary waves and reach the Earth's surface after primary waves. Secondary waves cannot travel through liquid layers in the Earth; rock particles move at right angles to the direction of the waves.

Seismologists measure the strength of an earthquake by estimating the amount of energy released at the focus. Seismic waves are detected, recorded, and measured by sensitive instruments called "seismographs". In 1935, Charles Richter, an American seismologist, developed the Richter Scale for measuring the size of earthquakes. For example, an earthquake of about 7 on the Richter Scale -- like the earthquake that hit California in 1989 -- is fairly strong. The 1989 earthquake lasted only 15 seconds but caused millions of dollars in damage. Most of the world's earthquakes occur in the "Ring of Fire", made up of the Pacific coasts of North and South America, the Aleutian Islands of Alaska, Japan, Indonesia, and New Zealand. Over a million earthquakes occur every year; most are hardly even felt.

Topics: Earth.

MATERIALS: Slinky; about 3 m of rope; ping-pong ball; golf ball; container of water.

DOING IT:

1. *Plate Pressure:* Hold your hands up, with the palms facing you. Press the sides of your hands together as hard as you can. This is like two of the Earth's plates bumping against each other. Still pressing very hard, try to slide one hand up along the other hand. Do you feel how hard it is to move the hand? Keep trying to slide one hand along the other until it breaks free. Do you feel a sudden burst of energy? When a giant Earth plate breaks free, the burst of energy causes an earthquake.

2. *Primary Wave:* One person holds one end of a Slinky and a second person holds the other end. Stretch out the Slinky. Now, one person should count about twenty coils at his or her end and compress the coils together. Let the coils loose, but still hold on to the very end of the Slinky. Watch the Slinky's back and forth, pushing and pulling motion. This is like a primary wave as it goes though the Earth.

3. *Secondary Wave:* One person holds one end of a rope and a second person holds the other end. Shake the rope from side to side. This is like the movement of a secondary wave, which arrives after a primary wave.

4. *Waves Through Liquid:* Hold a golf ball and a ping-pong ball about 30 cm above a container of water. What happens when you drop the golf ball into the water? What happens when you drop the ping-pong ball? The golf ball penetrates through the water like a primary wave. The ping-pong ball, which floats, acts like a secondary wave; it does not penetrate through the liquid.

5. *Waves Through a Solid:* Drop a golf ball onto a table. How many times does it bounce? Drop a ping-pong ball. How many times does it bounce? The golf ball acts like a primary wave; it penetrates deeply and loses a lot of energy to the table (feel the table vibrate as the golf ball falls against it). The ping-pong ball acts like a secondary wave; it does not penetrate as deeply.

More Than Just Little Rocks

Our lives depend on an ultra-thin layer of the Earth -- the soil. Take a soil profile to investigate soil layers in the ground.

MATERIALS: Magnifying glass; spade; white paper; measuring tape; glue.

DOING IT:

1. Find a natural area from which to take a soil profile (perhaps you can find a bank where the soil has already been exposed).

2. Look at the natural litter on the ground. Use a magnifying glass to examine the undersides of any leaves you find making up the litter. Do you see long, stringy, white threads? Or any tangled up ones? These are molds. Bacteria and molds help the leaves decompose; the nutrients contained in the leaves then return to the Earth.

3. Dig a small hole 30 to 60 cm deep. Cut one side of the hole straight up and down, and slope the other side. Scrape the steep side of the cut to ensure a smooth surface for examination.

4. How many separate layers can you see? What colour is each layer? How large are the rock particles in each layer? Which layer contains the most organic material?

5. Measure the height of each layer. Which layer is thickest? Why?

6. Take a handful of soil from each layer. Squeeze and ball the soil. Try to squeeze "ribbons" of soil between your fingers; the finer the particles in the soil, the easier it is to ribbon.

7. Does the top layer of soil look, smell, and feel the same as layers deeper down?

8. Make a permanent record of your soil profile. Crease a sheet of white paper down the centre, lengthwise. Run a wide, thick strip of glue along the crease. Add soil from each layer to the glue, making layers on the paper in the same order as the layers in the ground. Let the glue dry. Gently shake away any loose soil. Label the layers.

9. When you're finished, *fill the hole with soil.*

10. *Extension:* Compare soil profiles from different sites (e.g. field, forest, river bank).

A good soil -- one containing the right balance of air, nutrients, and water -- is what plants need to grow; we need plants to survive. Soil is created as part of the rock cycle. Magma rises up from the depths of the Earth and hardens. Erosion then wears the rock down. Eventually, the rock is reduced to bits and washed by rains, rivers, and streams into the ocean. Soil is the powdered rock part of the cycle. But soil is much more than bits of rock. Fertile soil is also made up of a rich mix of organic matter. Looking at the various layers, or "horizons", in the ground is useful for understanding the components that make up soil. The top layer on the ground is usually natural "litter". Leaves fall from trees and decay on the ground. They eventually form "humus", a black, sticky, nutrient-rich material found beneath the litter. The layer beneath the litter is the topsoil, generally dark and crumbly. The topsoil is the most fertile part of the soil. It can range in thickness from a few centimetres to over a metre. After the layer of topsoil comes a lighter brown layer of subsoil. Subsoil is not nearly as productive as topsoil because the subsoil contains less water and organic nutrients to offer plants. Underneath the subsoil comes several centimetres of partially broken-down rock. The fragments of rock are from the more solid layer of parent rock below. The parent rock (so named because it breaks down to add to the horizons above it) is usually gray-brown in colour.

Although many areas in the world can sustain some plant growth, only 8% of the Earth's surface is covered with topsoil good enough to grow crops. It takes nature hundreds of years to build a few centimetres of topsoil. Erosion can remove it quickly. Before farming began, erosion was probably around 8 billion tonnes of topsoil a year, slow enough to be replaced by the rock cycle. By the 1980s, erosion was estimated to be as high as 23 billion tonnes. Exposed soil erodes more quickly than does soil covered by vegetation. Plants help to hold soil in place with their fine meshworks of roots and their umbrellas of leaves, which protect against the wind, rain, and harsh light of the sun. Many farmers no longer leave fields bare if they are not growing a crop on them. Instead, they plant grass to help hold the soil in place.

Topics: Soil; Earth; Resources.

SOIL SAMPLING

Different mixtures of rock particles and organic material result in different kinds of soil. Compare the characteristics of different soil types.

In general, soil is half air and water (necessary for plants and animals to live) and half recycling organisms (fungi, molds, bacteria, earthworms), rock (mineral) particles, and humus (black or dark substance made up of decaying leaves, wood, and animal matter). The rock particles in a soil determine the soil's grain size, texture, and pH. The particles are the result of erosion. They vary depending on the parent material from which they eroded (e.g. sandstone, granite). Humus is very important in soil: it helps soil hold water, improves air circulation, makes soil easier to work with, encourages the existence and multiplication of recycling organisms, and helps store plant food. The formation of humus is dependent on decomposition by recycling organisms. Humus varies based on the type of material that has decayed (i.e. leaves from deciduous trees form a different type of humus than do evergreen needles).

Humus and rock particles mix together in different proportions to produce different types of soil. There are three basic types of rock particles; from largest to smallest grain size they are sand, silt, and clay. The dominant type of rock particle in a soil determines the soil's name and properties. For example, a "silt soil" contains 80% or more silt and less than 12% clay. Soils with a lot of clay tend to hold too much water. The clay particles also often stick together into big lumps into which neither air nor plant roots can penetrate. Soils with a lot of sand tend to be well-drained and easy to work. The relatively big spaces between the sand particles means that there is a lot of air in the soil. But the sand does not contain the nutrients that plants need to grow. A common soil name is "loam". In ordinary usage, the term refers to a rich, black, fertile soil containing a fair bit of humus. Technically speaking, loam contains about equal amounts of silt, clay, and sand, and is not necessarily fertile. If you know what's in a soil, you can usually make a good guess as to the kinds of plants and animals it sustains. One way to improve the fertility of a soil is to add manure or composted material.

Topics: Soil; Resources.

MATERIALS: Trowel; small containers to hold soil samples; sheets of paper or newspaper; water; small can; hammer and nail; measuring cup; watch which indicates seconds; small jars with lids; paper; pencil. Optional -- oven.

DOING IT:

1. Dig up soil samples from a variety of areas (e.g. under a bush, in a field, on a path, near some flowers, on a lakeshore). A good sample size is three or four handfuls. If you find some decaying surface vegetation (e.g. leaves), take it along. Make some notes about where you find each sample: What is each site like (e.g. amount of water and sunlight)? What types of plants grow at each site? What types of animals do you find?

2. Place each soil sample on a separate sheet of paper or newspaper. Make notes on each sample, using the following steps.

3. *General Appearance:* What does the soil look like? What's the grain size: large (the separate particles are readily visible), medium, tiny? Do you see any stones? These may indicate a sandy or rocky soil. Do you see decaying material, roots, or small animals? These may indicate a fertile soil.

4. *Colour:* Is the soil light, medium, or dark coloured? A darker colour may indicate a more fertile soil.

Make your own soil. Use a small plastic bag to collect materials such as leaves, water, sand, moss, seeds, lichens, rotting wood, and bits of dead plants. Squish and mix all the materials together. Compare your handful of soil with soil on the ground. Are you a good soil-maker? How is your soil different from the ground soil in terms of smell, colour, and texture?

MAKE TIME

5. *Smell:* How does the soil smell: no smell, foul, earthy/pine? The amount of humus in a soil affects its smell; often, a large amount of humus creates an earthy smell.

6. *Texture:* To investigate a soil's texture, moisten a bit and rub it between your fingers. Is the soil made up of many grains of sand? A sandy soil will feel rocky and coarse. Does the soil stick together in clumps? A clay soil will feel sticky and plastic, and it makes a smooth, continuous smear. Is the soil made up mostly of dead leaves and other organic material? A loam soil will feel gritty. It may also smear slightly on your fingers; but, when rubbed, it doesn't thin out like clay before becoming rough and broken.

7. *Spaces:* The amount of open space between particles has a lot to do with how easily water moves through a soil and how much water the soil will hold. Test a soil sample's "water percolation rate"; that is, see how long it takes water to ooze or trickle through the soil. Remove the top from a can. Use a hammer and nail to punch six holes in the bottom. Fill the can half full with soil. Hold the can level and pour a set amount of water (e.g. 200 ml) into the can. Time the number of seconds from when the water is added to when the first droplets pass through the holes in the bottom of the can. How quickly does water flow through the soil sample? The longer it takes for the water to appear, the greater the absorption capacity of the soil. Note: You may not get a completely accurate evaluation of the soil because it may have been wet to begin with, and will therefore hold less water. If possible, dry soil samples by heating them in an oven at a medium heat for about 15 minutes.

8. *Soil Separation:* What kinds of particles make up the different soil samples? Fill a jar about 3/4 full with water. Add enough of one sample of soil to raise the level of water so that the jar is almost full. Secure the jar's lid and shake the jar vigorously. Place the jar on a level surface and don't move it for a couple of hours. The particles in the soil will settle out into layers, with the heaviest particles settling first. Sand-sized particles will settle almost immediately and form the bottom layer. Silt particles will settle next. Clay may take over a day to settle on top of the sand and silt. Humus may act as silt- or clay-sized particles, or it may be partly decomposed material that will float. Different soils will settle out differently; for example, one sample may give you a thick layer of sand while another results in a thin layer of sand. Determine the relative proportion of each layer to the total. One soil may be 90% sand and 10% silt/clay, while another may be 5% sand and 95% clay. The particles present in the greatest amount will help you name a soil (e.g. 80% clay, call it a clay or clay-based soil).

9. Compare notes for the various soil samples. Which soils are most alike? Which are most different? What are the majority components in each soil sample? Which soils might be best for sustaining plant and animal life?

HARD AS ROCK

Soil can be amazingly hard and compact, which affects its important ability to absorb water. Use two simple tests to explore soil compaction.

MATERIALS: Long, sharpened pencil or dowel rod (sharpened at one end) about 25 cm long; tape measure; large can with top and bottom removed; water; measuring cup; stopwatch or watch which indicates seconds; paper; pencil. Optional -- hammer.

DOING IT:

1. Choose a patch of soil to test.

2. Measure the exact length of a dowel (or pencil). Jam the sharpened end of the dowel into the ground by pushing on the top of the dowel with the flat palm of your hand. Stop pushing when the dowel feels uncomfortable against your palm. (Note: To ensure accuracy when you repeat the test, remember exactly how the dowel feels against your hand when you stop pushing.) Another approach is to give the dowel fifteen uniform taps with a hammer.

3. Measure the length of dowel sticking out of the ground. Subtract this number from the total length of the dowel to get the depth to which the dowel can easily be pushed. In general, the farther down the dowel goes, the less compact the soil.

4. Push the dowel into the ground at least three times, in slightly different spots, to get an average depth.

5. Twist a can into the soil to a depth of about 5 cm; don't use any of the spots into which you pushed the dowel.

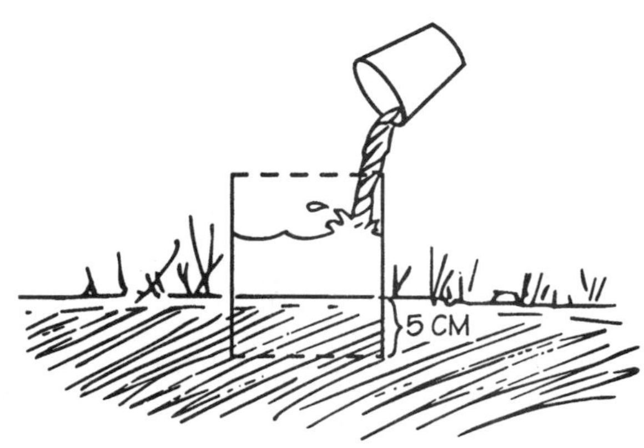

6. Pour a measured amount of water into the can (e.g. 500 to 1000 ml). Record the amount of time it takes for all the water to be absorbed into the soil. The longer it takes, the less able the soil is to readily absorb water. Is soil compaction the only factor in water absorption?

7. *Extension:* Compare the soil compaction at a variety of sites (e.g. lawn, field, forest, path). In general, is more compact soil less able to absorb water? Where do you find the most compact soil? What is the surface vegetation like in soil which is very compact? Which soils seem to be the most and the least likely to compact? Why? Is soil more likely to compact when it is wet or dry? Does topsoil differ from subsoil? Does soil on level ground differ from soil on a slope? Does soil near a pond hold as much water as similar soil elsewhere?

The composition of a soil gives it certain properties; however, some soil characteristics such as compaction are affected more by environmental factors than by composition. The major difference between hard and soft soil is the amount of space between particles: harder, more compact soils have less space between the particles. A certain degree of compaction helps soil retain water and prevents erosion. However, if the soil gets too compact, water runs off and the soil cannot sustain plant and animal life. Humans can cause soil compaction. Trampled-down nature trails are an excellent example of human-compacted soils. Compaction by humans can cause problems. When a building, a highway, or other solid covering is placed on soil, the particles in the soil are pushed together. The spaces between particles become smaller; water and air levels decrease; and living organisms can no longer live in the soil.

Topics: Soil; Measurement; Ecosystems.

PLANTS

"Botany", which comes from the Greek word meaning "plant", is the scientific study of plants. It is a branch of biology, the scientific study of living things. Until the invention of the microscope, botanists could examine and compare only the readily visible, physical features of plants. But the microscope now allows them to explore plant anatomy and cells.

In Arctic areas of Canada, there are little spruce trees which take more than 100 years to struggle to a height of 0.5 m.

Try drying wild flowers and garden flowers. Mix 6 parts white corn meal with 1 part Borax. Fill the bottom of a jar with the mixture. Take a flower with a longer stem and gently put the flower -- stem up -- into the mixture. Make sure the entire flower is buried in and covered by the mixture. After about two weeks, you'll have a beautifully dried flower.

Vegetable or fruit? Most plants are part of the vegetable world; a fruit is a special part of a seed-producing plant. After a plant is pollinated, the flower turns from an attractor to a protector. Seeds grow within the walls of the flower. In some plants, these walls become thick, fleshy, juicy fruit. Are the following fruits or vegetables: cucumbers, cherries, grapes, watermelons, string beans, bananas, squash, tomatoes?

Answer: They are all fleshy fruits, with seeds inside.

The potato is the world's fourth food staple after wheat, corn, and rice, yielding more food value per acre than the other three. Potatoes and milk products eaten together make a wholly nutritional meal. Europeans are the greatest consumers of potatoes. For example, the average German eats about 170 kg of potatoes a year; the average American eats only about 50 kg. Scientists estimate that about 10,000 varieties of potatoes grow throughout the world. Aside from eating, potatoes can be used to produce alcohol, which can then be used as a fuel.

For hundreds of years in Europe, people didn't eat tomatoes because they thought the fruit was poisonous. The French grew tomatoes as a hobby and called them "love apples" (fruits to be admired, but not eaten). Another name for the tomato was "wolf peach" (beautiful, but dangerous). However, the Indians of Peru and Ecuador had been eating tomatoes for thousands of years, and soon this practice spread to Europe and then North America.

WHAT IS IT?

Living things are grouped into five main kingdoms: Monera (e.g. bacteria), Protista (e.g. amoeba), Fungi, Plants, Animals. Use a game and simple key to classify plants.

MATERIALS: Measuring tape. Optional -- magnifying glass; plant identification guide.

DOING IT:

1. *Plant or Animal?:* Make two teams -- plants and animals. Teams stand facing each other, 3 to 5 m apart. Mark a safety area for each team, about 30 m behind the team. A leader calls out the name of a plant or an animal. If it's an animal, all plants chase animals until all animals are in their safety area. If it's a plant, the plants try to run to their safety area. Those who are tagged become members of the opposite team. Is it difficult to decide what's a plant and what's an animal? Why or why not?

2. *Plant Hunt:* Look for plants in your backyard or in a park. How many different kinds can you find? Use the simple key on the following page to classify plants (and differentiate them from algae, fungi, and lichens). Examine a specimen closely, perhaps using a magnifying glass. Into which one of the divisions does it fall? If a particular specimen doesn't seem to fit anywhere, you probably made a mistake; go back to the beginning of the key and try again. If both choices in a point seem possible, try going both ways and see which one works out better. To more precisely identify plants, use a plant identification guide.

What's the difference between a plant and an animal? Plants usually remain in one place; animals usually move around. Plants make their own food; animals obtain their food by eating plants or other animals. Most plants contain chlorophyll and are therefore green; animals do not have chlorophyll. Plants usually have branching bodies; animals usually have compact bodies. Plants have rigid, supporting cell walls containing cellulose; animals do not. Finally, plants, unlike most animals, do not have a nervous system or sensory organs.

Plants vary from small, simple mosses to larger, more complex systems like trees. "Taxonomy" is a system of classification for plants (and animals) based on hierarchy. Hierarchy is easy to understand using the example of a supermarket. When you walk into a supermarket, the first choice you make is whether you want a food or a nonfood item. You choose food. Then you decide whether you want meat or vegetables. You head toward the meat department. At the meat department, there's a wide selection: beef, pork, veal, chicken. Say you decide on beef. Then you have to decide what kind of beef: hamburger, steak, prime rib. You take the hamburger. All your choices can be ordered in a ranked series that becomes more and more specific: food, meat, beef, hamburger. Scientists take the same approach to ordering the plant, animal, and other kingdoms. Modern taxonomy is based on the work of Carolus Linnaeus, an 18th century Swedish botanist. He divided living things into eight different levels: kingdoms, phyla (or divisions, which are used by botanists), classes, orders, families, genera, species, and varieties or breeds.

Topics: Classification; Plant Parts.

A "cell" is the smallest living unit that makes up plants and animals. It can carry on essential life processes like producing energy and reproducing. A cell has three key parts: the cytoplasm; the cell membrane, which surrounds the cytoplasm and is the cell's outside wall; and the nucleus, which is the cell's control centre. Plant cells also have a thickened cell wall, made mainly of cellulose.

THE PLANT KINGDOM (MAJOR DIVISIONS)

DIVISION BRYOPHYTA (MOSSES): No roots or circulatory system. Roots replaced by thread-like "rhizoids" (root hairs) which anchor the plant. Most live in damp, shady areas, but a few mosses live at high elevations in direct sunlight. In general, mosses have tiny, upright stems surrounded by masses of tiny "leaves."

DIVISION HEPATOPHYTA (LIVERWORTS): No roots or circulatory system. Roots replaced by thread-like "rhizoids" (root hairs) which anchor the plant. They thrive in moist habitats and are small, broad, flat, green plants.

DIVISION FILICINOPHYTA (FERNS): Distinct roots, leaves, and stems with water-conducting tubes. When a fern first comes up from the ground, it is tightly curled, like the end of a violin.

DIVISION CONIFEROPHYTA (CONIFERS): Seed-bearing plants with distinct roots, leaves, and stems. Most are trees. Includes all coniferous evergreens (e.g. pine, spruce, cedar, hemlock, fir). Conifers are *gymnosperms* (means "naked seed"; seeds have no covering and can be found between the scales of a cone).

DIVISION ANTHOPHYTA (FLOWERING PLANTS): Largest division. Seed-bearing plants with distinct roots, leaves, and stems. They are *angiosperms* (seeds develop in a flower, which may later become a fruit). There are two types of angiosperms: 1) *Monocotyledons* have narrow leaves and one seed leaf (e.g. grasses, onions, lilies, palms); 2) *Dicotyledons* have broad leaves and seeds have a covering called a fruit (e.g. deciduous trees, most wild flowers, fruits, and vegetables).

ADDITIONAL NOTES: Algae, fungi, and lichens may look like plants, but they fall into other kingdoms. They do not have true roots, leaves or stems, no circulatory system, and no seeds or flowers. Many have a "holdfast" (anchor) which holds them to the ground or rock. *Algae* have green chlorophyll and can produce food by photosynthesis; many are aquatic; classified by colour -- blue-green, green, brown, red; e.g. seaweed. *Fungi* are not green, have no chlorophyll, cannot produce food, and must get organic food from other decaying plants; e.g. mushrooms, bread mold, yeasts, puffballs. *Lichens* are algae and fungi living together; fungi provide shelter and moisture for algae which carry on photosynthesis and provide fungi with organic food matter.

SIMPLE KEY: This key, together with some close observation, will help you classify plants and differentiate them from algae, fungi, and lichens. Using the key takes a little practice. Start with the first point; read parts "a" and "b" carefully. If part "a" fits, it will tell you where to go next (e.g. go to 2). If part "b" fits, it will tell you to go someplace else (e.g. go to 4). Note: Keep in mind that some plants may not have flowers or fruits because of the time of year.

1. a) A simple organism without obvious roots, stems, or leaves ➛ go to 2.
   b) An organism with roots, stems, and leaves ➛ go to 4.

2. a) A simple pigmented (coloured) organism growing in water or very damp places ➛ an ALGA.
   b) If not ➛ go to 3.

3. a) A brown, yellow, or white land organism ➛ a FUNGUS.
   b) A simple, dry, encrusting organism found on rocks, trees, and buildings ➛ a LICHEN.

4. a) A small land plant, up to 8 cm tall, which may have capsules ➛ go to 5.
   b) If not ➛ go to 6.

5. a) A tiny, erect plant with "leaves" growing right around the stem ➛ the plant is a MOSS.
   b) A small, flat, ribbon-shaped plant found in very damp places ➛ the plant is a LIVERWORT.

6. a) A green land plant with "fronds" (tightly-coiled, fuzzy leaves when young; unfold in spring), growing up to 2 m tall, and may have spores but never flowers ➛ the plant is a FERN.
   b) A leafy land plant with erect stems bearing buds, flowers, fruits, or cones in season ➛ go to 7.

7. a) The plant's seeds are in cones, not fruits ➛ the plant is a GYMNOSPERM.
   b) A plant with flowers, seeds in a fruit (seed case) ➛ the plant is an ANGIOSPERM ➛ go to 8.

8. a) A plant with narrow leaves and parallel veins ➛ the plant is a MONOCOTYLEDON.
   b) A plant with broad leaves and a network of veins ➛ the plant is a DICOTYLEDON.

FOOD FACTORIES

Green plants have tiny "food factories" in their leaves. Try these fascinating mini-investigations to explore photosynthesis, the food manufacturing process.

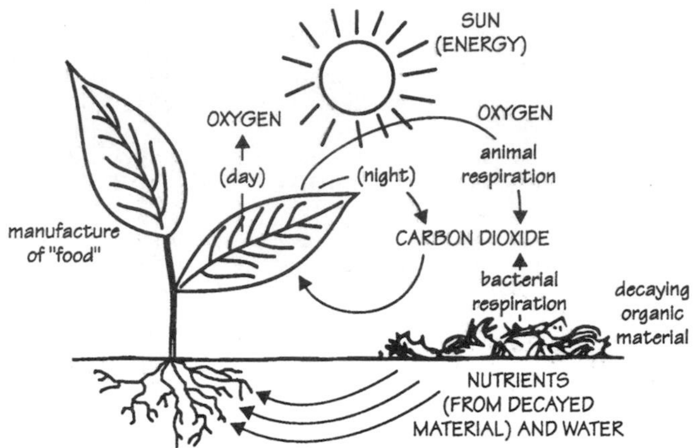

MATERIALS: Leaves; rubbing alcohol; paper clips; container; cardboard; scissors; petroleum jelly (e.g. Vaseline). Optional -- boiling water.

Green plants are "autotrophic" (self-nourishing). With energy from the sun, water and nutrients from the soil, carbon dioxide from the air, and the help of "chlorophyll" (the green colouring matter in leaves and other parts of plants) a leaf produces "food" consisting of sugars and starches. The food then circulates throughout the plant in the sap. Some of the food is used by the plant right away for energy. Some is sent off to the roots for storage. And some is used to create more of the plant itself (roots, leaves, stems, and fruit). The food manufacturing process is called photosynthesis ("photo" means light and "synthesis" means putting together).

If you tear a leaf into two parts and look closely along the tear, you should be able to see a thin, film-like layer on the underside of the leaf. If you look at a piece of this layer under a microscope, you will see tiny openings called "stomata". Plants breathe through the stomata. During photosynthesis, plants take in carbon dioxide and give off a waste product, oxygen. Much of the oxygen animals and humans require is made by green plants. At night, when there is no light and photosynthesis cannot take place, plants give off carbon dioxide. Humans, of course, continually breathe in oxygen and give off carbon dioxide.

Topics: Plant Processes; Ecosystems; Plant Parts; Atmosphere; Chemical Reactions; Energy.

DOING IT:

1. *Shades of Green:* Collect some leaves. Arrange them according to their shade of green (light to dark). Why are different leaves different shades? Is there a relationship between where leaves are found (e.g. top branches of a tree, on a shrub in the shade) and their shade of green?

2. *Extracting Chlorophyll:* Place a *fresh* leaf in a container with a small amount of rubbing alcohol (note: dipping the leaf in boiling water first speeds the extraction). Examine the leaf after a few hours. The leaf's green colouring (chlorophyll) is in the alcohol. Try a variety of leaves.

3. *Blocking Sunlight:* Cut pieces of cardboard, each just large enough to make a "patch" on a leaf of a shrub or a tree. Use paper clips to attach patches to several leaves. After four days to a week, remove the patches and examine the lighter-coloured spots on the leaves. The patches prevent light from reaching the spots and photosynthesis cannot take place.

4. *Blocking Carbon Dioxide:* A plant gets much of its carbon dioxide through the stomata. Another important part of a leaf's surface is the cuticle, a waxy coating. The cuticle is waterproof, keeps moisture inside the leaf, and is transparent so that the sun can shine through. Cover a leaf with petroleum jelly. The jelly blocks the stomata but, like the cuticle, allows sunlight through. What happens after a few days? Does this happen to leaves at other times of the year?

AIR CONDITIONERS

Plants act like air conditioners; as water evaporates from their leaves, the surrounding air is cooled. Use a plastic bag to see how much water evaporates from leaves.

MATERIALS: Plastic bag; small pebble; twist tie; measuring cup.

DOING IT:

1. Find a healthy tree or shrub. Inflate a plastic bag to make sure it doesn't have any holes. Put the bag over a small twig covered with leaves; count the number of leaves enclosed in the bag. Drop a pebble into the bag so that the bag hangs down. Use a twist tie to securely close the plastic bag around the base of the twig.

2. Examine the plastic bag after 24 hours. Why is there water in the bag?

3. Carefully pour the water from the plastic bag into a measuring cup. How much water evaporated from the leaves? Divide the amount of water by the number of leaves enclosed by the plastic bag to estimate how much water would transpire from one leaf.

Plants will react if you talk to them. But they don't react to what you're saying. When you talk, you breathe out carbon dioxide and water, two things plants use.

4. Count the number of leaves on a small tree. Multiply the number of leaves by the amount of water transpired by one leaf. How much water evaporates from the tree in one day? How would transpiration affect the temperature and humidity in a forest area? What effect would trees have on the environment in a polluted, urban area?

5. *Extension:* Compare the amount of water transpired in daylight hours and during the night. Compare a cloudy day with a sunny day.

The sundew is a pretty, innocent-looking little plant that grows with its leaves pressed close to the ground. There are many hairs on the leaves, and each hair is covered in droplets of sticky liquid. The droplets shine like dew and give the plant its name. An insect which lands on the hairs is trapped by the sticky liquid. The hairs bend over, enclose the insect, and the insect is digested.

"Transpiration" occurs when a plant's roots absorb moisture from the soil. The water passes through the plant's stem or trunk, through the branches to the leaves. Inside the leaves, the plant uses some of the water to make food for itself and grow. But there is more water in the leaves than the plant needs. This extra water evaporates into the air from the surface of the leaves. When water evaporates, it changes from a liquid to a gas. The change uses up heat energy in the surrounding air, so the air becomes cooler. On a hot, sunny day, many litres of water can evaporate into the air from a large tree. Desert plants, like cacti, have adapted so that they do not transpire as much water as other plants. The pull of transpiration is one cause of fluids flowing up through a plant from its roots; capillary action is another cause.

Topics: Plant Processes; Measurement.

LOOKING AT LEAVES

Leaves come in different shapes and sizes and with different edges. Get to know the leaves around you.

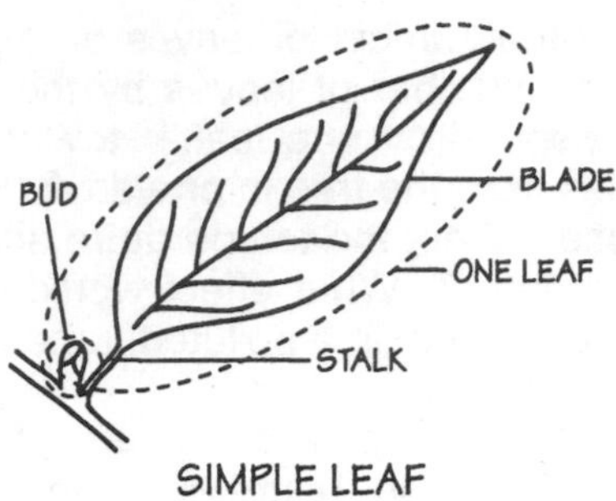

SIMPLE LEAF

MATERIALS: Ruler; paper; pencil.

DOING IT:

1. Examine the illustrations showing common leaf shapes and edges.

2. Go out to your backyard or a park and look for leaves. *Never strip leaves from trees.* How many different leaf shapes can you find? How many types of leaf edges can you find? Can you find a tooth within a lobe? Can you find a simple leaf? Can you find a compound leaf?

A typical leaf consists of a flat blade and a stalk which connects the blade to the plant's stem. Leaves come in a variety of shapes. Although some leaves have smooth outside edges, most are toothed to some degree. Sometimes, you can find a tooth within a larger lobe on a leaf (a lobe has a primary vein; a tooth has only a secondary vein). Leaves are divided into two main types: simple and compound. A simple leaf usually has one blade, a stalk, and a bud at the base of the stalk. A compound leaf has two or more leaflets and a bud at the base of a single stalk. To figure out whether you have a leaf or a leaflet, check the bud; a leaf always has a bud at its base, a leaflet doesn't. Leaves play an important role in determining a plant's outline, particularly a tree's shape. Some trees have only a thin sprinkling of leaves, which means you can easily see the branches. In other trees, the leaves form a solid barrier, concealing most of the branches. When these trees shed their leaves for winter, they can look startlingly different.

Topics: Plant Parts; Classification.

3. Compare leaves. What shape of leaf is most common in your area? What type of leaf edge is most common? Are most leaves simple or compound? What are the differences between leaves? Are leaves from the same plant, or even the same branch, exactly alike? How many veins do different leaves have? Do the top and bottom surfaces of a leaf feel different?

4. Measure the lengths of different leaves. How many different leaf lengths are there? Which length is most common? Which length is least common? Why are leaves different lengths? What's the largest leaf -- both in length and width -- you can find?

5. *Variation:* Prepare a set of leaf rubbings made from plants in the area. The challenge then becomes matching the leaf rubbings to real leaves.

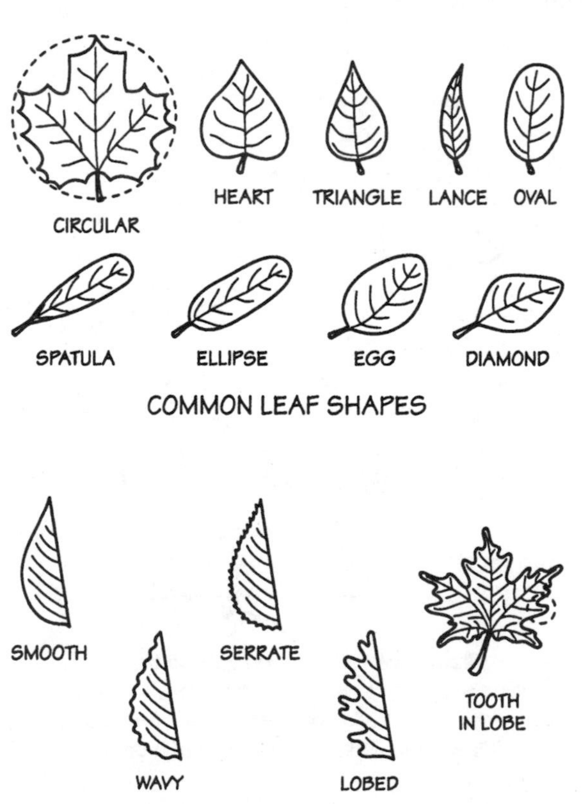

COMMON LEAF SHAPES

COMMON LEAF EDGES

FLOWER POWER

Stop and smell the flowers! While you're at it, examine the different parts of a flower, compare different types of flowers, and explore the pollination process.

MATERIALS: Flower (e.g. lily, tulip, violet); knife; magnifying glass. Optional -- plant identification guide.

DOING IT:

1. Start by examining and dissecting a flower. Lilies and tulips are easy flowers to dissect. If you pick a wild flower to dissect, try to use a violet. Violets can be picked without harming the species because they have a second, small flower hidden at the base of the plant, which takes over if the main flower disappears.

2. Dissect the flower by first carefully plucking off the petals. How do the petals feel? What colour are they? Are they the same colour all over? Next, look for the stamen and/or pistil. Compare the stamen or pistil to the illustrations on this page. Can you find all the parts? Cut open a pistil's ovary to see the tiny "eggs" (which will become seeds).

3. Go to a park or other area with flower gardens. How many different flowers can you find? *Remember just to look, and not to pick or trample!*

4. Find three examples of one type of flower. Count the number of pistils, stamens, petals, and sepals on each. Not all plants are the same and the number of each part can vary. Do all the parts look the same? Are all the petals the same size? Are all the stamens the same shape? What colour are the sepals?

5. Try a pollination demonstration. Pretend your finger is an insect. You've come to a flower to get nectar. By accident, you hit the anther. Take a close look at the yellow, powdery substance on your finger. Then your finger "flies" to another plant to get more nectar and the pollen lands on that flower's stigma. Pollination completed!

6. Look at the ways flowers grow to aid pollination. With snapdragons, for example, an insect entering the flower in search of nectar must first brush against the stigma (where the insect will deposit or pick up pollen). Plants that depend on insects for pollination are usually colourful and have a sweet-smelling nectar to attract the insects. Wind-pollinated plants have no need for colour or odour. They may have stamens that stick up from the flower or stigmas that are large and branched. The pollen grains are often small, light, and dry.

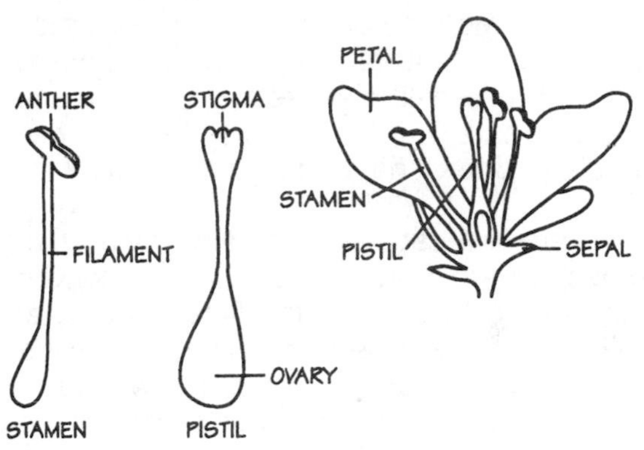

The flower is the part of a flowering plant that takes care of reproduction. The "stamen" is the male, pollen-producing part of a flower. It's made up of an anther (tiny, bag-like structure) and a filament (thread-like stalk). The "pistil" is the female, seed-bearing part of a flower. It consists of a stigma and an ovary (hollow structure at the base containing "eggs"). "Pollination" occurs when a pollen grain is transferred by insects, birds, or the wind from the stamen to the pistil. The grain swells as it absorbs water, sugar, and other materials from the pistil's stigma. The pollen then "germinates" -- it grows a tube downward to the pistil's ovary and, after reaching the ovary's "eggs", produces seeds. Seeds stay in the ovary until they are ripe and ready to be scattered by the wind, animals, humans, water, or expulsion. Some flowers have both a pollen-bearing stamen and a pistil with an ovary; these are called "perfect" flowers. "Male" flowers have only the stamen; "female" flowers have only the pistil. All flowers have petals, which attract insects and protect the stamen and pistil. Sepals -- which are really specialized leaves -- encircle the petals of a flower and also protect it. Sepals are often green, as in roses, or they can be the same colour as the petals, as in tulips.

Topics: Plant Parts; Plant Processes; Insects.

BRANCHES AND BUDS

Winter and spring are good times of the year to explore branches and buds. Dissect a bud. Then, count bud scale scars to estimate the age of a branch or twig.

MATERIALS: Knife; magnifying glass.

DOING IT:

1. Choose an interesting twig with a large terminal bud. A lilac bush twig is a good choice.

2. Is the twig long or short (the length may give you a clue about its age)? What colour is the twig (e.g. green, brown, reddish)? Is it smooth, rough, or fuzzy? Is it round or flat? Is the twig straight or does it have many crooks in it?

3. There are usually enlargements on the twig (nodes) where leaves occur. If the leaves are out, there will be tiny buds (lateral buds) at the stalk of each leaf (the bud remains when the leaf falls off). How many nodes or leaves are there? There are spaces (internodes) of various lengths between nodes (or leaves). Which is the largest? What's the leaf pattern -- are the nodes/leaves directly *opposite* each other, on the same level, or do the nodes/leaves *alternate* (i.e. one bud and then a little further up another bud)?

4. Where's the terminal bud? What colour is it? What shape is it? Is it sticky, hairy, or smooth? Usually, a waxy or fuzzy coat prevents water loss. How many scale leaves (at base of bud) does the terminal bud have?

5. Dissect *one* large terminal bud. Very carefully, remove one layer at a time. Line the layers up in a row. Use a magnifying glass to examine the pieces of the bud. What shapes do the pieces have? They should look like tiny leaves. Is there anything in the centre of the bud? There may be a tiny flower.

6. Examine the twig for a rough thickening of the stem or bark (bud scale scar) at places where the terminal bud used to be. The distance between rings indicates the amount of growth in one year. Did the twig grow the same amount each year? Count the growth areas between bud scale scars (or the number of bud scale scars, minus 1) to get the age of the twig.

7. Examine several other twigs and calculate their ages. How old is the oldest twig? How much older is it than the other twigs you find?

During the summer, trees and other plants use the sun's energy to manufacture food and grow. They also produce "buds" from which next year's leaves and flowers develop. A bud is an immature, miniature plant stem. Depending on the type of bud, the miniature stem may develop leaves, flowers, or both.

Plant stems and branches generally perform two functions: they support leaves and flowers, and they carry water and food from place to place within a plant. The typical stem or branch is either soft or woody. This activity works best with woody twigs on shrubs and bushes, and with twigs and branches on trees. There are scars on each twig. The scars are formed when the "terminal bud" -- the large bud at the end of the twig -- opens. When the scales that grow around the new bud fall off, they leave a thickened, circular ring around the twig. This is called a "bud scale scar". You can calculate the age of the twig by counting the bud scale scars.

Topics: Plant Parts; Plant Processes; Measurement.

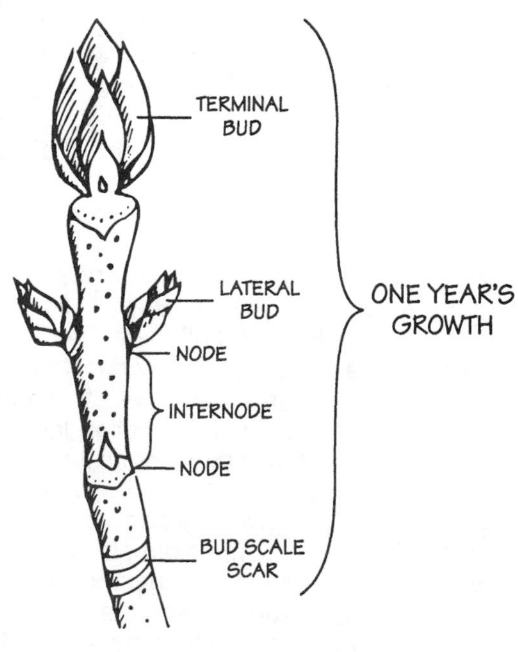

Up The Tubes

The way plants suck up water is similar to the way you suck liquid through a straw. Use a celery stalk and some coloured water to explore capillary action.

MATERIALS: Fresh celery stalk (with leaves on it); knife; drinking glass; water; red or blue food colouring. Optional -- fresh, white carnation.

DOING IT:

1. Cut about 2 cm off the bottom of a long stalk of celery.

2. Half fill a drinking glass with water. Add several drops of food colouring. Put the cut end of the celery into the glass.

3. Leave the celery in the glass for a few hours. Check it occasionally. You should be able to see the colour gradually travel up the stalk to the leaves.

4. When the colour has reached the leaves, cut a small piece off the bottom of the celery stalk. You will see coloured spots along the edge. These are the ends of little tubes that take water up the stalk to the leaves.

5. Cut the celery stalk lengthwise and try to follow a tube up to the leaves.

6. *Variation:* Put the cut stem of a white carnation into some coloured water. What happens to the carnation after a few hours?

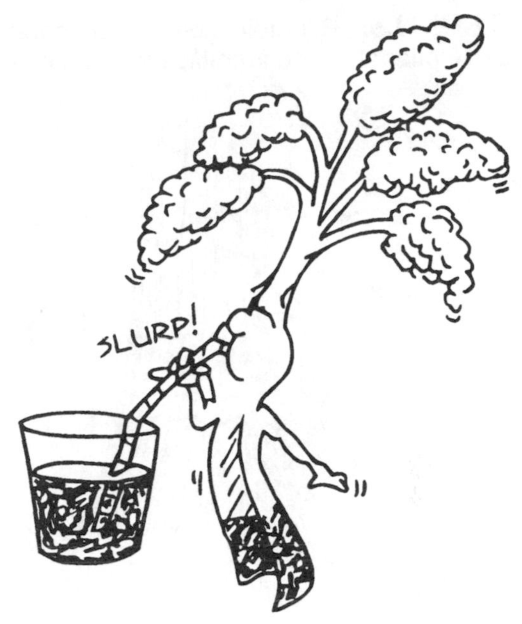

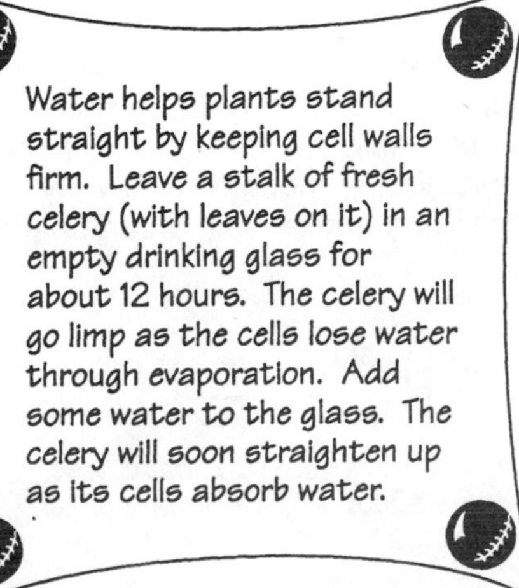

Liquids travel up plant stems. A plant stem carries water and nutrients to the leaves where they are used in the manufacture of food. A large tree can pump as much as 900 litres of water to its leaves on a hot day. Fine tubes running up the roots, stems, and leaves of plants help to draw water from the ground to the top of even the tallest trees through "capillary action". Capillary action is the tendency of water to be pulled into very thin tubes. The thinner the tube, the higher into the tube capillary action draws the water. Capillary action is based on attraction between molecules, the same attraction that causes surface tension. When water is in a tiny tube, water molecules at the top are pulled up the tube and then pull the molecules behind them. If you dip the end of a paper towel strip into some water, you can watch the water creep slowly up the strip. The paper towel has long, narrow, tube-like gaps between its fibres and the water travels up these gaps. Sponges soak up water through capillary action. A sponge is filled with many narrow spaces that act like thin tubes. Note that capillary action works with transpiration to help water flow through a plant.

Topics: Plant Processes; Forces.

TREE I.D.

Trees are some of the easier types of plants to identify. Compare two very different approaches to tree identification.

MATERIALS: Blindfold; paper or notebook; pencil. Optional -- tree identification guide.

Trees are flowering plants that produce woody tissue, continue to grow year after year, and have a main stem from which branches and twigs extend to form a characteristic shape. *All* trees have flowers. Some trees, such as fruit trees, have obvious flowers; other trees, like elms and some maples, have flowers which lack petals and are harder to see. There are two main types of trees: coniferous and deciduous. Deciduous trees have broad leaves that are shed at the end of each growing season (usually in the fall). Conifers are also called evergreens because their narrow needles do not turn brown and drop to the ground every fall. Conifers lose their needles slowly throughout the whole year. Some broad-leafed shrubs follow the coniferous pattern, and the larch sheds its needle-like leaves deciduously. Generally speaking, the wood of coniferous trees is softer than that of deciduous trees. Therefore, conifers are sometimes referred to as "softwoods", while deciduous trees are "hardwoods". Trees come in a variety of heights. Some trees attain heights no greater than 5 m (shrubs), while taller trees can reach into the sky for more than 100 m. Trees are an important source of wood, food, and products such as resins, rubber, cork, quinine, turpentine, and cellulose.

Topics: Classification; Plant Parts; Resources.

DOING IT:

1. *Identification Through Experience:* People work in pairs. One partner is blindfolded. The sighted partner chooses a tree, leads the blindfolded person to it, and ensures the blindfolded person's safety as he or she examines the tree. The blindfolded person has about 5 minutes to get to know the tree. Hug the tree. How big is it? Can you reach around it? Run your hands up and down the tree. Press your cheek against the tree. Does the bark feel rough, smooth, uneven, or even? Sniff the tree. How does it smell? What does it remind you of? Can you find any leaves? How do they feel? Is the tree straight or crooked? Is the tree alive? After a few minutes, the sighted person leads his or her partner back to the starting point, but takes an indirect route (e.g. take some unnecessary turns, step over imaginary logs). The blindfolded person removes the blindfold and must then find the tree. How easy is it to "identify" the tree?

2. *Identification Through Analysis:* Choose a tree. Use the tree identification key on the following page to get to know the tree and to make a guess about what kind of tree it is. You may want to use a formal tree identification guide to precisely name the tree.

3. What's the difference between the two approaches to identification? When is one approach preferable to the other? In general, a single experience allows a person to identify a particular tree or a limited variety of trees. Analysis can help many people identify a large number of trees. A tree key is also helpful in communicating to people what they should look for if they're unfamiliar with a certain type of tree.

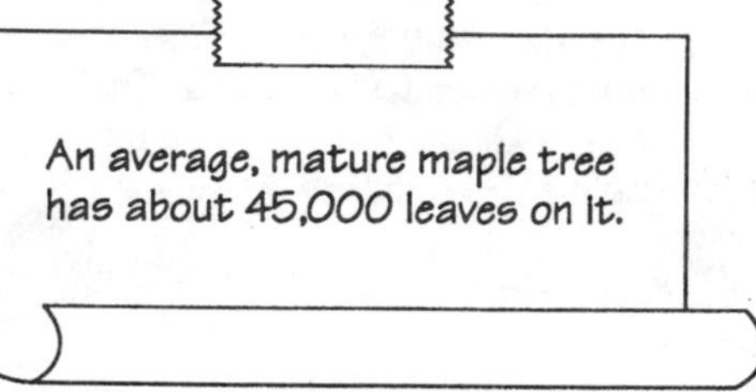

TREE IDENTIFICATION KEY

HEIGHT: How tall is the tree? Have someone whose height is known stand next to a tree. He or she becomes the "standard" unit of measurement. Walk about twenty paces away from the tree. At arm's length, hold up a straight stick or pencil. Sight the top of the stick with the top of the person's head. Move your thumb down along the stick until your thumb appears even with the person's feet. Now move the stick upward one "standard" unit at a time. Multiply the person's height by the number of "standards" to get the approximate height of the tree.

SHAPE: What is the tree's general shape?

ANGLE OF BRANCHES: Branches are the arms that give a tree its typical shape. Examine how the branches grow from the trunk. Do more branches grow in one particular direction? If so, which direction? Does this pattern occur in other trees of the same type? Could other trees or buildings block the sun and therefore affect the branch pattern?

BARK: Do the grooves in the bark run up and down or sideways? Can you see different shades in the colour of the bark? The following are some example barks and trees: shaggy, in long, loose strips ➔ shagbark hickory; gray, mottled with yellow ➔ sycamore; white, peeling ➔ white birch; light gray, smooth ➔ American beech.

LEAVES/NEEDLES: Does the tree have needles or leaves? If the tree has leaves, what is the general shape of the leaves?

If the tree has needles, pick up a needle from the ground under the tree. Place the needle between your thumb and index finger and feel its shape. Does it roll easily? Is it round, square, or flat? Look at the needles on a branch to see how they grow. Do the needles grow alone, in twos, threes, or clusters?

- If the needles grow alone and the needle feels *square* ➔ the tree is a *spruce*.
- If the needles grow alone and the needle feels *flat* ➔ the tree is a *fir*.
- If the needles grow in clusters of two or more on a branch and the needle is semicircular so that when you put two needles together they form a complete circle or *pie* ➔ the tree is a *pine*.
- If the needles grow in clusters of ten to forty so there are *lots* of needles on a short spur-shoot (and the tree loses its needles deciduously) ➔ the tree is a *larch*.

Notice that the characteristic and the tree begin with the same letter (e.g. square and spruce).

TYPE OF LEAF: Leaves are divided into two main types: simple and compound. A simple leaf usually has one blade, a stalk, and a bud at the base of the stalk. A compound leaf has two or more leaflets and a bud at the base of a single stalk. To figure out whether you have a leaf or a leaflet, check the bud; a leaf always has a bud at its base, a leaflet doesn't.

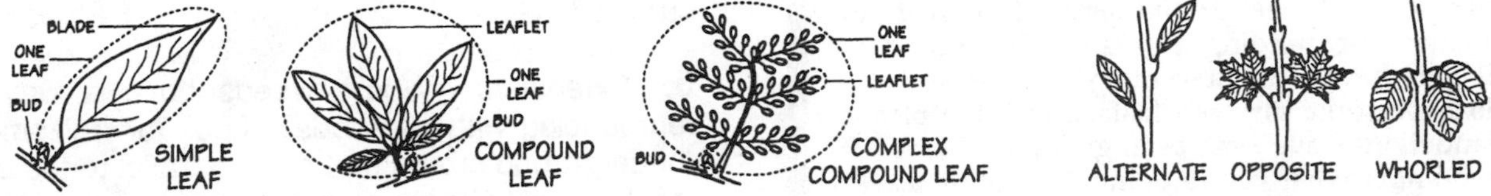

LEAF PATTERN: There are three typical patterns: alternate, opposite, or whorled. Only four common trees have the opposite leaf pattern: *m*aple, *a*sh, *d*ogwood, and *horse* chestnut. Here's a simple way to remember the trees: MAD Horse.

FLOWERS: All trees have flowers. The following list describes some common trees: obvious flowers ➔ fruit trees and magnolia; lacking petals, harder to see ➔ elms and some maples; catkins ➔ alders, birches, oaks, and nut trees; many small flowers surrounded by white or coloured bracts ➔ dogwood.

FRUIT: The fruit occurs after the flower and contains seeds. The following list describes some common trees: fleshy fruit ➔ apple, cherry, pear; winged fruit ➔ maple, elm, hoptree; cone ➔ conifer; nut ➔ beech, hickory; acorn ➔ oak.

THE HARDY DANDELION

A weed is a "weed" only if we say it is. Weeds are usually wild plants thriving where we don't want them to thrive. Explore the dandelion's hardy characteristics.

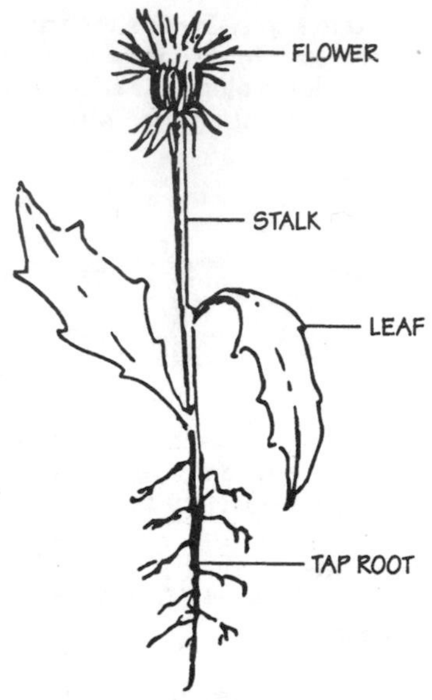

Weeds are just plants whose virtues we haven't yet discovered -- but they can be so annoying until their virtues are found! How are weeds better able to survive than most plants humans cultivate? All plants survive by remaining alive and reproducing. Weeds tend to do both well. Weeds have sturdy bodies and extensive root systems, which means that, in general, you can't kill a weed just by snipping off its top. Weeds often grow faster than other plants. Weeds tend to be plentiful and produce huge numbers of seeds. Finally, weed seeds are able to last longer without sprouting than other seeds. An interesting example of a hardy weed is the dandelion. The dandelion is found almost everywhere. Its long tap root reaches deep into the soil. The dandelion's circular leaf arrangement close to the ground serves to crowd out smaller surrounding plants. Although dandelions have frustrated many a gardener, they do have some virtues. In fact, in some places, dandelions have even been grown as a crop. If you know what you're doing, the young leaves are good in salads or can be boiled and taste a little like spinach. The milky juice in a dandelion's stem makes an excellent wine. Last but not least, the roots may be roasted, pounded down to a powder, and used as a substitute for coffee.

Topics: Plant Parts; Measurement.

MATERIALS: Trowel; measuring tape; string; stakes; magnifying glass.

DOING IT:

1. *Roots:* Dig up a dandelion and try to get most of the long tap root. If parts of the root break, dig out the pieces remaining in the soil. This can be quite a challenge! Measure the tap root and compare its length with the part of the plant above ground? How does root length help the plant to survive?

2. *Number:* Mark off an area of 10 square metres in a field with stakes and string. Divide the area into ten plots of 1 square metre each. Working in teams of two, people should count the number of dandelions in a plot. How many dandelions are in the total 10 square metres? Compare the results of each plot. Why are there more or less dandelions in certain plots?

3. *Seeds:* Estimate the number of seeds each dandelion produces. Carefully count the number of seeds per flower (use a magnifying glass) and multiply by the number of flowers. How many seeds would have to survive for a plant to maintain itself as a species? Is it likely that all plant seeds will grow? Does the number of seeds a plant produces help its survival?

4. *More on Seeds:* If the flower head has turned into a white puffball, examine the silvery parachute seeds. How easily can they be blown off? Are some seeds carried long distances by the wind? How can this help the dandelion to survive?

5. *Extension:* Which weeds have a way of reproducing without seeds? Look for "rhizomes" (underground stems that grow parallel to the surface). Aerial shoots come off the rhizomes at intervals, producing new plants. Crabgrass is a good example of a plant that reproduces by rhizomes as well as by seeds. What are the advantages of this type of reproduction?

NEIGHBOURS

Plants can be found almost everywhere on Earth -- in fields, on mountains, in cracks in sidewalks, and in the water. Visit a plant community.

MATERIALS: Paper; pencils; measuring tape. Optional -- plant identification guide.

DOING IT:

1. Pick a plant community: a clump of trees, a group of shrubs, a lawn, a grassy field, the edge of a stream, the steep slope of a hill, a vacant lot, or cracks in a sidewalk. Get ready to make notes and sketches (these don't seem important until you can't remember something later!).

2. What's the dominant plant in the community you're exploring? In every plant community, certain plants dominate. The dominant plants are the ones that determine what other kinds of plants grow around them (i.e. they affect the sunlight and water available). Dominant plants are usually the largest, most numerous types present. For example, ragweed might be the dominant plant in a field, while oak may be the dominant plant in a forest.

3. How many layers can you find in the plant community? Most plant communities have at least two layers of life. The highest layer is usually the one in which the dominant plant is present. What types of plants are present in each layer? For example, the upper layer in a field may be ragweed, and the lower layer may be grass of some sort.

4. Keep an eye out for non-plants, like mushrooms, growing on decaying leaves or branches.

5. Take a plant census. How many different plants can you find in the plant community: more than 10? more than 50? How similar are they in height, colour, and number? You may want to identify plants using a plant identification guide.

6. *Extension:* Explore and compare several plant communities.

Certain plants enjoy growing next to each other. The plants seem to grow better together than they do apart. "Companion planting" is putting good friends together in the garden. Corn and beans are good companions (other plant combinations seem to cause these plants to be weak). Peas and onions aren't compatible at all; gardeners avoid putting these two together.

A lichen is two living things in one: a fungus that provides shelter and retains water, and a blue-green/green alga that makes food. Search on dead branches, logs, and rocks for lichens. Examine a lichen with a magnifying glass. How would you describe it? Lichens can withstand extremes in temperature and are found in deserts as well as polar regions.

When you find one plant, you'll usually find another. Different plants living together in the same area form a "plant community". The fact that the plants are neighbours means they affect each other in certain ways. Plants can compete for the same water and nutrients in the soil. One plant may block out another's sunlight. One type of plant may crowd out another type.

Topics: Habitat; Ecosystems.

PLANT DYES

Long before synthetic dyes were invented, people used natural dyes made from parts of plants. Make and use your own natural dyes.

MATERIALS: Plant parts; knife; water; containers (nonmetal); pots (glass or enamel); heat source (e.g. stove); spoon; strainer; 100% natural wool (it takes the dye easily); rubber gloves. Optional -- alum and cream of tartar (available from a drugstore); teaspoon; laundry detergent.

DOING IT:

1. **This activity should be done with adult supervision.**

2. Collect plant parts to make natural dyes (you may want to start with one colour). Examples:

- dandelion roots, beetroot, cherries, red cabbage, strawberries, or red raspberries -- red/pink
- goldenrod flowers, onion skins, ragweed, carrot skin, sunflower seeds, or birch leaves -- yellow
- instant coffee, walnut shells, or bark -- brown
- blueberries, elderberries, black raspberries, or red rose petals -- purple/blue
- grapes -- violet
- spinach or dandelion greens -- green

If you're collecting plants from a natural area, *take only what you need.* **Don't taste the plants.**

3. Keep each type of plant separate. Rinse off any dirt. Finely chop all leaves, roots, skins, stems, etc. Crush berries.

4. Soak each plant material in water -- in separate containers -- overnight. Put enough water over the plant material to cover it; the more water you use, the lighter coloured the dye.

5. Simmer (stirring occasionally) each plant material and its water in a clean pot for half an hour. Strain each dye.

6. If you want to use a mordant, completely dissolve about 2 ml (1/2 teaspoon) of alum in every 470 ml of warm dye liquid. You may have to experiment with the amount of alum (too much can make the wool sticky).

7. Wet the wool. Then put it in a pot with a dye so that the wool is completely covered. Simmer (don't boil), stirring occasionally, for at least half an hour or until the colouring of the wool is deep enough (remember, it looks darker when wet). If you've used a mordant: After the initial 20 minutes, add cream of tartar (in same amount as the alum) and simmer until colour is deep enough.

8. Let the wool cool in the dye. Wring out the wool and rinse it in baths of lukewarm water. Hang the wool to dry (not in direct sunlight).

9. *Extension:* Test your dyed wool for colourfastness by heating it in soapy water for about 15 minutes. Does the colour look the same?

10. *Extension:* Experiment with dyeing variables: dye with and without a mordant; dye other materials (e.g. cotton; vary the amount of mordant); vary dyeing time; vary dye temperature; try different kinds and amounts of plants.

Over 5,000 years ago, probably because of accidental staining, people discovered that leaves, flowers, fruits, stems, bark, roots, and some animal and mineral substances can be used to permanently colour clothes, pottery, and other objects. Dyes add colour to other materials because they can mix completely in a liquid, and then easily enter and cling to the material being dyed. To create a stronger bond between a dye and the material being dyed, dyers often use "mordants". Mordants are chemical substances like alum, iron, and chrome that attach themselves to fibres and help the dye take. The dyed material then becomes more "colourfast", which means the dye will not fade, bleed, or run easily.

Topics: Plant Parts; Chemical Reactions; Scientific Method.

RUBBINGS

You can create rubbings using stumps, bark, and leaves. The rubbings are a permanent record of plants -- and make attractive wall decorations.

MATERIALS: Crayons or artist's charcoal; lightweight white paper; masking tape; newspaper.

DOING IT:

1. *Stump Rubbings:* Smooth a sheet of paper across a stump and use masking tape to secure the paper in place. Use the full length of a crayon or piece of charcoal to rub across the paper. Rub in just *one* direction across the stump. The rings and other markings on the stump will show on your paper.

2. *Bark Rubbings:* Find a tree with interesting bark. Securely tape a sheet of paper to the tree using masking tape; make sure the spot you choose is free of moss and lichens because these will distort your bark pattern. Use the full length of a crayon or piece of charcoal to rub across the paper. Rub in just *one* direction. The bark pattern will show on your paper.

3. *Leaf Rubbings:* Collect a variety of leaves; include different leaf shapes and edges, as well as simple and compound leaves. Stack several layers of newspaper on a flat surface to make a padding for the rubbing. Arrange the leaves in an attractive pattern on the newspaper, taking up just enough space to fill a sheet of paper. Place a sheet of paper over the arrangement; you may want to tape the paper in place. Use the full length of a crayon or piece of charcoal to lightly rub over the paper. The rubbing should reveal a fair bit of detail.

4. *Extension:* Put together a collection of identified stump, bark, and leaf rubbings. Compare the rubbings of different plants.

The world's tallest trees are redwoods in California. The trees can grow to be more than 110 m high, or twice the height of Niagara Falls.

"Cork" is the protective, waterproof, outer covering of the stems and roots of all woody plants. Water from a plant's roots can't pass through the cork, so all the cells outside it die off to form the rough outer layer of a tree called bark. Cork is light; it floats; and it is an excellent insulating material. The cork oak, which has a thick cork layer, is the source of commercial cork.

Nature's beauty and complexity can often be more readily appreciated by taking an artistic approach to observation. Rubbings can help you notice things you might not otherwise notice. For example, tree bark rubbings can make patterns in the bark more apparent. Flat-barked trees work best for rubbings. Young gray birch trees produce a strong, obvious rubbing pattern. The red oak has whitish "ski trails" that run vertically down its trunk. Slippery elm and butternut trees have bark that looks like it has been ironed. The sycamore has one of the most beautiful, intricate bark patterns of any tree.

Topics: Plant Parts.

SPORE PRINTS

Spores continuously fall from the gills of mature mushrooms. Spore prints make interesting works of art.

MATERIALS: Knife; paper; bowl; hair spray, varnish spray, or other fixative.

DOING IT:

1. Look for mushrooms growing in shady, moist areas.

2. Cut a mushroom cap off its stem. Place the gills down on a sheet of paper. Cover the cap with a bowl (to protect the spores from air currents) and let it sit overnight. **Always wash your hands after handling unidentified mushrooms!**

3. Carefully remove the mushroom cap from the paper in the morning. Spore print designs will always be interesting. The spores of some mushrooms may also be beautifully coloured.

4. To preserve a spore print, carefully spray it with hair spray or another fixative like varnish. Be sure to aim the nozzle at the print **only**! Also, don't hold the spray container too close to the paper or the spray will blow away the spores.

The first things to grow on jagged surfaces of rocks torn by earthquakes or after catastrophes like landslides, avalanches, and fires are hardy growths like algae (on rocks, on bark, in ponds), mushrooms. lichens, mosses, horsetails, and liverworts.

Mushrooms (part of the Fungi Kingdom) are characterized by spore-bearing gills on the underside of an umbrella-shaped or cone-shaped cap. Mushrooms reproduce through the production of spores. One of the first steps in identifying a mushroom is to find the colour of its spores; spore prints make identification easier. Once considered a delicacy, mushrooms are now grown commercially. A variety of mushrooms are available in stores. Although mushrooms contain some protein and minerals, they are largely water. Inedible, or poisonous, mushrooms are often referred to as "toadstools".

'arts.

Most algae are tiny -- less than a millimetre long -- single-celled organisms that belong to the Protista Kingdom. Seaweeds are algae which have developed into a many-celled form. Some seaweeds grow up to 60 m long, but most are about 1 m. Seaweeds have no real roots, stems, or leaves, like most plants do. They are rich in protein. You probably eat seaweed without knowing it. Agar, from red seaweed, goes into candy, ice cream, sherbet, canned meat, and fish products. Seaweed can also be dried and burned as a fuel.

LIVING CREATURES

"Zoology" is the scientific study of animals. It is a branch of biology, the scientific study of living things. Modern zoology studies cell structure and function, as well as psychological, anthropological, and ecological aspects of animals.

What's the difference between a living and a nonliving thing? There are five basic life processes (processes that make living things living): getting and using food (metabolism); releasing energy (respiration); removing waste (elimination); growth; and reproduction.

Birds can't stand the taste of Monarch butterflies. The butterflies taste the way they do because they eat milkweed when they are larvae (young insects). Since the Viceroy butterfly looks very much like the Monarch (this is called "mimicry"), birds avoid it too -- even though it is, to birds, quite tasty.

A cat will always land on its feet. Cats have an amazing sense of balance due to the very sensitive balancing mechanism in their inner ear and the suppleness of their bodies. Their tail also helps cats keep their balance.

It takes 9 whole months before a human baby is born. It takes only 1.5 months for a baby dog, about 1 month for baby rabbits, and the American opossum normally carries its young only 12 to 13 days. On the other hand, it takes 11 months before a baby horse is born, and just over 20 months for a baby Asiatic elephant!

The carpet beetle is a great cleaner-upper. It will eat anything -- even woollen carpets. The beetle's favourite meal, however, is leftover bits of dead animals that no other creatures want, like hair. The beetle leaves nothing of rotting animals except the bones (they're a bit tough even for this champion chomper!).

Words for animal babies are plentiful. Everyone knows a baby cat is a kitten, but did you know that a baby swan is a cygnet? A baby kangaroo is a joey; a baby turkey is a poult; and a baby mackerel is a spike, blinker, or tinker. Whelp is one name for a baby dog or tiger. A baby pig is a shoat or a farrow. A baby fox, beaver, rabbit, or cat is a kit.

CREATURE TREE

Rather than looking at thousands of animals one at a time, it's more useful to understand the characteristics of groups of animals. Play the creature tree game.

MATERIALS: Following page; paper; pencil.

DOING IT:

1. Write up a fact sheet for each of the dots making up the creature tree illustrated. The detail on the fact sheets depends on the age of the players. Fact sheets might contain the formal and/or informal name of a phylum and two or three points about the phylum and/or class.

2. Make a creature tree by having people sit or stand in the positions of the dots. In general, animals go from simple to more complex up the tree trunk. Chordates (having a cord) are at the top of the trunk, with each major class of vertebrates as a "branch" above it. Mammals make up the tree's crown. Each person has a fact sheet about his or her position.

3. Begin the game by having each part of the tree introduce itself; people can read aloud the points on their fact sheets.

4. A leader, who has a copy of all the fact sheets, uses the sheets to call out a series of directions. For example: Wave your arms if you live in salt water. Clap your hands if you have stinging tentacles. Who is a worm? Who has a shell? All mammals jump up and down and count to five. Shake hands with animals most like you (animals next to you in the tree).

5. If someone who should respond doesn't, or someone doesn't know an answer, or a response takes "too long", the leader yells "scatter!" Everyone runs to a predetermined spot (e.g. a fence 50 m away, or the furthest corner of a room), runs back, and reforms the tree as quickly as possible. The leader can count out loud to time how quickly the tree reforms.

6. The game goes on as long as you wish. Rotate positions to help players become familiar with all parts of the tree.

7. *Variation:* Make a creature tree by putting the fact sheets in the position of each of the dots. People can play the game individually or in groups. Individuals or groups take turns following the leader's directions (e.g. point at certain parts of the tree, find certain information). When the leader yells "scatter!", he or she scrambles the sheets of paper and players must work together to quickly arrange them again.

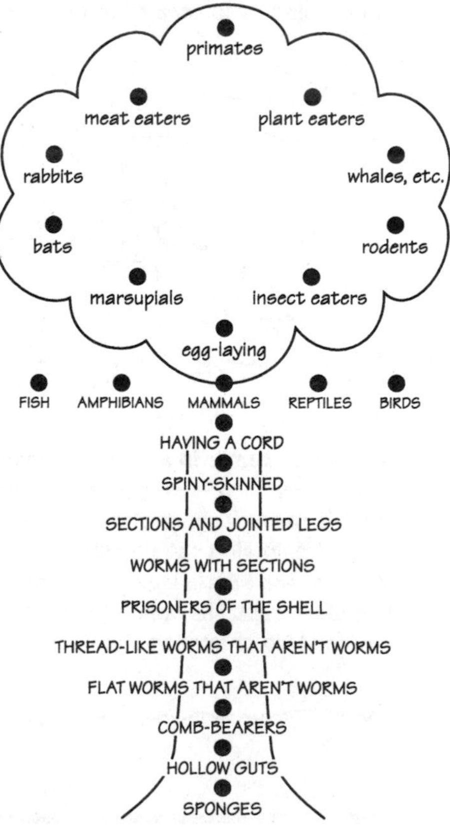

Different classifications break down the Animal Kingdom slightly differently. The following page lists ten major phyla. The animals that make up a given phylum may live in every part of the environment and differ in size and behaviour. The one thing they have in common is their basic structure. For example, the Arthropods phylum includes lobsters, spiders, millipedes, centipedes, and all insects. Their common structure is that their bodies are divided into segments and their legs are jointed. No other phylum has this structure.

Topics: Classification; Animal Characteristics; Mammals; Birds; Insects.

THE ANIMAL KINGDOM (MAJOR PHYLA)

PHYLUM PORIFERONS (SPONGES): Animals with large pores. All live in water -- some in fresh, but most in salt water. Attach themselves to a permanent structure like a rock. Filter water filled with microscopic organisms through their body to obtain food.

PHYLUM CNIDARIA (HOLLOW GUTS): Water animals with stinging tentacles. Most live in salt water. If you poked your fist into the top of a round balloon partially filled with water, what you would see would be the general form of these animals. The deep pit or cavity created by your fist would be the hollow gut. The gut is lined with cells that digest food. The water within the balloon would represent the body fluids. Examples: jellyfish, Portuguese man-of-war.

PHYLUM CTENOPHORES (COMB-BEARERS): Animals that look like "hollow guts", but have a slightly different structure. Have a small, transparent body. Rows of little combs cover the body. These combs help the animals to get food and move about. Appear in both fresh and salt water.

PHYLUM FLATWORMS (FLAT WORMS THAT AREN'T REALLY WORMS): Animals that are flat and ribbon-thin. Occur either in fresh water or as parasites (e.g. tapeworm) in the bodies of other animals.

PHYLUM NEMATODES (THREAD-LIKE WORMS THAT AREN'T REALLY WORMS): Roundworms. Animals with an outer coat made of noncellular material. Have a fluid-filled chamber separating their body from their insides. Many look like tiny pieces of moving thread. Found in water, soil, and as parasites in the bodies of other animals. Examples: pinworm, threadworm, eelworm.

PHYLUM MOLLUSCS (PRISONERS OF THE SHELL): Soft-bodied animals which require a shell to protect themselves. All have a mantle that covers their body and secretes the shell. Most occur in salt and fresh water. Examples: snail, oyster, clam, squid, octopus.

PHYLUM ANNELIDS (WORMS WITH SECTIONS): Segmented worms. No legs. If you take a close look at the body of a worm, you'll see that it seems to be divided into a series of rings or ring-like grooves. Each part of the body is like a tiny compartment. Largest number of these animals live in salt water, but many species live in fresh water, moist soil, or as parasites in the bodies of other animals. Range in length from 0.5 mm to 3 m. Examples: earthworm (occupies a central position in the Animal Kingdom between the very simple and the very complex), bristleworm, leech.

PHYLUM ARTHROPODS (SECTIONS AND JOINTED LEGS): Animals with jointed legs and a segmented body. No backbone (horny exoskeleton instead). 80% of all animals belong to this phylum. Major classes: *crustaceans* (e.g. lobster, crab, shrimp); *millipedes* (four legs per body segment) and *centipedes* (two legs per body segment); *spiders* (eight legs, two body sections); *insects* (six legs, three body sections -- head, thorax, and abdomen).

PHYLUM ECHINODERMS (SPINY-SKINNED): Animals with many spines projecting from their body. Slow-moving creatures. All are found in salt water. Examples: starfish, sea urchin, sand dollar, sea cucumber.

PHYLUM CHORDATES (HAVING A CORD): Vertebrates are a subphylum. Vertebrates are animals with a spinal cord and a backbone (internal skeleton). An external skeleton can be bulky and must be thick to be strong; an internal skeleton can be strong while also being light and flexible. All animals in the vertebrates subphylum have a central heart and never more than four appendages (legs). Major classes of vertebrates: *fish* (cold-blooded animals that live and breathe in the water); *amphibians* (cold-blooded animals start in water and as they grow older spend more time on land; e.g. frog, toad, salamander); *reptiles* (cold-blooded and covered with scales; e.g. snake, lizard, turtle, alligator, crocodile); *birds* (warm-blooded, winged, covered with feathers); *mammals* (warm-blooded, have some hair on body, nurse their young, and have highly developed brain).

SPECIAL NOTES ON MAMMALS: *Egg-laying mammals* include the spiny anteater and duck-billed platypus; *marsupials* are pouched animals whose young are cared for in the pouch (e.g. opossum, kangaroo); *insect eaters* use underground tunnels (e.g. mole, shrew); *bats* are the only flying mammals; *rodents* have large, chisel-like teeth in the front of their mouths that grow constantly (e.g. squirrel, mouse, beaver, woodchuck, porcupine); *rabbits* aren't rodents because they have four incisor teeth in their upper jaw as compared to the rodents' two; *whales, dolphins, and porpoises* are mammals that live in the sea; *carnivores* are meat eaters (e.g. cat, wolf, bear, otter, skunk, weasel); *single-toed herbivores* are plant eaters (e.g. horse); *two-toed herbivores* are also plant eaters (e.g. sheep, cow, deer, moose); *primates* have eyes in the front of their head, an opposable thumb, and a large, well-developed brain (e.g. ape, humans).

ANIMALS WITH BACKBONES

There are five major groups or "classes" of animals with backbones. Get to know these animals through this vertebrate game.

"Vertebrates" are animals with a spinal cord and a backbone (internal skeleton). Three out of the five major vertebrate "classes" are cold-blooded. *Fish* live and breathe in water. They use "gills" to extract oxygen from the water. Some fish also breathe air with a lung. All fish lay their eggs in the water. Most fish have fins to help them swim and eyes located on the sides of their head. Fish are usually covered with scales. *Amphibians* start out in water and, as they grow older, they spend more time on land. They are similar to reptiles but, unlike reptiles who have scales or armour, most amphibians have a smooth skin. All amphibians take in oxygen through their skin and most also breathe with lungs and/or gills. Examples of amphibians include the salamander, toad, and frog. A frog starts out as an egg that hatches into a tiny "tadpole". The tadpole has gills and gets its oxygen the way fish do. Slowly, the tadpole grows legs, loses its tail, and, eventually, breathes with lungs. *Reptiles* are covered with scales and breathe air with lungs. They usually lay hard- or soft-shelled eggs. Many reptiles spend most of their lives in the water. For example, some sea turtles rarely come on land; they have flippers, which help them swim well but are poor for walking on land. Other turtles, or tortoises, live mostly on land; they have feet with toes and claws instead of flippers. Examples of other reptiles: snake, lizard, alligator, and crocodile.

Birds and mammals are warm-blooded vertebrates. *Birds* are covered with feathers and have wings. Not all birds can use their wings to fly (e.g. ostrich, penguin, kiwi, emu). Hollow or partially hollow bones make birds lighter than if they had more solid bones like mammals. Birds have large appetites; they need great amounts of energy to fly. *Mammals* have some hair on their body, nurse their young, and have a highly developed brain. Most, but not all, mammals give birth to live young (instead of incubating an egg). Mammals have a very efficient metabolism. Their blood cells, pumped through a powerful heart, can carry more oxygen than the blood cells of any other type of animal. Mammals are also the only animals with a "diaphragm" -- a muscle in the chest that allows more air to enter the lungs.

Topics: Classification; Mammals; Birds; Animal Characteristics.

MATERIALS: Information on these pages; large, hand-drawn or cut-out (from magazines) pictures of the sample animals illustrated; cardboard; scissors; tape; paper; pencils.

DOING IT:

1. Write up a fact sheet identifying the major characteristics of each of the five groups of vertebrates. The detail on the fact sheet depends on the age of the players.

2. Each player should have a copy of the fact sheet. Discuss the five vertebrate groups.

3. Make a cardboard stand for each of the five sample animals. The animals each represent one of the five vertebrate groups. Label the animals: fish, amphibians, reptiles, birds, mammals. Place the sample animals in a row on the ground.

4. Divide players into two equal teams. The teams face each other across the row of animals; teams should each be the same distance from the animals (e.g. 10 m). Players on each team are given sequential numbers, starting at 1; each player must remember his or her number.

"Warm-blooded" animals have a constant body temperature and must eat a lot of food so they have the energy to maintain that temperature. "Cold-blooded" animals, such as insects and reptiles, have a body temperature close to the temperature of their surroundings. A fish, for example, has a body temperature similar to the water in which it swims. Cold-blooded animals experience big swings in their body temperature. When the temperature warms up, cold-blooded animals become more active. If the temperature is too cold, these animals aren't active at all.

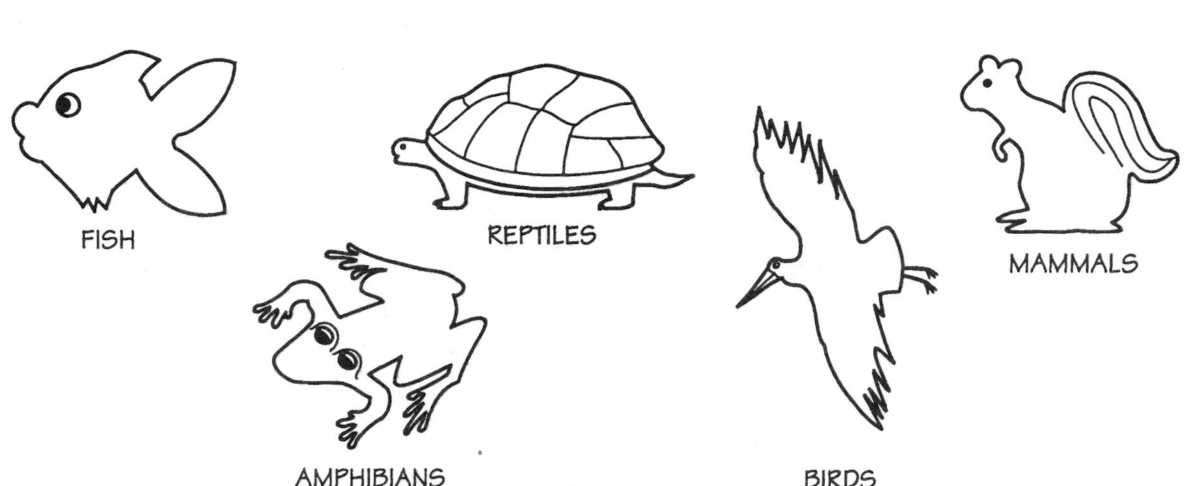

5. A leader then begins calling out clues based on the information on the fact sheet. Start each clue with the statement "I am a vertebrate." For example: "I am a vertebrate. I can't fly but I have wings."; "I am a vertebrate. I am warm-blooded."; "I am a vertebrate. I have hair."; "I am a vertebrate. I have scales and lay eggs."; "I am a vertebrate. Some in my group lay eggs, but I give birth to live young." After saying a clue, the leader pauses and then calls out a player number.

6. The players on each team with the number called must run to grab the animal representing the group described by the clue and then run back "home". The player who does not grab the animal can chase the other player and try to tag him or her to score a point.

7. Points can be awarded as follows: 2 points for grabbing the correct animal and making it home; *minus* 2 points for grabbing the incorrect animal and making it home; 1 point, for each team, for grabbing the correct animal and getting tagged; *minus* 1 point, for each team, for grabbing the incorrect animal and getting tagged. Some clues may have more than one correct answer; in this case, both teams could score 2 points.

8. After each run, the sample animal is returned to the centre row. Play can continue as long as you wish.

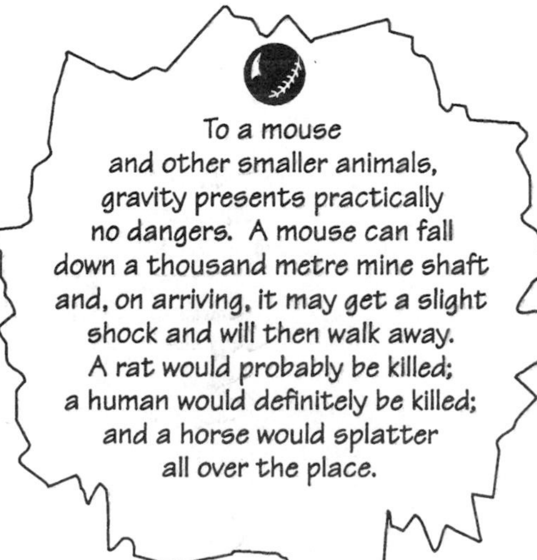

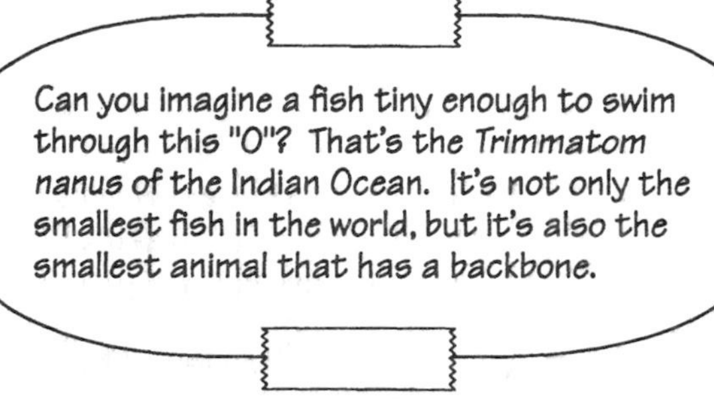

Hair helps to keep many mammals warm. The "underfur", which is closest to the body, is dense and woolly and insulates the animal. The outer layer, or "guard hair", is rough and keeps the animal dry by shedding moisture. The guard hair also gives certain animals their smooth, sleek appearance.

Camouflaged Creatures

In order to survive, living things must be able to adapt. Play a game that shows how worms and insects have adapted so that they can "hide" from birds.

The colour a head louse is as an adult depends on the colour of the person's hair in which it's living. For example, a louse living in blond hair is usually a light colour, while one living in black hair is dark.

"Adaptation" is a gradual, but continuous process of change from one generation of a species (a group of similar animals) to the next. When the environment changes, animal species must change with it. If animals don't adapt, they are eaten or starve and species become extinct. Sudden, major changes in an environment can cause animals serious problems because they are not able to adapt quickly enough. Forms of adaptation are numerous. For example, predatory birds such as eagles, hawks, and condors have a hooked beak that can rip and tear food. Seed-eating birds like the sparrow, parakeet, and nut hatch have short, pointed beaks that can crack open seeds. Water birds like ducks or geese have longer, flat beaks which allow them to strain water for food or scoop up vegetation from the bottom of shallow lakes.

Body colour is a form of adaptation that protects animals by allowing them to blend into their surroundings, to be "camouflaged". When an animal is camouflaged, it is harder for enemies to find it. Deer and mice are extremely difficult to see when they're standing still in their natural environment. Polar bears are white, which allows them to blend in with the snow. Some rabbits are white in the winter, but their fur changes to brown in the summer months. A tiger's stripes and a giraffe's patches help the animals become part of the bushes and trees around them. The female of most bird species is dull and drab, which serves as protection while the bird is on the nest. On the other hand, the male bird is often very brightly coloured so that it stands out from its environment; the male bird attracts the attention of predators to lure them away from the nest.

Topics: Animal Characteristics; Birds.

MATERIALS: Approximately 100 coloured toothpicks, pipe cleaners, or pieces of wool, made up of about 25 of each of four colours (one colour should blend into the game area -- like green objects on a green lawn).

DOING IT:

1. Scatter coloured objects throughout an area of about 20 square metres.

2. People play the role of birds looking for "worms and insects" (coloured objects) to "eat". Each person has a "nest" (a place to collect coloured objects) about 25 m from the feeding area.

3. One at a time, birds run to the feeding area to find food. Each bird takes its turn and makes several flights. The rules: only one worm or insect can be caught per flight; birds don't care what colour worms or insects they eat, so they grab the first food they see; birds can't run their hands over the ground, so they pick up worms or insects only after spotting them; birds keep moving while they look for food.

4. After several flights, how many of each colour of worm or insect has each person collected? What colour of food is hardest to find? Why?

SMALL CHANGES

Scientists believe that animals are different today than they were millions of years ago -- that they constantly, gradually change. Explore the theory of evolution using paper.

MATERIALS: Paper; scissors; pencil crayons.

DOING IT:

1. Make four piles of paper, each containing five sheets of paper. Number the sheets in each pile 1 through 5.

2. These are the basic steps for each pile (specific instructions in 3 to 6 below): cut a triangle from all five sheets and put sheet 1 aside; cut a circle from the four remaining sheets and put sheet 2 aside; cut a long rectangle from the three remaining sheets and put sheet 3 aside; cut half a circle from the two remaining sheets and put sheet 4 aside; cut a square from sheet 5.

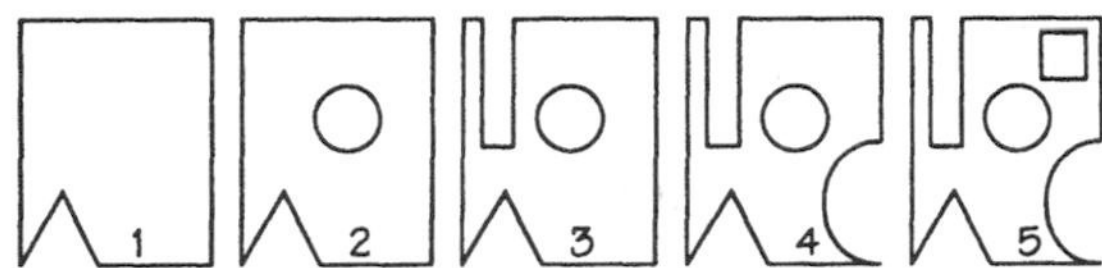

Follow the same basic steps for each pile of paper; but, for each pile, make shapes different sizes and cut them from different areas of the paper.

3. For the first pile of paper, follow all the steps above without any change.

4. For the second pile of paper, before you make any cuts, cut the sheets in half. Then follow all the steps using only one pile of five half-sheets.

5. For the third pile of paper, after you follow all the steps, cut the pile of sheets in half and discard the half-sheets without a sheet number.

6. For the final pile of paper, don't cut out the shapes. Instead, use a coloured pencil to draw and colour the shapes on the paper.

7. Put a sheet of blank paper on the floor. Use your completed piles of paper to make a cross (+) shape, with the blank sheet in the centre and each pile of paper making up one arm of the cross. For each arm, arrange sheets in a row with number 1 sheets closest to the blank sheet.

8. All the sheets in the cross started off blank; the blank sheet in the centre is their common ancestor. Compare the blank sheet to the sheets at the outer edge of the cross. Can you see how small changes add up? How are all the sheets on the outer edge the same? How are they different? Can a change like cutting the sheet in half make a big difference? Does it matter when you cut the sheet in half (i.e. before or after making the other cuts)? How might animals develop in the same way as the sheets of paper?

Charles Darwin was an English naturalist living in the 1800s. As he travelled the world and observed the similarities and differences between the animals he saw, he collected information which helped to form the modern theory of "evolution". Evolution involves the way in which living creatures change and adapt to a changing environment. An important idea in evolution is "natural selection" or "survival of the fittest" -- animals best suited or adapted to their environment survive and reproduce, while those least fitted do not. Evolution occurs very slowly, with small changes adding up. Similar animals in different environments can evolve very differently. Major events like an ice age can dramatically affect an evolutionary path.

The theory of evolution states that all present living creatures gradually developed, over millions of years, from simpler forms of life. Mammals are one of the youngest groups of animals around, in terms of evolutionary history. Scientists believe the first mammals evolved from mammal-like reptiles that lived about 200 million years ago. These mammal-like reptiles had some characteristics of reptiles, but they also had many characteristics of mammals (e.g. mammal-like teeth, skulls, and limbs). Many mammals have changed dramatically over the years. For example, seals today seem to have evolved from land animals that had legs. Scientists don't think that bats were always able to fly. However, other mammals, such as the opossum, don't seem to have changed very much at all.

Topics: Animal Characteristics.

DINO

Dinosaurs are animals that lived millions of years ago but no longer exist because they couldn't adapt to changes around them. Construct some dinosaur models.

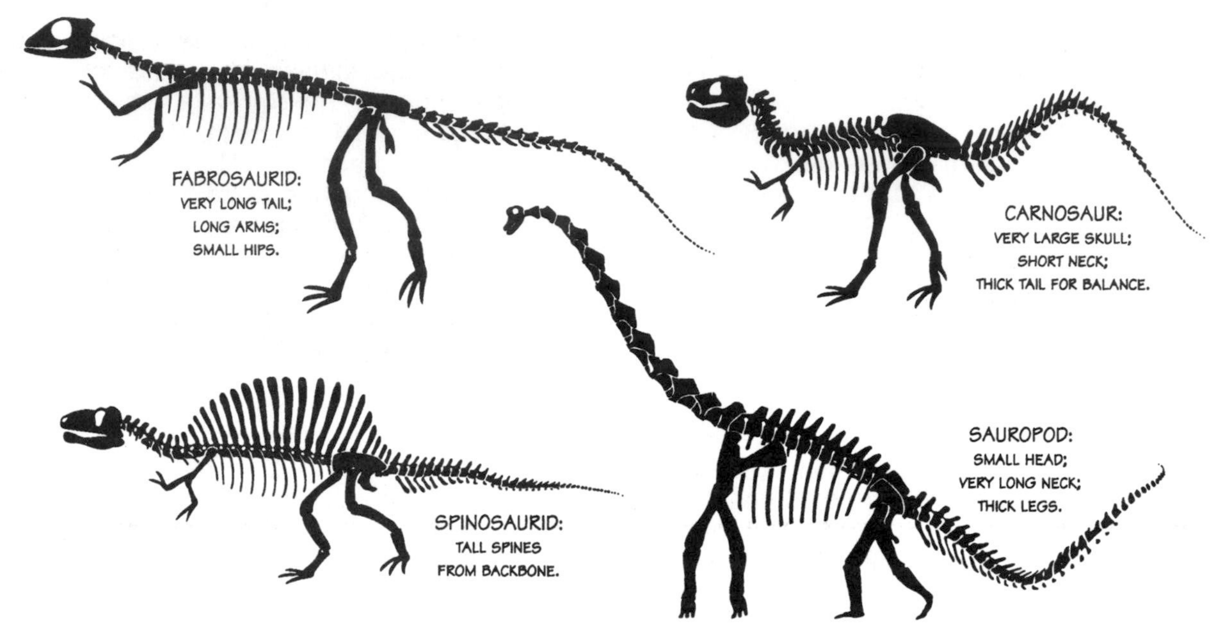

Dinosaurs were reptiles that appeared about 200 million years ago and became extinct about 65 million years ago. Scientists have learned about dinosaurs from fossilized skeletal remains, footprints, droppings, and eggs. They have discovered hundreds of different kinds of dinosaurs and believe there may still be hundreds more to find. Different types of dinosaurs existed at different times. The largest dinosaurs were 27 m long and the smallest were about the size of a chicken. Scientists believe a few dinosaurs could glide, but none could fly. Some dinosaurs could swim, but none spent all their time in the water. There were dinosaurs that were herbivores (plant-eaters) and dinosaurs that were carnivores (meat-eaters). The large herbivores walked on four legs, while the smaller ones walked on only two.

Scientists aren't sure why dinosaurs became extinct. Changes in geography, climate, and sea level may have been responsible. One theory suggests that an asteroid impact caused the changes that led to their extinction. Whatever happened, dinosaurs simply weren't able to adapt quickly enough to the environmental changes.

Topics: Animal Characteristics; Earth.

MATERIALS: Pipe cleaners; scissors. Optional -- paper; glue; coloured pencils.

DOING IT:

1. Use pipe cleaners to make skeletal models of the dinosaurs shown. Start with a dinosaur's backbone. Add the appropriate head size. Add the front and back legs in the correct relative positions (make sure the neck is the right length). Then model the ribs. If you wish, you can add other details with bits of paper.

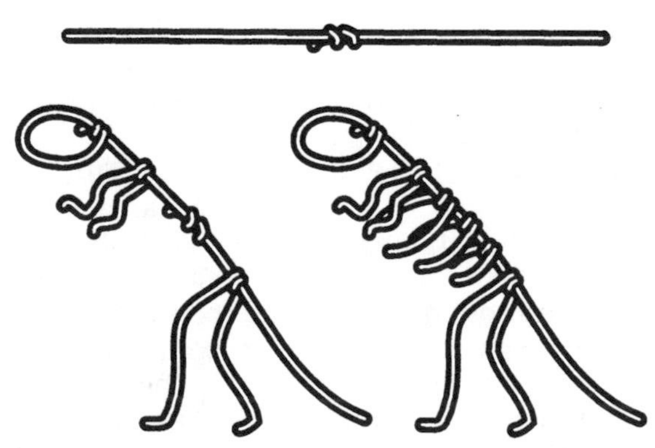

Creative Creatures

What would a duck-billed pigeon look like? How about a jumping bee? Mix and match insect or bird parts to invent new creatures.

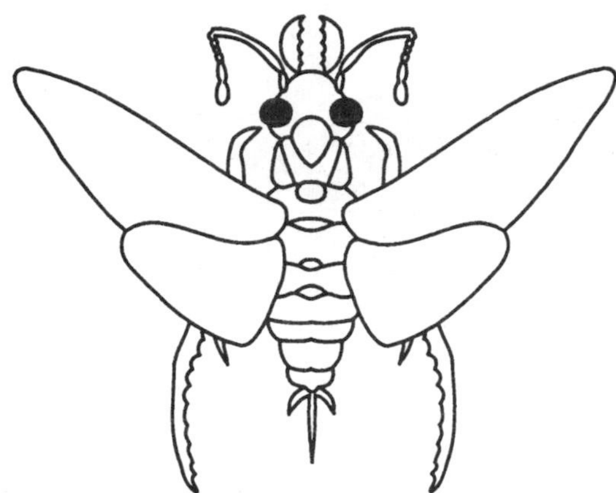

MATERIALS: Following pages; paper (graph paper, if possible); ruler; scissors; glue or tape; pencil; coloured pencils.

DOING IT:

1. The easiest way to draw creative creatures is by using graph paper. If you don't have graph paper, make a faint grid of 1 to 3 cm squares (depending on how large you want the final creature) on a sheet of blank paper.

2. Use the grid to help you draw the body parts shown on the following pages. Choose a body first. Then choose any combination of other body parts (e.g. wings, legs) you wish. Make sure each of your squares for a body part looks exactly like the original body part's squares. You don't have to draw the parts so that they form a completed creature on your paper; but it's easier later if you draw some of the smaller parts (e.g. mouth, tail) so that they are attached to the body.

3. Colour your body parts. Insects and birds have many colours, so be creative. If you're stuck for ideas, look at a real insect or bird.

4. Cut out the body parts. Lay them on a fresh sheet of paper and experiment with different ways of arranging and overlapping them. Then, paste them in place.

5. Name your new creature. Make a list of its characteristics based on what each body part enables it to do.

6. *Variation:* Create your own insect and bird parts. Or, mix different grid sizes for the same creature (e.g. so that you have huge feelers on a tiny body).

7. *Extension:* Draw pictures of and make up stories about funny animals like the cowbird, great horned owl, hairy woodpecker, pintail duck, and whistling swan. What does each animal look like? What does it do? Where does it live? What does it sound like?

Many living creatures act as their own doctors. A cat or dog will eat grass if its stomach is upset. Other animals also eat certain leaves and grasses for their medicinal value. The animals seem to know exactly which plants to eat -- and which ones to avoid.

The atlas moth of India is one of the world's largest insects. It measures 30 cm from wing-tip to wing-tip.

Many animals have some basic body parts in common. For example, most animals have a distinct body and legs. But there are different kinds of bodies and different kinds of legs. Different body parts have evolved in special ways to do special tasks. Legs used for jumping are different than legs used for walking. Body parts can also be combined in different ways to result in different animals. Getting to know basic body parts not only helps you to invent new creatures, but it will help you identify real animals and understand why they have the body parts they do.

Topics: Insects; Birds; Animal Characteristics.

INSECT PARTS

TYPICAL INSECT: A true insect has six legs. The three main body parts are: head (holds brain, two feelers or antennae, mouthparts, and eyes); thorax (holds large muscles which work legs and wings); and abdomen (most insects breathe through tiny holes called "spiracles" along the side of their abdomen). Insects have two kinds of eyes -- small, "simple" eyes with only one lens and larger, "compound" eyes made up of many tiny, six-sided lenses that fit together like the cells of a honeycomb. Insects have no bones; they have an external skeleton called an "exoskeleton". A tough material called "chitin" covers and protects insects like a suit of armour.

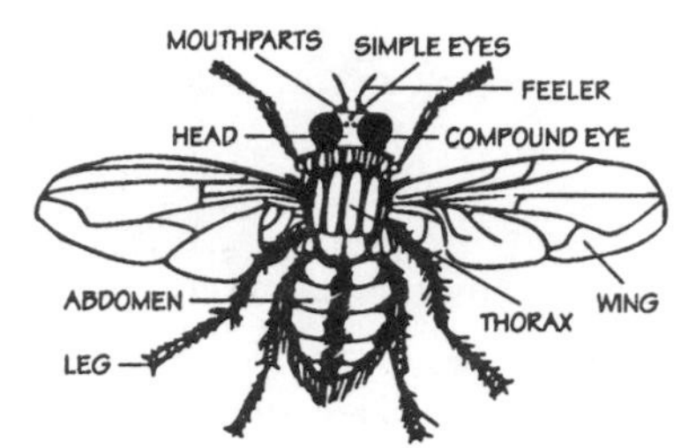

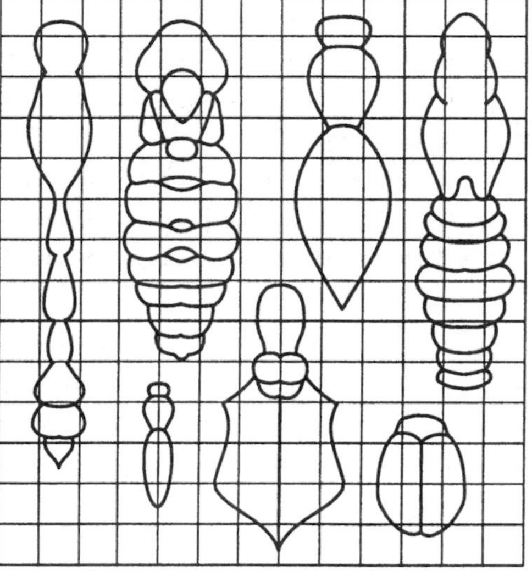

BODIES: Have three main parts -- head, thorax, abdomen. Can be streamlined (e.g. far left) for flying, or round and armour-plated (e.g. bottom, right) for a defensive life on the ground.

LEGS (clockwise from top, left): Swimmer; crawler; jumper; swimmer/jumper.

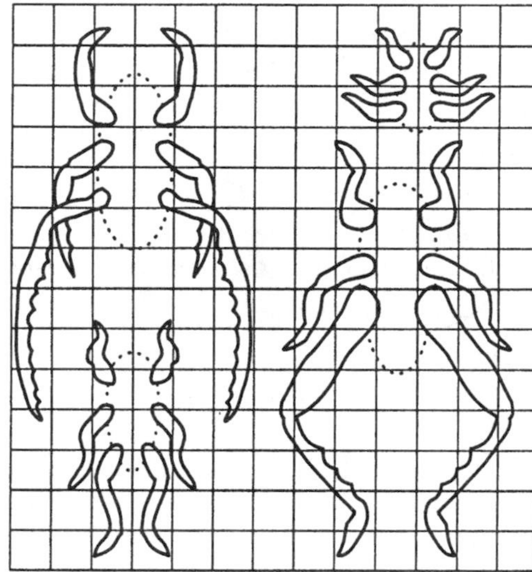

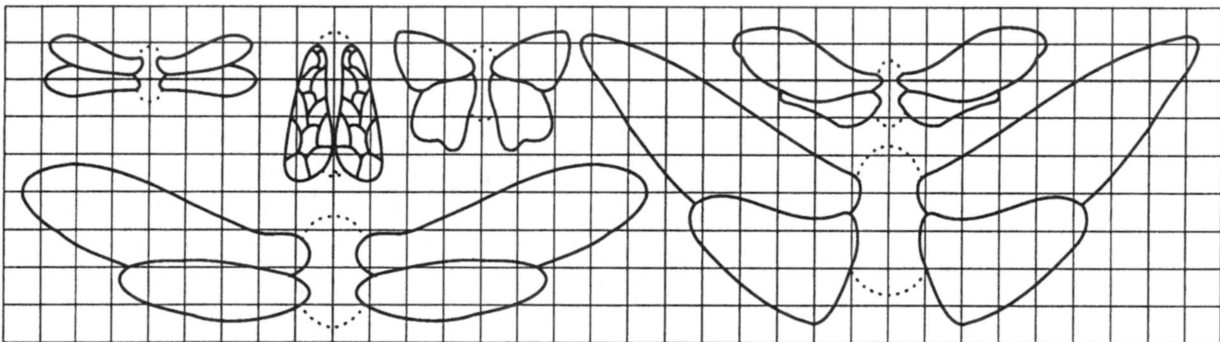

WINGS: A soft, fuzzy wing is used for fluttering (e.g. bottom, right), while a clear, lacy wing (top, second from left) is more for buzzing. Some wings are hidden under a protective covering and come out only when needed.

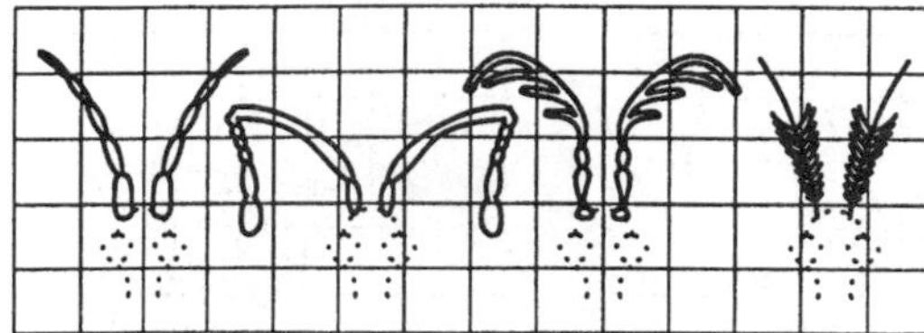

ANTENNAE/FEELERS (left to right): Dragonfly; ant; beetle; moth. Insects use their antennae or feelers for feeling, smelling, tasting, and sometimes hearing.

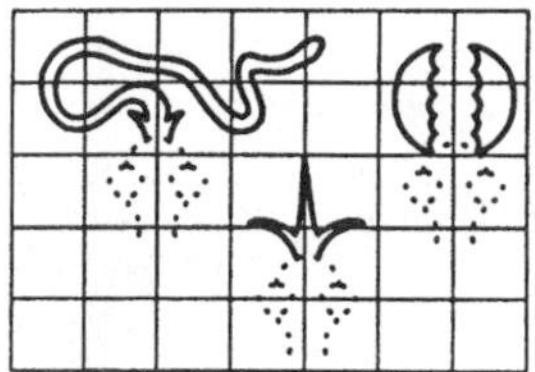

MOUTHPARTS (left to right): Suction tube; prober; crusher.

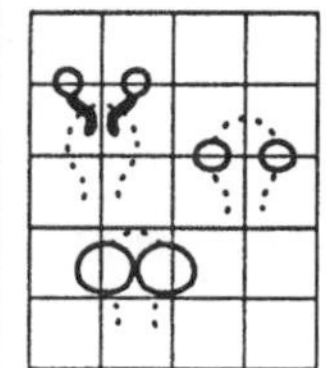

EYES: Large, compound eyes.

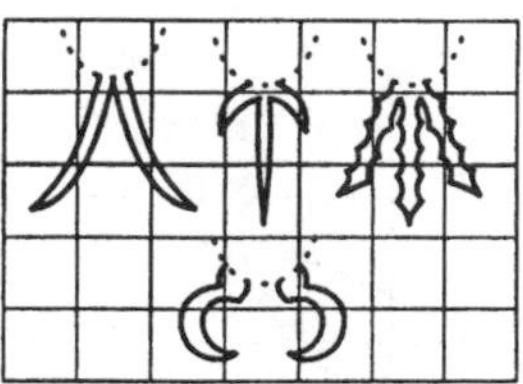

TAILS (clockwise): Fuzzy; smooth stinger; barbed stinger; pincers.

Bird Parts

Typical Bird: Wings and feathers are the two most obvious features of birds. A bird has hundreds of feathers over its body. One kind of swan has over 25,000 feathers, and even the tiny hummingbird has almost 1000 feathers. Differences in bills/beaks and feet are important for identifying different types of birds.

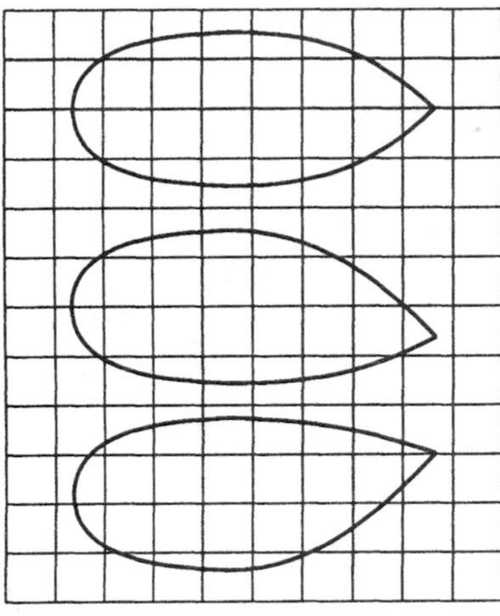

Bodies (top to bottom): Tail falls in middle of body; tail points downward; tail points upward.

Bills Or Beaks (clockwise from upper, left): Long, slender bill (for probing mud); heavy, conical beak (for cracking seeds); wide bill (for scooping and straining water); straight beak (for snatching insects from the ground); strong, hooked beak (for tearing meat).

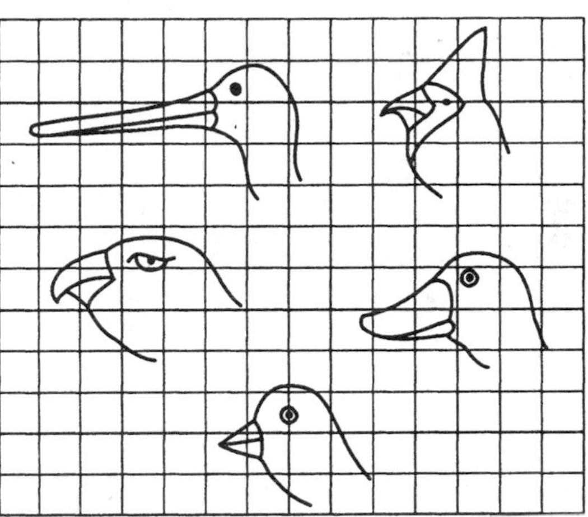

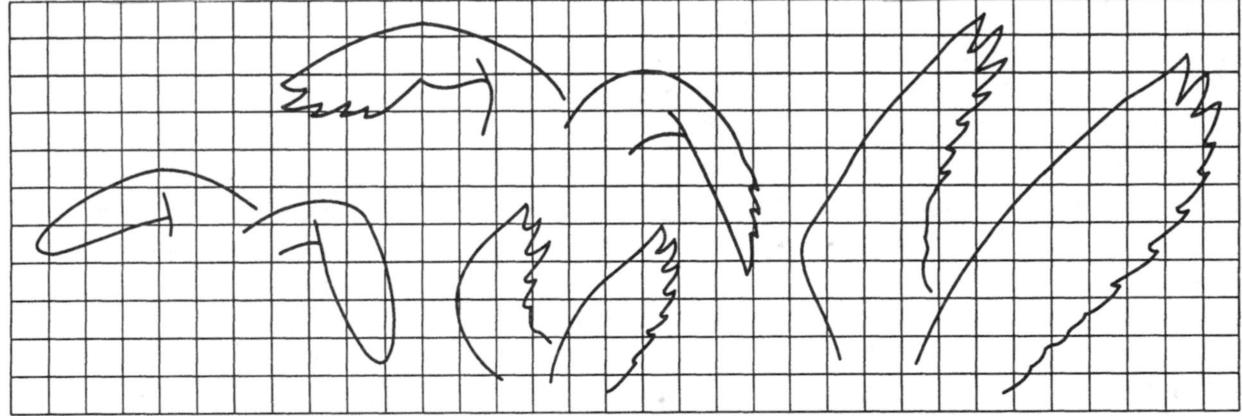

Wings (clockwise from left): Flipper-like wings; long, narrow wings (for graceful flight and gliding); large, broad wings (for powerful flight and soaring); stubby wings (for short, rapid flight).

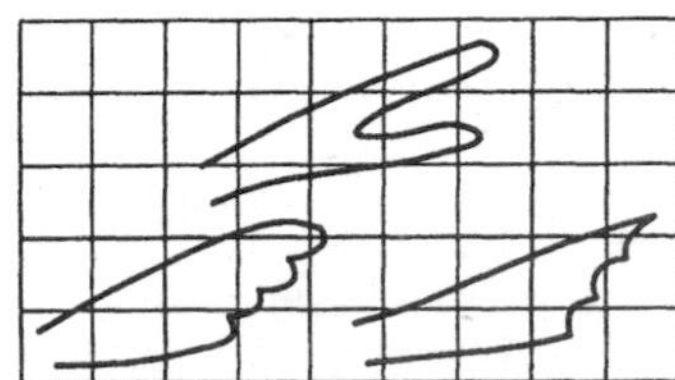

Tails (clockwise from top): Forked tail; spine-tipped tail (aids perching); fan-like tail (aids gliding).

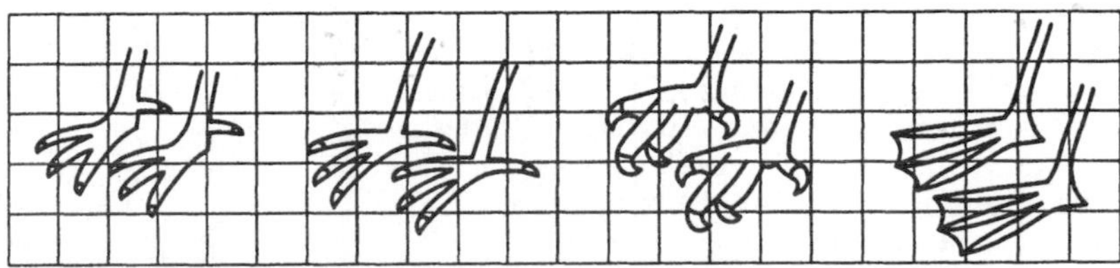

Feet (left to right): Long, strong toes of pedestrian birds (rear toes don't touch ground); feet for perching, hopping, and climbing; gripping, meat-hook feet for catching and killing; webbed feet for swimming.

MAKE TIME

Words And Animals

Have you noticed that "hiss" sounds like the animal noise it describes? These three puzzles explore other interesting words that describe and name animals.

MATERIALS: Following page; pencil.

DOING IT:

1. *Insect Word Search:* Hunt through all the letters in the puzzle to find the words listed. Circle each word as you find it. The words can overlap, run in any direction, or be spelled backwards. After you've found all the words, write down the leftover letters starting from the top, left-hand corner and moving from left to right. What secret message do the words form?

2. *Animal Noises:* Can you find 23 animal noises in the puzzle? For each noise, start at any letter and move to an adjoining letter, then to a letter beside that letter, and so on. You can go in any direction (vertically, horizontally, or diagonally) and you can even return to a letter you've used before. But you must always move from one letter to a letter beside it.

3. *Animal World Crossword:* Fill in the crossword using the clues.

Word puzzles are a great way to introduce animal names and information. They get you thinking about the words we use to name and describe animals. We also have a lot of animal-related sayings. For example, when you say that someone is as "busy as a beaver" you mean that they're working hard. Beavers always seem to be working. From early spring to late fall all members of a beaver colony can be observed busily cutting trees, building and repairing dams and lodges, and cutting twigs for their winter food supply. Beavers are very intelligent and successful animal engineers. Not all animal-related sayings are true -- like "blind as a bat". All bats can see; a few even have better vision than people. Most, though, don't have an exceptionally keen sense of sight. They rely on their ability to "echo locate" (to listen to how echoes bounce off surrounding surfaces) to help them navigate. The idea of a "lone wolf" is also incorrect. Wolves live together in very close family groups and hunt in packs. They keep the same mate for life and are good parents, taking care of their cubs until the cubs are grown. Wolf packs even care for members of the pack that are too old or sick to hunt. Perhaps the idea of the lone wolf came about because single wolves were spotted from time to time raiding flocks and herds of animals.

Topics: Animal Characteristics; Insects; Mammals.

Insect Word Search Hidden Message: One acre of soil can contain one billion insects.

Animal Noises Solution: bark, bawl, cackle, chirp, cluck, croak, crow, cry, growl, hiss, honk, hoot, howl, meow, mew, moo, neigh, oink, roar, sing, squeak, squeal, whine.

Animal World Crossword Solution:

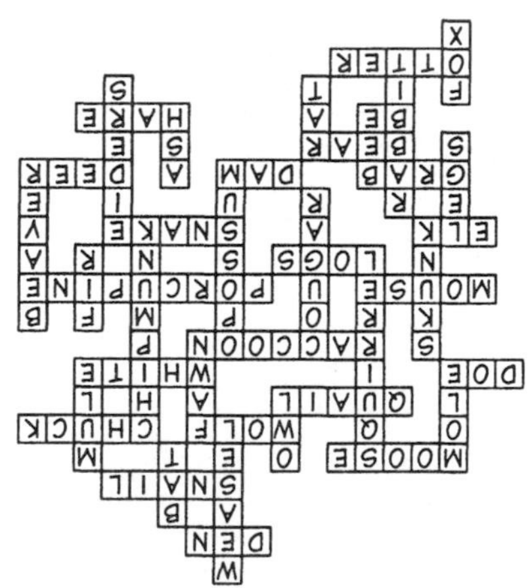

Animal Puzzles

Insect Word Search

O A S S A S S I N B U G
N W E T A N G A E C C R
D B A E O F U D S O O T
R T E S O W B U G C E I
I E L E P U E C A K G Y
B N M N G C N T C R U L
Y R O M N G U A N O B F
D O T A I I J I N A K E
A H M R O W D U B C N R
L P O N O R S E B H I I
I L H L T A L K T I T F
O N L I I E L O C U S T
I E C N D C M S E A C T
Y K Y L F R E T T U B S

ANT
APHID
ASSASSIN BUG
BACKSWIMMER
BEDBUG
BEE
BEE
BUDWORM
BUTTERFLY
COCKROACH
EARWIG
FIREFLY
GNAT
HORNET
JUNE BUG
LADYBIRD
LICE
LOCUST
MOTH
SOWBUG
STINKBUG
TICK
WASP
YELLOWJACKET

Animal Noises

Animal World Crossword

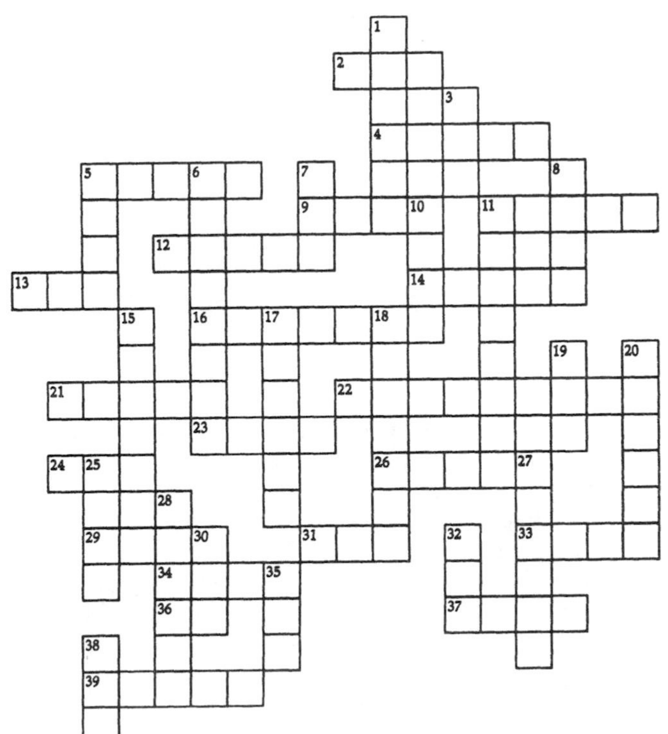

DOWN

1. A pointy-nosed mammal; rhymes with measle.
3. Looks like a mouse with wings.
5. This furry tunneller seldom comes out by day.
6. A bushy-tailed nut lover.
7. What a hoot!
8. The offspring of an ass and a horse.
10. A baby deer.
11. Looks a bit like a small, striped squirrel.
15. Phew! Don't alarm this animal.
17. A mountain lion.
18. This furry mammal hangs upside down.
19. An evergreen; rhymes with purr.
20. This animal chomps down trees.
25. Many animals have four of these.
27. Soft down from these ducks fills sleeping bags.
28. A hippety-hopper.
30. Honey-making insect.
32. A tree; rhymes with gnash.
35. It followed the Pied Piper.
38. The hunter in 29.

ACROSS

2. A winter home for bears.
4. This slowpoke wears a shell.
5. Rhymes with goose.
9. A wild relative of the dog.
11. A wood _____ is often mistaken for a groundhog.
12. This bird's name rhymes with whale.
13. A female deer.
14. In winter, several normal animals turn _____.
16. This animal looks as if it's wearing a mask.
21. A cheese-lover.
22. A prickly animal.
23. Small animals sometimes sleep in hollow _____.
24. A large deer with spreading antlers.
26. It slithers.
29. Watch out, mouse! A fox might _____ you.
31. Beavers build this.
33. A buck is a male _____.
34. This hibernates in 2 across.
36. _____ prepared! The Boy Scout's motto.
37. The snowshoe _____ has big furry feet.
39. A sleek, web-footed river mammal.

WHO GOES THERE?

It may be rare to actually see mammals in the wild, but you can find their tracks. Identify animal tracks and make plaster casts or footprint papers.

MATERIALS: Lightweight cardboard; scissors; tape; talcum powder; petroleum jelly (e.g. Vaseline); plaster of Paris; water; container; spoon; paper; potatoes; small knife; poster paint or ink pad.

DOING IT:

1. Look for tracks in cultivated fields, muddy lake and stream banks, sandy beaches, or at the base of trees or bushes. You may want to make a special "track-catching spot". Find a piece of level ground with fairly soft, fine, textured soil. Smooth it over and wet it. Come back later to see which creatures have visited the spot.

2. When you find tracks, try to identify the animal that made them. How many feet does the animal have? Are the front and back feet alike? What's the shape, length, and width of a single track? Do you see pads, webs, cleaves, or claws? How many toes are there and how are they arranged? Does the animal look like it was walking, trotting, running, galloping, bounding, or hopping? In what direction was it headed? Can you tell if the tracks are fresh?

3. *Plaster Cast:* Choose a single, sharply-outlined track at least 1 cm deep. Carefully brush away any loose soil or leaves. Sprinkle the track lightly with powder; if the track is in snow, spray it with water to form a thin ice crust. Make a round cardboard frame (i.e. tape the ends of a strip of cardboard together) about 8 cm high and large enough to encircle the track. Rub petroleum jelly on the inside of the frame. Place the frame around the track and press it firmly into the ground. Mix plaster of Paris with water until the mixture is thick and creamy. Pour the mixture into the frame to about 3 or 4 cm deep. Let it set for about 20 minutes. Remove the frame, lift up the "negative" mold, and gently brush it clean. Allow the mold to dry completely (about 24 hours). To make a "positive" mold, apply petroleum jelly to the surface of the negative mold. Make a second, higher frame and rub petroleum jelly on the inside. Place the frame around the negative mold. Fill the frame with plaster. When the plaster has dried, separate the positive and negative molds.

4. *Footprint Papers:* Cut off and discard about a third of a potato. Choose a footprint from the following page and use a knife to scratch the general shape into the potato. Then *carefully* cut away everything that isn't animal track to make a stamp (always cut away from your body or hands). Apply a smooth and even coat of paint or ink to the stamp. Stamp tracks on paper to make wrapping paper, book covers, or stationery.

When an animal moves across a soft surface it leaves foot impressions called "tracks". A sequence of tracks, together with accessory marks such as tail or feather drag, form a "trail". Tracks look different depending on the type of surface. Distinct tracks with well-formed claw and paw shapes show up in mud, moist sand, and in freshly fallen, shallow snow. Tracks become blurred in deep snow and don't show up well at all in hard sand and soil.

Tracks and trails can help you identify an animal. For example, many mammals that live in trees (e.g. squirrels) hop when they're on the ground such that their larger hind feet land ahead of their smaller front feet. The tracks of hopping animals that live on the ground (e.g. rabbits, certain mice) are different. The hind feet still land ahead of the front feet; but instead of the front feet being side by side, they are found one in front of the other. Tracks can also reveal subtle differences between animals. For example, all mammals have basically the same foot structure; however, they use their feet in different ways, which results in different tracks. Some animals walk on their hands (e.g. raccoons, bears). Others walk or run on their toes (e.g. cats, coyotes). Still others walk on their "toenails" or hooves (e.g. deer, elk). Raccoons, skunks, coyotes, foxes, and dogs often leave claw marks; the marks point in the direction the mammal was going, just as your toes point in the direction you're going. But most cats -- including house cats, cougars, and lynx -- pull in their claws so they can walk or run more easily. If you can't see any claws in the tracks, look for soil or snow pushed back by the movement of the animal's feet.

Topics: Mammals; Birds.

Animal Tracks

These drawings show the tracks of several common animals. Although the tracks are drawn quite small, their approximate actual size is noted beside each drawing; use the ruler to get an idea of the actual size.

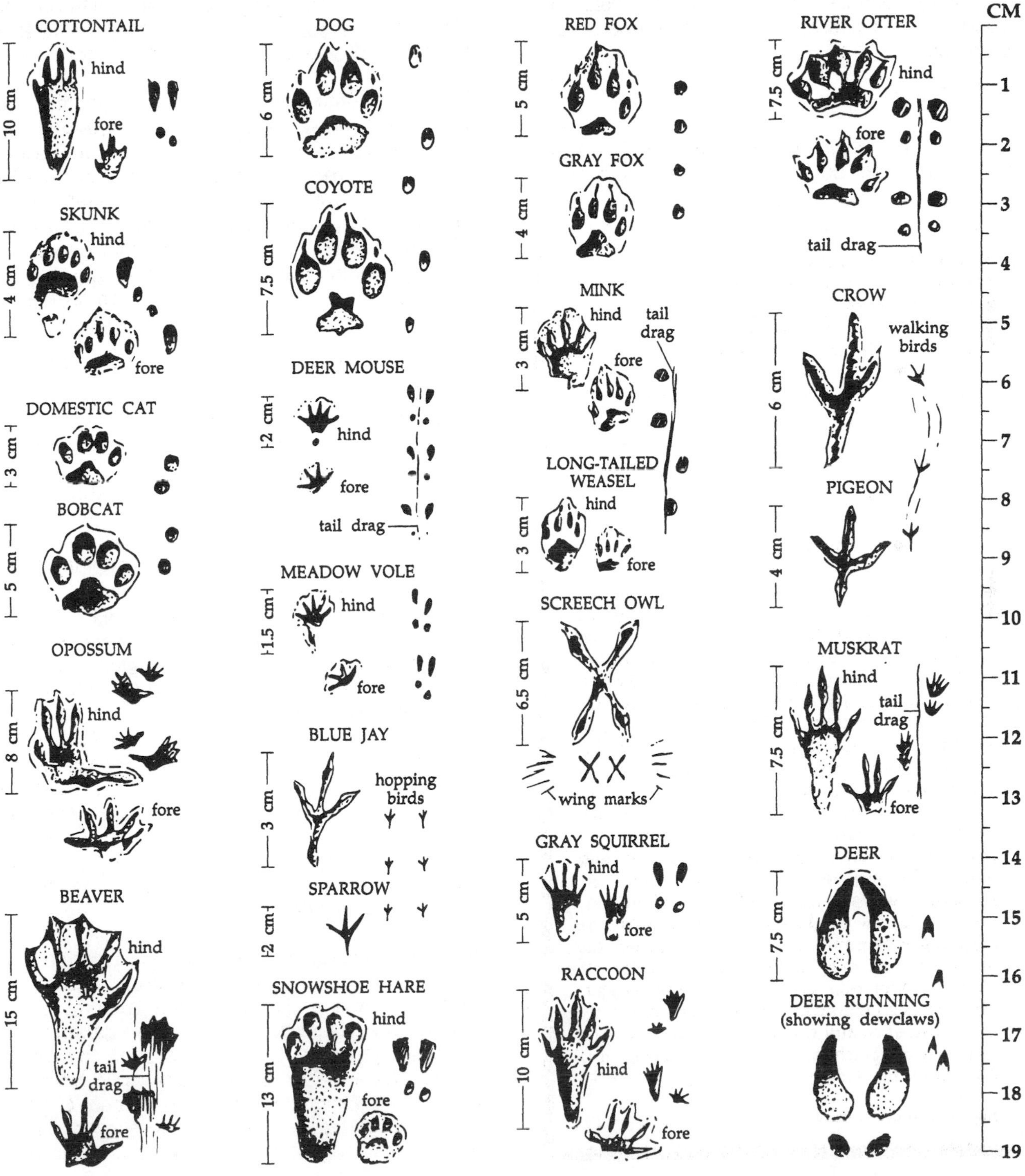

COTTONTAIL
10 cm
hind
fore

SKUNK
4 cm
hind
fore

DOMESTIC CAT
3 cm

BOBCAT
5 cm

OPOSSUM
8 cm
hind
fore

BEAVER
15 cm
hind
tail drag
fore

DOG
6 cm

COYOTE
7.5 cm

DEER MOUSE
2 cm
hind
fore
tail drag

MEADOW VOLE
1.5 cm
hind
fore

BLUE JAY
3 cm
hopping birds

SPARROW
2 cm

SNOWSHOE HARE
13 cm
hind
fore

RED FOX
5 cm

GRAY FOX
4 cm

MINK
3 cm
hind
tail drag
fore

LONG-TAILED WEASEL
3 cm
hind
fore

SCREECH OWL
6.5 cm
wing marks

GRAY SQUIRREL
5 cm
hind
fore

RACCOON
10 cm
hind
fore

RIVER OTTER
7.5 cm
hind
fore
tail drag

CROW
6 cm
walking birds

PIGEON
4 cm

MUSKRAT
7.5 cm
hind
tail drag
fore

DEER
7.5 cm

DEER RUNNING
(showing dewclaws)

CM
1
2
3
4
5
6
7
8
9
10
11
12
13
14
15
16
17
18
19

MAKE TIME

ANTS ON THE RUN

Ants are fascinating little creatures -- and they're easy to find. Try an ant taste test and follow an ant to find out more about its life.

Bombardier beetles can shoot a hot, smelly liquid from their abdomen that is 100 degrees Celsius. That's as hot as boiling water!

All animals need food to survive. Animals eat food so that they have the energy they need to live. Some foods provide more energy than others. Ants -- and other insects -- are attracted to sweet foods, but not just any kind of sweet food. Ants know which foods are high in energy. Sugar and artificial sweetener taste the same to many people; but sugar has a much higher energy value. Ants can figure this out and this knowledge helps them to survive.

Ants are very determined creatures. They are also extremely strong for their size; they are able to lift 50 times their body weight. Ants are sensitive to changes in temperature. All ants show some degree of social organization; they nest in a system of tunnels under soil they pile into large mounds. Most ants are harmless to humans and other animals. Some ants have stingers, and some can spray poison from the end of their abdomen. Army ants travel in columns, overrunning and devouring any animals in their path.

Topics: Insects.

MATERIALS: Sugar; artificial sweetener; two small, shallow, identical bottle caps; two drinking glasses; water; teaspoon; pen; watch.

DOING IT:

1. *Ant Food:* Mix a spoonful of sugar with a little water in a glass to make a thick liquid. Clean the spoon. Mix a spoonful of artificial sweetener with a little water in another glass to make a thick liquid. Fill one bottle cap with one liquid and the other cap with the other liquid (mark the caps so you know what's in each). Place the caps close together where there are ants. The ants should be able to easily get to both caps. Which mixture attracts more ants? Why? What happens if you take away the sugar mixture? How does the ants' response help them survive?

2. *Follow That Ant:* Find an ant. Mark the spot where you first find it. Follow the ant for about 10 minutes. Where does it go? What does it do? Put an obstacle in the ant's path. What happens? Does the ant seem to move faster when the temperature is higher (e.g. in sunlight)? If you follow the ant long enough, you might find its anthill. If the ant leads you to other ants, watch the way ants move in a line. When your observation time is up, take a look at how far you and the ant travelled. Try to retrace your steps.

Not all animals detect the taste of their food through tongues. Ants, bees, and wasps can make taste tests with their antennae. In some butterflies and the honeybee, the tarsal, or foot, joints have a set of taste buds. Houseflies walk all over food so that they can taste it; they have chemical-sensitive cells in their feet. Some frogs and toads have taste-sensitive cells on their cheeks and lips, and some fish have them on their fins and tails.

CATERPILLAR RACE

A caterpillar has a lot of power for a little body. Run a caterpillar race and experiment with ways to make your favourite caterpillar run fastest.

MATERIALS: Caterpillars; short race course (e.g. a patch of ground with marked start and finish lines).

DOING IT:

1. Each individual or team should have a caterpillar. Finding the caterpillars is half the fun. They're easy to find if you follow the right clues. Look for holes in leaves or half-eaten leaves. Caterpillars should be nearby, either hidden in the leaves or on the ground below. **Caution: Some hairy caterpillars can cause skin irritation. Some large caterpillars can nip the skin.**

2. Make a race course. Each entry is placed at the starting line.

3. People can coax their racers along (e.g. put some tempting food ahead of a caterpillar), but can't actually touch them.

4. The winner is the caterpillar that crosses the finish line first. *Don't harm the caterpillars. After the race, return the caterpillars to the exact spots in which you found them.*

Many people around the world eat insects. Some cultures eat fat, juicy caterpillars, cooked like french fries. Other cultures fry or roast grasshoppers. Still others dry and grind up beetle grubs and fly maggots into flour. Insects are a good food source -- they are abundant and high in protein.

The South African hercules beetle is as big as a mouse.

Insects go through great changes, called a "metamorphosis", during their life cycles. Most insects begin as eggs until the "larvae" (young insects) hatch. After a period of time in which the larvae eat constantly, a covering forms that's like a tent protecting the insect during its next stage, the "pupa". The insect emerges from the covering as an adult. Not all insects go through all four stages of development. A grasshopper, for example, has only three stages in its development. It does not form a covering; it starts as an egg, hatches into a "nymph" (which looks like a miniature adult), and grows to an adult.

Caterpillars hatch from eggs the size of the dot at the end of this sentence. They grow rapidly, so rapidly that they outgrow and must shed their skin every 3 to 4 days. When butterfly caterpillars reach a certain size, they make a covering called a "chrysalis"; moth caterpillars form a pupa within a simple or elaborate "cocoon". When the moth or butterfly emerges as an adult, it lays eggs which will hatch to become caterpillars. This cycle continually repeats.

A caterpillar's power comes in large part from its 4000 different muscles (humans only have about 640). You might be tempted to think that a centipede, for example, is a better racer than a caterpillar. It may have more legs, but when a centipede gets nervous, it rolls up into a tight ball and won't go anywhere.

Topics: Insects.

SPIDER WEBS

Spiders look something like insects. But insects have six legs; spiders have eight. Preserve a real spider web or construct your own web.

MATERIALS: Can of white spray paint and dark construction paper OR dark spray paint and white construction paper; paper; pencil; string or cord; scissors.

DOING IT:

1. *Preserving a Web:* Spider webs are plentiful at certain times of the year and under certain weather conditions. A good place to find webs is between tree branches. When you find a web you want to save, spray it with paint so that it is completely covered. **Don't breathe in the paint.** Before the paint dries, carefully press construction paper into the web and on through the web. The paint causes the web to stick to the paper. With a little practice, you can neatly mount webs so that you can study their construction.

2. *Constructing a Web:* Imagine that you are an orb-web weaving spider. You must spin a web to catch food and survive. Draw some sketches of webs or examine real ones. Where would a spider build a web? Pick a location where the possibility of catching "food" is good (e.g. across a path). Use rope or cord to make the web. First lay out the radials.

Then weave strands back and forth between the radials.

Once the web is finished, sit very still beside the web for about 10 minutes, like a real spider waiting quietly for food. Does any food happen to come along? What must a spider's life be like?

Most spiders spend much of their time spinning webs. Webs are spun out of spider silk, the strongest fibre found in nature. Liquid comes out of glands at a spider's rear and solidifies as it hits the air. The spider starts a web by spinning long threads outward from a central point. Once these radial strands -- which anchor the web in place -- are finished, the spider weaves strands back and forth, or spirally, from radial to radial. The strands between radials are coated with a sticky substance from the spider's body. The radial strands aren't sticky; the spider walks on these so that it doesn't get caught in its own web. Webs built outdoors are quite intricate; webs built indoors -- cobwebs -- are often irregular and simple. Different kinds of spiders spin different webs. In fact, web type is one method of spider classification. Some spiders do not spin webs at all. Spiders that do spin webs can spin them even in space. Scientists thought that without gravity, spiders wouldn't be able to spin webs. But they can; the webs just aren't as neat as they would be on Earth.

Topics: Insects.

BIRD FLIGHT PATTERNS

Different species of birds have different flight patterns. Sit back, relax, and do some bird watching to draw flight patterns.

MATERIALS: Paper; pencils. Optional -- bird identification guide.

DOING IT:

1. Find an open spot, perhaps by a lake. Sit down and make yourself comfortable. This activity takes a little patience.

2. When you see a bird, observe its flight pattern as it flies by. Record your observations, along with a few notes to help keep different birds straight in your mind (e.g. bird was big and had red beak). A good way to record a flight pattern is to simply draw a line similar to the path taken by the bird.

3. Does each type of bird seem to have its own flight pattern? Which bird has the most graceful flight pattern? Does wing shape or body size affect a bird's flight pattern? Are there differences in the way different birds take off and land? How high do different birds fly? Select words from the following list to help you describe the flight patterns you see: jerky, bouncy, darting, circling, straight, bounding, erratic, twinkling, irregular, swooping, unsteady, soaring, zigzagging.

The tiny hummingbird may be mistaken for a moth, but it can outfly any insect or bird in the sky. A hummingbird's average mass is about equal to that of a penny. Wing muscles account for up to one-third of this mass. If the hummingbird's body was, for example, the size of a swan, its wings would span the length of a school bus. A hummingbird's wings move very quickly and the tiny bird needs a lot of energy to keep going. It sips half its own weight in nectar each day. An adult person with the same appetite would eat almost 900 hamburgers a day.

Only four groups of animals -- birds, insects, bats, and pterosaurs (prehistoric flying reptiles, now extinct) -- have the ability of flight in which the wings flap to produce lift and thrust. To fly through the air, a bird needs a lighter and more powerful body than other animals of the same size that only walk or swim. Birds move their wings in a figure eight shape when flying. As a bird flaps its wings, the tips twist around to thrust air backward. This forces the bird forward. As the wings move forward they keep the bird in the air. A wing's upper side is curved and its lower side is flattish. This makes air rush faster over the wing than under it. The pressure of the air above is lowered and the wing is sucked into the lower pressure air; at the same time, the wing is pushed up by the higher pressure air below. This gives the bird "lift". Each type of bird flies through the air in a particular way. Here are some examples of flight patterns: flap, flap, flap -- sails in a straight line; flap, flap, flap -- sails in circles; flap, flap, flap -- hovers and glides.

A bird's feathers serve many purposes. They give buoyancy and lightness, which aid flight. They provide colourful adornment for courtship and camouflage. And they retain body warmth. Birds have special muscles in their skin for fluffing out their feathers. Humans have similar muscles; they're the ones that give you goose bumps. The puffed-out feathers form a thicker, warmer covering and give the animal a larger appearance in the face of a fearful enemy. Birds usually "moult" twice a year, losing and growing new small, covering feathers in the spring and all their feathers in the fall.

Topics: Birds; Flight.

FRIGHT DISTANCE

One difference between wild and tame animals is how easily they are frightened. How close can you get to a bird before it flies away?

MATERIALS: Markers (e.g. rocks or pieces of cloth); paper; pencils. Optional -- bird identification guide.

DOING IT:

1. Take a walk. When you see a bird, make a mental note of the bird's exact location (finding a landmark, such as a large rock or oddly-shaped tree, is helpful).

2. Holding a marker in your hand, walk slowly toward the bird. The moment the bird flies away, drop the marker.

3. Pace out the distance between the marker and where the bird was just before it flew away. Record the fright distance and type of bird (e.g. big bird with red beak).

4. What is the average fright distance for a particular type of bird? What type of bird allows you to get closest? Which bird has the longest fright distance? How different are the longest and shortest fright distances? How does whistling or shouting change fright distance? Can one person get closer than another person to the same type of bird?

5. *Extension:* Can you find the fright distance of other wild animals (e.g. squirrels, rabbits)?

Birds are very timid creatures. Sudden or quick movements cause them to take flight. A bird will allow you to get only so close and then it will fly away. This distance is called the "fright distance". Some birds tend to be more timid than others. Fright distance varies with the type of bird and with whether or not a bird is used to having human beings around. Many animals, because they do not have the option of soaring into the sky to escape an enemy, will often freeze instead. Yet other animals are curious enough to cautiously investigate what caused the movement.

Topics: Birds; Mammals.

An egg is really a single cell, adapted to the task of producing a new creature. For most birds, egg laying stops after a certain number of eggs has accumulated in the nest. The house sparrow, for example, generally lays just 4 or 5 eggs. But if the eggs are removed as she lays them, the bird continues to lay until as many as 50 eggs have been laid in succession and the ovaries are exhausted. Apparently, the sparrow needs to see a certain number of eggs in her nest in order to stop laying. When the bird finds an egg missing, she lays another to make up for it. The same behaviour also occurs in chickens, which is the basis for the egg industry. There are two kinds of chicken eggs: those produced for you to boil or fry or bake a cake, and those produced to hatch chicks. Eggs which produce chicks have been fertilized by the male bird.

WEATHER

"Meteorology" is the study of the atmosphere, its composition, and the changes that take place in it.

The lowest temperature ever recorded on Earth was -89.2 degrees C for Vostok, Antarctica on July 21, 1983. Snag, Yukon Territory, Canada holds the North American cold record; it recorded a temperature of -63 degrees C on February 3, 1947. The highest temperature ever recorded was 58 degrees C in Al'aziziyah, Libya, on September 13, 1922.

Death Valley, California is both the lowest point on the American continent and one of the hottest places in the world. Temperatures there may be as high as 49 degrees C for several days straight, and on July 10, 1913 it reached 56.7 degrees C. Since hot air rises and cold air falls, and since the valley is surrounded by mountains with cold air at their tops, why isn't Death Valley a relatively cool place? (Some scientific guesses: The area has hot, dry winds which blow low across the valley floor, creating a desert; lack of shade and vegetation make the sandy valley floor act as a reflector that heats the air near the ground).

In Japan they're called "typhoons"; in Bengal they're "cyclones"; in Australia they're "willy-willies"; in North America, we talk about "hurricanes". To be classed as a hurricane, the wind speed of a storm must exceed 117 km/h. Hurricanes are produced in tropical regions and, when fully developed, are the most destructive of all storms. Meteorologists give human names to hurricanes in order to keep track of concurrent storms. Lists of names, both female and male, are prepared in advance for use during a hurricane season.

A tornado is the most violent of storms. It's like a hurricane, but much smaller, being only a few hundred metres across. The air moves around the central core very fast -- sometimes at speeds of 600 km/h. These fast winds are able to uproot trees, demolish houses, and even fling cars several hundred metres.

The rainiest place on Earth is Tutenendo, Colombia. It gets about 11,770 mm of rain a year. The greatest precipitation in one year in Canada, 8122.4 mm, fell in Henderson Lake, British Columbia in 1913. The driest place on Earth is Arica, Chile. Over a 59 year period, the average yearly rainfall was only 0.76 mm. The least precipitation in one year in Canada was 12.7 mm at Arctic Bay in 1949.

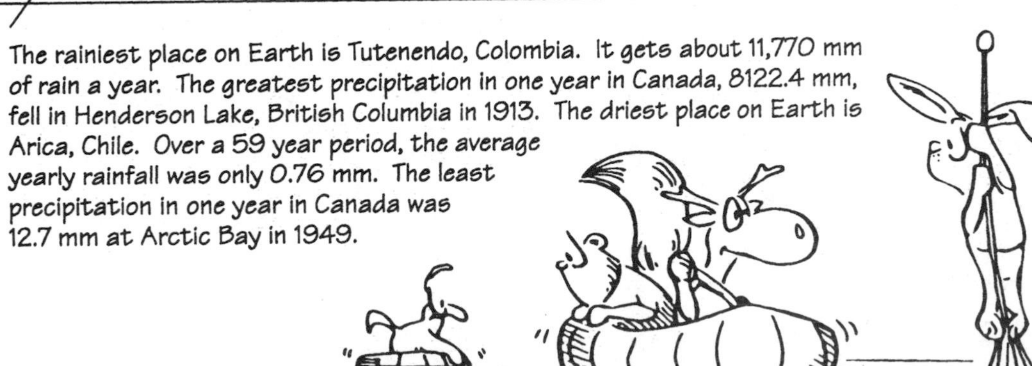

MAKE TIME

MAKING CLOUDS

There are two things needed for clouds to form: tiny particles (like dust, soot, or pollen) and warm, moist air that is cooled. Make your own "cloud" in a bottle.

MATERIALS: 2 litre, clear, plastic pop bottle with screw-on cap; warm water; match. Optional -- plastic bags; twist ties.

DOING IT:

1. **This activity should be done with adult supervision.**

2. Fill the bottom of a plastic pop bottle with 1 to 2 cm of warm water.

3. Lay the bottle on its side. Light a match and, after it burns for a couple of seconds, blow it out.

4. Hold the match in the opening of the bottle so that smoke drifts into the bottle. You may want to push down on and then release the bottle to help suck smoke inside.

5. Screw the cap on the bottle. Swish the water around to rinse down all parts of the bottle.

6. Hold the bottle up toward a bright window or lamp. Squeeze the bottle for a moment and then let it go. What do you see inside the bottle? You should see a faint "fog". How is this like a cloud in the sky? Does "fog" form each time you squeeze and release the bottle? Why?

7. *Extension:* Blow up two plastic bags and twist tie the bags shut. Each bag is filled with warm, moist air from your breath. Put one bag into the freezer and leave the other bag at room temperature. After about 15 minutes, take the bag out of the freezer. Compare the two bags. Which bag has condensed water vapour inside? Why? Leave both bags at room temperature for half an hour. What happens to the condensed water vapour? How does the temperature of air affect the formation of clouds?

You make clouds on cold days without even knowing it. When you breathe out warm, moist air, it cools in front of you and briefly forms a little "cloud".

Clouds form when warm, moist air rises and cools. Cooler air cannot hold as much water vapour as warmer air. As the air cools, the water vapour condenses (changes from a gas into a liquid) to form water droplets (or ice crystals); this is similar to water condensing on the outside of a glass of cold water on a hot, humid day. For clouds to form, the water vapour must have something to condense around. There are all sorts of microscopic particles in the air (e.g. dust, soot, pollen, bits of rock, salt from the oceans, as well as particles added by humans through car exhaust and smoke from factories). Billions of particles with tiny water droplets on them make up a cloud. When you make a "cloud" in a bottle, the smoke provides the microscopic particles. You condense the water vapour by lowering the air pressure in the bottle; squeezing the bottle increases the air pressure and then immediately releasing the bottle lowers the pressure. Air pressure is related to the formation of clouds because the higher into the atmosphere you go, the thinner the air and the lower the air pressure.

Water droplets may persist at temperatures well below freezing (such droplets are said to be "supercooled"). Clouds made up mainly of water droplets have sharp, well-defined edges. Those made up chiefly of ice crystals appear to be fuzzy and diffused. Clouds aren't as light as you might think. A mid-sized cloud can have the mass of as many as five elephants. The inside of a cloud is similar to what it's like on a very foggy day.

Topics: Atmosphere; Air; Weather Conditions.

Making Rain

Water in nature is always moving -- rising up to form clouds and then coming down again as rain. Simulate the water cycle with a kettle, pot, and some ice water.

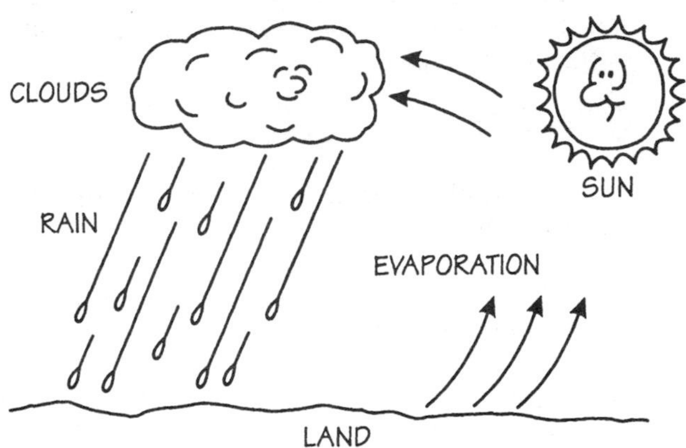

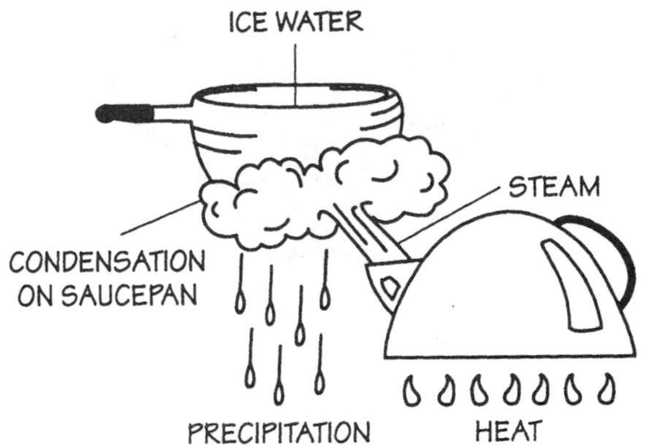

MATERIALS: Kettle (ideally electric, otherwise you'll also need a stove); small saucepan; shallow pan; water; ice cubes.

DOING IT:

1. This activity should be done with adult supervision.

2. Heat some water in a kettle.

3. Put some cold water and ice cubes into a saucepan.

4. When the water in the kettle is boiling, hold the saucepan full of cold water just above the steam. Put a shallow pan underneath the saucepan to prevent a mess. **Keep your hands out of the steam because it can cause severe burns.** Watch water droplets form on the bottom of the saucepan. Some of the droplets will become large enough to drip off. When this happens, it's "raining"!

5. How is your model of rain like the water cycle? What does the kettle of boiling water represent? Where are the clouds in the model? How can you make a "rain shower" develop more quickly? Can you affect the size of the drops that fall from the saucepan? Can you create a "downpour"?

When lakes, oceans, and rivers are heated by the sun, invisible water vapour rises into the air (some of the water turns from a liquid into a gas). This is "evaporation". There are a number of factors that affect evaporation. The hotter water gets, the faster its molecules move, and the faster it evaporates. When a greater surface area of water is exposed (e.g. shallow pan of water containing the same volume of water as a drinking glass), the water evaporates faster because more of it is in direct contact with the air. Finally, wind makes water evaporate faster because it "pushes" molecules on the water's surface into the air faster.

As water vapour rises, it cools and condenses into tiny droplets of water around microscopic particles floating in the air. Billions of particles with water droplets form a cloud. Precipitation occurs when droplets combine and become so heavy that air currents can no longer hold them up. Or, as a cloud grows and reaches up into the higher, colder parts of the atmosphere, some droplets turn to ice. The ice crystals grow at the expense of liquid droplets, which are attracted to the ice and freeze on it. The ice crystals eventually become too large to be held up by air currents, and begin to fall. Depending on the temperature near the ground, the moisture from clouds falls as either rain, snow, or sleet. Much of the precipitation that falls on land eventually flows back into lakes and oceans. So, the cycle continues.

Topics: Atmosphere; States of Matter; Snow.

A FRONT SEAT

Put together a motion booklet that shows the meeting of a cold front and a warm front to produce rain.

MATERIALS: Three copies of each of the following three pages; stapler.

DOING IT:

1. One motion booklet is made up of three copies of each frame on the following pages; you need multiple copies so that you have enough pages to flip and so that your eyes can catch the image of each picture.

2. Cut out each frame. Put the frames in order in a pile, with frame number 1 at the top of the pile. Place identical copies of a frame next to each other. Staple the pile of frames together along the left side to make the booklet.

3. What do you see as you flip the pages quickly and look at the pictures? It may take some practice, but you should see a cold front meet a warm front to produce rain. The booklet only shows one system, and represents a simplified version of one way that rain might develop.

4. *Extension:* Use an extra set of the pictures. Cut out each frame and black out the number. Mix up the frames. Can you put the frames in the right order to "make it rain"?

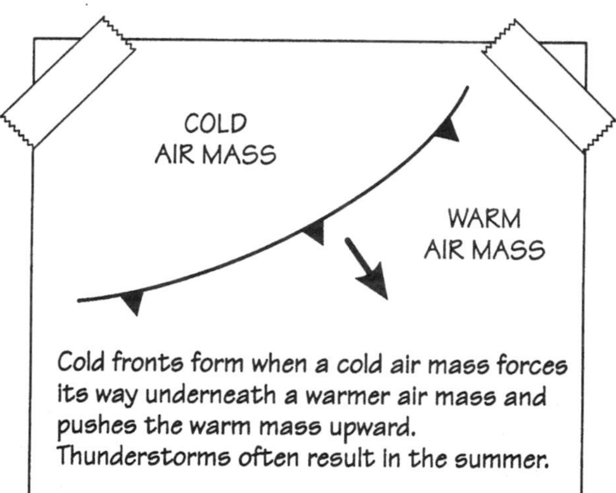

Cold fronts form when a cold air mass forces its way underneath a warmer air mass and pushes the warm mass upward. Thunderstorms often result in the summer.

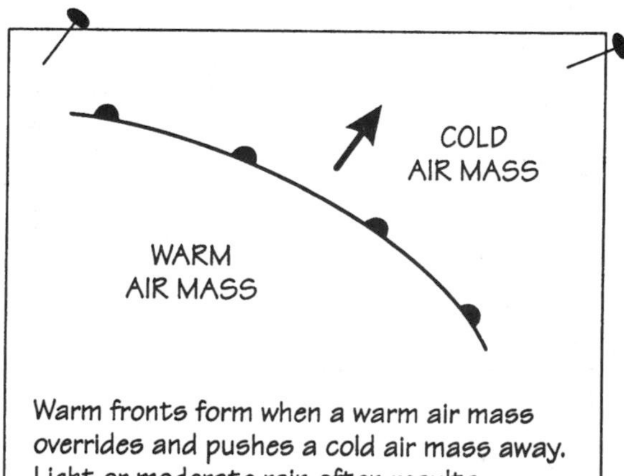

Warm fronts form when a warm air mass overrides and pushes a cold air mass away. Light or moderate rain often results.

Four times each day, year-round, weather observers around the world simultaneously read their instruments and look at the sky to record a weather observation. This is "synoptic" observation -- recording the state of the weather at a specific hour, at selected stations all over the world. Synoptic observations, together with information from weather satellites, are used to construct weather maps. Weather maps provide a general overview of atmospheric conditions at particular times over vast areas of the globe and form the basis of weather forecasts.

The following pages contain a series of very simplified weather maps. When a large body of air -- as large as 13 million sq. km -- remains over a certain area (e.g. snow and ice of Arctic regions) for a long period of time, it takes on the characteristic temperatures and humidities of the area and is called an "air mass". Cold air masses are usually associated with high pressure (cold air is denser; the air molecules are closer together, and so the pressure is higher) and warm air masses are associated with low pressure. When two air masses with different properties meet, they form a boundary zone called a "front". A "cold front" is the leading edge of an advancing cold air mass (a cold air mass pushing and moving under a warm air mass); advancing cold air masses usually move southward across the North American continent. A "warm front" is the leading edge of a retreating cold air mass (a warm air mass pushing a cold air mass); retreating cold air masses usually move northward. Fronts are frequently characterized by clouds and produce some of the stormiest weather.

Topics: Weather Conditions; Atmosphere; Air; Mapping.

1

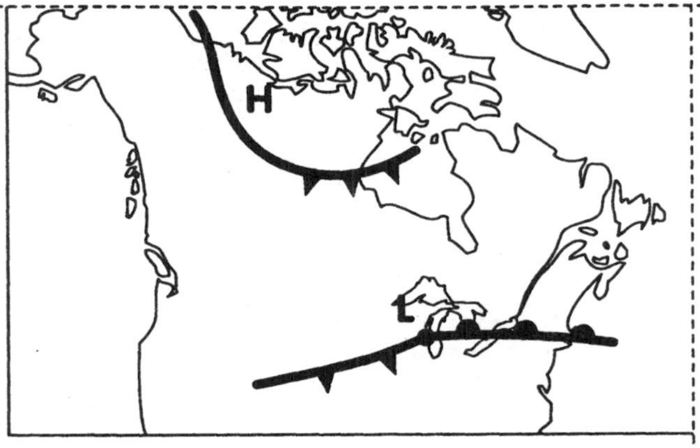

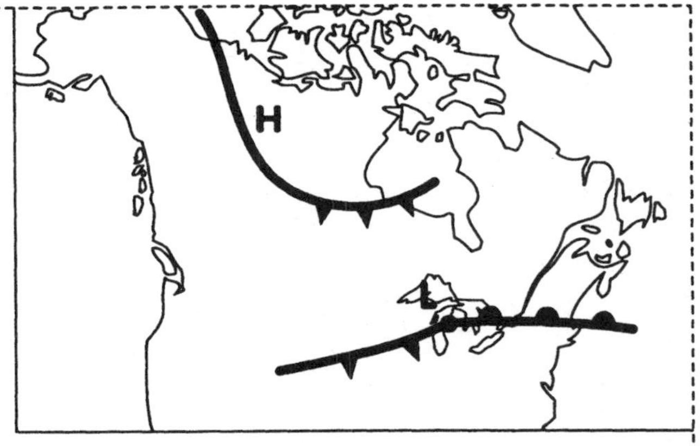

H High Pressure

L Low Pressure

Thundershowers

Cold Front

Warm Front

Rain

2

3

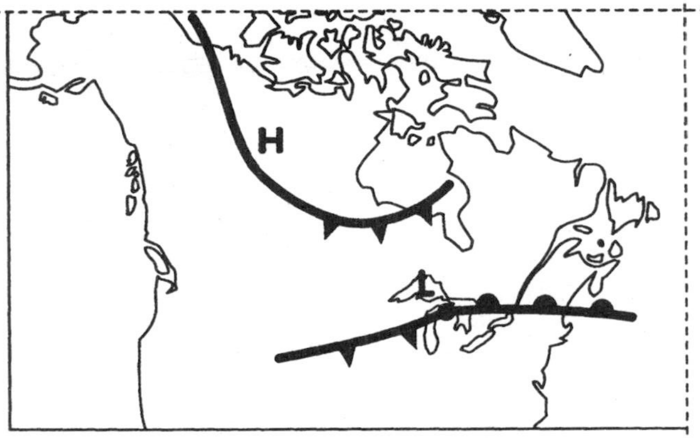

4

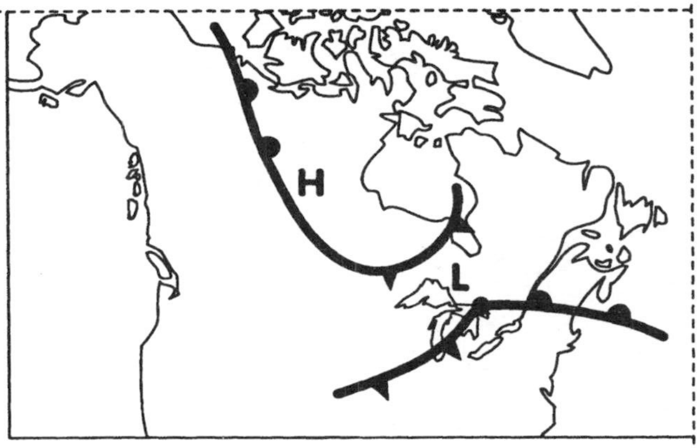

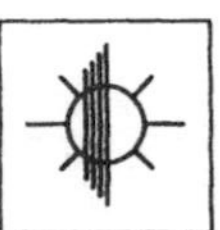

5

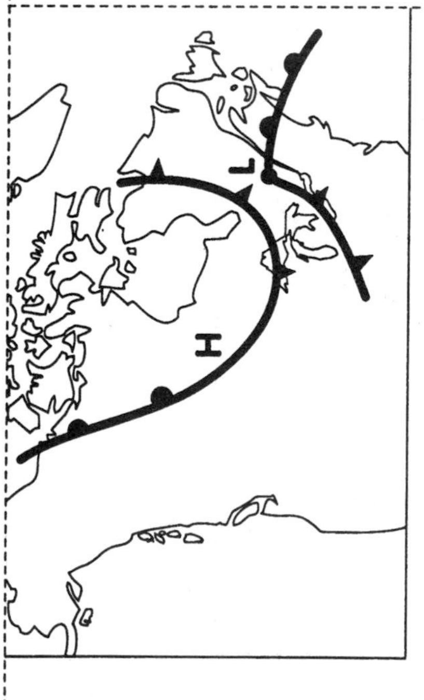

6

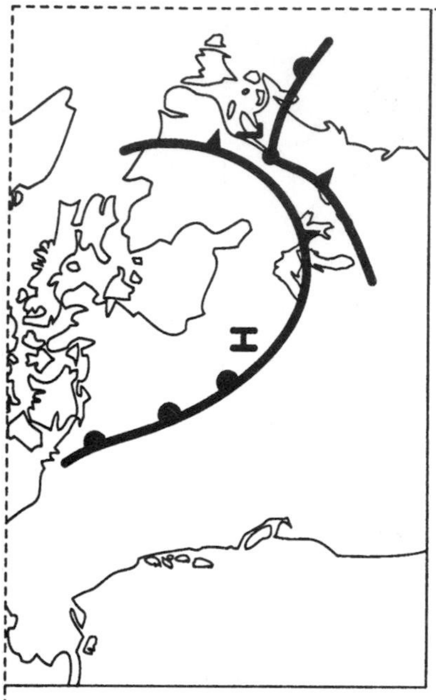

7

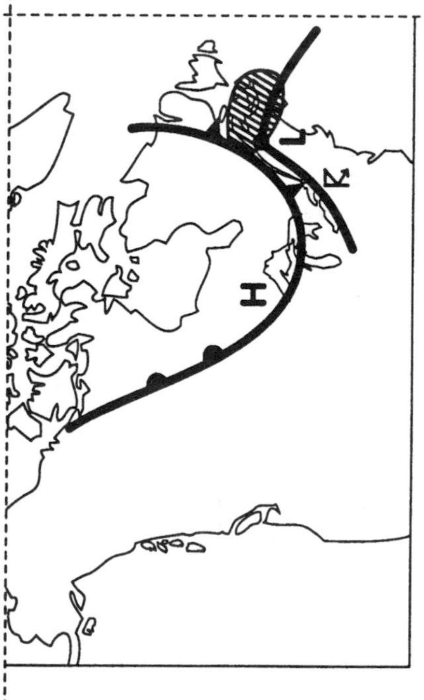

8

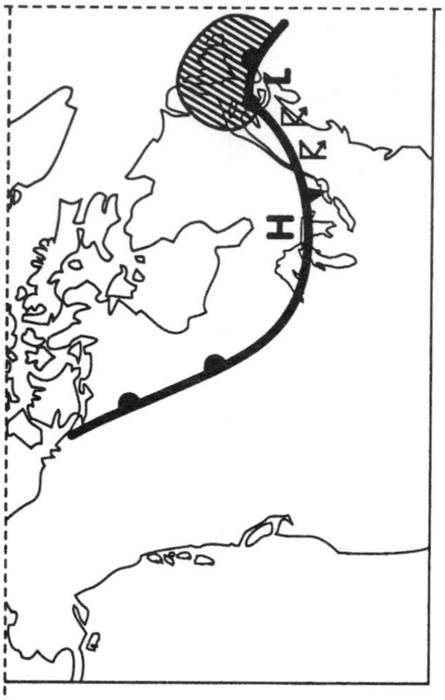

9

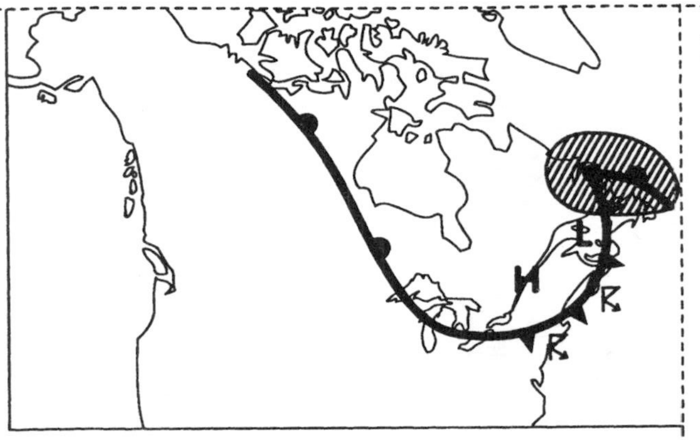

10

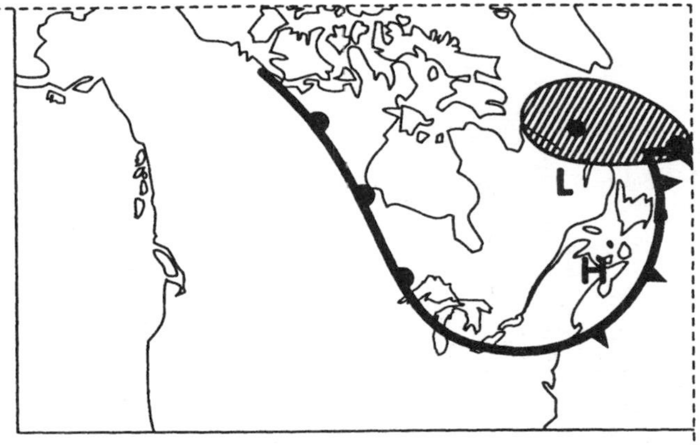

11

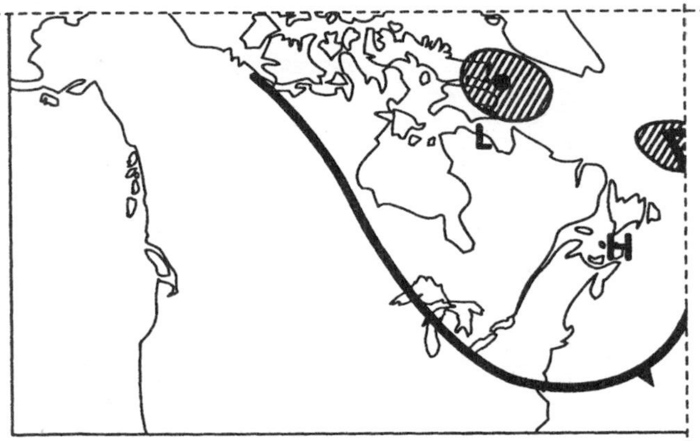

12

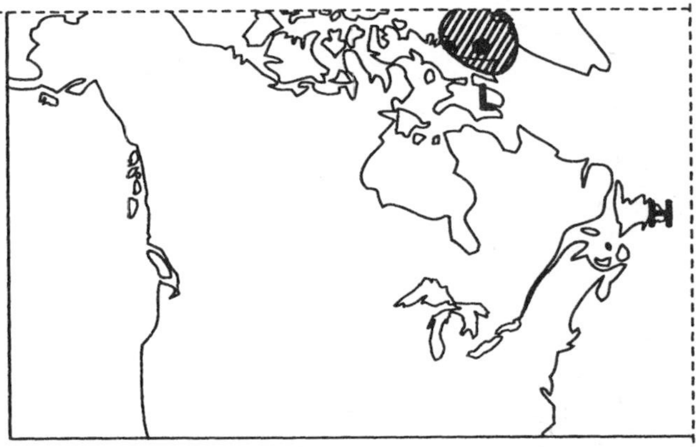

SNOW STUDIES

If the temperature near the ground is below freezing (0 degrees C), moisture will usually fall from clouds as snow. Get to know snow through these mini-studies.

MATERIALS: Small shovel; magnifying glass; ruler; thermometer; can (e.g. 284 ml soup can) with both ends removed; piece of metal or stiff cardboard; four containers (e.g. jars); masking tape; measuring cup; different colours of construction paper; rocks or other small weights; paper; pencil.

DOING IT:

1. *Shades of White:* Most people think of snow as white, but snow can be other colours. Go on a walk to see how many different colours of snow you can find; look for shades of white as well as soft, pastel colours. What makes particular areas of snow a certain colour? For example, snow can be coloured pink by algae in it.

2. *Snow Drifts:* Compare the depth of snow in different spots (e.g. in the open, under a shrub, under a tree, in a ditch, along the sides of a building). Look for snow drifts. Where do they form? How do obstructions (e.g. buildings, trees) affect the shape of snow drifts? How is wind direction related to snow drifts? What patterns or designs can you find in snow drifts? Carefully slice through a snow drift with a shovel. How many layers do you see? Use a ruler to measure the width of each layer. Are the layers different colours? Do the layers feel different (e.g. hardness, iciness, grittiness)? Use a magnifying glass to compare snow crystals in different layers.

Some areas of the world stay very warm all year round and do not get any snow. In other areas of the world, winter is a time of year when temperatures dip below freezing and snow is common.

If you're out in cold weather investigating snow, remember to dress warmly. Layers of clothing help to keep you warm. Wear a cap or hood (half a person's body heat is lost through his or her head!). And don't forget boots and mittens (mittens keep your hands warmer than gloves because your fingers can share heat).

Topics: Snow; Measurement.

3. *Snow Temperatures:* Snow can act as an insulating blanket. Prove this by taking the air temperature. *Measure the air temperature in shade so that the thermometer isn't heated by the sun. Whenever you take a temperature, hold the thermometer in place for several minutes to get a valid reading.* Then take the following readings: at the top of a snow drift; halfway down through the drift; under the snow at ground level. How does the temperature of the snow compare to the air temperature? Where is it coldest? Where is it warmest? Why?

4. *Snow Density:* Snow density (how compact the snow is) varies with the depth and age of snow, air temperature, and wind. Take four samples of snow: freshly fallen snow; snow that fell several days ago; snow from a drift; snow that has been walked on. Collect a sample by carefully pressing the full length of a can (both ends removed) into the snow until the can is level with the surface of the snow. Lift the can out of the snow; place a piece of metal or cardboard against the bottom of the can to hold the snow in. The snow should be level with both ends of the can; if it isn't, use a ruler to level it. Put each of your snow samples into a separate container and mark the containers. Bring the samples indoors and allow the snow to melt. Then, use a measuring cup to compare the water from each sample. Which sample produced the most water (and therefore had the densest snow)? Why?

5. *Snow Melt:* On a *sunny*, mild day, lay different coloured sheets of construction paper on the snow; use rocks or other small weights to keep the sheets in place. Each sheet should be exposed to the same amount of sunlight throughout the day. At regular intervals during the day, measure and record how deeply each sheet has melted into the snow. Why does colour affect melting? How does this relate to the colours of clothing we wear for different seasons? How does it affect the way snow melts in the spring? For example, why does snow melt more quickly on a black road surface?

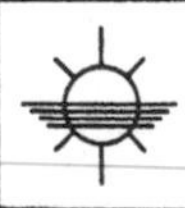

FLAKES OF SNOW

No two snowflakes are exactly alike. But snow crystals do have some similarities and can be grouped into general categories. Collect snowflakes during a snowfall.

MATERIALS: Black construction paper; magnifying glass; ruler. Optional -- sheets of white paper; scissors.

DOING IT:

1. Put a sheet of black construction paper into the freezer so that it cools before you use it. Go outside when it's snowing and collect snowflakes on the paper. Examine the flakes with a magnifying glass. Are they all alike? How many sides do they have? Are they the same size? Try to measure the size of snowflakes in millimetres. Look at individual snowflakes and decide into which of the ten general groups they fall. How many different kinds of snowflakes can you find? What happens to the shape of a snowflake as it melts?

2. *Variation:* Catch and examine snowflakes at the start of a snowfall, then when the snowfall is at its strongest and, finally, toward the end of the snowfall. Do the snowflakes change throughout the snowfall? Also compare flakes that fall when it's very cold outside to flakes that fall when it's mild.

3. *Extension:* Use a magnifying glass to compare the crystals in window frost, on plants, and in a freezer to snow crystals. How are they the same? How are they different?

4. *Extension:* Make your own snowflakes by folding a circular piece of paper in half, in thirds, and then in half again (as shown). Cut a pattern into the paper and open up the flake. Into which of the ten general groups do your snowflakes fall?

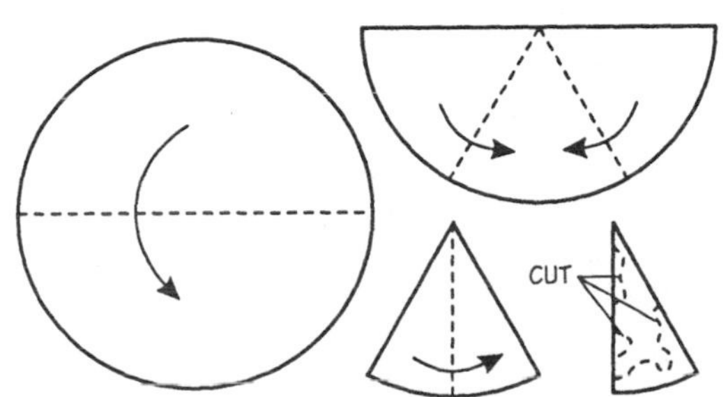

TYPES OF SNOW AND ICE CRYSTALS

Name	Symbol	Example
Hexagonal Plates		
Stellar Crystals		
Hexagonal Columns		
Needles		
Spatial Dendrites		
Capped Columns		
Irregular Crystals		
Graupel		
Sleet		
Hail		

Technically speaking, the term "snowflake" is defined as a cluster of snow crystals that have stuck together as they fall to the ground. The world's biggest snowflake was 38 cm in diameter. A large snowflake can fall at a speed of 5 km/h. Different kinds of snow crystals result from certain combinations of conditions -- particularly temperature and moisture level -- in the clouds and near the Earth's surface. There is an international system for grouping snow crystals into ten general categories. The system is based on the structure of the crystals. For example, "graupel" (snow pellets) refers to snow crystals with a thick, icy coating. "Sleet" consists of frozen rain drops, usually small, smoother, and transparent. "Hail" is solid precipitation made up of a solid centre and layer upon semi-transparent layer of ice. The international system applies to falling snow. Snow crystals change when they reach the ground and lose their original identity. As a snow crystal melts, its parts blend into a spherical shape and it ends up as a drop of water.

Topics: Snow; Classification.

ICE STICKS

An "icicle" is a hanging, tapering stick of ice formed by the freezing of dripping water. Explore existing icicles and then make your own.

MATERIALS: Magnifying glass; ruler; 2 litre plastic pop bottle with screw-on cap; water; scissors; string; paper; pencil. Optional -- food colouring; aluminum foil tart cup.

DOING IT:

1. Find a building with icicles. **Never stand directly underneath icicles and look up at them; they can fall and hurt you.** What colour is the roof? Of what material is the roof made? How might roof colour and material affect the formation of icicles? Which side of the building has the most icicles. Why? How would you describe the icicles? Why are they different lengths?

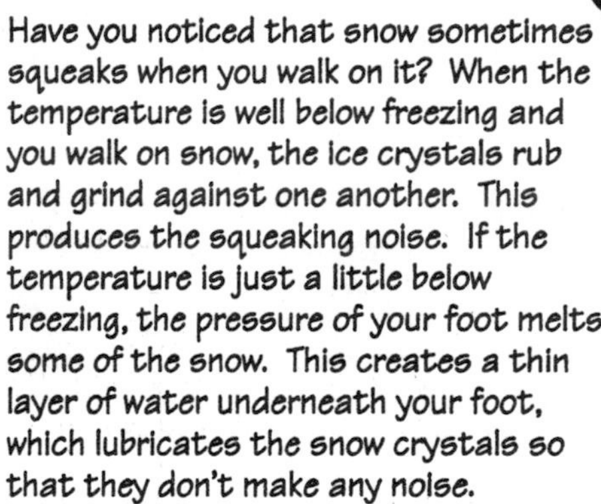

Icicles are both beautiful and interesting. In the right location and with the right temperature variations, you can see many different lengths and thicknesses of icicles. Icicles form and reform throughout the winter, and particularly in spring, as the temperature fluctuates.

Topics: Snow; States of Matter.

2. Examine icicles with a magnifying glass. What does the surface look like? Are icicles always smooth? Can you see through them?

3. Measure several icicles -- both their length and the diameter of their base. How long is the longest icicle you find? How thick is the thickest? How thin is the thinnest?

4. Break an icicle into two pieces. How does it break? Use a magnifying glass to look at the layers of ice. How do icicles form?

5. Fill a pop bottle 3/4 full with water (if you wish, you can add some food colouring to the water). Put the cap on the bottle. Make a very small hole in the side of the bottle, near its bottom. Use string to hang the bottle outside. As water drips from the hole, an icicle will form. How long does it take the icicle to form (check the bottle every hour or so)? How long is the icicle? What happens to the water in the bottle? Experiment with different hole sizes. How is hole size related to the icicle that forms? Air temperature will also affect the formation of your icicles.

6. *Extension:* How does ice form? On a cold day, fill a foil tart cup with water and place it outside in some snow. Use a magnifying glass to watch the water freeze. Where does ice form first? In what directions does the ice spread? What do the ice crystals look like? How long does it take for the water to freeze completely?

Weather records are very useful. For example, they can help determine whether a particular location receives enough snow to justify building a ski resort; whether a solar energy project will work in a certain area; or whether farming is practical in a given region. A climatologist can review historical weather records and give advice based on averages and extremes.

MAKE TIME

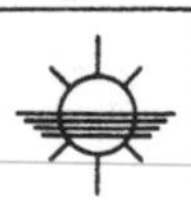

MICROCLIMATES

It may be hot in the sun, but much cooler in the shade under a tree. A microclimate study demonstrates the differences that can exist within small areas.

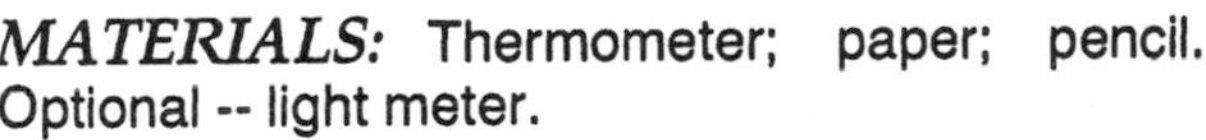

MATERIALS: Thermometer; paper; pencil. Optional -- light meter.

DOING IT:

1. How many different microclimates can you find within a few metres? Compare open, exposed spots to sheltered spots. Write down the location of each spot and its temperatures.

2. For each spot, measure the temperature just above the surface of the ground. Then, measure the temperature 1.5 m above the ground, in still-wind or low-wind conditions. *Whenever you take a temperature, hold the thermometer in place for several minutes to get a valid reading.* Look for holes in trees or in the ground. Is the air temperature in a hole higher than the air temperature just outside the hole? Look for different surface materials and textures. Take and compare temperatures near grass, pavement, gravel, wood, etc. Compare temperatures on slopes and in gulleys; or at the base of a tree, in the lower branches, and at the tip of the outer branches. Take light readings if you have a light meter.

3. As you take temperature readings, note animals and plants found in the various spots. Are the plants found in open, sunny spots the same as those found in the shade? Where are the greatest number of plants found?

4. What is the hottest microclimate you find? The coolest? The sunniest? The darkest? The driest? The dampest? How close together are the microclimates? Why are temperatures in the same area different at different heights?

5. *Extension:* Make a map showing the locations of the various microclimates.

"Weather" refers to the atmospheric conditions in a specific place at a specific time. "Climate" refers to the average weather conditions (e.g. temperature, wind, precipitation) of a place, usually taken over all the days throughout the year (e.g. an area which has high temperatures is said to have a hot climate). The difference between weather and climate is like when your friend, who is generally a very nice person (climate), is in a bad mood one day (weather). A major factor in climate is "latitude", the distance of a place from the equator. More of the sun's energy reaches the area close to the equator and so it is hottest there. Another important factor in climate is ocean currents. Newfoundland, Canada is at about the same latitude as Britain, but has a cooler climate because of the cold Labrador Current. Yet another factor in climate is height above sea level.

A "microclimate" is the combination of heat, light, and humidity in a *very* small area, like under a tree, near a pond, or in a field. This activity focuses on the temperatures of various microclimates. When someone talks about "temperature", they're usually referring to air temperature. General air temperature is an important factor in weather. However, the temperature *you personally experience* is very much a function of where you are. For example, it tends to be cooler higher above the ground. Temperature can vary a great deal in an area as small as a few metres. In one small site, temperature readings ranging from 16 degrees to 51 degrees Celsius were recorded, when the "official air temperature" was 31 degrees Celsius. The microclimate of a particular area determines the type and number of plants and animals found there.

Topics: Weather Conditions; Habitat; Measurement; Mapping.

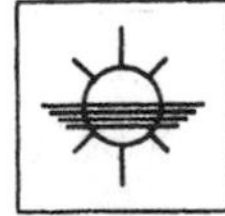

WARNING: FIRE DANGER

Calculating and reporting the fire-danger rating of your area emphasizes the close tie between weather and the environment, and encourages fire safety.

MATERIALS: Paper; pencil.

DOING IT:

1. Examine your surroundings and rate the fire danger from 1 (little danger) to 5 (great danger) along the following five dimensions:

- *Wind* -- 1 for a low wind to 5 for a high wind.
- *Relative Humidity* -- 1 for high humidity (very moist air) to 5 for low humidity (very dry air).
- *Ground Dampness* -- 1 for very wet to 5 for very dry.
- *Plants* -- 1 for plenty of green, moist plants to 5 for many dry, browning plants.
- *Days Since Heavy Rain* -- 1 for one day; 2 for two days; 3 for four days; 4 for six days; and 5 for eight days or more.

For example, if the wind is fairly light, you might rate it at a 2. If the relative humidity is moderate, you might rate it at a 3. For the "days since heavy rain" area, you may want to use the actual number of days as the rating instead of the usual 1 to 5 rating (e.g. if 6 days have passed since a heavy rain, use the figure 6 in your calculations instead of the usual rating factor of 4). This will depend on the constant factors of your area, such as slope and drainage. For example, if the land drains rapidly, you should put more emphasis on the rain factor.

2. Add the ratings and divide by 5 to obtain the average fire-danger index for the day. For example, if wind = 2, relative humidity = 3, ground dampness = 4, plants = 2, and days since heavy rain = 4, the total is 15. 15 divided by 5 equals a fire-danger index of 3.

3. A fire-danger index of 1 is low danger; 2-3 is medium; and 4-5 is high. Report the rating daily. How does the rating change over a period of a week or two? What causes it to change?

Very few forest fires are caused by lightning and campfires. Most are caused by careless smokers and people burning trash. Fire danger is influenced by both constant and variable factors. Constant factors for a given area of land include its slope, drainage, elevation, exposure to prevailing winds, and the density, size, quantity, distribution, and arrangement of fuels. The variable factors change from day to day and include wind velocity, humidity, flammability of green vegetation, and flammability and moisture content of dry fuels on the forest floor.

Topics: Weather Conditions; Habitat; Measurement.

"Rain before seven,
Fine after eleven."
This saying indicates a truth
about rain at any time,
not just before seven:
belts of rain brought by fronts
tend to last less than 6 hours.

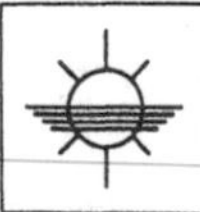

THE HEAVENS

"Planetology" is a new field, uniting the study of Earth with the study of space. Planetologists are trying to explain why Earth is so different from other planets. How is it that we alone have a gentle climate? Why are we the only planet covered by so much water? Why are we the only world in this solar system (as far as we know) that is home to life?

The typical lifetime of a star is 10,000,000,000 years!

There is one star in our solar system -- the sun. The sun's diameter is 1,392,000 km; a line of 109 Earths would be needed to equal the diameter of the sun. The sun is made almost entirely of hydrogen and helium gas. The sun's surface has a temperature of 6000 degrees C, and the temperature in its core is at least 10 million degrees!

The most exciting parts of many space movies are the fantastic battles between spacecrafts. The interesting thing is, every time you see a bright flash of light you also hear a blast. This isn't scientifically accurate. Space has no air; it's a vacuum. Sound doesn't travel through a vacuum, so the explosions should be silent.

On July 20, 1969, American Neil Armstrong was the first human being to walk on the moon. His famous words: "One small step for a man, one giant leap for mankind."

ANOTHER DAY, ANOTHER PLANET!

Scientists aren't as sure as they once were that life exists elsewhere. If the galaxy were filled with advanced civilizations, why haven't we had contact with them? There is no widely-accepted evidence indicating that Earth is now being -- or has ever been -- visited by creatures from other planets. Computer simulations show that a high-tech civilization, situated in the centre of the galaxy (where the stars are older) would -- even including 1,000 year colonization stops at each planet -- colonize the entire galaxy in 5.5 million years. That's a blink of the eye compared with the age of the galaxy. Where are the aliens?

HAVE A BALL!

There are nine planets, including Earth, in our solar system. A few balls and some physical activity combine for a great way to get to know the planets.

MATERIALS: Huge, 2 to 3 m diameter balloon (sun); two small marbles (Mercury, Pluto); two tennis balls (Venus, Earth); ping-pong ball (Mars); basketball (Jupiter); soccer ball (Saturn); two baseballs (Uranus, Neptune); string; stick markers. Note: Instead of balls, you can use pieces of cardboard cut to the sizes of the balls. Optional -- measuring tape; planet labels for stick markers.

DOING IT:

1. The following page provides background information on the planets.

2. One person is the "sun" and receives the gigantic balloon. Nine other people are "planets" and hold the appropriate balls. Get to know the planets by tossing the balls around. Which planets are about the same size? Which planet is smallest? Which is largest? Is it possible to hold more than one Mercury in your hand? More than one Jupiter? Mix up the balls. Can people toss the right ball back to each of the planets?

The "solar system" consists of the sun and all the objects -- nine planets and their moons, thousands of asteroids, meteoroids, thousands of comets, and particles of dust and gas -- that revolve around the sun. Each of the nine planets spins around an axis through its centre, while also travelling in a counterclockwise direction around the sun. The time it takes a planet to completely spin around on its axis is that planet's "day". The time it takes a planet to orbit around the sun is that planet's "year". The farther a planet is from the sun, the longer its year. A planet's distance from the sun also affects its climate and atmosphere. The exact distances between planets and the sun, and between planets themselves, vary because the planets move in oval orbits, which puts them closer to certain points at certain times. One of the units of distance used by astronomers is the "astronomical unit". One astronomical unit (AU) is equal to the average distance between the Earth and the sun, or approximately 150,000,000 km.

Topics: Planets; Earth; Measurement.

3. Planets and their balls go to their positions in a line from the sun: Mercury 4 paces; Venus 7 paces; Earth 10 paces; Mars 15 paces; Jupiter 52 paces; Saturn 95 paces; Uranus 191 paces; Neptune 301 paces; Pluto 395 paces (average orbital distance). Mark each planet's position using a stick. Note: You can do this on a smaller scale by moving the decimal point one unit left; this will also give you the approximate distance from the sun in astronomical units (e.g. Mercury 4 paces becomes 0.4 paces or 0.4 AU; Uranus 191 paces becomes 19.1 paces or 19.1 AU).

4. People can leave their balls at the appropriate stick marker and meet at the sun. Walk or run at a constant speed from the sun to Pluto; notice how quickly you pass by the first six planets. Can one person travel from, for example, Earth to Mars faster than another can travel (at the same pace) from Neptune to Pluto? Compare distances between the various planets.

5. The planets can return to their stick markers and try orbiting in a counterclockwise direction around the sun (real orbits aren't exactly circular, but close). Everyone should start orbiting at the same time, and orbit at the same pace. Why do some orbits take longer?

6. If there are enough people, some people can play moons. Moons can orbit their planets while planets orbit the sun (planets and moons also spin around an axis through their core, but keep things simple!). Does anyone bump into anyone else? This doesn't happen in reality.

7. Try a more exact demonstration of orbits. For example, tie one end of each of two pieces of string to the sun's stick. Stretch one piece of string from the sun to Earth and the other from the sun to Jupiter. Earth and Jupiter should then make one revolution around the sun. Earth and Jupiter start at the same time and hold their strings tight, but Earth moves twice as fast as Jupiter (closer planets orbit the sun faster than farther planets, in addition to having a shorter distance around). Does Jupiter take about twelve times as long as Earth (Jupiter's year is about twelve times as long as Earth's)? Repeat this idea with other planets.

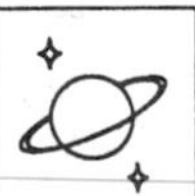

THE PLANETS OF OUR SOLAR SYSTEM

Planet	MERCURY	VENUS	EARTH	MARS	JUPITER	SATURN	URANUS	NEPTUNE	PLUTO
Relative Size	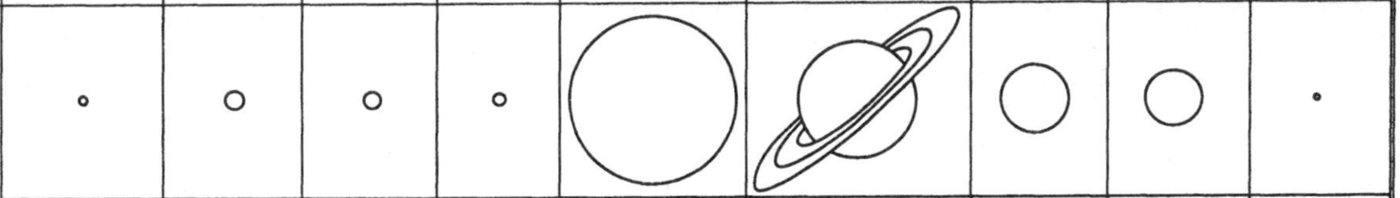								
Colour	Orange	Yellow	Blue & White (as seen from space)	Red	Yellow	Yellow	Green	Yellow	Yellow
Named For	Roman winged messenger god	Roman goddess of love	Greek, meaning "to the ground"	Roman god of war	Chief Roman god	Roman god of agriculture	Greek sky god	Roman sea god	Greek god of the under-world
Maximum Distance from Sun (millions)	69.7 km	109.0 km	152.1 km	249.1 km	815.7 km	1,507.0 km	3,004.0 km	4,537.0 km	7,375.0 km
Diameter	4,880 km	12,100 km	12,756 km	6,787 km	142,800 km	120,000 km	51,800 km	49,500 km	3,000 km
Average Surface Temperature	350 °C day, -170 °C night	480 °C	22 °C	-23 °C	-150 °C	-180 °C	-210 °C	-220 °C	-230 °C
Day Length (Earth Units)	58.0 days	243.0 days	1.0 day	1.0 day	10.0 hours	10.0 hours	16.0 hours	18.0 hours	6.4 days
Year Length (Earth Units)	88 days	225 days	365 days	687 days	12 years	30 years	84 years	165 years	248 years
Number of Moons	0	0	1	2	16	18	21	8	1

NOTES:

Mercury Planet closest to the sun. Resembles Earth's moon in size.

Venus Brightest planet. Earth's sister planet. All the planets spin around their axis in a counterclockwise direction, except Venus which spins in a clockwise direction.

Earth Home. Similar to Venus in size.

Mars Similar to Earth in mass and size. Appears to have two polar ice caps consisting of carbon dioxide and water, and a thin atmosphere composed largely of carbon dioxide.

Jupiter Largest planet. If all the other planets were rolled into one ball, the ball would be smaller than Jupiter. Has a mysterious big red spot.

Saturn Slightly smaller than Jupiter. Famous for its many distinct rings. Largest moon has a diameter of 5800 km, which is bigger than Mercury.

Uranus Third largest planet. Like Saturn, Uranus has rings, but they are not as thick.

Neptune Fourth largest planet.

Pluto Smallest planet. May be a lost satellite of Neptune. Its orbit hints there may be another, still more far-flung planet.

PLANETARY PLAY

What are the planets like? How is Venus different from Jupiter? Let the planets introduce themselves through this play about the solar system.

MATERIALS: Script on following pages; any sort of props and costumes you wish.

DOING IT:

1. The previous page provides background information on the planets.

2. Use puppets or real people to put on the following play. Adding costumes (e.g. wearing a shirt the colour of the planet) makes a play more interesting for those watching, and more fun for those acting.

3. You may have to add or take out characters depending on the size of your group. As written, the characters are: Sun, Mercury, Venus, Earth, Mars, Jupiter, Saturn, Uranus, Neptune, Pluto, Atmosphere. If there are enough people, add asteroids or meteoroids to the cast of characters. People in the audience can be made to feel like part of the play through such things as raising their hands when the voting takes place.

MAKE TIME

The "terrestrial" planets -- Mercury, Venus, Earth, Mars, and Pluto -- resemble the Earth in size, chemical composition, and density. The "Jovian" ("like Jupiter") planets -- Jupiter, Saturn, Uranus, and Neptune -- are much larger in size and have thick, gaseous atmospheres and low densities.

Human beings once considered themselves as the centre of the universe. The small patch of land over which they could walk was the limit of their world. As time went on, humans became aware of the Earth as a whole and it became the centre of the universe. Humans began to feel smaller when it was discovered that the Earth is one of many planets travelling in space around the sun. Then it was established that our sun is only one of billions of stars forming a huge cluster called a galaxy. Our galaxy is only one of millions of galaxies, each an island of stars in a sea of space. Human beings are a speck of dust in this sea.

Since the beginning of time, human beings have been fascinated by the heavens. We've looked up and imagined all sorts of things. We've even attributed human ideas and characteristics to heavenly bodies (everyone has heard of the man in the moon!). This play involves the imaginary personalities of the planets. "Planet" comes from the Greek "planetes", meaning "wanderer". Each planet was named for a different Roman or Greek god. The planets each have a different mythology, as well as different physical/scientific characteristics.

Topics: Planets; Earth; Atmosphere.

First Annual Meeting Of The Solar System

(Scene: The planets can be seated in a semicircle. They are chatting as they wait for the SUN to call the meeting to order.)

SUN: (Enters stage left and calls meeting to order.) Planets, I now call the First Annual Meeting of the Solar System to order. *(Pause.)* The purpose of this meeting is to promote diplomatic relations. We've been having some problems out there and it's time to deal with them. Let's start by getting everyone to introduce themselves. Some of us live quite far from one another. I am the Sun. *(Polite applause from group.)* We'll start with the planets nearest to me.

MERCURY: I'm Mercury, named after the Roman winged messenger god.

(Polite applause.)

VENUS: I'm Venus, named after the Roman goddess of love. *(Winks at group and throws a kiss.)*

(Wild applause!)

EARTH: I, of course, am your host today -- Earth.

(Long applause, one or two planets stand.)

MARS: It's none of your business who I am!

SUN: Now Mars, that's enough of that behaviour! Ladies and Gentlemen, may I introduce Mars, named after the Roman god of war. He gets a little testy sometimes and --

MERCURY: Yeah, that's what we want to talk about. I'm --

SUN: Please, let the other planets introduce themselves. Jupiter you're next, I believe.

(MERCURY sits and sulks.)

JUPITER: Hello. I'm Jupiter, named after the Chief Roman god.

(Polite applause.)

SATURN: I'm Saturn, named after the Roman god of agriculture.

(Polite applause.)

URANUS: I'm Uranus, named after the Greek sky god.

(Polite applause.)

NEPTUNE: I'm Neptune, named after the Roman sea god.

(Polite applause.)

MERCURY: And that's Pluto, named after the Greek god of the underworld. I bet he's behind this trouble with Mars! I know it!

PLUTO: Listen you puny little planet --

MERCURY: Puny! You're the smallest planet. You haven't given us all the information on your size, but we all know the truth. You're no bigger than I am!

SUN: Now that's enough! Obviously we have a problem here. It seems that Mars has been causing trouble.

MERCURY, VENUS, EARTH, JUPITER, SATURN, URANUS, NEPTUNE: *(All shake their heads in agreement.)* Yes!

(Planets begin whispering to each other. Then SATURN shouts out . . .)

SATURN: All you have to do is look at the red colour of Mars to know that he's an angry sort of planet!

URANUS: He's been using his colour just to get attention. Most of us are plainer shades of yellow, orange, green, and blue. Mars has been showing off at every opportunity he gets.

JUPITER: I think we should kick Mars out of the solar system! He doesn't deserve to be with us. He can be a hot shot by himself!

(All planets cheer and agree.)

NEPTUNE: Let's take a vote. All in favour?

(People begin to raise their hands to vote.)

SUN: Hold on a minute. QUIET! *(Pauses.)* Don't you planets realize what you're doing? All parts of the solar system depend on the gravitational forces of the different bodies. If Mars left, the gravitational forces would change. That could mean big changes in our orbits, and temperatures and atmospheres. Earth, you in particular should realize that. You might not be warm or have enough oxygen in your atmosphere any more.

MARS: *(Shouts.)* Don't you see that Earth is the problem!! *(All planets look at Mars.)* Earth has it all: warm temperatures and human beings to keep it company. I don't have anyone. My average surface temperature is -23 degrees Celsius. I guess I'm . . . well . . . jealous! That's why I wanted to get more attention.

PLUTO: You know, I have the same complaint. I lack heat and light. My surface temperature is -230 degrees Celsius! It's so cold and dark that life can't

exist on me. I'm terribly lonely having no living things around -- not even plants or animals!

NEPTUNE, URANUS, JUPITER, SATURN: *(All agree.)* That's true! We're all cold and lonely.

MERCURY: *(Looking at complaining planets.)* You can have some of my light and heat. They don't help one bit. You see, Sun, I get too much heat and light. Any living creature would bake on my surface!

VENUS: I have the same problem Mercury does.

ALL PLANETS, EXCEPT EARTH: Then what can we do, Sun? We want life to exist on us like it does on Earth.

(EARTH grins an embarrassed kind of grin. All other planets start making noise by pounding their fists or stomping their feet.)

SUN: Silence, please. Now, I realize how each one of you must feel, but I'm not totally to blame.

ALL COMPLAINING PLANETS: *(Astonished.)* Who then?

SUN: You yourselves are partially to blame.

ALL COMPLAINING PLANETS: *(Each say something different to each other and to SUN.)* How is that? What did you say? No way! This guy's off his rocker.

SUN: Mercury and Venus, you revolve too close to me; that's why you get so much heat and light. And you, Jupiter, Uranus, Neptune, Pluto, and Saturn, you revolve far away; not enough of my heat and light can reach you to warm you up way out there in space. Only Earth and Mars revolve at the right distance from me to make life possible on their surfaces.

MARS: Then why doesn't life exist on me?

SUN: You will have to talk to Atmosphere about that.

(Mars calls out for ATMOSPHERE.)

ATMOSPHERE: *(Enters and looks around. Yawns.)* Here I thought I could get some sleep while you planets argued. Who called for me?

MARS: I did!

ATMOSPHERE: Yes, Mars, what can I do for you?

MARS: I have a complaint, Atmosphere. You spread yourself so thin on my surface that no life can exist on me. If people came, they wouldn't be able to breathe.

VENUS: Atmosphere, I have the opposite problem. You spread yourself so thick on me that if someone were on my surface they wouldn't even be able to see big, bright Sun at all.

JUPITER: Yes, I have that problem also.

SATURN, NEPTUNE, URANUS: Yes, we do, too.

MERCURY: You should be thankful. Atmosphere doesn't even come to me at all. *(Sniffs.)*

ATMOSPHERE: It's too hot your way, Mercury. I can't survive in such conditions.

PLUTO: Atmosphere doesn't come to me either. *(Starts to cry.)*

ATMOSPHERE: Bunch of cry babies! Pluto you're too far away from the Sun. It's just too cold way out there. I can't survive in those conditions, either. Why, I'd immediately turn to ice.

SUN: Silence, please! You are such a noisy bunch. I can't understand how the universe stays as quiet as it is. Each of you has complaints except Earth.

ALL COMPLAINING PLANETS: Earth doesn't complain because living things are found there. How could Earth be lonely?

EARTH: I've been listening to all of this and I have something to say. It's true that having life is nice. It's got its problems though. Humans can make an awful mess with things like pollution. But, they're working on it. I do like having them around. What you don't realize is that humans are interested in each one of you. Sometimes I think they care more about you than they do about me! They spend millions of dollars sending up satellites and space probes to visit you. They buy telescopes, they study you, they take pictures. Next time you feel lonely, think of all of Earth's people looking at you.

VENUS: Why, maybe I could be a movie star! You know, in one of those ro-man-tic kind of films!

(All planets laugh.)

ALL COMPLAINING PLANETS: *(Smiling and excited. Certain planets can say certain lines.)* I guess we're not so alone after all, with all those people looking at us. We're more popular than we could of imagined. And maybe some day we can even do something to help those humans. Thank you, Sun, for talking to us, and thank you, Earth, for all your people.

(All planets take a bow.)

PHASES OF THE MOON

The moon is most visible at night; sunlight makes it difficult to see the moon during the day. This people model is useful for understanding the moon's phases.

MATERIALS: Flashlight; large ball (e.g. basketball). Optional -- signs for Earth, sun, moon.

DOING IT:

1. Do this activity in a dimly-lit room. A person holding a flashlight is the sun. The sun stands in one place.

2. A second person is Earth. Earth walks around the sun and *at the same time* spins around slowly (don't get dizzy!). The sun keeps the flashlight's beam pointed at Earth as Earth moves. When Earth sees a flash of light as he or she turns, it's "day". When Earth's back is toward the sun, it's "night".

3. Now try the phases of the moon. A third person holding a ball slightly above his or her head is the moon. The moon circles Earth and faces the Earth at all times. Sometimes the moon's back is toward the sun; other times the moon faces the sun. Earth must keep his or her eyes constantly on the moon to see the phases (i.e. Earth turns with the moon), but can skip rotating around the sun. The sun keeps the flashlight's beam on the ball as the moon moves. Freeze the motion of the model periodically. What does Earth see? For example, when the moon is between Earth and the sun, the sun's rays fall on the far side of the moon only, so Earth can't easily see the moon. This is called a new moon.

4. People should try different roles. What do observers see? What does the moon see? What does Earth see? Reality is more complicated than the model (e.g. the Earth spins on a tilted axis, and orbits aren't exactly circular), but people will get the general idea.

An "eclipse" occurs when one heavenly body obscures another. Close one eye. Hold out your finger at arm's length and look at it. Slowly move a finger from your other hand in front of your open eye. You'll reach a point where you block out the farther finger. This is what happens during a full eclipse.

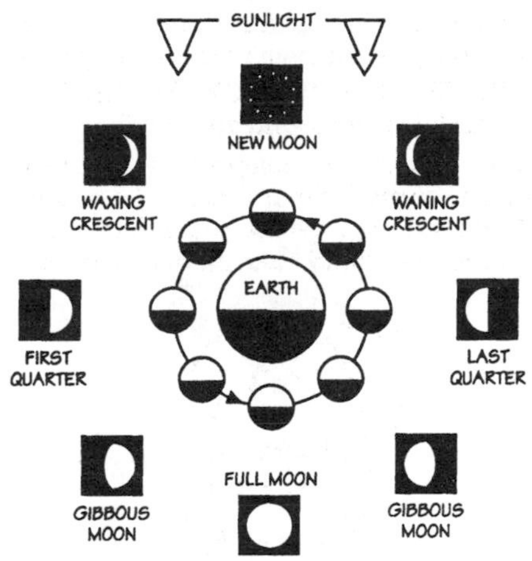

The Earth spins around an axis that passes through the centre of the globe. One complete rotation is one day (24 hours). The sun's rays reach only half of the Earth at any one time (the side in daylight). Half the moon is always illuminated by the sun; the moon's phase depends on how much of that illumination is visible from Earth. The lunar cycle moves from new moon phase (completely invisible) to full moon and back to new again. As the moon moves from new to full it's said to be "waxing". As it moves back to new moon again it's said to be "waning".

A "solar eclipse" occurs when the moon passes directly between the Earth and the sun and hides the sun from view. A solar eclipse can turn daylight to darkness in an instant. In place of the brilliantly shining sun, there is only a black disc with a sparkling circle of pearl-white light around it. The moon is almost 400 times smaller than the sun, but it can hide the sun because the sun is so much farther away and therefore appears smaller. The moon shines by reflecting light from the sun; if something blocks the sunlight, it ceases to shine. In a "lunar eclipse", the moon passes into Earth's shadow (i.e. Earth is directly between the sun and moon); the Earth blocks the sun's light from the moon. Lunar eclipses do not take place every month because the moon usually clears the Earth's shadow by passing above or below it.

Topics: Earth; Light.

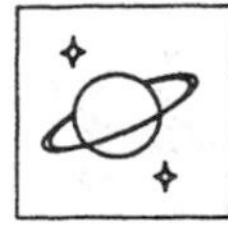

The Reasons For Seasons

There are four basic seasons: summer, fall, winter, and spring. Why? Use a globe and a lamp to explore the reasons for seasons.

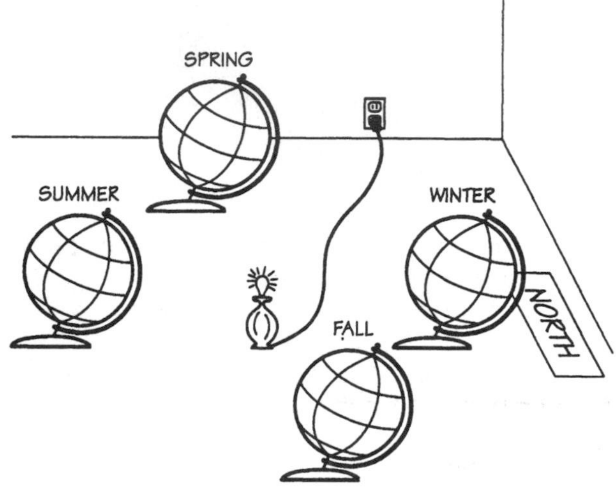

MATERIALS: Globe that rotates around a tilted axis; small table lamp; small nail with a large head; tape; flexible ruler; paper; pencil.

DOING IT:

1. Remove the shade from a small table lamp so that the bulb is exposed. Place the lamp on the floor and turn it on. The lamp represents the sun. There should be no other light in the room.

2. Choose a direction as north and put a sign down labelling north.

3. Find where you live on a tilted globe. Tape a small nail, head down, on top of the location.

4. Place the globe on the ground, about 1.5 m away from the lamp, on the side opposite north. The light bulb should be at the same height as the middle of the globe. The globe should tilt toward north. This is the summer position for the northern hemisphere.

5. Centre the nail in the light from the lamp. How does the nail's shadow look? Measure the length of the shadow. Rotate the globe; one rotation represents one day (24 hours). Note that for part of one rotation the head of the nail is in the light (representing daylight hours) and for the remainder of the rotation it is in darkness (representing night).

6. Repeat your observations for each of the three other positions -- fall, winter, and spring. Each time, make sure that the globe is tilted toward north.

7. During which season is the nail's shadow shortest? During which season is it longest? A short shadow indicates strong, direct sunlight; a long shadow indicates weaker sunlight coming toward your area at an angle. During which season do you get the most daylight (i.e. nail's head is in light the longest as you rotate the globe)? During which season do you get about the same amount of daylight and darkness? In general, the more sunlight during the day, the warmer the day.

The Earth rotates around a tilted axis (it is tilted by 23.5 degrees). The north end of the axis always points toward the North Star as the Earth circles the sun. The tilted axis of the Earth and the yearly orbit of the Earth around the sun cause variations in the amount of heat at different locations on Earth at different times of the year -- which causes seasonal changes.

The "solstice" refers to either of the two times of the year when the sun is furthest from the equator. The summer solstice is the time at which the sun is furthest north from the equator (it is directly above the Tropic of Cancer, latitude 23.5 degrees N), about June 21. In the northern hemisphere, this date marks the beginning of summer and has the most hours of daylight. The winter solstice is the time at which the sun is furthest south from the equator (it is directly above the Tropic of Capricorn, latitude 23.5 degrees S), about December 22. In the northern hemisphere, this date marks the beginning of winter and has the fewest hours of daylight. The seasons are reversed in the southern hemisphere.

Topics: Earth; Stars; Weather Conditions.

SUN TIME

The sundial is the oldest device known for measuring time (Earth rotation). Make a horizontal sundial, adjusted to your latitude.

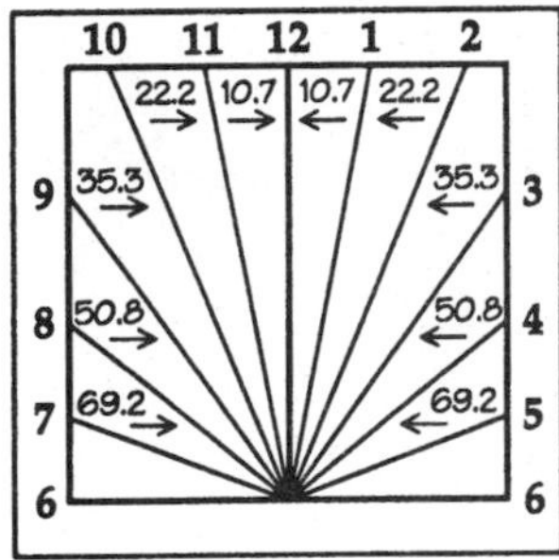

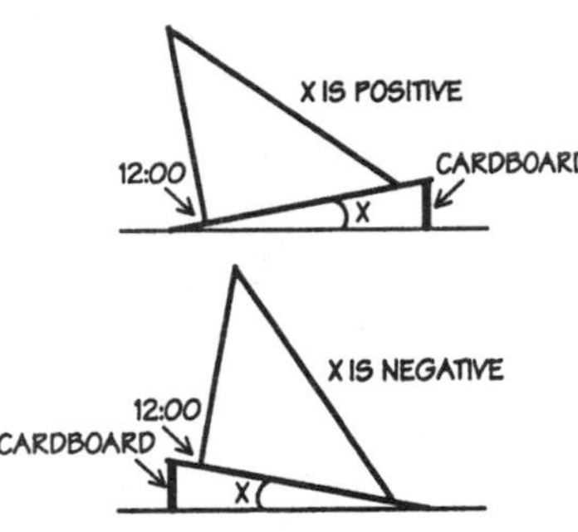

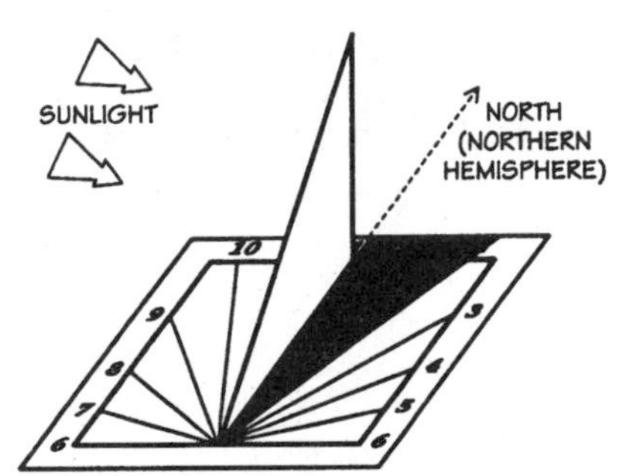

MATERIALS: Thick, stiff cardboard; thinner, stiff cardboard (for gnomon); scissors; ruler; pencil; protractor; tape; compass (to determine north). Optional -- atlas (to find your latitude).

DOING IT:

1. This sundial will be most accurate at 45 degrees latitude, and generally accurate up to 50 degrees and down to 40 degrees. You can also adjust the sundial to your latitude (see below).

2. Cut a 25 cm square of cardboard. This is the sundial's base. Within this cardboard square, draw a 20 cm square.

3. Divide the 20 cm square into two equal halves by drawing a straight (90 degree) line down the middle. This line represents 12:00. Using a protractor, draw lines to the angles indicated; angles are measured from the 12:00 line (i.e. first line is 10.7 degrees from 12:00; second line is 22.2 degrees from 12:00; etc.). Number the lines like a clock, as shown.

4. Use thin, stiff cardboard for the gnomon. Draw two 20 cm lines perpendicular to each other and join them, as shown. Cut out the triangle. Use tape to fasten the gnomon perpendicular to the sundial base, over the 12:00 line; use the protractor to check that the gnomon stands at exactly 90 degrees.

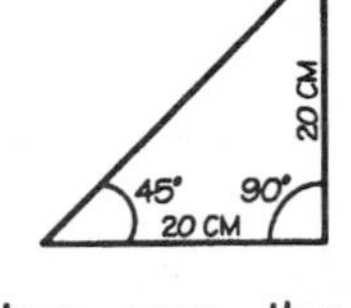

5. If you are located a distance from 45 degrees latitude, you must adjust the sundial to your latitude. Subtract your latitude from 45 degrees (i.e. 45 - your latitude = X). Then cut a piece of cardboard and tape it underneath the sundial to prop it up to an angle equal to the difference (X); you must tilt the sundial differently depending on whether X is a positive or negative number (e.g. 45 - 39 = 6; 45 - 51 = -6).

6. Put the sundial on level ground in a spot that is in sunlight all day. In the northern hemisphere, 12:00 points north; in the southern hemisphere 12:00 points south (also, reverse the morning and afternoon hours). The shadow cast by the gnomon indicates the approximate time. Why is there a difference between the time on the sundial and the time on your watch?

The time at a specific place according to the sun's position is called "solar time". This time is indicated by a sundial's pointer, the "gnomon" (Greek for "to know"). The angle of the gnomon must be adjusted based on your latitude. The Earth's axis is tilted, so the sun appears to be higher in the sky in summer and lower in the sky in winter. If the gnomon's angle is based on your latitude, the sun's shadow will fall on the sundial in the same way for each hour throughout the year. Some sample latitudes: Canada -- Vancouver 49 N, Toronto 44 N, Montreal 46 N; U.S.A. -- Los Angeles 34 N, Houston 30 N, New York 40 N; Australia -- Sydney 34 S; New Zealand -- Wellington 41 S; England -- London 51.5 N. The accuracy of solar time varies depending on your location (i.e. longitude) in your time zone; whether you are on daylight saving time; the time of year; and whether the sundial is pointing precisely at true (rather than magnetic) north/south.

Topics: Earth; Measurement; Light.

STAR CLOCK

Just as the sun can be used to tell time during the day, the stars can be used to tell time at night. Construct a nocturnal.

MATERIALS: Stiff acetate film (i.e. clear plastic covering on some folders or plastic used for overhead projectors); felt marker; scissors; single hole punch; brass paper fastener; masking tape.

DOING IT:

1. The pattern for the nocturnal appears on the following page. Lay a sheet of acetate film on top of the pattern and copy the pattern onto the film.

2. Cut out all the pieces. Stick a strip of masking tape to the part of the arm shaded in the pattern. Punch a hole through each black dot just big enough to use a brass fastener to put the pieces together as shown.

3. When you're using the nocturnal, make sure the pointer on the inner dial points to the correct date on the outer dial (i.e. date on which you're using the device). Hold the nocturnal vertically (handle down). Face north. Lift up the nocturnal and cover the North Star with the stud of the brass fastener. Move the arm of the nocturnal until the two pointer stars of the Big Dipper are just level with the lower edge of the arm. *Make sure the dials aren't moving around as you do this.* Read the time from the inner dial, along the lower edge of the arm. Note: If you're under daylight saving time, add 1 hour to the time shown.

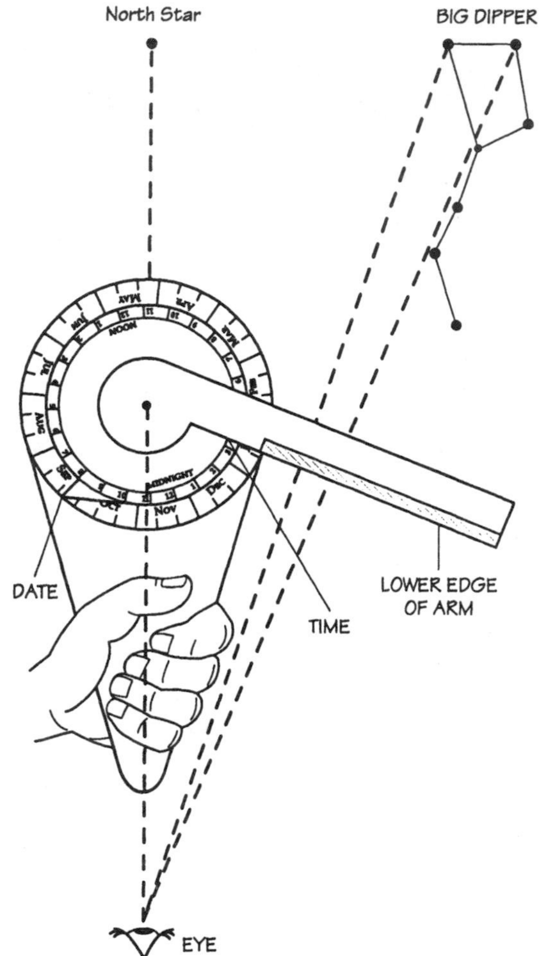

MAKE TIME

The Big Dipper appears to make a complete rotation around the North Star approximately once every 24 hours. Its starting point at a given time differs according to the season. These facts enable us to tell time using a device called a "nocturnal". The nocturnal only works in the northern hemisphere.

Topics: Stars; Measurement.

Check the moon's phase and its position in the sky to tell time. (Note: If you're under daylight saving time, add 1 hour to the times shown.)

PHASE	RISING	HIGHEST POINT	SETTING
new	6 a.m.	noon	6 p.m.
first crescent	9 a.m.	3 p.m.	9 p.m.
first quarter	noon	6 p.m.	midnight
first gibbous	3 p.m.	9 p.m.	3 a.m.
full	6 p.m.	midnight	6 a.m.
last gibbous	9 p.m.	3 a.m.	9 a.m.
third quarter	midnight	6 a.m.	noon
last crescent	3 a.m.	9 a.m.	3 p.m.

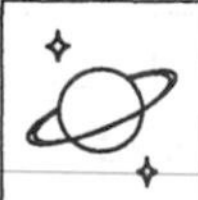

Pattern For Nocturnal

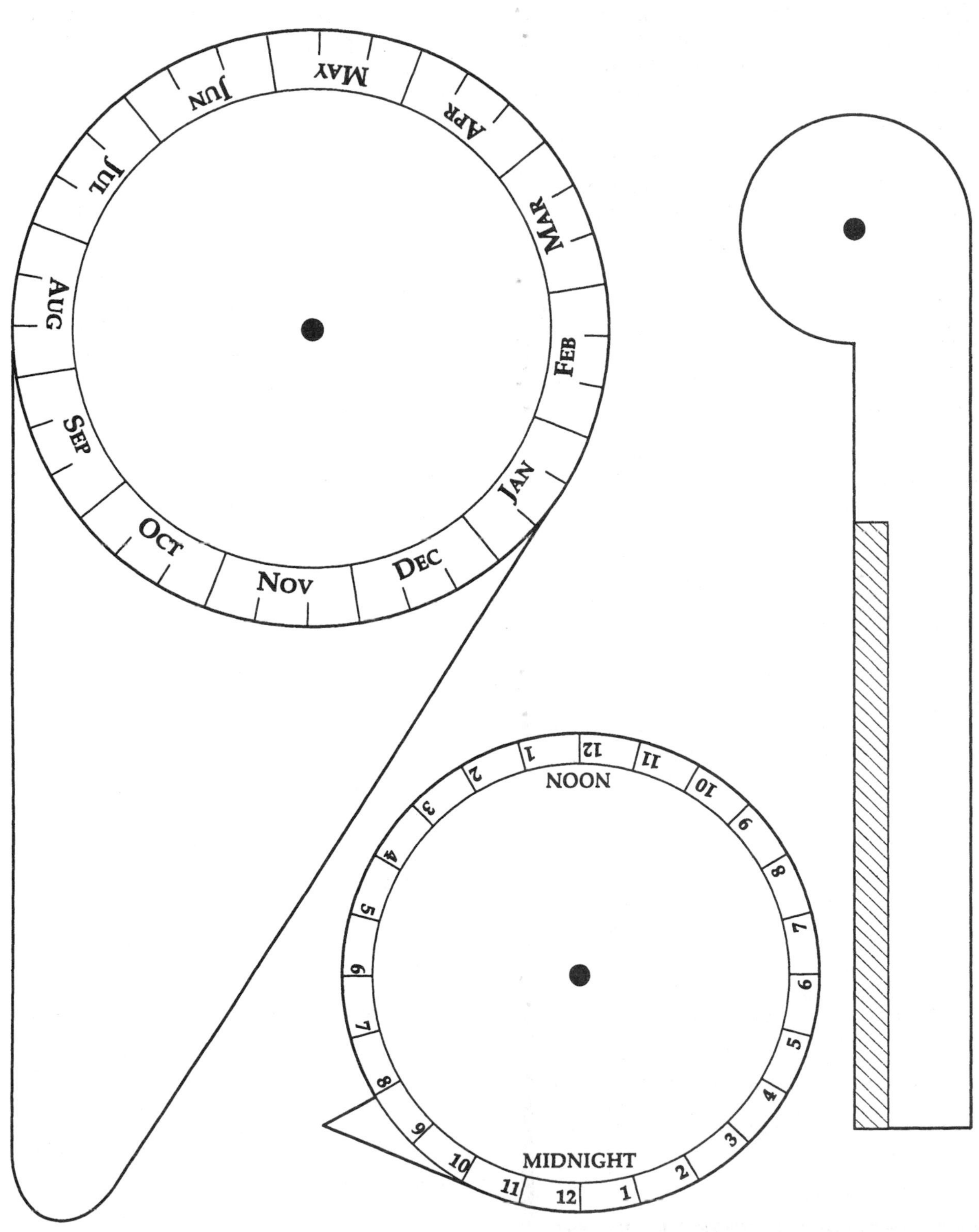

SIMPLE PLANETARIUMS

Here are some working models that show the positions and apparent motion of the stars much like a real planetarium.

Walking on the surface of the moon is something like hiking through talcum powder with stones in it. The moon is blanketed with finely powdered rock. Moon soil contains no water, or decaying plant and animal material. But it does contain small, glassy emerald-green and orange-red glass beads. These are created when a meteorite hits the moon's surface and sprays hot, liquid rock -- which later cools -- in every direction.

MAKE TIME

MATERIALS: Cereal boxes; flashlight; scissors; plain umbrella (preferably black); chalk, white pencil, or masking tape; star maps (see One Leads to Another section).

DOING IT:

1. Use star maps (a circumpolar map is particularly helpful) to place stars.

In general, a planetarium consists of half a hollow sphere on the inside of which have been placed the various stars in their relative positions. The half sphere spins slowly to give the appearance of stars moving through the night sky. Making mini planetariums is a good way to familiarize yourself with the constellations (groupings of stars) before you go stargazing to look for the real things. If you make the umbrella planetarium, there are several things to note. First, stars don't really move; they only appear to move because the Earth is turning. Second, the constellations shown circle the North Star and are always visible above the horizon. Constellations further from the North Star rise and set each day as the Earth turns. Finally, the ribs of the umbrella represent celestial meridians. Astronomers determine the celestial longitude of stars in the same way that longitude is used on Earth.

Topics: Stars; Mapping.

2. *Cereal Box Planetariums:* Remove the waxed paper bags from several cereal boxes. Each box can be used to show one or two constellations. Punch holes through the side of a box in the right positions for a given constellation. Cut a round opening at one end of the box for a flashlight. Take the box into a dark area. Shining a flashlight into the box makes the holes glow brightly. Take cereal box planetariums along on a stargazing trip to help you find constellations in the sky.

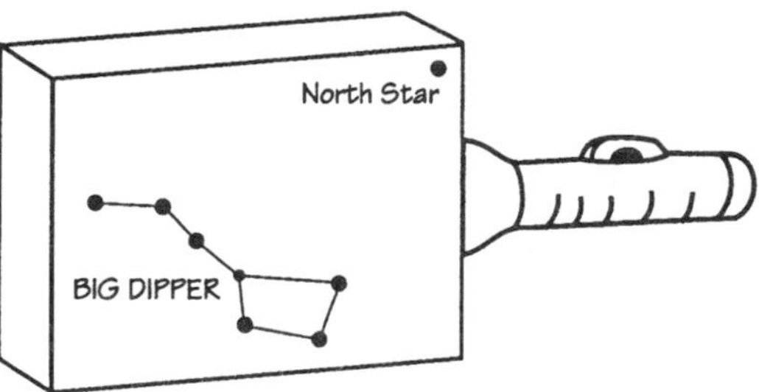

3. *Umbrella Planetarium:* Use chalk or a white pencil to draw stars onto an umbrella, or mark the stars with small pieces of masking tape. Put the North Star around the very centre of the umbrella. The North Star is at the end of the handle on the Little Dipper. Mark the positions of the other stars in the Little Dipper, as well as the stars in the Big Dipper, Cepheus, Draco, and Cassiopeia. Draw lines to connect the stars for each constellation. Turn the umbrella counterclockwise to see how the stars appear to move through the night sky.

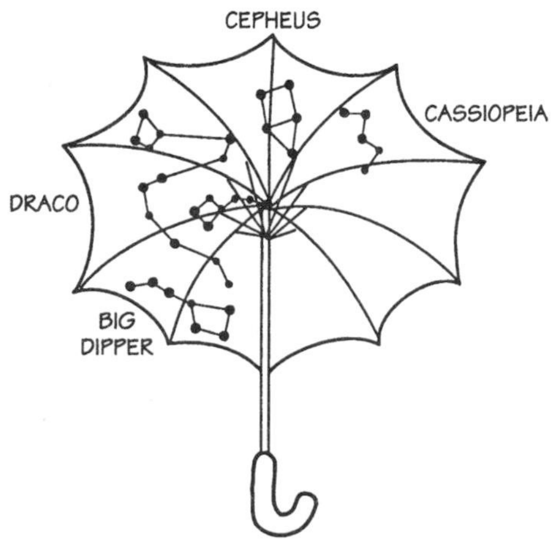

APPLYING SCIENCE

"Engineering" involves applying science in the design, building, and use of structures, machines, and other devices. Engineers search for faster, better, and less expensive ways to meet the needs of society. Buildings, televisions, bicycles, bridges, highways, airplanes, and video games -- among many other things! -- all involve the work of engineers.

American Thomas Alva Edison, a genius in the practical application of scientific principles, had 1093 inventions to his name. Some of his inventions: the microphone; the record player; and the electric light bulb.

Concern for
[human beings and their fate]
must always form the chief interest
of all technical endeavours in order that
the creations of our mind shall be
a blessing and not a curse.
Never forget this in the midst of
your diagrams and equations.
(Albert Einstein)

Thomas Edison invented the electric light bulb, right? Wrong. People had experimented with light bulbs at least 70 years before Edison did. Edison, however, was able to invent the first *practical* light bulb. He also developed the complete electrical distribution system (homes in his time did not have electricity) and headed the installation of the world's first central electric-light power plant in New York City.

Of all
the scientists
who ever lived,
95%
are alive today.

Thomas Edison's two New Jersey workshops were forerunners of the modern industrial research lab, in which teams of scientists, engineers, researchers, and technicians -- rather than a lone inventor -- work to systematically investigate a problem.

Playing with words can lead to ideas for inventions. For example, try reversing phrases. "Washing clothes" becomes "clothes washer". Another approach is to make a list of verbs (e.g. mixing, spreading, squashing, stretching, catching, walking) and a list of nouns (which are not names of people or places). Then, at random, choose one verb and one noun and put them together. Some combinations won't work, but others may give you some invention ideas. For example, "walking" and "rock" might have led to the invention of the pet rock. Choose the best idea and write a description of the possible invention.

MAKE TIME

BOSAK'S MOTOR

An electric motor changes electrical energy into mechanical energy. Susan Bosak used this basic motor design in her first science project in grade five.

MATERIALS: Shoebox; steel strip 2.5 cm x 46 cm x 0.2 cm; 11 m of insulated wire; steel bolt about 0.6 cm in diameter and 2.5 cm shorter than the width of the shoebox; one nut and two washers; lightweight wood dowel or foam rod (available at a hobby shop) about 2.5 cm in diameter and 1 cm shorter than the length of the shoebox; two thin nails without heads; wire cutters; pliers; knife; ruler; pencil; masking tape; two 6 volt lantern batteries. Optional -- hammer; drill.

The electric motor was developed in the 1800s. Its operation is opposite to that of the electric generator. Electric motors are used in a variety of machines and devices, from washing machines to hairdryers. The motor in this activity is a DC motor (direct current is supplied by the batteries). There are two electromagnets in the motor: one battery magnetizes the field structure; the other battery magnetizes the bolt that makes up part of the armature. The field structure is a stationary electromagnet; one side of the structure is the north pole and the other side is the south pole. The bolt is a rotating magnet. Current runs from the battery, through the commutator, to the bolt and magnetizes it. One end of the bolt becomes the north pole and the other end becomes the south pole. Like poles of the two electromagnets (e.g. the two north poles) repel each other and so the armature makes a half turn. When the north pole of the armature reaches the south pole of the field structure, the rotation would stop (unlike poles attract) if it weren't for the commutator.

The commutator has two parts -- the two separate ends of the wire around the bolt. At any given time, one brush touches one end of the wire and the other brush touches the other end, which sends current through the wire in a certain direction. As the commutator turns, the brushes each come in contact with the other end of the wire. The current flow through the wire reverses and the poles of the bolt reverse. So, the north pole of the armature becomes a south pole. That south pole is repelled by the south pole of the field structure and the armature makes another half turn. The current keeps being reversed, and the armature keeps turning.

Topics: Electricity; Magnetism.

MAKE TIME

DOING IT:

1. Start by making the field structure. Bend a steel strip into a U shape. When placed upright inside a shoebox, the base of the U-shaped strip should be about the same width as the box and the arms should extend a little above the sides of the box.

2. Wind two layers of insulated wire around the base of the U, leaving about 50 cm of wire free when you start and when you end. Start at one end of the base, wind the wire to the other end, and then wind it back again.

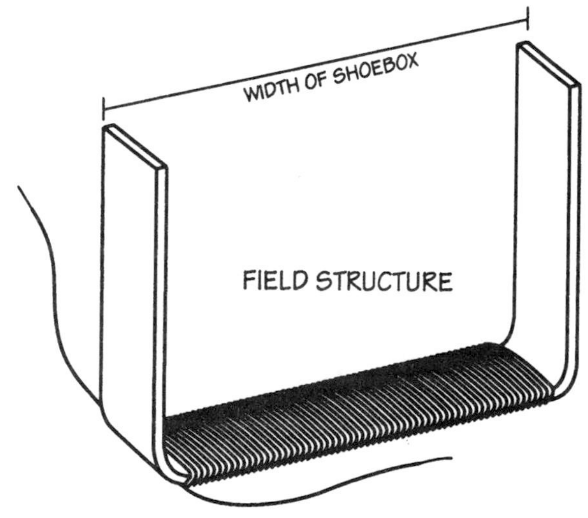

In the early 1800s, American Samuel Morse developed the first practical telegraph. The telegraph is basically a long electric circuit with a switch at one end and an electromagnet and iron bar at the other. Closing and opening the switch causes the electromagnet to attract and release the iron bar, making a "click-clack" sound. A system of "dots" (quick click-clack) and "dashes" (slow click-clack), called Morse code, enabled messages to be quickly sent over long distances.

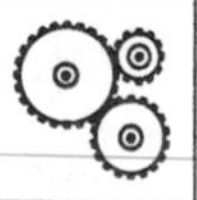

3. Use a wood dowel or foam rod as the armature shaft. A bolt makes up the other part of the armature. Put a washer on the bolt. Then put the bolt through the shaft, about 1/3 in from one end (you may need a drill to get the bolt through a wood dowel). The bolt should be wedged tightly in the shaft. Put a washer and nut on the open end of the bolt.

4. Wind insulated wire around the bolt, leaving about 30 cm of wire free when you start and when you end. Start winding near the shaft and wind outward to one end of the bolt. Then wind back to the shaft and cross over it. Wind to the other end of the bolt and back to the shaft.

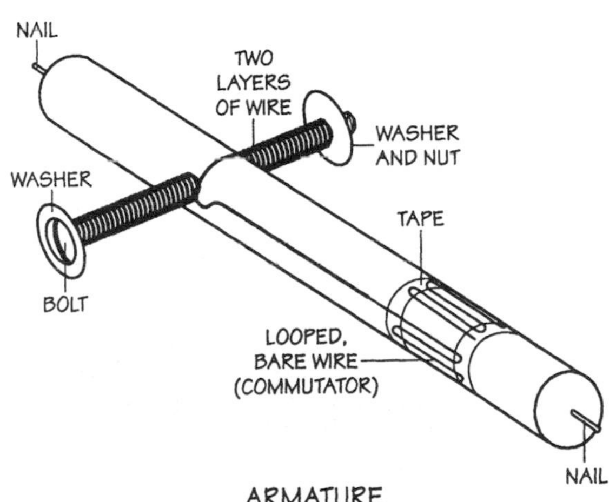

ARMATURE

5. Make the commutator by stripping off about 20 cm of insulation from each end of the wire from the bolt. Loop the bare wire back and forth. Tape the set of loops from one wire to one side of the armature shaft and the set of loops from the other wire to the other side of the shaft. The two sets of wire loops should not touch each other.

6. Secure a nail in the centre of each end of the shaft. The total length of the shaft and nails should now be *slightly* longer than the length of the shoebox.

7. Now you have all the basic parts of the motor. Place the field structure upright into the shoebox. It should be located so that it will line up with the bolt on the armature. You may want to secure the field structure in the box by running a couple of strips of tape over the base.

8. Make two small, reinforced holes in the ends of the shoebox, just below the rim and centred relative to the sides. Slip the nails at the ends of the armature shaft into the holes (you should be able to bend the box just enough to get the second nail through the second hole). The armature should turn freely. The bolt should line up with the field structure.

9. Make two small holes in the sides of the shoebox, in line with the commutator.

10. Cut two lengths of wire about 60 cm each. Strip off 2-4 cm of insulation from one end of each wire. Feed the wires through the holes in the shoebox. Make a loop in each of the bare wire ends. One wire loop should fall on top of the commutator and one should curve below, as shown. The loops should gently brush the bare wires of the commutator. Make sure the brushes and commutator are set up so that both brushes *never* touch the same end of the commutator wire at the same time. You may want to make supports for the brushes by taping pieces of cardboard to the shoebox, as shown.

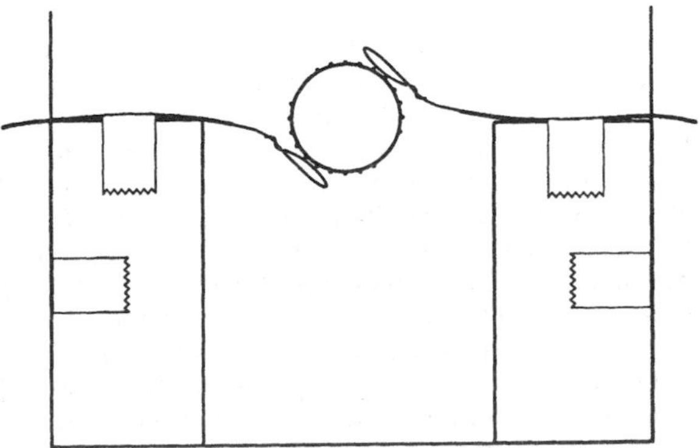
BRUSHES AND COMMUTATOR

11. Strip off about 2 cm of insulation from the free ends of the wires coming from the brushes. Attach the ends to a battery.

12. Strip off about 2 cm of insulation from the ends of the wires coming from the field structure. Attach the ends to a second battery.

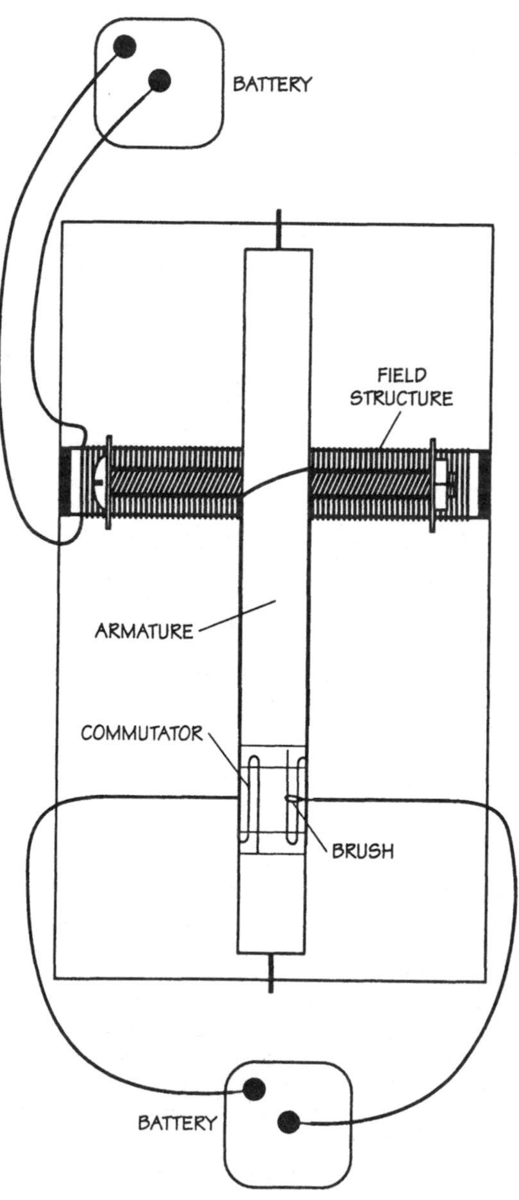

13. If the armature doesn't turn when the batteries are attached, nudge it to get it started. You may also have to curve or change the angle of the brushes relative to the commutator (the brushes should not, however, prevent the armature from rotating). How quickly does the armature rotate? How can you improve the motor's operation?

14. *Extension:* Reverse the connections on one or both of the batteries. How does the rotation of the armature change? Why does it change? Experiment with batteries of different voltages. Try making the field structure from different metals. Does the number of turns of wire around the field structure affect the motor's operation?

Alexander Graham Bell (who was born in Scotland but spent most of his life in Canada and the United States) invented the telephone in 1876. The telephone works in a way that's similar to the telegraph. When you speak to someone on the phone, the mouthpiece changes the vibration from the sound into an electric signal. The signal travels along wires to the other telephone where the earpiece -- which has an electromagnet in it -- changes the signal back into sound.

Canadian J. Armand Bombardier spent his winter days tinkering with machinery, searching for a way to travel easily over snowy roads. In 1922, at the age of 15, Bombardier developed the world's first snowmobile. He called the machine "ski-dog".

WATER WHEEL

Water power has been used for thousands of years. Construct a water wheel which produces mechanical energy for doing work.

MATERIALS: Aluminum foil pie plate; scissors; pencil; tape; ruler; piece of string about 45 cm long; eraser, nut from bolt, or other small weight; water source (e.g. faucet, hose).

DOING IT:

1. Cut out the circular bottom of an aluminum foil pie plate. Make eight equally spaced cuts (dotted lines in illustration below) toward the centre of the foil circle. End each cut about 2 cm from the centre.

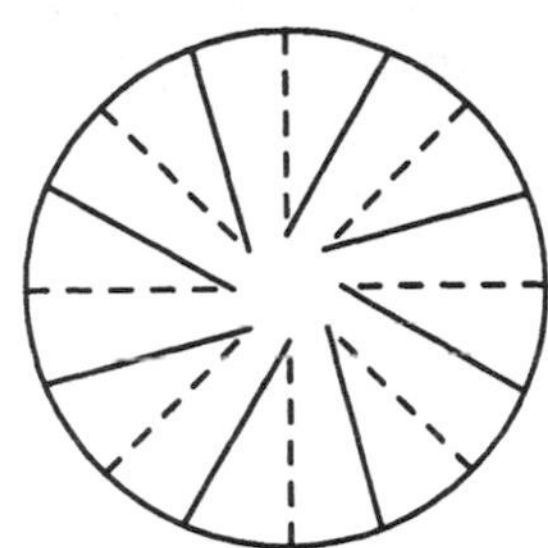

2. Use a ruler to fold one edge of each section of the plate (solid lines in illustration) to make small ledges.

3. Punch a hole in the centre of the plate and push a pencil through it. The pencil should fit snugly in the hole; secure the pencil in place with tape.

4. Hold the wheel under a slow stream of water (e.g. under a garden hose or kitchen faucet). Position the wheel so that water hits the blades. Let the ends of the pencil rest lightly between your thumbs and index fingers. The wheel should turn smoothly.

Television was invented in the 1920s, but it didn't begin to become a part of most homes until the 1950s. TV pictures are formed by streams of electrons scanning a fluorescent screen. The electrons build up a static charge on your TV screen, which is why it attracts dust.

5. What happens to the wheel when the water flows quickly? What happens when the rate of flow is reduced?

6. Tie one end of a piece of string to the pencil and attach a weight to the other end of the string. The water wheel should wind the string onto the pencil, lifting the weight. How much weight can be lifted? How do you know when the load is too heavy for the water wheel to lift?

Water power is based on the fact that water at a higher level has more "potential energy" (stored energy) than water at a lower level. Water gives up some of its potential energy when it flows from a higher level to a lower level. The potential energy changes to "kinetic energy" (energy of motion) as the water falls. The moving water can be made to turn a bladed wheel so that the kinetic energy is transformed into mechanical energy. The shaft of the bladed wheel is usually attached to gears, levers, and different types of machines. In the past, mechanical energy from water wheels was used to grind grain and saw timber. Today, moving water is used primarily in generating electricity. Power plants are built at the foot of high dams. Powerful jets of water shoot through pipes from a reservoir. The water hits the blades of dozens of water wheels, making them turn hundreds of times per minute. These wheels then turn electric generators.

Topics: Energy; Electricity.

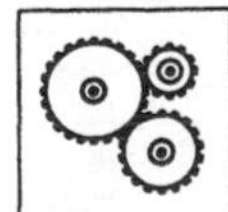

OBEDIENT CAN

A specially-constructed can returns to you when called -- except the can isn't *really* obeying you, it's obeying the laws of physics.

Technology has changed our world. The invention of the airplane didn't just mean we could travel great distances much faster. It meant airports had to be built. It meant that complex air travel schedules were needed. And it meant that you had to trust your safety to a long string of people -- the airplane manufacturer, the maintenance crew, the pilot, the air-traffic controller. The word "travel" means something completely different now than what it meant when people got around using a horse and buggy.

MAKE TIME

MATERIALS: Coffee or fruit drink crystal can with plastic lid; elastic bands; weights (e.g. lead sinkers, heavy nuts, heavy bolts); nails; hammer. Optional -- file; string; scissors.

DOING IT:

1. Punch a hole in the centre of the bottom of a can; you may want to smooth off the edges of the hole with a file. Punch another hole in the centre of the can's plastic lid.

2. Thread an elastic band through the hole in the bottom of the can. Slip a nail through the elastic band to secure it as shown.

3. Attach weights to the elastic band midway between the bottom of the can and the lid. Knot the elastic band around the weights to hold them in place, or secure the weights with string (tie string *tightly* to elastic band).

4. Pull the remaining end of the elastic band through the hole in the can's lid. Secure the elastic band with another nail, and snap the lid in place. The elastic band shouldn't be stretched too tightly inside the can.

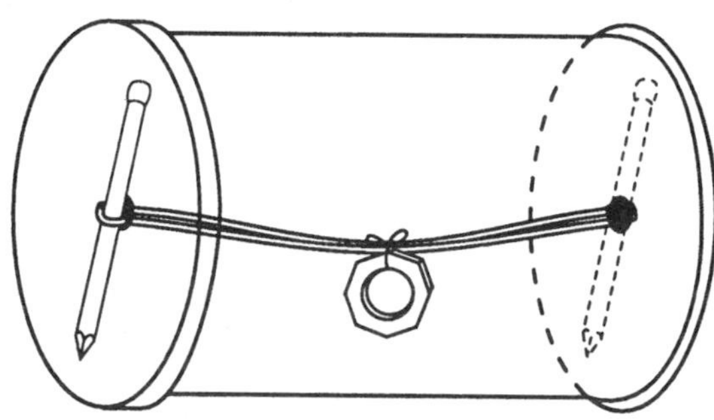

5. Roll the can gently on a hard, smooth, level surface. Just before the can stops rolling, command it to return. The can will obey!

6. *Variation:* Try relocating the weights, decreasing or increasing the number of weights, using different sizes and shapes of elastic bands, and changing the size of the tin can. How does the can perform in each case?

7. *Extension:* Redesign the obedient can. Punch two holes (a few centimetres apart) in the bottom of the can and two holes in the lid. Snip an elastic band so that you have a long elastic strip. Thread the strip through all four holes, in a figure eight. Tie the ends of the strip together. Fasten a weight to the centre of the elastic band (i.e. where the band crosses itself inside the can). How does this design compare with the original design?

Weights tied to the middle of an elastic band stretched inside a can cause the elastic band to twist when you roll the can. The harder you initially push the can, the more the elastic band twists and the greater the potential energy (stored energy). When the energy given the can by the initial push is used up, the can stops rolling. The stored energy in the twisted elastic band makes it unwind, causing the can to roll back to you. The potential energy becomes kinetic energy (energy of motion). When the elastic band completely unwinds and the potential energy is all used up, the can stops rolling.

Topics: Energy.

PROJECTILE LAUNCHER

A "projectile" is an object fired by force, like a missile. Make and experiment with a projectile launcher.

MATERIALS: Piece of wood 15 cm x 25 cm; elastic bands; three *new, unsharpened* pencils (or wooden dowels); three small nails; hammer; tape; measuring tape; stopwatch.

DOING IT:

1. Tape two pencils lengthwise on a piece of wood, as shown. Leave enough room between them for a third pencil.

2. Place two nails about 13 cm apart on the board, one on each side of the two pencils. Hammer the nails about halfway into the board.

3. Drive a third nail firmly into the third pencil.

4. Hook an elastic band between the two nails on the board. Place the third pencil, the projectile, between the other two pencils.

5. Place the launcher on an elevated surface (e.g. a table). A height of about 1.2 m would be ideal.

6. **Make sure no one is in the target area of the launcher. The launcher can be dangerous if it is misused.** Pull the nail on the projectile back against the elastic band to stretch the elastic band, and then release the projectile. How far does it travel? Change the amount you stretch the elastic band. What happens?

7. When an object falls freely from a height of 1.2 m, it hits the ground in about half a second. The time it takes the projectile to reach the ground is the same no matter how fast the object travels in a horizontal direction. Drop a pencil from the table at the same time you launch a projectile. Both should hit the ground at the same instant.

8. How fast is the projectile travelling? If it travels 3 m in half a second, then it would have travelled 6 m in one second (twice as far in double the time). Multiply 6 by 3600 (number of seconds in an hour). That gives you 21,600 m/hr, or 21.6 km/hr.

9. *Variation:* Try using two or three elastic bands. Try changing the size, mass, and shape of the projectile.

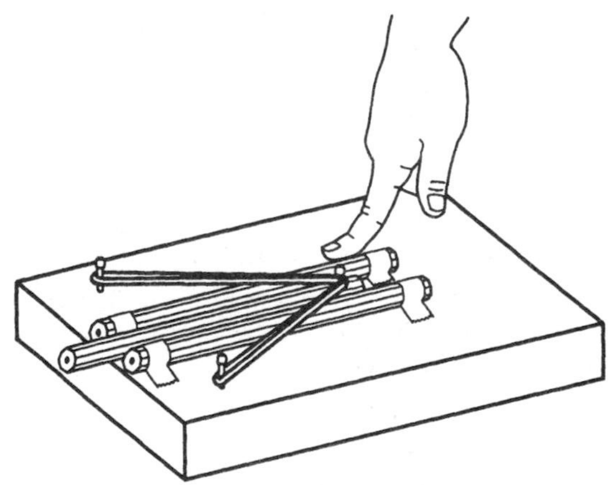

While the Americans and Japanese were perfecting the copying machine, Canadians came up with a paper treatment that makes a page virtually uncopyable.

A projectile launcher involves the Second Law of Motion, developed by Isaac Newton about 300 years ago. The Second Law states: 1) the greater the force on an object, the greater its change in speed or direction; and 2) the heavier an object, the less its change in speed or direction. This explains why, for example, you need more force to throw a baseball quickly (i.e. a "fastball") than you need to throw it slowly and gently. It also explains why it's easier to throw a light rock farther than a heavy rock.

Topics: Forces; Measurement.

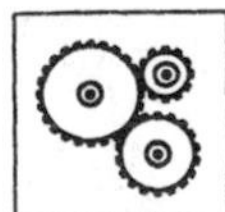

BIGGER IS BETTER

For thousands of years, people could study only what they could see with the unaided eye. Experiment with lenses that make it possible to make small things much bigger.

A camera is basically a dark box that holds light-sensitive film at one end and has a small hole at the other. Light enters the camera and passes through a lens which creates a small, upside-down image on the film.

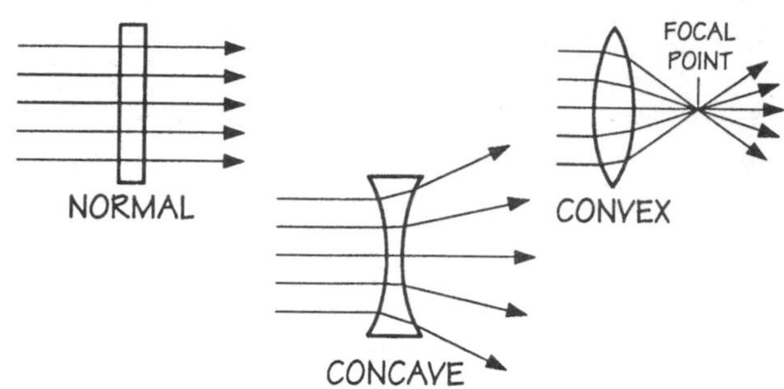

Light rays usually travel in straight lines. Lenses bend (refract) light rays. In its simplest form, a lens is a disc of glass or plastic with two surfaces curved or with one surface flat and the other curved. A "concave" lens curves inward and is thicker at the edges than in the middle; it bends light rays outward. A "convex" lens curves outward and is thicker in the middle than at the edges; it bends light rays inward. All rays of light passing through a lens are refracted except those that pass directly through a point called the "optical centre". When you look at an object through a concave lens, the object appears smaller. A convex lens can make objects appear larger. A water drop can act like a simple convex lens.

A magnifying glass is a convex lens. As the parallel light rays passing through it bend inward, they converge (come together) at the "focal point". Convex lenses not only bend light, but they concentrate light. The focal point is very bright. As a magnifying glass concentrates light rays, it also concentrates heat, or infrared, rays. The focal point for light is different than the focal point for heat because the lens bends light and heat rays slightly differently. A magnifying glass can make an object appear larger because you think the light reflected from the object is travelling in a straight line from the object (dotted lines in illustration); your eye is fooled because it doesn't know the lens has bent the light. As you use a magnifying glass to magnify an image, the image will flip upside down when you pass the focal point. This is because the light rays converge at the focal point, *cross* each other, and then continue on through the *opposite* side of the focal point.

Topics: Light.

MATERIALS: Water; plastic wrap; scissors; clear, round container with tight-fitting lid (e.g. jar, pill bottle); magnifying glass; coin; rock; plastic bag and twist tie; lined paper; graph paper; glass bowl; page with small text; pencil.

DOING IT:

1. *Water Drop:* Place a small square of plastic wrap over some small text. Put a single drop of water onto the plastic. Does the drop magnify the text? What kind of lens does the water drop look like?

2. *Homemade Magnifier:* Completely fill a clear, round container with water. Then carefully add a few more drops of water. Be careful not to spill any of the water as you put the lid on the container. If there's an air bubble in the container, try adding a little more water. Hold the magnifier sideways and bring it up to your eyes. How do your surroundings look through the magnifier? Hold the magnifier sideways over some text. Is the text larger? What other objects can you magnify? Look at an insect, a flower, a rock, and/or the writing on a coin. Try making another homemade magnifier by filling a plastic bag with water.

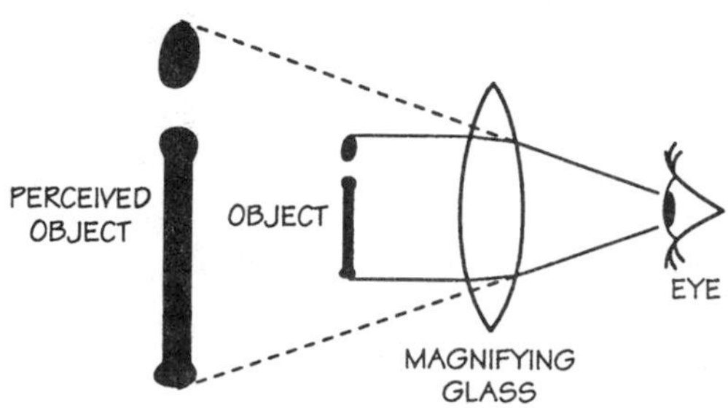

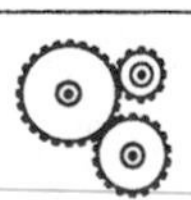

The electron microscope was developed in the late 1930s by Canadians James Hillier and Albert Prebus. In order to magnify a specimen, the electron microscope shoots electrons at it (instead of manipulating light rays like an ordinary microscope). The electron microscope greatly increased the resolution possible during magnification, and the microscope has revolutionized biological and medical research.

3. *Focal Point and Heat:* **This activity should be done with adult supervision. Never look at the sun with or without a magnifying glass because your eyes will be damaged permanently.** Go outside and find a spot in direct, bright sunlight, but out of the wind. Place a small square of paper in a glass bowl. Hold the magnifying glass over the paper so that sunlight passes through the magnifying glass and forms a bright spot on the paper. **Do not stare at this bright spot because it can damage your eyes.** What happens to the spot as you move the magnifying glass closer to the paper and then farther away? Hold the magnifying glass so that the bright spot is very small and bright, and then pull the magnifying glass back a centimetre or so. This will help you find the focal point for heat, which is past the focal point for light. What happens to the paper? Why?

4. *Focal Point and Images:* Put a page with text on the ground. Lay a magnifying glass directly on top of the text. How does the text look? Pick up the magnifying glass and slowly pull it away from the text. Do the letters get larger? Why? Keep pulling the magnifying glass away from the text. At what point do the letters become blurred? If you can get far enough away from the page, you may notice that the letters eventually flip upside down. The point at which the text flips is the focal point. A better way to see the flip effect is to hold the magnifying glass very close to your eye and look at an object several metres away. Slowly, steadily move the magnifying glass away from your eye. The object will blur and then flip over (you may have to move the magnifying glass up or down slightly to find the object after it has flipped).

5. *Magnifying Glass Tests:* Some magnifying glasses magnify objects more than others. Test the *magnifying power* of your magnifying glass using a sheet of lined paper. Close one eye and place the magnifying glass near the sheet. Slowly pull the magnifying glass up, as far from the sheet as you can without the lines getting blurred. As you hold the magnifying glass at this point, use a pencil to make two marks on the paper, one on either side of the rim of the magnifying glass. Then count the number of spaces (between lines) that you see through the magnifying glass. Put aside the magnifying glass and count the number of spaces (between lines) between your two marks on the paper. Divide the actual number of spaces by the number of spaces you saw through the magnifying glass. For example, 11 actual spaces divided by 5 magnified spaces equals a power of about 2x (i.e. magnified image is 2 times larger than original object; if original was 2 mm across, it now appears to be 4 mm across). Test the *quality* of your magnifying glass by looking at the squares on a sheet of graph paper. Move the magnifying glass up and down over the sheet until the squares are in sharp focus. Compare the view in the centre of the magnifying glass with the view on the outer edges. If the lens is a good one, the squares will be sharp no matter where you look. If the lens is of poor quality, the view will be sharp only in the centre; the squares toward the edges will look broken and crooked.

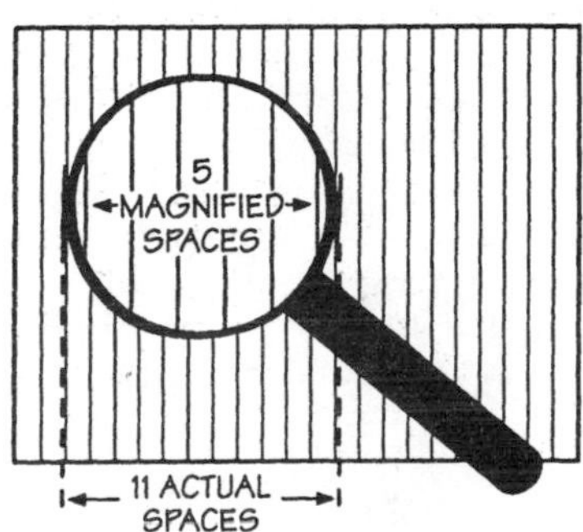

MAKE TIME

CATCH THE CRIMINAL

"Forensic science" involves using scientific methods to solve crimes. Use fingerprints to catch the criminal in this mystery game.

MATERIALS: Drinking glass; ink pad; paper; talcum powder, or black dust (graphite) scraped from a pencil using an emery board or fine sandpaper; fine, wide-tipped, "fluffy" paintbrush; kleenex; magnifying glass. Optional -- clear tape; shiny black paper (if you're using powder) or white paper (if you're using graphite).

DOING IT:

1. Set up the "crime scene" by having one person secretly touch a *clean* drinking glass in several places. Leave the drinking glass on a table. A "detective" must then work to "solve the crime": Who left the drinking glass on the table?

Your fingerprints are different from everyone else's in the world. Fingerprints are a good way to identify people. When a person touches an object, a small amount of perspiration and oil from the skin's surface is transferred to the object. The perspiration and oil are in the pattern of the person's fingerprints. Powder or dust stick to the perspiration and oil and help to make the prints visible. Powder and dust have been used since the late 1800s to reveal fingerprints, but they don't work on surfaces such as cloth and paper. Newer methods of revealing fingerprints make use of lasers. A laser beam can help police find fingerprints on a variety of surfaces. The light causes the perspiration and oil to shine with a yellow colour so that the print can be photographed. The laser will even reveal prints that are several years old.

Topics: Human Body; Scientific Method.

2. The first step is to make a record of suspects' fingerprints. Each person makes a print of each of their fingers. Roll your finger on an ink pad. Put the outside edge of your finger (the side furthest from your body) on a piece of paper. Roll your finger in toward your body to get a print of a large part of the finger. Roll the finger gently and evenly, in just one direction. Don't press too hard.

3. Now the challenge is to match one person's fingerprints with fingerprints found at the scene of the crime. Pick up the used drinking glass with a kleenex (don't get *your* fingerprints on the glass!) and examine it for fingerprints.

4. Place the glass on a sheet of paper. Dip a paintbrush into powder or graphite and gently dust one of the fingerprints. Brush in one direction only (stroke in the direction of the ridges). It takes some practice, but you should be able to reveal the pattern without damaging it.

5. If you want to keep a fingerprint you've found, press a piece of clear tape over it. Peel off the tape, making sure that the fingerprint is on it. This is called "lifting" a print. Stick the tape onto shiny black paper (for powder) or white paper (for graphite).

6. Use a magnifying glass to carefully compare the fingerprints on the glass with those in your records. Is there a match? Who is the "criminal"? Can you identify the exact finger (e.g. index finger, little finger) that matches a given print?

Back And Forth

A pendulum consists of a weight hanging so that it can swing freely. Learn the secret to a pendulum-based carnival game and make pendulum patterns.

MATERIALS: String with weight (e.g. ball of clay, ball) attached on one end; tape; small pop bottle; high table; paper; black construction paper; scissors; string; sand, salt, or sugar.

DOING IT:

1. *Carnival Game:* Get a length of string with a ball on one end. Make a pendulum by taping the free end of the string to the *side* (not the top) of a high table; the tape must come down to the bottom edge of the table so that the pendulum can swing freely in all directions. The pendulum should hang straight down to about the middle of a pop bottle directly underneath it. The challenge is to swing the pendulum so that it misses the bottle on the forward swing and then hits the bottle on the return swing. You can't aim directly at the bottle or throw the pendulum over the bottle.

2. *Pendulum Patterns:* Make a cone out of a sheet of paper; tape the cone together. The cone should have a *small* hole at its tip. Cut three pieces of string, each 15 cm long. Tape the pieces of string to the top of the inside of the cone; the pieces should be spaced apart evenly and should be *exactly* the same length when you pull them together over the cone. Use one end of a long piece of string to tie together the three loose ends of string. Tape the free end of the long string to the *side* (not the top) of a high table. The tape must come down to the bottom edge of the table so that the pendulum can swing freely in all directions, and the tip of the cone should hang about 3 cm above the ground. Lay sheets of black construction paper in a large area underneath the pendulum. Fill the cone with sand, salt, or sugar while you hold your finger over the hole. Start the pendulum swinging by pulling it back and then pushing it off to the side. What kind of pattern forms on the black paper? Why do the shapes get smaller?

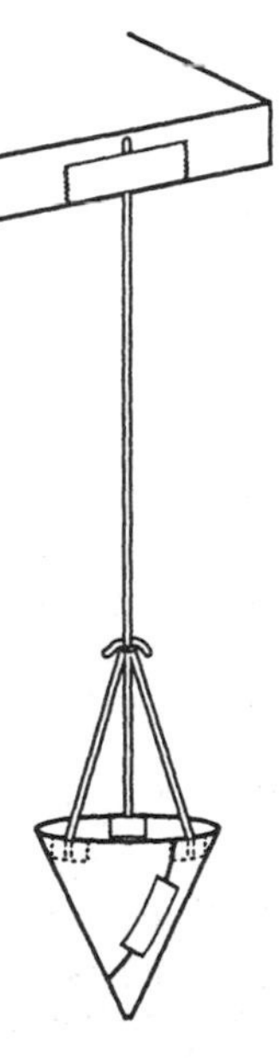

Playground swings are pendulums. As one person sits on a swing (no pumping allowed!), another person can push. How can you vary the way the pendulum swings? Does the position or weight of the rider make a difference? Can you predict how far the rider will swing when released from various heights? At what point in the swing does the rider feel he or she is going fastest? After a few pushes, does a pendulum swing longer with or without a rider?

There's an old *Carnival Game* in which players must swing a large ball suspended from a long string so that the ball misses a bottle on the forward swing and then hits the bottle on the return swing. The pendulum will orbit around the bottle, but won't hit it because the path of the pendulum is an ellipse (oval shape). If the pendulum swings to one side of the bottle on the way out, it will miss the bottle by the same distance on the other side on the return trip. Twisting the string before you release the pendulum makes the ball spin while it's in flight. With the right spin, the pendulum's elliptical path is flattened and the bottle can be knocked over on the pendulum's return swing. *Pendulum Patterns* makes the elliptical path of a pendulum more visible. The pattern gets progressively smaller as the pendulum slows down (due to friction). The pendulum doesn't go back and forth in a straight line because the weight at the end is unevenly distributed.

Pendulums are used to regulate the movement of some clocks because they swing back and forth at a regular rate under the influence of gravity. The swing can be made to take more or less time by changing the length of the pendulum; the longer the pendulum, the more time it takes to make one forward and one return swing. The bearing on which a clock pendulum swings must be as nearly frictionless as possible to maintain a regular swing. A device inside the clock gives the pendulum small, regular pushes to keep it swinging.

Topics: Forces.

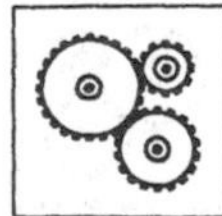

WHICH WAY?

The discovery of the compass made it possible for early explorers to travel the Earth, particularly the oceans. Make a compass like the one used by those explorers.

At one time, people depended on the North Star to help them find their way; when they headed toward the star, they knew they were going north. They also used the sun and moon to find directions. But none of these heavenly bodies were ideal; most change their position in the sky hourly and are frequently hidden by clouds. In old writings, the magnet is often referred to as a "lodestone", meaning "leading stone" or "directing stone". It was found that when a bar magnet is suspended so that it can turn freely, it swings into a north-south position (i.e. north pole of magnet points north). The Earth is like a giant magnet, and a smaller magnet simply aligns itself with the lines of force of the Earth's magnetic field. So, the magnet became a compass.

Chinese and Mediterranean navigators probably first used magnetic compasses on their ships in the 1000s or the 1100s. The compasses were pieces of magnetic iron floated on straw or cork in a container of water. The only problem with magnetic compasses is that if they are placed near a metal object, they're drawn toward that object. When iron and steel ships replaced wooden sailing vessels in the late 1800s, they affected the accuracy of their magnetic compasses. The "gyrocompass" was developed. It is not affected by magnetism and points toward true (geographic) north. Large ships now carry both magnetic compasses and gyrocompasses.

It may seem strange that the north pole of a magnet/compass is attracted to and points toward the north magnetic pole of the Earth. Don't like poles repel and unlike poles attract? There is a contradiction, but it's caused by history, not science. The poles of compasses were named before the laws of attraction and repulsion were fully understood. If we could change history, we might want to call the end of the magnet that points to the north its south pole, and the one that points to the south its north pole. In order to deal with this problem, the north pole of a magnet/compass is often called the "north-seeking pole".

Topics: Magnetism; Earth; Mapping.

MAKE TIME

MATERIALS: Bowl (not metal); water; sewing needle; strong bar magnet; *small* piece of styrofoam/polystyrene; sensitive compass. Optional -- paper clip.

DOING IT:

1. Stroke the length of a sewing needle in *one direction only* (from thick end to pointed end) with the south pole of a bar magnet. You should stroke the needle about 100 times.

2. Partially fill a nonmetal bowl with water. Stick the needle through the base of a small piece of styrofoam/polystyrene and float it in the bowl.

3. Does the needle slowly swing around and point in a certain direction? In which direction? Compare the north indicated by the pointed end of the needle with the north indicated by a store-bought compass. Use your finger to move the needle gently so that it points in another direction. What happens after a few seconds? What happens to the needle if you turn the bowl carefully? What happens if you hold the bar magnet near your homemade compass? Why?

4. *Variation:* What happens if you stroke the needle with the north pole of the bar magnet? Can you use an unmagnetized needle as a compass?

5. *Extension:* Hold a magnetized paper clip near a sensitive compass. What happens to the compass needle? Why? Try bringing other magnetic items near the compass (don't hold a strong magnet near the compass because it can pull the compass needle off its delicate support).

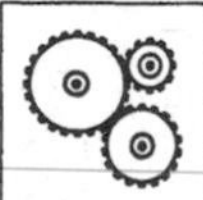

TREASURE MAP

A map is a model of the Earth's surface. Make a map and see if someone else can use it to find a "treasure".

MATERIALS: Paper; pencil; compass; ruler.

DOING IT:

1. You can make a map for someone to follow at a later time. Or, each person in a group can secretly make a map; then people can exchange maps and try to find the "treasures".

2. Map a relatively small area (otherwise, the mapping becomes too difficult). Start by writing an N at the top of a blank sheet of paper. Where are south, west, and east on the map? If north is at the top of the page, south is at the bottom; an easy way to remember where to put the W and the E is that they spell "we" across the page. As you make your map, remember that if, for example, one object is north of another in real life, you must draw that object north of the second object on the map.

3. Use a compass to find north from where you're standing in the mapping area. Mark the outside boundaries of the mapping area on your paper (e.g. long building at north edge, line of trees at east edge, street at south edge, etc.). Now all you have to do is "fill in" the centre of the map with the features you want to highlight.

4. Find something special within the boundaries as the "treasure" (e.g. an unusual tree, an animal home, animal tracks). An "X" on the map marks the treasure. The task then becomes making a map so that someone else can find the treasure.

5. Draw in any major landmarks (e.g. sidewalk, large boulder, group of tall trees, playground). If possible, draw them to scale. You can pace out distances rather than measure them; a pace is a normal walking stride, measured from heel to heel. The exact scale you use will depend on the size of your mapping area (e.g. you might want to make 20 paces equal 1 cm on your map).

6. Choose two or three trail markers for people to follow as they walk toward the treasure. Make up a symbol for each trail marker; explain what symbols mean in a key at the bottom of the map. For example, you might have two stacked rectangles as a symbol for a two-story building; then a person must walk 35 paces north to a crooked line, which is a symbol for a crooked tree. Number each trail marker on your map so a reader moves from one to the next to find the treasure.

7. Who can use your completed map to find your treasure? How can you improve your map?

The best model of the whole Earth is a globe. A flat map on a sheet of paper can distort the size and shape of areas, and the direction or distance between points. To minimize inaccuracies in flat maps, there are certain rules to follow when you're making them. Always include *directions* (i.e. north, south, east, west). "Up is north" is fairly standard on maps. The *scale* of a map refers to the ratio of distances shown on the map to actual distances on the Earth. One unit on the map is equal to some larger number of units on the ground. For example, the scale may be 1:500,000, which means that 1 cm on the map represents 5 km (500,000 cm) on the ground. *Landmarks* are obvious, stationary features of the area mapped (e.g. mountains, rivers). Landmarks don't disappear, unlike a small rock which may be moved. A map should contain at least two or three key landmarks to help readers orient themselves. *Symbols* are used to represent and pinpoint significant features or objects (e.g. road, railroad tracks, buildings, bridge over river). Symbols eliminate unnecessary writing or drawing all over a map and help to simplify the map. In this activity, symbols are used as "trail markers"; a treasure hunter moves from marker to marker toward the treasure. The *key* is the legend in the bottom corner of a map which explains what symbols mean.

Topics: Mapping; Communication.

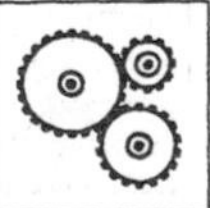

CONTOUR MAPPING

Hills are a physical challenge to climb and a mental challenge to map. Put your scientific/measuring skills to work making a contour map.

The metric system of units is used by all scientists throughout the world in their everyday work. The system was developed by the French Academy of Sciences in 1799.

MATERIALS: Large container (e.g. plastic dish pan); large, irregularly-shaped, smooth rock; water; ruler; chalk or felt pen; paper towels; two sharpened stakes (a little more than 1 m high); several shorter stakes; two flat pieces of wood (each about 45 cm long); hammer; nails; nuts or other weights; tape; string; straw; measuring tape; paper; large sheet of paper; pencil; protractor. Optional -- contour maps; compass; large ball of string.

MAKE TIME

DOING IT:

1. What are contour lines? Take a large rock and put it in a large container. Add water to a depth of 2 cm. Use chalk or a felt pen to draw a line on the rock -- all the way around it -- just above the water's surface. Add 2 cm more of water and draw a second line around the rock. Continue adding water -- 2 cm at a time -- and drawing lines around the rock until the rock is completely submerged or the container is full. Remove the rock from the water and gently pat it dry. Look at the rock from above. The lines on the rock would be the contour lines on a map. Which lines are on the highest part of the rock? Where would these lines be on a flat map? Draw all the lines, as seen from above, on a sheet of paper. You should end up with a series of rough oval shapes, one inside the other. To learn more about contour lines, you may want to examine some real contour maps.

2. Now you and a partner can try mapping a hill. You'll need to build two, identical sighting devices. For each device, use a sharpened stake (pointed at one end) slightly longer than 1 m. Make the crossbar by hammering a flat piece of wood about 45 cm long to the top of the stake to form a "T"; make sure the crossbar is level and at a right angle to the stake. Tape a straw along the length of the crossbar, close to the edge of one end of the crossbar. Make the plumb line by taping a string with a weight on it (e.g. nut) to the side of the crossbar.

A "contour line" on a map joins points of land at an equal elevation or altitude. A series of contour lines are used to describe a third dimension (height) on a two-dimensional scale (i.e. flat map). There are two important parts of a contour map: the vertical interval and the horizontal interval. The vertical interval is the change in elevation each successive contour line represents; the change is constant on a given map. For example, say you have three oval-shaped contour lines on a map; contour line A is inside contour line B, which is inside contour line C. Contour line A represents land that is 100 m higher than line B, and line B represents land that is 100 m higher than line C. The constant vertical interval for the map is 100 m. The horizontal interval is the distance between adjacent contour lines and varies with the steepness of the hill in various areas; the steeper the hill, the closer together the lines. For example, lines might be far apart on one side of a hill (indicating a gradual slope) and closer together on the opposite side of the hill (indicating a steep drop or cliff).

Topics: Mapping; Measurement.

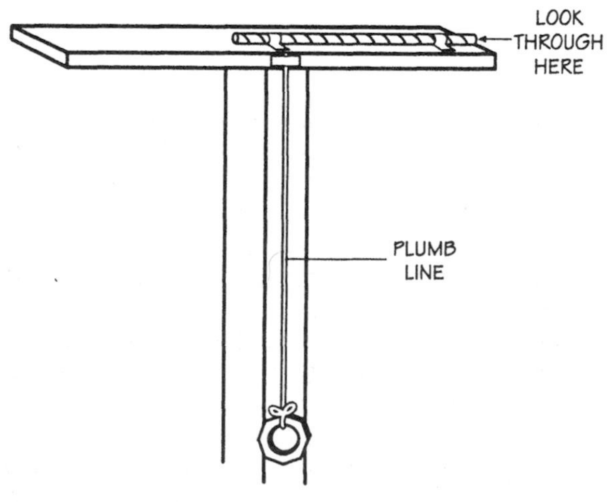

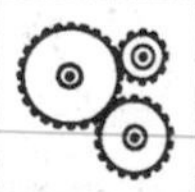

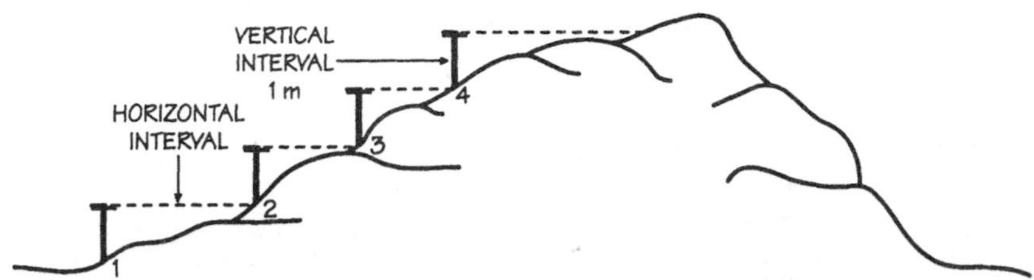

3. Choose a simple, gentle slope (e.g. a hill about four or five times as high as you are). Before you start mapping, imagine the top of the hill as the centre of a wheel. Spokes run down the hill from the centre. The spokes are "sighting lines". You should use at least three equally-spaced sighting lines. The map illustrated below shows six sighting lines, each 60 degrees apart. Decide how many sighting lines you want to use. Then put a short stake into the ground at the top of the hill (the centre of the wheel). Put short stakes at the bottom of the hill (the outside rim of the wheel) to represent your sighting lines; use a compass and a large ball of string to space them equally (i.e. run string from top stake to bottom stake), or simply do it by eye as you stand on top of the hill. All the first sighting points (short stakes at bottom of hill) must be at the same level to ensure the map's accuracy.

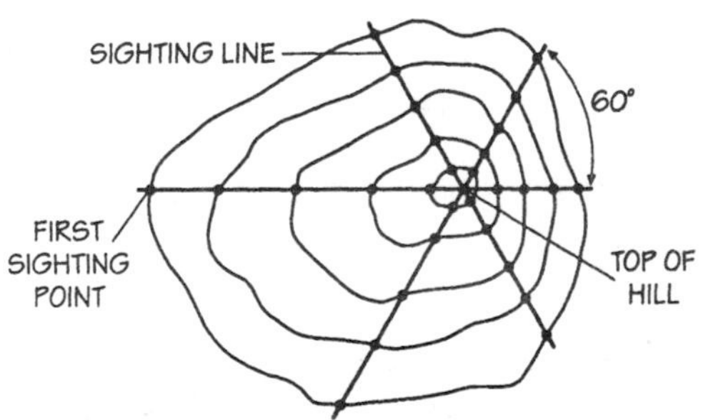

4. Map the first sighting line by going to the bottom of the hill and standing at the short stake. Push a sighting device into the ground deep enough so that it will stand by itself and so that *the top of the straw is exactly 1 m above the ground.* The height of the straw (1 m) is the vertical interval for your map. Make sure the stake is upright by using the plumb line; it should hang perfectly straight, parallel to the stake. This position is your first data point.

5. As you stand at the first data point, look straight up the hill to the stake at the top. Visualize the sighting line. Now look through the straw, along the sighting line. The point on the sighting line that you see through the straw will be exactly 1 m higher than your current position. As you direct your partner, he or she should push the other sighting device into the ground at this spot (which becomes your second data point); set up the second device the same way you set up the first one. Find the horizontal interval by measuring the distance from the top of the straw (directly above the stake) of the first device to the base of the stake of the second device. Write down the distance.

6. As you stand at the second data point, repeat what you did at the first data point. Keep moving from one data point to the next until you reach the top of the hill. It's okay if the last data point doesn't fall exactly at the top of the hill.

7. Collect data for the other sighting lines. In the map illustrated, there are six sighting lines; five of the lines have five data points, while the sixth, shortest line has only four.

8. Once you've collected data for all your sighting lines, you're ready to draw the map. Put a dot in the middle of a large sheet of paper. This centre dot represents the top of the hill. Choose an appropriate scale (e.g. 1 cm = 1 m actual distance). Draw the sighting lines from the centre dot, spacing the lines as you located them on the hill. Following your scale, plot the horizontal interval measurements along each sighting line. For example, if the highest data point along one of the sighting lines was 7.5 m from the top of the hill, convert the distance (7.5 m becomes 7.5 cm) and then plot the point 7.5 cm from the centre dot. Once you plot the horizontal intervals on all the sighting lines, connect the points on the different sighting lines that correspond to equal heights to make the contours (i.e. connect all first sighting points; all second sighting points; etc.). What is the vertical interval on your map? What is the largest horizontal interval? Where is the hill steepest? How high is the hill?

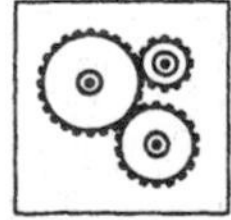

EXTINGUISH THAT FIRE

A fire extinguisher is a metal container filled with water or chemicals used to put out fires. Make your own fire extinguisher.

MATERIALS: Baking soda; vinegar; container with secure lid (e.g. jar with screw-on lid); hammer; nail; straw or other rigid tubing; ruler; scissors; small plastic container (e.g. *wide-mouth* pill bottle); tape; Plasticine; spoon; candle in a shallow glass or metal pan; matches.

DOING IT:

1. This activity should be done with adult supervision. Fire can be dangerous.

2. Fill a small, wide-mouth, plastic container with baking soda.

3. Use tape to attach the small container to the inside wall of a larger container, so that the top of the small container comes just above the middle of the large container. If the small container is tall enough, you can simply stand it in the large container.

4. Cut a straw so that it is about 6 cm long. Punch a hole in the large container's lid, just large enough so that the straw will fit *snugly* into the hole. Use Plasticine to secure the straw in the hole and plug any openings around the straw.

5. Fill the large container about halfway with vinegar, to below the top of the small container. Don't get any vinegar into the small container!

6. Secure the lid on the large container.

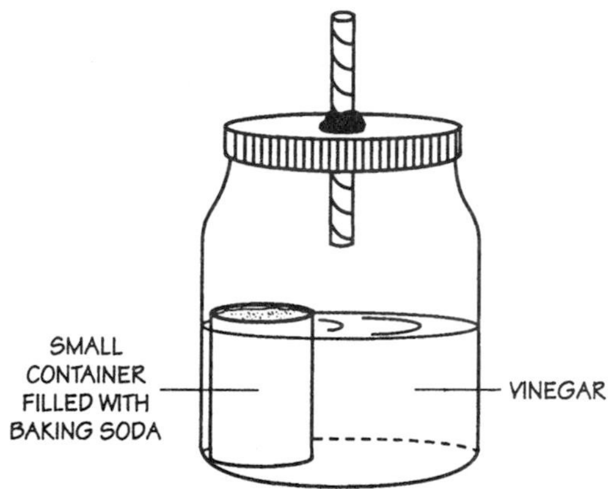

7. Light the candle. **It should be contained in a shallow pan and there should be no flammable materials nearby.**

8. Shake the large container briefly so that the baking soda and vinegar mix. Then quickly tilt the large container over the flame, so that foam spills out of the straw (but no liquid). The foam should put out the flame. Why? How quickly does the flame go out? How long does the foam keep spilling out of the container?

9. *Variation:* Does it matter how much vinegar and baking soda you put into the container? Should you put in equal amounts of each, or more of one than the other?

Fire extinguishers are portable and easy to use so that you can put out small fires before the flames spread. To operate most fire extinguishers, you pull the locking pin, squeeze the operating lever, and aim the nozzle at the *base* of the flames. There are three basic kinds of extinguishers: water, liquefied gas, and dry chemical. A water extinguisher is filled with water and can be used *only* to put out simple fires involving paper or cloth (Class A fires). A liquefied gas extinguisher contains either carbon dioxide gas or a gas called "halon" in liquid form under pressure. When you squeeze the handle, the liquid changes to a gas and flows out of the nozzle. This type of extinguisher can be used on gasoline or cooking grease fires (Class B fires) and on fires involving electrical equipment (Class C fires). A dry chemical extinguisher contains a chemical powder and can also be used on Class B and C fires.

In the homemade fire extinguisher, a chemical reaction takes place between the baking soda and the vinegar. When the two are mixed, the result is carbon dioxide gas. The gas bubbles turn the baking soda/vinegar mixture into a foam and also build up pressure inside the container. The pressure forces the foam out of the straw. As the carbon dioxide in the foam pushes the oxygen in the air away from the flame, the fire is smothered (fire needs oxygen to continue to burn).

Topics: Chemical Reactions.

STAIN AWAY

Science plays an important role in helping you get your clothes clean. Find out what kind of stain removers work best on different types of stains.

Bacteria don't grow well if it's too cold. Refrigerators keep foods safe from spoilage for much longer than foods kept at room temperature. Some frozen foods can be safe from spoilage for a year or more.

MATERIALS: White, 100% cotton cloth; scissors; staining substances (e.g. mustard, ketchup, grape jelly, strawberry jam, coffee, chocolate syrup, felt marker, lipstick); stain removers (e.g. milk, white vinegar, liquid detergent, various commercial stain removal products, bleach); spoons; pen; small pieces of sponge; water; paper; pencil. Optional -- different types of cloth; clean toothbrush (for scrubbing stains).

DOING IT:

1. Cut several pieces of cotton cloth (number of pieces depends on the number of stain removers you're testing), each about 10 cm wide and 30 to 40 cm long (length depends on the number of staining substances you're using).

2. Make a row of stains on each piece of cloth. There should be one stain from each staining substance and each stain should be a few centimetres away from the next stain. Use only a little of a staining substance on a spoon to make a stain. Label each stain with a pen. Let the stains set for about half an hour.

3. Make a chart to record your data. List staining substances along the top of the chart and stain removers along the side.

4. Once the stains have set, put one piece of cloth beside each of the stain removers you're going to test. Which stain removers do you think will remove which stains?

5. Using a small piece of sponge, apply a little of a stain remover to each of the stains on the cloth beside it. Apply each stain remover in the same way. **Be very careful using bleach; do not get it on your skin or your clothes**. You may want to rinse the pieces of cloth in water after you've applied stain removers.

6. Which stain removers remove which stains? Write your results on your chart. You can make comments like: works very well; works okay; does not work; leaves faint colour; changes colour of cloth. Does any one stain remover remove all the stains? How is the bleach different from the other stain removers?

7. *Variation:* Experiment with different ways of applying stain removers (e.g. soaking, gently blotting, scrubbing, applying a lot, applying a little). What happens if you soak stains in hot or cold water before applying a stain remover?

8. *Extension:* Stain different types of cloth (e.g. polyester, nylon, rayon). How does the type of cloth affect the stain and the effectiveness of a stain remover?

A stain occurs when a substance causes a chemical change in the colour of a material or in the fibres of a cloth. Different stains require different stain removers. For example, enzymes (e.g. in milk) "eat" protein stains (e.g. chocolate). There's one key thing to keep in mind when you're trying to remove a stain: the longer you let the stain set, the more damage it does and the harder it will be to get out.

Topics: Scientific Method; Chemical Reactions.

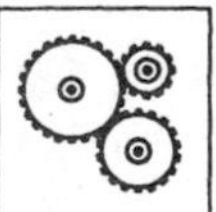

PAPER CHASE

Paper is used in books, for writing, and to make packaging and other items. There are more than 10,000 kinds of paper. Experiment with different types of paper.

One day, a Canadian farmer, Charles Fenerty, noticed some wasps chewing wood fibres to make paper for their nests. That gave him an idea. By 1838 he had made the world's first usable newsprint from ground wood fibres. His mechanical wood pulp process became the foundation of the Canadian pulp and paper industry.

MATERIALS: Sheets of different kinds of paper (e.g. writing, brown, waxed, tissue, photocopy, construction, newspaper, lightweight cardboard, gift wrap, paper towel); magnifying glass; pen; pencil; crayon; felt marker; chalk; two boxes; metre stick; tape; ruler; scissors; cups of water.

DOING IT:

1. *Appearance:* Compare the appearance of several different kinds of paper. What colours are they? Which papers are smooth? Are any of the papers smooth on one side and rough on the other? Do any of the papers look shiny? Are the papers the same thickness (feel them between your fingers)? Examine the surface of each type of paper with a magnifying glass. How do the papers look different? Can you see bits of fibres in any of the papers? What do all the types of paper have in common? How do you know they're all paper?

2. *Tearing:* How easily does each type of paper tear? Is it easier to tear a particular sheet along its length or its width? Can you tear the papers in a straight line? Examine torn edges with a magnifying glass. Do the edges look smooth or fuzzy? Can you see layers at any of the edges?

3. *Transparency:* One at a time, hold a sheet of each type of paper up against a window. Which sheets let a lot of light through? Which don't? Why? Can you see through any of the sheets? How much can you see?

4. *Writing:* Try writing or drawing on each type of paper with a pen, pencil, crayon, felt marker, and chalk. How easy is it to write on the papers? Do some things write on certain types of paper but not on others? Which writing is difficult to see? Why? Examine the writing with a magnifying glass. How does the writing look on the different types of paper? Does the writing cover the paper evenly or does it skip in spots? Why?

5. *Absorbency:* Cut a strip of each type of paper about 2.5 cm x 18 cm. Prop up a metre stick with two boxes, as shown. Tape the strips of paper to the stick. Put the bottom end of each strip into a cup of water (there should be the same height of water in each cup). How quickly does water travel up each strip? Which strips absorb the most water? Why?

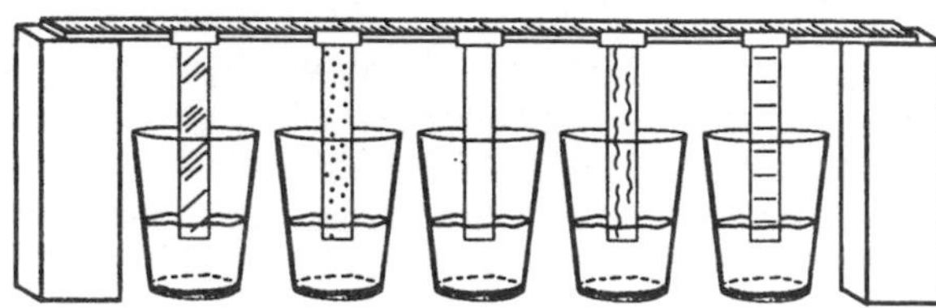

Paper gets its name from "papyrus", a reed used in ancient Egypt for making a writing material. Papyrus stalks were cut into thin slices and pressed into sheets. Paper as we know it was invented in China in AD 105 (that's less than 2,000 years ago). The Chinese found that the inner bark of the mulberry tree could be broken into fibres and pounded or matted into sheets. They also found that good paper could be made by pounding rags. For centuries, paper was made by hand from rags. Today, most paper is made mechanically and chemically in large paper mills from wood pulp. Glue, starch, and/or clay are sometimes added to give paper a smooth surface for writing or printing ink.

Paper can be pretty sturdy stuff. Chemical engineers have developed ways of treating paper to make it strong, fireproof, and resistant to liquids and acids. In some cases, paper can replace materials such as cloth, wood, and metal. For example, specially treated paper is used to make clothing, such as disposable diapers and hospital gowns.

Topics: Scientific Method; Resources.

Pen And Ink

Have you ever really thought about your pen? A pen is a pointed tool used in writing or drawing to apply ink to a surface such as paper. Make a "ballpoint pen".

MATERIALS: Knife; plastic squeeze bottle (e.g. dishwashing liquid or ketchup bottle); large marble; paper; water; food colouring; other available liquids (e.g. syrup, milk, dishwashing liquid).

DOING IT:

1. Carefully cut off the top third of a plastic bottle. Discard the bottom two thirds. Clean the bottle top thoroughly.

2. Find a marble that fits snugly into the small hole in the bottle top. The marble doesn't have to go into the hole, but it must be large enough to cover the hole.

3. Lay a sheet of paper on a table and put the marble on the paper.

4. Hold the bottle top over the marble and push it down onto the marble so that the marble is snugly against the small hole in the bottle top. Pour *a bit* of coloured water into the bottle top. Roll the marble along the paper. Does the marble spread the "ink"? How well does your "ballpoint pen" write? What happens if you apply more pressure to the marble? What happens if you apply less?

5. Try other available liquids as ink (add food colouring to each liquid to make your writing clearly visible). How does a thick liquid work in comparison to a thin liquid? Which liquid spreads the best on paper? Which liquid dries the fastest?

In 1880, a French scientist discovered that, when cut in a certain way, the mineral quartz moves back and forth at a constant rate when electricity is passed through it. Clockmakers first used quartz in the 1920s, with two results: accuracy and silence (the quartz replaced the moving parts in clocks that went "tick-tock").

Various types of pens have been used since ancient times. Pens have ranged from plant stems (reeds) and bird feathers (quills) to modern metal fountain pens, ballpoint pens, and felt- and fibre-tipped pens. Ballpoint pens were the first to write smoothly without causing ink blotches. Inventors first envisioned some sort of ballpoint pen about 100 years ago. Although there were a number of attempts to make a ballpoint pen, it took many years to come up with one that worked well. The first practical ballpoint pen was invented in 1938 by the Biro brothers. The two Hungarians combined their talents -- one was a sculptor/writer and the other was a chemist -- to come up with both a good pen design and an ink that wouldn't leak out of the pen.

The ballpoint pen is more complicated than it looks. It's much more than a tube with a rolling ball bearing at the end. An actual ballpoint pen is so small that it's difficult to see how the ink gets from the tube to the paper. This activity consists of a fairly close model of a ballpoint pen. Using the model, it's clear that the tip of a ballpoint pen has to be specially designed to take advantage of certain properties of liquids. Also, ink isn't just coloured water, but a liquid selected for qualities that result in uniform writing.

Topics: States of Matter.

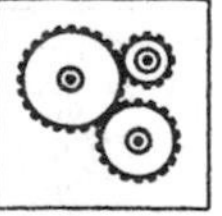

READING HANDWRITING

Handwriting is used for such things as legally identifying people. Analyse your handwriting or someone else's to see what personality characteristics it reveals.

MATERIALS: White, unlined paper; pen.

DOING IT:

1. You can analyse your own handwriting or someone else's. It's best to try to get a sample of "normal" handwriting; that is, handwriting that wasn't written specially to be analysed. If you're getting a sample from someone else, don't tell them why you want it until they're finished writing. This way, they won't think about their writing, which can change its characteristics.

One type of graphology involves scientifically analysing handwriting to detect forgery. Handwriting experts testify in court about whether or not something has been written by a certain person.

Another type of graphology involves examining a person's handwriting to get information about his or her personality. For example, Italian artist, engineer, and scientist Leonardo da Vinci's square, precise handwriting shows him to be inclined toward applied science and mathematics. British politician Winston Churchill's handwriting is fast, straight, and not as easy to read as da Vinci's, indicating a person who is used to being in charge and is self-assured. This approach to studying handwriting goes back to ancient times. Formal analysis techniques were developed in the late 1800s. The techniques are used more in Europe than in North America; some business firms consult graphologists before hiring new employees. Many people do not view this type of graphology as a science. Some principles of graphology are reasonable. For example, handwriting is affected by illness, aging, and stress. But the meanings that graphologists attach to various handwriting features are open to debate and can be somewhat arbitrary. If nothing else, looking at handwriting helps to develop skills of analysis and observation -- and it's fun! This activity provides a general introduction to the analysis of handwriting; graphologists go into much more detail.

Topics: Classification; Human Behaviour; Communication.

2. A handwriting sample should be on a sheet of white, unlined paper. Choose a specific topic to write about (e.g. what you did yesterday, a description of your home, your favourite sport, what you would like to do on your birthday). The topic itself doesn't really matter; what's important is concentrating on the topic you're writing about (not on your handwriting!). The sample should be made up of one or two paragraphs, and finished off with a signature. Now you're ready to analyse the handwriting.

3. *Letter Slope:* How do the words and letters slant? This feature gives insights into a person's sociability. The greater the slant, the more extreme the personality characteristic.

- Right: Outgoing, open to other people's ideas and experiences.
- Left: Shy, doesn't feel comfortable with people.
- Straight: Very independent, little concern about other people or what they think.

4. *Line Slope:* How do the lines of handwriting slope (i.e. from left to right) on the page? This feature is influenced by a person's mood at the time he or she wrote the sample.

- Rising: Optimistic and energetic.
- Falling: Worried, lack of confidence.
- Straight: Self-controlled, reliable.

5. *Flow:* How are letters in words connected to each other? This feature gives insights into the way a person thinks.

- All connected: Rational, logical.
- Some connected, others not: Imaginative, depends on hunches and intuition.
- Few connected: Dreamer, not always practical.

6. *Pressure:* How hard does the person press the pen when he or she is writing? Check this by using your finger to feel for grooves and ridges on the underside of the page. This feature gives insights into health and will-power.

- Heavy pressure: Healthy, forceful, can be stubborn.
- Light pressure: May be physically weak, sensitive.

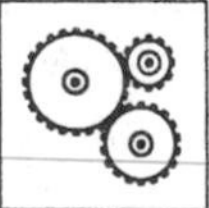

7. *Capital Letters:* How do capital letters look relative to other letters? This feature gives insights into how someone views himself/herself.

- Very large: Conceited, arrogant, perhaps dishonest.
- Same size as small letters: Modest, humble.

8. *"T":* Some letters are key in analysing handwriting. What does the "t" look like? How is it crossed? This feature helps a graphologist put other features/personality characteristics into context.

- Long line: Aggressive, passionate, may anger easily.
- Short line: Fixed ideas, can find it difficult to make decisions, lacks passion.
- Thick line: Wants to be in charge.
- Thin line: Timid, weak will.

9. *"I":* What does the "i" look like? How is it dotted? This feature helps a graphologist put other features/personality characteristics into context.

- Dot is high above stem: Unrealistic, focuses on tiny details instead of bigger picture.
- Dot close to stem: Doesn't share easily.
- Dot centred above stem: Pays attention to details, over-precise.
- Dot to the right of stem: Tends to act very hastily, dynamic.
- Dash-like dot: Anxious, sense of responsibility.
- Circle dots: Stubborn, fussy.
- No dot: Careless, poor memory.

10. *Signature:* Signatures aren't usually like normal handwriting. Most people develop and practice a particular signature. Your signature is your own personal stamp. A signature often reveals what a person *thinks* they are like or would *like* to be like. Compare the signature to the rest of the handwriting sample. Do letters look the same? What about capital letters? Is the signature decorated in any way? Is it larger than the rest of the handwriting? Is the full first and second name included? Are initials used? What insights can you get into personality?

11. Do you agree with the analysis? Do you think it's scientific? Do you think that handwriting can tell you something about a person's personality? Why or why not?

12. *Variation:* Collect handwriting samples over several days or weeks. Analyse and compare the samples. Does handwriting change? Why?

13. *Extension:* Get several people to write the same one or two sentences on the same type of paper with the same pen. Don't look at the handwriting samples as you collect them. Scramble the samples and then try to identify who wrote which sample. Everyone writes differently, so you should be able to see differences in the samples.

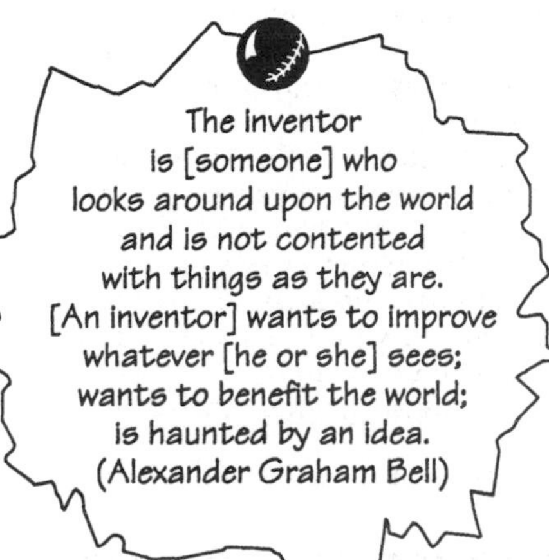

MAKE TIME

One Leads to Another activities in a particular subject area build on one another. They may emphasize a key theme for the subject area or result in a completed project (e.g. weather station). One Leads to Another activities require a little planning.

There are ten subject areas. An activity's subject area is shown by a symbol in the lower, outside corner of the page. Each subject area begins with a short overview for the series of activities and some general tips.

Activities begin with a two-line introduction. A materials list and detailed description follow. Background information and facts are provided in the shadowed boxes.

If you aren't interested in all the activities in a certain series, then just do individual activities here and there. Topics listed for each activity will help you combine activities to suit your interests and needs.

ONE LEADS TO ANOTHER

ONE LEADS TO ANOTHER

SCIENCE OLYMPIC GAMES

The Discovering Science subject area has nine One Leads to Another activities. Complete the activities as a series over a period of several days or do all the activities on a special Science Olympic Games day.

Science Olympics cover a broad range of scientific areas. The Games emphasize problem-solving. Each activity combines imagination, creativity, the practical application of science, and a little competitive spirit. Competing in or judging the Science Olympic Games requires no special scientific background. The events are designed to be fun -- for everyone!

The activities which follow have been selected for the Science Olympic Games because they are well-suited to team competition. Activities found elsewhere in this book could also be adapted for use in the Games. In general, order events so that activities which stress physical effort are mixed with those that stress mental concentration. Some activities can be more difficult versions of ones that participants have completed earlier.

A large-scale version of the Science Olympic Games can be organized so that teams compete against one another at all the events or teams rotate between the various events. A good team size is five people, but the size can vary with your situation. The length of time spent completing each event should vary between half an hour and an hour. If all the activities which follow are used, end the Games with the Modelling Competition and the Instant 3-D Poster. The activities are good climax, tie-breaker events.

Required materials and scheduling should be planned well in advance of the Science Olympics. Judges should familiarize themselves with the activities, and participants should be told about each activity. Events can be judged out of a possible 100 points each. Sample point breakdowns are provided.

The object of the events is to have fun, so awards don't have to be the focus of the Games. All participants should receive some memento of their involvement in the Games. Winners should get some special recognition, but this recognition need not be elaborate or expensive. An awards ceremony can be held at the end of the day. Winners of each individual event should be announced, as well as an overall winner and runners-up. Participants can also be judged within age groupings. Awards can consist of anything from ribbons, certificates, or medals to buttons, magazine subscriptions, or a celebration meal.

The Great Egg Race

The relay team which makes it through an obstacle course and most accurately determines the volume of an egg, in the least amount of time, is the winner.

MATERIALS: Measuring cups; buckets of water; *fresh* eggs; obstacle course (made up of boxes, chairs, hula hoops, stairs, etc.); paper; pencils; stopwatch or watch which indicates seconds.

DOING IT:

1. Lay out the course. Check eggs to ensure that they *all sink completely.* If the eggs aren't fresh, they will float.

2. A relay team consists of five people. Teams run the course one at a time. The clock starts running as the first person in a team begins the relay course.

3. *First Person:* Relay an egg 20 m to second person. You may run with the egg, throw it, roll it, etc. If the egg breaks, it must be replaced by an unbroken egg and a 10 second time penalty is assessed.

4. *Second Person:* Use a measuring cup and water to determine the volume of the egg. You must fill the cup to a level that allows you to completely submerge the egg without causing the water to spill over the rim of the cup. Subtract the initial water level from the new level to determine the egg's volume. (Estimate, or interpolate, the volume if the water level falls between two scale lines on the measuring cup. *Do not round off the value to the nearest scale marking.*) Write the volume on a slip of paper and fold the paper twice.

5. *Third Person:* Wait beside the measurement station until second person is done. Take the folded slip of paper. Run an obstacle course and deliver the egg and paper to the fourth person.

6. *Fourth Person:* Wait beside the second measurement station until third person arrives. Repeat volume measurement procedure. Write the volume on the outside of the folded paper. *Do not look at the first volume* written inside the folded paper.

7. *Fifth Person:* Wait beside the second measurement station until fourth person is done. Take egg and paper. Run 20 m to last station. Look at both volume measurements, average the two values, and present the average volume and the egg to the judge. The timer records the team's relay time when the judge takes the egg.

8. The judge measures the volume of the egg, and notes the percent difference between his or her measurement and the relay team's measurement (subtract team's value from judge's value, divide result by judge's value, then multiply by 100).

9. The highest possible score is 100 points. 50 points is given to the team with the best relay time. Each subsequent team loses 2 points from this 50 points for every second it is behind the fastest team. In addition, 50 points is given to the team with the lowest percent difference between its volume measurement and that of the judge. Each subsequent team loses 2 points from this 50 points for every percent that it is above the best team's percent difference.

Two types of measurement error can occur in scientific experiments: 1) Measuring instruments are only accurate to a certain degree; 2) Different people may read the scale on a particular instrument slightly differently. Scientists overcome these kinds of errors through repeat experimentation and averaging techniques.

Topics: Measurement.

HIGH RISE

The goal is to build a free-standing framework which will support weight one metre above the ground. The framework which can support the most weight is the winner.

MATERIALS: Straws; pins, tape, paper clips, and/or elastic bands; scissors; metre stick; set of objects of varying weight.

DOING IT:

1. The framework is built using straws. Straws can be joined together in many different ways. You can make a long straw by squeezing one end of a straw and placing it inside another. You can use pins or tape to hold straws together. You can bind straws where they intersect with elastic bands. Straws can also be put together with paper clips, as shown. Participants may be told which method to use, or they may choose a method for themselves.

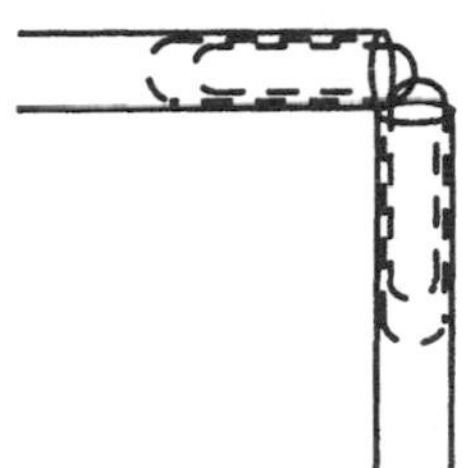

2. Each team receives thirty straws and has access to the remaining materials. Note: Thirty straws may be too few for younger tower builders. Teams have 20 minutes to construct a free-standing framework which will support weight one metre above the ground.

3. When the time is up, a judge tests each structure. Which structures can support the lowest weight object one metre above the ground? From the structures that pass, which structure can hold the most weight (keep adding weight until all but one structure collapses)? The highest possible score is 100 points. The structure supporting the most weight is the winner. Teams are ranked in relation to this structure. In other words, the team with the most stable structure receives the 100 points, while subsequent teams receive 10 points less than the team ahead of them.

Have you ever watched a house being built? Under the bricks or siding, there's a frame of wooden beams -- the skeleton of the house. A frame provides both strength and stability to a structure.

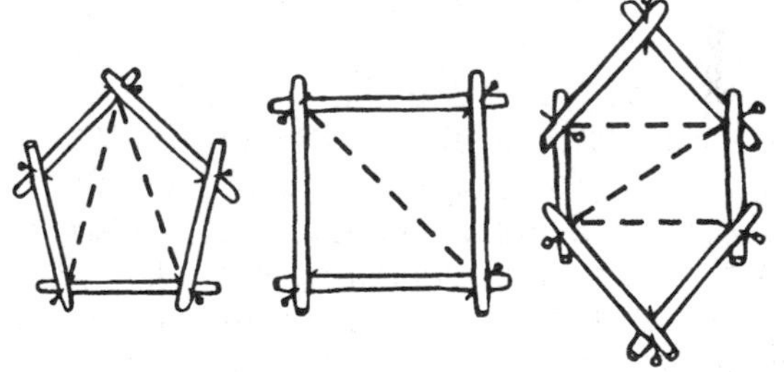

What if the shapes in the illustrations were made of straws? The dotted lines indicate what you would need to do to make each shape rigid (i.e. shape would not sway back and forth when handled). If you look closely, you'll see that each shape becomes divided up into triangles. The triangle is a very stable arrangement, and it's the key to building frames which are both strong and stable. When a force is exerted on a triangular shape, all the sides work together to hold it in place. In this activity, stability is emphasized. The key is to put together a tall, rigid structure that will not topple.

Topics: Problem-Solving; Forces.

FRAME WORK

The goal is to construct a framework to support a full cup of water. The framework with the *fewest* number of straws that can still support the water is the winner.

MATERIALS: Straws; pins, tape, paper clips, and/or elastic bands; foam or plastic cups; ruler; scissors; water.

DOING IT:

1. The framework is built using straws. Straws can be joined together in many different ways. You can make a long straw by squeezing one end of a straw and placing it inside another. You can use pins or tape to hold straws together. You can bind straws where they intersect with elastic bands. Straws can also be put together with paper clips, as shown. Participants may be told which method to use, or they may choose a method for themselves.

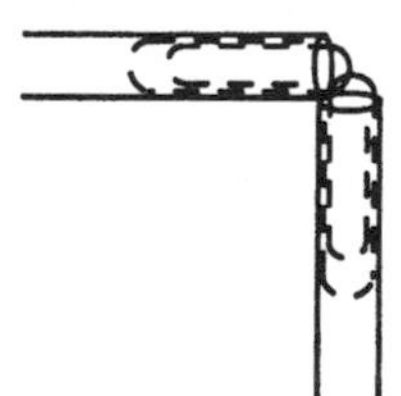

A structure's frame gives the structure both strength and stability. In this activity, strength is emphasized. Straws are used to construct a framework which must support a full cup of water. Each straw has the same strength. The key is to come up with a configuration that utilizes as much of each straw's strength as possible and ensures that straws work together to support the weight applied.

Topics: Problem-Solving; Forces.

2. Each team receives a cup with a straw through the top (use scissors to punch the holes necessary for the straw). Teams have 25 minutes to construct a framework which will support a full cup of water at least 5 cm off the ground. Participants should imagine that each straw is worth $1000, so they must build their frames with as few straws as possible.

3. Teams are allowed to test their frames as they build them using *only half a cup of water.* Tests should be made out of sight of other teams. The half cup of water will give participants an idea of weaknesses in their design. However, participants must still use their judgement to estimate the mass of the full cup of water and the effect it will have on their straw framework.

4. The framework which is made up of the fewest straws, yet still supports a full cup of water at least 5 cm off the ground, is the winner. The winning team receives 100 points. The framework with the second fewest number of straws (yet still able to support the water) receives 90 points, and so on. Frames which cannot support the water receive 50 points or 20 points less than the lowest score (whichever is lowest).

BEST RAFT

Each team designs and constructs a raft made of paper or foil. The raft which can support the most weight without sinking in a pail of water, is the winner.

MATERIALS: Sheets of paper or aluminum foil; weights; tape; a large pail of water.

DOING IT:

1. The object of the raft-building contest is to build a raft that will support as much weight as possible without sinking. Teams have 15 minutes to construct several different raft designs. Teams use identically-sized sheets of paper or aluminum foil. They may not cut the sheets to make them smaller or tape sheets together. They may go through as many sheets as they wish to try different designs. Rafts are made by bending up the sides of one sheet of paper or aluminum foil, folding around the corners, and securing the corners with tape.

2. Teams are *not* allowed to actually test their raft designs before the competition begins. The idea is to think through each design, and to make modifications based on any foreseen problems. Teams must choose only one design for entry into the competition.

3. When the construction time is up, the competition begins. A judge tests the rafts one at a time. More and more weight should be slowly added to a raft until it begins to sink. The weights should be put onto the rafts evenly. The highest possible score is 100 points. The raft supporting the most weight is the winner. Teams are ranked in relation to this raft. In other words, the team with the best raft receives the 100 points, while subsequent teams receive 10 points less than the team ahead of them.

4. What type of raft design works best? After the judging, it can be interesting to test rafts which weren't entered into the competition. Do any of them do better than the designs entered?

The idea in this activity is to think about different raft designs. If people fold the paper or foil only a few centimetres in from the edge, the raft will be long and wide, but not very deep. If they fold the paper or foil several centimetres in from the edge, the raft will be short, thin, and deep. The object is to determine which is best: a broad, shallow raft; a narrow, deep raft; or a design between the two extremes.

Topics: Problem-Solving; Forces.

PAPER ARCHES

Each team designs and constructs a bridge made of newspaper. The bridge which can support the most weight is the winner.

MATERIALS: Newspapers; paper clips; glue; stapler; scissors; ruler; set of objects of varying weight.

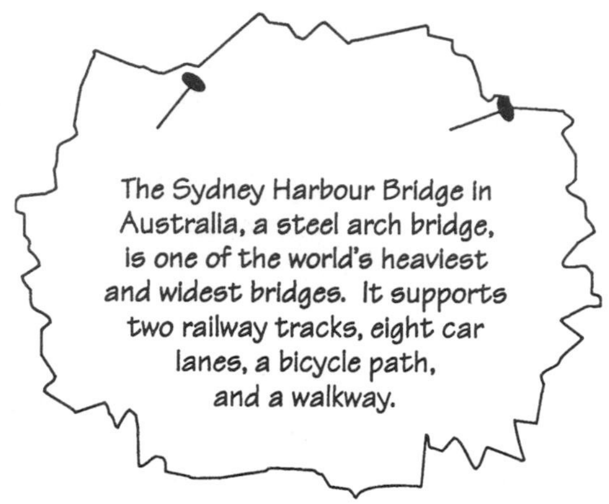

DOING IT:

1. Each team receives five full sheets of newspaper. Participants may use as many of the remaining materials as they wish.

2. Teams have 25 minutes in which to design and construct their bridges. No preassembly is allowed. The bridges may not be fastened to any structure (e.g. chair, table), and must span 1 m in length. The weights to test the bridges will be applied to the centre of the span.

3. The bridges are judged as two team members (one at each end) hold their team's bridge above the ground (or rest the bridge on two chair backs). A judge places successively heavier objects at the centre of the bridge. The heaviest object which can be placed on the bridge, without causing it to collapse, is the weight which the bridge can support.

4. The highest possible score is 100 points. The bridge supporting the most weight is the winner. Teams are ranked in relation to this bridge. In other words, the team with the best bridge receives the 100 points, while subsequent teams receive 10 points less than the team ahead of them.

The key to this activity is designing and constructing a bridge which most efficiently distributes weight along its entire length. There are many designs for bridges.

Some of the very oldest bridges are arches. The arch bridge was first built by the Romans. The Roman bridges were made of stone or brick. A brick arch bridge gets its strength from the support each brick gives to the one on either side of it. The bricks are often wedge-shaped. The middle brick, right at the top of the semicircle, is called the "keystone" because of its importance. The keystone is usually larger than the other bricks in the bridge and is supported by *all* the bricks on either side of it. This prevents the keystone from being squashed outward when a heavy load passes over it. The weight of an arch bridge and a load passing over the bridge push downwards. The arch form turns the downward force into an outward force along the curve of the arch. The "abutments", the walls on either end of the arch, have to be strong to withstand the pressures on them. Arches make safe, strong bridges that can be built to spans of well over 60 m.

Topics: Problem-Solving; Forces.

Paper Plane Flight Tests

Participants construct one paper airplane for competition in four categories: duration aloft; distance; accuracy in hitting a target; and aeronautical stunts.

MATERIALS: Letter-size sheets of paper; strips of masking tape 50 cm long; scissors; straight edge; stopwatch or watch which indicates seconds; measuring tape; target.

DOING IT:

1. This event can be an individual or group competition. If the event is completed by individuals, individual scores are combined and averaged for a team score.

2. Participants receive five sheets of paper and one strip of masking tape. Scissors and a straight edge are available if needed. Everyone has 15 minutes to design and construct *one* airplane for the four competitions.

3. In each area of competition, planes must be hand-launched. Participants are allowed three launches in each category. Each category is worth 25 points. Ties are permissible. The highest possible score for the entire event is 100 points.

4. *Duration Aloft:* Use a stopwatch to determine the length of time a plane stays in the air. Launches can be made from a high place so that flights are more spectacular (planes can be expected to fly five to ten times farther than the height from which they're launched). The plane which stays in the air the longest is awarded 25 points. The plane with the next longest time receives 20 points, the third-longest receives 15 points, and so on.

5. *Distance:* Measure the straight-line distance from launch spot to landing spot. The plane which travels the greatest distance overall receives 25 points. Other planes are ranked relative to the greatest distance, with the second-best plane receiving 20 points, the third-best plane receiving 15 points, and so on.

6. *Accuracy in Hitting a Target:* Participants aim for a target (e.g. a chair) placed 5 m from the launching point. A plane which hits the target automatically receives 25 points. Planes which land within predetermined distances of the target receive lower scores, with units of 5 being subtracted from 25 (e.g. plane within 0.5 m of target receives 20 points, within 1.5 m receives 15 points, etc.).

7. *Aeronautical Stunts:* Points are awarded for paper plane acrobatics. A judge evaluates all three launches of a plane to determine the plane's score. A maximum of 25 points are awarded at the judge's discretion. There are several ways to run this category: planes can simply be launched; participants can describe what they plan to do and be judged on whether or not they accomplish their goal; or a judge can instruct participants on what stunts the planes must perform. The latter approach is, of course, the hardest. Possible stunts include upward or downward loops, graceful landings, and turns around specific objects.

Characteristics that help a plane fly long distances may not make it capable of many stunts. One plane is used for each of the four competitions in this event, but participants are allowed to make minor alterations -- to ailerons, vertical stabilizers, rudders -- to tailor the plane to a category.

Topics: Flight; Problem-Solving.

BALLOON ROCKETS

Teams must construct a balloon rocket which will carry a sheet of paper as far as possible. The rocket which carries the paper the farthest is the winner.

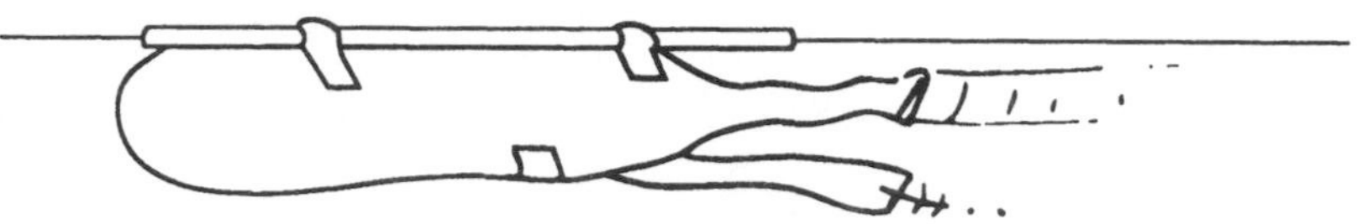

MATERIALS: Sausage-shaped balloons (all of equal size); sheets of letter-size paper; about 10 m of string or fishing line; straws; tape; scissors.

DOING IT:

1. Each team receives sheets of paper, a balloon, and a straw. Tape and scissors should be made available.

2. The goal is to construct a balloon rocket which will carry one sheet of paper as far as possible along a string or fishing line. Teams have 10 minutes to determine the best way to fold a sheet of paper and attach it to a balloon, and then attach the balloon to a straw. Teams may not alter their entry in any way once the 10 minutes is up.

When the air inside a balloon escapes, it pushes the balloon forward. The principle on which the balloon rocket works is Newton's Third Law: For every action (in this case, air escaping from the balloon), there is an equal and opposite reaction (the balloon is propelled forward).

This activity requires that participants not only consider the best way to fold or crumple the sheet of paper (making a paper airplane from the paper or folding the paper into a long, thin strip can reduce the air resistance), but they must also consider the best way to attach the balloon to the straw (the balloon shouldn't be taped to the full length of the straw because the balloon must be able to shrink as the air escapes).

Topics: Problem-Solving; Flight; Forces.

As the fuel inside a spacecraft burns, hot gases expand and then rush from the rocket at tremendous speed through the only opening available -- the exhaust nozzle. The force of the gases rushing in one direction sends the rocket in the opposite direction.

3. Each team takes a turn at launching its balloon rocket. Two people can hold the ends of the string or fishing line, or the ends can be attached to chairs or posts. One member from each team slips the team's straw onto the end of the string and releases the air from the balloon at the appropriate signal.

4. The team whose rocket travels the furthest receives 100 points. Teams are ranked in terms of the distance travelled by their rocket, with each team receiving 10 fewer points than the team above it.

Popcorn and rockets have a lot in common. When you heat kernels of corn, you heat the white fibres of starch inside the tough yellow hull. The small amount of water in the starch turns to steam, which builds up pressure, and POP! If you let it, the popping corn will not only burst into a fluffy white treat but will also go shooting into the air.

Modelling Competition

Teams construct a model of a given area for scoring in four categories: physical accuracy; attention to detail; effective use of available materials; and creativity.

MATERIALS: Pieces of cardboard, boxes, paper plates, paper cups, straws, toothpicks, paper clips, cotton balls, paint, pencils, and/or any other available materials. Optional -- rulers; measuring tape.

DOING IT:

1. The area to be modelled should be fairly small (e.g. a room, a building and surrounding yard). Each team should have an opportunity to walk around the area and make notes on objects and features it wishes to include in its model. Teams may want to make certain team members responsible for reconstructing certain parts of the area to be modelled.

2. Models must be larger than the human brain and smaller than a car. Participants can be required to use only certain materials as they construct their models, or they can be allowed to choose whatever materials they wish. The models may or may not be to scale, depending on the age and skill of participants.

3. Teams should have at least half an hour, and preferably an hour, to construct their models. They should be encouraged to include as much detail as possible.

4. The highest possible score is 100 points. A maximum of 25 points is awarded in each of the following four categories: physical accuracy (e.g. buildings are the right size relative to one another, trees are in the right positions); attention to detail (e.g. windows are the right shape, a deciduous tree is represented differently than an evergreen); effective use of available materials (e.g. a cotton ball is used for a tree's crown instead of just a piece of cardboard, toothpicks are used for window frames); and creativity (e.g. participant makes a model of himself or herself standing beside a tree). Points are awarded at a judge's discretion. The team receiving the most points is the winner.

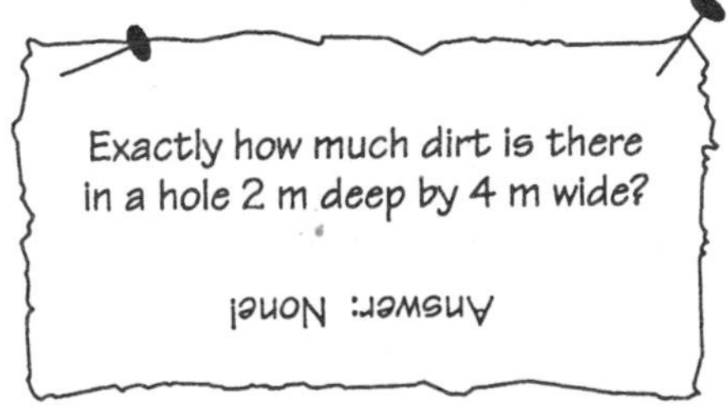

When you make a model, you make something that represents something else. Once you try to model something, you begin to realize how complicated it really is. Model construction requires creativity, effective use of available materials, physical accuracy, and close attention to detail.

Topics: Mapping.

Instant 3-D Poster

The goal is to make a 3-D poster which hangs on the wall with a set amount of tape. The winning poster is the one which receives the highest score from four categories.

MATERIALS: Large sheets of paper; tape; aluminum foil, coloured construction paper, straws, paper plates, paper cups, toothpicks, paper clips, cotton balls, paint, pencils, and/or any other available materials.

DOING IT:

1. Each team is given one sheet of paper and access to the available materials.

2. Teams have 30 minutes to put together their 3-D posters. The posters should be related to some type of science theme (e.g. How to Build a Better Mousetrap; Exploring Space; Our Fragile Earth).

3. 3-D figures may extend out in front of a poster, but should not extend beyond the edges of the paper. A poster must be able to hang on the wall supported by only four 4 cm strips of tape (one in each corner of the paper). Participants are not allowed to hang their posters before the judging begins.

4. The highest possible score is 100 points. Posters must first pass the hanging test. Posters that fail the test automatically lose 25 points. Posters are then judged in the following categories: visual appeal (25 points); originality and creativity (25 points); skill and use of materials (25 points); appropriateness to theme (25 points).

Poster presentation is an effective way of expressing ideas quickly and concisely. The 3-D addition prompts participants to exercise their creativity while dealing with mass limitations.

Topics: Communication.

THE SCIENCE SHOW

The Matter & Energy subject area has five One Leads to Another activities. When the activities are done as a series, they make up a show that is approximately an hour long.

Science and magic have been linked for thousands of years. Humans have turned to both in an attempt to make sense of the world around them. Often, because people could find no other answers, they explained certain occurrences as "magic". Both magic and science are based on people's belief that a particular act will result in a particular effect. Some magic uses science to achieve surprising effects.

To put on The Science Show, one person can act as the magician-scientist, or several people can each learn a trick and take turns in the show. No matter how you put the show together, The Science Show is just as entertaining as an ordinary magic show -- and maybe even more interesting because the audience learns how tricks are done.

The following two pages contain the suggested patter for The Science Show. An entertainer's patter is the rapid speech that he or she uses as tricks are performed. The patter keeps the show going, explains what's happening, and is a large part of the entertainment value of the show. The patter can also set a theme for the show. The theme for The Science Show is the quest for the answer to the question, "What's the world made of?". The entire show is the magician-scientist's attempt to answer the question.

The patter indicates the way in which the following five activities are related to one another. The first four activities each deal with one of the four elements -- earth, air, water, and fire -- that for 2500 years were believed to be the basic elements of which the world was made. It wasn't until the 1700s that the concepts of matter and energy started becoming popular. The final activity in the series gives the modern answer to the question "What's the world made of?" and also gives a "bonus answer" -- something you may have always wanted to know but were afraid to ask!

Activities from elsewhere in *Science Is . . .* can also be used in The Science Show. The five which follow have been selected for the show because they are well-suited to working with an audience and offer variety (e.g. some use audience participation, others are puzzlers, yet others are "hey wow!" types of tricks). The show works best with a small audience. A young audience and an older magician-scientist, perhaps even an adult, complement each other well.

SUGGESTED PATTER FOR THE SCIENCE SHOW

Welcome, welcome to The Science Show! *(Hold your hands up and apart to welcome the audience, or walk onto the stage area and swirl around in a cape.)*

This show will entertain you! This show will amaze you! And this show will show you the secrets to tricks that you too can do! Now on with The Science Show . . .

I have a question. It's a question that's been bothering me for years -- and I mean years and years. What's the world made of? What are the basic things from which everything is made? What do a building, a tree, a mountain, a car, my body, your body all have in common? For thousands of years, people have asked the same question I'm asking. And today, right here on this stage, you and I are going to find the answer!

(Look around mysteriously, then begin to whisper . . .) I went to look in some books. They were really old books. I started to sneeze because of all the dust -- ACHOOO! You know what? I found out what a lot of people *used* to think the world was made of.

(Use normal voice . . .) People used to think that the world was made of four things: earth, air, water, and fire. That seems to make sense. You see, earth meant solid things like metal, wood, and rock. There are a lot of solid things around us -- like that chair over there. Speaking of earthy, solid things, I've got this great trick I just have to show you.

Magicians say a man named Yan Poz invented this trick, but no one seems to know who he was. Some think he was an Italian performer; others say Japanese. But I personally think he was a science teacher, because I found this trick in an old science book when I was looking through those other old books. The trick involves hard, solid things like a broom handle, some salt, and a kleenex. *(Do first Earth trick, and then give scientific explanation.)*

That kleenex is pretty sturdy stuff! I've got another trick with some other hard, solid things: a bottle, a strip of paper, and some coins. Want to see it? *(Put a mysterious twinkle into your eye.)* I'll need your help though. This one is called Bottle Teaser. *(Do second Earth trick, and then give scientific explanation.)*

Okay, what were we doing? Ah, yes. We were answering the question, "What is the world made of?" I told you about the book that said that people thought the world was made of four things: earth, air, fire, and water. Earth was everything that's solid. Now air is, well, air. Air meant anything that's a gas, like the oxygen we're breathing right now. Steam is a gas, and so is the helium that makes helium balloons float in the air.

Now I know I have some air tricks. Let's see, what were they? While I'm thinking, could someone come up and give me a hand? I want to get ready for another trick. *(Pick a person from the audience.)* Could you blow this card over for me? Just blow under it so that it flips over. I'd really appreciate it.

(While the person blows on the card, stand and scratch your head, as if you're trying to remember the air tricks. Every couple of seconds, pay attention to the person blowing on the card and say something like, "Blow harder!" or "Gee, that's taking you a long time." or "You sure don't seem to be trying very hard." No matter how hard the person tries, the card will not flip over. When the person starts to get really frustrated, stare at him or her for a moment and then look as if you just remembered something important.)

Oooops! I just remembered one of the air tricks. You know that card you've been trying to blow over? Well -- now don't get upset -- but as I recall, it's impossible. Great trick, eh? You see . . . *(Give the scientific explanation for the first Air trick.)*

I know another trick that involves air pressure. I have here several ordinary sheets of newspaper -- no strings attached! . . . *(Do second Air trick, and give scientific explanation.)*

I have one more really great air trick! This water fountain is a perfect cooler on a hot day. Anyone want a shower? *(Do last Air trick, and give scientific explanation.)*

Well that takes care of air. So far we've looked at two of the four basic elements people thought the world was made of. We've looked at earth and air. My last trick also involved the third element: water. Water meant everything that was liquid, from water in lakes to milk to orange juice to really, really hot metals that can be poured from one container to another. *(Make pouring motion from one imaginary container to another.)*

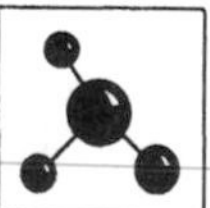

SUGGESTED PATTER (CONT.)

My water trick is very exciting. *(Bend forward toward the audience as if you're telling a secret.)* This trick was passed down to me from my great-great-great-great grand uncle -- from my mother's side, of course. It involves a family recipe for special water -- water that moves all by itself! This water is absolutely amazing. When you least expect it, the water jumps from one place to another. And today, just for you, I've brought along some of this very special water. I'm going to demonstrate just how amazing it is with a little challenge. *(Do Water trick, and give scientific explanation.)*

Now, this little birthday candle reminds me of the last of the four elements. The fourth element that people thought the world was made of was fire. Fire meant energy. Energy is what's needed to change each of the other three elements into each other. For example, if you heat ice (a solid) you get water (a liquid). If you keep heating the water until it starts to boil, you get steam (a gas).

There are lots of amazing fire tricks. Ever seen the one where performers eat fire? People are always amazed by that trick from India. It's not something you or I should try, but I do know how it's done. Nothing magical about it; just pure science. The performers bring a burning wad of cotton close to their lips and hold it there as flames leap in front of their face. Then the performers place the cotton wad in their mouth and fire shoots out. Unharmed, the performers go on to another feat. Well the explanation is simple. The cotton wad is soaked in alcohol, which burns with a cool flame. As the performers stuff the cotton in their mouth, they exhale and blow the flame away. *(Blow air out of your mouth to give people the general idea.)* The alcohol stops burning and the "fire-eater" is unharmed. The trick takes a lot of practice -- to get your technique right so you don't end up looking like a roasted marshmallow -- but there's nothing magical about it. Now don't tell anyone I told you that! *(Wink at the audience.)*

On with my fire tricks. I think we need more light here on stage. Don't you agree? *(Light two candles.)* Hmmmmmm. *(Look as if you're evaluating the amount of light.)* I think now we have too much light. It's too bright. Well, I'd better blow out the candles. *(Do first Fire trick, and give scientific explanation.)*

I love that leaping flame trick. Now, since we have candles that just won't go out, why not really get some flames going? *(Do second Fire trick, and give scientific explanation.)* This fire seesaw will keep going up and down for hours. So let's just leave it here.

For a long, long time, people thought the world was made of four basic things: earth, air, water, and fire. They were things you could see, they were easy to understand, and they made sense. But today we know that there are even more basic things than earth, air, water, and fire that the world is made of. These magic squares are going to tell us the two basic things the world is made of.

(Do the final activity. Everyone can get a blank set of squares and fill in their own numbers, people can get a set of filled-in squares, or the group can work together to fill in one big set of squares on a piece of poster board. The general idea is that the audience participates in finding the two letters which represent the two things that make up the world.)

So the world is made of Matter and Energy. Matter is anything that takes up space and has mass. That means matter is anything from a piece of wood to a puddle of water. Energy can change matter into different forms. That's what happens when heat energy melts ice and turns it to water. If you keep heating the water, the water boils and you get steam. People had the right idea when they said that the world was made of earth, water, air, and fire. Earth is a solid; water is a liquid; and air is a gas. All of these are states of matter. And from fire you get energy. The ideas of matter and energy are just a little more exact than the old ideas.

M and E. Matter and Energy. But did you notice that the letters M and E spell a word? The two letters give a bonus answer -- to another question I've been wondering about. Maybe you've been wondering about it too, because this is The Science Show. What's science all about, anyway? It's about numbers and formulas and test tubes and things, right? Wrong! The letters M and E, which stand for matter and energy, also spell ME. Science is all about me -- and you! Science is about people. Science is people asking questions like "What's the world made of?", and then looking for the answer in an organized way. We looked for an answer in an organized way by adding up different numbers in the "magic" squares until we found the right letters of the alphabet.

And science is about people because I couldn't have done this show without you. You've been a great audience. I think we should clap for each other!

(Show ends with everyone clapping.)

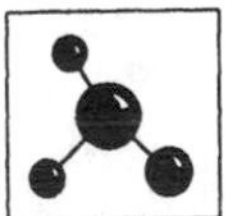

EARTH

Earth is the first of the four elements people used to think made up the world. Earth represented all things that are solid.

MATERIALS: Tissue (i.e. kleenex); cardboard tube (e.g. from roll of paper towels); elastic band; salt; broom handle; empty pop or ketchup bottle (or any other kind of bottle with a small top); paper; scissors; several coins.

DOING IT:

1. *Yan Poz Trick:* Separate the two plies of a tissue in front of the audience. You may want to punch a hole through one ply to demonstrate how delicate it is.

Stretch a single ply over one end of a cardboard tube and hold the ply in place with an elastic band. Pour salt into the tube to a depth of at least 8 cm. Announce that you will ram a broom handle down into the tube without breaking the tissue. Then do so with all your strength. Invite others to try. (Note: Some tissues are weaker than others. You may find that you need both plies of a tissue for the trick to work. But, before you decide to use an unseparated tissue, try adding more salt.)

2. *Bottle Teaser:* Cut a strip of paper about 4 cm x 12 cm. Lay it across the top of a bottle. Then stack some change -- several quarters, a nickel, a penny, and a dime, in that order -- on top of the paper strip. As long as there is some stability to the stack, a higher coin stack works better (because there's more inertia) and makes the trick look more difficult. Make a big show of how easy it is to knock over the coins. Dare someone from the audience to remove the paper strip and leave the coins in place. The person is not allowed to touch the bottle or the coins, or to permit or cause them to be touched by anything. No matter how gently the person tugs and jiggles at the paper, the coins will fall down. Now you do the trick. The key is to remove the paper strip quickly: moisten your index finger (so it sticks briefly to the paper, providing better contact); grasp the longer end of the strip between your index finger and thumb; bring your hand down fast.

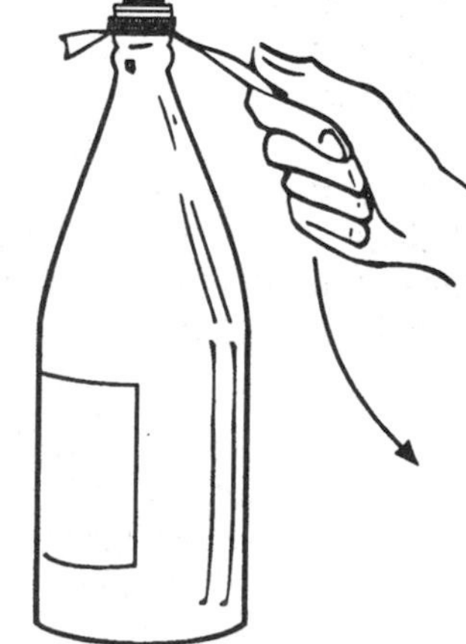

In the *Yan Poz Trick,* a tightly-stretched tissue doesn't tear when you ram it with a broom handle because the tissue is protected from the force by some salt. There are many tiny air spaces between salt particles. When the broom handle rams down on the salt, the salt grains are packed closer together. The force of the collision is distributed evenly and the friction between salt grains absorbs the energy (energy is converted to heat). So, there's nothing left to tear the tissue.

The *Bottle Teaser* trick involves inertia. Newton's First Law of Motion states that moving objects remain in their state of motion and resting objects remain at rest, unless an outside force acts upon them. For example, the outside force that makes a ball rolling on a level surface stop is friction. Friction is the force that makes two surfaces in contact with each other resist moving past each other. In the Bottle Teaser trick, you can pull a strip of paper from under some coins without disturbing them because of the inertia of the coins (they want to stay put). When the strip of paper is pulled away very quickly, the frictional force between the bottom coin and the paper is too brief to overcome the inertia of the coins. The force needed to move the paper can only move the coins through friction, because there's no other force acting directly on the stack of coins.

Topics: Forces.

Air is the second of the four elements people used to think made up the world. Air represented all the different types of gases.

MATERIALS: Piece of cardboard or an index card about 8 cm x 13 cm; table; two full sheets of newspaper; ruler or slat of wood; hammer or broom handle; straws; scissors; drinking glass; water. Optional -- food colouring.

DOING IT:

1. *The Card:* Fold a piece of cardboard or an index card as shown. For best results, put the card about 10 cm back from the edge of a table. The challenge is to blow underneath the card to make it flip over (the card cannot be moved or touched!). No matter how hard someone blows, the card just won't flip.

2. *Newspaper and Ruler:* Place a ruler, or slat of wood, on a table so that approximately a third of the ruler extends over the table's edge. Cover the rest of the ruler with two full sheets of newspaper. Smooth down the newspaper, stroking from the centre of the paper out to the edges (the idea is to make sure there is as little air as possible between the paper and the tabletop). What do people think will happen if you strike the ruler quickly, as hard as possible, with a hammer or broomstick? Everyone probably expects the newspaper to fly up, but the ruler will break before the newspaper moves. The idea is to deliver the force so swiftly that the wood is broken before it has a chance to act as a lever and lift the paper.

3. *Water Fountain:* Fill a glass with water (colouring the water makes this trick more dramatic). Place a straw in the water and cut its length so that just a bit of the straw extends above the water. Take another straw and, holding it perpendicular to the first straw, blow through it across the top of the first straw. A spray of water should flow from the first (vertical) straw.

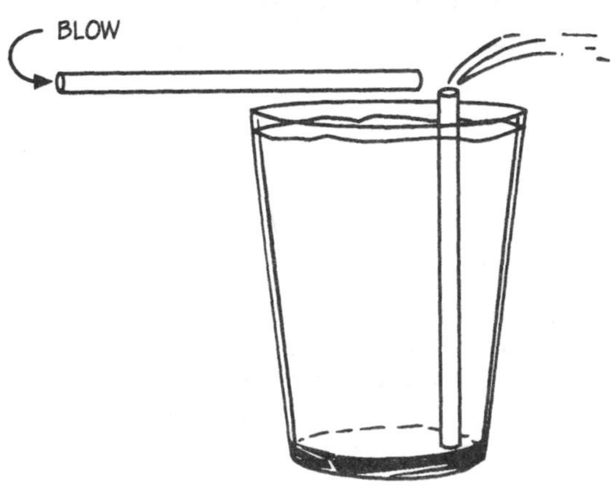

Each of these tricks involves the properties of air, and in particular air pressure. Air constantly exerts tremendous pressure, but we don't feel it because the pressure is directed in all directions and is balanced by the pressure inside our bodies. In *The Card,* blowing underneath a card lowers the air pressure under the card. The greater pressure of the air surrounding the card then pushes down and keeps the card in place. In *Newspaper and Ruler,* the pressure of the air pushing down over the large surface of the newspaper is so great that the air resists being squeezed up suddenly and holds the ruler down. In *Water Fountain,* the water rises through the vertical straw because the moving air stream from the horizontal straw lowers the air pressure above the vertical straw. The greater pressure of the surrounding air pushes the water in the glass up the straw.

Topics: Air; Forces.

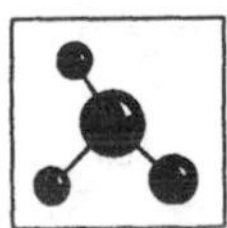

WATER

Water is the third of the four elements people used to think made up the world. Water represented liquids.

MATERIALS: Birthday candle; a bit of Plasticine or a small candleholder; coin (dime works well because it's thin); shallow dish (e.g. glass pie plate); water; food colouring; matches; drinking glass (with smooth rim).

DOING IT:

1. Place a coin in a shallow dish. Fill the dish with coloured water so that the water barely covers the coin (if you put in too much water, this trick won't work).

2. Challenge members of the audience to rescue the coin without getting their fingers wet. The water may not be poured off the coin nor tilted away from it. No instrument of any sort can be used to fish the coin out of the water. When everyone has run out of ideas, announce that you will accomplish this feat with the aid of a birthday candle, a match, and a glass.

3. Get a small candleholder (or make one out of Plasticine) and place the candle in it. Put the candle in the dish as far from the coin as possible. Light the candle.

4. Cover the lit candle with a drinking glass. When the candle goes out, the water will be pushed up into the glass. The dish is now dry and you simply reach in and pick up the coin. (Note: If the trick doesn't work, try rubbing the dry dish *lightly* with a bar of soap or a finger moistened with detergent to make sure the water film won't break.)

If you empty a pail of water onto the ground, the water quickly flows everywhere, even into the tiniest cracks and crevices. The same idea applies to air. Air flows into spaces not already occupied by air. The sound you hear when you open a vacuum-packed (air removed) jar of coffee or peanuts is made by air rushing in as the seal is broken. The motor of a vacuum cleaner creates a partial vacuum in the dust-collection bag. As air rushes in to fill the space in the bag, it sweeps up solid material in its path. In this trick, you create a partial vacuum by burning a candle in a closed space. As the candle burns, it uses oxygen (oxygen makes up about 20% of the gases in air). The flame goes out when almost all the oxygen has been used up. The pressure of the air left in the closed space once the oxygen has been used up is less than the pressure of the air outside. A layer of water is between this partial vacuum and the outside air. Like dirt being swept into a vacuum cleaner, the water is pushed up into the closed space by the pressure of outside air.

Topics: Air; Chemical Reactions; Forces.

FIRE

Fire is the fourth of the four elements people used to think made up the world. Fire represented energy.

MATERIALS: Two or three large candles; waxed paper; matches; knife; two nails; paper clips; two drinking glasses; two saucers; ruler. Optional -- baking sheet.

DOING IT:

1. Use extreme caution with fire. These tricks should be done with adult supervision.

2. *Leaping Flame:* Spread a piece of waxed paper on a flat surface to catch candle wax as it drips (you may also want to use a baking sheet to protect the surface). Light two candles. Hold a candle in each hand (watch that hot wax doesn't drip on your hands). When the flames are burning strongly, turn the candles sideways so they are burning near each other. Blow out the flame of one candle and move it some distance below the other, still burning, candle. Make it look as if you're doing some sort of juggling act. The column of smoke from the unlit candle should rise to meet the flame. The reaction quickly travels down the smoke, causing the wick of the unlit candle to reignite. The flame "jumps" through the air! (Note: This trick must be viewed up close, because the distance you can hold the candles apart is small.)

3. *Variation to Leaping Flame:* Light a candle. Blow out the flame. Quickly put a lighted match into the smoky streak. A flame will shoot down.

4. *Fire Seesaw:* Blow out and use one of the candles from the previous trick, or use a new candle. Cut away the wax from the bottom of the candle until the wick is exposed. Measure the candle to find the middle. Push two nails into the candle, one on each side. Rest the ends of the nails on the rims of two glasses to make a seesaw. Slip paper clips over the rim of each glass, one paper clip on each side of each nail, to keep the nails from sliding off the rims. Put a saucer under each end of the candle. Light both ends of the candle. The candle will seesaw up and down for hours.

Energy makes things happen -- like changing a solid into a liquid and the liquid into a gas (e.g. ice into water and then into steam). All chemical reactions involve energy. A familiar chemical reaction takes place when a candle burns: candle wax reacts with oxygen in the air to form water vapour and carbon dioxide. Heat energy and light energy (which you see as a flame) are involved in the burning candle. The match needed to initially ignite the candle supplies the heat energy that makes the wax hot enough to combine with oxygen. After that, the heat given off in the reaction is enough to keep it going so additional wax reacts. When you blow out a candle, some of the hot wax leaves the wick as smoke. This wax vapour burns if you bring a flame close to it.

In the *Leaping Flame* trick, a flame travels down a column of hot wax vapour to reignite the wick from which the vapour comes. It looks as if the flame is jumping through the air. The *Fire Seesaw* trick is perfect as the last fire trick and provides a good backdrop for the final activity in The Science Show. As wax drips from both ends of the candle, one side soon becomes lighter than the other. The heavier end goes down and drips a large amount of wax on the saucer. This makes it lighter. As it goes up, the other end goes down and deposits a blob of wax; then it goes back up again. And on and on it goes!

Topics: Chemical Reactions; Energy.

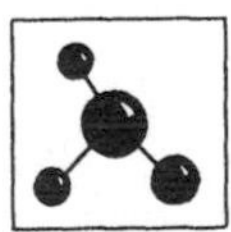

THE ANSWER(S)!

The "magic" squares uncover the modern answer to the question, "What is the world made of?" and give a bonus answer, for the question, "What's science all about?"

MATERIALS: Paper; pencils.

DOING IT:

1. Draw a large square; divide it into three equal columns and three equal rows.

2. Now you want to put numbers into the nine small squares. If you work them out correctly, the numbers in the "magic" squares will always add up to the same total -- whether you add the numbers horizontally, vertically, or diagonally. The magic squares in this activity should always add up to 18. Figure out the number for each square as follows:

- *centre square* -- 18 divided by 3;
- *top middle* -- add 4 to centre number;
- *bottom centre* -- subtract 4 from centre number;
- *right middle* -- add 2 to centre number;
- *left middle* -- subtract 2 from centre number;
- *lower right* -- add 1 to centre number;
- *lower left* -- add 3 to centre number;
- *upper right* -- subtract 3 from centre number;
- *upper left* -- subtract 1 from centre number.

5	10	3
4	6	8
9	2	7

Matter and energy are the two basic things that make up the world. Matter is anything that takes up space and has mass. The same amount of matter has been around since the beginning of time. Matter cannot be created or destroyed; it can only be changed in form. The old idea of earth, water, air, and fire making up the world wasn't too far from the truth. After all, earth is a solid, water is a liquid, and air is a gas. Solid, liquid, and gas are the three states of matter. And fire is energy. The ideas of matter and energy are just a little more exact than the old ideas.

Topics: Numbers.

What's science all about, anyway? It's about numbers and formulas and test tubes and things, right? Wrong! The letters M and E, which stand for matter and energy, also spell ME. Science is all about me -- and you! Science is about people. Science is people asking questions like "What is the world made of?", and then looking for the answer in an organized way.

3. Two numbers which add up to 18 also represent the letters of the alphabet which lead to an answer for the question, "What's the world made of?". Since each row has three numbers, you'll have to add together two of the three numbers to get only two numbers total. For example, from the middle row you could get a 10 (4 + 6) and an 8. Keep going through combinations of two numbers until you find two letters which spell a word. The word is the bonus answer, and the letters stand for the two things of which the world is made.

Answer: The two key numbers are 13 and 5 (e.g. top row has 5 and 10 + 3 = 13, or left column has 5 and 4 + 9 = 13). M is the thirteenth letter in the alphabet and E is the fifth letter. The answer to "What's the world made of?" is M (matter) and E (energy). M and E also spell the word ME, which is a bonus answer (to the question, "What's science all about?").

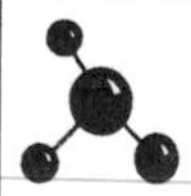

SENSING THE WORLD AROUND YOU

The Humans subject area has nine One Leads to Another activities. The series of activities focuses on the basic human senses.

We generally identify five basic human senses: sight, hearing, touch and feeling, smell, and taste. Your sense organs -- eyes, ears, skin, nose, and mouth -- provide information about what's going on "out there" in your surroundings, so that you can act or react appropriately. Your sense organs tell you that fire is hot and that a knife is sharp. "Reality" for any creature is constructed in its brain according to its capacities and the information it has available. Some creatures depend on only one or two basic senses. For example, fish depend on pressure-sensitive nerve endings along their sides. Their reality is thought to consist of nothing more than an ever-changing blur of the shape and motion of the watery space around them. Certain senses are very acute in some creatures. For example, birds have keen eyesight; bears have discriminating noses. In humans, no individual sense is extremely developed. We're unique because we have several fairly-developed senses, and because we're able to use our senses very effectively to complement one another.

The senses function through "receptors". A receptor is a specialized nerve cell that converts physical stimulation into electrical information the brain can use. Receptors can be stimulated in only two ways: chemically, as in taste, smell, and vision; or mechanically, as in touch and hearing. Information is carried from receptors to the brain along the nervous system.

The way we make contact with the world around us is complicated. "Perception" is the process by which the brain constructs an internal representation of the outside world. We can't directly know or experience the world around us; we only experience what our senses and brain allow us to experience.

The following activities provide an introduction to the ways in which humans sense the world around them. The first three activities look at vision and the amazing human eye. Hearing has some similarities to vision -- at least from the standpoint that you have two eyes and two ears -- and hearing is explored in the fourth activity. The fifth and sixth activities involve the ways in which skin senses warmth, cold, touch, and pain. The seventh activity focuses on the nose, while the eighth activity looks at the tongue. The final activity provides an example of how the senses help each other; it explores how the tongue and nose work together to help humans taste food.

Quickies and Make Time activities for the Humans subject area can be used to provide a complete picture of how the human body functions. For example, an activity on digestion (from Make Time) is an effective complement to the sense activity about tasting food.

THE EYES HAVE IT

You can touch, taste, and smell only those things that are close to you; you can see things that are near and far. That's why vision is so important. Make a model eye.

MATERIALS: Round, glass bowl; a sheet of black cardboard or paper; a sheet of white cardboard or paper; water; scissors; small table lamp (shade removed).

DOING IT:

1. Make a small hole in the middle of a black sheet of cardboard or paper. The hole is like the pupil.

2. Fill a round glass bowl with water.

3. Hold the black sheet against one side of the bowl of water.

4. Hold a sheet of white cardboard or paper on the other side of the bowl of water, opposite the black sheet. The white sheet is like the retina.

5. Place a table lamp in front of the hole in the black cardboard.

6. The room should be fairly dark. Turn on the table lamp. Move the white sheet and/or the lamp until you can see an image of the lamp on the white sheet. How is this set-up like your eye? What does the bowl represent? How is your eye different?

All light entering your eye passes through the small black "pupil" in the centre. The coloured "iris" around the pupil automatically adjusts to limit or increase the amount of light that enters; the iris contracts in bright light and expands in dim light. The "cornea", a thin, clear disc, protects the pupil. The "lens" is just inside the pupil. Your lens operates much like a camera lens, forming an image of objects. However, a camera lens zooms in or out to focus the image; muscles attached to the lens in your eye actually change the curvature of the lens to focus the image. Images are formed on the back of your eye ball, on the "retina". The retina is covered with tiny receptors, called rods and cones, which send signals to your brain when light falls on them. The signals include information on the brightness and colour of the light. The size of an image on the retina is affected both by the size of the original object and its distance from your eye. For example, if two people of the same height are standing at different distances from you, the retinal image of the nearer person will be larger. Just as with a camera lens, the image formed on your retina is upside down. Your brain turns the image right side up.

Normally, the lens in your eye focuses images directly on your retina. "Nearsighted" people can't focus on objects far away because their lens focuses the images in front of their retina. Glasses with a "concave" (curved inward) lens correct this problem. "Farsighted" people can't focus on objects close to them because their lens focuses the images behind their retina. Glasses with a "convex" (curved outward) lens correct this problem.

Topics: Senses; Light; Brain.

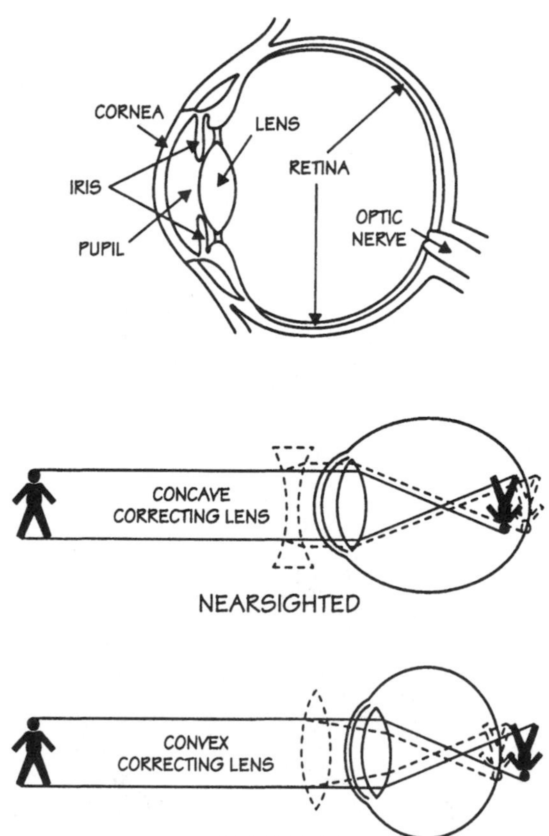

TWO EYES ARE BETTER THAN ONE

One key reason that your eyes are so useful is that there are two of them. Try these experiments to find out how your eyes work together.

MATERIALS: Paper; pencil; ball; ruler.

DOING IT:

1. *Hole in Hand:* Roll a sheet of paper into a long tube. Hold the tube up to your right eye and look through the tube. Hold up your left hand, palm toward you. Put your hand beside the tube, touching the tube, in front of your face. Your brain receives very different information from each eye; it combines the information so that there appears to be a hole in your hand.

2. *Touch the Dot:* Use a sharp pencil to draw a tiny dot on a sheet of paper. Put the paper on a table, about 80 cm in front of you. As you sit at the table, cover one eye with your hand. Use your other hand to try to touch the dot with the tip of your pencil. It's difficult to touch the dot because it's hard to judge distance with only one eye.

3. *One-Eyed Catch:* Stand about 8 m away from a partner. Use both eyes to catch a ball your partner throws at you. You get ten tries. Write down how many catches you make. Then, close one eye so that you can't see through it. You get ten tries to see how many catches you can make with only one eye open (if you find this too easy, try making one-handed catches). How many catches do you make the second time? It's harder to judge distances with only one eye.

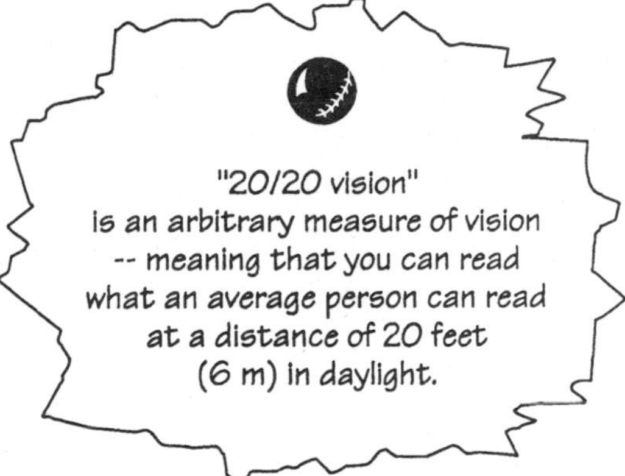

Blinking is an automatic reflex. You blink an average of twenty times per minute -- that's over 15,000 times each day. Only four blinks per minute are really needed to keep the eyes moist and clean.

The eye is an intricate structure that does a number of things: it receives and transmits thousands of visual messages per minute; it automatically adjusts its iris to changing light conditions; it focuses incoming light; and it produces its own fluids for lubrication, cleansing, and fighting off infection. The human eye is very sensitive. It is possible for an eye to detect a candle flame 48 km away. Your eye is also very versatile. Your central vision enables you to read this page, while your peripheral vision lets you see a person entering a door to your right or left, without turning your head. A single eye is amazing; two eyes working together are doubly amazing. You see through each eye separately; each eye sees objects from a slightly different angle. But your brain is able to combine the information it receives from both eyes to give you "stereoscopic" vision. Stereoscopic vision provides a picture of your surroundings that makes sense, gives you three-dimensional depth perception, and helps you to judge distances. When you cover one eye, you no longer have stereoscopic vision and you see the world like a photograph, in two dimensions.

Topics: Senses; Brain.

IN FULL COLOUR

Look around you. What do you see? Colours -- all sorts of colours. Change the colours in this drawing with a single movement of your eyes.

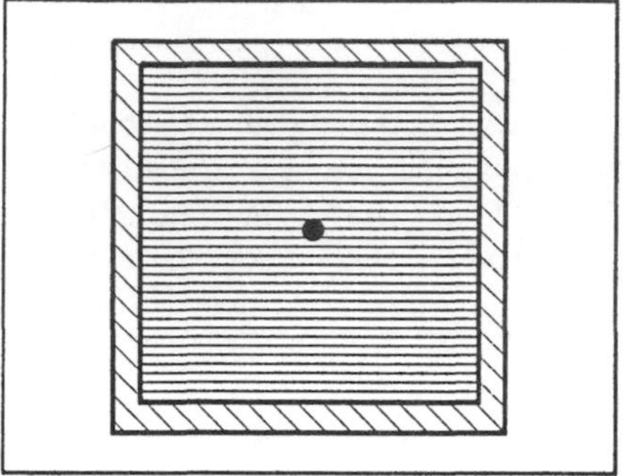

MATERIALS: White paper; coloured pencils.

DOING IT:

1. Make a drawing of a square (or other shape) with a yellow border, a green interior, and a small black dot in the centre. Use intense colours.

2. Stare at the dot in the coloured square for about 40 seconds, in bright light, without blinking your eyes. When the time is up, look quickly at a blank sheet of white paper. What colour is the square's border? What colour is the interior? Why?

3. *Extension:* Try other shapes. Also try other colour combinations.

The cones are the part of your retina that enable you to see colour. Your eye has only three types of cones: "red", "blue", and "green". From the messages these three colour receptors send, your brain is able to "see" all the colours you know. The exact colour you see at any given time depends on the number of each type of receptor and the combination of different receptors which have been excited by the light hitting your eye. When no cones are excited, you perceive black (an absence of colour). People who are missing one or more of the three colour receptors are called "colour blind". The most common kind of colour blindness is the inability to tell the difference between red and green -- which can be a problem when you come to a traffic light. These people are not truly colour "blind" because they can see other colours, such as blue and yellow.

"Afterimages" occur when certain cones are excited for a long period of time and become "tired". The green square bordered in yellow becomes a red square bordered in blue because of an afterimage effect. When you stare at the green square, the colour receptors that are most sensitive to green light send "green" messages to your brain. When you glance at a sheet of white paper, the light reflected from the surface of the paper contains all the colours of the rainbow. The tired cones in the square-shaped area on your retina which had been responding to green now fail to react to the green portion of light from the white paper. What you see is white with green subtracted from it, a situation your brain interprets as red. The same explanation applies to the yellow changing to blue.

Topics: Senses; Light.

Rods are a part of the eye that do a poor job of defining details. But, at night or in dim-light situations, rods are far more useful than cones. Cones are clustered in the centre of your eye; there are more rods away from the centre. At night (after your eyes have adapted to the darkness), site a star that is barely visible. Look at it directly. Then look at it out of the corner of your eye. See anything more?

GOOD VIBRATIONS

Perhaps the most important function of hearing is that it makes human speech possible. Explore the ways in which your ears enable you to hear sounds.

MATERIALS: Piece of waxed paper; a hard plastic comb; small radio.

DOING IT:

1. *Feel the Vibrations:* Fold a piece of waxed paper in half. Slip a comb into the waxed paper so that the teeth are against the fold. Put the comb into your mouth so that your lips rest gently on the folded edge of the waxed paper. Blow and hum. Can you feel the vibrations produced by this homemade kazoo?

2. *Listen:* Tap around your ears with one finger. Relax. Breathe deeply. Close your eyes. Listen. What do you hear? Don't identify where the sounds are coming from (e.g. dog barking, train whistling); just experience the sounds. Count all the different sounds you can hear -- rustling, whistling, swishing, shuffling, hissing, thumping, buzzing, etc. Which are natural sounds and which are human-made? Imitate the sounds, exactly as you hear them.

3. *Moving Music:* Close your eyes as a partner moves a radio to different spots in a room. How accurately can you point to the location of the sound? Do you improve with practice? How easy is it to locate the sound if the radio is directly in front or behind you?

When you put your ear to a large seashell, you hear a dull roaring sound. That's the echo of the blood moving in your ear.

The sounds you hear are vibrations of the air around you; the louder the noise, the more the air vibrates. The human ear is so sensitive to vibrations that it is possible for a person to sit in a quiet room and detect the ticking of a watch 6 m away. The outer part of your ear (the part that sticks out the side of your head) channels vibrations down to a thin membrane that's stretched so tightly it's called the "ear drum". The ear drum then vibrates and the vibrations are amplified by three tiny bones (the hammer, the anvil, and the stirrup) as they go into the inner ear, deep inside your head. The inner ear consists of a 34 mm long, coiled tube called the "cochlea". The cochlea is filled with fluid and divided down its length by a flexible membrane. Along the length of the membrane are thousands of tiny receptor cells, called "hair cells" because stiff hairs stick up from their top surface. The hair cells are very sensitive to the vibrations of the membrane. The hair cells translate the vibrations into nerve impulses which your brain registers as sound.

Just as you need two eyes to work out where objects are in relation to each other, you need two ears to locate sounds. If, for example, a sound is on your left, the vibrations of the air reach your left ear just before your right ear and are less intense at the right ear because your head is in the way. Your brain is able to detect the slight differences in what each ear "hears". When a sound is directly in front or behind you, the sound reaches both ears at the same time and you can have difficulty locating the sound. Blind people can become quite good at locating sounds, and can often make a sound and listen to it echo back from objects to locate the objects.

Topics: Senses; Sound; Brain.

KEEP IN TOUCH

Some parts of your skin have a lot of nerve endings and are very sensitive to touch, while other parts are less sensitive. Try these touch tests.

MATERIALS: Matched pairs of small objects (e.g. chalk, pencils, leaves, erasers, crayons, nails, coins, elastic bands, pieces of cloth, rocks, paper, aluminum foil); box; paper clip; ruler; paper; pencil.

DOING IT:

1. *Matched Set:* Gather matched pairs of small objects. Put one of each of the objects into a small box and put the other in a pile outside the box. Close your eyes. A partner should choose an object from outside the box and let you feel the object. Then, using only one hand, you have to feel through the objects inside the box. Can you find the object that matches the one your partner chose? Match all the objects, one at a time. When you're done, count how many objects are correctly matched. Which objects are hard to tell apart? Which are easy? Why? Is it easier to identify objects using two hands? How is sight related to your sense of touch?

2. *Two Pricks or One?:* Open up and bend a paper clip into a "U" shape; both sides of the "U" should be exactly the same length. Push the two tips of the "U" together so that they touch. Have a partner close his or her eyes. Touch the tips lightly to the palm of your partner's hand. Does your partner feel one prick or two? Separate the tips a little bit. Does your partner feel two pricks? Keep spreading the tips, a bit at a time, until your partner feels two pricks. Measure the distance between the two tips with a ruler and write the measurement down. Test different parts of the body: back of hand, fingertips, forearm, back of knee, thigh, back of neck, tip of nose, under nose, lips. For some, less sensitive parts of the body, the tips may be far apart and still feel like one prick.

How well do you really know the back of your hand? A 2 cm square patch of skin can contain: 30 hairs, 2.5 m of blood vessels, 12 m of nerves, 4 oil glands, 300 sweat glands, 9000 nerve endings, 600 pain receptors, 6 cold receptors, 36 heat receptors, and 76 pressure receptors.

Why doesn't it hurt when you get a haircut or clip your fingernails? The feeling of pain arises from harm to nerve endings in the body. There are no live cells or nerve endings in the hair shaft or fingernail plate. Hair and nails are made of a hard protein called "keratin".

When something comes in contact with your skin, you may feel one or more of the following basic sensations: warmth, cold, touch, or pain. When you open the door to the freezer, you feel the sensation of cold. When you take an ice cube out of the freezer, you not only feel cold but you feel the sensation of touch. Each of the basic sensations comes from electrical impulses triggered by a particular kind of receptor cell. Some receptors, when stimulated, result in a feeling of warmth; others result in a sensation of cold; still other receptors are sensitive to touch or pain. Human skin isn't uniformly sensitive or sensitive in the same way in all places. Fingertips are one of the most sensitive parts of the body; they have a high concentration of nerve endings. That's why you use your fingers so much to feel objects. You can tell objects apart by different touch-related characteristics such as size, texture, shape, and hardness. It's important not to look when you're doing touch tests, because what you see can alter what you feel. Limiting sight can also heighten the sense of touch.

Topics: Senses; Human Body.

Cold, Hot, and Wet

Some parts of your skin sense heat, others sense cold. Explore your hot and cold receptors and learn how to fool your body's ability to sense temperature.

MATERIALS: Three drinking glasses; hot (not scalding) water; lukewarm water; cold water; two large bowls; rubber gloves.

DOING IT:

1. *Cold or Hot?:* Place three glasses of water in a row: hot water on one side, cold on the other, and warm in the middle. Put a finger from one hand in the hot water and a finger from your other hand in the cold water. Is it easy to tell which water is hot and which is cold? Leave the fingers in the water for about one minute. When the time is up, quickly put both fingers into the warm water. How does the water feel to your left finger? How does it feel to your right finger? Take the two fingers out of the warm water and put in two other fingers. Does the water feel warm now?

2. *Wet or Not?:* Put on rubber gloves. Put your hands into a bowl of cold water. The gloves keep your hands dry, but do they feel dry? Put your hands into a bowl of warm water. How do they feel now?

Your nerves, which are long, thin fibres, produce small electric charges. The charges travel very quickly along one nerve and on to the next one -- like electricity passing through wiring in a circuit. If you step on a pin, the message from your foot takes only 0.05 of a second to reach your spinal cord, then your brain, return to your foot, and make your muscle move the foot.

Your body can sense temperature because you have temperature receptors in your skin. There are separate hot and cold receptors. As with all the senses, your perception of temperature is affected by the receptors *and also* by how your brain interprets the information it receives from receptors. You trust your senses to tell you the "truth" about your environment, but your senses can be fooled. For example, we say that seeing is believing; but seeing *isn't* believing when you're looking at an optical illusion.

One way to fool your senses is to expose receptors to the same, strong sensation for a while. That's what happens when you put one finger in hot water and another finger in cold water. When you then put both fingers into warm water, the water feels hot and cold at the same time. The finger that was in the hot water was conditioned to sense "hot", so when it's placed in the warm water, the water seems cold by comparison. The finger that was in cold water was conditioned to sense "cold", and so the warm water seems hot by comparison. The sensation of "wetness" is interesting because it involves a feeling of both coldness and pressure on the skin. When your hand is in a rubber glove and you put it in cold water, your skin receptors sense the coldness and the pressure from the gloves; your brain is fooled into interpreting the information as wetness.

Topics: Senses; Brain.

The Nose Knows

Many animals have a keener sense of smell than humans. What would it be like if you had to depend on your nose the way animals do? Follow a scent trail and find out.

MATERIALS: Several different scents (e.g. vanilla, peppermint, lemon, orange, banana, strawberry, maple, coconut, root beer, chocolate, cinnamon, onion, garlic); cotton balls; string; blindfolds; paper; pencil.

DOING IT:

1. Make scent markers by soaking cotton balls in various scents, one scent per marker. Most scents should be distinct (e.g. lemon and garlic), but a couple should be similar (e.g. lemon and orange).

2. Choose a trail. The trail can be indoors or outdoors. It should wind for 5 m to 10 m. The start and finish should be clearly marked and the trail should not involve any obstacles.

The receptors for smell lie in the upper, inside part of your nose. There are about 30 million smell receptors in each nostril, which means humans have a fairly sensitive sense of smell. It is possible for a human being to detect one drop of perfume in a three-room house. Humans can identify thousands of different odours. Some individual smell receptors detect a wide variety of smells, while others pick out only one smell. Sometimes, a faint odour can be difficult to detect. If you're having trouble smelling something, it's helpful to sniff a little; sniffing gets more air into your nose. A moist nose is also supposed to help you smell.

Topics: Senses.

3. Place the scented markers in different spots along the trail. Assign each marker a number. You can make the trail more difficult by having it double-back and/or by having some markers low to the ground and others high up. Make a list of the numbers and their associated scents.

4. People work in teams of two. One partner is blindfolded and must sniff his or her way along the trail. The other partner has the list of scents and the order in which they must be found. The sighted partner serves as a guide, reading from the list, checking off scents as they are found, and preventing any mishaps.

5. How quickly can the blindfolded sniffers find all the scents, in the correct order, and get to the end of the trail? Partners should switch roles after completing the trail once.

6. How does it feel to use just your sense of smell? Do some people perceive odours better than others?

"Synesthesia" is a rare condition in which a person's senses are mixed together. People with synesthesia "see" sounds or smells. For example, when they hear a person's name, they may see a colour. Or, when they taste a certain food, they see shapes.

When you sneeze, the air that comes out of your mouth travels at about the same speed as a hurricane-force wind.

STICK OUT YOUR TONGUE

Your tongue is important for helping you to detect different tastes. Can you taste salty foods all over your tongue, or just in certain places? Make a tongue map to find out.

MATERIALS: Four drinking glasses; water; salt; sugar; vinegar; unsweetened grapefruit juice or strong instant coffee; tablespoon; teaspoon; cotton-tipped swabs; four different colours of pencils; paper; paper towels.

DOING IT:

1. Fill three glasses about 1/3 full with warm water. Stir a tablespoon of sugar into one glass (sweet solution). Stir a teaspoon of salt into the second glass (salty solution). Stir a teaspoon of vinegar into the third glass (sour solution). Put a little grapefruit juice or instant coffee into a fourth glass (bitter solution).

2. Draw a large "U" on a sheet of paper as a tongue diagram.

3. Dip a swab into one solution and touch the swab to different parts of your tongue: the tip, then to each side, and finally to the back. Wherever you can taste the solution, mark the spot on your tongue diagram in one colour of pencil.

4. Rinse your mouth out well with water. Repeat the testing process with each of the three other solutions. Rinse your mouth out after trying each solution. Use a clean swab each time. Use a different colour of pencil for each solution as you mark spots on your diagram.

5. How does your tongue map look? How does your tongue map compare to another person's? Which of the four basic tastes do you like the most? Which do you like the least? Why?

6. *Extension:* Dry off the end of your tongue with a paper towel. Sprinkle sugar on your tongue. Can you taste the sugar? The sugar won't taste sweet until it mixes with saliva.

The only time most people notice their tongue is when they accidentally bite it. Usually, the tongue manages to stay out of the way and still perform all the fine movements needed to make words. Try talking while you hold your tongue. When does it want to lift? Widen? Thicken? Curl? Touch your teeth? Talk, but don't move your lips. Talk, but don't move your jaws. Try talking while holding a clean marble or pebble (don't swallow it!) under your tongue.

The rosy bumps you can see on your tongue are "taste buds". There are thousands of taste buds on the tongue. Each bud contains ten to fifteen individual receptor cells. Each receptor lasts for only about four days before it wears out and is replaced by a new receptor. In very simple terms, your tongue can detect four basic tastes: sweet, salty, sour, and bitter. Scientists believe individual receptors are sensitive to certain tastes, although recent research has shown that things may be more complicated than this. In general, the back of the tongue is where bitter receptors are found. The sour receptors are along the sides of the tongue, toward the front. The sweet receptors are concentrated at the tip of the tongue. Further back, along the sides of the tongue, are the receptors for salt; sometimes, the tongue's tip can also taste salt. How sensitive is your sense of taste? It is possible for a human being to detect one teaspoon of sugar dissolved in 7.5 litres of distilled water. Your tongue only works when it's wet; "saliva" -- the watery liquid in your mouth -- helps you to both taste and digest food.

Topics: Senses; Mapping.

TASTE THIS

When you have a cold and your nose is stuffed, food seems tasteless. That's because your sense of smell is out of order. This taste test shows the importance of smell.

MATERIALS: Equal-sized, peeled chunks of raw carrot, apple, onion, potato, pear; plate; drinking glass; water; toothpicks; vanilla extract, peanut butter, or cinnamon.

DOING IT:

1. Spread the food chunks out on a plate. Get a glass of water ready.

2. Close your eyes and use your fingers to plug your nose firmly.

3. A partner should use a toothpick to feed you one chunk of each type of food. Carefully chew each chunk. Rinse out your mouth between chunks of different food. Can you identify the foods? Why is it so difficult? Trade places with your partner. Does he or she have any better luck?

4. Try the taste test again. The taster has eyes closed and nose *unplugged.* Any trouble identifying the foods?

5. Try the taste test one more time. The taster has eyes closed and nose unplugged. Rub a little vanilla extract, peanut butter, or cinnamon on the taster's upper lip. Now how do the food chunks taste?

Your senses help each other in different ways. Tasting food involves more than just the receptors on your tongue. The smell, texture, feel, temperature, and look of food also contributes to how good -- or bad -- it tastes. Smell is an important helper to taste. The "olfactory nerve" carries "smell" information from your nose to your brain. Your brain receives this smell information before it receives taste information from receptors on your tongue. Often, you're smelling food when you think you're tasting it. You can taste the salt on a peanut, but you can't actually taste the peanut; you smell the peanut. Your sense of taste is most sensitive when food is close to body temperature.

You learn, or "acquire" tastes, just as you learn to use your other senses. Some tastes, like spinach or anchovies, are not immediately appealing. But, if you try the food several times, you adapt to the new taste sensation. That's why some people enjoy foods that others find revolting, and why people from different cultures enjoy different kinds of foods.

Topics: Senses; Brain.

Often, when people imitate the action of jaws chewing, they make both the top and bottom move up and down. That's not quite right. Chew some food while resting your nose on the edge of a table. Then, chew some food while resting your chin on a table. Which way is it easiest to chew? When your lower jaw can't move, what must your head do so that you can chew?

THE ENVIRONMENT

SOLVING OUR ENVIRONMENTAL PROBLEMS

The Environment subject area has thirty-one One Leads to Another activities. Done together, the activities provide an overview of the environmental problems facing the Earth and some possible solutions to the problems.

Humans are causing problems for themselves, for the other living things on Earth, and for the environment -- the air, water, and land. Only we can solve the problems. The following series of activities deals with each part of these two statements.

The series of activities begins with a look at human population growth and limited resources. Endangered animals are then discussed. Issues related to the air are introduced through activities on the destruction of trees (in particular, the rainforests) and the greenhouse effect. Forms of air pollution, holes in the ozone layer, and acid rain are explored. Then, there's a shift to energy -- the polluting effect of burning fossil fuels, energy conservation, and alternative energy sources. The next group of activities deals with water as a limited resource. Water conservation and pollution (e.g. chemicals, oil spills) are explored. Land pollution, in particular garbage, is up next. Composting and recycling activities are included. The One Leads to Another series ends with five activities addressing social and personal factors related to solving environmental problems. Three activities involve the concept of trade-offs. Issues have many sides and decisions require a lot of thought and cooperation between people. The fourth activity looks at personal knowledge and action. The last activity is a powerful experience in personal responsibility. People must care for and protect an egg (which represents the Earth) for a day.

Caring for the planet is a team effort. Being an effective, active member of the team begins with knowledge. The environment is a complex subject area. Quickies activities cover basic awareness experiences. Make Time activities deal with the workings of the natural world and topics such as ecosystems and habitats. Quickies and Make Time activities, together with this One Leads to Another section, provide a solid knowledge base.

COOKIE CONCERNS

The world's population increases by about 160 babies/minute. More people need more resources. But resources are limited -- just like the cookies in this activity.

In the last forty years, the human population has doubled from 2.5 billion people to over 5 billion people. The growing human population affects plants and animals around the world, directly and indirectly. More people clear more land to make room for houses, roads, shopping malls, and other developments, which means less land for plant and animal homes. More people generate more waste, which takes up space (e.g. landfills) and can pollute the environment. And more people place more demands on limited resources such as energy, food, and water.

The problem of limited resources is compounded by the fact that resources are not always fairly and effectively managed. Rich western countries, with only 20% of the world's population, use 70% of the world's energy. Many wealthy countries get more food than they need, while poorer countries often don't get enough. Population growth is greatest in poorer countries in Asia, South America, and Africa; they can least afford to support more people. Some farmers in poorer countries grow "cash crops" -- coffee, tea, cotton, bananas, tobacco -- to sell to wealthy countries instead of growing much needed basic food crops. Poor farming practices in poorer countries can turn good land into desert and worsen the effects of drought.

Topics: Resources; Decision-Making.

MATERIALS: One cookie for each person.

DOING IT:

1. Start with two cookies and two people. How much cookie should each person get? Add two more people. How much of the two cookies should each of the four people get? Add four more people. How much cookie should each of the eight people get? How does this example relate to the world's growing population? How should the cookies be divided up? What's "fair"?

2. People form two groups: one group is made up of two people and the other group is made up of everyone else.

3. Make two equal piles of cookies (total number of cookies equals total number of people). The group of two people gets one pile and the other pile goes to the other group.

4. Is the distribution "fair"? How do people in each group feel? Compare the cookies to world resources, like food or energy.

5. How does the large group want to divide its cookies? What might the larger group do to get some of the smaller group's cookies? What can the small group do to more fairly distribute the cookies (e.g. sharing, bartering, breaking cookies apart)? Does the small group want to share its cookies? Why or why not? Does anyone think it's a good idea to save some cookies for a snack later? Why or why not?

6. People should work together to decide on a "fair" cookie distribution -- and then eat away!

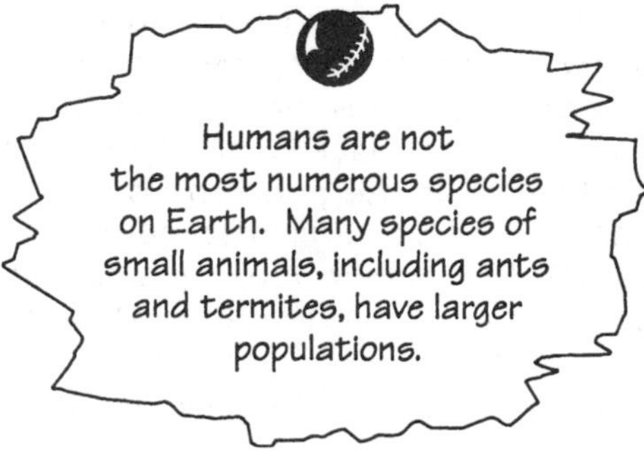

EATING LOW

Using resources wisely can involve "eating low on the food chain". Explore energy loss in a food chain with playing cards and popcorn.

MATERIALS: Deck of playing cards; paper; pencils; large bowl of popped popcorn.

DOING IT:

1. *Card Pyramid:* Each person secretly writes down the name of a plant or animal on his or her slip of paper. Once everyone has done this, the task is to build a card tower. Each card represents one of the plants or animals from the slips of paper. The Earth gets its energy from the sun. Plants are the first living things to make use of the sun's energy, so they are all at the bottom of the tower. Herbivores and carnivores make up the second and third levels of the tower. Are there enough plants to form a wide, stable base for the card tower? There will nearly always be many more animals (it's more fun to be an elephant than a dandelion!). So, the real task becomes reassigning cards plant and animal names in order to build a stable structure. Why are so many plants necessary? What would happen if plants were pulled out of the card tower?

2. *Popcorn Energy:* One person is the sun, twelve people are plants, six people are herbivores, and two people are carnivores. Plants, herbivores, and carnivores sit in an upside-down pyramid facing the sun (i.e. plants are closest to sun). Plants get their energy directly from the sun; herbivores get their energy from plants; and carnivores get their energy from herbivores. The sun passes a bowl of popcorn to the row of plants. Each plant takes one handful of popcorn. Plants eat at least half of the popcorn in their hand. They pass the rest of the popcorn back to the herbivores; each herbivore gets popcorn from two plants. Herbivores eat at least half of the popcorn in their hand. They pass the rest of the popcorn back to the carnivores; each carnivore gets popcorn from three herbivores. Carnivores eat at least half of the popcorn in their hand. Why do plants pass back some of their popcorn? Why do herbivores get popcorn from more than one plant? Why do carnivores get their energy from more than one herbivore? If a human being entered the picture, would he or she get more popcorn by going to a carnivore or by going directly to the six original plants in the carnivore's food chain?

A food pyramid illustrates differences in size and numbers of different forms of life at the different parts of a food chain. The base of a food pyramid is the largest and is made up of green plants. Then come herbivores (plant eaters), followed by carnivores (meat eaters). Creatures at the top of the pyramid, such as scavengers (e.g. vultures), are found in the fewest numbers.

A food pyramid also shows energy loss. As energy moves from the sun to plants and on to animals, much of it is lost. An animal gains only 10% of the energy of the plant it eats; 90% is lost to heat or is never digested. Eating an animal is like "eating sunshine" third-hand. "Eating low on the food chain" means eating more plants -- grains (e.g. corn, wheat, rice), fruits, and vegetables -- than meat and dairy products. North Americans eat a lot of meat, eggs, and milk. The animals from which we get this food are the first to eat plants. It would be more efficient if *we* ate the plants. "Eating low" is also an efficient approach to feeding a growing world population. 4000 sq. m of crops can feed 1000 people for a day; the same crops fed to animals eaten as meat feed only 50 people for a day. However, efficiency isn't the only consideration. The meat and dairy industries employ many people and provide us with a variety of nutritious products. And there are larger problems involving the politics of world food distribution. Using resources wisely involves difficult choices and creative problem-solving.

Topics: Resources; Energy; Ecosystems.

THE ENDANGERED HOPPIT

Every week, more than 20 kinds of living things disappear from the Earth forever. In this game, an imaginary creature called a "hoppit" is threatened with extinction.

MATERIALS: Masking tape; a large number of similar, small objects (e.g. several decks of playing cards; several dozen bingo chips).

DOING IT:

1. Mark off a small "home" area with masking tape. Spread small objects throughout a larger playing area.

An "extinct" animal is one which no longer exists anywhere on Earth. An "endangered" animal is one which is threatened with immediate extinction due to the activities of humans. A "threatened" animal is likely to become endangered if human activities do not change. An "extirpated" animal no longer exists in the wild, but exists elsewhere, like in a zoo. Zoos try to recreate animals' natural habitats, and many types of rare animals -- like jaguars and bald eagles -- are even able to raise families.

People and wildlife have the same basic needs: a home, enough food and water, and space and freedom to carry out daily activities. Unfortunately, humans often needlessly kill animals, pollute the environment, destroy animals' natural habitats (by clearing land for farming, roads, or buildings), and upset ecosystems by adding foreign plants and animals. The passenger pigeon once darkened the sky as it migrated in its millions; hunting and destruction of its summer habitat made it extinct. Martha, the world's last passenger pigeon, died in the Cincinnati Zoo in 1914. About 10 years ago, there were 1.5 million African elephants. Today, only about 400,000 are left. Their numbers are getting smaller because "poachers", illegal hunters, kill them for their ivory, used in jewellery and ornaments. There are only about 5,000 wild tigers left. Too many have been killed for their fur, and their habitat is being destroyed. We are also in danger of losing animals like whales, parrots, monkeys, rhinoceroses, sea turtles, and gorillas. When we lose animals, we don't know how it will affect the delicate balances in ecosystems.

Topics: Habitat; Ecosystems.

2. Everyone becomes a "hoppit". Hoppits are imaginary creatures which hop. Their life consists of gathering as much food (small objects) from the ground as possible. The object of the game is for hoppits to keep hopping and gathering food. Hoppits collect their food in a small pile in the home area; they can also stop hopping and rest in the home area.

3. To start the game, hoppits hop about on two legs and gather food. They can pick up only one piece of food (object) at a time and take it to their food pile. Each hoppit has its own food pile in the home area, and tries to keep the pile at least as large as other piles.

4. After about 10 minutes, hoppits are told that bad weather has made it harder to get food. This harder life is represented by hoppits now being able to hop on one leg only. If a hoppit hops on two legs, it "dies" and is out of the game. The one-legged hoppits should hop about and gather food for another 5 to 10 minutes.

5. Hoppits are now told that humans have built a shopping plaza on their home. Hoppits can leave their food piles where they are, but can no longer stop and rest in the home area. To stay alive, hoppits must *continuously* hop on one leg, while adding to their food piles.

6. How many hoppits survive after 5 minutes? 10 minutes? 20 minutes? At least two hoppits must survive for the species to continue.

SAVE AN ANIMAL

In this four-person game, players must ensure the survival of their three species while dealing with problems like habitat destruction, pollution, and natural disasters.

MATERIALS: Large version of game board shown; 21 red cards; 19 blue cards; 30 green cards; 4 sets of three animal markers (e.g. use coins labelled with animal and player name); die.

DOING IT:

1. Each person receives a set of three animal markers. The goal of the game is to ensure that each of the animals survives (i.e. reaches the outside of the playing board with food). The game is over when there is only one person left who has animals still living on the board. The winner is the person who saves the most species from extinction by reaching the end of the board. If two players save the same number of species from extinction (i.e. players reach end of the board with same number of species), the player who still has living animals on the board wins.

2. The game begins as animals are born. For an animal to be "born", a player must roll a 6. The animal moves to the born space and starts from there. A player can play as many animals at one time as he or she wishes.

3. Players take turns rolling the die. When someone lands on a coloured space, he or she picks up the top card of that colour (make sure card piles are shuffled well before starting).

4. Make up cards as follows:

Red cards: Represent major events that can help (advance), endanger (move back), protect (stay in same place) or make an animal extinct (remove from board). Number of cards: HABITAT DESTROYED extinct (one card); NUCLEAR WAR extinct (one card); ICE AGE extinct (one card); GLACIER MELT extinct (two cards); HUNTING LAWS advance 2 (two cards); ANIMAL PROTECTION stay put (three cards); FIRE miss a turn (three cards); EARTHQUAKE move back 2 (four cards); VOLCANO ERUPTS move back 3 (four cards).

Blue Cards: Represent weather conditions and can cause an animal to advance or move back. No extinction cards. Number of cards: CALM DAY advance 1 (two cards); HURRICANE move back 1 (two cards); FLOOD move back 2 (three cards); DROUGHT move back 3 (four cards); NEEDED RAIN OCCURS advance 2 (four cards); PLENTY OF SUN advance 3 (four cards).

Green Cards: Consist of sixteen food cards, seven pollution cards, and seven famine cards. If a player does not have a food card when an animal reaches the end of the board, the animal has starved and is extinct. Players keep green cards until one of two things happens: 1) Famine cards destroy food cards. When a player has a food card and a famine card at the same time, they cancel each other out and both must be shuffled into the pile. 2) If a player has 3 pollution cards, one of his or her animals becomes extinct and is removed from the board. Pollution cards are then shuffled back into the pile.

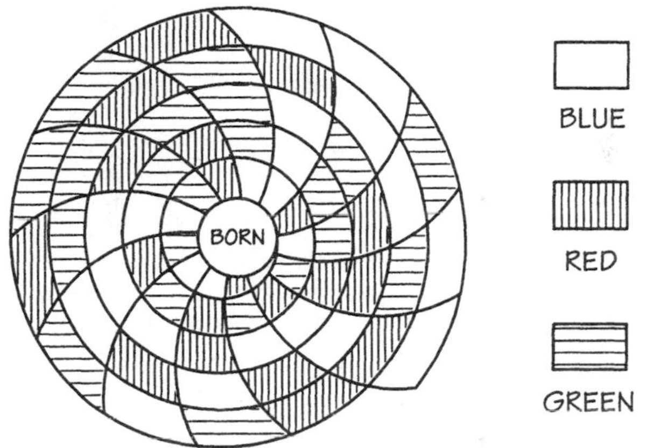

Over 90% of all living things that ever lived are extinct. Scientists believe extinction is the natural end of all species. The end of a species does not mean the species is a failure; it just means the world has changed. It normally takes millions of years for a species to disappear. But the rate of extinction has *increased significantly* -- largely as a result of human activities. A hundred years ago, about one species a year became extinct. Now at least one species a day is lost.

Humans can solve extinction problems. Bald eagles, whooping cranes, and alligators -- to name a few species -- are doing better than they were a few years ago. In the mid-1960s, scientists concluded that too many polar bears were being killed for meat, fur, and/or sport. Polar bear hunting in areas was limited to native peoples using traditional weapons and hunting techniques. Polar bears are now doing much better in some areas, but are still vulnerable.

Topics: Habitat; Pollution.

PLANT A TREE

When we lose trees -- particularly in large areas like the rainforests -- we lose animal habitats and air quality. Plant a tree and make a positive contribution to planet Earth.

MATERIALS: Tree; shovel; water; mulch; stakes; soft, flexible plastic tubing.

DOING IT:

1. Visit a local nursery to choose a seedling. Ask a person who works at the nursery for help. What kinds of trees grow fast and need little extra water? What kinds attract birds and animals? What kind of tree is best for your area? What kind of soil and how much space does the tree need? Where is the best spot for the tree?

2. Some General Tips on Location: Plant deciduous trees on the south, southwest, or west side of a building. They will provide shade during the summer months and still allow winter sun through (because they lose their leaves in fall). Plant coniferous trees on the north and northeast to protect the building from winter winds. Choose a spot for the tree with the right amount of sunlight and good soil drainage. Too much drainage and the soil will be dry; too little drainage means the soil will stay damp and the tree roots might rot. Make sure there are no power lines overhead (which could be a problem when the tree grows taller).

3. Once you've decided where to plant your tree, dig a hole as deep as the tree's root ball and about twice as wide as the root ball.

4. Place the tree gently into the hole. Carefully spread out the roots.

5. Fill the hole halfway with soil. Soak the soil with water. When the water has seeped in, add the remaining soil and press it down.

6. Spread out a thickness of 6 to 10 cm of mulch around the tree trunk, but not touching the trunk.

7. Water the tree again.

8. Put two stakes, one on each side of the tree, into the ground about 30 cm away from the tree. Attach a length of soft plastic tubing to each stake and loop each piece of tubing around the tree. The tubing should brace the tree, but shouldn't be pulled too tight. The tree should be able to bend with the wind. You can remove the stakes after several months, when the tree is stronger.

9. Water the tree regularly. Don't over water it.

Trees are places for animals to live. They produce fruit, nuts, and seeds. They can be used to make paper and lumber. They provide shade and cooling (a cluster of trees can cool the air surrounding them by as much as 6 degrees Celsius). Trees prevent topsoil from being blown away. They use the carbon dioxide in the air and they produce oxygen for humans to breathe. The problem is that we're cutting down too many trees -- and not planting enough to make up for it.

"Rainforests" are lush forests growing near the equator, in Brazil, Africa, Asia, and parts of Australia. There are also cool rainforests in places like southeast Alaska. The vegetation in rainforests is very dense. There are so many trees that they actually affect the climate around the world. The trees also generate about 40% of the world's oxygen.

Although rainforests cover only a small area of the Earth, they are home to more than half the world's plants and animals -- many of which are losing their habitats as the forests are cut and burned down. It's estimated that we lose 100 acres of rainforest per minute. That's fast enough to destroy all the world's rainforests in just a few decades. Rainforests are cut and burned to grow crops. Unfortunately, the soil of the rainforests isn't very fertile, so a few years later the farmers have to clear more rainforest to continue farming. Ranchers clear rainforests to make pastures for raising cattle. Logging companies cut down large areas of rainforests for wood (e.g. mahogany, teak). Rainforests are also being flooded behind hydroelectric dams.

Topics: Resources; Plant Processes; Ecosystems.

Too Hot

The Earth seems to be getting warmer. Too few trees and too much carbon dioxide are part of the problem. Find out how the Earth is warming up.

MATERIALS: Two identical glass jars, one with a lid; two pieces of dark cloth; two thermometers; paper; pencil; sunshine.

DOING IT:

1. Place two jars on their sides, in the sunshine. Put a piece of dark cloth into each jar.

2. Place a thermometer on each cloth so that you can read the thermometer through the glass.

3. Put the lid on one jar. Turn both jars so that their lids face away from the sun.

4. Watch the thermometers. Record the temperatures every minute. *When a thermometer gets close to its highest temperature, stop the experiment; the thermometer may break.*

5. In which jar does the temperature rise fastest? How much faster does it rise? Why? How is this like a greenhouse?

6. *Variation:* Try the same experiment on a cloudy day.

7. *Extension:* On a warm summer day, get into a car that's been parked in the sun, with the windows closed. The car's interior should be very hot -- even if the outside air temperature is just pleasantly warm. The closed car acts like a greenhouse.

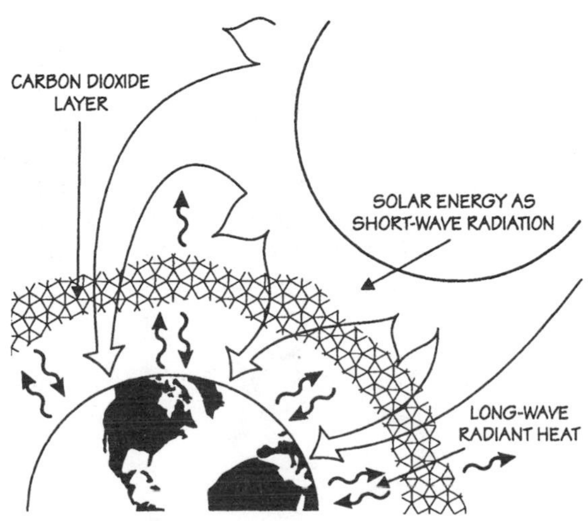

Try a living Christmas tree. Nurseries sell small evergreens that can be decorated indoors for Christmas and then planted outside. A living Christmas tree does double duty: it means one less tree cut down, plus one more tree planted.

In a "greenhouse" (used for growing plants), sunlight comes through the glass roof and walls and is turned into "heat rays". Heat rays are shaped differently than light rays and cannot easily get back out through the glass. So, the inside of the greenhouse stays very warm. The "greenhouse effect", or "global warming", is the gradual warming of the Earth because carbon dioxide and other gases prevent heat from escaping to space. The layer of gases is supposed to keep some heat close to Earth. The problem is that the concentration of carbon dioxide in the atmosphere has doubled in the last 100 years and so the layer of gases is holding *too much* heat. Millions of cars and factories all over the world are burning fossil fuels (e.g. coal, gasoline), which puts more and more carbon dioxide into the atmosphere. At the same time, millions of trees that could have helped to absorb the carbon dioxide are being cut down.

During this century, the average global temperature has increased just over 0.5 degrees Celsius. The six warmest years in the last century occurred in the 1980s. A global temperature change of only a few degrees could make a big difference; the average world temperature during the last Ice Age was only 3 degrees C lower than it is now. Global warming of 1 to 4 degrees C could cause a major shift in weather patterns (e.g. more droughts and tropical storms, warm areas would become unbearably hot), a melting of polar ice caps, a rise in sea level, flooding of low-lying areas (e.g. state of Florida, country of Bangladesh), and habitat changes. What can we do to prevent global warming? Reduce the burning of fossil fuels and ensure that we have lots of trees. A growing tree can take in more than 20 kg of carbon dioxide a year.

Topics: Pollution; Atmosphere; Ecosystems; Earth.

IT'S IN THE AIR

There are things in our air that we don't want there. Use an air-particle collector to make pollution more visible.

MATERIALS: Several drinking glasses or plastic cups; an equal number of large cans with both ends removed; petroleum jelly (e.g. Vaseline); masking tape; magnifying glass; paper; pencil. Optional -- flashlight.

DOING IT:

1. How clean is the air around you? Choose several test sites, both indoors and outdoors. Some sites should be areas where you think the air is fairly clean (e.g. your classroom, your backyard). Other sites should be areas that might have a pollution problem (e.g. by a busy road, near a construction site, near a fireplace).

2. Put an air-particle collector at each site. To make a collector, smear a thin layer of petroleum jelly on the outside of a drinking glass. Write the name of the test site on a small piece of masking tape and stick the tape inside the glass. Place the glass upside down at the test site. Put a can over the drinking glass (the height of the can will help to keep ground dust away from the glass). Some collectors should be on the ground, while others should be higher up. If possible, outdoor collectors should be in spots where they are protected from rain.

3. Check your collectors every day, over a week. *If it's going to rain, you should bring in outdoor collectors that might get wet.* When you check collectors, use a magnifying glass to take a quick look at the outside of the glasses. How does a glass look when you first smear on the petroleum jelly? How does it look after the first day? How does it look after a week?

4. After a week, bring in all the collectors for close examination with a magnifying glass. You might want to shine a flashlight inside the glass to make particles more visible. Which collectors have a lot of particles stuck to them? Which particles seem "unnatural"?

5. Mark off a 0.5 cm square on each glass. Using a magnifying glass, count all the particles visible in a square. If there are 15 or fewer particles, the air is probably free of particle pollution; if there are more than 100 particles, the air may be badly polluted with particles. Mark off a second square on each glass and compare the particle counts for the first and second squares. Are the counts about the same? Why or why not? Which test site seems most polluted?

Air isn't as plentiful as you might think. The layer of air around the Earth is only about 15 km thick, which is comparable to the thickness of a human hair on a globe with a 45 cm diameter. Of this layer of air, only the first 5 to 6 km contains enough oxygen to be of use to most living organisms, particularly human beings. If we continue to pollute the thin layer of air around the Earth, it will eventually be of little use to us.

Air pollution can consist of visible gases, invisible gases, and particles of matter (such as soot). There are always gases and particles in the air (e.g. oxygen and pollen), but air pollution is those gases and particles which affect the quality of the air around us, which are harmful to the environment, and/or which enter the atmosphere at highly concentrated levels. A simple example of air pollution is the smoke from burning trash, which can make air "smell bad" and unpleasant to breathe. A more complicated example involves carbon, a natural element that enters the atmosphere primarily as carbon dioxide. The burning of fossil fuels (e.g. coal, oil) has significantly increased atmospheric carbon dioxide levels.

Topics: Pollution; Atmosphere; Measurement.

Smog Alert

One way that air pollution becomes more visible is when certain weather conditions create smog. Create your own smog in a jar.

MATERIALS: Glass jar; water; aluminum foil; two or three ice cubes; paper; ruler; scissors; matches.

DOING IT:

1. This activity should be done with adult supervision. Do not breathe in the "smog".

2. Cut a strip of paper about 15 cm x 1 cm. Fold the strip's length in half and twist the paper.

3. Make a "lid" for a glass jar by shaping a piece of aluminum foil over the open end of the jar. Remove the foil and put it aside.

4. Put some water in the jar and swish it around so that the inside walls of the jar are wet. Spill out the water.

5. Place two or three ice cubes on top of the foil lid to make it cold.

6. Light the strip of paper and drop it and the match into the damp jar. Put the foil lid on the jar and seal it tightly. Keep the ice cubes on top of the foil, in the middle. You must do all of this very quickly.

7. What do you see in the jar? How is this like real smog? **When you're finished, release the "smog" outdoors.**

8. *Extension:* Does your local newspaper or weather channel have a pollution index or other type of report on pollution in your area? Record this information over several days and see how it changes.

"Ozone" is a colourless gas made up of three atoms of oxygen, rather than the usual two. It can be a part of car and factory pollution. Near the ground, it's one of the more dangerous components of smog. But 16 to 40 km above the Earth's surface, it forms a layer than keeps out the sun's most damaging ultraviolet rays (a sunburn is a painful example of what these rays can do). Ozone that pollutes our ground air can't get into the protective ozone layer. And human-produced gases like "CFCs" (chlorofluorocarbons) -- used for some insulation, mattresses, food packaging, air conditioner and refrigerator coolants, and as cleaners for electronic equipment -- are "eating" holes in the ozone layer. It takes up to one hundred years for CFCs to disappear from the environment, so we should use much less of them now. We should also produce less ozone at ground level.

Smog occurs with heavy concentrations of smoke and chemicals near ground level. The term "smog" was first used in the early 1900s to describe the combination of smoke and thick fog that at times hung over London, England. London-type smog occurs when moisture in air condenses on smoke particles, forming tiny smog droplets. Today's smog also contains chemicals "baked" by the sun. Weather conditions such as lack of wind or a "thermal inversion" can cause smog to build up in an area. A thermal inversion occurs when a layer of warm air settles over a layer of cool air that lies near the ground. This condition prevents the smog from rising and scattering. Mountain ranges near cities may also trap smog in an area.

Smog is a visible example of air pollution. There are also kinds of air pollution that you can't see or smell. Some of this pollution is made up of poisonous chemicals. Other types of air pollution are naturally-occurring gases, like carbon dioxide, that become harmful when there is too much of them. Air pollution is harmful to people, animals, plants, and buildings.

Topics: Pollution; Atmosphere; Weather Conditions; Chemical Reactions.

Sock It To Me

Car exhaust contains invisible gases that add to the greenhouse effect, smog, and acid rain. Use a sock to take a closer look at what's coming out of a car tail pipe.

MATERIALS: White sock; car; magnifying glass.

DOING IT:

1. This activity should be done outdoors with adult supervision. Make sure the tail pipe is cool (the car should not have been running recently). Do not breathe in the car exhaust.

2. Put a white sock over the tail pipe of a car.

3. An adult should turn on the car and allow it to run for a minute or so. Then turn the car off. The adult should remove the sock from the hot tail pipe.

4. What do you see on the sock? Examine the sock with a magnifying glass. Imagine millions of cars spewing exhaust into the air. Why is this a problem?

5. *Extension:* Compare the exhaust of different types (makes and years) of cars. Does it make a difference when a car got its last tune-up?

We get a great deal of our energy from burning fossil fuels. Fossil fuels are a limited resource; there's only so much of them around. Over millions of years, given the right conditions of heat and pressure, layers of dead plants and animals covered by layers of soil and rock turn into fossil fuels -- coal, oil, and natural gas. When these fossil fuels are burned, the carbon trapped in them is released as carbon dioxide.

Cars are one of the biggest sources of pollution on Earth. They use fossil fuels in the form of gasoline and oil. Car exhaust contains both invisible gases (e.g. carbon dioxide, carbon monoxide, hydrocarbons, and nitrogen oxides) and particles that pollute the air. The United States has more cars -- more than 140 million of them -- than anywhere else in the world. In some countries, many people use bicycles instead of cars. In Japan, for example, there are special parking garages for bicycles so that people can use bicycles to get to work. Other big air polluters are factories (which may burn fossil fuels to get heat for their production processes) and coal-burning power plants.

Topics: Pollution; Energy; Resources.

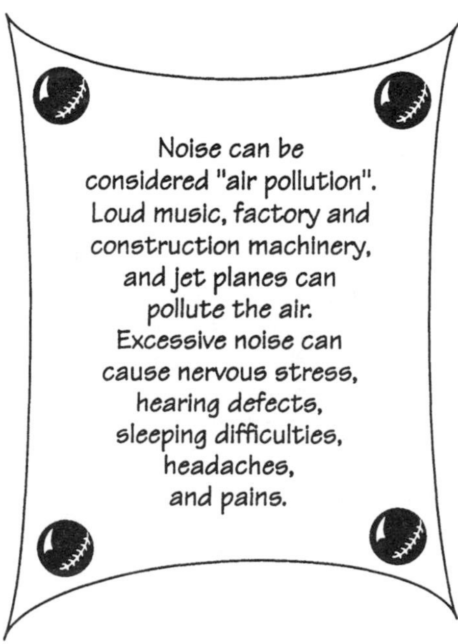

Rain, Rain Go Away

Acid rain is one of the results of air pollution. Measure the pH level of rain and other water samples from your area.

MATERIALS: Clean containers; litmus paper (narrow-range); a variety of test substances (e.g. milk of magnesia, baking soda solution, milk, tomato juice, vinegar); rain water; various other water samples.

DOING IT:

1. Use litmus paper to test the pH of various substances. Dip the end of the paper into the substance for a few seconds. The paper will gradually change colour. Compare the colour obtained with the colours printed on the package in which the litmus paper is sold. Which substances are acidic? Which are basic?

2. Right before a rainfall, place a clean container outside, away from trees and buildings. After you've collected some rain water, use the litmus paper to test it. If the pH is much less than 6, there may be an acid rain problem in your area.

3. Collect a variety of water samples (e.g. tap water, pond, stream, lake, puddle). Test each sample to determine its pH level. Compare pH levels. **Note: Standing water can contain dangerous bacteria. Do not touch or drink any of the water you collect, and wash your hands thoroughly after working with the water.**

pH	Substance	
14.0		ALKALINE
13.0	LYE	
12.4	LIME	
11.0	AMMONIA	
10.5	MILK OF MAGNESIA	
8.3	BAKING SODA	
7.4	HUMAN BLOOD	
7.0	NEUTRAL -- DISTILLED WATER	
6.6	MILK	ACIDIC
5.6	UNPOLLUTED RAIN	
4.5	TOMATOES	ACID RAIN
4.0	WINE AND BEER	
3.0	APPLES	
2.2	VINEGAR	
2.0	LEMON JUICE	
1.0	BATTERY ACID	
0.0		

The strength of acids and bases is measured on the "pH scale". The scale runs from 0 to 14. 7 is the neutral point. A solution rated below 7 is acidic; the lower the pH, the stronger the acid. A solution rated above 7 is basic, or alkaline. Because the scale is "logarithmic", each whole number increases by a factor of 10. In other words, a solution with a pH of 6 is 10 times more acidic than pure water (pH 7).

Rainfall is normally slightly acidic. It might have a pH around 6. However, rainfall in some parts of the world has a pH of 3 or 4. The term "acid rain" is used to describe overly acidic precipitation of any kind: frost, dew, mist, fog, rain, sleet, snow. When factories burn coal or oil, many gases are given off, including sulphur dioxide. In the atmosphere, sulphur dioxide can react with water vapour to form sulphuric acid. Car exhaust contains nitrogen oxides, which can react in the atmosphere to form nitric acid. The acids are carried back to Earth with precipitation; sometimes, they can even fall to the ground on dry days as dust-like little particles. Nothing will happen to you if you go for a stroll during a rain shower; but the indirect, long-term effects of acid rain are serious. Acid rain can kill plants and fish, damage buildings and roads, and contaminate public water supplies.

Topics: Pollution; Atmosphere; Chemical Reactions; Measurement.

ACID RAIN AND PLANTS

The long-term effects of acid rain on living things -- animals and plants -- might be hard to imagine. Try this experiment with three potted plants.

MATERIALS: Three small and healthy potted plants of the same type; three large jars with lids; vinegar; water; measuring cup; masking tape; paper; pen.

DOING IT:

1. Fill one jar with 960 ml of tap water. Use a piece of masking tape to label the jar "tap water".

2. Fill a second jar with 60 ml of vinegar and 900 ml of water. Use a piece of masking tape to label the jar "slightly acidic".

3. Fill the third jar with 240 ml of vinegar and 720 ml of water. Use a piece of masking tape to label the jar "very acidic".

4. Label one plant "tap water", one "slightly acidic", and one "very acidic". Use the jar with the matching label to water a given plant.

5. Place all three plants in the same spot so that they get the same amount of light. Water the plants when they need it (every 2 to 4 days). Examine the plants every day. Write down what they look like: What colour are they? Are their leaves drooping? Do they look healthy?

6. What happens to the plants watered with the acid solutions? How long does it take to see the effects of the acid? How do the plants differ in colour? Is the plant watered with the "very acidic" solution affected most? Why?

The effects of acid rain may not be immediately apparent. For example, at a glance, a lake might look clear and beautiful. But when you look more closely, you might begin to see some problems. Where are the fish? Why are there few or no plants? Where are the frogs? The lake's water has been made acidic because of acid rain; living things are dying off. Nature can cope with some changes in acidity. Areas with limestone or sandstone rock (which reacts with acid) are able to neutralize acidic rainfall so the damage is reduced. However, large parts of the world do not have this acid rain coping ability and, in any case, no area can handle very large amounts of acid rain.

Acid rain can affect plants in many ways. It takes nutrients away from the soil so that plants can't grow. It weakens trees so that they become diseased more easily. Branches at the top of trees lose their leaves. Tree leaves might be an unusual colour. Trees may not have as many leaves or may lose their leaves earlier each year. Eventually, the trees die. In this experiment with potted plants, the more acid in the plant water, the sooner a plant dies. The plants are watered with solutions that have a lower pH than most rainfall. But rain is becoming more acidic all the time.

Topics: Pollution; Ecosystems; Plant Processes; Scientific Method.

Each spring, many areas experience "acid shock". As snow melts, pollutants stored in the snowpack are abruptly released. Meltwater has been measured to be as much as 100 times more acidic than normal. This happens at the worst possible time for most fish and amphibians -- at spawning time.

The acidity of water affects different animal species in different ways. At a slightly acidic pH of 6, some fish, such as lake trout and smallmouth bass, have trouble reproducing. Some clams and snails can't survive at all. At a pH of 5, most crayfish, brook trout, walleyed pike, and bullfrogs die.

ACID RAIN AND BUILDINGS

Statues that have been around for thousands of years are now being eaten away by acid rain. See how acid rain affects some statues and buildings.

MATERIALS: Chalk; two small bowls; water; vinegar; ruler; masking tape; pen. Optional -- lemon juice.

DOING IT:

1. Use masking tape to label one bowl "water" and another bowl "acid".

2. Put a piece of chalk about 3 cm long into each bowl.

3. Fill the bowl marked "water" with tap water and the bowl marked "acid" with vinegar.

4. Watch the bowls for several minutes. What happens? Do you see bubbles in the bowl marked "acid"? Are there bubbles in the bowl of water?

5. Leave the bowls overnight. In the morning, are there still bubbles in the bowl marked "acid"? Take the pieces of chalk out of both bowls. Is one piece of chalk smaller than the other? Why?

6. *Variation:* Try lemon juice instead of vinegar. Also, cover a piece of chalk with acid, watch for bubbles, then spill out the acid and cover the chalk with water. Do the bubbles stop?

Areas that have many factories may not be immediately or directly affected by acid rain. Pollutants are injected high into the atmosphere from tall smokestacks; by the time the pollutants have undergone the chemical reactions responsible for acid rain, they have drifted downwind.

Chalk is a "calcium carbonate" mineral. Acid "eats away" at calcium carbonate. When acid reacts with calcium carbonate, calcium ions and carbon dioxide gas, among other things, are produced. The bubbles you see coming from chalk in a bowl of vinegar (a weak acid) are carbon dioxide.

Acid rain affects some stone and metal buildings and statues the same way that vinegar affects the chalk. Chalk is similar to a rock called "limestone". Limestone is used in the construction of some buildings. Limestone has also been used to make statues and monuments. Some thousand-year-old Greek statues are made of limestone. The only way to control acid rain is to reduce the air pollution that causes it.

Topics: Pollution; Chemical Reactions.

LESS IS BETTER

We can reduce air pollution and other harmful effects on the environment if we use less energy. Here are three energy conservation investigations to get you started.

MATERIALS: Smooth tissue paper (or other light-weight paper); scissors; long pencil; tape; two similar-sized pots, one with lid; water; measuring cup; stopwatch or watch which indicates seconds; stove.

A lot of energy is produced by burning fossil fuels, which is a major cause of air pollution. If we use less energy, if we "conserve", we will produce less pollution. We waste a great deal of energy. When you throw away two aluminum cans, you "throw away" all the energy that went into making the cans; a lot of energy will also be required to replace the cans. Instead of energy being put into making *two* new aluminum cans, the same amount of energy could be used to make *twenty* recycled cans. The amount of energy used to produce *one* sheet of new paper can instead be used to make *two* sheets of recycled paper. Conserving energy means being more efficient -- being smarter.

Think of ways you can conserve energy at home. For example, can you put on a sweater instead of putting up the heat? In colder climates, more than half the energy we use at home is for heat. And more than half of that may be wasted. Heat escapes under doors, around window frames, through the attic, up the chimney. If we conserve by plugging all the leaks, we can heat two homes with the amount of energy we now use for one. If you're leaving the room, does the light need to be on? To produce enough energy to power a 100 watt light bulb all day, every day for a year, you would need to burn about 400 kg of coal. The typical light bulb is also a big energy waster. 90% of the energy the bulb draws is lost as heat. There are light bulbs called "compact fluorescents" that can replace some regular bulbs; compact fluorescents use only 25% of the energy used by a regular bulb and can last 10 times longer. Are you opening the refrigerator more often than you need to? How long do you keep it open? The average refrigerator is opened 22 times a day; that's over 8,000 times a year. Every time you open the refrigerator and let warm air in, the refrigerator has to use more energy to cool itself back down again.

Topics: Resources; Energy.

DOING IT:

1. *Draft Detection:* Try this on a cold, windy day. Cut a piece of tissue paper 15 cm x 13 cm. Tape the short end of the paper along the length of a pencil. Test the draft detector by opening the refrigerator *a little* and holding the detector at the opening. Does the detector wave in the breeze? Hold the detector near windows and doors (sides and bottom), fireplaces, or anywhere else you think there's a draft. Where there's a draft, there's a good chance that heat is escaping. How can the leaks be fixed?

2. *Bulb Count:* How many light bulbs do you use in your home? Count all the light bulbs -- inside and out. Now imagine millions of homes using the same number of light bulbs. That's a lot of energy!

3. *Water Test:* **This activity should be done with adult supervision.** Fill two pots with 500 ml of water each. Cover one pot and leave the other uncovered. Put both pots on the stove, on burners they cover completely (no sense wasting energy!). Start heating both pots at the same time; make sure the heat level is the same for both (e.g. "high" setting). Which pot boils first? Why? Which uses more energy?

North Americans use 2 billion batteries a year. It takes 50 times more energy to make a battery than the battery will ever provide. Batteries can contain very toxic materials such as cadmium, mercury, lead, and sulphuric acid. A lot of chemicals end up in the environment when batteries are made -- and when they are thrown away. Batteries should never be thrown into the regular garbage; they are considered "hazardous waste" and must be taken to a special site. Whenever you can, use things like solar calculators that don't need batteries. And, buy rechargeable batteries, which can be reused.

BLOWING IN THE WIND

Scientists are working to develop energy sources that aren't as environmentally harmful. Explore wind power using sheets of different materials and a mini windmill.

MATERIALS: Several different weights of flat material (e.g. waxed paper, writing paper, construction paper, cardboard, plastic sheet, thin metal sheet, thin wood sheet); ruler; cord; scissors, tin snips, and saw; stiff paper; pencil with eraser top; straight pin with head.

DOING IT:

1. Cut 15 cm squares out of several different materials. Punch two holes, spaced about 13 cm apart, at the top of each sheet. Use pieces of cord to hang the sheets from a long length of cord. Two people (one holding each end of the cord) should hold the sheets in the breeze. Which sheets move most easily with the breeze? Why? Which flutter uncontrollably? Which keep their shape?

2. Cut a 10 cm square from a sheet of paper. Cut the square diagonally from each corner to within 1 cm of the centre. Bend every other point back to the centre of the square. Insert a straight pin through the centre of the pinwheel and into the eraser on a pencil.

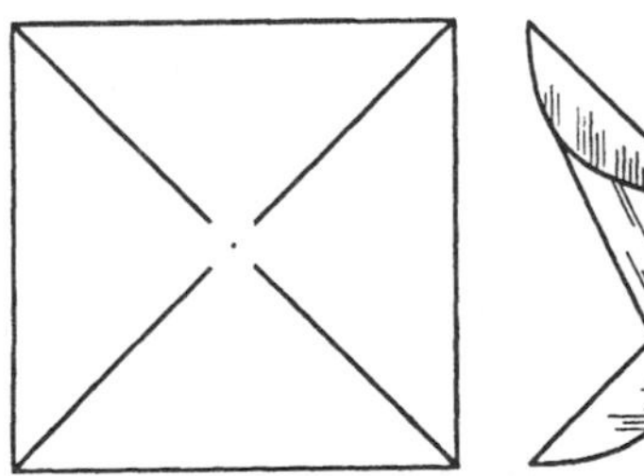

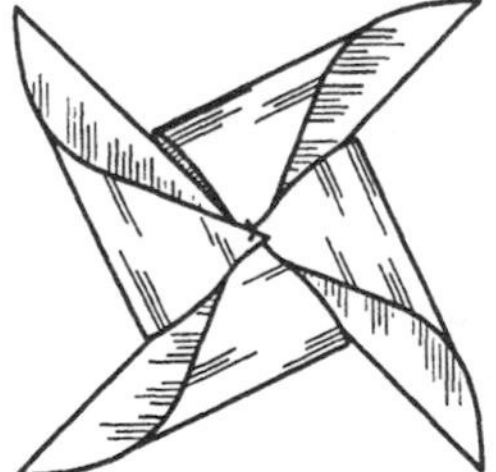

Oceans can be used to generate electricity. Ocean currents like the Gulf Stream can turn turbines deep underwater. Or, as special "rafts" rise and fall with the waves, they can drive electric generators. Dams can also be built across bays; as the water behind the dam rises with the tide, the water can be let through the dam to turn turbines.

3. Hold the pinwheel into the wind. How easily does it turn? Does it turn if you face away from the wind? How can you make the pinwheel turn faster (e.g. run with it)?

Energy sources like coal and oil (fossil fuels) are "nonrenewable" because there's only so much of them on Earth. After we use up the supply, that's it. Energy sources we won't run out of are called "renewable" or "alternative" sources.

Aside from burning fossil fuels, there are two methods used right now to produce large amounts of energy. More than 16% of the world's electrical energy comes from *nuclear* power. Nuclear energy -- produced when atoms are split -- doesn't put invisible gases into the air, which means it doesn't add to the acid rain problem or the greenhouse effect. But it does result in small amounts of radioactive waste that is very harmful to living things. The waste must be stored safely for thousands of years until it loses its radioactivity. Nuclear energy is not a renewable energy source because there is a limited supply of the uranium needed by nuclear power plants. *Hydroelectric* power stations make use of falling or running water. As water falls from a higher to a lower level, it drives large electric generators. Unfortunately, not all rivers are suitable for hydroelectric dams and the dams can cause flooding.

Other renewable energy sources -- wind, tidal, biomass, geothermal, and solar -- are not presently feasible for widespread use. For example, windmills have been used for centuries to pump water and grind grain. Modern windmills are designed to turn even in the lightest winds and are attached to electric generators. California has large "wind farms" that produce electricity. But problems with wind power include the noise produced and the large amounts of land needed. There is no "one" solution to our energy problems. Many solutions will have to be combined and we may need to move away from large power stations to local "energy units" making use of renewable energy sources appropriate for the area.

Topics: Energy; Resources; Weather Conditions; Electricity.

SOLAR ENERGY

The sun is a source of both heat and light energy. Solar energy doesn't pollute, it's safe, and there's lots of it. Experiment with collecting solar energy.

Biomass energy is obtained from organic matter such as plants and manure. Sometimes, as in the burning of wood (which gives off heat energy), the energy can be obtained directly. Energy is obtained more indirectly by using bacteria to decompose manure. Methane gas is given off, and this gas can be used to power cars or can be burned to produce heat.

People have used the sun for centuries to heat water. Today, some people have solar heat collectors in their homes. A solar collector can consist of a shallow box with a clear glass or plastic top. Sunlight passes through the glass and heat is trapped inside the box, much like it is in a greenhouse. A dark plate at the back of the collector absorbs the heat. Air or water can be run over the plate and used to heat a home or produce hot water. The sun's energy can be successfully turned into small amounts of electricity using a "photovoltaic cell". The cell is usually made with silicon, a material which allows electricity to pass through it in one direction only. The sun's energy drives electrons from their normal places in the atoms that make up the silicon; that flow of electrons is electricity. Photovoltaic cells are used to power things like calculators. However, the cells are not yet practical for large-scale use. Silicon is very expensive and the numerous cells required would have to cover a lot of land. Another problem with solar energy: it doesn't work when the sun isn't shining.

There are certain "basics" to efficiently capturing the sun's energy. A pie tin painted black absorbs more heat than an ordinary tin. The shiny surface on the ordinary tin reflects the sunlight away. A large pie tin heats water to a higher temperature than a smaller pie tin because the larger surface area collects more heat. The water in the larger tin will also heat faster because the water is not as deep as it is in the smaller tin.

Topics: Energy; Measurement.

MATERIALS: One large and two small aluminum foil pie tins, with the large tin and one small tin painted inside with flat black paint; two measuring cups; two thermometers; plastic wrap; water; paper; pencil; sunshine.

DOING IT:

1. Never look directly at the sun because it can damage your eyes.

2. Fill a measuring cup with 200 ml of water. Take the temperature of the water and write it down. Pour 100 ml of water into an ordinary, small pie tin and 100 ml of water into a small pie tin painted black. Carefully secure plastic wrap over each tin. Put the pie tins in direct sunlight for about 20 minutes. Which pan do you think will heat the water to a higher temperature?

3. When the 20 minutes is up, carefully but quickly spill the water from each tin into separate measuring cups. Take the temperatures of the water in both cups. Subtract the initial water temperature from the final temperatures. Did the black tin heat the water to a higher temperature? How much higher? Why?

4. Fill a measuring cup with 200 ml of water. Take the temperature of the water and write it down. Pour 100 ml of water into a small pie tin painted black and 100 ml of water into a large pie tin painted black. Carefully secure plastic wrap over each tin. Put the pie tins in direct sunlight for about 20 minutes. Which pan do you think will heat the water to a higher temperature?

5. When the 20 minutes is up, carefully but quickly spill the water from each tin into separate measuring cups. Take the temperatures of the water in both cups. Subtract the initial water temperature from the final temperatures. Did the large tin heat the water to a higher temperature than the small tin? How much higher? Why?

6. *Variation:* Change some of the other variables, such as the depth of the water or the presence of a plastic cover.

SOLAR COOKER

Instead of simply collecting solar energy, concentrate the sun's rays with a solar cooker to cook a marshmallow. Here are two solar cooker designs.

MATERIALS: Mixing or salad bowl (wooden salad bowls are good because they are often rounded without the flat bottom usually found in plastic or glass bowls); aluminum foil; double-sided tape; 20 cm x 35 cm sheet of flexible cardboard; 1 m of string; scissors; marshmallows; long forks or skewers. Optional -- Plasticine.

DOING IT:

1. Never look directly at the sun or at reflected, focused sunlight. It can damage your eyes permanently.

2. *Design One:* Line the inside of a large bowl with aluminum foil, shiny side up. Use several small pieces of double-sided tape to secure the foil. Press the foil close to the bowl and make it as smooth as possible.

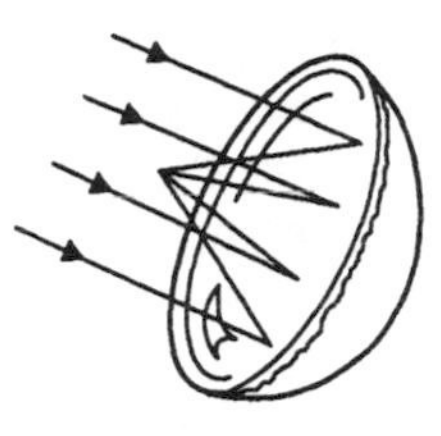

3. *Design Two:* Cover one side of a sheet of cardboard with aluminum foil (shiny side up), securing the foil with double-sided tape. Bend the cardboard into a semi-circle, with the foil on the inside of the curve. Wrap a length of string twice around the cardboard semi-circle and knot the string at the back.

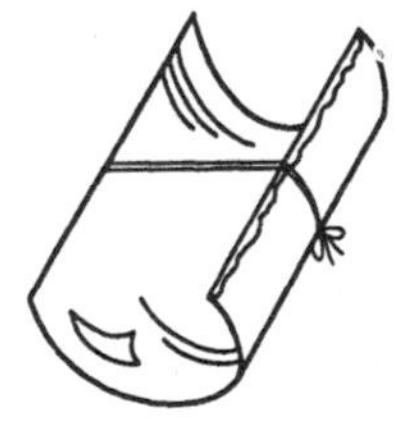

4. Face both cookers into the sun. You may want to prop up and angle the cookers by making a base with Plasticine. Find each cooker's "hot spot", the spot where the sun's reflected rays criss cross. Different cookers have different hot spots. To find the bowl cooker's hot spot, slowly put your open hand into the bowl until you feel the hot spot; **don't hold your hand in the hot spot!** You'll probably find the cardboard cooker's hot spot near the middle of the string, closer to the foil.

5. Put marshmallows on the end of long skewers and hold a marshmallow in each cooker's hot spot. Which cooker cooks a marshmallow the fastest? Can you alter a cooker to make it work better (e.g. change curve of cardboard)?

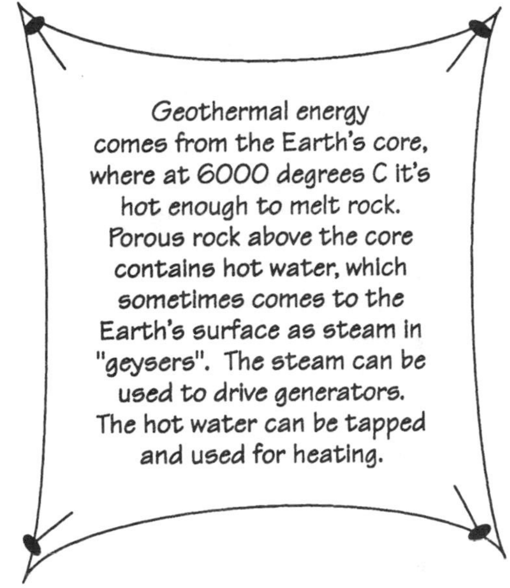

It's possible to fry an egg on a sidewalk, but you need a very hot, sunny day and the cooking process takes awhile. Using a solar cooker is more efficient. You've probably taken a magnifying glass and focused sunlight through it to burn paper. The curved reflector in a solar cooker does about the same thing, concentrating all the sunlight that strikes it into a very hot spot near the centre of the cooker. The efficiency of a cooker made from a bowl is affected by the size and shape of the bowl; a continuous curve shape will focus the parallel rays of sunlight better. Both homemade solar cookers will be affected by how smoothly you're able to apply the aluminum foil. And be aware of things you can't control, like the movement of the sun (you can tell the sun is moving by watching the cooker's shadow). As the sun moves, so does the cooker's "hot spot", so adjust the cooker accordingly. Ideally, the reflector should point directly at the sun at all times.

Topics: Energy; Light.

PURIFYING WATER

The sun is an important part of a natural process that provides pure drinking water. Make a solar still to purify muddy water.

MATERIALS: Large pan (e.g. dish pan); plastic cup or drinking glass shorter than the pan; plastic wrap; several clean marbles; a rock or marble; masking tape; muddy water.

DOING IT:

1. Put about 4 cm of muddy water into a large pan. Put a cup in the centre of the pan; use a few clean marbles at the bottom of the cup to keep it weighted down.

2. Cover the pan securely with plastic wrap, but leave a little slack. Use your finger to put a little water around the rim of the pan so that you can make a good seal between the plastic and the pan. You may want to use masking tape to keep the plastic in place.

3. Put a rock or marble on the centre of the plastic so that there's a slight dip in the plastic over the cup. The plastic should not touch the cup. Water that condenses on the plastic will drip into the cup.

4. Put the still in direct sunlight. Over several hours, pure water should collect in the cup.

5. *Variation:* If you ever need clean drinking water, a survival still is a handy thing to know how to make. Dig a hole large enough to sink a clean container into the ground. Surround the container with *plenty* of fresh, leafy, green plants. Place a large piece of plastic wrap loosely over the hole; secure the plastic wrap by putting stones or soil on top of the edges. Put a stone in the centre of the plastic so that the plastic sags toward the container. Water caught on the plastic will run into the container. Replace the plants daily. When you no longer need the still, be sure to fill the hole and leave the area as you found it.

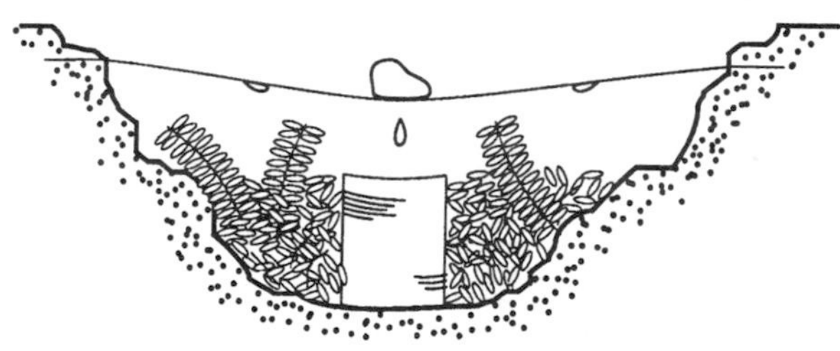

A human being can live for as long as thirty days without food, but can last for only three or four days without water. Pure drinking water is essential to human life. A solar still uses the natural process of evaporation and condensation to purify water. The sun heats muddy water in a large container. The water turns into vapour; the mud is left behind. The vapour is captured on a plastic sheet covering the container. The plastic sheet is cool because of the cooler air outside the container. So, the water vapour condenses. The water droplets drip into a smaller, clean container. A survival still works on the same principle as a still designed to purify muddy water. The key difference is that the survival still makes use of the process of "transpiration". Transpiration occurs when the roots of plants absorb moisture from the soil. The water passes through a plant's stem or trunk, through the branches to the leaves, and then evaporates into the air from the surface of the leaves.

Topics: Resources; States of Matter; Plant Processes.

There's a lot of water around, but most of it is salty. Water can be desalinated (salt removed), but the process is expensive. There's fresh water in polar ice caps, but we can't drink ice and we just can't melt the ice caps. Only 3% of the world's water is appropriate for human consumption. That water is in lakes, rivers, streams and underground. "Groundwater" is water deep in the Earth under layers of rock and sand; it is pumped to the surface in wells. Most people in the world depend on groundwater supplies.

FILTERING WATER

The first step in cleaning water for human use is to filter out large particles. Try filtering a variety of water samples.

MATERIALS: Clean containers for collecting water samples; clean jar; paper towels or filter paper; funnel; magnifying glass; a variety of water samples. Optional -- snow.

DOING IT:

1. Collect water samples from a variety of sources (e.g. shower, lake, puddle, rain). Examine each sample for the water's clarity, colour, and smell. Use a magnifying glass to look for small particles in the water. **Note: Standing water can contain dangerous bacteria. Do not touch or drink any of the water you collect, and wash your hands thoroughly after working with the water.**

2. Filtering can remove solid particles from water and is one step toward purification -- **but filtering alone does not make the water safe to drink.** To make a filter from paper towelling, fold a paper towel in half, lengthwise. Fold the towel in half again so that it's in four layers. Fold over three of the layers from the corner toward the side. Turn the towelling over and fold the remaining corner toward the side. Pull away one layer from the rest to open a cone (the cone shouldn't have a hole at the bottom).

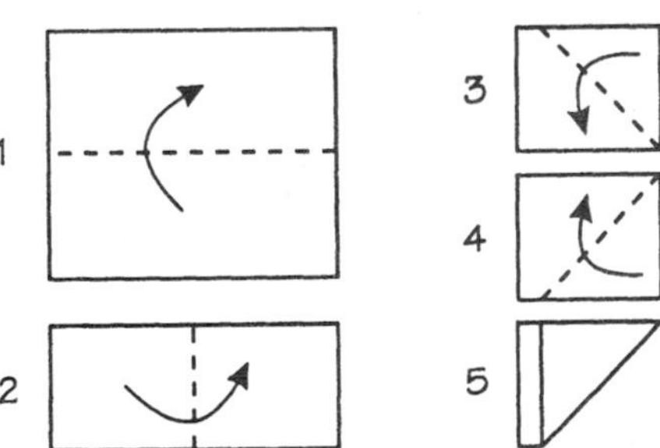

3. Put a filter into a funnel and place the funnel into the mouth of a jar. Run a water sample through the funnel. Each time you filter a new sample, clean the jar and funnel and use a new filter. How do filtered samples compare to the originals? Use a magnifying glass to look for particles left on filters. Compare the filters from different samples. Are most of the filters covered with particles? Are the particles similar?

4. *Extension:* How clean is snow? When it is snowing, place a clean container outside, away from trees and buildings. When the container is full, bring it indoors. Cover the top of the container so that no dust gets inside. Let the snow melt. Pour the melt water through a filter. Examine the filtered melt water and the filter with a magnifying glass.

Even under the best natural conditions, water is not completely pure. It contains bits of sand, dirt, various salts, and tiny organisms; these must be filtered out. Pollution often makes water so dirty that filtering is only the first step in a complex purifying process. More disturbingly, some water can be so badly polluted that it is almost impossible to clean. When water isn't clean, not only are humans affected, but plants and animals are affected. Some fish may be able to survive in polluted water, but their bodies are filled with chemicals and it becomes dangerous for us to eat the fish. Water pollution also clogs up lakes and ponds, causes disease, and destroys the beauty of natural areas.

There are a number of stages involved in getting clean water. The natural water cycle involves evaporation and condensation: water in lakes and rivers is heated by the sun and evaporates into the air; the vapour condenses and forms tiny droplets around microscopic particles in the air; clouds begin to form; when the droplets grow to a certain size they fall back to the ground as rain. Humans have added to the natural water cycle: water purification plants take in water from sources like lakes, rivers, or the ground; water is filtered and purified (fluoride and/or chloride may also be added); pumping stations pump water into pipes; pipes carry water to homes; the water is used for drinking, cooking, washing, or the toilet; water goes down the drain; sewer pipes carry water to the sewage treatment plant; some contaminants like human waste are removed from the water before it is put back into the natural water cycle.

Topics: Pollution; Resources; Snow.

Water Down The Toilet

Water is a limited resource and so it is important to conserve it. Learn how toilets use more water than any other place in the home -- and why a lot of that water is wasted.

MATERIALS: Brick or some other heavy object (e.g. plastic container filled with some rocks and water); food colouring.

DOING IT:

1. *Toilet Watching:* An adult can take the lid off the toilet tank to provide a good view of how a toilet works. Watch what happens when you flush the toilet. Watch as the arm inside lifts and the water flows from the tank into the bowl.

2. *Less Water:* Put a brick or other heavy object into the toilet tank to take up space (don't obstruct the toilet mechanism). Then there will be less room in the tank and the toilet will use less water.

3. *No Leaking:* Put 10 to 15 drops of food colouring into the toilet tank. Don't let anyone flush the toilet. After about 20 minutes, check the water in the toilet bowl. Do you see any food colouring? If you do, the toilet is leaking -- and it should be fixed.

We use a lot of water. Huge amounts of water are used daily for agriculture and industry, and in homes. The average North American uses about 300 litres of water a day. The most water is used in toilets, with bathing coming second. Much smaller amounts of water are used for drinking, cooking, and cleaning. A lot of water is wasted. For example, every time you flush the toilet you use around 20 litres of water. The water used in toilets is valuable; it starts out as drinking water. Fresh water flows into the toilet tank at the back. When you flush the toilet, the water flows into the bowl to clean it out and then goes into the sewer. The tank then fills up with more fresh water. Many toilets use more water than they have to; some simple conservation measures can fix this. And did you know that 20% of the toilets in North America are leaking right now? Most people don't even know their toilet is leaking. Over a year, one leaky toilet can waste *thousands* of litres of water.

Topics: Resources.

When you use less hot water, you save both water and energy. The water that goes to people's homes is cold drinking water. When a water pipe gets to your home, it splits into two branches: one that takes cold water to all the "cold" faucets and one that takes water to the hot water tank. Tanks can hold nearly 200 litres of water. A heater in the tank stays on until the water gets hot. When hot water leaves the water tank, cold water takes its place. Then the tank starts heating the water all over again. A lot of energy is needed to make hot water, so use hot water carefully. For example, rinse clothes in cold water when you wash them.

You don't flush a composting toilet, which means big water savings. Human and kitchen wastes decompose in this special toilet to form a rich humus soil. A composting toilet is a high-tech version of an "outhouse".

Water Down The Drain

Every tap everywhere is a potential water waster -- pouring out too much water too quickly or dripping when it's turned off. Be a water conservation detective.

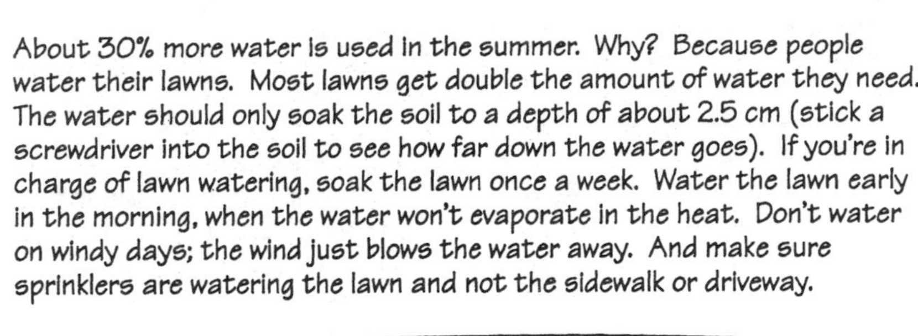

About 30% more water is used in the summer. Why? Because people water their lawns. Most lawns get double the amount of water they need. The water should only soak the soil to a depth of about 2.5 cm (stick a screwdriver into the soil to see how far down the water goes). If you're in charge of lawn watering, soak the lawn once a week. Water the lawn early in the morning, when the water won't evaporate in the heat. Don't water on windy days; the wind just blows the water away. And make sure sprinklers are watering the lawn and not the sidewalk or driveway.

MATERIALS: Paper; pencil; pot; stopwatch or watch which indicates seconds; large measuring cup.

DOING IT:

1. *Leak Hunt:* Check every faucet in a certain building (e.g. home, school). Remember to check faucets inside and outside the building. Watch each tap for a few seconds. Is any water dripping out? Make a list of all the dripping taps. When you find a dripping tap, try to tighten it. Does it stop dripping? If not, put a star beside it on your list; the tap needs to be fixed!

2. *How Fast?:* Hold a pot under a water faucet. How long do you think it will take to fill the pot with water? After you've made your guess, have someone turn on the *cold* water tap and time how long it takes until the pot is full. Water comes out of the faucet faster than you might think. *Don't waste the water by spilling it out; make use of it in some way, like watering a plant.*

3. *How Much?:* Put a large measuring cup under a faucet. Turn the *cold* water tap so just a few drips of water are coming out. After 10 minutes, write down how much water dripped out. Empty out the measuring cup *(don't waste the water!)*. Now turn the tap so the drips come out faster. After 10 minutes, write down how much water dripped out. Compare the amount of water from each test. How much water would be wasted if the taps were each left dripping for 24 hours?

People used to think they could dump garbage and other waste into large bodies of water, like oceans, without doing them any harm. We now know this isn't true -- yet we keep polluting the water. Some cities spill untreated sewage -- containing harmful bacteria -- directly into rivers that lead to oceans. Pesticides and other chemicals are making their way into the oceans. And some air pollutants can settle in the ocean.

Taps make it easy to waste water. A simple turn and out pours the water. The water may come out more quickly than you need. You might let the tap run longer than you need. Or, the tap might be dripping when you're not using it. A shower can pour forth with the equivalent of forty big glasses of water a minute. If you leave the water running while you brush your teeth, you can waste enough water to fill more than ten pop cans. If you leave the water running while you wash the dishes, you can waste enough to wash a whole car. Besides being more careful about using water, there are devices which can help reduce water flow. A "low-flow showerhead" can cut the amount of water flowing from the shower-head in half -- but the shower still works and feels just fine.

Topics: Resources.

NATURALLY CLEAN

Chemicals washed down the drain can end up in bodies of water from which people get their drinking water. Mix up some natural cleaners to replace chemical cleaners.

"Nonpoint pollution" is pollution that can't be traced to a single source but comes from many places. An example is the water pollution from pesticides that wash off farm fields. Because there is no single, concentrated source, nonpoint pollution is difficult to control. A lot of people have to work together to make a change.

Bodies of surface water can be polluted in many ways. Garbage may be dumped into rivers and lakes. Human sewage -- containing dangerous bacteria -- may spill straight into rivers. Pesticides run off farm fields. Household wastewater contains detergents, bleaches, and other household chemicals, and paper products such as toilet tissue. Industrial wastewater may contain concentrated, dangerous chemicals. All this pollution can affect bodies of water directly -- and indirectly. For example, "phosphates" (chemicals found in some laundry and dishwasher detergents) and "nitrites" (found in human and animal waste, as well as in many farm and lawn fertilizers) promote the fast growth of algae in ponds and lakes. The algae use up all the oxygen in the water and cause other living things to die. Even something that seems innocent -- like hot water -- can pollute water. Some factories and nuclear plants use cool water from lakes or rivers to cool their equipment. The water heats up as it is used. The hot water is then spilled back into the lake or river. Some kinds of algae grow faster in the warm water. As well, some fish can't live in warmer water.

Groundwater is also vulnerable to pollution. Just dumping common, everyday things on the ground can pollute groundwater because the Earth is like a sponge that soaks everything in. A couple of litres of paint, motor oil, or gasoline can seep into the Earth and pollute hundreds of thousands of litres of groundwater. Pesticides and fertilizers can seep into the ground and affect groundwater. Toxic chemicals from dump sites and even the salt used on slippery winter roads can affect groundwater supplies.

Topics: Pollution; Resources.

MATERIALS: Cooking oil; lemon juice; baking soda; vinegar; water; measuring cup; storage bottles; rags.

DOING IT:

1. *All-Purpose Cleaner:* Store-bought cleaners can contain chemicals that are dangerous -- even in small quantities -- to people and animals. They can also contain chemicals that "eat away" at materials -- including human skin. For a natural alternative, mix together 50 ml of baking soda, 125 ml of vinegar, and 4 litres of warm water. Store in a labelled bottle.

2. *Glass Cleaner:* Store-bought glass cleaners can contain chemicals that are dangerous to people and animals. They can also contain harmful chemicals. For a natural alternative, mix one part vinegar with five parts water. Store in a labelled spray bottle. Try cleaning some windows. How well does the natural glass cleaner work?

3. *Scouring Powder:* Store-bought powders made to deal with tough stains and messes can contain chemicals that are dangerous to people and animals. They can also contain harmful chemicals. For a natural alternative, sprinkle some baking soda on the stained surface and rub with a damp cloth. It may involve a little more work than store-bought powders.

4. *Wood Polish:* Store-bought polishes can contain chemicals that are dangerous -- even in small quantities -- to people and animals. The polishes can also catch fire easily. For a natural alternative, mix one part lemon juice with two parts cooking oil. Use a soft cloth with the polish.

5. *Extension:* Compare the performance of natural cleaners to store-bought cleaners. Set up a scientific experiment. Why do you think people use store-bought cleaners instead of natural ones?

AN OILY MESS

No form of water pollution is easy to clean up. But oil spills are particularly difficult. How hard is it to clean up an oil spill? Find out for yourself by creating a mini spill.

MATERIALS: Two aluminum foil pie tins; water; used motor oil (or cooking oil, although it is not as visible); dropper; cotton balls; nylon; string; paper towels; dishwashing liquid; feather. Optional -- salt.

DOING IT:

1. Fill a pie tin halfway with water.

2. Create an "oil spill" in the water by putting in five to ten drops of oil. Does the oil mix with the water?

3. Create waves on the "ocean" in the pie tin by blowing on the water or moving the tin. What happens to the oil? Why would it be important to clean up an oil spill quickly?

4. Dip a feather into the "oil spill". What happens? How would oily feathers affect a bird?

5. Which material -- cotton ball, nylon, string, or paper towel -- cleans up the "spill" best? Test each material; make new "spills" as needed. How much oil is cleaned up by each material? How quickly can you clean up the "spill"? What problems do you have? What happens to the oil as time goes on? How difficult would it be to clean up the spill if there was a terrible storm?

6. Create an "oil spill" (five to ten drops of oil) in a second pie tin half-filled with water. Add five drops of dishwashing liquid. What happens to the oil? Where would the oil go in a real ocean? How "clean" is the water now that it has dishwashing liquid in it? What's worse -- oil or the cleaner?

7. *Variation:* Repeat the steps using salt water. How is salt water different?

Oil spills -- like the one off the coast of Alaska in 1989 or the ones during the Gulf War in 1991 -- attract a lot of attention. But these spills are only a small part of the oil that's polluting bodies of water. More than 50% of the oil in the oceans comes from land-based, nonpoint sources such as leakage from industrial processes. Tanker spills contribute about 10%. The remaining oil gets in the water through ordinary marine operations, such as tankers cleaning and flushing tanks at sea. The most disturbing fact is that at least 40% of the land-based, nonpoint oil pollution may result from car owners changing their own oil and disposing of it improperly (oil should be taken to a service station for recycling). Oil kills aquatic animals and plants. If the oil sinks to the bottom of a body of water or covers beaches, it does not allow animals like oysters and clams to reproduce; if the animals are able to reproduce, the offspring are usually affected. Birds that get covered in oil are unable to fly and their feathers lose the ability to keep the birds warm.

Oil in water isn't easy to clean up. Some oil spill clean-up methods can be as damaging to the environment as the oil itself. "Chemical surfactants" act like detergents to break up oil. They are often dropped on large spills from airplanes. In many cases, these surfactants are the only feasible solution to an oil spill, particularly in rough seas. Mechanical clean ups (where oil is contained by booms and absorbent materials such as straw, cotton, or nylon) are more expensive and take longer to implement than surfactants. A third, more controversial approach to cleaning spills involves "oil-eating microbes".

Topics: Pollution; Resources.

PILES AND PILES OF GARBAGE

The average North American makes enough garbage in one year to fill a dump truck. Collect all your garbage for one week to see how much you generate.

MATERIALS: Garbage; large trash can with lid and plastic liner; several large boxes; paper; pencil; bathroom scale. Optional -- two small plastic bags per person; large plastic garbage bags.

DOING IT:

1. This can be a group activity for a classroom or family. Each person collects *all* the garbage they make over one week. The group's garbage can be piled into separate containers for different materials (food waste, metals, glass, paper, and plastic). If people won't be near the containers all the time, they can carry two small plastic bags with them -- one for food waste and one for all other garbage -- and empty the bags into the containers later.

2. Use a large trash can with a lid and plastic liner for food waste and food-contaminated garbage (e.g. the paper box from a hamburger). If you normally use a garbage disposal, put that garbage in the food can.

3. Use separate large boxes for plastics, glass, metals, and paper. Rinse glass, plastics, and metals so they don't smell. *Be careful not to cut yourself on the glass or metal.*

Is plastic a big part of our garbage problem? Plastic makes up 5-7% of our municipal solid waste. Most plastics don't biodegrade (those that do need strong light and leave behind a plastic dust which may be harmful), but they can be recycled. They are made from nonrenewable fossil fuels; but materials like paper and glass are also made using precious resources. Plastic garbage, like other garbage, should be reduced as much as possible -- through things like buying products in large containers with minimal packaging, and refilling/reusing containers.

There was a time when people used things over and over again. They would have never thought of using something just once and then throwing it away. But today we are surrounded by things that are made to be tossed away: plastic bags, paper bags, aluminum foil, plastic wrap, paper towels, paper clips, disposable lighters, cereal boxes, gum wrappers, chocolate bar wrappers, . . . Millions of kilograms of materials -- made by factories using precious fossil fuels and energy -- are made to be thrown away. And all this garbage just keeps piling up. More than a third of our garbage is paper. The rest is made up of yard waste, food, metals, glass, and plastics. About a third of what we throw out started as packaging. Some packaging serves a purpose, but most is just there to attract your attention so that you buy one product instead of another -- or buy something you may not really need at all.

Topics: Pollution; Resources.

When you throw something into the garbage can, it doesn't just disappear. Some garbage is taken to "incinerators" and burned. But not all materials burn easily. Dangerous gases can also be produced as some materials burn (modern incinerators can be built to remove these gases from the smoke before it's let into the air, but there's still the problem of the smoke). Finally, the ash that's leftover after incineration can contain dangerous metals such as lead and cadmium.

4. There are some types of garbage -- like toilet paper and kleenex -- you can't collect for sanitary reasons. Keep a list of this garbage -- count every sheet of toilet paper and every kleenex -- over the one week.

5. At the end of one week, weigh all the garbage. Climb on a bathroom scale while holding a container of garbage. Then subtract your weight from the total weight to get the approximate weight of the garbage (the weight of the garbage will be most accurate if you have it in lightweight plastic garbage bags). Depending on the type of scale you're using, you may be able to weigh the trash can full of food waste directly. What's the total weight of all the garbage? What type of garbage is there the most of?

6. How much garbage does each person throw out each day? Divide the total weight of the garbage by the number of days (e.g. 20 kg of garbage in five days is 4 kg of garbage a day). Then divide the weight per day by the number of people in the group (e.g. 4 kg a day tossed by four people equals 1 kg per day).

7. Discuss what should be done with the garbage. Perhaps you can compost the food waste (see next page). Does your area have a curbside recycling program or recycling depot that might take some of the other materials? Sort the paper into two piles: paper that has been completely used and paper that can be used again in some way. Can you make use of any of the plastics in some way (e.g. artwork, storage containers)?

8. *Extension:* Collect large items that would ordinarily be thrown away. Can the item be fixed -- lubricated, sanded, glued, painted, straightened, part replaced -- to make it useful again? For a major restoration project, learn how to fix an item such as a clock or toy.

Plastic garbage in the oceans kills thousands of sea creatures every year. For example, strong winds often blow helium balloons out to the ocean. When the balloons lose their helium, they fall into the ocean and the salt water washes off their colour. The clear, floating plastic can look like food to animals and birds. Whales sometimes accidentally swallow balloons which then get stuck inside the whale's stomach and can kill the creature. Another dangerous form of plastic garbage are the rings used to hold together six-packs of canned drinks. Sea turtles, dolphins, fish, seals, and birds can get the rings caught on their noses or beaks, necks, and flippers. They can't get the rings off, and they often die. Before you put six-pack rings into the garbage, cut them into small pieces.

BURY IT

We get rid of most of our garbage by burying it. Some of the garbage might break down and disappear; much of it won't. Try burying different kinds of garbage.

MATERIALS: Garbage samples (e.g. different types of paper -- toilet paper, writing paper, newspaper, paper towel; egg shell; apple core; lid from can; plastic packaging; piece of nylon stocking; aluminum foil; piece of bread; 100% cotton cloth); large cardboard box; aluminum foil or plastic sheeting; soil (don't use sterilized potting soil because it doesn't contain the required microorganisms); popsicle sticks; water; rubber gloves; paper; pencil. Optional -- dishpan; hangers; clothespins; trowel.

Most garbage is taken to a garbage dump, or "sanitary landfill", where the garbage truck empties it onto the ground. The garbage used to be left in piles that smelled horrible and attracted rats and flies. Today, the garbage is compacted and covered with a layer of dirt. Landfills are made up of alternating layers of trash and fill. Eventually, the landfill builds into a "mountain" and is landscaped with trees and grass.

Landfills aren't a great solution to our garbage problems. We are running out of land to use; sometimes, valuable farmland or delicate ecosystems are destroyed for landfills. People throw hazardous household waste -- like batteries, medicines, and oven cleaners -- into the trash without realizing they can poison the environment. In some landfills, "leachate" forms as rainwater and runoff seeps through the landfill. Leachate can contaminate groundwater supplies. Finally, you would think that things which are supposed to "biodegrade" -- rot and become part of the Earth again -- would do so when buried in a landfill. But, deep underground with little oxygen and moisture, they don't. Scientists have dug into landfills and found carrots and ears of corn still intact after 20 years and newspapers still readable after 30 years. And then there are things that don't biodegrade at all, things made from Earth's resources we've changed so that they can never become part of the Earth again. The bottom line: the best solution to our garbage problem is to stop producing so much garbage.

Topics: Pollution; Ecosystems.

DOING IT:

1. Gather equal-sized pieces of garbage.

2. Line a large cardboard box with foil or plastic. Fill the box halfway with soil.

3. Place each garbage sample in its own spot on the "landfill". Cover each sample with a mound of soil, pressing down firmly. Label mounds with popsicle sticks.

4. Put the "landfill" in a sunny, warm spot (e.g. near a window). Keep the soil moist, but not wet.

5. Every two weeks, dig up the samples. Wear rubber gloves. Examine the samples closely. What biodegrades quickly? What doesn't? What does this tell you about garbage? Continue observing the "landfill" until you think materials have degraded as much as possible.

6. *Variation:* For each garbage sample, dig a hole about 15 cm deep outside in some soil. Wet the hole. Put in the sample and fill the hole. Mark each hole. Dig up the garbage in a month. What has decomposed and what hasn't?

7. *Extension:* What happens to garbage thrown into a lake? Follow the steps above, but instead of a "landfill" use a dishpan filled with water. Replace the water as it evaporates. What happens if garbage is thrown on the street, out in the open? Use clothespins to attach suitable garbage samples to hangers. Put the hangers outside in direct sunlight (windows filter the ultraviolet light needed for photodegradation).

Different materials take different amounts of time to biodegrade. A piece of paper might biodegrade in about a month. It could take a wool sock a year to completely break down. A pop can laying on the ground won't disappear for a couple of hundred years.

A SOIL FACTORY

Composting is one way we can get something good from our garbage and reduce the garbage in landfills. Make your own composter.

MATERIALS: Plastic garbage can with lid; knife; soil (not sterilized); grass clippings (not recently sprayed with a herbicide) and other organic matter (avoid meat and bones because they attract animals; avoid walnut tree leaves and droppings from evergreen trees); pitchfork or shovel. Optional -- worms (red worms are good; you can buy them at a bait shop).

DOING IT:

1. Make holes all over a garbage can and its lid. The holes allow air to circulate through the composter.

2. The composting recipe is simple: combine soil, food and yard waste, along with moisture and air. You can start your composter with three thin layers. The first layer should be made up of 2.5 cm of grass clippings and soil. The next layer can contain kitchen wastes. To speed up composting, shred kitchen wastes. The third layer can be made up of decaying leaves. Sprinkle some soil on top of the heap. Throwing in a few decomposers -- like worms -- will help the material to biodegrade.

3. Put the lid on the garbage can and locate it in a sunny, out-of-the-way spot. Don't put it near a wall; the organic matter should be able to get air from all sides.

4. You can add more kitchen waste as you generate it. Your composter needs a balanced diet to produce top-quality compost. Add some soil, leaves, or grass clippings every time you add kitchen waste.

5. Keep the organic matter damp, but not wet. To get rid of odours and help the composting process, mix the layers regularly with a pitchfork or shovel.

6. When the garbage can is three-quarters full, stop adding organic matter and let the composting process work.

7. If your ingredients have been shredded and the composting process gets off to a good start, the compost can be ready in as little as two to three weeks. How does the end product compare to the original garbage? Dig the compost into house plant soil or a garden (compost can also be a nice gift for a gardener).

At least 20% of the garbage that ends up in landfills is organic (things that were once alive). "Compost" forms when organic matter decays or rots. The decay is brought about by decomposers like bacteria, fungi, earthworms, and snails. Possible ingredients for a compost heap include: leaves and grass clippings; straw and hay; vegetable and fruit peelings; coffee grounds; used tea bags; peanut and nut shells; and small amounts of eggshells, sawdust, and newspaper. Farmers often use manure in their compost heaps. It's not uncommon to see piles of composting manure literally steaming on a cold winter or spring morning. The "microbiological" processes involved in composting generate so much heat that some of the moisture is vapourized. The vapour condenses to steam when it hits the cold air. Compost is ready when it's fairly dark and crumbly. You might still be able to see some leftovers from the original organic material.

Topics: Resources; Soil; Microorganisms.

Recycling

If you think of used materials as garbage, you'll throw them away. If you think of used materials as a resource, it makes sense to recycle them. Try recycling paper.

Energy has to go into recycling materials, but recycling is a lot better than throwing the materials away. Less trash ends up in landfills, which means more room for materials that can't be recycled. Half of the stuff people throw away can be recycled. Many communities now have curbside recycling programs for newspapers, glass, pop cans, corrugated cardboard, and plastics. Some industries are recycling by swapping wastes -- what one company might throw out, another can use as a raw material.

Paper is recycled in factories that shred and mash the paper into pulp, which is then turned back into paper. Recycling about 54 kg of newspaper saves an entire tree from being cut down. Not only does recycling save trees, but it also uses 30% to 40% less energy than producing paper from new wood pulp. Glass is recycled at factories where bottles and jars are broken into tiny bits. The bits are melted down and mixed with new glass. Aluminum can be recycled over and over and over again. Pop cans and other aluminum products like cat food cans and aluminum foil are ground into little metal chips. The chips are melted down and turned into solid aluminum bars. The bars are rolled into sheets of aluminum, which are then sold to can makers -- who make new cans out of them. Oil is a nonrenewable resource that can easily be recycled. Recycled motor oil is as good as new. Used oil is cleaned, filtered, and new additives are mixed in.

Topics: Resources; Energy.

MATERIALS: Newspaper; peelings from one potato or carrot; water; measuring cup; blender; large cake pan or other shallow pan; window screening; rolling pin. Optional -- food colouring.

DOING IT:

1. Tear some newspaper into tiny pieces. Pack the paper bits tightly into a measuring cup until you reach the 100 ml mark.

2. Put 300 ml of water into a blender. Add some newspaper bits and vegetable peelings. Cover the blender and blend until smooth. Add more newspaper bits and peelings. Cover and blend. Continue until all the ingredients are used up and the pulp is as smooth as possible.

3. Lay a piece of window screening on the bottom of a cake pan. Pour 400 ml of water into the pan.

4. Put half the pulp into the pan (you can use up the rest of the pulp when you finish with the first half). Use your hands to spread the pulp evenly in the water, over the screen. Pat the pulp down and fill in any holes.

5. Open a thick newspaper section to the middle and lay it on a table. Lift the screen carefully out of the pan and let the water drain away. Place the screen with the pulp on one half of the open newspaper.

6. Close the newspaper. Carefully flip the newspaper section over so that the screen is on top of the pulp -- *this is important!*

7. Run a rolling pin over the newspaper to squeeze out extra water from the pulp. Go back and forth several times and press hard.

8. You now have wet, recycled paper. Open the newspaper and carefully peel the screen off the recycled paper; if the recycled paper sticks, you need to press out more water.

9. Once you get the screen off, lay a sheet of dry newspaper on the recycled paper and use the rolling pin to flatten the recycled paper. Leave the recycled paper to dry on the newspaper.

10. It may take as long as two days for the recycled paper to dry. When the paper is dry, carefully peel it away from the newspaper. The dry, recycled paper may look and feel like cardboard. Write a letter on the recycled paper and send it to a friend!

11. *Variation:* Add food colouring to the pulp to make coloured paper.

A tree that has been growing for about 15 years can be used to make approximately 700 paper bags. A big supermarket can give out all 700 bags with groceries in less than an hour.

Look for and use products with recycled paper in them. Some cereals, crackers and cookies come in boxes made of recycled cardboard; the cardboard is probably recycled if it's gray on the inside. Buy recycled paper for writing. Don't use just one side of a piece of paper -- use the other side for scrap paper; that's recycling too. And did you know that schools buy more books than anyone else in the country? Check how many textbooks are printed on recycled paper.

AND A SIDE ORDER OF GARBAGE

Many people feel that fast-food restaurants are hard on the environment because of the food packaging they use. Eat your way through this activity to learn more.

MATERIALS: Money and an appetite!

DOING IT:

1. This is a good activity for a group of people who are hungry. Each person goes to a different fast-food restaurant (try for a sample of four or five restaurants) and orders about the same thing (e.g. the same size and general kind of hamburger, the same size and type of milkshake, the same size of french fries, and an ice cream sundae). "Take out" the order.

2. Each person eats their meal and keeps their garbage -- all of it. Keep everything the server gave you -- even the napkins and salt packet you didn't use. Keep the garbage from each restaurant separate.

3. Sort through all the garbage. Which restaurant sold the most garbage with the meal? Which sold you the least? Did the hamburgers each come in the same type of package? What about the other foods? How much of the garbage is paper? How much is plastic? Are any other materials used? Are you surprised at how much garbage there is?

4. Read the story on the following page. What do you think about what the fast-food chain did? Do you think paper hamburger containers or wrappers are better than polystyrene containers? Why do fast-food restaurants use disposable packaging? Would it be possible for the restaurants to operate without throw-away packaging? What are the alternatives? What if these alternatives made the food more expensive?

Would you like that wrapped? Think about some items you've bought recently. Now think about the packages they came in. Think about the type, the size, and the weight of different packages -- including plastic or glass bottles, cans, boxes, cartons, sacks -- and combinations of different types of packaging for one product. Advantages of packages include convenience, sanitation, security, and durability in distribution. The disadvantages of packages are that the hidden costs of packaging can exceed 50% of the total cost of a product and packages most often end up as garbage. A lot of attention has been focused on the garbage created by fast-food restaurants. The restaurants use tonnes of paper and plastics for packaging their food. The sad part is that all of the packaging is thrown away within fifteen minutes after the food is purchased. The packaging may be handy for keeping food warm and taking it home, but are the benefits worth the cost to the environment?

Very little is known about the trade-offs involved in making, using, and getting rid of packaging. What we need are thorough "cradle-to-grave" scientific studies. These studies can take years of research and a lot of money. They look at *everything* involved in a package from the time it's made to the time we're done with it. For example, one type of package may create more garbage in the end but may require less energy to make than another type of package. Which package is "better"? Making decisions about packaging involves looking at costs, at how much to cut back how quickly, at what will be lost (e.g. will it be sanitary?), and at which packages are better than others from an environmental standpoint.

Topics: Resources; Decision-Making; Pollution.

A Short Story About Fast Food

(THIS STORY IS BASED ON A REAL SITUATION)

Once upon a time, there was a fast-food chain with restaurants all over the world. For years and years, this chain -- which shall remain nameless -- served billions and billions of shakes, fries, and hamburgers (their sign said so, so it must be true) -- along with billions and billions of paper wrappers, plastic cartons and boxes, cardboard trays, plastic and paper cups, plastic straws, paper napkins, salt and ketchup in paper packets, plastic forks and spoons.

There came a day when people started worrying about the environment. All that garbage wasn't going to just disappear with a flick of a fairy godmother's wand (fairy godmothers are pretty scarce, you know). What a mess. So people started to protest. Adults marched in front of the fast-food restaurants with signs saying "Don't Eat Here!" Kids protested by showing up at restaurants with their own reusable plates and cutlery. The news was all over the newspapers, television, and radio.

The fast-food chain responded by saying that people weren't being fair. It took out big, expensive ads saying that the garbage it creates is a very small part (a quarter of 1%) of all the garbage that ends up in landfills. The fast-food chain was quite right about that. The fast-food chain also wondered why people were picking on the restaurants when, probably, each one of the people -- at home, work, and school -- did lots of other things that weren't good for the environment.

But people still shouted, marched, wrote letters and -- basically -- complained. The fast-food chain had to *do* something. So it started a restaurant recycling program. It had two bins for people to throw away their garbage: one bin for recyclables and one bin for everything else. Nice idea -- said a few people. Bad idea -- said many more people. People got confused about what belonged in which bin. And, people still complained that the fast-food chain was creating too much garbage -- recyclable or not.

The fast-food chain had to do something else. It took a big step: it changed its hamburger containers. Hamburger containers were one of the things people shouted about most. The chain switched from "polystyrene" (a type of plastic) containers to paper containers and wrappers.

Suddenly, some people stopped shouting bad things about the fast-food chain and starting shouting "YAHOOO!" They said they had won. They said paper containers were much better for the environment. But this isn't the end of the story. No way.

Other people started shouting "Hold it!" (Boy, there's a lot of shouting going on!) They said that paper containers *weren't* better for the environment. Now it starts to get complicated:

1) Polystyrene containers can be recycled easily. The leftover food can be cleaned away in a low-energy, water-conserving wash. You can't wash paper containers. If the paper has ketchup or mustard on it -- which aren't exactly strange things to find on a hamburger -- it can't be recycled. If most of the paper containers are dirty, it won't be worth it to have a restaurant recycling program for the paper. So, the paper containers will just end up in a landfill.
2) Paper biodegrades; polystyrene doesn't. But, once a container is in a landfill, it may not make much difference whether it's paper or plastic. Landfills don't have enough moisture and air to help things biodegrade. 20-year-old carrots have been dug up from landfills and they still look like carrots.
3) Some people said that the way polystyrene containers were made hurt the environment; but new ways of making them are much better. Making both paper and plastic containers creates pollution and uses energy.
4) It's true that polystyrene containers are made of nonrenewable fossil resources. But, paper containers are made from trees -- and we have too few of those already.
5) A paper box can weigh more than a polystyrene box. More material goes into it, which means more garbage is actually created by one box.

When people heard all of this, the shouting just got louder. Some people said the fast-food chain should just use and reuse washable dishes. But that had problems of its own: washing billions of dishes could create water and sewage problems.

So, did the fast-food chain do a good thing? Some people say it did. The fast-food chain *listened* to the people and at least tried to do something. Other people say it didn't because the fast-food chain won't win, the people won't win, and -- most of all -- the environment won't win. We shouldn't do things just to keep people quiet. We should do them because they're smart. We have to really think everything through.

People are still shouting. The story doesn't have an end yet. The environment is still in trouble, and the fast-food chain -- along with you and me and everyone else -- is still part of the problem. We have to do some more work before we get the ending we want: And they all lived happily ever after . . . in peace and quiet.

It's All About Choices

Whenever you do something, you have to look at what you get out for what you put in. These paper-collecting races show that making choices isn't always easy.

MATERIALS: Paper; two bags; measuring tape; stopwatch or watch which indicates seconds.

DOING IT:

1. The first race represents chopping down trees and making new paper. Scatter ten sheets of paper close to each other at the end of a 50 m distance. Who can run the distance, collect the paper, and run back in the shortest amount of time?

If the solutions to environmental problems were simple, then all the problems would have been solved by now. It's not as simple as making a choice between "right" and "wrong" or "good" and "bad". For example, disposable diapers are the choice of many parents, and as a result are a large component of city garbage. The environmental impact of disposable diapers versus reusable cloth diapers is very different. Disposables are made using precious resources and create solid waste, while cloth diapers require large amounts of water and energy for washing. Which diapering method is "better"?

While practices like recycling are a good idea, they can be hard to make work in our world. Factors involved include the cost of a large-scale recycling program versus the cost of making new products; how much energy is used in each case; what resources are used in each case; the pollution created in each case; and how the size of the population might affect the activity. For example, does it take more money and energy to recycle paper than it does to chop down trees and make new paper? The costs involved in collecting and transporting large quantities of scrap paper for recycling are significant. Water removed from the recycled paper may be dirty and contaminated. Where or how should it be disposed of? These types of practical points must be taken into consideration, in addition to convenience and product quality. Making good decisions means balancing the good and the bad, the advantages and disadvantages, for everybody today and tomorrow.

Topics: Decision-Making; Resources.

2. Unemployment is high and people need work. So, try putting two people to work. They start the race together, collect the sheets of paper, and run back together. The clock stops ticking when the last person in the pair finishes the return trip. How long does the race take now? In terms of getting the task done in the shortest amount of time, is one or two people best? Does the second person really do anything to "help"?

3. The second race represents collecting old newspapers from homes throughout a community to recycle the newspaper. Tear five of the sheets of paper into several dozen *small* pieces. Scatter the pieces in an area about 5 m x 5 m. One person must collect *every single scrap* of paper in a bag. How long does this task take? Does it take longer than simply running a 50 m distance and collecting the whole sheets of paper? Is it easier to collect the whole sheets of paper or the pieces?

4. Unemployment is still high. Maybe it makes sense to put two people to work at the recycling job. Rescatter the pieces of paper. Two people work together to gather the paper. How long does the task take? Is it easier to collect the pieces of paper when two people are at work? Is the second person more effective in this task than he or she was in the first race?

5. Which race is "better"? What are the advantages and disadvantages of each? Which race takes the least amount of time? Which takes more energy? What do you have to be good at to do well in the first race? What do you have to be good at to do well in the second race? Which race is better if there's high unemployment? What if the people who are unemployed only know how to pick large sheets of paper, not small ones. Which race is best for them? In the second race, only five sheets of paper are used; five sheets (i.e. trees) are saved. Is that good or bad? Which race is the most fun?

POINTS OF VIEW

One of the reasons that environmental problems are hard to solve is because different people see things differently. How do you see some of the issues?

MATERIALS: Following two pages.

DOING IT:

1. Read through the situations described on the following pages. You might even try role-playing the various situations.

2. How do you feel about each situation? What do you think is the "best" solution in each situation? Why? Try to use the nine steps for evaluative action.

Why do certain people think and behave in certain ways? The "social sciences" involve looking at the way people act and interact. The social sciences are an important part of working to solve environmental problems. The problems often involve conflict between different groups of people. People see things differently -- sometimes very differently. People have different needs and different values.

How do you make decisions when there are different points of view? There are two basic approaches: judgement or evaluative action. Judgements often involve saying that something is good or bad, desirable or undesirable, beautiful or ugly. They often emphasize making a decision considering only two extremes; people aren't forced to think through all the alternatives. Also, judgements tend to reinforce the human tendency to label things and then do nothing. Evaluative action, based on thinking things through, can be more helpful. It involves putting forward ideas for solving a problem. Take evaluative action by following these steps:

1. Understand the situation (get as much information as possible).
2. Check your feelings (i.e. what gut-level reaction do you have?).
3. Consider any information you may have on the needs, motives, or intentions of the people involved.
4. Write down the conflicts (e.g. the need for a job versus the need to preserve the environment).
5. Write down all the alternatives you can think of, even those that don't initially seem practical.
6. Go through each alternative and write down what might happen if you did it.
7. After looking at all the alternatives and their consequences, decide what you think should be done.
8. Explain why your choice is the best one and why you chose it over the others.
9. Take action.

Topics: Decision-Making; Human Behaviour.

What Would You Do?

Environmental Issue: The human population is growing faster and faster.

Situation: Two friends are talking about whether or not they want to have children.

Points Of View:

First Person -- knows that in the last forty years the human population has doubled from 2.5 billion to over 5 billion people and that resources are limited; feels population growth is out of control; sees hungry people from throughout the world on the evening news; does not want to have children and add to the world's population problem.

Second Person -- wants very much to raise children; loves large families; argues that raising a child to be a concerned, well-educated, responsible citizen might help to solve some of the world's problems.

Environmental Issue: Animal habitats are being destroyed and many animals are endangered.

Situation: A young screech owl, taken in by a family when it was sick, has been raised to maturity and can no longer live in the family's small apartment.

Points Of View:

Son or Daughter -- has been very responsible in caring for the animal; loves it very much; wants it to have a good home; would like to keep it, but if can't keep it thinks it should be released to the wild because it was "born free".

Father or Mother -- owl was more expensive to care for than the family initially thought; believes that owl has become pampered by living with the family; doubtful that owl could survive in wild; thinks owl should be given to the local zoo; doesn't know a lot about what to do in a situation like this.

Environmental Issue: Animal habitats are being destroyed and many animals are endangered.

Situation: Three people are fishing together on a quiet, secluded lake.

Points Of View:

Law-abiding Citizen -- hasn't been fishing in years; fishing has been great fun and relaxing; catches ten fish during first day; catches five fish in the first hour of the second day, all of which are bigger than yesterday's fish; the law allows a total of only twelve fish (therefore, the total has already been exceeded by three fish).

Close Friend of Law-abiding Citizen -- is getting a nice tan sitting in the boat; says should continue to fish; keep the biggest fish to stay within limit, and eat the rest for lunch.

Biologist -- is concerned about the fish population being depleted; has seen acid rain take its toll on the fish and knows that the fishing limit is set based on the fish population.

Environmental Issue: Animal habitats are being destroyed and we are cutting down too many trees.

Situation: A farmer and his or her son or daughter are looking at clearing a piece of land for farming and are visited by a naturalist.

Points Of View:

Farmer -- farm has been in family for decades; times are tough; doesn't want to clear land, but has to; can plant a crop which may bring in enough money to keep the farm going and support the family.

Son or Daughter -- has just studied about the greenhouse effect in school; very worried about the environment; has decided that individuals must stand up for what they believe in; also wants an expensive CD player and sneakers for next birthday.

Naturalist -- the land is covered with beautiful, mature trees; the land is home to several species of birds which will have no place to live if the land is disturbed; these species of birds are in danger of extinction, and there are very few natural habitats still in existence for them; has the support of the government in setting aside the land as a natural area.

Environmental Issue: The air is becoming more and more polluted and the Earth is getting warmer (greenhouse effect).

Situation: City council is meeting to discuss closing all downtown streets to personal cars.

Points Of View:

Councillor -- downtown streets are very congested; it can take an hour to travel a few blocks; public buses can't get through because the streets have so many personal cars on them; wants to be re-elected and knows that people are concerned about the environment; brings out statistics showing high levels of air pollution downtown.

Citizen -- housing prices are too expensive downtown, so has to live outside of the city; has to bring car to work downtown because there is no public transit from home; often works late at night and feels safer in own car.

Another Citizen -- points out that high pollution levels downtown could be caused by all the factories nearby; angry about several recent increases in transit fares; wants better public transit for the money; suggests allowing cars downtown only if they have at least three people in them.

WHAT WOULD YOU DO?

ENVIRONMENTAL ISSUE: Animal habitats are being destroyed. Land is a scarce resource and must be used carefully.

SITUATION: City council is meeting to discuss how a piece of land will be used.

POINTS OF VIEW:

Councillor -- very tired and overworked; wants to make a fair decision; has small children waiting at home to be tucked into bed and meeting is running late; sometimes thinks about environmental mess world is in.

Motorcycle Club Owner -- club made a large donation to local charity last year and is respected in the community; club wants to turn land into dirt-bike raceway; club's members have no place to ride, and this piece of land is away from residential areas; not many pieces of land available that are as large as this one.

Naturalist -- land is home to several species of birds which will have no place to live if the land is disturbed; these species of birds are in danger of extinction, and there are very few natural habitats still in existence for them; the area would make a good wildlife preserve, and could be opened to the public for bird-watching and hiking.

Hunter -- wants to maintain the natural environment, but wants hunting and fishing to be allowed; area has a lot of wildlife; close enough to the city so that it's a short trip, but far enough away so there's no danger to people from guns.

Real Estate Developer -- wants to build housing development; employment opportunities are booming in the city, and there's a housing shortage; people are on waiting lists and are willing to pay top dollar for homes; this area of land would open up a whole new section of the city.

ENVIRONMENTAL ISSUE: Chemicals are polluting the air and water.

SITUATION: A home owner is spraying a chemical on the lawn.

POINTS OF VIEW:

Proud Owner -- has lived in neighbourhood for many years; concerned about local property values and beauty of neighbourhood; is very proud of own front lawn and flower bed; has back problem so can't bend and weed a great deal; uses weed killer because it's easy and cheap.

Neighbour -- also proud of neighbourhood; promptly runs over when sees the weed killer; concerned about neighbourhood children inhaling the poison; worried about runoff into the pond at the end of the street.

ENVIRONMENTAL ISSUE: Our air, water, and land are all being badly polluted.

SITUATION: A president of a large company is in a meeting to decide on pollution control measures for the company.

POINTS OF VIEW:

President -- very interested in pollution control; had a task force in the company review the pollution the company's plant is creating; task force reports that the plant is barely within the legal requirements, but is adding more than its share of pollution to the community; to add the necessary equipment to reduce pollution would cost so much that fifty employees would have to be fired.

Concerned Citizen -- very interested in environmental issues; lives near plant; concerned about children inhaling pollutants; also a consumer of company's products; doesn't want price of products to rise.

Employee -- has three children to support; does not want to lose job or see any friends lose their jobs.

Government Representative -- warns that tougher government regulations and controls may soon be put into effect; company could be in position of having stiff fines imposed on it, and being forced to put in more pollution controls.

ENVIRONMENTAL ISSUE: The environment is in trouble and we have to educate people to take action.

SITUATION: The government has just given a major grant for environmental education and a group of interested people is discussing the best use for the money. There is only enough money for one project.

POINTS OF VIEW:

Naturalist -- public needs more information on the long-term effects of problems like acid rain and habitat destruction; believes the media gives very biased news coverage by covering only sensational stories and not including the small stories which involve damage that can add up; feels that public doesn't know a lot of the things it can be doing.

Business Owner -- money should be spent on informing big business about government grants available to reduce pollution and increase energy efficiency within factories; feels this is the first priority because industry is a large air polluter.

Inventor -- has just developed a new pollution control device which can be attached to any car and significantly reduces its emissions; feels public must be informed about these and other devices which are available but which do not receive the media attention they should; many devices are developed by individuals who cannot pay high promotional costs and hire an advertising agency.

Elementary School Teacher -- feels money must be spent on school programs for children; young people are our hope for tomorrow, and they must be educated so that they are knowledgeable and concerned about the environment; future generations cannot take the environment for granted.

THE BIG PICTURE

We are all caretakers of planet Earth. We have a job to do. Here's a way to start thinking about the big picture so that you can do your job well.

MATERIALS: Large sheet of paper; sheets of letter-size paper; pencils.

DOING IT:

1. This group activity works best with five or more people.

2. Before people know anything about the activity, give these instructions: "Think about ten things you need to do or want to do. They can be anything at all. Write down the ten things and beside each one write down when you think you should do it." Don't give any other instructions or information.

3. Once everyone has made their list, draw a big rectangle on a large sheet of paper. Make five rows and five columns in the rectangle.

4. Each of the columns has to do with time. Label the columns: tomorrow, next week, sometime this year, sometime in my life, sometime in my children's life.

5. Each of the rows has to do with people. Label the rows: family, friends/neighbourhood; city/ region; country/ethnic group; world.

6. Everyone should put dots in the boxes where their thoughts belong. For example, if someone thought about going to the shopping mall with friends tomorrow, a dot belongs in the box where the "friends/neighbourhood" row meets the "tomorrow" column. If someone thought about joining the park clean-up campaign next week, then a dot belongs in the box where the "friends/neighbourhood" row meets the "next week" column.

7. When everyone has filled in their dots, step back and look at the big picture. Where are most of the dots? Why do most of the thoughts involve things close to you? How easy is it to think about doing things many years from now? How easy is it to think about solving the world's problems?

8. Read the "12 Steps to Being a Good Caretaker of Planet Earth". How many of the steps will you follow? How can these steps help you to "think globally, act locally"? Even though you concentrate on things in your immediate life, you can do those things in a way that will help the world for many years to come.

Have you heard the expression "you can't see the forest for the trees"? It means that sometimes we get so overwhelmed by the little things of daily life -- by all the "trees" around us -- that the bigger picture, like the "forest", gets lost. For example, your Walkman battery is dead. The trash can is right beside you. You know you shouldn't throw the battery into the can because the battery is hazardous waste. The battery shouldn't end up in a landfill. But, it's just one battery. What's it going to hurt? It's a lot of trouble to get the battery to a special waste site. What should you do? Think globally, act locally. Think about poisoning the environment, and make the extra effort to dispose of the battery properly. Then, purchase a rechargeable battery. It can be hard to always keep the big picture in mind, but it's important. It's normal to think about those things that are closest to you. But with some practice, you can also think about the bigger things.

Topics: Human Behaviour; Decision-Making; Environmental Awareness.

If you've decided to do a few little things -- like walking or biking instead of taking a car, or turning off the lights when you don't need them, or recycling -- then you're already helping to stop the greenhouse effect, acid rain, energy waste, and landfill overflow. Everything every person does counts.

12 Steps To Being A Good Caretaker Of Earth

(USE THESE TO GET STARTED!)

1. Follow the "Three Rs" -- Reduce, Reuse, Recycle:

Reduce by buying only what you really need and by using as little of everything as possible. Some examples: Buy quality products that will last a long time. Instead of using wrapping paper, wrap a T-shirt around a present; then the wrapping becomes part of the gift.

Reuse everything as often as possible and avoid products that are used once and thrown away. Some examples: Take cloth bags with you when you go shopping instead of getting plastic bags when you buy things. Use a lunchbox instead of a paper or plastic bag to carry your lunch to school. Use wrapping paper more than once.

Recycle materials that you can't reuse. Some examples: Newspapers and other types of paper, aluminum cans, glass bottles and jars, and plastic can be recycled. If you don't have a recycling program, help to start one.

2. Conserve precious resources like water and energy. Some examples: Can you bike where you're going? Can you turn down the thermostat? How about turning off the water when you're brushing your teeth?

3. Throw garbage into trash cans, not on the ground. If you see trash laying on the ground, take the time to pick it up.

4. Avoid using chemicals that will pollute the environment. Some examples: Try natural cleaners and body care products. Don't spill liquids like paint or oil onto the ground; if no one can use them, they should be taken to a special waste depot.

5. Keep an eye out for the sky. Some examples: Help the ozone layer by avoiding products made with CFCs. Instead of using the car air conditioner, open the window. Conserve energy to reduce the greenhouse effect and acid rain.

6. Watch for signs of pollution, like unusual smells, strangely-coloured liquids, piles of garbage, sick animals, or dying plants. *Don't touch or go near these things yourself*, but report them to officials who can do something.

7. When you're in a natural area, take only notes and pictures and leave only footprints. Some examples: Don't disturb animals, pick up their eggs or young, pick flowers, strip bark from trees, or trample vegetation. Don't leave any garbage behind.

8. Be on a wildlife alert. Some examples: Don't kill even the smallest of insects; all creatures have a job on Earth. Don't buy pets taken illegally from the wild. Support your local zoo, if it's a good one. Animals should have room to roam, should be healthy, and should be treated with respect by zoo keepers and the public. If the zoo isn't treating animals properly, write a letter to the zoo director.

9. Learn as much as you can about environmental issues. Join an environmental group or subscribe to an environmental magazine. Listen carefully to everyone's point of view and then make your own decisions.

10. Write to local and national leaders telling them what you're concerned about, why, and what you think should be done about it. Be polite, use your own words, and don't forget to ask for a reply. Encourage other people to write letters too. More letters will get more attention.

11. Talk to other people about the environment. What do they think about certain problems? Can you give them any information they didn't already know?

12. Take it slow! Learn to stop, to look at, and to appreciate the wonderful world around you.

World In Your Pocket

The world is rather like an egg. It's fragile and we must take care of it. Take care of an egg for one day -- and the world for all the rest of your days.

Humans gave themselves a very choice name: "Homo sapiens" is Latin for "wise men". Other species of animals might not agree with this name. To a large animal like the moose, which can move its bulk through the bush without cracking a twig, a human being stumbling and crashing through a forest probably doesn't seem very wise. Yet, as a species, humans are wise in many ways. We have learned to use the resources of the world to make our lives easier and more comfortable. But, at the same time, we have caused a lot of damage and destruction. No other living creature is able to influence and change the environment as humans can. That means that humans have a big responsibility in the world. Humans are indeed wise; but the real question is, "Are we wise enough?"

The world is like an egg. The world houses life, just as an egg can contain a baby chicken. The world sustains life, just as we can obtain nourishment from an egg. The world is strong, just as an egg's shell is tough enough to protect a developing chick. But the world is also fragile, just as a forceful blow will crack an egg's shell and cause its contents to spill out. The world is a human responsibility, just as caring for an egg for the day is a responsibility.

Topics: Environmental Awareness; Human Behaviour.

MATERIALS: Eggs. Optional -- pencil, pen, or crayon to mark eggs.

DOING IT:

1. First thing in the morning, choose your very own egg. You might want to mark the egg so that you can tell it's yours. How is the egg like planet Earth?

2. The challenge: Carry the egg with you all day and make sure it stays whole. You can't put the egg in any sort of protective packaging. Do all the things you would normally do. Take the egg everywhere you go. You only get one egg. If the egg cracks, there are no second chances.

3. How do you feel at the end of the day? Did the egg survive? How did you change your activities to protect the egg? Is it a big responsibility to care for an egg? How difficult is it? How well do other people do at caring for an egg for a day?

ROCKHOUNDING

The Rocks subject area has five One Leads to Another activities. The series takes a step-by-step approach to collecting rocks.

Rocks come in all shapes, sizes, and colours. They can be found almost everywhere. Have you ever picked up a rock because you liked its colour or shape? Did you take the rock with you and hold on to it? If you did, you might make a good rockhound. Rockhounds look for rocks. Some rockhounds collect rocks to see how many different types they can find. Some look only for special kinds of rocks. Often, rockhounds keep adding rocks to their collections until they lack only three or four of a certain type of rock. Then, the search for the missing few rocks becomes exciting and consuming. Other rockhounds get the most fun from showing off their collections. And still other rockhounds think the most fascinating part of searching for rocks is the curiosity -- wondering what rock is just over the hill or a few metres away.

At one time or another, most people have gathered rocks and may have even started collections. But, the collections are often nothing more than accumulations of unlabelled and unknown specimens thrown into a cardboard box. It's no wonder people lose interest in rockhounding! The following series of activities begins at the beginning: putting together a good rock-collecting kit so you have everything you need to dig and chip away at interesting finds. The next activity deals with finding rocks and actually taking specimens. The third activity presents a rock key for identifying the three basic types of rocks: igneous, sedimentary, and metamorphic. The fourth activity describes a number of tests for exploring the properties of rocks and minerals. Finally, preparation, display, and care of rock collections is discussed.

The Quickies and Make Time sections in *Science Is . . .* contain activities which provide valuable background information about rocks. The best way to learn more about rockhounding is to get in touch with a local club of rockhounds. Clubs can give you tips on finding rocks, identifying specimens, and caring for a rock collection. Clubs are also great places to talk with other people interested in rocks and to engage in rock trading.

GETTING READY

Gathering the equipment for rock collecting and becoming familiar with its use is an activity in itself. Put together a rock-collecting kit.

MATERIALS: Discussed below.

DOING IT:

1. Gather and examine the following rock-hounding equipment.

- *Crack hammer or small sledge hammer* -- useful for cracking large rocks. The best kind of hammer has a hard steel head and a steel handle (hammers made of cast iron break and scratch easily when hitting rock).
- *Rock pick or geologist's pick* (with a flat head on one side and a pick on the other) -- something to think about if you become a dedicated rock hound. You don't need one to begin rockhounding. The kind called a "hardrock pick" is best, and is found in mineral or rock shops, or at a hardware store. Use the blunt end for breaking off medium-size pieces from larger rocks. Use the pointed end to chip off small pieces and to pry rocks apart. Aim the hammer blows carefully; otherwise, you'll just get a lot of small rock chips and a chipped pick head.

A responsible rockhound follows a few simple rules. For safety -- and fun -- go rockhounding with at least one other person; work with someone older or more experienced. Don't climb up rock faces and quarry walls. Be careful around loose material on hillsides. Don't work below someone else. Never enter an abandoned mine (often, the only thing holding up an old mine is rotten timber). For your first few trips, choose familiar areas. Cause no damage to fences, signs, buildings, and so on. Treat the environment with respect; don't disturb wildlife or destroy vegetation. Fill in all holes you dig, because they may pose a danger to humans, wildlife, or livestock. Don't take larger specimens than you can reasonably use. Don't walk across or dig in cultivated land, especially if crops are growing on it. Always obtain permission to collect on private property. Property doesn't have to have "no trespassing" signs posted on it, and there are fines for trespassing. Tell the owner that you plan to collect rocks and will not damage his or her land. Know the boundary lines of property on which you plan to collect.

Topics: Rock Types.

- *Cold chisels* (the kind used on metal) -- useful for prying crystals out of cracks and for chipping away small pieces of rock surrounding crystals. Buy two: one with about a 2 cm cutting edge and one with about a 0.5 cm edge. If you can only afford one, buy a 1 cm chisel.
- *Safety goggles* -- very important for protecting your eyes from sharp, flying chips of rock. **Always wear goggles when you hammer or chip rocks.** Make sure that people near you are also wearing goggles. Rock chips can fly quite a distance.
- *Gloves* -- to protect your hands when you're digging or chiselling.
- *Crowbar or wrecking bar* -- useful for prying up small boulders, or for prying apart a rock that has a large crack in it.
- *Spade* -- use for digging. The best kind of spade is the small, folding type, which is also called an entrenching tool or a boy scout shovel.
- *Magnifying glass* -- useful for examining small crystals and seeing differences in very similar rocks. Get one that does not magnify more than ten times (10x).
- *Steel-bladed pocket knife, a piece of window glass, and a penny* -- handy for testing hardness.
- *Sturdy canvas bag or knapsack* -- for carrying equipment and rock samples. Don't get one that's too large or you may put more into it than you can carry!
- *Old newspapers* -- use to wrap each sample separately before it goes into the knapsack. This prevents samples from chipping/scratching each other.
- *Small plastic bottles or an egg carton* -- handy for carrying and protecting small crystals. Put cotton or crumpled paper in the bottoms of the containers.
- *Notebook, pencil, and labels* -- essential for keeping track of your rocks. They help you to make sense of your collection, especially when it becomes large. Masking tape makes a good temporary label.
- *Compass* -- useful for finding direction, especially if you're in unfamiliar territory.
- *Outdoor clothing* -- should be comfortable and provide protection from insects, temperature, etc. Shoes or boots should give you a secure grip on rocks.

FINDING SPECIMENS

Where should you look for rocks? What do you do when you find something interesting? Here are some approaches.

MATERIALS: As discussed on the previous page. Optional -- map of collecting area.

DOING IT:

1. Choose a safe area and follow the general rules on the previous page.

2. Don't just collect several pieces of the same rock. Look for a variety of rocks. Don't be discouraged if you can't find dozens of different kinds of minerals in one area. Different kinds of minerals are found in different parts of the world.

3. Rocks exposed to rain, wind, and extreme temperatures may be hard to identify because of changes in colour and appearance (e.g. surface of rock turns yellow or brown). Look for freshly broken pieces of rock, or use your hammer or chisel to break apart a large rock.

4. It's easiest to pick up loose specimens lying on the ground or in cracks and hollows. Chipping away a specimen, like a crystal, from a large piece of rock takes more patience and skill.

5. A good specimen size is about 10 cm wide by 10 cm long and perhaps 5 cm thick. This size is large enough to show the rock's properties, but small enough to carry and store easily. Use a hammer or chisel to chip out a specimen. **Always wear safety goggles when chipping rock.** First, place the rock you want to break solidly on top of another large rock. Then, look for a crack and try to hit along that line. This takes some practice.

6. When you chip away a crystal, chip off an amount of rock surrounding the crystal that is several times as large as the crystal itself. You can trim when you get back to home base.

7. Besides the specimen itself, take a few chips. You can use the chips for testing hardness and other properties without harming your main find.

8. Take only the best specimens. A knapsack full of rocks can be heavy!

9. When you find a specimen you want to keep, put a small numbered label on it. In your notebook, record the number of the specimen, date, area in which specimen was found (you may want to mark the spot on a local map), and general surroundings (e.g. kinds of rocks around specimen). Include anything else you feel is important (e.g. is specimen similar to the bedrock?).

Rockhounds try especially hard to find crystals. They look for large, perfect crystals, but these are very rare. Most crystals are found broken or chipped. It's easier to find small crystals that are almost perfect. So, always look into even the tiniest cracks and crevices. Look carefully at the sides and bottom of hollows in large rocks. Use a magnifying glass. You may find some very good crystals that are less than 1 cm long (these are called micromounts and are valued by rockhounds).

There are some places which are especially good for rockhounding: rock exposures along cliffs and along the shores of seas, lakes, or streams; landslide areas; gulches; dry ravines; beaches; stream beds; quarries; mine site dumps; building excavation sites; and rock cuts (on the side of highways and railroad tracks).

Topics: Rock Types.

Classifying And Identifying

Start working with specimens by grouping them into the three basic rock types -- igneous, sedimentary, and metamorphic. Use this simple rock key.

MATERIALS: Rock specimens; magnifying glass; vinegar. Optional -- rock and mineral identification guide.

DOING IT:

1. Examine your rock specimens. In what ways are they alike? In what ways are they different? Look at characteristics such as shape, texture (related to where found; e.g. wearing effect of water in motion can make rocks smooth), odour, and weight.

2. Use a magnifying glass to get a close look at specimens (most crystals are rather small and buried within rocks). Hold the magnifying glass close to your eye. Then move the specimen toward the magnifying glass until the specimen is in sharp focus.

3. Use the following rock key to decide if a rock is igneous, sedimentary, or metamorphic. Working with a key takes practice. Start with part "a" of the first point. If the characteristic fits, it will tell you where to go next (e.g. go to point 2). If the characteristic doesn't fit, go to part "b" of the same point. It will tell you what to do.

1. a) Rock is made up of mineral grains that you can see → go to 2.
   b) Rock is not made up of visible mineral grains → go to 5.
2. a) Rock is made up of mineral grains that look melted together (interlocked) → go to 3.
   b) Rock is made up of mineral grains that look glued together (noninterlocked) → go to 6.
3. a) Mineral grains in the specimen all look to be the same kind → the rock is METAMORPHIC.
   b) Mineral grains in the specimen are of two or more different types → go to 4.
4. a) Mineral grains in the specimen are *not* lined up; they are distributed in a random pattern, as shown in illustration A → the rock is IGNEOUS.
   b) Mineral grains in the specimen are lined up; they show a definite arrangement or bonding, as shown in illustration B → the rock is METAMORPHIC.

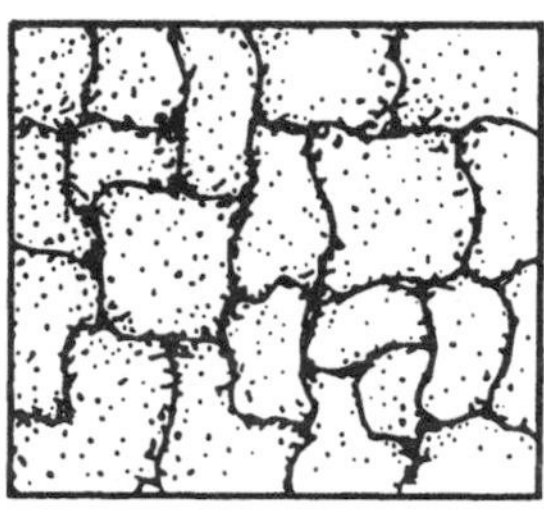

A

B

5. a) Rock is either glassy or frothy (has small holes) → the rock is IGNEOUS.
   b) Rock is made up of strong, flat sheets that look like they will split off into slate-like pieces → the rock is METAMORPHIC.
6. a) Rock is made of silt, sand, or pebbles cemented together; it may also have fossils → the rock is SEDIMENTARY.
   b) Rock is *not* made of silt, sand, or pebbles but contains a substance that fizzes when vinegar is poured on → the rock is SEDIMENTARY.

4. After classifying rocks using the rock key, use the charts on the following page to try to identify specimens. The charts provide only examples of more common possibilities. Use a rock and mineral identification guide for more detailed information.

Classifying and identifying rocks involve the minerals within them. Rocks are made up of minerals, but rocks themselves are not minerals. Rocks are mixtures of minerals. Some rocks are mostly one mineral with small amounts of other minerals. Other rocks contain equal amounts of several different minerals. Certain rocks are even made from other rocks that have been naturally cemented together. The minerals that make up rocks are usually found in the form of particles or grains. Sometimes the grains are too small to be seen, even with a magnifying glass. Mineral grains in rocks can be scattered about or arranged in layers. The size and arrangement of mineral grains help to classify and identify rocks.

Topics: Classification; Rock Types.

The Three Basic Rock Types

IGNEOUS (formed from cooled and hardened magma from deep inside the Earth)				
Rock	**Texture**	**Colour(s)**	**Mineral Content**	**Notes**
Breccia	coarse ↓	green-gray	feldspar, quartz	Cemented together by volcanic dust and ash. Individual grains visible.
Pegmatite		light	feldspar, mica, quartz	Very large, readily visible grains.
Granite		pink, buff, white-gray	feldspar & quartz, mica or hornblende	All mineral grains about the same size. Magma that cooled slowly; large crystals formed. Hard to scratch with a fingernail.
Basalt		black, dark green	feldspar, olivine	Solidified volcanic lava. Found in dikes, sills, and other intrusions. Hard to scratch with a fingernail.
Pumice		buff-gray	glass	Full of tiny holes. Solid, ash-like lava containing trapped volcanic gases. Floats on water.
Obsidian	fine	red-black	glass	"Natural glass". Volcanic lava which cooled so quickly that no crystals were able to form.

SEDIMENTARY (formed when layers of sediment have cemented together)						
Rock	**Texture**	**Hardness**	**Colour(s)**	**Content**	**How Formed**	**Notes**
Conglomerate	coarse ↓	hard ↓	tan, red, white	rounded mass of pebbles; much quartzite and feldspar	coarse rock fragments carried by river, deposited, cemented together	Also called "puddingstone". Held together by brownish muds of sand or clay. Hard to scratch with a fingernail.
Tillite			tan, gray, white	both sharp and rounded stones of all sizes; much quartzite	stones carried by glaciers and dropped when ice melted	Held together by a coarse mud cement. Larger boulders may show glacial scratches.
Sandstone			red, gray, brown	quartz grains	sand carried by rivers, then deposited	Coarse or fine sand cemented together. Surface like sandpaper. Hard to scratch with a fingernail; can scratch off grains.
Limestone			black, gray, white, tan	calcite	built up in shallow seas from skeletons of tiny animals	May be rough or smooth. Fizzes in acid (e.g. vinegar, lemon juice). May contain fossils.
Shale	fine	soft	red, brown, gray, black	clay, mud, and silt	fine mud and silt carried by rivers, then deposited	Smooth surface. Can be split into layers. Often has alternating dark and light layers. Easy to scratch with fingernail.

METAMORPHIC (rock changed by heat, pressure, and/or chemical action)				
Rock	**Colour(s)**	**Mineral Content**	**Rock Formed From**	**Notes**
Quartzite	pale, whitish	quartz	sandstone	More compact than sandstone. Crystalline. One of the hardest rocks.
Marble	white, pink, gray, black	calcite	limestone	Smooth and soft. Fizzes in acid (e.g. vinegar, lemon juice). Crystalline. May have intermixed, coloured bands. May scratch with a fingernail.
Slate	red, gray, green, black	clay	shale	Very fine grain. Tiny mica flakes may be visible. Splits into flat layers.
Phyllite	variable	feldspar, quartz, mica, chlorite	shale and granite	Fine texture. Silky lustre. Irregular layers.
Schist	black, silver	mica, garnet, hornblende	slate, felsite, granite	Often soft; coarse grain. Thick layers. Flakes of mica come off on hands. Easy to scratch with a fingernail.
Gneiss	variable	garnet, feldspar, quartz, hornblende, mica	shale, sandstone, granite, conglomerate	Medium to coarse texture. Irregular bands. Hard to scratch with a fingernail.

Exploring Properties

Mineralogists have developed tests to classify and identify minerals. Use the tests to explore the properties of your own specimens or a pre-identified set of minerals.

There are a number of mineral tests you can do. For example, streaks can be used to identify minerals because a streak is usually constant even though the colour of a mineral might be quite variable, and because a streak may not be the same colour as the mineral. Gold and pyrite (fool's gold) are both yellow and have a metallic lustre. But gold has a yellow streak and pyrite has a greenish-black streak. The streak test can be open to interpretation though; not all mineralogists agree on the difference between a white and a colourless streak.

Most rockhounds and mineralogists agree on the hardness test. The resistance a mineral offers to scratching is its hardness. Hardness is useful for distinguishing between minerals that look alike. In 1812, Friedrich Mohs devised a hardness scale based on the ability of one mineral to scratch another. The scale is set up so that each mineral is followed by a mineral harder than itself. Minerals are ranked in a range from 1 to 10; 1 is very soft and 10 is extremely hard (see table below). Every mineral can be scratched by itself, and by minerals harder than itself. Therefore, a given mineral will scratch minerals with a lower ranking and will be scratched by minerals with a higher ranking. For example, fluorite will scratch calcite, but it will be scratched by (and cannot scratch) apatite. Diamonds are the hardest minerals, with a rating of 10; nothing can scratch them. A Mohs' hardness scale collection (available in rock shops) is helpful for determining hardness.

Hardness	Mineral Example	Test Material
1	Talc	soft pencil lead
2	Gypsum	blackboard chalk; fingernail (2.5)
3	Calcite	copper penny (3.5)
4	Fluorite	brass; iron nail (4.5)
5	Apatite	steel knife blade (5.5)
6	Feldspar	window glass; steel file (6.5 to 7)
7	Quartz	flint sandpaper
8	Topaz	spinel (7.5 to 8)
9	Corundum	emery sandpaper; coarse aluminum oxide sandpaper
10	Diamond	carborundum sandpaper (9.5)

Topics: Rock Types; Classification; Measurement; Magnetism.

MATERIALS: Specimens you have collected or a pre-identified set of rocks and minerals; magnifying glass; small hammer; copper penny; dull steel knife blade; piece of window glass; streak plate or unglazed bathroom tile (the backs of most are unglazed); black construction paper; thread; magnet. Optional -- newspaper; rock and mineral identification guide.

DOING IT:

1. *Colour:* Minerals come in a rainbow of colours. You can start by looking at a mineral's colour, but colour isn't a key characteristic in identification because many minerals exist in more than one colour.

2. *Texture:* Use a magnifying glass to look at the size of the mineral grains in a rock specimen. Large grains or chunks represent a coarse texture, and often make the mineral easier to identify. Small or indistinguishable grains represent a fine texture.

Try panning for gold. You'll get the best results by panning sand and pebbles from the bottom of a stream (dry or wet). Gold is in the heaviest sediment in a stream. Probe a stream's cracks and collect the bottom sediment in a gold pan. When the pan is half full with sand or gravel, dip it in water and shake it back and forth. Sand and other light materials should wash away. Remove any large pebbles. Eventually, you'll be left with a patch of black sand and other minerals. Add a bit of water, swirl the concentrate across the bottom of the pan, and the gold, if any, can be picked out. Of course, prospectors never throw out the concentrate; you can use a magnet to further separate magnetic black sand from nonmagnetic gold dust. An important part of finding gold is making sure it is gold, not fool's gold (pyrite).

3. *Form:* If a specimen has flat, clean surfaces that are -- or look like -- crystal faces, then it's "crystalline". Most minerals are crystalline. If a specimen is of irregular shape, having no crystal faces, it's "massive". If a specimen looks powdery or soil-like it's called "earthy" or "granular".

4. *Lustre:* Lustre is the appearance of minerals in reflected light. If a mineral looks shiny (like a piece of foil or a new nickel), it has a metallic lustre; if it doesn't, it's nonmetallic. Gold, silver, and copper have metallic lustres. There are several kinds of nonmetallic lustres: sparkly (like a diamond); glassy (like the broken edge of glass); waxy; pearly; silky; greasy (like beef fat); and earthy (e.g. clay), which means it doesn't really have a lustre.

5. *Transparency:* Transparency is the degree to which minerals transmit light. Hold a specimen up to the light; if you can see clearly through it, it's transparent. If you can barely see through it, then it's translucent. If you can't see through it at all, it's opaque.

6. *Hardness:* Do some simple hardness testing using your fingernail (2.5), a penny (3.5), a dull steel knife blade (5.5), and a piece of window glass (6.5 to 7). First try to make a small scratch on the specimen with your fingernail. If a scratch appears, the specimen is softer than your fingernail. If no scratch appears, try scratching the specimen with a penny. If the penny scratches the specimen, the specimen is softer than the coin and has a hardness less than 3.5 (but greater than 2.5). If no scratch appears, continue until you find a substance that will scratch the specimen. The scratches you make on your specimens shouldn't be longer than 3 mm so that you don't ruin them. After you make a scratch, rub your finger over it to make sure it actually is a scratch. Good minerals for initial hardness explorations: fluorite, talc, quartz, alabaster, and calcite.

7. *Streak and Crush:* If you push down on a mineral as you rub it across a streak plate, the mineral will leave a powdery streak. Since a streak plate has a hardness of about 7, you can't use it to make streaks of minerals with a hardness of more than 6.5. However, you can take a small piece of a harder mineral and crush it with a hammer or pick (but not on the streak plate!). The finer pieces will have the same colour as a streak of the mineral. If you're in doubt about whether a streak is white or colourless (a colourless streak on a white streak plate is likely to look white), make three or four streaks of the same mineral on a streak plate. Brush the powder off the plate and onto a sheet of black construction paper. Then, examine the powder with a magnifying glass to discover whether it's white or colourless. Good minerals for initial streak explorations: galena, malachite, magnetite, hematite, pyrite, limonite, talc.

Meteorites are prized by rockhounds. They are pieces of rock and metallic iron that have fallen to Earth from outer space. They vary from the size of a pinhead to masses weighing several tonnes. Meteorites can be found anywhere, and may or may not be near the surface (depending on the amount of time since impact and the force of impact). At first glance, a meteorite may look like an ordinary rock or human-made material; but it will have a number of distinctive characteristics. Meteorites usually have a fusion crust, which is dull black to brown in colour and very soft. This crust may have partly flaked off. Some meteorites contain a lot of nickel and are strongly magnetic. They are irregular in shape and their surfaces have smooth pits (the pits look something like thumb prints). Certain meteorites contain metallic iron in the form of scattered grains that are visible on broken or polished surfaces. Many meteorites have small spheres of silicate minerals called "chondrules" that are visible to the naked eye on broken or polished surfaces. Because meteorites come from space, universities and museums are very interested in obtaining authentic specimens.

8. *Magnetism:* Suspend a small chip of a specimen by a piece of thread. Is the specimen attracted to a magnet? Good minerals for initial magnetic explorations: lodestone, magnetite, talc, graphite.

9. *Rupture (Cleavage and Fracture):* The way minerals break is an important characteristic. If possible, wrap a specimen in newspaper and strike it with a hammer. Examine the rock fragments. Alternatively, closely examine the surfaces of the original specimen. If a specimen breaks so that it always leaves smooth, flat surfaces, mineralogists say the mineral "cleaves". Minerals that do not cleave, still break; specifically, they "fracture". There are several kinds of fractures: conchoidal (leaves a series of parallel curves, like a conch shell); splintery (leaves surfaces that are roughened by splinters); fibrous (leaves surfaces that are roughened by fibres); uneven or irregular (leaves rough, bumpy surfaces); and hackly (leaves surfaces that are jagged with sharp points).

10. *Heft:* Heft is an informal assessment of a specimen's specific gravity. The specific gravity of a mineral is its mass divided by the mass of a volume of water equal to the volume of the mineral. If a mineral has a specific gravity of 2, that means it has a mass twice that of the same volume of water. It's possible to make a crude approximation of specific gravity on a relative basis. Place a mineral specimen in the palm of your hand and move your hand up and down, feeling the mass of the specimen. Then do the same thing with another specimen. You'll soon be able to feel the difference between minerals. Most common minerals have a specific gravity of 2.5 to 3.0. Minerals less than 2.5 feel "light" and those more than 3.0 feel "heavy" for their relative size. A good initial comparison is galena and mica.

11. Compare the test results for a variety of specimens. Can you use the test results and the chart on the following page to identify any specimens? Use a rock and mineral identification guide for more detailed information. Do a specimen's properties make it good for a particular use (e.g. jewellery, insulator)?

Some Common Minerals

Mineral	Hardness	Colour(s)	Lustre	Transparency	Streak	Specific Gravity	Notes
Talc	1.0	white, gray, pale green	earthy, pearly	translucent to opaque	white	2.7-2.8	Feels greasy. Can be cut easily. Used for talcum powder, face powder, and carvings.
Gypsum	2.0	colourless, white, gray	glassy, silky	opaque	white	2.3	Used to make plaster of Paris and as a building material.
Biotite Mica	2.0-2.5	black, brown, green	glassy to pearly	transparent or translucent	white, gray	2.7-3.1	Thin, elastic sheets.
Muscovite Mica	2.0-2.5	colourless, gray, white, yellow	glassy to pearly	transparent	white	2.7-3.0	Thin, elastic sheets.
Halite (Rocksalt)	2.5	when pure, colourless or white; when impure, red, blue, or purple	glassy	transparent to translucent	white	2.1-2.6	Salty taste. Fractures.
Gold	2.5-3.0	yellow	metallic	opaque	yellow	16.0-19.0	Can be hammered flat or pulled out into thin strips. Excellent conductor of electricity.
Serpentine	2.4-4.0	green, white, brown, red, yellow	silky, waxy, greasy	translucent to opaque	greenish-black	2.2-2.6	No crystals. Fractures.
Calcite	3.0	usually colourless, tinted by impurities	glassy to earthy	transparent, opaque	colourless	2.7	Fizzes in acid (e.g. vinegar, lemon juice). Often chalky-white in rocks. Cleaves.
Apatite	5.0	white to brown, green, yellow, or violet	glassy	translucent to opaque	colourless	2.7	Looks like many other minerals. Human bones and teeth are made of apatite. Fractures.
Augite	5.0-6.0	dark green to black	glassy	opaque	grayish-green	3.2-3.4	Cleaves perfectly. Short, stubby crystals.
Diopside	5.0-6.0	white, light green, dark green, brown	glassy	translucent to transparent	white	3.0-3.5	Cleaves perfectly.
Hornblende	5.0-6.0	green, bluish-green to greenish-black	glassy	opaque, but translucent to transparent on thin edges	colourless, gray, gray-green, brown	2.0-3.4	Very common. Cleaves.
Orthoclase Feldspar	6.0	white, pink, gray, red	glassy to pearly	translucent	white	2.4-2.7	Large, hard. When found in rock, appears dull. Cleaves.
Pyroxene	6.0	olive green, brown, white, black, gray	glassy to pearly	translucent to opaque	grayish-green to white	3.1-3.5	Short, stubby crystals. Like Amphibole.
Amphibole	6.0	dark green, brown, black	glassy	translucent to opaque	dark green, brown	2.9-3.5	Long, narrow crystals. Like Pyroxene.
Pyrite	6.0-6.5	pale brass-yellow	metallic	opaque	greenish- or brownish-black	4.5-4.6	Also known as "fool's gold". Fractures. Often found with other metallic minerals (e.g. zinc, lead, gold).
Garnet	6.5-7.5	shades of red-brown to near black	glassy	transparent	colourless	3.5-4.3	Fractures.
Quartz	7.0	usually colourless, or any colour	glassy, waxy	transparent to opaque	white	2.7	Very common. Does not fizz in acid. Fractures.
Olivine	7.0	yellow-green to green-yellow	glassy	translucent	pale green, white	3.2-3.6	Granular, sugary, glassy grains. Weathers easily; leaves rock brown with iron oxide stains.

Displaying a Rock Collection

Specimens should look their best if you want to develop a rock collection and show it off. Follow these basic steps to prepare specimens for display.

MATERIALS: Chisel, iron nail, sewing needle, or other sharp tool; hammer; pick; water or rubbing alcohol; cleaning cloth; penknife; stiff brush (e.g. toothbrush); white paint; fine-tipped pen; cardboard labels. Optional -- vinegar.

DOING IT:

1. Free any crystals surrounded by rock. Carefully pick and chip away the rock using a small chisel or other sharp tool. Leave a bit of the rock attached to the crystal as a base on which the crystal can stand. Freeing a crystal is a long and tedious task. Do a little at a time.

2. Clean specimens carefully. One of the best ways to clean rocks and minerals is to soak them in water for a few hours and then wipe them with a cloth. However, some minerals dissolve in water. Test a small piece of a specimen by soaking it in water for a few hours to see if it gets smaller or disappears. If you can't soak your find in water, you'll have to chip and then brush off hardened mud or clay. Use a penknife and a stiff brush. If the specimen has a hardness of more than 5, you can use a wire brush. Some minerals which dissolve in water are fine in alcohol; test a piece first before you soak the whole specimen.

3. Some specimens may have ugly reddish-brown rust stains. The stains indicate that the rock or mineral was in soil that contained iron. You may be able to get rid of the stains by soaking the specimen in vinegar for a few hours. Again, first test a small piece. If bubbles form around it or it changes colour (besides losing the stains), you shouldn't use vinegar to clean it.

4. You should put a *permanent* identification number on each specimen. The number is the one you first gave the specimen when you found it. Paint a small spot on the specimen. When the spot is dry, write in the identification number with a fine-tipped pen.

5. Organize specimens in any way you wish (e.g. by type, colour, size, collection location). Make a display label for each specimen. Use cardboard rather than paper (paper tends to curl). Put on the specimen's name, where and when it was found, and any other information which will make the display more interesting.

6. *Extension:* Micromounts are prized by many rockhounds. It's hard to beat their perfection and beautiful colour. The crystals are often so small that you need a magnifying glass or a microscope to get a good look at them. There are no specific rules for displaying micromounts. Simply choose a specimen, trim it, clean it, and glue it to a pedestal (e.g. popsicle stick). Then mount several pedestals in a box and label them.

Displaying your rock collection enables you to enjoy what you've found. It also helps to keep the collection organized. Use any available cases to display specimens -- egg cartons, cardboard boxes, boxes constructed out of wood. Each specimen should be in an individual compartment, and perhaps surrounded by some tissue or cotton. Use an aquarium tank for a really fancy display case. Set up a few boxes or pieces of wood as a series of steps to place your specimens at different levels. A piece of felt or velvet material, draped over the steps, gives the display a rich look. To keep dust out, use a lid or cut a piece of plastic so that it fits on the top of the tank.

Many rockhounds get into rock polishing. Polished rocks are really an example of speeded-up erosion. Rock tumblers can be purchased at a hobby store.

Topics: Rock Types.

PLANT A PLANT

The Plants subject area has twelve One Leads to Another activities. Do the activities as a series or choose just those individual activities which interest you.

Growing is the thing plants do best -- and one of the most fascinating things they do. A tiny, lifeless seed is plopped into the ground. With the right combination of water and temperature, the little seed begins to sprout. A seedling peeks out of the soil. The plant's stem stretches toward the sky. The plant uses sunlight, water, and nutrients to manufacture food. Before you know it, leaves and flowers appear, and new seeds begin to form. The transformation from seed to plant is nothing short of amazing. The transformation is almost miraculous in the case of the Californian sequoia. This tree is one of the largest living things on Earth. At its base, the tree's circumference is 31 metres; it would take 22 people standing fingertip to fingertip to encircle the tree just once. The tree contains 1200 cubic metres of wood, enough to build 40 average-sized houses. The seed of the sequoia has a mass of only 0.01 grams. Its growth to a mature tree therefore represents an increase in mass of 100,000 million fold (that's ten times the increase of the mass of a human egg cell to the mass of a fully-grown man).

The following series begins with a couple of activities exploring the little packages from which plants grow: seeds. The third activity moves to sprouting beans for a tasty sandwich and salad enhancement. The fourth activity looks at growing plants without seeds. The next two activities focus on roots, including the tendency of roots to grow with gravity, toward the centre of the Earth. Then comes an activity providing directions and suggestions for testing your green thumb by planting and caring for plants. The two activities that follow explore two key things plants need to grow: light and water. Plants also need nutrients to grow, but the nutrients don't necessarily have to come from soil. The tenth activity deals with hydroponics, growing plants without soil. The final two activities deal with close cousins to plants: fungi. One activity involves growing a mold garden and the other investigates the best food for yeast.

Plants need air, warmth, light, water, and nutrients to grow. And plants need time. Growing certain types of plants takes awhile, which means having a little patience. Examine a plant every day; make notes and take measurements. You might even want to take pictures. This will help make the wonder of the growing process more visible.

The Quickies and Make Time sections have other interesting plant activities that deal with plant types and plant parts.

Seed Search

A seed carries a "baby" plant, stores food for the tiny plant, protects the plant, and helps the plant travel to its sprouting spot. Take a sock walk to collect seeds.

Seed "dispersal" -- seeds being scattered over wide areas -- is a survival technique for many plants. It prevents overcrowding near parent plants and the competition of too many seedlings in too small an area. Also, if the parent plants are somehow destroyed, the farther away seeds land, the better their chance of survival. Seeds get around in a number of ways.

Plants like milkweed, dandelion, and cattails release seeds attached to light, parachute-like puffs that are easily carried by the wind over great distances. The seeds of the maple, linden, and ash -- with their helicopter-like "wings" -- also drift in the wind. Some seeds catapult into the air through "expulsion". Touch the pod-like seed containers of the jewel weed and they spring open into two halves, flinging seeds into the air. Witchhazel and violets also disperse their seeds this way. There are a number of seeds -- like those of the coconut, American lotus, bladder nut, and cranberry -- that travel by floating on water. Drop a few cranberries into a bowl and see how easily they float. The berries have a waxy, waterproof covering. Cut a berry open to find four air pockets, each containing a seed.

Animals and people help seeds get around. Some seeds, like those of the burdock, are "hitchhikers". The seeds are in burrs with little hooks that cling to human clothing and the fur of animals. Squirrels are known for their habit of burying acorns for winter food. Acorns that the squirrels can't find later have, in effect, been planted by the squirrels. Some fruits and seeds are eaten together by birds and other animals. The seeds have a tough, indigestible coating, and later reach the ground as waste. Farmers' fence lines often become rows of berry bushes. Birds sit on the fences and excrete seeds; the seeds germinate and grow into plants. Humans can carry seeds across continents and oceans. Oranges originally grew only in China, cucumbers came from India, corn originated in Central and South America, and tomatoes are native to Peru. Colonists brought seeds from their homelands, both deliberately, for planting, and accidentally (e.g. in bales of hay).

Topics: Plant Parts; Flight.

MATERIALS: Magnifying glass; white paper; fuzzy, woollen socks. Optional -- packets of various seeds.

DOING IT:

1. Visit a natural area, a garden, a vacant lot, or a school yard. Look for different plants. Can you figure out how each of the plants disperses its seeds?

2. Take a sock walk. Put a pair of old, fuzzy socks *over your shoes*. Walk around in a grassy field or bushy area. When you remove the socks, you can pick off a variety of seeds. Examine them with a magnifying glass. The seeds will be easier to look at if you place them on a sheet of white paper. How are the seeds different? How are they the same? Can you take a seed and find the plant it came from? What would happen if the socks were a rabbit's foot or a fox's tail?

3. *Variation:* Purchase a number of different seeds from a store. Compare the seeds in terms of colour, shape, and size. How are the seeds different? How are they the same?

4. *Extension:* Plant the weed seeds you collect on the sock walk to see what will sprout. The plants will grow better if you put the seeds in a plastic bag in the refrigerator for a week before planting them (the seeds are used to going through a cold winter before sprouting).

Some of the largest seeds in the world come from a palm plant called the coco de mer. The seeds can grow to be bigger than beachballs, with weights of as much as 23 kg.

JUST ADD WATER

Many plants reproduce through seeds. A seed forms when pollen from the male part of a flower and an egg from the female part of a flower combine. Bring seeds to life.

MATERIALS: Bean (e.g. lima bean) and corn seeds; drinking glasses or jars; water; paper towels; toothpicks; knife; magnifying glass. Optional -- pea, sunflower, pumpkin, peanut seeds.

DOING IT:

1. *Inside Seeds:* Soak some dried bean and corn seeds in a glass of water overnight. Examine the seeds closely in the morning. How do they compare to seeds that have not been soaked? Are their coats still tough? Are they larger than the night before? Look for the scar on the side of a seed, which shows where it was attached to the parent plant. The seed coat should slip easily off the beans. Use a toothpick to carefully split a bean into two halves -- the seed leaves, or cotyledons. Examine the embryo with a magnifying glass. Roots will grow from the bottom of the embryo; stems and leaves will grow from the top. Compare the bean seed to a corn seed. Can you easily split the corn seed in half? What's inside the corn seed?

2. *Seed Germination:* Soak several dried bean seeds overnight. Line the inside of a drinking glass or jar with a wet, folded paper towel. Stuff wet, crumpled paper towels into the centre of the glass to hold the other towel against the glass. Place the seeds between the paper and the glass. Watch the seeds over several days, adding water as required to keep the paper towels wet. What happens to the seeds? Which plant parts can you see first?

3. *Variation:* Soak three equal-sized, dried beans overnight. Before putting the beans into a glass stuffed with paper towels, vary the amount of food available to each. Place one whole seed between the paper and the glass. Carefully remove one of the seed leaves from one of the remaining beans without injuring the embryo. Then place the seed leaf containing the embryo between the paper and the glass. Cut the seed leaves of the last bean so that only half of one seed leaf remains with the embryo. Place this seed between the paper and the glass. Watch the seeds over several days, adding water as required to keep the paper towels wet. What happens to the seeds?

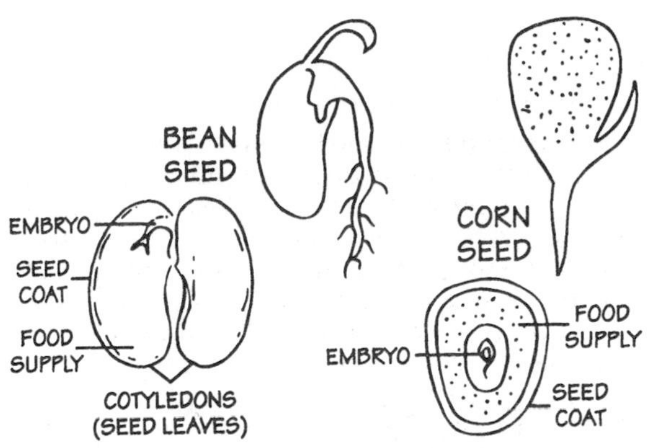

4. *Extension:* Soak and open other kinds of seeds. Look for similarities and differences.

There are two kinds of seed-bearing plants: flowering plants called "angiosperms" and non-flowering plants called "gymnosperms". Most seed plants are the flowering kind; there are some 250,000 species of flowering plants and only about 600 nonflowering species. All seeds have three parts in common: a tough covering, a "baby" plant, and a food supply. The tough covering of a seed is the "seed coat". The "embryo" is the tiny plant inside the seed. Surrounding the embryo is the food supply. The food supply is the seed's only source of nourishment as it pushes up through the soil and grows into a young plant. When the food supply is gone (for a bean, this takes about two weeks), a green plant begins to manufacture its own food through photosynthesis. Beans, sweet peas, and peanuts have seeds that divide into two halves and are called "dicotyledons". Seeds that are a single unit (e.g. corn, oat) are "monocotyledons".

Once a seed reaches its sprouting spot, it begins to grow with water and the right temperature. Water causes the seed to expand. "Germination" is the process through which the embryo inside the seed begins to grow. As a seed germinates, it develops roots, a stem, and then leaves. The food supply is very important to the seed as it germinates. A bean seed without its food supply grows poorly, if at all. A seed with half its food supply grows better, but a seed with both halves does best of all.

Topics: Plant Parts; Plant Processes.

Little Sprout

You start with dry beans and in a few days you have tasty bean sprouts. It's magic! At least plant growth can *seem* magical.

MATERIALS: 60 ml of dried beans (mung beans are the kind used in Chinese cooking; soybeans don't sprout as easily as other beans); bowl; water; colander or strainer; towel.

DOING IT:

1. Spread out the beans you've decided to use. Pick through them carefully. Use only whole beans; throw away any that are in pieces or are split.

2. Wash the beans thoroughly. Soak them overnight in water.

3. In the morning, drain the beans in a colander or strainer. Spread out the beans in the colander or strainer to make a single layer. Cover with a towel.

4. To sprout properly, the beans must be in a dark, moist (not wet) place. Keep the beans covered with the towel, and rinse them with warm water two or three times a day. Make sure you drain the beans well.

5. In about three days, the sprouts will be 5 to 8 cm long. Then you can eat them! If you wish, store them in the refrigerator in a closed container. The sprouts will stay fresh for about a week.

When a plant is just beginning to peek out from the seed, it's said to be "sprouting". Beans, peas, and other plants can be eaten just as they're sprouting. Bean sprouts are especially crunchy and tasty. They are often used in Chinese cooking. They also add crispness and flavour to salads and sandwiches, and are easy to grow in a short period of time.

Topics: Plant Processes.

Watermelon seeds come in two colours: black and white. How do the two compare in terms of size, shape, and texture? Use a knife to remove the skin from one white seed and one black seed. Split the seeds in half, lengthwise. Examine the seeds through a magnifying glass. Does each contain the tiny embryo necessary for the growth of a new plant? Plant some black seeds and some white seeds to see which grow.

If it's too cold outside to grow a garden, grow one inside. Fill a shallow box with soil. Plant salad cress or parsley by sprinkling seeds on the soil and then roughing up the soil to mix in the seeds. Cover the box with plastic wrap for a few days. Make sure the soil stays moist, but not wet. When the plants are about 5 cm high, clip and use them in salads and sandwiches. You can also try growing beets this way.

Look Ma, No Seeds!

Many types of plants can be grown without seeds. Grow a carrot and a potato without seeds. Then try other plants to see what will grow.

MATERIALS: Carrot; white potato (a "boiling" potato with a thin skin and several eyes is good; thicker-skinned "baking" potatoes may have a reduced budding capacity); knife; drinking glass or jar; toothpicks; clay pot; plate; potting soil; water; watering can. Optional -- sweet potatoes, beets, turnips, parsnips, onion, and/or garlic.

DOING IT:

1. *Carrot:* The carrot is easy to grow -- even if it has been out of the ground for a while. Remove the green sprouts from the top of the carrot (leave the green base). Cut the carrot so that only about 5 cm remains below the green base. Put the carrot in a drinking glass or jar filled with water. Keep the carrot in place by pressing three or four toothpicks into it and resting the toothpicks on the rim of the glass. The water should cover only the bottom 1 cm of the carrot. Put the glass in a bright spot, but not in direct sunlight. Add water as required. In about one week, thin, feathery, green sprouts will appear from the top of the carrot. The green top will continue to grow if you keep the carrot in water. What happens to the carrot as the new growth flourishes?

2. *Potato:* Fill a clay pot almost full with potting soil. Put the pot onto a plate and water the soil slowly until water leaks onto the plate. Cut off a piece of potato that has a bud. Poke a hole in the soil; make the hole slightly deeper than the size of the potato piece. Bury the piece of potato, bud up. Keep the soil moist, but not wet. What happens after a week or so?

3. *Variation:* Using the carrot set-up, try sprouting sweet potatoes, beets, turnips, parsnips, onions, and/or garlic.

4. *Extension:* Try planting a piece of potato without a bud. What happens if you plant *only* the bud? What would happen if you planted a whole potato?

5. *Extension:* Try planting carrots, beets, sweet potatoes, turnips, parsnips, onions, and/or garlic in soil.

Some plants produce more of themselves through "runners". Runners are special growths that develop on the stems of the plants. The runners grow away from the main stem, take root, and then form new plants. Many common grasses reproduce this way. Newly-seeded grass may start as only a thin covering, but it soon thickens into a lush lawn. Strawberries and some forms of ivy also reproduce through runners.

You need neither seeds nor flowers to grow potatoes. Although potato plants produce both, and scientists use the seeds to produce new varieties of potatoes, farmers grow new crops from "seed potatoes". Certain plants can reproduce from specially-adapted roots and stems. The roots and stems have large amounts of stored energy that nourish the new plant. A carrot that grows to produce a new plant will, at first, use energy stored in the carrot itself. Only after a set of green leaves have developed will the plant manufacture energy from the sun. Potato sprouts grow from the "eyes", or buds, on a potato's skin. The starchy white part of a potato nourishes potato buds; it acts like the food supply in a seed. Once the stalk and leaves appear, photosynthesis allows the plant to continue to grow. Each bud can grow into a plant with many potatoes.

Topics: Plant Processes; Plant Parts.

Root Watching

Cuttings are a way to produce new plants without seeds. They also provide a good opportunity for root watching. Grow a new plant from an existing leaf.

A single rye plant can have so many roots that, if joined in a straight line, they could stretch for more than 570 km.

MATERIALS: Healthy plant (e.g. echeveria, African violet, rex begonia, coleus geranium, impatiens, Swedish ivy); knife; water; tall, thin, glass jar or large test tube; magnifying glass; black construction paper. Optional -- charcoal chips (available from pet store); water-soluble house plant fertilizer; potting soil; clay pot; plate.

DOING IT:

1. Water the parent plant well before taking a cutting and make sure the plant is healthy (never take a cutting from a stem that is becoming woody). Carefully cut a healthy leaf (including the leaf's stalk) from the plant.

2. Place the stalk of the leaf in a jar or test tube filled with some water. The leaf itself should be propped up above the water. You may want to add a few charcoal chips to the water to absorb toxic chemicals that may build up.

3. Keep the cutting in a warm spot, near a window (but not in direct sunlight). Add water as required.

4. After a few days, you should see roots growing from the end of the stem. Study the roots with a magnifying glass. Put the roots on black construction paper so that the extensive network of fine, white root hairs is more visible.

5. You can keep the cutting in water for several weeks. Once a month, add one drop of water-soluble house plant fertilizer (before adding, dilute the fertilizer to one-third of the manufacturer's mixing instructions).

6. *Extension:* Plant the cutting once it has developed a good root system. Fill a clay pot almost full with potting soil. Make a small hole in the soil and place the cutting in the hole. Pack the soil firmly around the stem. Place the cutting near a window. Keep the soil moist, but not wet. Eventually, the cutting will sprout new leaves and you will have a complete plant.

Roots serve two key functions: they anchor a plant and they gather raw materials such as water and nutrients. Roots do not grow in dry soil; they require moisture. Most often, roots grow underground and you have to dig through the soil to see them. Growing plants through cuttings allows the roots to be visible.

"Cloning" is a way of reproducing using only one parent. Part of a parent plant's stem or leaves can be cut off and put into water. The plant part grows roots and can become a complete plant, identical to the parent plant. For example, all of the small spider plants hanging from a parent spider plant are clones; they can be cut off and developed into new plants. A more complex form of reproduction is "grafting", a process in which cuttings are joined to other plants. Usually, a branch or stem is cut from one plant and grafted (inserted) into the stem or roots of another plant. Seedless orange trees are grown this way.

Topics: Plant Parts; Plant Processes.

Some trees have a long, tapered "tap root" that looks like an underground trunk. The longest tap root ever found belonged to a huge fig tree in South Africa -- the root went straight down for over 130 m! Other trees, such as oaks, have surface roots that fan out underground in the same shape as the branches above ground.

Root Flip

You don't have to worry about planting seeds in a certain position because plants know which way is up and which way is down. Try to fool plant roots.

MATERIALS: Bean seeds (they grow quickly); two large drinking glasses or jars; water; paper towels.

DOING IT:

1. Soak eight to twelve bean seeds overnight.

2. Line the inside of two drinking glasses or jars with wet, folded paper towels. Stuff wet, crumpled paper towels into the centre of the glasses to hold the folded towels against the glass.

3. Put half of the beans in one glass and half in the other. Place the beans between the paper and the glass. Put them in different positions -- level, straight up and down, on an angle. Make sure there is space between the beans.

4. Watch the seeds over several days, adding water as required to keep the paper towels wet. What happens to the seeds? Which way do the roots grow? Does it matter how you placed the beans?

5. Once the roots have grown to a few centimetres, carefully lay one of the glasses on its side.

6. Watch the seeds over several days, keeping the paper towels wet. What happens to the plants in each glass? In which direction do the roots grow? In which direction do the stems and leaves grow?

The banyan is a one-tree forest, and its roots are in the air! It grows something like this: A bird eats one of the fig-like fruits and drops a seed in some treetop. Out from the seed sprouts a root, which winds down to the ground, takes on strength, and becomes a trunk. The seed, still perched up in the air, puts out branches and leaves. New "air roots" come out of the branches and find their way to the ground, until, in some cases, the tree has spread over several acres. Whole marketplaces have been built under single banyan trees in India.

"Geotropism" (Greek for "turning to the Earth") involves the way plants grow relative to gravity. Negative geotropism is the tendency of stems, etc. to grow away from the centre of the Earth. Positive geotropism is the tendency of the roots to grow toward the centre of the Earth. Seeds respond to gravity. No matter which way you plant a seed, it always manages to grow roots downward and a shoot upward. Little granules in the growing tips of plants react to gravity and help orient a seedling's growth. Plants depend on gravity so much that when they're put in a zero-gravity tank, they get confused and grow any which way.

Topics: Plant Processes; Forces.

TEST YOUR GREEN THUMB

Pick a seed, plant it, and watch it grow. It may take some time before the seedling emerges, but if you care for your plant properly, your patience will be rewarded.

The peanut sprouts easily and grows into a lovely plant. The trick is to find fresh, *unroasted* peanuts. Look for them in seed stores or in some vegetable stores. Remove the shells before you plant the peanuts. As the plant grows, watch its leaves fold together at night; they open again in the morning.

MATERIALS: Seeds (collect them from the outdoors or from foods you eat, or purchase them); clay pots or other containers; soil (potting soil is good); plates; trowel; water; watering can or spray bottle; masking tape or popsicle sticks to label plants. Optional -- hammer and nail; pebbles; plant food; bean seeds; egg carton.

DOING IT:

1. Decide what type of seeds you'll plant and where you'll get them. Salad greens, herbs, and flowers are good plants for beginners. There are lots of different kinds of salad greens to choose from, such as red leaf lettuce or butter lettuce. You'll get a fresh, tasty salad for your efforts. Many herbs used to flavour foods are easy to grow from seeds -- like chives, parsley, oregano, and dill. Certain flowers are easy too, like alyssum, petunias, and marigolds.

2. Dried seeds (seeds purchased from a store are usually dried) should be rinsed, soaked overnight, and then planted immediately. Fresh seeds can be planted without soaking. If you decide to plant something like a peach pit, crack the pit slightly with a nutcracker so that the new plant will have an easier start.

3. Clay pots are good for growing plants, but you can use any kind of container. If you use plastic or metal containers, take a hammer and nail and punch a few holes in the bottom of the containers. For added drainage, drop in a few small stones before you put in the soil.

4. Fill each pot almost full with soil. Water the soil. Let the soil settle in the container. The soil should be moist like a wrung-out sponge, but not wet. Put a plate under the pot to catch water that drains out of the soil.

5. Plant a seed by placing it on the soil and then pushing it under the surface with your finger. Be careful to plant seeds at the right depth; seeds that are buried too deeply won't sprout. If you buy seeds at a store, read the back of the package to find out how deep to bury the seeds. In general, large seeds, like lima beans, do well when planted deeper in soil (e.g. 5 cm). Small seeds, like radish, onion, and carrot, should be planted at shallower depths (e.g. 5 mm).

Plants need air, warmth, light, water, and nutrients to grow. They make food using these things. Nutrients are generally obtained from the soil in which a plant grows. Potting soil is best for small, potted plants. However, beginners who are just going to grow a few plants may simply want to dig up a bit of soil from the ground. If the soil is dark and crumbly, the grass and other things growing in it look healthy, and the soil contains earthworms, it's probably good.

Topics: Plant Processes.

Plant seeds from the fruits and vegetables you eat. Some seeds that are easy to grow are orange, grapefruit, watermelon, squash, and green pepper. Rinse any pulp off the seeds before planting them. If you can't use the seeds right away, dry them for a couple of days and save them for later. It's best to avoid drying out orange, grapefruit, and lemon seeds; if necessary, soak the seeds in water until you're ready to plant them.

6. Many of your seeds may not sprout. The more you plant, the better chance you have of something coming up. Put at least four or five of one type of seed in each pot. Space the seeds out. Once the seeds sprout, you can give the strongest ones room to grow by taking out all the other seedlings.

7. Once you've planted your seeds, pat the soil down gently. Water the soil again, being careful not to disturb any tiny seeds. It's best to use a soft, fine spray of water from a spray bottle.

8. Label each pot by writing the type of plant and date of planting on a piece of masking tape or on a popsicle stick.

9. Check the soil every day and keep it moist. If the seeds dry out, they won't sprout. It may take a week or so before you see anything. Watering soil when you can't see a plant may seem a little odd, but patience pays off.

10. When the seeds sprout, place the pot near a window. Keep plants in a bright spot, but out of direct sunlight. You can keep them outdoors, but bring them inside if there's a heavy rain or if birds and animals disturb the plants.

11. Water your plants regularly, keeping the soil moist (but not wet). You may want to feed your plants with fertilizer every two weeks or so.

12. At first, seedlings look a lot alike. The plants become more interesting as they grow bigger. As plants grow taller, they may need support (e.g. use a popsicle stick).

13. *Variation:* The growing process can be so gradual that it may be difficult to appreciate the changes that occur as a plant grows. Fill all twelve holes in an egg carton with soil. Plant a bean seed (or other seed) every day in *one* of the holes (remember to soak dried seeds overnight before planting). Water the plants daily (you may want to make drainage holes in the egg carton). After twelve days, you'll have twelve plants growing, each at a different growth stage.

14. *Extension:* You may want to transfer a plant from a small pot into a garden. Transplanting must be done carefully or the plant will die of shock. Dig up and transfer as much of the root system as possible; try to leave a ball of soil around the roots. Dig the new hole large enough to take the root system without crowding or folding the roots. When you replant the plant, work the soil between the roots or under the curve of the root ball, patting down the soil from time to time to avoid air pockets. Water the plant well.

Apple, pear, peach, plum, and cherry seeds come from trees that grow where the winters are cold. The seeds go through a cold period before they sprout in the spring. To imitate this cycle, put the seeds in a plastic bag containing moist peat moss (you can buy peat moss in a plant store). Place the bag in the refrigerator for three months or so. Then take the seeds out of the peat moss and plant them. Treat and plant at least ten seeds because tree seeds do not sprout as readily as seeds of other plants.

LIGHT THE WAY

Light is one of the things plants need to grow. Experiment with seeds and light. Then make a plant grow through a maze to find light.

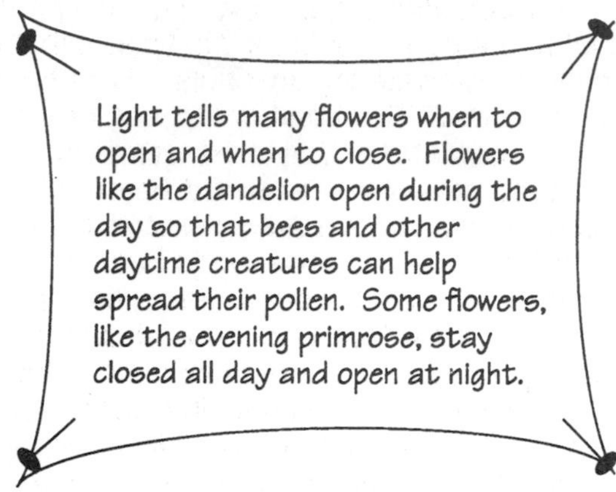

MATERIALS: Bean seeds; two drinking glasses or jars; water; paper towels; black construction paper; tape; box (e.g. shoebox with lid) divided into sections; scissors; small, healthy, potted plant (a bean plant is a good choice because it grows quickly); watering can.

Grow two identical plants. Put them in the same soil and give them the same amount of water at the same times. But make one important thing different: place one plant near a window and the other in a dark closet. It won't take long before you see how important light is to plant growth. Plants need light to manufacture food and grow. Plants need light so much that they will grow toward even the faintest light source, as is demonstrated in a plant maze. "Heliotropism" is the tendency of plants to grow toward light. House plants often lean toward the light of a nearby window; the leaves all seem to turn so that each gets the maximum amount of light.

Plants may need light to grow, but seeds don't. Seeds are planted underground where it's dark. A seed grows because it uses its own stored energy. If the seed is kept in darkness, it will grow a long stem in search of light. This long stem will often make the plant very hardy once it does develop into a seedling that needs light for photosynthesis.

Topics: Plant Processes.

DOING IT:

1. *Seeds in Darkness:* Soak several dried bean seeds overnight. Line the inside of two drinking glasses or jars with wet, folded paper towels. Stuff wet, crumpled paper towels into the centre of the glasses to hold the folded towels against the glass. Place several seeds into each glass; the seeds should be between the paper and the glass. Wrap one glass in black construction paper so that it is *completely* covered; leave the other glass exposed to light. Water (keep the paper towels wet) and watch the seeds over a couple of weeks, unwrapping the one glass only briefly to add water and examine it. Which seeds germinate faster? How do the sprouts compare? Do seeds need light to grow?

2. *Plant Maze:* Can a plant (e.g. bean plant) get through a maze when light is its reward? Get or make a divided box. Cut holes in the dividers to create a path from one corner of the box to the far corner. Cut a fairly large hole in the side of the box at the far corner. Put a small, healthy plant in the corner where the path starts, away from the large hole. Cover the maze so that sunlight streams in only through the hole. Remove the cover briefly to water the plant regularly. What happens after about a week? Does the plant grow in the box? What happens to the green colour of the leaves? Does the plant grow toward the light?

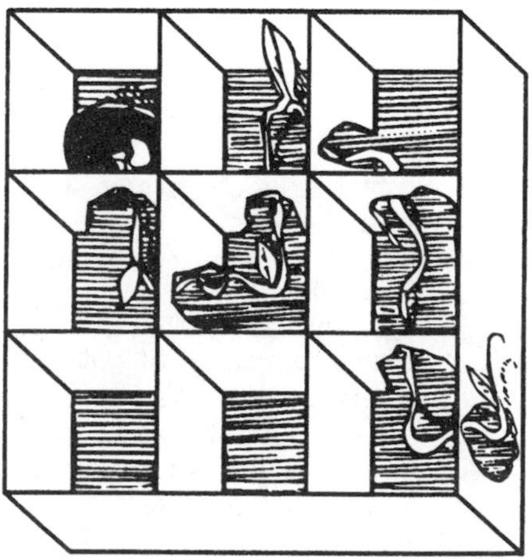

WATERLOGGED

Water is one of the things that plants need to grow. Can plants get *too much* water? Do this experiment to find out.

MATERIALS: Bean seeds; radish seeds; ten clay pots or other containers; plates (for drainage); potting soil; water; watering can; paper; pencil; masking tape to label pots. Optional -- large container.

DOING IT:

1. Soak radish and bean seeds overnight.

2. Fill ten clay pots or other containers almost full with soil.

3. Plant radishes in five of the pots and beans in the other five pots. Plant to the depth recommended on the seed packages.

4. The conditions (i.e. soil, light, temperature) for all of the pots should be identical, with the exception of the watering schedule. Place the bean pots in a row. The bean pot at one end should receive no water. The next bean pot should receive some water. The third bean pot should receive a little more water, perhaps more often than the second pot. The fourth bean pot should receive a fair bit of water, more often than the third pot. The final bean pot should sit continuously in water; if the pot has drain holes, seal them or put the pot, rim deep, in a large container of water. The idea is to move in increments from no water to continuous water. Set up the radish pots in the same way. Label all the pots.

5. Keep a record of the amount and frequency of water each pot receives each day.

6. Dig up the seeds after a week or so. What do they look like? Compare the radish and bean seeds. How much water do seeds need? What is the best watering schedule?

Grow greenery over an ordinary sponge. Wet a sponge and place it in a deep container. Scatter seeds (e.g. radish or grass seeds) thickly and evenly on top of the sponge. Water the sponge daily. Use a spray bottle to sprinkle the water on very lightly; add just enough water so that a small amount drains down to the bottom of the container. You may want to cover the sponge with a clear dish or some plastic wrap to keep in warmth and moisture. Within a week or so, you should have a sponge garden. How long will the plants continue to grow?

Most plants take a fair bit of time to grow -- but not bamboo grass. It's the world's tallest grass. It can grow at a rate of 1 m a day.

Water is necessary for proper germination of seeds. Water is also necessary for plant growth. But seeds and plants that get too much water die. Too much water can cause a seed to rot instead of grow. A plant's roots may need water, but they also need oxygen; too much water blocks the oxygen needed for growth.

Topics: Plant Processes; Scientific Method.

NO SOIL NEEDED

Nutrients are one of the things plants need to grow, but plants don't have to get the nutrients from soil. Try this special way to grow plants without soil.

MATERIALS: Bean seeds (they grow quickly); *plastic or clay* pot; *plastic* container (e.g. juice pitcher) with a rim slightly wider than the base of the plastic or clay pot; water; large, *plastic* watering can; masking tape; vermiculite and hydroponic fertilizer (available from a garden store).

DOING IT:

1. Soak a few bean seeds in water overnight.

"Hydroponics" is the growing of plants without soil. The nutrients plants need are added to the water. Modern hydroponic techniques began to be developed over 100 years ago. Today, there are both hydroponic gardens outdoors and hydroponic greenhouses. Hydroponics has a number of advantages. It's useful when soil conditions are not good for growing plants. It can result in larger, healthier yields of commercial crops. It requires the use of less water than conventional growing because the water is recycled. It also almost eliminates weeds and pests. On the negative side, hydroponics is expensive.

Aside from supplying nutrients, soil holds plants up. In hydroponics, vermiculite (granite rock that has been expanded under pressure) can be used to support plants. Some hydroponic gardeners also use gravel, wood chips, crushed brick, and coarse sand. Plants need to grow in something that will support them and hold moisture, but which will also allow the roots to get air. So, drainage is important in hydroponics. Roots should be submerged in the special hydroponic nutrient solution only briefly, but regularly. There's a delicate balance between water, air, and nutrients. In large hydroponic greenhouses, feeding and drainage are taken care of mechanically. The nutrient solution is continuously pumped in and out of the growing beds. Whatever hydroponic gardeners choose to grow plants in, it must be sterile to prevent disease. Also, the containers used (e.g. pot, watering can) shouldn't be metal; the metal may interact with the nutrient solution and harm the plants.

Topics: Plant Processes; Soil; Resources.

2. Wash all the containers you're using.

3. Use masking tape to reduce the size of the drain holes in the bottom of the pot; the holes must be small, otherwise the vermiculite will spill through. Fill the pot almost full with vermiculite.

4. Plant the beans in the pot. Plant to the depth recommended on the seed package.

5. Wedge the pot into the top of the plastic container. The idea is to set up the pot so that water drains completely through the bottom holes, into the container.

6. For the first week, you can water the beans with ordinary tap water (the seeds have their own food supply). Water carefully, once or twice a day, so that the seeds are kept moist but not wet. Pour water into the pot until it fills the pot almost to the surface of the vermiculite. The water should drain slowly (over several minutes) out of the pot.

7. After the first week, mix some hydroponic fertilizer according to the directions on the package. The bean sprouts now need the nutrients in the fertilizer. Water once or twice a day so that the vermiculite stays moist; never water at night (photosynthesis stops at night). Pour the fertilizer solution into the pot until it fills the pot almost to the surface of the vermiculite. The solution should drain slowly (over several minutes) out of the pot. Collect the solution from the container and reuse it.

8. Mix up fresh fertilizer solution once a week.

9. When the seedlings poke through the vermiculite, place them in a bright spot, but out of direct sunlight. Give the strongest ones room to grow by pulling out all the other seedlings.

10. Your beans will grow just like beans potted in soil. How is vermiculite different than soil?

11. *Variation:* Set up two pots as described. Water one with tap water only and the other with hydroponic solution. Compare the plant growth.

MOLD GARDEN

Fungi have their own kingdom, separate from plants, but they have some similarities to plants. Cultivate your own mold garden.

MATERIALS: Various bits of food (e.g. fruit, vegetables, bread without preservatives, cheddar cheese); plastic bags; twist ties; paper towels; water; soil or dust; magnifying glass. Optional -- can of tomato soup; small containers; plastic wrap; tape; bread crumbs; soil.

DOING IT:

1. Gather together bits of food. Inflate several plastic bags to ensure they *don't have any holes.*

2. Place each kind of food in its own bag. Put a damp (not soaking wet) piece of paper towel into each bag. You can also put in a pinch of soil or dust to provide spores for producing the mold.

3. Let some air into each bag (so the bags don't lay flat) and use twist ties to *securely* close the bags. Keep the bags in a warm, dark place.

4. After several days, molds should appear in the bags. Use a magnifying glass to examine the molds carefully. **Don't open the bags! Throw the bags away without opening them when you're finished examining the molds. Wash your hands after handling the bags.**

5. How many different colours of mold do you grow? What do the molds look like? Do different kinds of mold grow on different foods? Is there more than one kind of mold in each bag?

6. *Variation:* Pour some tomato soup straight from the can into several small containers. Sprinkle a few bread crumbs into one container. Rub your finger over the floor and then dip it into the soup in another container. Sprinkle a pinch of soil into a third container. Seal the containers with plastic wrap and tape. Put them in a warm, dark place for several days. What happens?

"Lemon" drops? Perhaps they should be called mold drops. These days, most citric acid (lemon flavour) is made from a black mold known as *Aspergillus niger.*

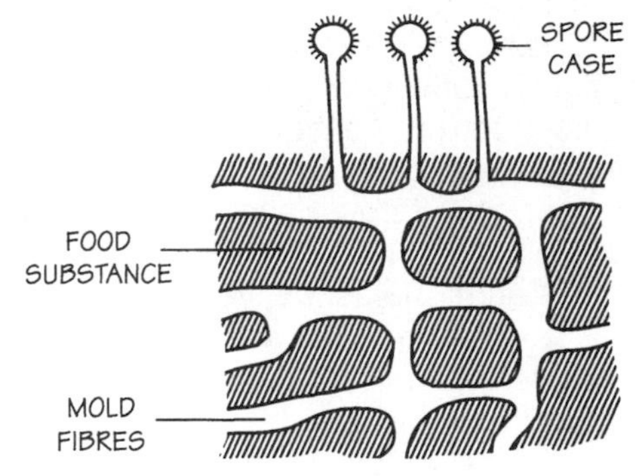

7. *Extension:* Can you grow a prize-winning mold crop? Try different combinations of food, water, light, and heat to determine the conditions under which mold grows best. Label each plastic bag to keep track of the conditions you use.

Fungi don't have any chlorophyll and therefore can't manufacture their own food (like plants can). Many things that make up our garbage serve as food for different kinds of fungi. That's why milk sours, meat rots, cheese gets moldy, cider gets hard, and eggs develop that "rotten egg" odour. Green plants need water, warmth, and sunlight to grow. Fungi need moisture and warmth, but they tend to like darkness. It's estimated that there are 1.5 million species of fungi. Examples of fungi include molds, mushrooms, puffballs, rusts, smuts, yeasts, and lichens.

Molds are particularly interesting because they come in many colours: white, black, green, red, orange, pink, yellow, purple, blue, and gray. The colour and dry, dull, powdery appearance of the surface of most mold colonies is due to millions of spores. Spores work the same way seeds do; each spore can grow into a new fungus. When conditions are right, some fungi make a "fruiting body" (e.g. mushroom) which contains spores. However, most molds don't grow a fruiting body; they have spore cases the size of a pinhead, each of which holds thousands of tiny spores. Molds provide many benefits to humans. Molds are used in making cheese. Penicillin, made from *Penicillium* mold, is an important medicine.

Topics: Microorganisms.

BALLOON BLOW-UP

Yeast needs food to grow; it doesn't manufacture its own food like green plants. What kind of food is best for yeast? Use balloons to find out.

MATERIALS: Three packets of yeast; corn syrup; flour; unflavoured gelatin; unsweetened grape juice; large measuring cup; jar or other container; tablespoons; four *clean*, 750 ml glass pop bottles; four large balloons; masking tape; pen; string; large towel. Optional -- milk; tomato juice; cornstarch; molasses; vegetable oil; coffee.

DOING IT:

1. In a jar or other container, mix together 240 ml of warm water and three packets of yeast.

2. In a measuring cup, mix 120 ml of corn syrup and four tablespoons of the yeast solution. Pour this mixture into a pop bottle. Label the bottle with masking tape.

"Yeast" is the name given to microscopic, single-celled fungi. The oval or round yeast cells reproduce mainly by "budding" (a small bump on the cell's surface increases in size until a wall forms and it separates to form a new cell), and sometimes by means of spores. A packet of powdered yeast doesn't look very alive, but it is. With the right conditions (sugar, water, air, and warmth), the yeast will grow and multiply. In this experiment, the yeast is given four different kinds of food: syrup (partially processed sugar); flour (high in starch); gelatin (high in protein); and grape juice (natural sugar). The balloons expand because of carbon dioxide gas produced by the yeast as it grows. The more growth, the more gas, and the more a balloon expands. Therefore, the biggest balloon indicates the best food for the yeast.

Yeast is used in making bread and the production of alcohol. As yeast grows, it produces "enzymes" which break down sugars and starches into simpler compounds (e.g. carbon dioxide, alcohol). This process is called "fermentation". Yeast makes bread lighter and better tasting. When yeast is added to bread dough, the yeast cells produce enzymes that change the starch in the flour into sugar, and then into alcohol. The alcohol evaporates away as the bread bakes.

Topics: Microorganisms; Scientific Method; Chemical Reactions.

3. Wash the measuring cup. Mix 120 ml of flour, 120 ml of water, and four tablespoons of the yeast solution. Pour this mixture into a second pop bottle and label the bottle.

4. Wash the measuring cup. Mix 120 ml of gelatin solution (prepare the solution according to the directions on the gelatin package) and four tablespoons of the yeast solution. Pour this mixture into a third pop bottle and label the bottle.

5. Wash the measuring cup. Mix 120 ml of grape juice and four tablespoons of the yeast solution. Pour this mixture into the last pop bottle and label the bottle.

6. Loosen up four balloons by blowing them up and then releasing the air. Slip a balloon over the mouth of each of the pop bottles. Wind string around the bottle necks so air can't get in or out of the bottles.

7. In a warm place, lay all the bottles on their sides (use a rolled towel to prop them up so that liquid doesn't flow into the balloons). Check the bottles every half hour. Pick up each bottle, shake it gently to mix the liquid inside, and lay it down again. What happens in each bottle? Do you see small bubbles in any of the bottles (indicating that the yeast is active)? After a couple of hours, which balloon is largest? What is the best food for the yeast? Open the bottles and smell the liquids inside; can you smell alcohol? **Don't taste any of the liquids.**

8. *Extension:* Try other foods (e.g. milk, tomato juice, cornstarch, molasses, oil, coffee).

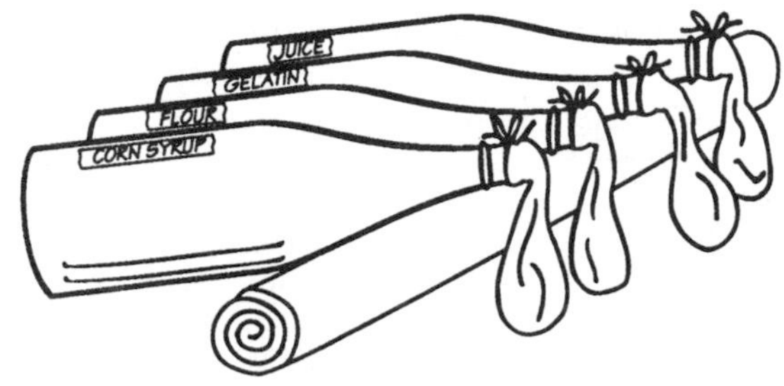

LIVING CREATURES

WILDLIFE WATCHING

The Living Creatures subject area has thirteen One Leads to Another activities. Do the activities as a series, or choose just those activities which interest you.

You can't just read about living creatures. You have to get to know them personally to really appreciate them. You have to visit them in their natural habitat or invite them to visit you. You can also go to a good zoo. Wildlife watching takes patience, but it's worth it. Many people are amazed at the animals around them that they never noticed before.

Any time you're watching an animal, look for answers to the same basic kinds of questions: What colour is it? How big is it? How does it move? How does it see? How many eyes does it have? How does it hear? How does it eat? What does it eat? How does it breathe? How does it sleep? Where does it sleep? How does it defend itself? What kind of animal is it? A good animal identification guide can help you with this last question -- but keep in mind that the names of animals are not necessarily that important. Names mean little until people can appreciate the differences between and uniqueness of various animals.

The series begins with making a Berlese funnel to find simple soil animals. After a brief look at amphibians and reptiles, the series moves to a focus on mammals, birds, and insects. The third and fourth activities involve taking an animal census, making a wildlife map, and constructing a nature blind for watching animals without disturbing them. The next two activities look at mammals, with general hints on finding them and instructions for a squirrel house. The activity that follows contains information on attracting birds and constructing birdhouses and feeders. The eighth and ninth activities provide bird and insect identification tips. The tenth activity involves putting together your own insect zoo. The next two activities look at setting up an ant colony and a worm farm. The final activity involves exploring creatures of the night.

Quickies and Make Time activities in the Living Creatures subject area can complement the wildlife watching series. For example, the activities cover animal body parts and tracks, and introduce basic concepts such as classification, adaptation, and predator/prey relationships.

As you watch wildlife in their natural habitats, keep in mind one basic rule: Take only notes and pictures, and leave nothing but footprints.

Starting Simple

Nematodes are very simple animals that look like pieces of moving thread. Construct a Berlese funnel to find nematodes and other soil animals.

MATERIALS: Can (with both ends removed); funnel; wire mesh (e.g. 3 to 6 mm screen); jar; spoon; water; paper towels; magnifying glass.

DOING IT:

1. Moisten some paper towels with water (don't soak them!) and use them to line the bottom of a jar.

2. Rest a funnel in the mouth of the jar. Cut a round piece of wire mesh and insert it into the top of the funnel.

3. Rest a can (both ends open) on the wire mesh. Put several spoonfuls of soil into the can.

4. Leave the Berlese funnel (named after the scientist who invented it) in full sunlight for a day or so. The funnel works by driving the moisture-loving soil animals away from the heat and light; the animals tunnel deeper into the soil and fall through the wire mesh into the jar.

5. After a day has passed, look for nematodes on the paper towels. Examine the tiny creatures with a magnifying glass. Can you find any other soil animals?

6. *Variation:* Sample soil from different areas (e.g. woods, garden, shoreline). Put leaf litter into the Berlese funnel instead of soil.

7. *Variation:* During winter, bring a chunk of hard-frozen soil indoors and allow it to warm up. Then put it into the Berlese funnel. Place the funnel under a lamp (if possible, one with an inverted, funnel-shaped reflector). You should be able to awaken dormant soil insects, nematodes, and other animals. Soil from areas covered by water in the spring may contain large numbers of mosquito eggs. You can hatch the eggs by placing the soil in a dish of water for a day or two. Other forms of life may also appear when you do this.

Nematodes are eel-like creatures that are cousins of the worm. Despite their tiny size, nematodes come complete with nerves, muscles, and mouths. They are found in water, soil, and as "parasites" in the bodies of other animals, including humans. A parasite is an organism that lives on or in another organism and, by doing so, harms the other organism. Some organisms can live as part of another organism and both organisms benefit; this is usually called a "symbiotic" relationship.

Topics: Soil; Animal Characteristics.

You can start an aquarium to watch fish. Or, you can go to their natural habitats. Lie on your stomach and look into a stream or pond. Look for fish nests, bunches of eggs, or a leftover skeleton.

FROG HIDE-AND-SEEK

Amphibians -- and reptiles -- can be difficult to find. Going on a frog search might be your best bet for finding an amphibian in its natural habitat.

MATERIALS: Plastic zip bags; aquarium or jar.

DOING IT:

1. *Finding Frogs:* Listen for the peeps and croaks of frogs, toads, and bullfrogs. The spring peeper has a high, jingle bell-like whistle; it has a dark brown X on its back. The green frog's call is a dull twang that sounds like a tuned-down banjo; it has a yellowish throat and its ear drums are about equal to the size of its eyes. The American toad's call is a long trill; toads do not cause warts, but they do have warts on their backs. The wood frog's call is a duck-like quack. Wood frogs are usually the first to call in spring; they have a black mask, like a bandit.

2. *Finding Eggs:* Look closely for eggs. Toad eggs are found underwater in quiet pools; look for long spirals with eggs encased in jelly. Wood frog eggs are underwater attached to plants; they are individual spheres in a mass about 10 cm across. Spring peeper eggs are also underwater attached to plants; they are single eggs.

3. *Hatching Eggs:* Collect a string of toad eggs and place them in a jar or aquarium along with pond water. Keep the water cool and fresh. Make sure there are plenty of algae and other plant material from the pond so that when the tadpoles hatch they have food. Once legs begin to form on the tadpoles, it's best to release them in the pond where you found them. Frogs and toads are hard to keep in captivity and they play an important role in ponds and streams by keeping insects under control.

Reptiles include lizards, alligators, crocodiles, snakes, and turtles. The painted turtle is one of the more common species. It has a bright yellow and red edge on its shell and often basks in the sun on exposed logs. The musk turtle is also common, but because it spends most of its time in water, it can be hard to find. It can be very hard to find other types of reptiles. Look for snake skins between rocks and in the grass, and signs of digging along shorelines (you may find egg masses).

The word "amphibian" is Greek for "double life". It refers to the fact that these animals spend part of their lives in water and part on land. For example, frogs start out as eggs. Frog (and toad) eggs are found in jelly-like clumps. The eggs hatch into tiny "tadpoles" or "polliwogs". The tadpoles spend their time in water and have gills to get their oxygen the way fish do. Over a few weeks, the tadpoles grow legs, lose their tail, and, eventually, spend their time on land and breathe with lungs. They capture insects and other food with a sticky, forked tongue. Frogs are able to obtain some oxygen from the water through their skin. This allows them to survive the winter months buried in the mud at the bottom of lakes and streams. When the ground and water warm up in the spring, they return to the surface.

Most amphibians feed on insects and other invertebrates, although sometimes bullfrogs eat other frogs. Tadpoles feed on algae. Amphibians are cold-blooded animals. They are similar to reptiles. One difference between amphibians and reptiles is that reptiles have scales or armour and most amphibians have smooth skin. Another difference is that while amphibians depend on gills in the early stages of their life cycle, reptiles use lungs throughout their lives.

Topics: Habitat; Animal Characteristics.

WHERE ARE THEY?

As you begin watching mammals, birds, and insects, it's a good idea to keep track of where you find certain animals. Take a wildlife census and make a wildlife map.

MATERIALS: Measuring tape; stakes; string; paper; pencils.

DOING IT:

1. A census is a count. When you take a wildlife census, record information such as the types of animals you find, the population levels (i.e. number of each type of animal), and the locations of the various animals.

2. Begin the census by choosing and defining the area to be included. Use stakes and string to mark out a large square around the area. To make your "survey squares", mark lines running vertically and horizontally at equal intervals (e.g. 1 m apart, 10 m apart) within the large square.

3. Survey one square at a time. If a group of people are working on the census, each person can be responsible for surveying one square. Count "what, how many, and where". For example, if you spot some caterpillars, write down how many you find and on which plants in which spots you find them. If you spot a mammal or bird, make a few notes to help identify it (e.g. bird with yellow tail and red beak). Actual sightings of animals should be recorded, as well as signs of animals (discussed on the following pages). Make a note of food (e.g. types of plants, other animals) and water sources. Be thorough.

4. On separate sheets of paper, make a sketch of each square based on the census information collected. Use symbols for different types of shrubs, trees, and potential feeding areas. Put the sketches of the survey squares together to make a large, complete map of the area. You may want to make three separate maps: one for mammals, one for birds, and one for insects.

5. Examine a map to see what wildlife was found. Are you surprised at the variety or number of animals that were found? Can you find certain animals in certain spots on another day?

6. *Extension:* Anytime you spot a new animal, add the information to your wildlife map. Repeat the census periodically to update the map.

Whenever you see a wild animal, the chances are that you are in its home range. Animals are creatures of habit; they travel the same paths again and again. Many animals spend their entire lives in a very small area. Getting to know the ranges of the animals in your area has many advantages. You'll know where to find certain animals and which animals have overlapping ranges. Mammals, in particular, come out of hiding to eat. Get to know their feeding habits if you want to watch them over a period of time. If you come across a spot where an animal has eaten before, and if the area has plenty of food available, the animal is likely to return. One way to watch birds up close is to go to an area they frequent, and sit quietly and wait for them. You'll blend into the area and the birds may not be overly concerned about you being there.

Topics: Mapping.

One way to do population counts with insects is as follows: Collect 50 grasshoppers in a given area. Dab fingernail polish on the inside of one back leg of each. After half a day, catch 50 grasshoppers in the same area and note the number of recaptures. Use this formula to estimate the population: $P = (50 \times 50) / R$, where P = population and R = recaptures.

NATURE BLIND

Mammals and birds won't be frightened away if they don't see you. You can crouch in some bushes or even sit quietly in a car. Or, you can construct a nature blind.

MATERIALS: Large piece of burlap; four wooden stakes; box of tacks; scissors; hammer; brown spray paint; string.

DOING IT:

1. Cut out a piece of burlap to the dimensions shown.

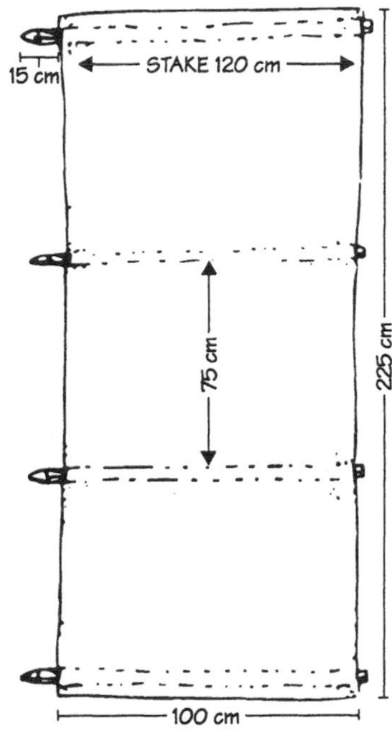

2. Rub the burlap fabric with grass or leaves to help mask the "human smell".

3. Lay the burlap on the ground and slide stakes under it, in the positions shown.

4. Tack the burlap to the stakes, making sure that the stakes stay straight and parallel to one another.

5. Use scissors to cut a window 10 cm x 15 cm in the centre of each burlap wall, at a comfortable viewing height.

6. Use a hammer to lightly tap the stakes into the ground so that the burlap stands up and stretches tight.

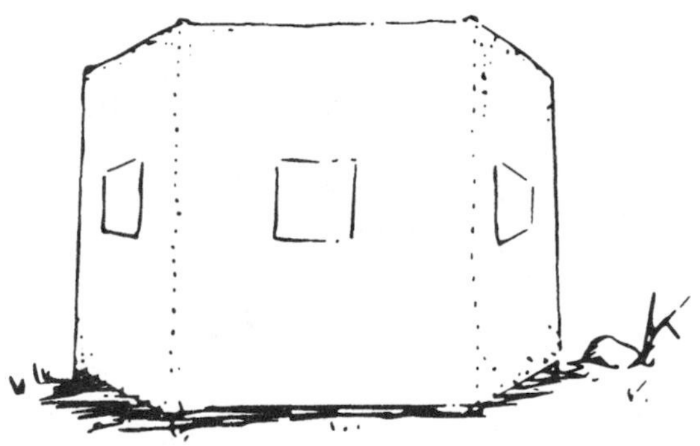

7. Spray-paint brown spots on the burlap to camouflage the blind. Let the paint dry.

8. Pull out the stakes and roll up the blind. Tie the roll with string for easy carrying to your observation sites.

Many animals are shy, and you have to be a little tricky to get close to them. A "blind" is a structure which resembles the natural surroundings and in which you can hide and watch animals. It helps you blend into the surroundings. The ideal place for a wildlife observation site is near a body of water, in a wooded area. Whenever you set up a blind, you should leave it alone for a couple of days so that animals can get used to it. The animals will eventually accept the blind as a part of the environment. Place the blind so that the prevailing wind blows away from the animals and toward you -- otherwise animals will pick up your scent. When going into the blind, be quiet and sneaky to avoid drawing attention to yourself. Try to enter and leave when wildlife activity is slow. Carry something to snack on and to read while you're waiting for animals. Wildlife watching takes patience and involves sitting quietly for a period of time.

Topics: Habitat.

MAMMAL SEARCH

Mammals are generally shy, quiet, dull-coloured, and, frequently, nocturnal (they come out only at night). Here are some tips for finding them in their natural habitats.

MATERIALS: Optional -- binoculars; animal identification guide.

DOING IT:

1. Start a mammal search by walking through woods, fields, or along a shoreline. Pay special attention to areas where water meets land or field meets forest. In these areas, sunlight stimulates a variety of plant growth which attracts animals.

2. Be as quiet as possible; step softly and try not to brush against bushes. Many animals have keen hearing. If an animal becomes alert and you think it has heard or seen you, freeze in your tracks. You may want to crouch down to disguise your human shape. Most animals watch for movements; if you're still, they're likely not to see you.

3. If you listen carefully, your ears will often give you the first clue that a mammal is nearby. Listen for the sound of feet scampering across dried leaves or a body brushing against shrubs.

Some common mammals include the badger, beaver, caribou, cat, deer, dog, fox, gopher, groundhog, moose, mouse, raccoon, skunk, squirrel, and woodchuck. Look for the animals themselves or signs that the animals have been in the area.

Topics: Mammals.

4. To use your vision effectively, begin scanning an area by holding your hands around your eyes like binoculars. This narrows your concentration. Once you've spotted an animal, you might want to look at it more closely with real binoculars. Get an overall view, then focus on hair, head, eyes, feet, and other details. Can you tell the animal's sex? Deer are the easiest animals to identify on sight; only male deer, elk, and moose have antlers.

5. Stay downwind of animals to keep your scent behind you and away from the animals you're watching. Stay at a comfortable distance for both you and the animals. Never approach baby animals or an animal with its young. Avoid male deer during mating season, as they are unpredictable.

6. If you're watching an animal and it suddenly disappears, it may simply have stopped and blended into the scene. Carefully examine the spot where you last saw the animal. The animal may be standing still and watching you!

7. If you can't find many animals, look for animal signs. Look up, down, and under things. Signs include "scats" (animal droppings), tracks, trails, hairs, bones, partly eaten food, stores of surplus food, signs of digging, nibble or scratch marks on trees, holes *(never reach inside!)*, and mounds on the ground. Some types of mammals leave distinctive markings behind when they've been in an area. Look for browse lines (all the available branches and foliage in a hedge or group of trees are stripped away up to as high as the browsing species concerned can reach). Many mammals make marking points along the boundary of their territory. Squirrels mark by gnawing and stripping sturdy trees near the roots or on the underside of the lowest branches. Other animals deposit urine, feces, and scent at marking points, giving rise to a dark, strong-smelling patch on a tree or the ground.

Inviting Mammals To Visit

You can visit mammals in their homes -- or invite them to visit you. Set up a watering and food site, put out food to attract mammals, and build a squirrel house.

MATERIALS: Brush (i.e. twigs, branches, and logs); large container or trough of water; wild hay and other foods described below; a board approximately 1 cm thick x 25 cm wide x 2.4 m long; two hinges with screws; screwdriver; hammer and nails; saw; pencil; ruler. Optional -- drill; binoculars; animal identification guide.

DOING IT:

1. *Watering and Food Site:* To attract larger mammals, build a brush pile about 3 to 5 m at the base and about 2 m high. Pile twigs and branches over a heavier log base. The brush pile gives animals a place to scratch and to sharpen their teeth. Make a rack of some sort to hold wild hay and other suitable foods. Set up a large container or trough full of water.

2. *Foods That Attract:* A common small mammal mixture consists of 1 part suet (melted beef fat), 1 part peanut butter, and 1 part oatmeal. Mix the ingredients well; spread the mixture on the ground, on rocks, or on tree trunks. Other "attractive" foods: apples, fresh vegetables (rabbit); fish, meat scraps, fresh vegetables (muskrat); sunflower seeds, peanuts (chipmunk and ground squirrel); corn, nuts, sunflower seeds (tree squirrel); stringbeans, corn, lettuce, apples, potato (woodchuck); dog food, meat scraps, eggs, fruits (raccoon); salt block, apples (deer).

3. *Squirrel House:* Build a house for squirrels (with variations, it can also be a birdhouse; described on following pages). Mark (i.e. write front, side, etc.) and cut a board as follows:

TOP 30 CM	FRONT 38 CM	SIDE 38 CM	SIDE 38 CM	BACK 51 CM	BASE

25 CM

240 CM

Cut a 7.5 cm x 7.5 cm square from the top, right corner of the front as an entrance. Nail the front and the sides together. Nail on the back so that it's higher at the top of the box. Measure the exact size needed for the base; it should fit snugly inside the other pieces. Cut out the base and nail it in place.

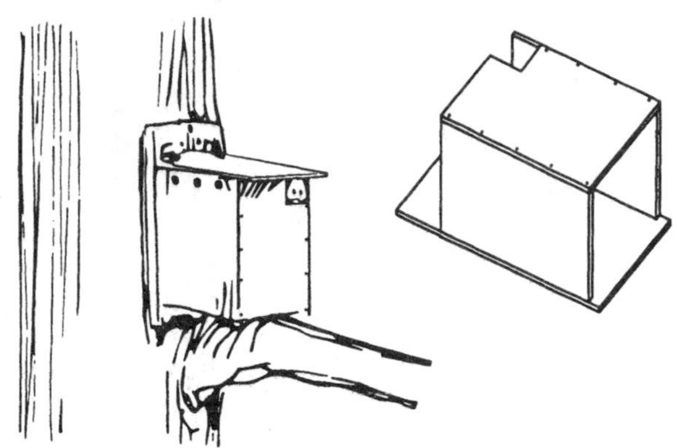

Hinge the top to the back. Hammer (or drill) two or three holes (ideally, 1 cm diameter) just under the roof on each side of the box for ventilation. Also, make five small holes in the base for water drainage. If you wish, you can paint the outside of the house a natural colour. *Never paint the inside!* Attach the house to a tree or post, 3-5 m above the ground; you can set the base on a branch for support. The house should be in a shady spot so that the inside won't get too hot.

Simulating mammal habitats not only makes observation more convenient, but also gives you some insights into the habitat needs of various animals. There are a few important points to keep in mind as you invite mammals to visit. Whenever possible, handle food with gloves and rub materials with grass or leaves to mask the "human smell". Once you start feeding animals, you should continue to do so. Animals will expect food in a certain place. And if there are bears in your area, be careful that you don't attract more than you can handle!

Squirrels are easy mammals to attract, particularly in winter. The squirrel family covers a wide variety of mammals, including woodchucks, marmots, prairie dogs and chipmunks, as well as the common tree squirrel. If you have bushes with berries or seeds, squirrels will be attracted to these. Squirrels and chipmunks will also often raid bird feeders. Flying squirrels feed at night; shine a light on some sunflower seeds in a feeder to attract them.

Topics: Mammals; Habitat.

Inviting Birds To Visit

Birds can be difficult to approach because they have keen eyesight and are very timid. It's best if you use a nature blind or encourage them to come to you.

MATERIALS: As described on the next page; foods described below. Optional -- binoculars; bird identification guide.

DOING IT:

1. *Birdhouses and Feeders:* Locate birdhouses, birdbaths, and feeders close to trees and shrubs to provide birds with refuge from predators. The location of a birdhouse is almost as important as its dimensions. For example, chickadees like a house at the edge of woods. Fill the box with sawdust or wood chips; chickadees like to clean house. A bluebird house should be in an open area. If bluebirds don't nest there, tree swallows probably will. Wrens will nest almost anywhere, but they prefer a house at the edge of woods or in an orchard. Make sure all birdhouses are firmly attached to trees or poles. Face the entrance away from the prevailing wind. Clean the houses once a year -- when you're sure they're not in use.

2. *Foods That Attract:* Birds are always hungry. They use up so much energy that they need to eat all the time. Feed birds suet (melted beef fat), bread crumbs, sunflower seeds, crushed corn, chicken feed, squash seeds, or peanut butter. Hang orange peels or unsalted peanuts in their shell by strings from a tree branch. You can also gather some "natural" bird food. Look for lamb's-quarters in unweeded gardens. Knotweed grows in hard-packed soils (it has reddish seeds and spear-shaped leaves). Dock and ragweed are common weeds found in meadows and on roadsides. Hang a bunch of weeds (with seeds) from a tree near bushes, or strip the seeds and put them into a feeder you've made. Watch to see which seeds attract which birds. If you start feeding birds in the fall, continue to spring. Birds will come to depend on the food supply, and if it's stopped suddenly they may starve before finding a new source.

Birds are found everywhere and getting them to come to you is easy. If you do look for birds in their natural habitats, sound is a sure giveaway that they're nearby. Also look for foot tracks in mud, lost feathers, old nests, broken egg shells, white droppings, pellets of bone and fur (owls), and holes in trees (woodpeckers).

Birds do a lot of beneficial things, including waging a constant war on insects, destroying thousands of tonnes of weed seeds annually, and keeping down rat and mice populations.

Topics: Birds; Habitat.

At some times of the year, it's possible to find a bird's nest which is no longer in use. *Before you take a nest, make sure the birds are finished with it; you should never disturb a bird or its eggs during the nesting season!* Place the nest in a shallow pan of water for a couple of weeks. Watch for seeds to sprout. What did the bird eat? What was its favourite food? Do any of the nesting materials themselves start to grow? What is the nest made of? Where did the bird get the materials?

IDEAS FOR ATTRACTING BIRDS

BIRDHOUSES: Follow the general instructions in the previous activity for making a squirrel house; use the specifications below as a guide for adapting the house to attract particular birds. The illustration gives you an idea of what the finished birdhouse should look like; be sure to place a piece of dowel or bark just under the entrance hole to help birds get a firm footing.

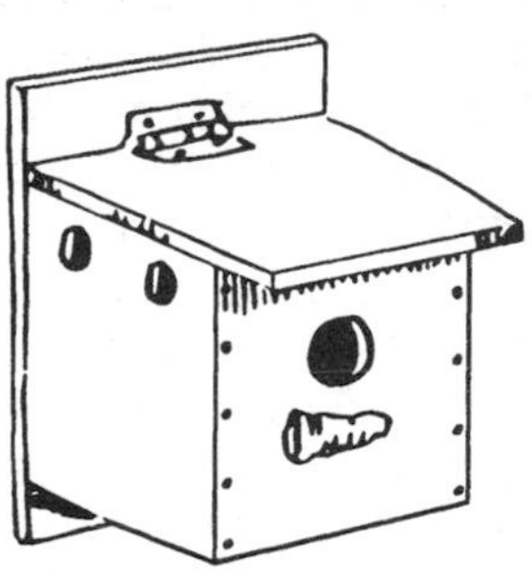

Species	Size of Base (cm)	Height (cm)	Entrance Above Base (cm)	Diameter of Entrance (cm)	Height Above Ground (m)
Bluebird	13 x 13	25	20	3.8	1.5-3.5
Chickadee	10 x 10	20-25	15-20	2.9	2.0-4.5
Nuthatch	10 x 10	20-25	15-20	3.2	4.0-6.0
House Wren	10 x 10	15-20	3-15	2.5-3.2	2.0-3.0
Tree Swallow	13 x 13	15	3-15	3.8	3.0-5.0
Purple Martin	15 x 15	15	2.5	6.4	5.0-6.0
Flicker	18 x 18	41-46	35-41	6.4	2.0-6.0
Downy Woodpecker	10 x 10	23-30	15-20	3.2	2.0-6.0
Hairy Woodpecker	15 x 15	30-38	23-30	3.8	2.0-6.0

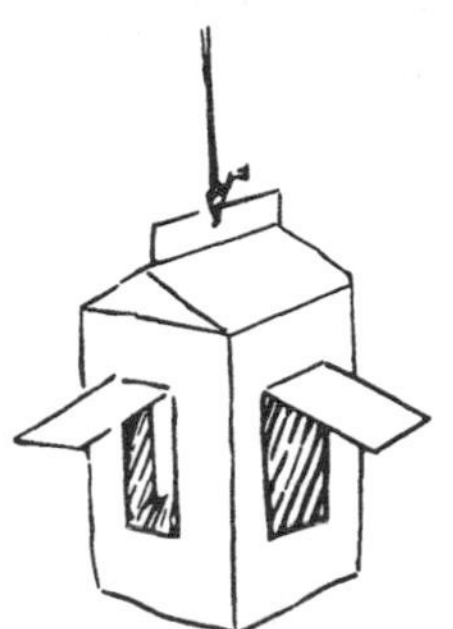

BIRD FEEDERS: Make a basic feeder by filling an upside-down plunger with bird food. Use two pie plates on a pole for a high-rise feeder. To make hanging feeders, suspend milk cartons or plastic bottles from tree branches. For a feeder that's a little more unique, tie a string securely around a pinecone. Smear the cone liberally with peanut butter (fill up all the spaces!), then roll it in mixed seeds. Hang the feeder on a tree branch.

HUMMINGBIRD FEEDER: Hummingbirds love red flowers. Draw a large flower on a 12 cm x 12 cm piece of white cardboard. Cut out the flower and paint both sides *bright* red. Stand the open end of a tall, thin, tube-like container on the middle of the flower and draw around it. Cut out the shape you've drawn. Slide the flower over the container and tape it in place about 1 cm from the open end. Tie or tape the feeder to a small stick and push the stick into the ground, among some flowers (hummingbirds are attracted to petunias, morning glories, and snapdragons). Make a honey solution to fill the feeder (one part honey to three parts warm water; stir well). Check the level of the solution every few days and refill the container when it's half empty.

DONATIONS TO A BIRD'S NEST: Bend a wire hanger into a square shape. Attach a mesh material (e.g. onion bag, nylon net) to the wire frame. Loosely weave yarn, strips of fabric, and string through the mesh. Birds will pick the materials from the mesh. Most birds build their nests in the spring.

BIRDBATHS: Make a simple birdbath out of an upside-down plunger. Or, use a flat pan on a wooden platform raised on a high pole. Avoid a metal pan because it can get hot in summer. The pan should have a rim birds can rest on. Fill the pan with about 5 cm of water. Barbed wire around the bath's stand prevents predators from reaching birds.

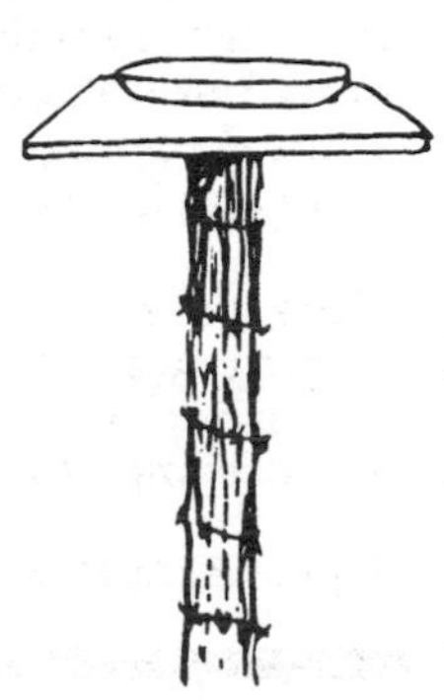

Bird I.D. Tips

If an animal has feathers, you know it's a bird. There are other things you can look for to narrow down your identification.

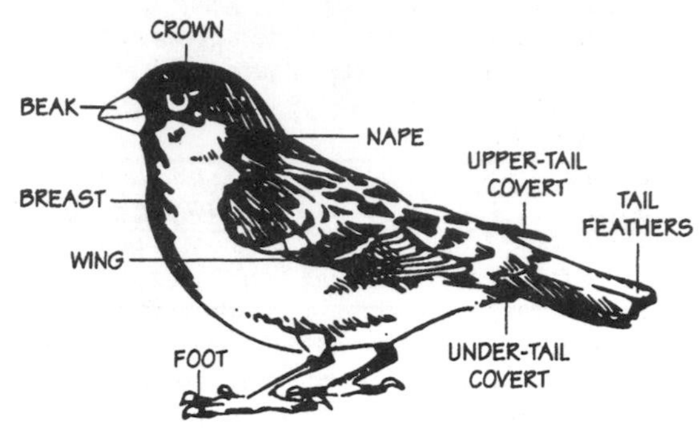

MATERIALS: Optional -- binoculars; a bird identification guide.

DOING IT:

1. *Size:* Is the bird larger than a sparrow (length = 15 cm), a robin (length = 25 cm), or a crow (length = 50 cm)?

2. *Body:* Is the body plump, bulky, sleek, thin, short and stubby, or streamlined? Does the tail point up or down? Is the tail rounded, wedged, squared, or notched? Are the wings long and graceful, or short and stubby? Are they rounded, pointed, or ragged? Is the beak thick, thin, heavy, wide, long, short, curved, hooked, or pointed? Are the legs long or short? Are the feet webbed or clawed?

3. *Shading:* Look at variations in colour on the throat, belly, wings, tail, and markings of feathers. Does the bird's head have a crest, crown patch, or crown stripes? Is the breast striped, spotted, or unmarked?

4. *Song:* What type of noise does the bird make? Can you imitate the sound?

5. *Surroundings:* Where is the bird located (e.g. treetop, vertical position on tree trunk, meadow, wooded area, prairie, shoreline, in water)?

6. *Flight:* What are the bird's flying characteristics (e.g. jerky, darting, swooping, irregular)?

7. *Males, Females, and Babies:* Male birds are easy to recognize by their brilliant colours and well-defined markings, while females are camouflaged by earthy tones. Even if the male and female are similar, the female will be the plainer of the two. A dull or plain colouring helps to protect (hide) the female bird while she is sitting on the nest. All baby birds have large, brightly-coloured mouths so that their parents can easily find them.

8. *Feathers:* Since feathers are the distinctive feature of birds, it's interesting to look closely at the feathers of different birds. The most common feather found along many woodland trails comes from the blue jay. Smash a blue jay feather and it will turn black; the feather's blue colour results from reflected light. Doves have gray-brown feathers with white tips; these feathers are also frequently found along trails. The flicker has sharply pointed and stiff feathers; each feather has a yellow shaft with a black tip. Flickers use their stiff tail feathers to rest against tree trunks. Owls have striped feathers, a little like a brown tiger. Crows have large, black feathers with white shafts.

Birds lay eggs with hard shells. The eggs are usually laid in a carefully prepared nest, and then incubated until the young hatch. The parents feed the young and teach them to fly. Many young birds never leave the nest; of those that do, only about two-thirds live through the first year. The life span of the average small bird is short (less than two years). Many birds that nest and rear their young in northern areas migrate farther south in the fall to escape the cold winter weather and inadequate food supply. Vast numbers of birds eat insects. Taste and smell are poorly developed in birds. The sense of touch is somewhat deadened by a bird's feathers and by the nature of the hard beak and claws. Sight and hearing, on the other hand, are exceptionally keen.

Topics: Birds; Classification.

INSECT I.D. TIPS

A true insect has six legs and three main body parts -- the head, thorax, and abdomen. There are other things you can look for to narrow down your identification.

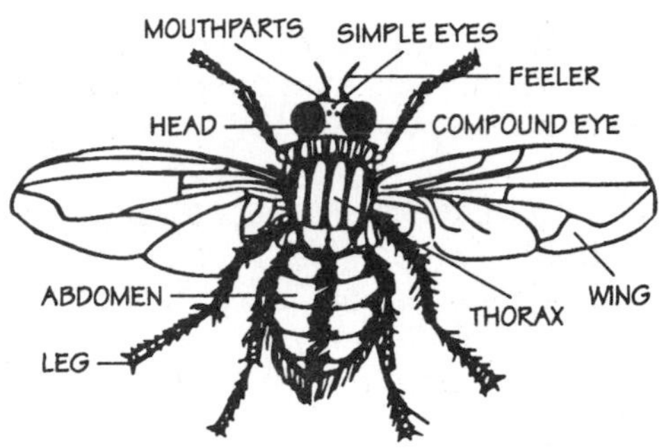

MATERIALS: Magnifying glass. Optional -- an insect identification guide.

DOING IT:

1. *In General:* In their immature, worm-like forms (larvae), many insects can be difficult to identify. Also, don't confuse insects with their relatives (e.g. a spider isn't an insect because it has eight legs and only two main body parts).

2. *Body:* Is the insect's body streamlined and delicate, or rounded and armoured? Does it have any special markings or unique features? Is it the same colour all over?

3. *Wings:* Does the insect have wings (the wings may be hidden from view)? If so, are the wings large and fuzzy, or short and lacy?

4. *Antennae or Feelers:* What kind of antennae does the insect have? Do they look like little clubs? Do they look feathery?

5. *Legs:* Does the insect look like a swimmer, a crawler, or a jumper?

6. *Mouthparts:* How does the insect eat: by chewing (grasshopper); sucking (butterfly); lapping (bee); sponging (fly); or piercing (bugs)?

7. *Colouring:* Does the insect's appearance mimic flower colours or bark patterns?

8. *Nine Common Insect Orders:*

- *Odonata:* Dragonfly, damselfly. Carnivorous; chewing mouthparts; huge eyes; two pairs of equal-sized wings.
- *Orthoptera:* Cricket, roach, grasshopper, katydid. Herbivorous; chewing mouthparts; two pairs of wings (front wings narrow and leathery, back wings broad and folded under front wings when at rest), although some wingless.
- *Isoptera:* Termite. Social; chewing mouthparts.
- *Hemiptera:* True bugs (other insects are often mistakenly called bugs); includes chinch bug, bedbug, many aquatic species. Piercing-sucking mouthparts; wings, if present, overlap back over abdomen.
- *Homoptera:* Aphid, leafhopper. Piercing-sucking mouthparts; wingless or one or two pairs of wings.
- *Lepidoptera:* Butterfly, moth. Sucking mouthparts; two pairs of scaly, usually broad wings; caterpillar larvae. Butterflies tend to be more brightly coloured. A butterfly's antennae are clubbed or enlarged at the tip, while a moth's are tapering and threadlike or plumy.
- *Diptera:* Fly, mosquito. Piercing-sucking or sponging mouthparts; large eyes; front wings transparent; hind wings replaced by short, knobbed structures.
- *Coleoptera:* Beetle, ladybug, firefly, many aquatic insects like whirligig. Chewing mouthparts; hard body parts and wings.
- *Hymenoptera:* Bee, wasp, ant, hornet. Many social; chewing or chewing-lapping mouthparts; some have a stinger.

Every year, more than 7,000 new species of insects are discovered and described by scientists. Almost all insects start out as tiny eggs. Some insects (e.g. butterfly, moth) undergo four distinct changes (egg, larva, pupa, adult); this is called "metamorphosis". Other insects (e.g. grasshopper) undergo a more gradual development in which each consecutive stage is only slightly different from the preceding one, but the overall change is significant; this is known as "incomplete metamorphosis". Insects have a short life, generally a year or a single season. Insects do not have bones. They have an external skeleton called an "exoskeleton". Insects probably function more on instinct than by senses. For example, they have eyes, but it's likely that they do not see as well as many other animals. "Simple" eyes are made up of only one lens and probably see little more than light and dark. "Compound" eyes are made up of dozens, even thousands, of separate lenses. They are superior to simple eyes, but still provide far from excellent vision.

Topics: Insects; Classification.

Insect Zoo

Put together your own insect zoo. Collect and keep small creatures for a short time to get a close-up view of how they look and what their lives are like.

Insects are easy to find and collect because they're everywhere. The main reasons that insects are so plentiful are that they reproduce very quickly and can adapt to many types of environments.

If you keep *caterpillars* long enough, you may see them change into butterflies or moths. For a caterpillar home, place soil on the bottom of a jar and a piece of bark at a slant against the side of the jar (in case the caterpillar goes into its pupal stage). Take a twig with leaves on it from where you find the caterpillar and place the twig in a small container of water in the jar so that the leaves stay fresh longer. How many legs do caterpillars have? For *millipedes,* start with a layer of moist soil, followed by a layer of green leaves, and then a layer of bits of fruit (e.g. apple, banana, orange). How many legs do millipedes have? For *slugs,* start with a layer of moist soil, followed by a layer of dead leaves, and then bits of fruits or vegetables (e.g. carrot, apple, potato, pear). Slugs like a dark environment. For *sow bugs,* start with a layer of moist soil followed by a layer of damp leaves. Lay a piece of bark in the home as a place to hide. Sow bugs also like a dark environment. A *cricket* home should have a layer of soil followed by moist clumps of leaves or grass. Crickets also like to hide under rocks. Does the cricket chirp? Only male crickets chirp, to attract a female mate. Female crickets have a spike at the end of their abdomen (for storing and burying eggs). A *grasshopper* home should have a layer of soil or sand followed by a layer of grasses. You might also put in bits of a raw corn cob. Add a wet cotton ball. How does a grasshopper's colour help camouflage it? For *houseflies,* place moist sawdust at the bottom of the jar. Tie a piece of meat or a cotton ball soaked with honey or sugar to a piece of string. Hang the food in the jar and tape the other end of the string to the outside of the jar. A hint for getting flies into their home: put them in the freezer for a few seconds to slow them down. For *ladybugs,* place a wet cotton ball in the jar. Add a piece of plant (e.g. rose) that has live aphids. Do all ladybugs have the same number of spots on their back? Do they walk in a straight line or zig-zag?

Topics: Insects; Habitat.

MATERIALS: Jars with lids; 1 m x 1.5 m piece of old, white bed sheet or other fabric; cardboard; wire coat hanger; broom or hockey stick handle; netting or cheesecloth; scissors; needle and thread; stapler; string; tape; can (top removed) or plastic container; hammer and nail; trowel; sugar, honey, jam, or similar sweet bait; piece of meat or similar solid bait; large glass jars (ideally, wide-mouth); elastic bands; black construction paper; window screening; large plastic bottle bottoms of the same circumference and depth or round cake pans; felt marker; cardboard box; small plastic containers (e.g. pill bottles); glue; cotton balls; toothpicks; ruler; magnifying glass; spray bottle; water; foods and simulated habitats described. Optional -- nylon stockings; plaster of Paris; insect identification guide.

DOING IT:

1. *Finding Insects:* A great place to look for insects is around plants, particularly under leaves. Look for egg cases glued to twigs, irregular blotches on leaves, swellings (galls) in plant stems, empty cocoons, tiny holes and tunnels in tree trunks and branches, and nibbled flowers and leaves. *As you collect insects, leave an area as undisturbed as possible. Capture only a few insects.*

2. *Catching Insects:* Many insects can be caught by simply scooping them into jars. Don't worry about putting holes in the jar lids; there's enough air in a jar for tiny creatures to live for several hours. Open a jar every few hours for a couple of seconds to replenish the air supply. To catch a flying insect, wait until it's busy at a flower or sitting on a leaf. Hold the jar over the leaf or

flower. As the insect flies upward, put on the lid. To capture crawling insects, lay a piece of cardboard in their path and, once they're on the cardboard, drop them into the jar. Another way to catch insects is to use a beating cloth. Spread out a piece of old bed sheet under a bush or tree. Gently knock or shake the plant. Catch insects on the cloth as they fall. To make an insect collection net for capturing flying and hopping insects, start by straightening the hook on a coat hanger. Bend the rest of the hanger into a circle. Sew or staple some netting or other cloth onto the wire loop to make a deep bag (use pattern below). Securely tape the straightened part of the hanger to a broom or hockey stick handle. Use the net to sweep through lighter grasses. Once an insect is in the net, grasp the upper part of the net so that the insect can't get out. Remember, you may catch stinging insects -- *be careful!* Also, it takes great skill to catch flying insects -- particularly dragonflies -- without hurting them.

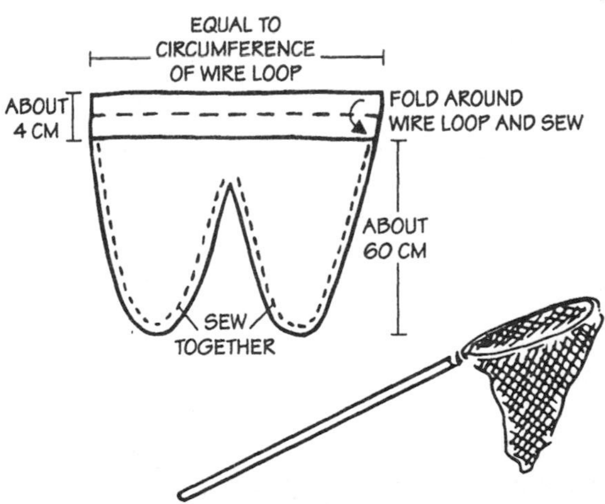

Finally, you can catch insects using an inground trap. Punch a few holes in the bottom of a can or plastic container. Sink the container into the ground so that its top is level with the ground. For bait, use a tiny piece of meat left to decay, or a couple of drops of molasses or honey. Cover the container with a rock or a piece of wood (allow some air space) to protect captured insects from the rain. Experiment with different baits to see which foods attract which insects.

3. *Insect Homes:* Once you've captured insects, they need a comfortable temporary home. Don't make homes from metals, which can corrode. The simplest home is a large, wide-mouth glass jar covered with netting or nylon stocking secured with an elastic band.

CATERPILLAR HOME

To make a larger home ideal for butterflies and moths, use window screening and two straight-sided, round cake pans or the bottoms of large plastic bottles. Measure the circumference of the pans with a piece of string; allow 2 cm of overlap. Use the string to measure a length of window screening. A rule of thumb for determining the height of the home is a ratio of one (height) to one and a half (length of screening); homes that

are too tall will be unstable. Cut out the piece of screening. Punch a few drainage holes in the pan that will form the bottom of the home. Put the home together as shown, using staples to fasten the screening into a cylinder (use a needle and thread to fasten any part of the screen you can't staple). To make the home sturdier, pour plaster of Paris into the bottom, insert the screen cylinder, and allow the plaster to harden overnight.

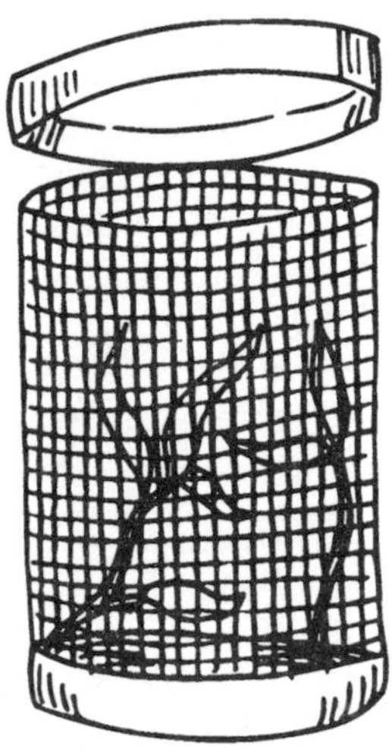

Make another type of small creature home out of a cardboard box. Use nylon net or window screening to make windows and a top. The home illustrated has plastic containers inserted through the side to hold food and drops of water; glue cotton balls inside the box, directly under the containers, to help insects crawl in.

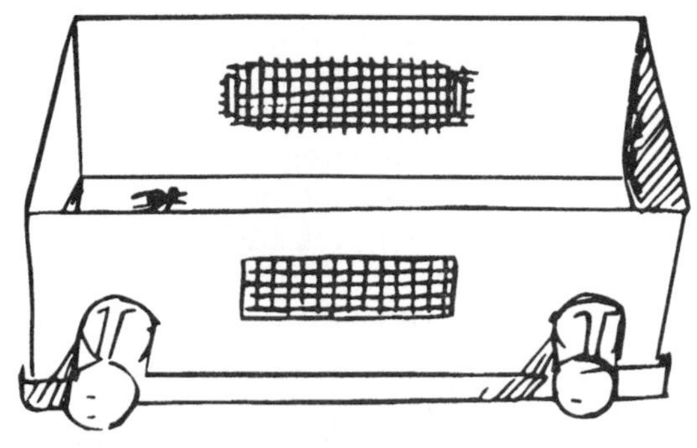

4. *Simulating Natural Habitats:* Tips for simulating natural habitats for particular small creatures are described on the first page of this activity. In general, try to duplicate a creature's natural habitat as much as possible (e.g. wet, dry, shady, sunny, warm, cool). Examine the area from which you take a creature and gather soil and plants from that area. For creatures that like a damp environment, don't forget to use a spray bottle to sprinkle a little water (not too much!) into their home daily. Tape black construction paper around jars housing creatures that like the dark. Clean homes regularly to prevent food from rotting.

5. *Food:* Fill a home with bits of grass, bark, twigs, and leaves from a creature's natural habitat. Creatures like caterpillars like fresh leaves as their food. Different creatures may also eat honey, small pieces of fruit, whole-wheat bread, cooked meat, and freshly-killed insects. All creatures need water; put a small container of water into some homes, a wet cotton ball in others, and for some others sprinkle in a little water every day to keep the environment moist.

6. *Examining Insects:* Use a magnifying glass to examine insects. Look at legs, antennae, eyes, wings, mouthparts, and colouring. Use a ruler to measure the length of a creature. What happens if you put a drop of water in a creature's path? What happens if you put a toothpick in its path? Put a piece of moist paper towel in front of a creature to see if it prefers to be on top of or underneath moist places.

7. *Releasing Insects:* Keep most insects in their temporary homes for only a short period of time. Return them to where you found them when you've finished making your observations.

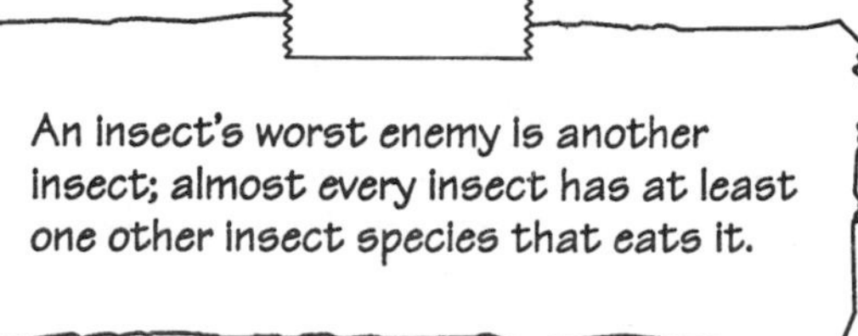

ANT COLONY

Ants are social insects. It's fascinating to watch them work together. Set up an ant colony in a jar.

MATERIALS: Trowel; plastic zip bag; large, wide-mouth glass jar; smaller glass jar or plastic container (with lid) which fits into larger jar; netting, cheesecloth, or nylon stocking; elastic band; black construction paper; masking tape; small piece of sponge; water; spray bottle; honey; magnifying glass. Optional -- paint; toothpick.

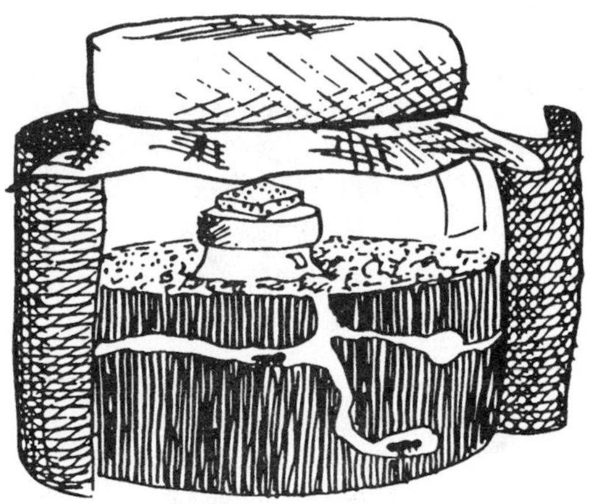

DOING IT:

1. Find your ants in good soil. Ant hills look like mounds of loose earth. Look carefully for a queen (she's bigger than other ants). Quickly and carefully place her, some soil, any white eggs and larvae, and as many ants as possible into a plastic bag and seal it. Take all your ants from one hill or nest.

2. Put the lid on a small jar and place the jar inside a larger jar. Scoop the soil and ants into the space between the small and large jar. Don't pack down the soil too much.

3. Keep a moist (not wet) piece of sponge lying on top of the small jar at all times. Also, every day, use a spray bottle to keep the soil slightly moist (not wet).

4. Provide the ants with a little food. Overfeeding will kill the ants; one drop of honey will feed 50 ants for a week. Experiment with different kinds of food.

5. Cover the large jar with netting, cheesecloth, or nylon stocking and secure it with an elastic band. Tape black paper around the outside of the jar so that the ants will tunnel close to the glass. Remove the paper only for observation purposes. Observe the colony in dim light.

6. Keep the ant colony in a dim, cool place. If, after a few days, the ants are busy making new tunnels, they are happy. Any other activity means they're unhappy and should be returned to their natural habitat.

7. How do the ants spend their time? How do social insects work with one another? What do the tunnels look like? What do two ants do when they meet each other? How do ants use their antennae? Examine ants through a magnifying glass.

8. *Extension:* Bring in a strange ant from another colony (a little paint will help identify it). What happens?

Ants belong to the same insect order as bees and wasps. An ant colony functions much like a family, with a division of labour among workers, individuals cooperatively caring for the young, and an overlapping of two or more generations. Ant colonies are usually made up of three groups of ants: winged, fertile females; wingless, infertile female workers; and winged males. Female worker ants each have a specific job: some obtain food; some care for the young; some construct the nest and dig the tunnels; others keep the nest clean. The males are present only for mating and die after the queen has been fertilized. Each nest has one or more queens to lay the eggs. Ants communicate with each other using their antennae and chemical odours. They protect themselves by escaping and biting. They are essentially helpful insects because they clean up the garbage humans leave behind.

Topics: Insects; Habitat.

Worm Farm

An earthworm is a soft, segmented animal that lives in the ground. Set up a worm farm in a jar.

An earthworm's reddish tinge is caused by "hemoglobin" -- which also gives human blood its red colour.

An earthworm is both male and female, so it can reproduce without ever meeting another worm.

Worms aren't insects because they don't have six legs and three main body parts. Worms aren't snakes because they don't have a backbone. And worms aren't lizards because they don't have legs. There are little bristles on the underside of each segment, or division, of a worm's body. A worm uses these bristles to crawl. An adult worm is around 20 cm long and has 100-200 segments along its body. The worm's brain is located in segment three; its five primitive hearts lie between segments five and eleven; and its mouth is between segment one and the worm's knob end. A worm is something like a water bed. It has what is called a "hydrostatic skeleton", which is a cavity between its muscles and its guts that contains fluid. This fluid gives the body shape and makes the worm a flexible animal.

Earthworms are able to force their way through soft earth; they must eat their way through harder soil. The earth a worm eats passes through its alimentary canal (digestive system) and is deposited on the ground's surface as castings. Castings improve the ability of the soil to grow plants. Earthworms also turn rotting plants and animals into rich fertilizer. And, as they burrow through the soil, they create spaces for air and water to penetrate.

Topics: Habitat; Soil; Animal Characteristics.

MATERIALS: Plastic zip bag; trowel; two large, wide-mouth jars; sand; soil; netting, cheesecloth, or nylon stocking; elastic band; black construction paper; masking tape; spray bottle; magnifying glass; paper towels; newspaper; water; foods described below. Optional -- flashlight covered with red cellophane.

DOING IT:

1. To find earthworms, look on the ground after a rain shower, preferably in the evening. Cover a flashlight with red cellophane (worms can't see red light) and walk softly (so the worms won't feel the ground vibrate). Another way to find worms is to dig in a shady, damp area. Scoop up about five earthworms and as much of the soil from their home site as possible into a plastic bag.

2. Separate the worms from the soil. Pack a jar firmly about 3/4 full with alternating layers of sand and soil; soil layers should be thicker than sand layers. Place the worms on the top layer.

3. Use a spray bottle to sprinkle the soil with a little water so that the soil is damp but not wet. If an earthworm drys out, it will die. Be sure to sprinkle a little water in the worm farm every day.

4. Sprinkle in bits of food. Try cornmeal (mashed corn), fats, decaying leaves, manure, straw, peat moss, moist leaf mold, sugar, coffee grounds, fruit, and vegetables. Put food in the farm once a week.

5. Cover the jar with netting, cheesecloth, or nylon stocking and secure it with an elastic band. Tape dark paper around the jar. Remove the paper only for observation purposes. Keep the jar in a dim, cool place.

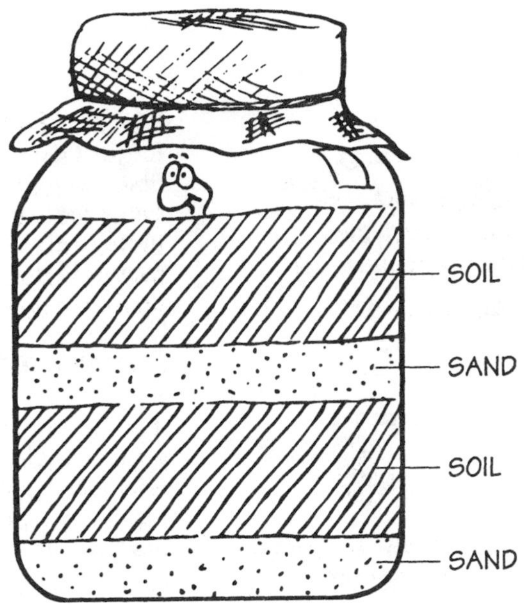

6. For the first week or so, let the worms settle in. Only disturb the jar for watering or feeding.

7. After the worms have settled in, take a look at the layers in the jar. What has happened to them? How do earthworms move? How sensitive are they to light and vibrations? Place a worm on a sheet of moist paper towelling and examine it with a magnifying glass. Which end of its body is the head and which end is the tail? How can you tell? Does the worm have a top and a bottom? How does the worm respond when you put a drop of water on it? Can you hear a worm move on a piece of newspaper?

8. Every 21 days or so, you can harvest earthworm eggs! In bright light, turn the soil from the worm farm onto a sheet of newspaper. Put fresh, moist soil and sand in the worm farm and return the worms to the farm. Then, carefully sift through the old soil to find lemon-shaped worm eggs. The eggs are about 5 mm long. They begin as a lemon colour, darkening later to a purple shade. You may also find eggs of other soil animals; discard these. Put the soil in a clean jar and "plant" the eggs about 5 cm deep. Keep the soil damp. Very soon, the eggs will hatch and the worms will help to enrich the soil; you can add the soil to a garden.

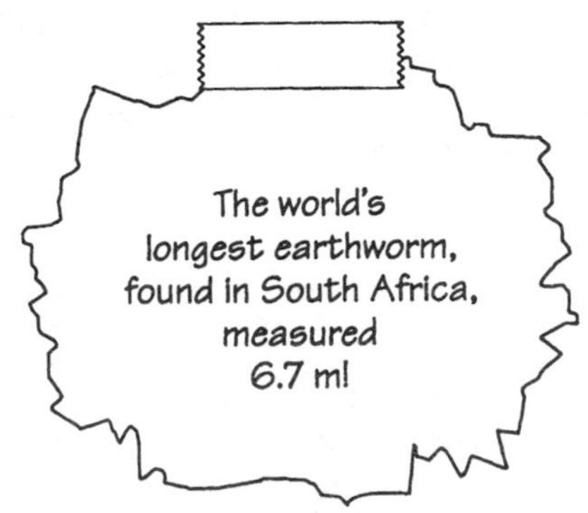

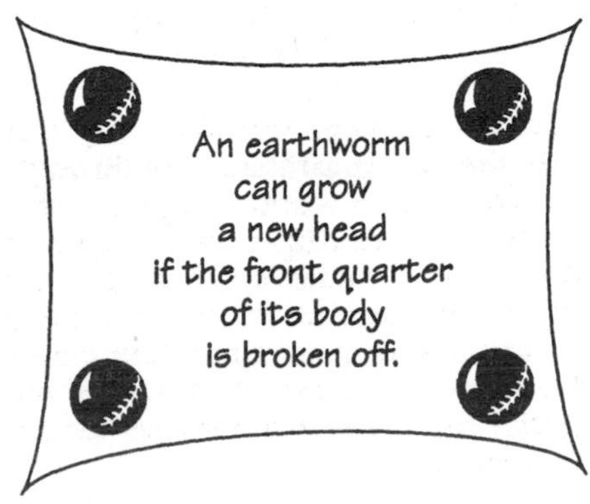

CREATURES OF THE NIGHT

Some animals come out only at night. Wildlife watching at night can be interesting and exciting.

MATERIALS: Regular and/or pen flashlight; jar with lid; stale beer, very ripe banana, and sugar, molasses, or honey; large spoon or flat stick; lamp without shade; different colours of light bulbs; white sheet; tacks. Optional -- fermented fruit juice; tennis balls; string.

DOING IT:

1. When you go wildlife watching at night, you should be familiar with the area you're walking through (walk through the area during the day to get to know it). Walk as silently as possible. Keep all your senses open -- you'll need them all because your eyes aren't as effective in dim light as they are in bright light.

2. Listen for the calls of nocturnal animals. Foxes make high-pitched yipping and yapping noises, and a strange sound that resembles a cat crying. Female owls have a deep hoot, while males have a more high-pitched hoot. Common night insects include katydids (which say their name over and over again) and snowy tree crickets (which make a dull, whistle-like sound; they often call in unison).

3. Use a flashlight for "night-lighting". Try to catch the gleam of a raccoon's or a cat's eyes, or a glimpse of a flying squirrel. When it's warm enough outside, spiders can be found on the ground and on low-lying plants. If you hold the non-lighted end of a flashlight against your forehead, the angle of the beam is just right for spotting the emerald-green reflection from a spider's eyes. You may see this reflection up to 9 m away if the spider is facing you.

4. Some animals make their own light. Collect fireflies in a jar. How much light do they emit? *Release the creatures when you're finished.* Look for the glowing larvae and eggs of fireflies on the ground. Fireflies have certain chemicals in their bodies. They can mix these chemicals together to produce light. Nothing burns to produce the glow so, unlike most light sources, there's no heat. The light isn't used to see, but is used to attract mates or prey. Male fireflies "talk" to females by flashing light. Different types of fireflies use different codes of light flashes. Use a pen flashlight to try to "talk" to a firefly.

5. Mix together stale beer, a ripe banana, and sugar, molasses, or honey. You might also want to add some fermented fruit juice. Spread the mixture on tree trunks, fence posts, stumps, and logs. Or, tie tennis balls to lengths of string, dip the balls into the mixture, and tie the balls from tree branches. Within an hour, you should attract moths and other animals. Try the mixture during the day to see if you can attract different animals.

6. You can attract a number of species of moths with light. Use tacks to spread an old, white sheet on the side of a building or between some trees. Use a lamp without a shade to shine bright light onto the sheet. How quickly do moths appear? Try white, red, blue, and yellow light bulbs in the lamp. Which colours of light attract night creatures and which do not?

> In order to hunt and survive in the darkness, animals have developed many marvellous ways of seeing and sensing their environment. For example, in the human eye, the retina absorbs only a fraction of the light reaching it through the pupil. Many nocturnal animals have a membrane behind their retina which reflects light back into it, just like a mirror. This allows these animals to see in light that would be too dim for the human eye to function effectively.
>
> **Topics:** Environmental Awareness; Animal Characteristics.

WEATHER STATION

The Weather subject area has ten One Leads to Another activities. If you do the entire series of activities, you'll have all the instruments needed for a complete weather station. However, you don't need all the instruments to begin weather forecasting. A general forecast can be made using only wind direction and some observations; the forecast will be more accurate if you also use a thermometer and a barometer.

In the past, weather forecasters based their predictions on measurements of such variables as air temperature, air pressure, and wind speed and direction. They would use this information to draw complicated weather maps, and would then analyse the maps. By repeating this process every 6 to 12 hours, they could estimate the speed, direction, and movement of weather systems. Weather satellites have changed things considerably. Meteorologists are now able to observe cloud formations over large areas of the globe. Successive satellite pictures are easy to obtain and provide complete, accurate information on the movement of and changes in weather systems over a period of time. Satellite information is still supplemented by information from traditional instruments such as the thermometer and barometer. In addition, many amateur forecasters and people who earn their living in weather-sensitive occupations (e.g. farmers) use traditional instruments and become quite good at "reading the sky".

The weather station described in the following pages includes all the traditional instruments used in weather forecasting. The series begins with a thermometer activity. The thermometer is a familiar, easy-to-use instrument, which provides results quickly. The activities then increase in difficulty, although none of the instruments are extremely hard to construct or use. Information for determining wind speed, wind direction, cloud movement, cloud type, atmospheric pressure, humidity, dew point, and precipitation levels is presented. The series ends with tips for weather forecasting and a Weather Conditions Record sheet. The record sheet will help you to maintain a daily log of weather information and to examine weather changes over a period of time.

Quickies and Make Time activities in the Weather subject area can complement the weather station. For example, the Make Time section provides background information on the formation of clouds and rain.

Once you've put together your weather station, why not visit a real weather station in your area? Your local government weather service can help you make the necessary arrangements.

TEMPERATURE

A thermometer is a key part of any weather station. Start with some basic air temperature explorations and then construct your own thermometer.

"Temperature" is a measure of the degree of heat in the air. An area gets hotter when it is heated (by the sun), and cools when the heat leaves the area (spreads out over the land and up into the atmosphere). The coldest time of the 24 hour day is just before sunrise, after the Earth has been losing heat all night. Temperature is measured in degrees Celsius (or degrees Fahrenheit, as in the United States; to convert degrees C into degrees F multiply the degrees C by 1.8 and then add 32). A store-bought thermometer consists of a narrow glass tube containing mercury or coloured alcohol (alcohol, plastic-backed, recessed thermometers are safest for this activity). As the temperature increases, the mercury or alcohol expands and its level in the tube rises. The number corresponding to the liquid's level at any given time is the temperature reading. A homemade, water thermometer works on the same principle; heat causes the water to expand up the straw.

There are two things to keep in mind as you take air temperature. First of all, the thermometer should be in the shade. The idea is to measure the temperature of the surrounding air, not the temperature of a thermometer heated by the sun. Secondly, each time you take a reading, keep the thermometer in place for several minutes to get a valid reading.

"Wind chill" is related to air temperature. Have you ever noticed that you feel much colder on a winter day when there's a strong wind blowing? Wind has a cooling effect, and the degree of that cooling effect is expressed as a wind chill factor. The wind chill factor indicates how chilly you feel when wind of a particular speed is blowing air of a particular temperature. The wind doesn't actually lower the air temperature -- it changes how the temperature *feels*. For example, when you hold a wet finger into the wind, you can tell the direction of the wind because one side of your finger feels cooler. The wind causes the water on the surface of your finger to evaporate quickly and that makes the finger feel cooler. A high wind chill can have a number of serious effects: water freezes more quickly; more energy is required to heat buildings; and exposed areas of skin freeze more rapidly.

Topics: Weather Conditions; Measurement.

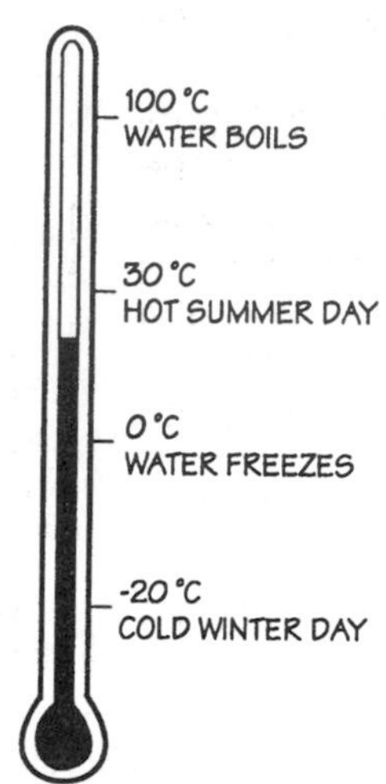

MATERIALS: Two thermometers; shoebox; tape; ruler; pop bottle; plastic straw; water; red food colouring; paper towel; Plasticine; stiff paper or cardboard; paper; pencil. Optional -- graph paper; light machine oil.

DOING IT:

1. *Sunlight Versus Shade:* Take the air temperature in direct sunlight in several different spots. Then take the air temperature in the shade in several spots. Which temperatures are higher? Why? Why should a thermometer be located in the shade?

2. *Time of Day:* Take the temperature at five different times during the day: early morning; mid-morning; noon; mid-afternoon; and late afternoon. What time of day is hottest? What is the temperature reading? What time of day is coolest? What is the temperature reading? What is the average temperature for the day (add the readings and divide by 5)? What adjectives would you use to describe the day's temperature?

3. *Wind Effect:* On a day when there's a steady wind blowing, use two thermometers to determine the effect wind has on the temperature you experience. Compare the readings of the thermometers indoors to ensure they are similar. Then tape one thermometer to the outside of an

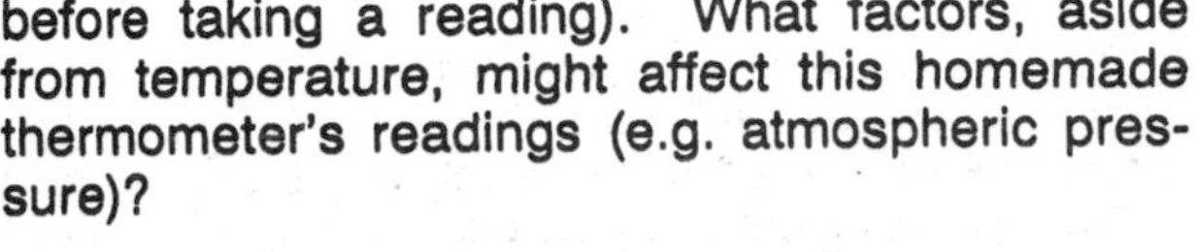

open shoebox and the other inside the box. Take the box outdoors and hold it so that the wind is blowing directly on the thermometer on the outside of the box; the thermometer inside the box should be sheltered and no wind should be blowing on it. Neither thermometer should be in direct sunlight. Compare the temperature readings. Try this test in several areas. Which thermometer provides the lower reading? Why? Note: A cold day will give you more dramatic results; if the day is warmer, the effect of wind can be more visible if you wet the thermometers.

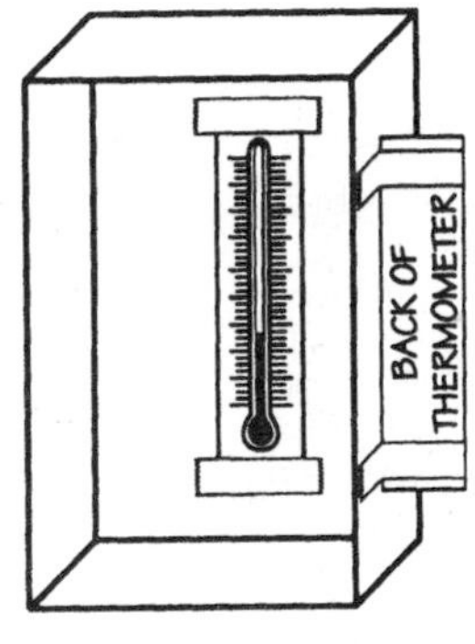

4. *Making a Thermometer:* Fill a pop bottle almost full with water at about room temperature. Add red food colouring to the water. Wipe the bottle's mouth with a paper towel. Hold a straw about halfway into the bottle and use Plasticine to wedge the straw in the bottle's mouth; plug the entire opening with Plasticine. Press the Plasticine down into the bottle so that the water rises up the straw to midway between the Plasticine and the top of the straw. If it doesn't, move the straw up or down and then press the Plasticine down tightly again. To reduce water evaporation, put a few drops of light machine oil down the straw. Cut a piece of stiff paper to equal the length of the straw above the bottle. Make horizontal lines on the paper, each about 1 cm apart. Number each mark, with the highest number at the top and the lowest at the bottom. Tape the paper to the straw. Now you have a scale to help you measure the temperature; the higher the reading on your scale, the warmer the temperature. Experiment with the thermometer in various warm and cool locations, both outdoors and indoors (a large volume of water can take a significant amount of time to gain and lose heat; leave the thermometer in place for several hours before taking a reading). What factors, aside from temperature, might affect this homemade thermometer's readings (e.g. atmospheric pressure)?

5. *Variation:* Using a store-bought thermometer, measure the temperature throughout the day by taking a reading every hour from 9:00 a.m. until 5:00 p.m. Draw a simple line graph of the results. What is the temperature pattern? When is it hottest?

6. *Extension:* Record the hourly temperatures each day, over a week. What patterns do you see? How much does the temperature usually rise each day? For the second week, see how closely you can predict the noon temperature based on the early morning temperature. How closely can you predict the mid-afternoon temperature based on the noon temperature?

7. *Extension:* During the winter, calculate the approximate wind chill. Determine the wind speed (see following page). Then, take the air temperature in a sheltered spot. Use the Wind Chill Chart below to determine the wind chill. For example, a wind speed of 30 km/h with an air temperature of about -15 degrees C results in a wind chill of a cold -32 degrees C (i.e. it feels like -32 degrees C).

WIND CHILL CHART

Air Temperature (degrees C)	Wind Speed (km/h) 10	20	30	40	50	60
5	4	-2	-5	-7	-8	-9
0	-2	-8	-11	-14	-16	-17
-5	-7	-14	-18	-21	-23	-24
-10	-12	-20	-25	-28	-30	-32
-15	-18	-26	-32	-35	-38	-39
-20	-23	-32	-38	-42	-45	-47
-25	-28	-39	-45	-49	-52	-54
-30	-33	-45	-52	-56	-60	-62
-35	-39	-51	-59	-64	-67	-69
-40	-44	-57	-65	-71	-74	-77

WIND SPEED

Wind is air in motion. Determine wind speed using the Beaufort Wind Scale and/or an instrument called an anemometer.

Air moves from areas of high pressure to areas of low pressure. The larger the pressure difference between two areas, the stronger the wind. In a hurricane, for example, the low pressure in the centre of the storm means that air rushes inward with great speed and causes high winds. The flow of air from high to low eventually evens out the pressure in both areas and the storm dissipates. Wind speed is measured in kilometres per hour. An "anemometer" is an instrument which measures wind speed. A common anemometer design consists of three or four cups attached to spokes on a rotating shaft. The spokes turn the shaft as the wind blows. The wind speed is indicated by the speed of the spinning shaft.

Wind speed can also be determined using the Beaufort Wind Scale. In 1805, Sir Francis Beaufort developed a scale which estimates wind speed by the wind's effect on the surroundings. The table provided is for use over land. A version of the scale also exists for use at sea; the scale is based on the appearance and height of waves.

Topics: Weather Conditions; Measurement.

MATERIALS: Wood; hammer and nails; long nail; stiff cardboard; compass; tacks; aluminum foil; masking tape; scissors; pencil.

DOING IT:

1. Build a fan anemometer. Nail a wood post to a small base. Draw a large circle on a piece of stiff cardboard and cut a quarter section from the circle. Tack the section to the post, as shown. Hammer in a long nail at the top of the post. Fold a wide strip of aluminum foil around the nail so that the foil hangs down and moves freely; carefully tape the two halves of the foil together.

Winds high above the Earth's surface are measured by sending up large, helium-filled balloons. The balloons move with the same speed and in the same direction as the wind. A balloon's motion is measured by sight or by radar.

Beaufort Wind Scale		
Beaufort Force	**Wind Speed (in km/h) 10 m above ground**	**Description**
0	Less than 1	Calm: Smoke rises vertically.
1	1 - 5	Light Air: Not enough to move a wind vane, but smoke drifts with the wind.
2	6 - 11	Light Breeze: Wind felt on face, leaves rustle, and wind vane moves.
3	12 - 19	Gentle Breeze: Leaves and small twigs move and light flags extend.
4	20 - 28	Moderate Breeze: Raises dust and loose paper. Small branches move.
5	29 - 39	Fresh Breeze: Small trees in leaf sway.
6	40 - 50	Strong Breeze: Large branches move. Difficult to use an umbrella.
7	51 - 61	Near Gale: Whole trees sway. Uncomfortable to walk against the wind.
8	62 - 74	Gale: Twigs break off trees. Difficult to walk against the wind.
9	75 - 88	Strong Gale: Slight damage to buildings. May blow shingles off roof.
10	89 - 102	Storm: Trees uprooted. Considerable damage.
11	103 - 117	Violent Storm: Widespread damage.
12	118 and over	Hurricane: Very rare inland. Violent destruction.

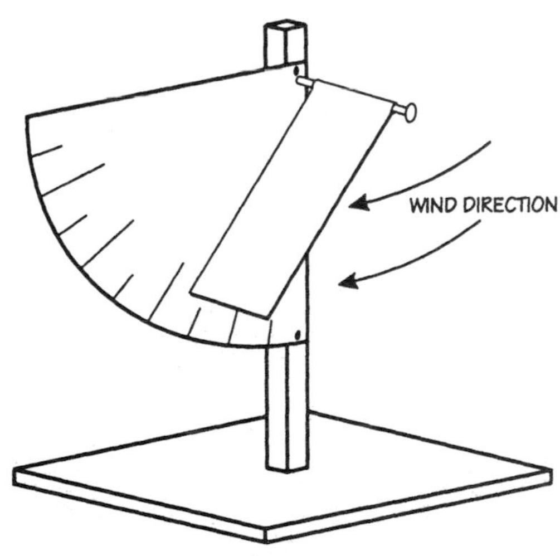

2. The foil flap will be blown easily by light winds. By layering strips of masking tape on the foil flap, you can make it heavier so that it can be used for stronger winds. You may have to build two anemometers -- one to measure low wind speeds and one to measure high wind speeds.

3. You can calibrate an anemometer in a number of ways. One approach is to use daily official weather information. When you know the wind is blowing at a certain speed, simply make a mark on the quarter circle to correspond to that speed. You can also calibrate the anemometer using a car. Choose a windless day and an area without traffic. While an adult drives, hold the instrument out the car window at arm's length. The car should begin travelling at 5 km/h and increase its speed by fives until reaching a speed of about 50 km/h. **Do this with extreme caution.** Mark the foil flap's position on the quarter circle at each 5 km/h increment. To check your calibrations, repeat the readings with the car travelling in the opposite direction.

4. Locate the anemometer as high as possible and away from any trees, buildings, or other obstructions. Position the instrument so that the wind blows against the foil flap. The stronger the wind, the more it will push the flap. Wind speed is determined by noting the position of the flap.

5. Estimate the wind speed using the Beaufort Wind Scale. Compare your estimate to the reading on the anemometer.

WIND DIRECTION

Wind direction is one of the most important factors in weather. Use a wind vane to determine the direction of the wind.

MATERIALS: Straw; cardboard; scissors; pin; pencil (with eraser top); tape. Optional -- small bead; paper clips; compass; ruler; paper; pencil.

DOING IT:

1. Construct the wind vane as shown. Slit the straw to insert the pieces of cardboard; secure the cardboard with tape. The straw should rotate easily around the pin and remain level, regardless of which way it points. The tail should extend farther from the pivot than the head and should be much larger than the head; this allows the wind's force to have the greatest turning effect on the tail. You can add paper clips to the pointer for balance. A small bead between the eraser and the straw will lower the friction between them and help the wind vane turn more easily.

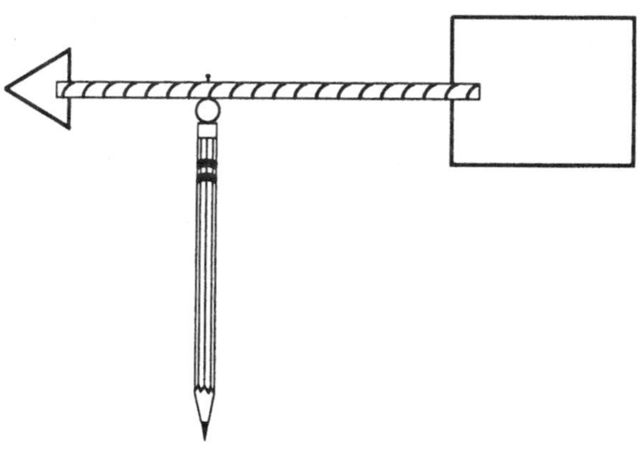

2. The arrow points in the direction from which the wind originates. Use the wind vane in an open area, away from trees and other objects which will block or deflect the wind. The wind vane should be well above the ground. If the arrow changes position from minute to minute, the vane is probably located where there are gusts and eddies caused by surrounding obstructions.

3. *Extension:* You may want to make a base on which to stand the pencil. Mark N, S, W, and E on the base so that once you orient the base, you can quickly and easily determine the direction the wind vane is pointing.

4. *Extension:* A "wind rose" is useful for showing the direction from which the wind most often comes (prevailing wind direction). Use a compass to draw six or more equally-spaced, concentric circles. Use a ruler to divide the circles into eight sections, as shown. Determine the wind direction daily over a few weeks. Each day, draw a bar along the appropriate directional radial, counting one circle as one observation. In the illustration, the wind blew from the west 6 times; from the southwest 5 times; from the south 3 times; and from the southeast, east, and northeast 2 times each (for a total of 20 observations). The wind rose shows that west/southwest winds dominate. Make several wind roses to determine how the wind pattern in your area changes throughout the year.

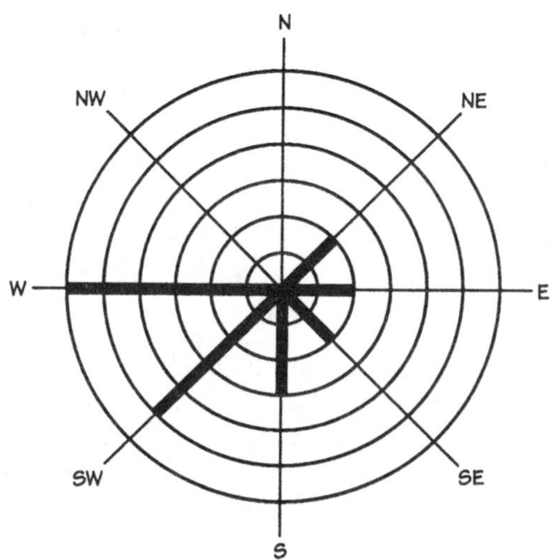

Wind carries with it changes in weather. The nature of these changes depends on the wind's direction. Winds are named after the direction *from* which they blow; for example, a wind blowing from the west, toward the east, is called a west wind. Wind vanes are used for determining wind direction. The tail on a wind vane is pushed by the wind so that the arrow points into the wind and indicates the direction from which the wind is blowing (e.g. a wind vane pointing westward indicates a west wind).

Topics: Weather Conditions; Measurement.

CLOUD MOVEMENT AND TYPE

Determine wind direction at cloud height -- which can be different from wind direction at ground level -- and get to know different cloud types.

MATERIALS: Mirror; paper; pencil; compass; scissors; tape; cloud type illustrations on following pages. Optional -- cotton puffs; dark blue or black paper; glue.

DOING IT:

1. Make a nephoscope to track cloud movement. Cut out and discard a large circle from the centre of a sheet of paper. Mark the cardinal points of a compass (i.e. N, S, W, E), and perhaps the intermediate points, around the circumference of the circular hole. Tape the paper on top of a mirror so that the mirror's surface fills the open circle.

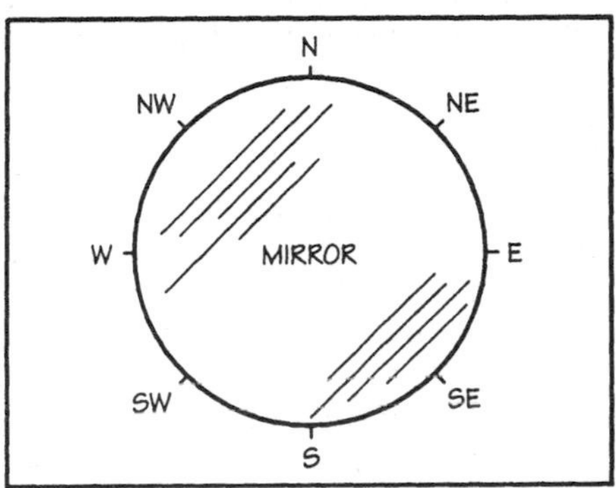

2. Use the nephoscope by placing it on level ground with N facing north. Look in the mirror and follow the path of a cloud as it passes across the circle and past the edge of the mirror's surface. The point on the nephoscope at which the cloud begins its journey across the circle indicates the wind direction. For example, if clouds are moving toward the east, the wind is coming from the west. Is the wind direction the same at higher altitudes as it is at ground level (use a wind vane to determine the wind direction at ground level)? Why might the wind directions be different? Why are high-altitude winds important for weather forecasting?

3. Use the cloud illustrations on the following pages to classify clouds in the sky. What do the clouds look like (e.g. high, low, thick, thin, fluffy, bumpy, white, gray)? What type of clouds are they? Is their name appropriate (think about the meaning of the name)? What kind of weather might they bring? Is there more than one type of cloud in the sky? How many clouds (not types) can you see? Watch a particular cloud for a few moments and see how it moves and changes. Make a picture of the sky in your mind, close your eyes and, when you open your eyes again, see how the sky has changed.

4. *Extension:* Make cloud pictures on dark paper using cotton puffs and glue. Try to make each of the different cloud types. Pay attention to the details that make clouds different from one another (e.g. thickness, formation). Some clouds will require large pieces of cotton while others will require only wisps of cotton.

High-altitude winds affect the cloud movements that bring changes in weather. Therefore, the direction of these winds can be very important. High-altitude winds do not necessarily blow in the same direction as ground winds. Winds at ground level tend to be light and variable because they're affected by hills, trees, buildings, and other obstructions. At higher altitudes, winds can have considerable velocity and a definite direction. A "nephoscope" indicates the direction of high-altitude winds by tracking cloud movement. Weather balloons are also used to determine the direction of upper winds.

Clouds are classified by shape and altitude. The two basic types of clouds are stratus (meaning "sheet" or "layer") and cumulus (meaning "heap"). Nimbus (which means "rain-bearing") is sometimes included as a basic cloud type. Prefixes are added to the names of the basic cloud types for a more accurate description of a particular cloud formation. Cirrus or cirro (e.g. cirrostratus) refers to high clouds, usually with a base above 6 km, consisting of tiny ice crystals. At middle levels, 2 to 6 km, are alto clouds (e.g. altocumulus). Below are the basic cumulus, stratus, nimbus, cumulonimbus, and so on, the tops of which may go up to higher levels. Clouds are seldom seen at altitudes higher than 10 km, which is why large airplanes usually fly higher than 10 km. If there are various types of clouds in the sky, those which appear to move faster are usually the lower ones.

Topics: Weather Conditions; Atmosphere; Classification.

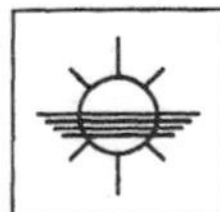

Cloud Types

Stratus: "Spread sheet". Low, horizontal sheet of lifted fog (becomes fog on water's surface). Base often low enough to hide tops of low hills or high buildings. Sun's outline clearly visible through the cloud. When torn apart, known as "stratus fractus". Often present during a light, steady rain or snow.

Cumulus: "Wool pack" or "heap". Dense, huge masses of varying height. Bulging upper parts can look like sections of a cauliflower. Bright when opposite the sun; on the same side as the sun, dark with bright edges. Fair weather cloud.

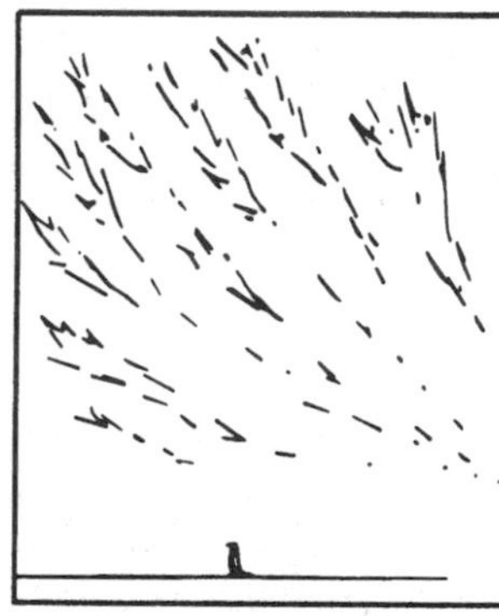

Cirrus: "Feather". Highest of formations. Fibrous, hair-like, silky in appearance. Sometimes shaped like a comma with a hook at the top. Slowly drifting indicates fair weather; moving rapidly and followed by more cloud indicates foul weather.

Cirrostratus: "Tangled web". Veil of high, thin, whitish cloud totally or partly covering the sky. May form a whitish ring or "halo" around the sun or moon. Rain or snow develops when thickens.

Cirrocumulus: "Mackerel" (looks like scales on a fish). Small flakes arranged in groups, lines, or ripples (merged or separate). Grainy appearance. Transparent enough to show sun or moon. Indicates changeable weather; often followed by strong winds.

CLOUD TYPES

ALTOCUMULUS: "Sheep". Large, white and/or gray masses or groups often spread into lines. Occurs most commonly as an extensive sheet of cloudlets, fairly regularly arranged. Transparency varies considerably. If dome-shaped, rain possible; if isolated and irregular, good weather.

ALTOSTRATUS: "Curtain". Thick, grayish, or bluish cloud. Often shows a bright patch where sun or moon hides. Precipitation may evaporate before reaching the ground.

STRATOCUMULUS: "Twist". Dark colour. Not very thick. Low. Blue sky may show in spots. Transparency varies considerably. May precede or follow precipitation.

NIMBOSTRATUS: "Umbrella". Thick, dark, and spread out. Little visible structure. Usually covers the entire sky and completely covers the sun. Small, ragged pieces floating at lower levels are known as "scud". Continuous rain, sleet, or snow.

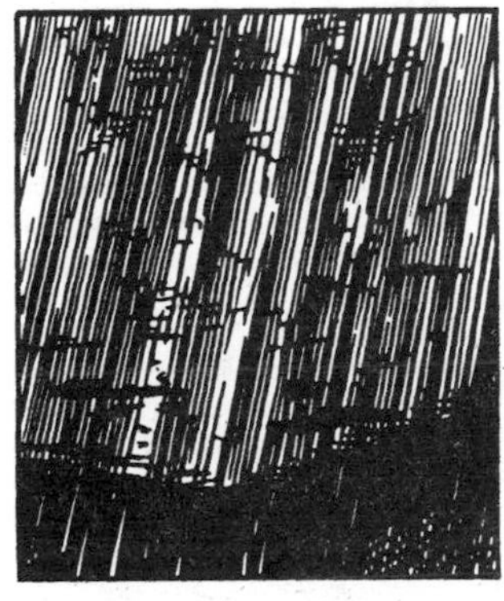

CUMULONIMBUS: "Thunder". Like cumulus, but much larger. Heavy, dense cloud which may look like a mountain or huge tower. Lower portion is dark; whiter top is often flattened into an anvil shape. Entire cloud can be seen only from a distance. Top may spread out and create "false cirrus", with nimbus and scud underneath. Storm cloud (weak or strong). Passes quickly and covers only a small area.

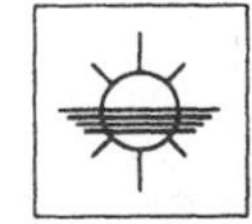

ATMOSPHERIC PRESSURE

A barometer is a relatively simple instrument that measures the pressure of surrounding air (atmospheric pressure).

MATERIALS: Clear bottle (e.g. pop bottle); clear, wide-mouthed jar (bottle should fit snugly -- but not airtight -- into the mouth of this jar); water; food colouring; permanent marker.

DOING IT:

1. *You must make this barometer when it is raining or snowing! The barometer will not work unless it's made when there is low pressure.*

2. Add a bit of food colouring (red looks rather nice!) to some water.

3. Pour enough coloured water into the jar so that when the bottle is inverted into the jar a little of the water rises up into the neck of the bottle.

4. Once you have the right level of water in the jar, let the barometer (bottle inverted into jar) sit for about 15 minutes.

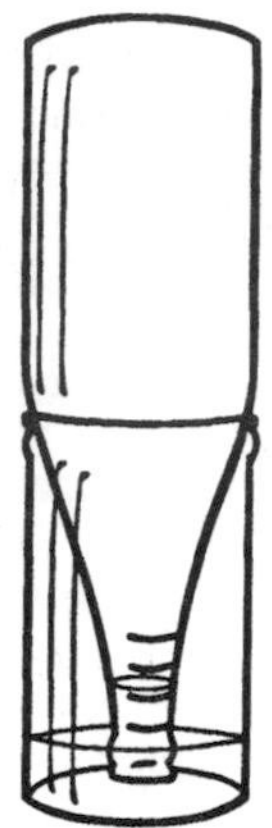

5. Take a look at the water level in the bottle's neck. Mark the level with a marker. This is the low pressure mark. Add three more marks, 1 cm apart, above the lowest mark. The top mark indicates high pressure.

6. Take a barometer reading at least a couple of times a day (i.e. once in the morning, once in the evening). Water at the lowest mark indicates wet, stormy weather; on the second or third mark it indicates a change in weather; and at the fourth mark it indicates settled, dry weather.

7. When the water in your barometer begins to evaporate away, you will need to make the barometer again.

"Atmospheric pressure" is measured in terms of large -- as large as 2.5 million square kilometres -- high pressure or low pressure areas. In a high pressure area (air molecules are closer together), the air in the atmosphere is heavy and therefore falling gently. This produces clear skies and fair weather. By contrast, the air in a low pressure area (air molecules are further apart) is gently rising. As it rises, the air cools. Water vapour condenses into tiny water droplets around microscopic particles floating in the air, and clouds result. If more and more water vapour continues to condense, it will eventually rain or snow.

In the homemade barometer, air pressure forces water up the neck of the bottle. The further up into the bottle that the water moves, the higher the air pressure -- and the drier the weather. The homemade barometer can be sensitive to the immediate air temperature and other conditions and, therefore, may not always correspond to official atmospheric pressure readings.

Topics: Weather Conditions; Air; Atmosphere; Measurement.

Because air at higher altitudes compresses air below it, about half the total weight of the atmosphere is concentrated in the 5 km layer closest to Earth. As you climb a mountain, there is less and less air above you. For example, at the top of Mount Everest (8,848 m) the weight of the air is only one-third that at sea level. "Thinner" air at high altitudes makes it difficult for humans to breathe, and also affects the temperature at which water boils (which means it takes longer to cook food).

HUMIDITY

You can measure the amount of moisture in the air, the humidity, using a simple, hair hygrometer.

MATERIALS: Straight, thick human hair (preferably blonde) approximately 20 cm long; soap and water; straw; tape; glue; cardboard box (e.g. shoebox); pencil; scissors. Optional -- large pot; water; stove; blow dryer.

DOING IT:

1. The hair you use in a hygrometer should be as thick as possible. Wash the hair with soap and rinse it well to remove all traces of oil and dirt. Dry the hair thoroughly.

2. If the box you're using has a lid, discard it. If the box has flaps, cut away the flaps. Turn the box on its side, as shown (side of box now becomes bottom).

3. Loosely tape one end of a straw to the bottom of the box. Tie and glue one end of the hair closer to the taped end of the straw (as shown) so that the shrinking and stretching of the hair are amplified as much as possible. Attach the other end of the hair to the top of the cardboard box. Stick a small weight (e.g. ball of tape) on the straw so that the hair remains taut.

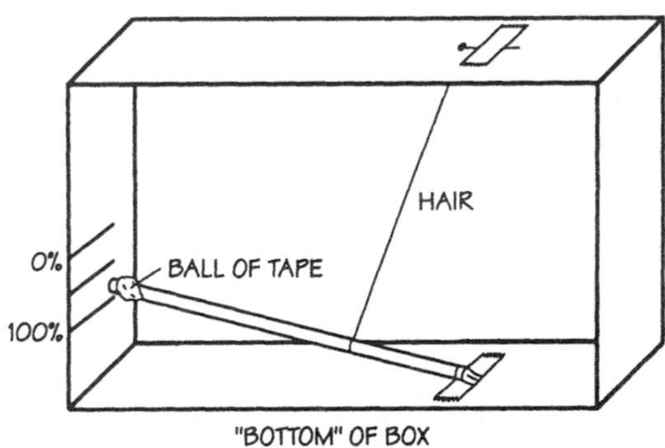

4. Calibrate the hygrometer by putting it in an area with a great deal of moisture in the air. For example, you can put it in the bathroom while you're taking a hot shower with the windows and door closed. Another option is to hold the hygrometer in the steam rising from a large pot of boiling water (**this should be done carefully, with adult supervision**). Mark the straw pointer's position on the side of the box. The mark represents 100% humidity.

5. Find the 0% mark by putting the hygrometer in a very dry place, such as near a heater. You can also use a blow dryer to dry the hair.

6. Take a hygrometer reading at least once a day. Is the humidity higher before a rainstorm than it is afterwards?

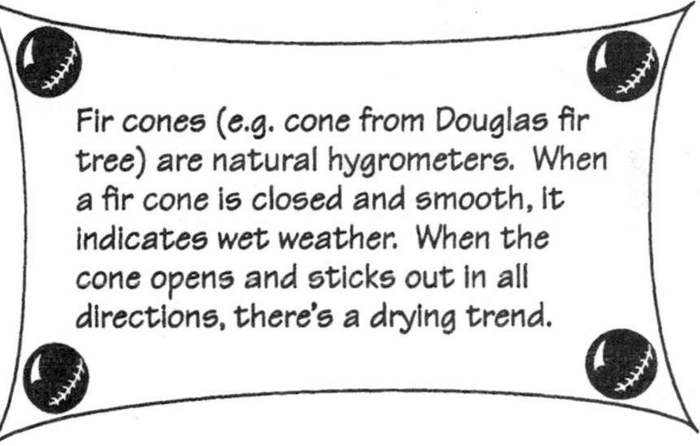

Temperature is the major factor affecting the amount of (invisible) moisture air can hold at any given time. Warm air can hold more water vapour than cold air; thus, it's often more humid on a warm day. In general, humidity increases just before rain and decreases afterwards. Meteorologists measure "relative humidity". Relative humidity is the amount of water vapour actually in the air, compared to the amount the air would contain if it was "saturated" (held all the moisture it possibly could). When air holds all the moisture it can, the relative humidity is 100%; if more moisture is added or the temperature goes down, some moisture condenses out as liquid water droplets (this is similar to what happens on the outside of a cold glass on a humid day). When air holds only half the maximum amount of moisture, the relative humidity is 50%. The hair hygrometer works because humid air causes hair to stretch and dry air causes it to shrink. The hair hygrometer will always be less accurate than the psychrometer described on the following page.

Topics: Weather Conditions; Air; Measurement.

MORE ON HUMIDITY

A psychrometer -- an instrument made up of one wet-bulb and one dry-bulb thermometer -- measures relative humidity more accurately than a hygrometer.

MATERIALS: Two thermometers; two elastic bands; cotton shoelace or gauze bandage; a container or box on which to mount the thermometers; a smaller container; scissors; water. Optional -- pot; water; stove.

DOING IT:

1. If you're using a shoelace, boil it for a few minutes to wash out any chemicals (**this should be done carefully, with adult supervision**).

2. Wrap one end of the shoelace or gauze around the bulb of a thermometer. This is the wet-bulb thermometer.

3. Mount the wet-bulb thermometer on the psychrometer stand, as shown. Push the loose end of the shoelace or gauze through a hole to the inside of the stand. Place the end in a small container filled with water. The container should be checked periodically to ensure that it's full and that the shoelace or gauze is soaked with water.

4. Mount a second thermometer, the dry-bulb thermometer, beside the wet-bulb thermometer.

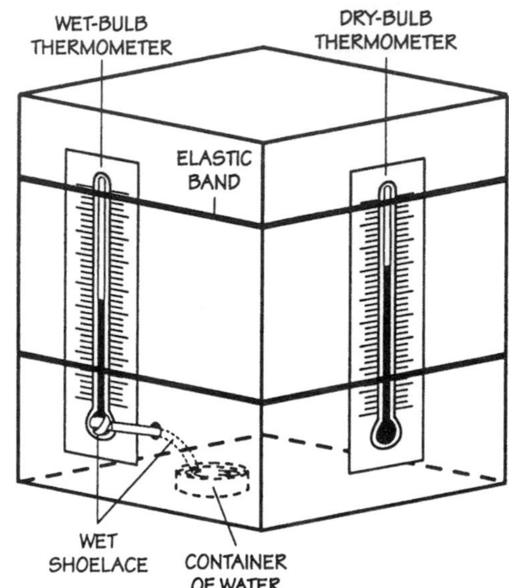

5. Locate the psychrometer in the shade, out of the wind. In general, the smaller the difference in temperature between the two thermometers, the greater the humidity in the air. Before reading the wet-bulb thermometer, fan it for about a minute to take full advantage of the cooling effect.

6. Use the graph on the following page to get a precise relative humidity reading with the psychrometer. For example, say the dry-bulb temperature (the normal temperature of the air) is 20 degrees C. Follow an imaginary line up from the 20 degrees C marking until you reach the curved line representing the approximate wet-bulb temperature. Say the wet-bulb temperature is 5 degrees C. Then follow an imaginary horizontal line to the other axis of the graph. In the example, the relative humidity is about 40%.

7. Compare your relative humidity readings to official readings.

The psychrometer works on the same principle that makes perspiration an effective method for cooling off the human body. When perspiration (water) evaporates from human skin, it cools the skin off. The "wet-bulb" thermometer is cooled the same way; water from the shoelace or gauze evaporates and lowers the "wet-bulb" temperature.

Dry air permits a great deal of evaporation, and thus a lot of cooling. The greater the amount of moisture in the air, the less cooling takes place -- and the closer the readings of the wet-bulb and the dry-bulb thermometers. If there is 100% relative humidity, the two thermometers in the psychrometer indicate exactly the same temperature.

Topics: Weather Conditions; Air; Measurement.

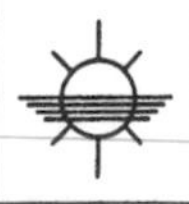

Psychrometer Graph

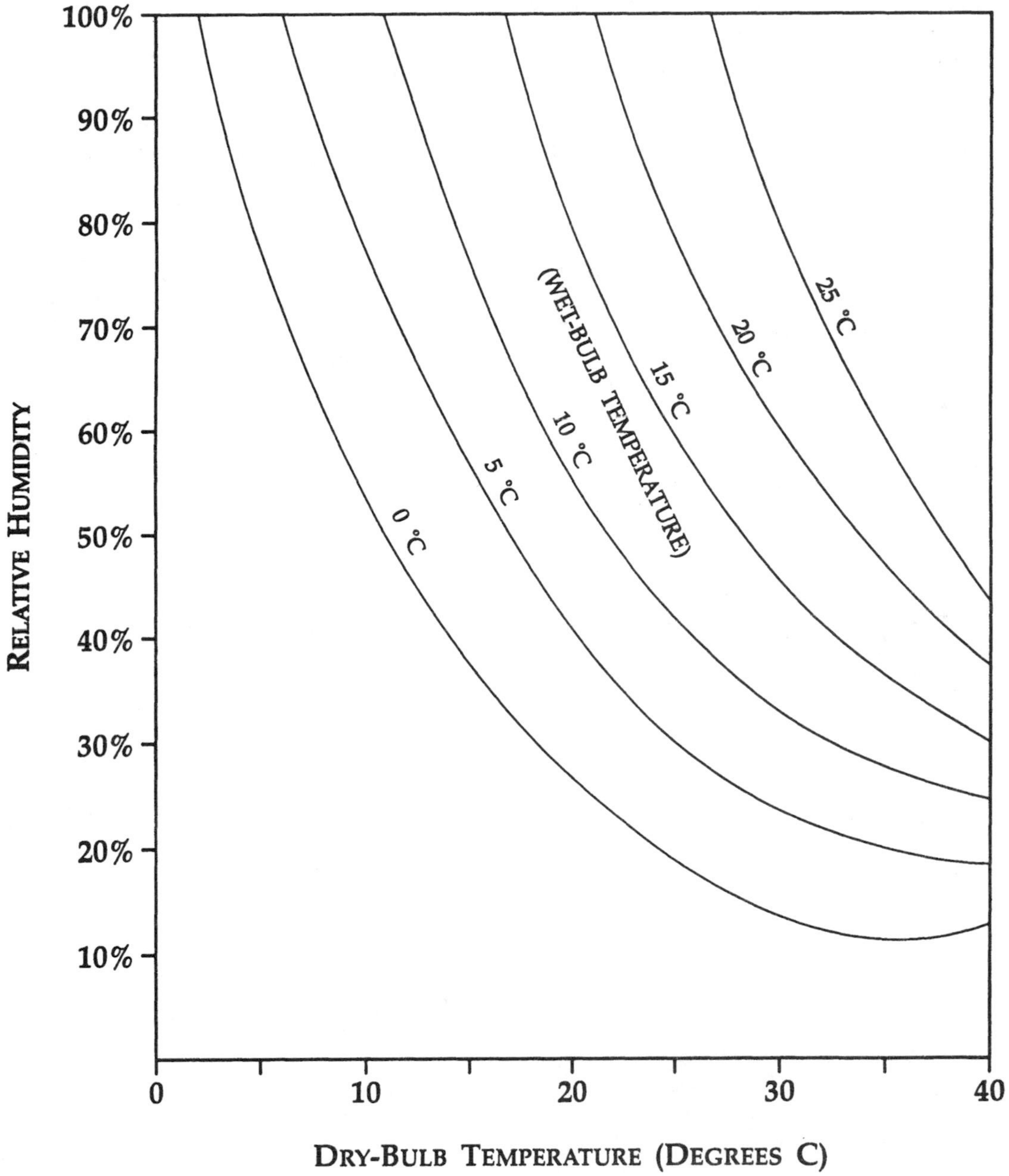

Relative Humidity

100%
90%
80%
70%
60%
50%
40%
30%
20%
10%

(Wet-Bulb Temperature)

0 °C
5 °C
10 °C
15 °C
20 °C
25 °C

0
10
20
30
40

Dry-Bulb Temperature (Degrees C)

Dew Point

Dew point -- the point at which air at a given temperature can hold no more (invisible) moisture -- can be measured with a can and some ice water.

MATERIALS: Can; thermometer; spoon; ice; water in container; paper; pencil.

DOING IT:

1. Let a container of water sit for a couple of hours at room temperature.

2. Use a thermometer to measure the air temperature (always take temperature readings in the shade).

3. Fill a can almost completely with the room temperature water. Place the thermometer in the water and hold it against the side of the can to get the temperature of the can.

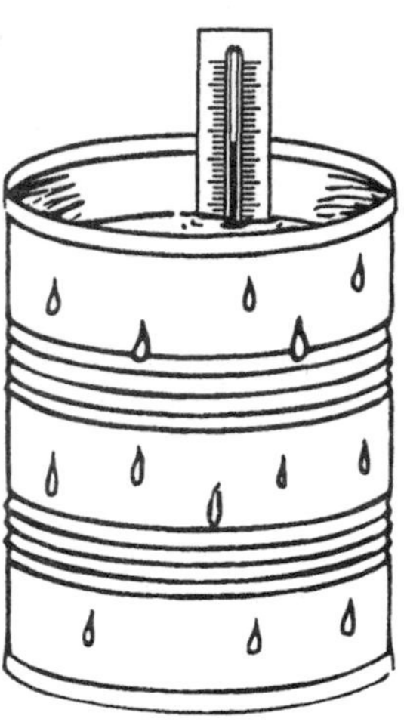

As air cools throughout the night after a hot day, it's able to hold less and less moisture. One result is drops of water condensing onto blades of grass to form dew. As the air becomes even cooler, water may condense onto dust particles floating in the air and form fog. The temperature at which the air becomes saturated with moisture is the dew-point temperature. This is also the temperature at which the humidity is 100%. The dew point can be used to determine the possibility of dew or frost, to calculate relative humidity, and even to determine the height at which clouds will form in the atmosphere.

Topics: Weather Conditions; Air; Measurement.

4. Put some ice into the water. (Note: On a really hot day, omit the ice and just use cool tap water.) Stir the mixture.

5. The dew point is the temperature registered on the thermometer when the *first sign* of moisture begins to appear on the outside surface of the can. As the can cools, more and more water will condense on the outside surface; the thin layer of air around the can has been cooled to its saturation point.

6. If the air temperature is near the dew point, dew or fog is likely to occur. If the air temperature and the dew point are far apart, the air is dry and the humidity is low.

7. *Extension:* The graph on the following page can be used to calculate the relative humidity from the air temperature and dew point. Compare the relative humidity figure found this way with that found using a psychrometer (previous page).

8. *Extension:* Cumulus clouds form when a parcel of air breaks away from the ground (because the surface is warmer than the air surrounding it) and rises. As the air rises, it cools. The relative humidity increases, and eventually the dew point is reached. Water vapour starts to condense and clouds result. The height at which cumulus clouds begin to form (i.e. the base of the clouds) on any given day can be calculated using this simple formula:

$$H = (T - DP) \times 120$$

H is the height in metres, T is the air temperature in degrees Celsius, and DP is the dew-point temperature.

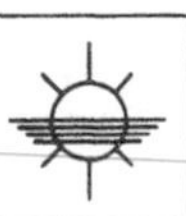

Using Dew Point To Determine Relative Humidity

Use this graph to figure out relative humidity. For example, say the air temperature is 25 degrees C. Say that the difference between the air temperature and the dew-point temperature (air temperature - dew-point temperature) is 2 degrees C. Follow an imaginary line sideways from the 25 degrees C point and another up from the 2 degrees C point until the lines intersect. The point at which the two lines intersect is the approximate relative humidity figure. In the example, the two lines intersect near the 90% relative humidity line and so the relative humidity is about 90%. If the air temperature was 25 degrees C and the difference was 3 degrees C, the two imaginary lines would intersect between the 90% and the 80% relative humidity lines; you can estimate the relative humidity to be about 85%.

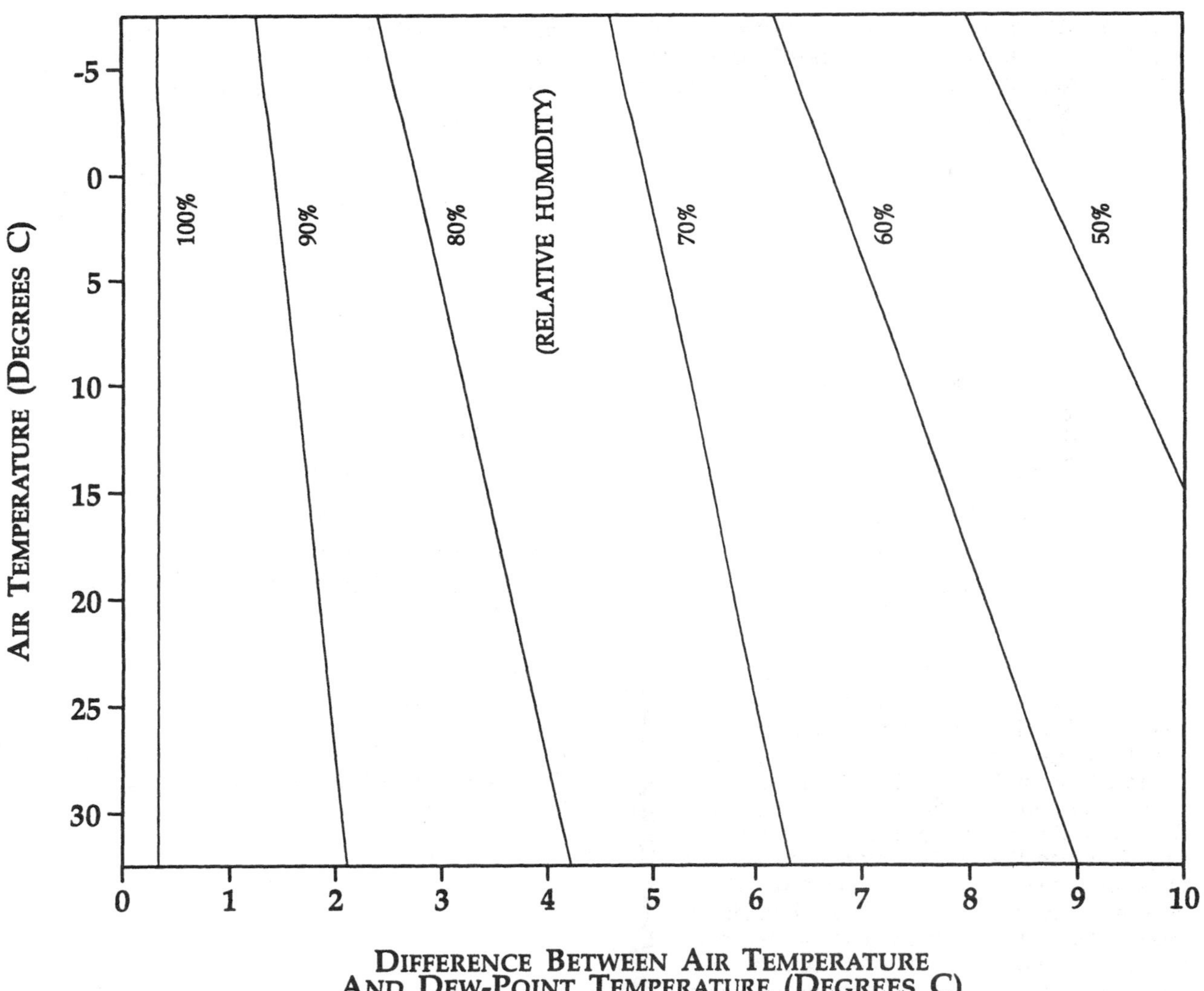

PRECIPITATION

In warm weather, use collecting and measuring containers to measure the rainfall in a given period of time. In cold weather, use a ruler to measure snowfall.

MATERIALS: A wide-mouth container (e.g. large can, open at top); a clear, straight, narrow container (e.g. tall drinking glass, olive jar); water; ruler; marker, tape, or paint. (Note: There should be a considerable difference in the size of the openings of the wide and narrow containers.)

DOING IT:

1. *Collecting Rain:* A wide-mouth container is the collecting container. Keep it outside, in an open area away from trees, buildings, fences, and other objects which might interfere with rain collection. You can partially bury the container in the ground to keep it sturdy and upright. However, the mouth of the container should be high enough off the ground so that raindrops won't splash from the ground into the container (this will give you misleading readings).

2. *Measuring Container:* Calibrate a narrow container for measuring rainfall. Pour water into the wide-mouth container to a depth of 1 cm (use a ruler to measure the depth). Then pour this water into the narrow container and mark the water level. This is the mark for 1 cm of rain. Divide the space between the mark and the bottom of the narrow container into ten equal divisions. Each division is 1 mm of rain. Measure the distance between the bottom of the container and the 1 cm mark. Measure this exact distance above the 1 cm mark and make a second major mark (representing 2 cm of rain). Divide the space between the 1 cm and 2 cm marks into ten equal divisions. Continue this procedure all the way to the top of the narrow container. This will allow you to easily read off the rainfall in millimetres. After a rainstorm, pour the rain from the collecting container into the measuring container. How much rain falls during a day? During a week? Compare your rainfall measurements with official rainfall readings.

3. *Measuring Snowfall:* You can use your rain collecting container to collect snow (sprinkle some water around the base so that the container is frozen in place). After a snowfall, stick a ruler into the container to measure the height of the snow in millimetres; make sure that the snow is level and that you hold the ruler straight. You can also stick a ruler directly into snow that has fallen onto the ground. Take several measurements (to overcome the problem of uneven depths caused by drifting) and then calculate the average (i.e. add up all the measurements and divide by the number of measurements). When fresh snow has fallen on old snow, dig a hole until you can see the line dividing the two layers. Then measure the new snowfall. How much snow falls during a day? Over a week? Compare the snowfalls from storms throughout a season. 10 cm of freshly-fallen snow is considered about equal to 1 cm of rain. When you melt 10 cm of snow, do you get about 1 cm of water? If not, why (e.g. relate to snow density)?

"Precipitation" is the moisture that falls from clouds in the form of rain, snow, sleet, or hail.

Raindrops can range in size from 1 mm to as much as 8 mm. Raindrops start out large, but as they fall, they break into smaller droplets. Droplets may then collide with others and grow in size again. Raindrops aren't shaped like tear drops; they're actually shaped like tiny hamburgers. They start out round, but as they fall to the ground, air resistance flattens them.

It's never too cold to snow. The heaviest snowfalls occur in relatively mild weather (the warmer the air, the more moisture it can hold), and the snow is in rather large flakes. As the air becomes colder, snowflakes become finer. However, no matter how cold the air becomes, it still contains a tiny amount of moisture, which can fall in the form of snow crystals.

Topics: Weather Conditions; Atmosphere; Snow; Measurement.

Watch rain as it falls on a window.
What shape are raindrops?
Are all drops the same size?
What colour are the drops?
Which drops move fastest?
Which drops join together?
What does the rain sound like?

FORECASTING

Use some or all of the instruments described on the previous pages together with your observational skills to keep weather records and prepare forecasts.

You don't need a special instrument to determine visibility. Select prominent objects at the following approximate distances from your location: 0.5, 1.0, 1.5, 5, 10, 15, and 20 km. Try to choose objects which have good silhouettes, such as trees, flagpoles, spires, and large buildings. Determine the visibility at a given time by noting the object which is farthest away and still visible. For example, if you can see the 5 km mark, but not the 10 km mark, then record the visibility as 5 km. Make visibility observations in the morning and afternoon. Always include a note about why visibility is reduced (e.g. fog, snow).

MATERIALS: Some or all of the instruments on the previous pages; copies of following pages. Optional -- wood, nails, paint and other building materials; plastic sheet protectors.

DOING IT:

1. You don't need an instrument box for forecasting, but it can be a handy place to store instruments. A general design for the box is shown. The box should be painted white to reflect sunlight, and should have holes which will let air circulate.

2. Locate the box in an open, flat, grassy area. Face the open side of the box northward so that direct sunlight won't reach the thermometers. You can keep instruments and papers inside the box, with the exception of the rain/snow collector and wind detection instruments. The rain/snow collector can sit on the ground a few metres away from the box. The wind detection instruments may be mounted on top of the box; make the instruments out of wood or plastic so that they are durable. Several of the pages in this One Leads to Another series contain graphs or listings of weather signs; photocopy these pages and mount them in plastic in or on the instrument box.

3. Enter daily weather information on photocopies of the Weather Conditions Record sheet.

4. Use the information on the following pages to help you make weather forecasts. Weather predictions are generally valid for 12 hours. At times, the results from some of the instruments may seem contradictory; use your intuition and past experience to resolve the contradictions.

5. *Extension:* To help you keep track of trends, graph or chart certain readings. A large calendar can be useful for tracking general weather conditions. Each day, draw a picture to represent the weather (e.g. sun for a sunny day). At the end of a month, cut the calendar into its individual days. Glue the days that show similar weather in columns to produce a bar graph.

Weather is the supreme activity director. Since humans can't control the weather, our only option is to schedule our activities around it. Unfortunately, no weather forecast is perfect -- there are many things that meteorologists don't know. This activity gives you some tips on forecasting. A description of an instrument box is included; the instrument box can act as the focal point for weather forecasting. A Weather Conditions Record sheet is also provided so that you can maintain a daily log of weather information and examine changes in weather over a period of time.

Topics: Weather Conditions; Measurement.

General Rules For Predicting Weather Changes

(MAY VARY WITH GEOGRAPHICAL LOCATION)

Look for a change to cloudy, unsettled weather when:
- The temperature rises abruptly, and at night is higher than usual.
- Air pressure falls steadily.
- The wind shifts to a southerly or easterly direction.
- Clouds move in different directions at different levels.
- Clouds get thicker and darker.
- After a day or two of westerly or northerly winds, the wind velocity drops at sunset and the sun sets clear with a few cirrus clouds in the west.
- A large ring (halo) appears around the sun or moon, and remains until clouds thicken and cover it up.
- There is a flow of moist air from the south. Fog may form.
- You suspect that a warm or cold front is approaching.

Look for steady precipitation when:
- The wind is south to southeast, and the air pressure is falling. If the pressure is falling slowly, rain will occur within a day. If it's falling rapidly, it will rain within a few hours and wind speeds will increase.
- The wind is southeast to northeast, and the pressure is falling. It will rain within a few hours.
- Thunderclouds develop against a south or southeast wind.

Look for showers when:
- Thunderclouds develop in a westerly wind.
- Cumulus clouds develop rapidly during early afternoon.

Look for clearing weather when:
- The temperature falls rapidly, especially in the afternoon.
- Air pressure rises.
- The wind shifts to a westerly or northwesterly direction.
- Clouds appear to break up and clear patches of sky show.
- The bases of clouds increase in elevation.
- You suspect that a cold front has passed.

Look for continued bright weather when:
- The temperature is normal.
- Air pressure remains steady or rises.
- A light breeze blows from the west or northwest.
- Cloudiness decreases after 3 or 4 pm, and the sunset is clear.
- Morning fog breaks within two hours after sunrise.
- There is dew or frost at night.
- A red sunset occurs.

Look for colder weather when:
- Air pressure is low and falling rapidly, and the wind is east or northeast and backing slowly into the north (the fall in temperature will be gradual).
- The wind swings from the southwest to the west or from the west to the northwest or north.
- A westerly wind drops in speed at night, and the sunset is clear.
- Clouds break up after a storm (if they clear in the morning, it will be warmer in the afternoon).
- You suspect that a cold front has passed.

Look for warmer weather when:
- Air pressure falls (in summer, falling barometer may indicate cloudy weather, which will be cooler than clear weather).
- The wind swings away from the north or west to the southwest or south.
- It's cloudy at night.
- The morning sky is clear, except if the wind is strong from the north or west.
- You suspect that a warm front has passed.

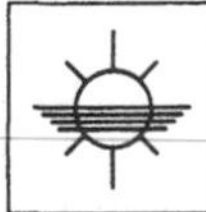

Forecasting Tables

(May Vary with Geographical Location)

Weather Changes Associated With Fronts				
Weather Element	Cold Front		Warm Front	
	Before	After	Before	After
Temperature	warm	cold	cool	warm
Wind Direction	southwest	northwest	southeast	southwest
Wind Speed	moderate	high	low	moderate
Clouds	cirrus/cumulus	cumulus/clear	stratus/nimbus	cumulus/clear
Air Pressure	low	high	high	low
Humidity	high	low	moderate	high
Precipitation	showers/thunderstorms	none/showers	moderate	showers/none

Quick Reference		
Wind Direction	Barometer Activity	Resulting Weather
west	low and rising	clearing and cooler
east to north	low and falling fast	gales with heavy rain
east to northeast	high and falling fast	storm with high winds
east to northeast	high and falling slow	rain within a day
south to southeast	low and falling fast	storm
south to southeast	high and falling slow	rain within a day
south to southeast	high and falling fast	rain, high winds soon
south to southwest	low and rising	fair weather soon
southwest to northwest	high and steady	continued fair weather
southwest to northwest	high and falling slow	rain in a day or two
southwest to northwest	very high and falling	temperature rising for a day
southeast to northeast	high and falling fast	high winds and rain
southeast to northeast	low and falling fast	storm with high winds
southeast to northeast	low and falling slow	continued rain
southeast to east	high and falling slow	rain within a day

Weather Conditions Record

DATE AND TIME							
Temperature (degrees C)							
Wind Speed (km/h)							
Wind Direction							
Cloud Movement Direction							
Cloud Type							
Amount of Cloud Cover (%)							
Atmospheric Pressure							
Relative Humidity (%)							
Dew Point (degrees C)							
Precipitation (mm)							
Visibility (km)							
FORECAST (and notes)							

THE HEAVENS

STARGAZING

The Heavens subject area has seven One Leads to Another activities. The series introduces novice stargazers to the night sky.

Gazing up into the night-time sky is the only way to fully appreciate the heavens. Stargazing takes time and patience, but nothing beats the excitement you feel when you finally find things you've heard so much about, like the North Star or the Big Dipper. There's also the possibility that you'll come across something new or completely unexpected. Amateurs and people making routine observations have made some fantastic discoveries and play an important role in the field of astronomy. For example, two young amateur astronomers carried their homemade telescope to a hilltop near their home in Texas to test out the optics. That very night they discovered a comet now named after them. A few hundred years ago, a group of astronomers from a monastery were observing the moon when they saw a bright, bursting light on its surface. Today's astronomers believe that the monks were lucky enough to see a meteor strike the moon and form a large crater. Of the billions and billions of people who have ever lived, those monks may be the *only* humans to have seen this kind of meteor strike.

Louis Pasteur once said that "chance favours the prepared mind". The following activities will help you to be prepared. Although the northern hemisphere is the focus, some information on the southern hemisphere is included, and much of the information is general enough to be useful in both hemispheres.

The first activity deals with basic guidelines for stargazing. The next activity outlines methods for locating stars. The third activity helps you on your first night out by describing prominent heavenly bodies visible year-round in the northern hemisphere. The next two activities involve making an instrument for investigating star brightness and constructing a constellation finder. The sixth activity is a guided tour around the summer sky (most people start stargazing in the summer because it's warmer); some information on spring, fall, and winter constellations is also provided. The final activity contains tips for buying and using binoculars.

Quickies and Make Time activities in The Heavens subject area can supplement the stargazing series. In particular, the Make Time section contains a pattern for making a nocturnal to help you tell time using the stars and instructions for making mini planetariums to help you become familiar with the shapes of constellations. Many of the activities contain interesting facts and background information which can be discussed while stargazing.

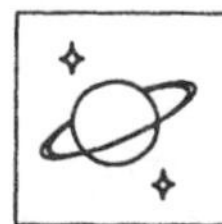

GETTING READY

Even though the stars are trillions of kilometres from Earth, we can see many of them. These suggestions will help you to get the most out of stargazing.

MATERIALS: Flashlight; red sock or red cellophane; notebook; pencil. Optional -- blanket; pillow; binoculars and/or telescope; star maps.

DOING IT:

1. Choose a clear, dark night for stargazing. Clouds, haze, dust, or mist will make it difficult to observe much. A bright, full moon can also block out faint stars. On the other hand, pitch-black skies can reveal such a multitude of stars that a beginner may feel overwhelmed and confused. The best time to make your first stargazing trip is just before or after a new moon.

2. When you're a beginner, it's best to go stargazing just after sunset. Only the brighter stars are visible, which prevents confusion.

3. Get as far away as possible from the bright lights of large cities.

4. Dress warmly. Nights can be very chilly, even in summer. No one enjoys stargazing when they're cold.

5. Always take a flashlight to find your way and read star maps. Cover the bulb end of the flashlight with a red sock or red cellophane (red light doesn't ruin your eyes' adaptation to the dark). If a group of people are stargazing, one person may want to use a strong, concentrated flashlight beam (not covered) as a pointer in the sky.

6. Find a place that's as dark as possible, away from a large city and out of direct light from buildings and street lamps. A hill makes a good observation site. Make sure you know the direction of north, south, east, and west.

7. Give your eyes at least 10 and preferably 20 minutes to adjust to the dark.

8. Lie on your back, if possible (here's where a blanket and/or pillow comes in handy). Get up and take a break every once in a while to get rid of restless energy.

9. Keep star maps and resource books close by to check locations of stars. Make notes or drawings in a notebook. Always include the date and place in your notes. Keep track of the time that elapses; make notes every five minutes or so on new things you've spotted and how your vision changes. When you first begin stargazing, make notes on everything you see -- planes, the moon, planets, bright stars, "UFOs", satellites, fireflies, clouds, meteors, Northern Lights, comets, halos around the moon, and the twinkling (scintillation) of bright stars. As you become more comfortable with stargazing, you can record star details such as size, colour, brilliance, position in relation to other stars, and movement, if any.

10. Watch lights carefully! If a light moves steadily, it may be a satellite, meteor, or plane.

11. Experiment with looking at objects in different ways. For example, look directly at a star and then look at it out of the corner of your eye. Which way can you see more?

There are billions of stars in the sky. From the heart of a big city, with bright lights all around, probably only about 250 stars are visible. But, outside the city, on a clear night, you can easily see 3,000 stars without a telescope. 99% of these stars are bigger and brighter than our sun.

Topics: Stars.

Over There!

You can't point to a star in the dark, so how do you tell others about it? How do you describe distances between stars? Here are some methods for locating stars.

MATERIALS: None.

DOING IT:

1. To indicate the direction of a star, you can simply say "north" or "northwest". To be more precise, you can pretend you're in the middle of a large clock. 12:00 is north. You can then indicate direction by saying, "I'm looking at a star at 10:00."

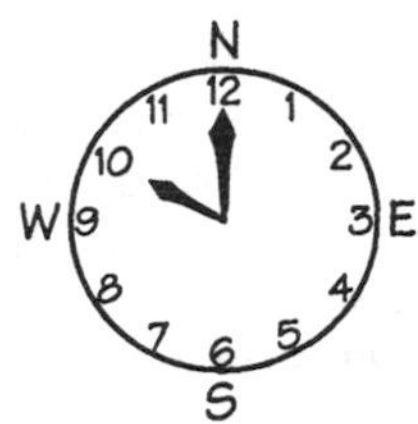

2. To find a star's altitude, look at the point in the sky directly over your head, called the "zenith". Don't just look up with your eyes; lean your head as far back as possible or lie down and look up. All visible objects in the sky are found between the horizon (0 degrees) and the zenith (90 degrees). For example, if a star is exactly halfway between the horizon and the zenith, it's at 45 degrees. You can also use your hands to find a star's altitude. Hold out one hand at arm's length, palm toward you, with fingers together and thumb straight up. Move your hand down until the bottom of your little finger "rests" on the horizon (ignore any buildings, trees, etc. blocking the horizon). The top of your index finger is "one hand high". Steadily move hand over hand until you reach the star you're observing. For example, a star may be an even "two hands" above the horizon, or it may be three hands plus two fingers.

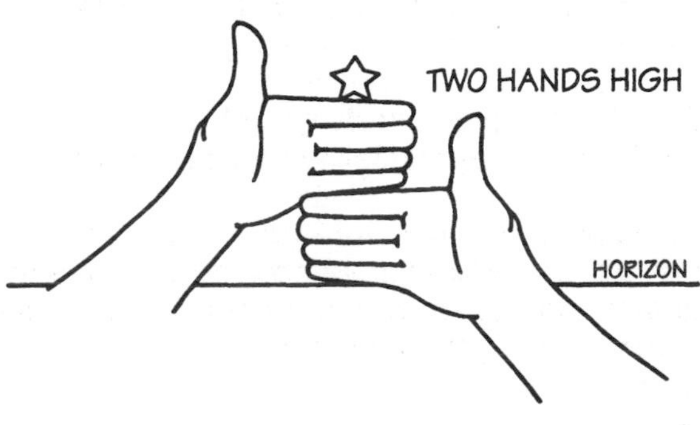

3. To point out a star, combine the imaginary clock and the divisions of 90 degrees (or the hands). For example, suppose you're looking at a star in the southeast, about halfway between the zenith and the horizon. You could explain where the star is by saying, "I'm looking at a star at 5:00, 45 degrees".

4. Use your hands to determine the apparent distance between stars in degrees. Hold out your hand at arm's length. The width of the tip of your little finger is about 1 degree. The illustrations below show the degrees made up by finger combinations and spans. The Big Dipper is a good way to test this measuring system. For example, the distance between the two "pointer stars" in the Big Dipper's bowl is 5 degrees (three middle fingers). The distance across the top of the bowl is 10 degrees (one fist). The distance from one end of the Big Dipper to the other is about 25 degrees (two fists plus three middle fingers, or span from little finger to thumb).

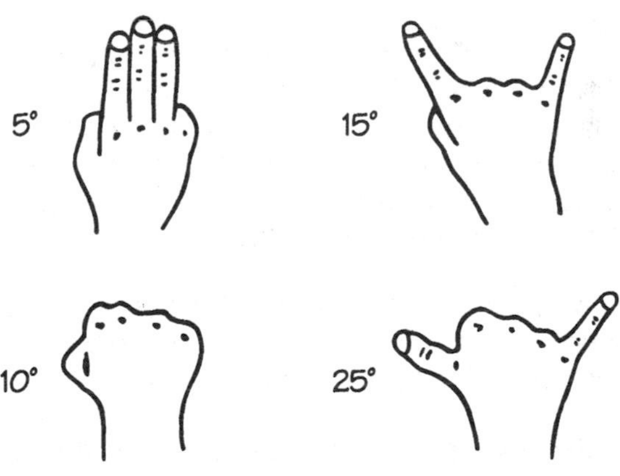

When you're stargazing, the important thing isn't the distance of stars from Earth, but their location in the sky and apparent distance from each other. The "azimuth-altitude" method is a simple way to describe the location of a star. First, you give the direction (azimuth); then you give the star's height in the sky (altitude). You can also describe a star's location in terms of the degrees between stars.

Topics: Stars; Measurement.

First Time Out

Introduce yourself to the night sky over the northern hemisphere. Once you're familiar with the basic stars, it's easy to build on your knowledge and find others.

The North Star (Polaris) is located almost directly above the North Pole; it indicates geographic north (which differs somewhat from magnetic north). The North Star's height in the sky depends on your latitude. Closer to the North Pole, the North Star appears almost directly overhead; closer to the equator, it appears near the horizon. The North Star is not a particularly bright star, but it's special because it changes its position very little. All the stars seem to turn counterclockwise around the North Star. The location of the Big Dipper at about 9:00 p.m. through the seasons in the middle latitudes of the northern hemisphere is illustrated; the Big Dipper shifts from almost directly overhead in spring to close to the northern horizon in fall. You can see the Big Dipper all year anywhere up from 40 N latitude (between 25 N and 40 N, it disappears for a few weeks in the fall).

A "constellation" is a group of stars. Early astronomers divided the sky into regions that had fairly distinct groups of stars. They named these groups of stars after the figures the stars seemed to form and associated the figures with stories about heroes, heroines, and beasts. The stars in a constellation do not necessarily have any relationship with one another. In 1930, the International Astronomical Union officially set the constellation names and boundaries. There are 88 constellations; each star is associated with only one constellation. A quarter of the constellations are visible only from southern latitudes, and half of the remainder are quite faint. As the Earth orbits the sun, many constellations can be seen only during certain times of the year.

For your first time out, concentrate on key "circumpolar" constellations (visible year-round). The easiest-to-find circumpolar stars are in the Big Dipper (part of Big Bear/Ursa Major constellation); the Little Dipper (Little Bear/Ursa Minor constellation); Draco (the Dragon); Cassiopeia (the Queen); and Cepheus (the King).

Using the Big Dipper, as well as Orion (the Mighty Hunter), it's possible to find every major star and constellation visible from Canada, the United States, or Europe. The key limitation of Orion is that it is visible only from late November to early April.

Topics: Stars; Planets.

The telescope opened the heavens. In the early 1600s, Dutch optician Hans Lippershey invented lenses that formed a magnified image of a distant object. Italian physicist and astronomer Galileo then fashioned such lenses for himself and pointed them toward the stars.

MATERIALS: As discussed in first activity.

DOING IT:

1. *The Big Picture:* Start by just looking. Enjoy the whole display of the night sky before you look for specific things.

2. *The Moon:* The moon is the brightest and most easily seen object in the night sky. On some nights, the moon shines so brightly that few stars or planets can be seen. Where is the moon? How would you describe its position in the sky (use the star location methods discussed on the previous page)? At arm's length, the width of the tip of your little finger is about 1 degree. Try to cover the moon -- which is less than a degree across -- with your little finger. In what phase is the moon? While the four main phases (first quarter, full, last quarter, and new) are enough detail for wall calendars, astronomers describe the phases of the moon in terms of the moon's "age" in days after the new phase (moon not visible). One complete cycle from new moon to new moon takes 29.5 days. First quarter occurs at 7 days; full moon at 14 or 15 days; and last quarter at 22 days. Around the first quarter phase, age 6 to 9 days, the moon is at its prime for amateur stargazers.

3. *Planets:* On a dark night, many stars and planets become visible. Planets usually appear first; not until the sky is completely dark do the stars come out. You should be able to find four planets fairly easily (it helps if you have binoculars or a telescope). *Venus* is brilliant white. It gets closer to Earth than any other planet. At its brightest, it outshines everything except the moon and can be seen in the east around

sunrise or the west around sunset. *Jupiter* is a big, bright, yellowish-white planet. With binoculars, you can see four of Jupiter's brightest moons (there are sixteen in total); the moons look like bright spots lying to one side of Jupiter in an almost straight line. *Saturn* appears pale yellow and, in terms of brightness, may be mistaken for a star; don't expect to see rings unless you have a telescope. *Mars* shines with a reddish light and slowly drifts in front of the stars. Once you spot a planet, watch it for a few nights in a row; it will move westward with the whole sky. Planets' positions depend on the year and the time of year, so consult a newspaper or monthly star bulletin to get exact locations.

4. *Stars:* Fix your eyes on a random star and watch it for a while. Then pick another star and do the same thing.

5. *Big Dipper:* The Big Dipper, visible in the north sky, is made up of seven stars, which are fairly bright and not hard to spot. The Big Dipper is shaped like a saucepan or a bowl with a handle on it. It is part of a larger constellation called Ursa Major (Big Bear). The Big Dipper is used as a guide around the sky and it's important to be able to find it easily. Find it, look away for a few moments, then try to find it again. Which of the Big Dipper's stars has a little star right next to it? The answer is Mizar, the second star from the end of the handle. The faint star is Alcor. The Indians used the two stars as an eye test; they called the large star the squaw and the other on her back the papoose.

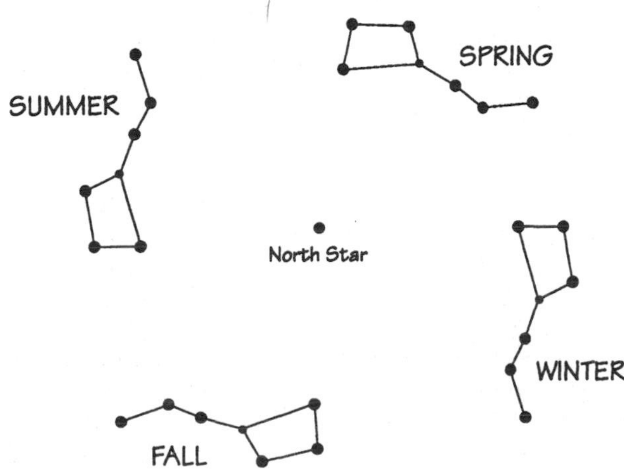

6. *North Star:* Extend a line outward from the two "pointer stars" in the Big Dipper, Merak and Dubhe. The stars point in the direction of the North Star (Polaris). The North Star has no stars around it, so it's easy to see even though it's not very bright. When you face the North Star, you face true north.

7. *Little Dipper:* The North Star is the end star of the Little Dipper's handle. The Big Dipper and the Little Dipper face each other. The Little Dipper forms the constellation of Ursa Minor, the Little Bear.

8. *Draco:* Draco, the Dragon, wraps its tail around the cup portion of the Little Dipper and comes between the Big Dipper and the Little Dipper.

9. *Cassiopeia:* Cassiopeia and the Big Dipper are on opposite sides of the North Star, about the same distance from the star. Follow the pointer stars of the Big Dipper to the North Star and continue on until you come to a W-shaped constellation of five stars. Named after a mythical queen, the constellation looks like points in a crown.

How can you tell a planet from a star? First of all, planets move in relation to the stars and each other. Secondly, planets shine more steadily and twinkle less than stars. Stars appear to twinkle because of the effect of Earth's atmosphere on the paths of light from the distant stars. Starlight hits molecules of air and microscopic particles in the atmosphere and is bent one way and then another way; so, stars appear to shimmer. Planets are closer to Earth than stars, and the greater amount of light from them isn't as affected by the atmosphere. A final way to tell a planet from a star: when you look through a telescope, a planet shows as a disc while stars are just pinpoints.

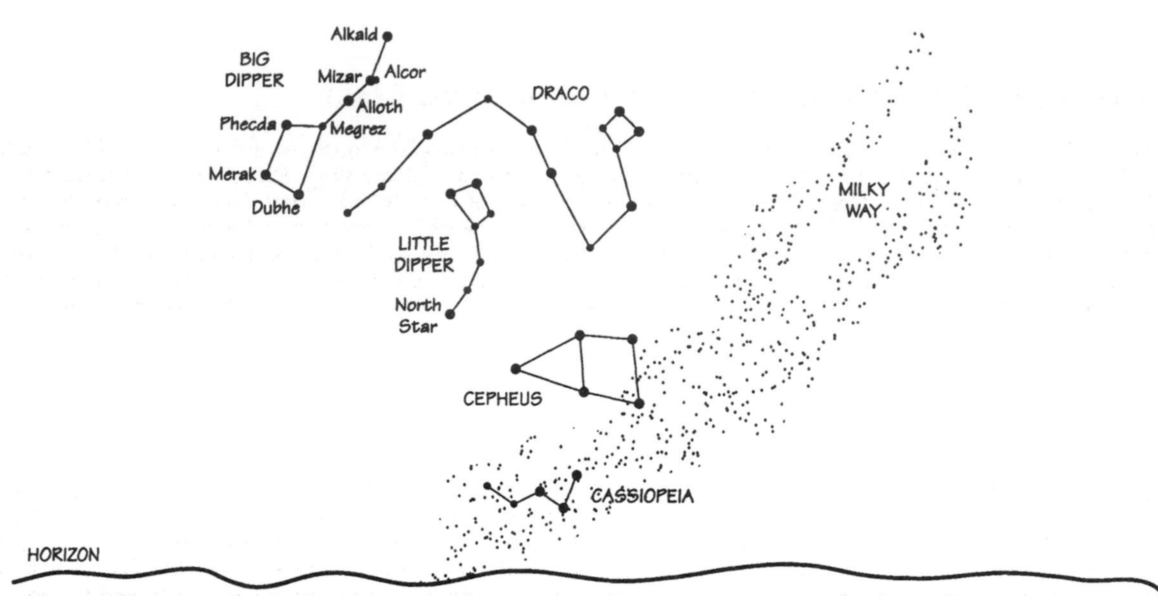

CIRCUMPOLAR CONSTELLATIONS, NORTHERN HEMISPHERE. SUMMER SKY, LOOKING NORTH.
MOST ACCURATE FOR THE FOLLOWING DAYLIGHT SAVING TIMES:
MAY 1, 1 A.M.; MAY 15, 12 P.M.; JUNE 1, 11 P.M.; JUNE 15, 10 P.M.; AND JULY 1, 9 P.M.

10. *Cepheus:* The constellation of Cepheus is found between Cassiopeia and the North Star. Cepheus is more difficult to see because of its fainter stars. Cepheus was named after a mythical king, but looks nothing like a king. It actually looks like a poorly drawn roof from a house.

11. *Orion:* Orion, the Mighty Hunter, is very important for finding other constellations, particularly those in winter. Look for Orion while facing south, between November and April. It is a dominant constellation made up of seven blue-white stars. Three evenly-spaced stars in the middle of the constellation form the hunter's "belt". Hanging down from the belt is a "sword", the Orion Nebula, a glowing mass of gas. Rigel, the brightest star in Orion, is also one of the most luminous stars known.

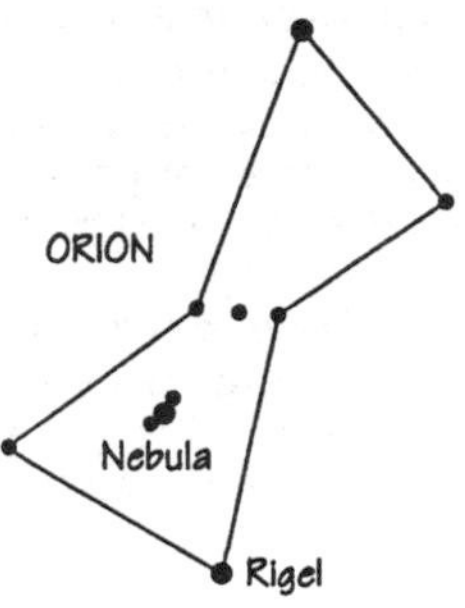

12. *Star Stories:* An interesting addition to star-gazing is to read about the mythology behind the constellations. Some stories are provided on the following page.

The stars move relative to one another, but the motion is very slight; stars remain in their place in constellations for thousands of years. However, the sky as a whole seems to move because the Earth rotates around its axis and orbits the sun. We see different stars at different times of the night, and different stars at different times of the year. Observe the motion caused by the Earth rotating around its axis by standing in a spot so that a bright star is just above a marker object (e.g. pole, tall tree). Note the star's position. Return to the exact spot in half an hour or an hour. The star will probably have moved quite a distance. In general, stars sweep across the sky from east to west, just as the sun does each day.

STAR STORIES

THE BIG DIPPER AND THE LITTLE DIPPER (BIG BEAR AND LITTLE BEAR):

One of many Greek legends tells the story of a nymph named Kallisto (meaning "the most beautiful"). She had the misfortune to have Zeus, king of the gods, fall in love with her. Zeus loved to hear Kallisto sing.. Every day he would leave his throne to listen to her in the forest. Hera, Zeus' wife, was very jealous of Kallisto. One day, Hera flew into one of her habitual jealous rages and turned Kallisto into a shaggy bear. Not content with this revenge on the innocent nymph, Hera put Kallisto in a part of the forest where Kallisto's son, Arcas, was hunting. Arcas did not recognize his mother; he drew his powerful bow and took aim. In another second he would have pierced Kallisto's heart. But, just in the nick of time, Zeus saved Kallisto by changing Arcas into a bear as well. Zeus placed mother and son into the sky so they could be near each other forever.

DRACO:

The Greeks had several stories about Draco, the dragon. In one story, a hero named Cadmus slew Draco on orders from the goddess Athene. The goddess then told Cadmus to extract the dragon's teeth and sow them in the ground. As soon as Cadmus had done this, the dragon's teeth sprouted into armed soldiers, unpleasantly ready for a fight. Rattling their swords against their shields, the soldiers looked at Cadmus in a way he didn't like at all. But Athene told Cadmus to toss a stone into the midst of the armed crowd. The stone struck one of the soldiers, and he immediately attacked the soldier standing next to him. The soldiers next to them joined in the fight, and in no time at all the whole army was fighting each other. Soon, only five soldiers were left alive, and they were too weary to fight any more. Cadmus persuaded them to lay down their arms, and they later became his helpers. Ever since this incident, "sowing dragon's teeth" has meant stirring up trouble. Draco was placed high in the sky so that no one could plant his teeth and cause trouble again.

CASSIOPEIA AND CEPHEUS:

Andromeda was the beautiful daughter of Cepheus and Cassiopeia, the King and Queen of Ethiopia. Cassiopeia was a very beautiful woman herself, and together she and her daughter made a stunning pair. Unfortunately, Cassiopeia was also very vain, and she unwisely boasted that she and Andromeda were more beautiful than the Sea-Nymphs, or Nereids. The Nereids heard of this and flew into a sulk. They ran to their protector, the Sea-God Poseidon, and whined that they had been insulted. The Sea-God decided that he really must put these uppity mortals in their place. So he created a hideous sea-monster named Cetus and sent it off with orders to devastate Ethiopia. "Cetos" is the Greek word for "whale", but this Cetus was not at all like a whale. It was a long, snake-like creature with a vicious-looking head and tusks like a wild boar.

Programmed for destruction, Cetus swam off for the coast of Ethiopia, snorting with bestial glee. It paddled along the rocky shore, darting its long, snake-like neck many feet inland and snatching people in its sharp-toothed jaws. Many of the people of Ethiopia were devoured by Cetus. The rest hid in their houses and refused to come out. Cepheus ordered his soldiers to shoot the beast full of arrows. But the sharp, iron-headed arrows only glanced off the monster's tough scales. In despair, Cepheus went to an oracle and was told that the only way to get rid of the monster was to placate Poseidon by sacrificing Andromeda. So Cepheus had Andromeda chained to a rock on the shoreline and stood back sadly to await her fate.

Just then the hero Perseus appeared, flying through the air with his winged sandals. Seeing the beautiful girl chained to the rock with a crowd of weeping people standing a safe distance away, he swooped down to ask what the trouble was. Andromeda quickly told him her story. No sooner had she finished than the monster was seen in the distance, making playful leaps out of the water in anticipation of its next meal. Perseus asked Cepheus and Cassiopeia if they would give him Andromeda for his wife if he killed Cetus. They said yes, edging back nervously from the approaching monster. Perseus soared up in the air, circled over the monster, and swooped down and beheaded it with his magic sickle.

Cepheus and Cassiopeia tried to wriggle out of their promise to give their daughter to Perseus, but Andromeda, who had fallen in love with her handsome young rescuer, insisted on going through with the wedding. On their deaths, Cepheus, Cassiopeia, Andromeda and Perseus were placed among the stars to reenact their story. The proud Cassiopeia was punished by being tied in a chair in a rather uncomfortable position. As her stars circle around the North Star, she suffers the humiliation of dangling upside down for half the year.

STAR BRIGHTNESS

Stars are not equally bright. Use this simple instrument to get a general idea of the brightness (magnitude) of different stars.

MATERIALS: Lightweight cardboard; nickel; scissors; ruler; pencil; clear, unwrinkled cellophane; stapler; tape.

The brightness of stars can be described in two ways: actual and apparent. Differences in actual brightness are caused by temperature differences between stars themselves. Apparent brightness involves how bright a star *appears* from Earth. A bright star that is very far away may seem to be just as bright as a weaker star that is closer to Earth.

The Greek astronomer Hipparchus classified the stars by their apparent brightness. He divided stars into six categories: brightest stars were given a "1"; very faint stars a "6" (the faintest stars visible on a very clear night with the unaided eye); and the rest of the stars fell in between. The lower the "magnitude" (i.e. the lower the number on the 1 to 6 scale), the brighter the star. The system has been refined since it was first developed, but it's still basically the same. A step of one magnitude is an increase or decrease in brightness by a factor of 2.5 times. For example, a first-magnitude star is 2.5 times brighter than a second-magnitude star, and is 2.5 x 2.5 (about 6) times brighter than a third-magnitude star. The numbers 2.5, 6, 16, 40, and 100 are usually used to describe the difference in brightness between 1, 2, 3, 4, 5, and 6 magnitude stars respectively. The magnitude scale has been extended (into higher positive numbers for faint stars and into negative numbers for bright stars) because some stars have been found to be too bright or too dim for their original magnitude, and new stars have been discovered. Using the world's most powerful telescopes, 28th magnitude stars have been found. At the opposite extreme, the brightness of the sun is a magnitude -26, six trillion times brighter than a sixth-magnitude star. There are only 22 stars of the first magnitude or brighter, and these are the ones that usually attract the attention of a casual observer. Sirius, the brightest star in the night sky (visible in winter), is magnitude -1. Planets that are brighter are Jupiter at -3, Venus at -4, and Mars, which varies from +2 to -3.

Topics: Stars; Measurement.

DOING IT:

1. Cut two strips of cardboard 27 cm x 7 cm.

2. Draw a faint line lengthwise, down the centre of one of the strips of cardboard. Make a small mark along the centre line every 4.5 cm. Use a nickel to draw a circle centred around each mark. Cut out the circles so that you have five holes.

3. Lay the strip of cardboard over your other strip of cardboard and trace the holes onto the second strip. Cut out the holes.

4. Cut fifteen 4 cm x 7 cm cellophane squares.

5. Lay one strip of cardboard on a table. Cover the first hole with one square of cellophane; the second hole with two squares; the third hole with three squares; the fourth hole with four squares; and the fifth hole with five squares. Use bits of tape to help hold the cellophane in place.

6. Carefully lay the other strip of cardboard on top of the pile, lining up the holes. Staple around the edge of the cardboard to hold the cardboard strips and cellophane together.

7. Label the holes from 1 to 5, starting with 1 for the hole with five squares of cellophane.

8. First, look at a star without the instrument. Then hold the instrument up and look at the star through hole 1. Can you see the star? If you can see the star through hole 1 (the hole with the most layers of cellophane), it is a bright star, first-magnitude or brighter. If you can't see the star, move down the row and look at the star through each of the other holes. If the star is visible through, for example, hole 3, it is around a third-magnitude star. If you can't see the star through hole 5, but you can see it with your eye alone, then it is a sixth-magnitude star.

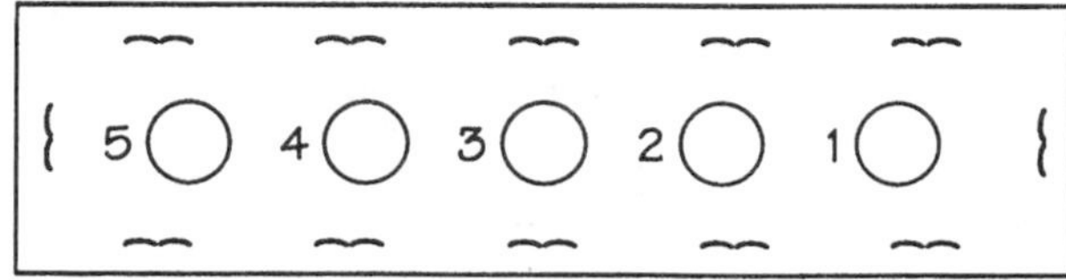

FINDING CONSTELLATIONS

Make a constellation finder to help you find constellations visible on a particular night in the northern or southern hemisphere.

MATERIALS: Photocopies of the maps and frame on following pages; lightweight cardboard; glue; pencil; tape; scissors; *small* brass paper fasteners.

DOING IT:

1. Examine the maps on the following pages. Which constellations are visible from your hemisphere? Which constellations visible in your hemisphere are also visible from the other hemisphere? Which constellations are visible from the other hemisphere only? Why?

2. You can use the maps alone to help you find constellations, or you can make a constellation finder. To make a finder, photocopy the map of your hemisphere and the finder frame. Stiffen the copies by gluing them onto cardboard.

3. Cut away any excess cardboard around the circular map. Cut out the frame, following the dotted lines. Lay the frame on a sheet of cardboard and trace around its outside edge. Then, cut the frame shape from the cardboard; this forms the finder's base.

4. Punch a small hole in the centre of the map (North Star for northern hemisphere, open circle for southern hemisphere) and the centre of the base. Place the map onto the base and push a brass paper fastener through the hole in the map and the hole in the base. Position the frame over the map so that the dates on the map are clearly visible through the slots in the frame. Tape the top two corners of the frame onto the base. The map should turn freely between the frame and the base.

5. The constellation finder is helpful if you're in the middle northern latitudes or the middle southern latitudes; it is set for standard time. Rotate the map so that the date of observation is lined up with the hour of observation on the frame. The stars within the oval on the frame will give you a *general* idea of the stars visible at that date and time. Hold the constellation finder over your head with the north arrow pointing north. The centre of the oval represents the skies directly above your head (the zenith). The outside edges of the oval show the stars in the north, south, west, and east skies around you. For example, if you're using the map of the northern hemisphere and set the constellation finder for November 1, 10 p.m., the Big Dipper will be shown on the north horizon. Andromeda will be almost overhead; Orion will be on the east horizon; and Aquila will be on the west horizon.

6. *Variation:* Put together one constellation finder for the northern hemisphere and one for the southern hemisphere. Turn both finders to the same date and time. Compare the visible constellations.

When you first look for a constellation, it can be difficult to find because of all the stars in the night sky and because constellations look different than when they are drawn on a map. A constellation finder can be helpful for initially orienting yourself. Once you find a constellation, it will be easier to find it again. The maps on the following pages show only the more important, readily-visible stars in each hemisphere and, as a result, the shapes of constellations may differ slightly from more detailed maps.

People at different latitudes have different views of the night sky. A person at the North Pole can never see the stars visible from the South Pole and vice versa. At the equator, a person can see all the stars during the course of the year. Some basic constellations in the northern hemisphere are discussed on the previous and following pages. In the southern hemisphere, look for Octans (faintly visible) and Crux. In both hemispheres, look for Orion, Pegasus, Virgo, Canis Major, Gemini, and Aquila. Everyone on Earth can also see a band of light in the night sky called the Milky Way. The Milky Way is a group of stars, gas, and dust that make up the galaxy of which our sun is a part. One nearby galaxy, in the constellation Andromeda, is faintly visible in the night sky of the northern hemisphere. People in the southern hemisphere can see two other galaxies, the Large and Small Magellanic Clouds.

Topics: Stars; Mapping; Earth.

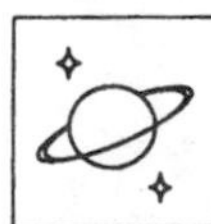

Stars Of The Mid-Northern Hemisphere

This map shows some key constellations in the northern skies, with the North Star directly overhead. Different latitudes give you different views of the sky. To use the map on its own, face *north* and turn the map so that the current month is at the bottom. Many of the stars in the top two-thirds of the map will be visible during some time of the night from the middle northern latitudes (including southern Canada and most of the United States).

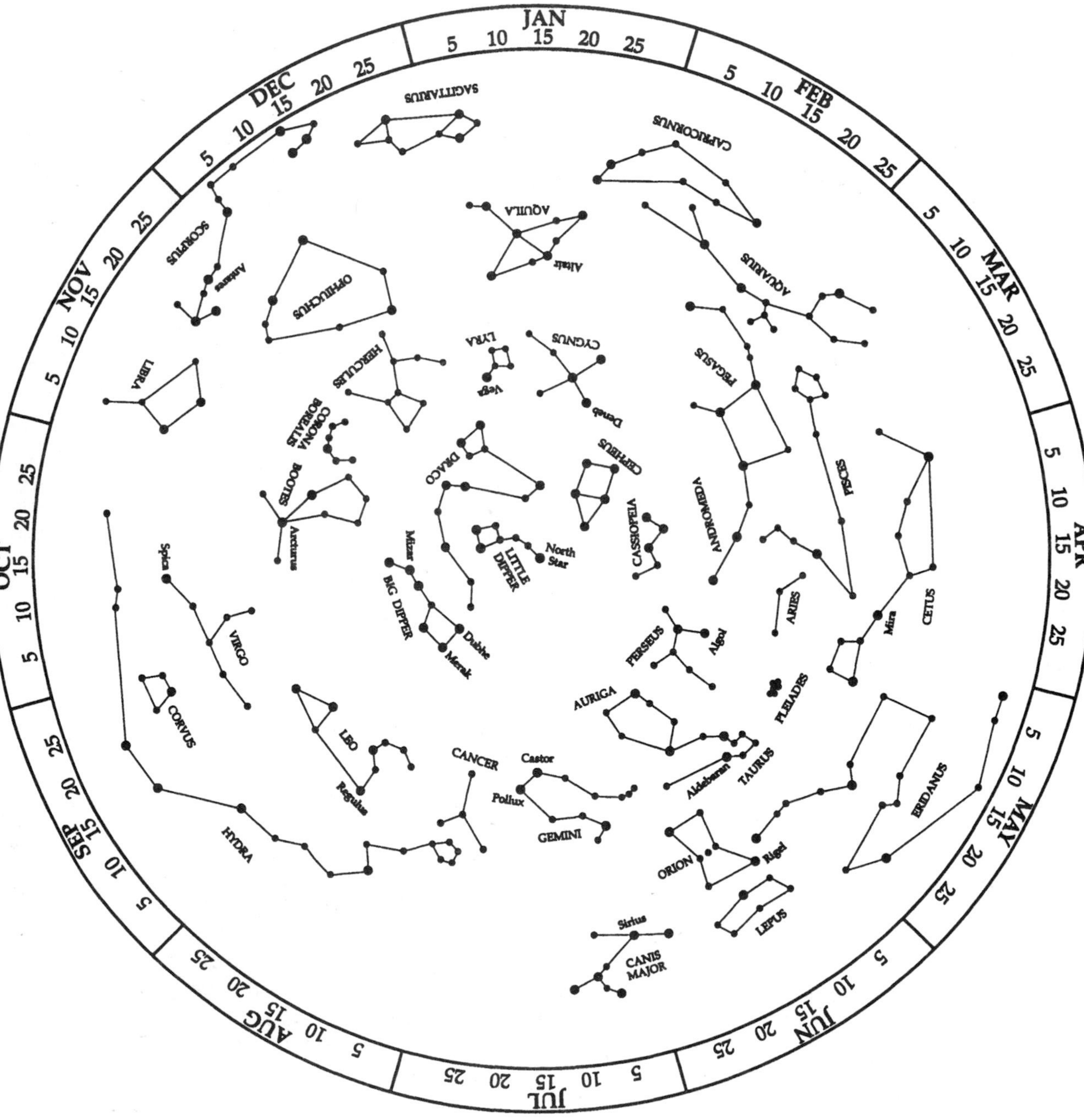

STARS OF THE MID-SOUTHERN HEMISPHERE

This map shows some key constellations in the southern skies. There is no "south star"; the constellation Octans is most directly overhead. Different latitudes give you different views of the sky. To use the map on its own, face *south* and turn the map so that the current month is at the bottom. Many of the stars in the top two-thirds of the map will be visible during some time of the night from the middle southern latitudes.

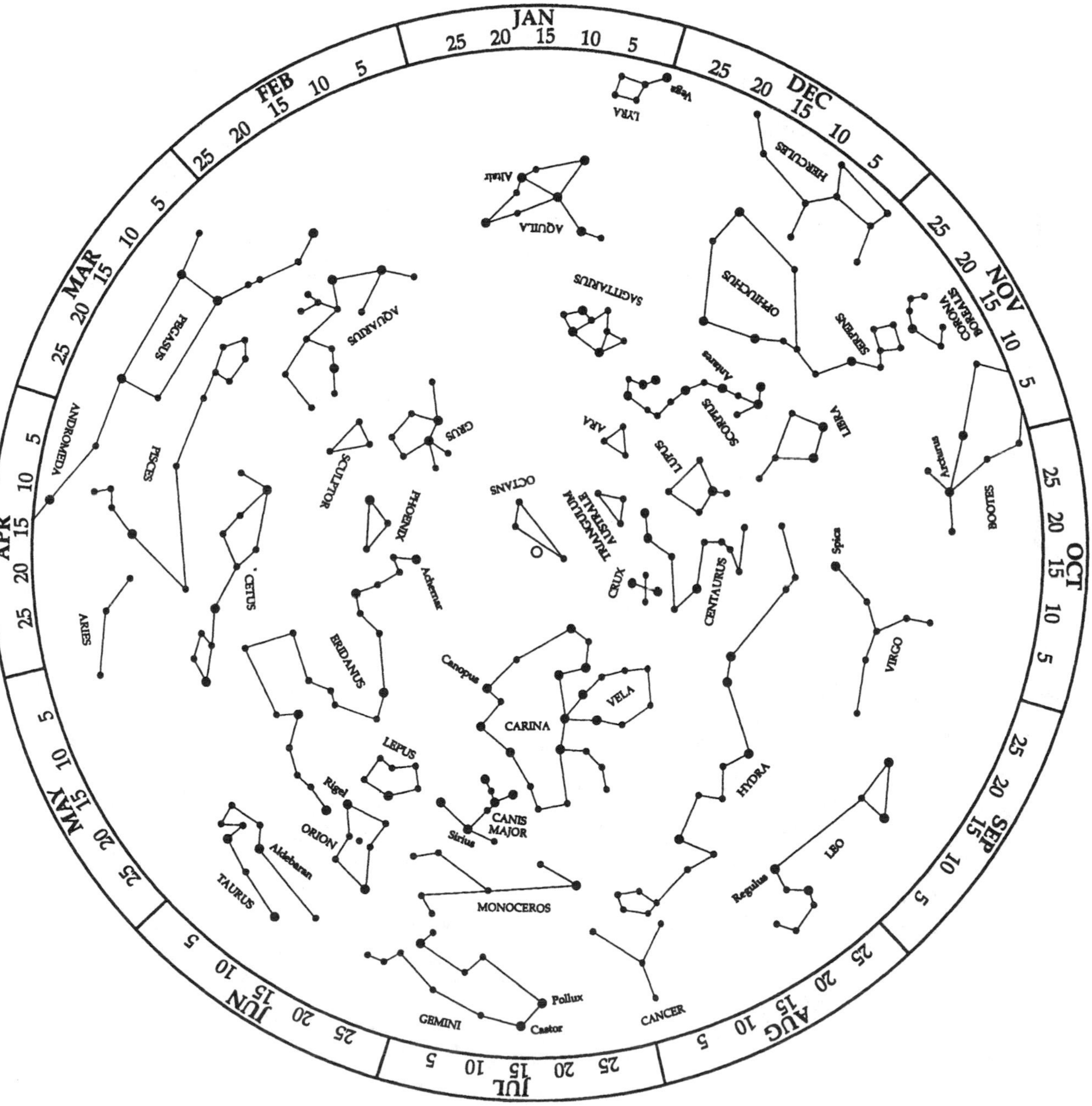

Constellation Finder Frame

This frame is designed for standard time in the northern hemisphere. To use the frame in the southern hemisphere, switch north and south (i.e. cross out N and write in S) and then switch west and east (i.e. cross out W and write in E). You must also change the times shown. Midnight and noon remain in place, but the rest of the times switch to the opposite side of the frame (e.g. 1 a.m. and 11 p.m. switch; 5 a.m. and 7 p.m. switch; 10 a.m. and 2 p.m. switch).

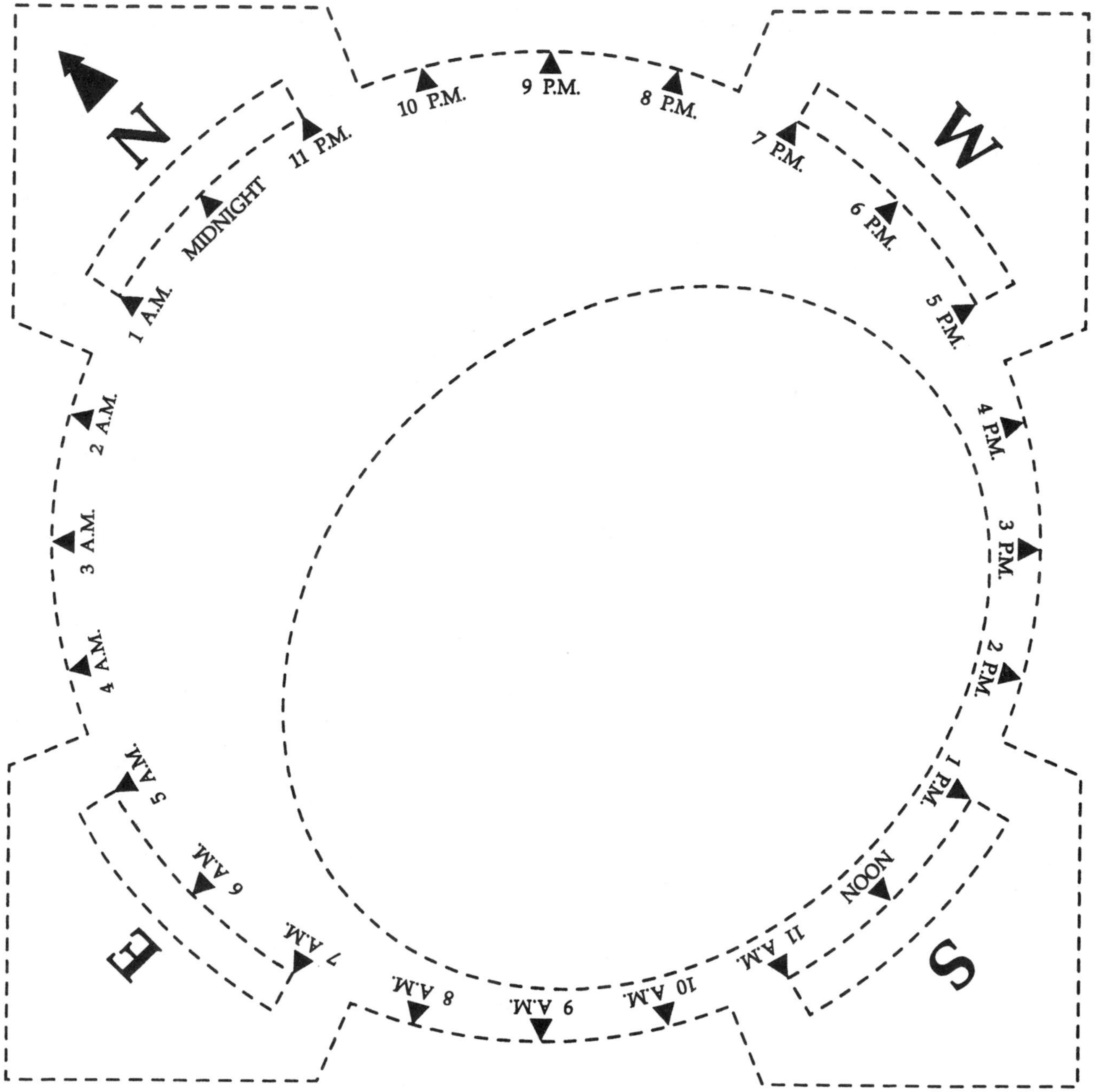

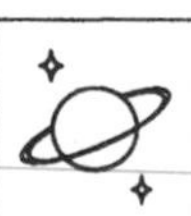

Getting Into More Detail

Take this guided tour (designed for middle latitudes in the northern hemisphere) to see many stars readily visible without binoculars or a telescope.

If you look carefully at stars, you should see faint tinges of colour. Colour is a hint of a star's physical condition and temperature. Red stars are coolest; blue stars are hottest; and yellow stars are in between.

MATERIALS: Flashlight; red sock or red cellophane; notebook; pencil. Optional -- blanket and/or pillow; binoculars and/or telescope; star maps; star brightness instrument and constellation finder (described on previous pages).

DOING IT:

1. *Bootes:* Start your summer star tour at the Big Dipper. Follow the curved line of the handle around until you come to the first-magnitude star Arcturus. Arcturus is about 25 times the diameter of our sun, is the brightest summer star, and has a red-orange colour. It's part of the constellation Bootes (the Herdsman). Next to Bootes is a half circle of stars which aren't particularly bright; they are the Corona Borealis (Northern Crown).

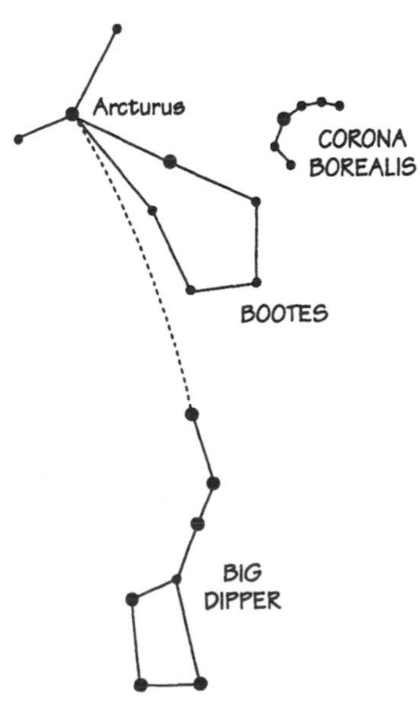

2. *Virgo:* Go back to the Big Dipper's handle and follow the curve again, but this time continue through Arcturus to the next brightest star, Spica. A verse for remembering this: "Follow the arc to Arcturus and speed on to Spica." Spica is a little over first magnitude. It's the brightest star of the constellation Virgo (the Virgin). In late summer, Virgo is very low on the western horizon.

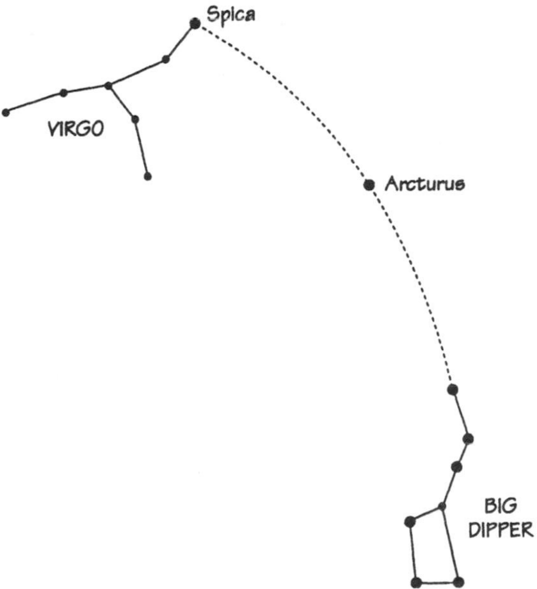

Always work from the known to the unknown. When you're trying to find a star or constellation, begin by finding the nearest, brightest known star; link stars by locater lines, arcs, and triangles; then fill in the details. Be patient -- it takes awhile to become completely comfortable with star identification. Note that the shapes of constellations can vary on different maps because some fainter stars may be omitted for clarity.

The Big Dipper is an important pointer for finding constellations visible in summer; this tour focuses on spring/summer stars. Orion is useful for finding winter constellations, which are mentioned toward the end.

Topics: Stars.

Comets look like stars with tails of faint light. A comet looks fuzzy to the naked eye, and often remains fuzzy when viewed with binoculars or a telescope. If possible, watch a comet from day to day; see the tail grow as the comet nears the sun and then shrink as the comet leaves. Check a newspaper or monthly star bulletin to find out when to expect a comet.

3. *Leo:* Return to the Big Dipper. Follow the pointer stars Merak and Dubhe in the opposite direction from the North Star until you locate the sickle (or backward question mark) which makes up the head and mane of Leo (the Lion). Regulus, a bright star in the constellation, is Leo's heart. Leo can be seen near the western horizon in July, but not in August.

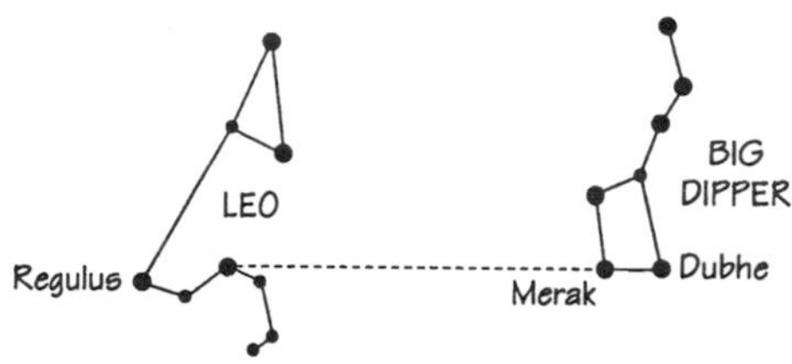

4. *Summer Triangle (Lyra, Cygnus, Aquila):* Go back once again to the Big Dipper. Follow the pointer stars to the North Star and then Cassiopeia. Using the two stars on the end arm of the "W" as pointers, follow a line through Cepheus to the very bright (zero magnitude), white star Vega. Vega is part of the constellation Lyra (the Lyre). Moving across slightly from Vega, you come to the first-magnitude star Deneb. Deneb is in the tail of the constellation Cygnus (the Swan). Slightly up from Deneb and across from Vega is the first-magnitude Altair. Altair is part of Aquila (the Eagle). The Summer Triangle is seen by connecting Vega, Deneb, and Altair. The Summer Triangle is visible during the summer months and into the winter. It covers a patch of sky a bit larger than the area blocked by a hand held at arm's length, fingers spread.

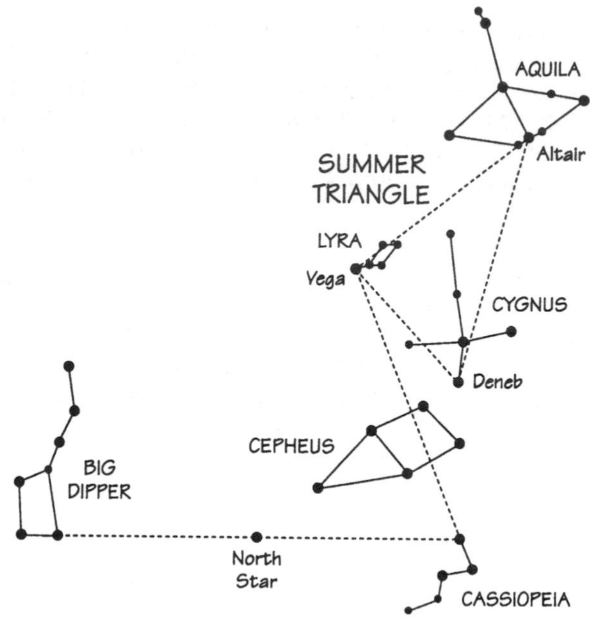

5. *Sagittarius:* While at Cygnus, follow a line through its length down to the southern horizon. Sitting on the horizon you'll find a group of bright stars forming the image of a giant teapot. The teapot's spout is on the right, its handle to the left. This is the constellation Sagittarius (the Archer). It may be difficult to find Sagittarius because it's so low in the southern sky.

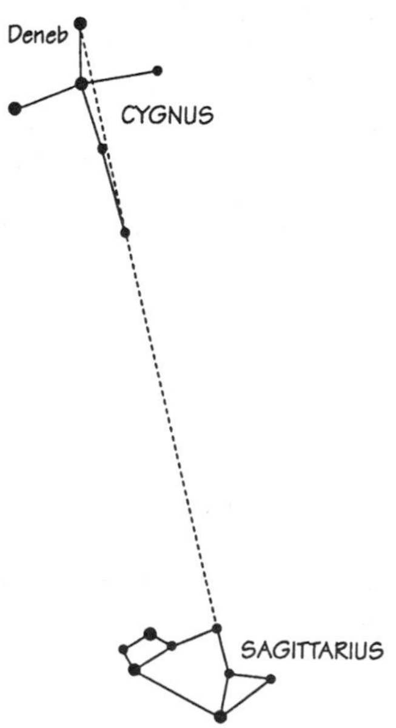

6. *Milky Way:* When you look at Sagittarius, you're looking into the centre of our galaxy. Look carefully to see some hazy patches of light in this region (binoculars will reveal these patches to be clusters of stars). This is the Milky Way. Follow the Milky Way across the sky through Cassiopeia.

7. *Scorpius:* West of Sagittarius is the winding constellation Scorpius (the Scorpion) with the super-giant, orange Antares near its head (in Arabic, Antares means "rival of Mars"; when the reddish planet is near Antares, the two look almost identical). Scorpius barely comes above the southern horizon on summer evenings.

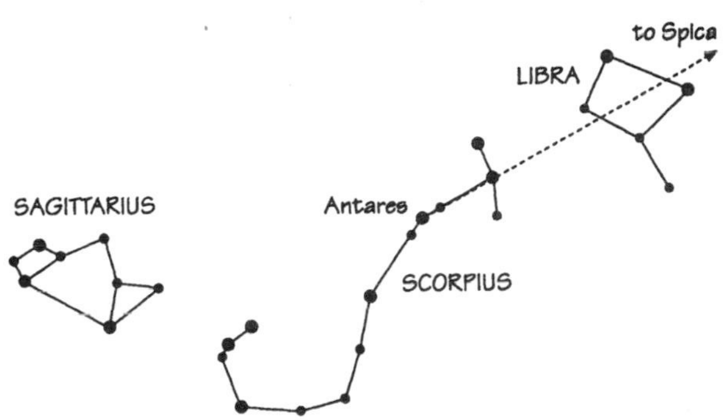

8. *Libra:* Follow a line from Antares through the head of Scorpius, past the diamond-shaped Libra (the Scales or Balance) with its faint stars, and you arrive back at first-magnitude Spica. Go up to Arcturus and around to the handle of the Big Dipper. Then go through the pointer stars and finally stop at the North Star. Your summer tour is complete.

Watch the reflection of the night sky on a still body of water. The reflection can often help you see things you otherwise wouldn't notice.

Meteors appear as a streak in the sky for a brief moment and then disappear. An average of seven meteors per hour can be seen on any night of the year. At certain times of the year, large numbers of meteoroids cross the Earth's orbit and create a meteor shower.

9. *Gemini:* In spring, follow a diagonal line across the Big Dipper's bowl toward second-magnitude Castor and first-magnitude Pollux in the constellation Gemini (the Twins). Gemini is made up of two roughly parallel chains of stars. Gemini is an important link between the spring and winter sky, largely because it can be found from either the Big Dipper or Orion (described on following page).

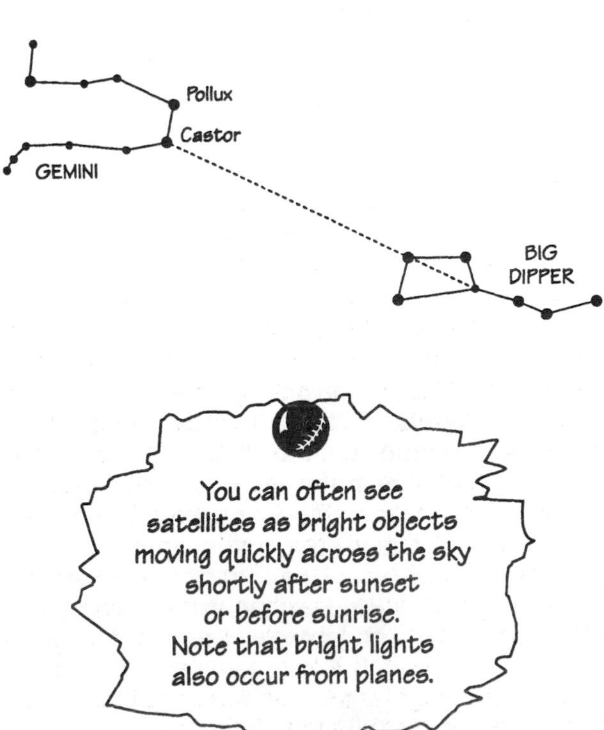

10. *Pegasus, Andromeda:* You can view Pegasus (the Winged Horse) in the fall. Find Cassiopeia. Using two stars in the inner part of the "W" as pointers, follow a line through to Pegasus. Four fainter stars in this constellation form a large square known as the Square of Pegasus. On a dark night, how many stars can you count inside the square? If you're able to see twelve or more, your eyesight is very good. Move from the left, corner star in the square to a string of fourth-magnitude stars making up Andromeda (you can also return to Cassiopeia, and use the partial triangle of stars closest to Pegasus as a pointer to Andromeda). The Andromeda Galaxy is the most distant object visible to the unaided eye.

11. *Orion, Canis Major, Gemini, Taurus:* The number of bright stars visible in winter is greater than any other season. Look to the south in the winter to see the dominant constellation Orion (the Mighty Hunter). Orion's belt points toward Sirius, the brightest star in the night sky (magnitude -1). Sirius is part of the constellation Canis Major (the Big Dog), which is most visible in January and February. Follow Orion's belt in the opposite direction to find the orange-red star Aldebaran, part of the V-shaped constellation Taurus (the Bull). Near the head of Taurus lies a cluster of stars called the Pleiades (the Seven Sisters). Six to seven stars can be seen with the unaided eye; binoculars or a small telescope bring many more into view. Follow a line from Orion's belt through Orion to blue-coloured Castor, part of the constellation Gemini.

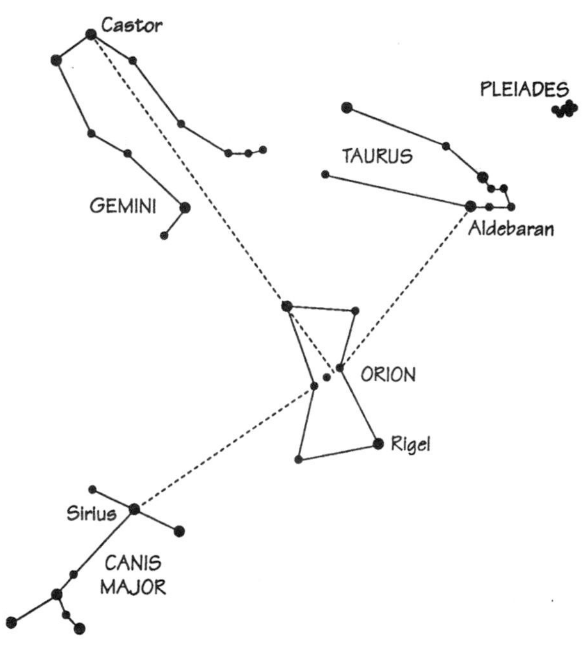

12. *Star Maps:* Use the star maps on the following page as an additional guide for finding constellations at certain times of the year. The dates and times for which a map is most accurate are listed underneath it. One side of the page illustrates the sky if you're facing north; the other side shows the view facing south. The top of each map is the sky directly overhead (the zenith). The maps are useful for the northern latitudes indicated; the sky below a given latitude mark falls below the horizon and is not visible from that latitude.

STAR MAPS

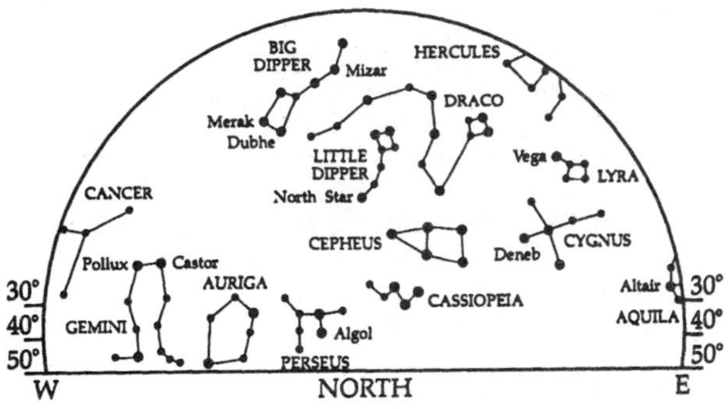

Most accurate for the following standard times:
April 1, 1 a.m.; May 1, 11 p.m.; June 1, 9 p.m.

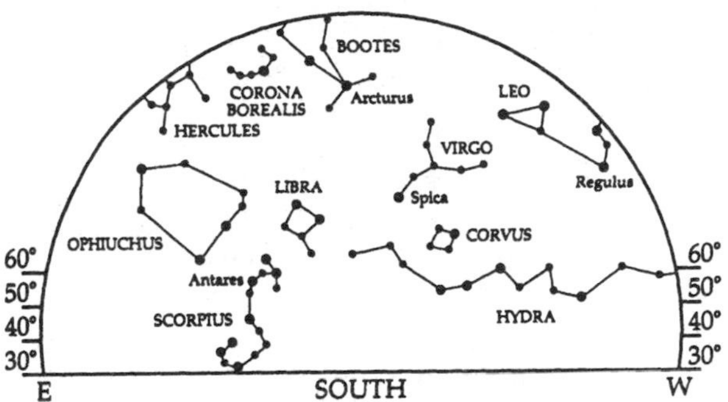

Most accurate for the following standard times:
April 1, 1 a.m.; May 1, 11 p.m.; June 1, 9 p.m.

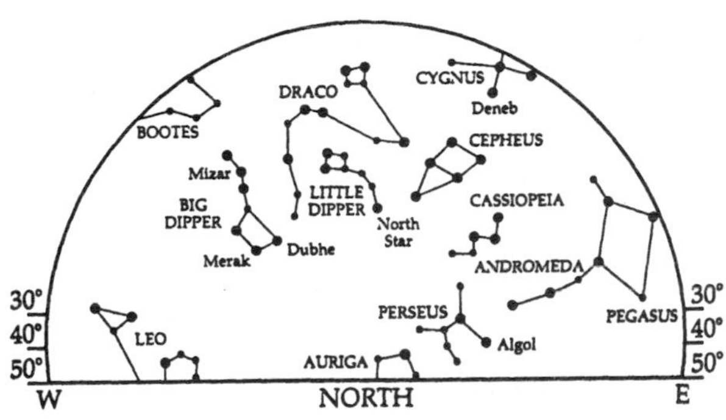

Most accurate for the following standard times:
June 1, 1 a.m.; July 1, 11 p.m.; August 1, 9 p.m.

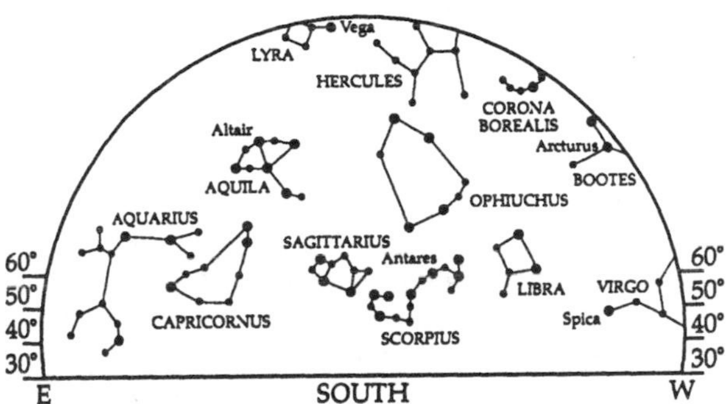

Most accurate for the following standard times:
June 1, 1 a.m.; July 1, 11 p.m.; August 1, 9 p.m.

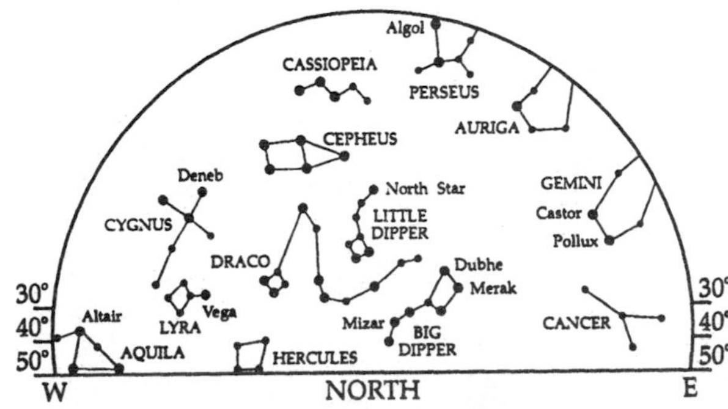

Most accurate for the following standard times:
October 1, 1 a.m.; November 1, 11 p.m.;
December 1, 9 p.m.; January 1, 7 p.m.

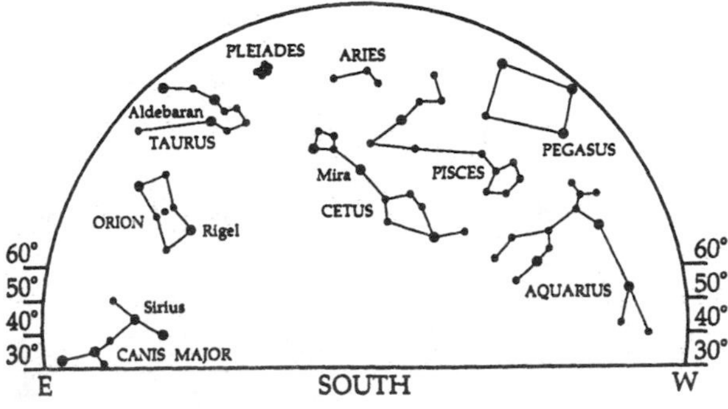

Most accurate for the following standard times:
October 1, 1 a.m.; November 1, 11 p.m.;
December 1, 9 p.m.; January 1, 7 p.m.

Zoom In

Once you're familiar with the night sky, binoculars can be helpful for zooming in on certain heavenly bodies. Here are a few hints on buying and using binoculars.

MATERIALS: As on previous pages; reclining lawn chair with arms.

DOING IT:

1. *Buying:* The best-selling binoculars are the 7 x 35 size (the eyepieces magnify an object seven times compared to normal vision, while the main lenses are 35 mm across). These binoculars bring in the Milky Way and provide a good view of a number of star clusters. Better performance, however, will be provided by 7 x 50 or 10 x 50 binoculars. However, the higher the power, the narrower the field of view. A small field of view means that you see less at one time and that the binoculars are more difficult to aim. Overall, for the beginner, the 7 x 50 size seems a good bet. They provide a balance between light-collecting power, field of view, weight/ease of handling, and adaptability to other uses. Stay away from the least and most expensive brands.

2. *Using:* Binoculars *must* be held steadily or supported in some way; movement makes the stars jiggle and difficult to see. You may want to use a comfortable lawn chair with arms for observation; hold the binoculars in both hands, resting your elbows on the arms of the chair. This provides a steady, adjustable mount. Focus the binoculars as required.

3. *Viewing:* Once your eyes have adapted to the dark, look up into the sky for a few minutes without binoculars. What do you see? Then, sweep the sky from east to west with your binoculars. Sweep from west to east. Now what do you see? Here are some things you can focus in on using binoculars:

- The view of the moon with binoculars is startlingly sharp and clear, with a few dozen craters, rugged mountain peaks, and dark plains readily visible. Lunar detail is most distinct along the "terminator", the line dividing the illuminated and the unilluminated portions of the moon. This is because of the sharp relief effect caused by the shadows. The full moon is the worst phase to observe because the strong relief effect is absent. The days around the first and last quarter are best for detailed viewing.
- Jupiter is the best planet to observe with binoculars because it's possible to see its moons. Saturn's rings may show up with high-powered binoculars.
- Take a closer look at any of the stars and constellations described in the previous activities.
- In the summer constellation Lyra, binoculars reveal a star closest to Vega (in the direction of Deneb) as a beautiful twin star.
- Scan inside the Square of Pegasus (visible in the fall). You should be able to see many more stars than are apparent with the unaided eye.
- Many double stars are revealed in Taurus, a constellation visible in winter.
- The Pleiades (or Seven Sisters) has only six to seven stars visible to the unaided eye, but the sky lights up with binoculars. The cluster is most visible in winter.
- Scan the Milky Way. With the unaided eye, it looks like a cloud-like ribbon through the sky. Binoculars transform the Milky Way into a glittering river of thousands and thousands of stars.
- Nebulae are big clouds of gas in the Milky Way. Two interesting nebulae are the Orion Nebula (just below the three stars of Orion's belt) and the Crab Nebula (near one of the horns of Taurus; not connected with the constellation of Cancer, the Crab); these nebulae are visible in late fall and winter.
- The Andromeda Galaxy (most visible in fall) is the farthest point visible to the unaided eye. Its galaxy shape becomes apparent with binoculars.

Binoculars or a telescope aren't essential for stargazing. In fact, a novice astronomer will probably be confused by seeing a narrow view in such detail. However, once you're familiar with key stars and constellations, using binoculars -- which are really like two small telescopes -- can add interest.

Topics: Stars; Light.

APPLYING SCIENCE

REACH FOR THE SKY

The Applying Science subject area has fifteen One Leads to Another activities. Do the activities as a series, or choose just those activities which interest you.

The series of activities focuses on flight. From the time that people first observed birds and flying insects, human flight has been the subject of speculation and dreams. The desire for human flight (coupled with the awe and fear of trying) appears in the art, literature, and mythology of so many cultures that it has probably been universal. The sky was finally opened to humans through science and technology.

In 1783, the Montgolfier brothers, two paper manufacturers from France, designed a practical hot-air balloon. For the first time, a machine was available (to those who were daring) that could lift people off the surface of the Earth and carry them on the wind. But a balloon is at the mercy of the winds (to this day, a free balloon has the right-of-way over any other flying machine); it was airplanes that made control of directional movement possible.

Englishman Sir George Cayley is often called the father of flight for having discovered many of the basic principles behind flying. He studied birds for hours trying to figure out what enabled them to fly. Cayley tested his ideas about flight in several gliders which looked very much like kites. American Samuel Langley was a pioneer in airplane development. He built two small flying machines. In 1896, one of these machines flew over a kilometre. This first airplane was too small to carry a person. By 1903, Langley had made a bigger flying machine that could take a passenger, but the machine crashed at takeoff. On December 17, 1903, two brothers, Wilbur and Orville Wright, managed to make the first successful manned flight near Kitty Hawk, North Carolina.

The following series begins with two activities that look at the basic forces important in flight. The third activity involves a key part of many airplanes, the propeller. The fourth activity deals with a special application of the propeller, the helicopter. After a look at some flying oddities, the series moves to seven activities dealing with paper airplanes. Included are detailed construction directions, as well as design and flying tips. The final three activities are made up of kite designs and flying guidelines.

Reaching for the sky is only one example of how humans apply science. But it's an example that symbolizes the human need to explore, to question, to challenge, to grow, and to reach for the "impossible". Who knows what we'll reach for next!

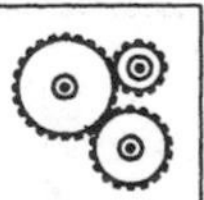

PARACHUTE

A parachute is affected by two of the forces important in flight: gravity and air resistance. Make a simple parachute and experiment with its characteristics.

MATERIALS: Paper; plastic wrap; lightweight cotton cloth; string; tape; ruler; scissors; small weight (e.g. box containing a couple of marbles, unbreakable toy).

A parachute is a device that slows an object's fall from a great height, such as from an airplane. A parachute is affected by two forces: gravity pulls it down, toward the centre of Earth, while air resists its movement. The pull of gravity is much greater than the air resistance, so the air only slows the parachute's fall. The larger a parachute's surface area, the more air resistance it meets and the slower it falls. The part of the parachute that catches the air is called the "canopy". For many years, parachutes had a round canopy that looked like an umbrella. Today, most canopies have a rectangular shape, rather like an airplane wing. Parachute canopies used to be made of silk. Nylon, which is stronger and cheaper, has been used since the 1940s.

A human being with a parachute falls at a rate of about 5.5 m/sec. French physicist Sebastien Lenormand made the first known parachute jump from a tower in 1783. The first parachute jump from a balloon was made in 1797 and the first parachute jump from a damaged airplane was made in 1922. Parachutes are used as escape systems from planes unable to land safely. They can be used as a braking system for airplanes and high-speed land vehicles. Finally, they are used to deliver cargo; airplanes drop food and medicine by parachute to areas that cannot be reached easily by other means. Parachute jumping for sport is called "skydiving".

Topics: Flight; Air; Forces.

DOING IT:

1. Drop a small weight from a high place (e.g. drop it while standing on a chair, or from the top of a stairwell). How quickly does the object fall?

2. Crumple a sheet of paper into a ball. Cut four pieces of string of equal length. Tape one end of the pieces of string to the paper ball. Tape the other end of the pieces of string to the small object. Drop the object from the same height that you dropped it before. How quickly does it fall? Does this design of parachute work? Why or why not?

3. Cut four pieces of string of equal length. Make a simple parachute by taping one end of a piece of string to each of the four corners of a sheet of paper. Tape the other end of the strings to the object. Drop the object. How well does your parachute drift to the ground? Why does the parachute make the object fall more slowly?

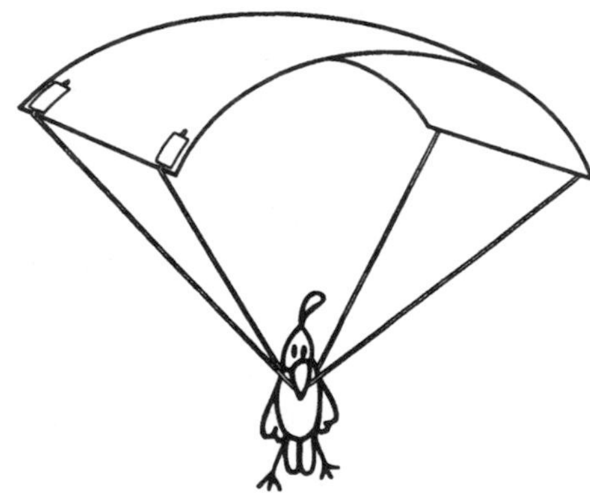

4. Experiment with different lengths of string. What length of string makes the best parachute? Why?

5. Use different materials for the canopy. Does paper, plastic, or cloth work best? Why?

6. Try different shapes and sizes for the canopy. Does a larger canopy work better than a smaller one? Why? Does a round or square canopy work better?

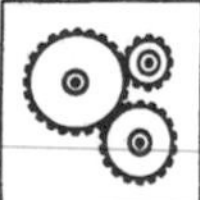

GETTING A LIFT

Every airplane is in the centre of four forces: lift, thrust, gravity, and drag. Here's a chance to get a first-hand look at how planes fly.

Blow at a lighted candle with half an apple in the way. If the rounded side of the apple faces you, it looks like you blow out the candle *through* the apple. As air passes around the curved surface, it speeds up and its pressure is lowered. The greater pressure of the surrounding air forces the two streams of air from each side of the apple together, and the flame is blown out. What happens when the flat side of the apple faces you? Why?

MATERIALS: Paper; scissors; pencil; tape.

DOING IT:

1. To feel the same forces that affect an airplane, take a running jump. You provide the thrust by running and the lift by jumping. Gravity pulls you down. You feel drag as air rushes against your face.

2. Cut a paper strip about 5 cm x 15 cm. Hold one end of the strip against your lower lip. The strip will sag. Now blow hard over the paper. Blowing over the strip reduces the pressure of the top air, so that the paper can take advantage of lift.

3. Bend a strip of paper 5 cm x 15 cm into the shape of an airplane wing (i.e. flat on bottom, curved on top). Tape the ends of the paper together.

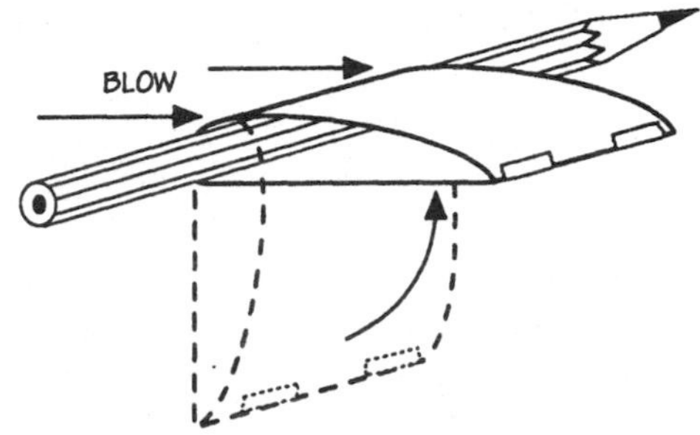

4. Put a pencil through the wide end of the wing and let the paper wing hang down. Blow over the paper wing. What happens? What happens if you blow under the paper wing?

What makes a plane go up? Air. A plane flies if the air below its wings pushes up harder than the air above pushes down. The airplane is held up by a difference in pressure between the top and bottom air. Air pressure can be reduced if air moves very quickly. Bernoulli's Principle states that as the speed of a gas increases, the pressure it exerts decreases. An airplane wing is curved so that air travelling over the top of the wing has farther to go than air travelling below the wing. The top air must go faster to reach the back edge of the wing at the same time as the bottom air. Because it's going faster, the top air has much less push than the slower bottom air. So, the bottom air gives the wing a lift. An airplane also gets lift from its speed and the angle of its climb. The wings of an airplane have adjustable flaps that can be extended or retracted. When extended, the flaps increase the curvature of the wings on the upper side and provide greater lift for takeoff and landing.

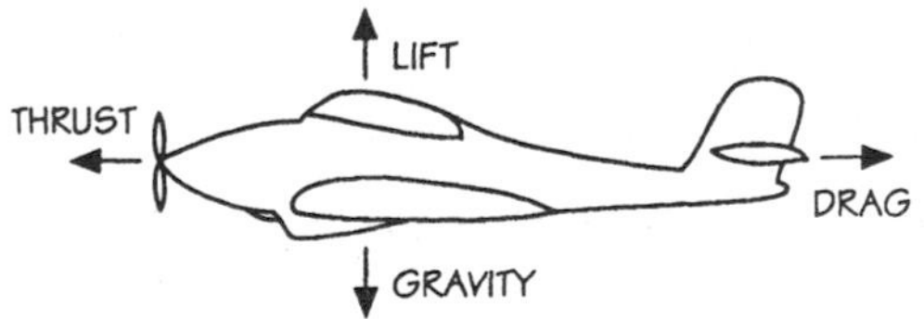

As it flies, a plane is in the centre of four forces. *Lift* (upward force) and *thrust* (forward push, provided by a propeller) get a plane into the air. *Gravity* and *drag* (air resistance, which is friction caused by air rubbing against the plane) try to pull the plane down and slow its speed. A plane must be built so that lift and thrust are stronger than the pull of gravity and drag by just the right amount. Speed is used to overcome the force of gravity. Shape is important in overcoming drag. For example, the nose of a plane is pointed and rounded so it can push through the air more easily. The front edge of each wing is rounded too. An airplane built like a railroad boxcar just wouldn't fly.

Topics: Flight; Air; Forces.

Propelled Upward

All airplanes except jet planes have propellers. This little device shows the power of a propeller.

MATERIALS: Stiff, bendable plastic (e.g. milk jug, shampoo bottle); large plastic spool from thread; dowel about 15 cm long (e.g. piece of broom handle); two paper clips; thin nail; long nail (smaller diameter than centre hole in plastic spool) with large, flat head; 1 m length of cord; hammer; scissors. Optional -- glue; tape.

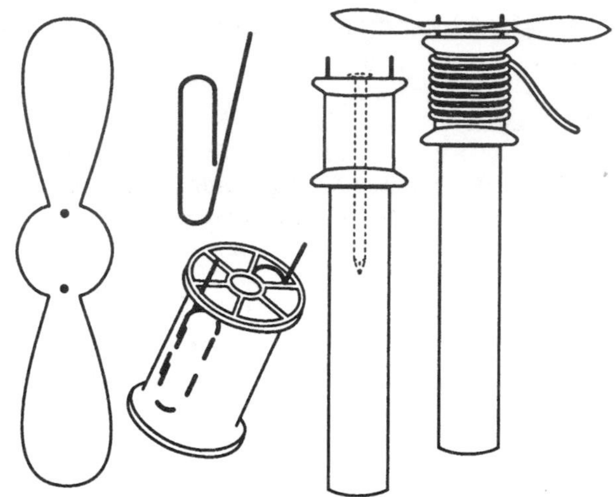

DOING IT:

1. Use scissors to cut a propeller 10-15 cm long (shape shown) from a piece of plastic. Twist one blade down to a slight angle. Twist the other blade up, to the same angle. A propeller must have blades that are of the same size and shape. You'll see why if you make a lopsided propeller!

2. Remove the paper label from one end of a plastic spool. Bend two paper clips as shown. Wedge the paper clips between the ribs inside the spool, on opposite sides of the centre hole. You may need to use glue or tape to secure the paper clips in place.

3. Use a thin nail to punch two holes near the centre of the propeller so that the propeller can slip easily on and off the ends of the paper clips in the spool.

4. Slip a large nail through the centre hole in the spool. Hammer the nail partway into the end of a piece of dowel. The spool should spin freely around the nail.

5. Wind some cord around the spool. Slip the propeller into place on the spool. Hold the dowel so that it points **away from your face and other people**. Pull on the cord. The propeller should spin fast and fly into the air.

6. What factors affect the propeller's flight? What happens when you pull the cord quickly? Slowly? What happens when you wind the cord the other way? What happens when you change the angle or shape of the blades?

A propeller is actually a twisted wing designed so that when it is rotated by an engine, it produces a force like lift but aimed in a forward direction. This force (thrust) pulls an airplane through the air so that its wings can develop lift and hold the airplane up. A propeller works because the blades have a thin edge, like a knife. The propeller "cuts" through air. Propeller blades are also at an angle, so that as they "cut" the air, they push it backward. When air is pushed back, it gives a little kick forward. This kick enables the airplane to go forward, takeoff, and fly. Propellers can also be used for landing a plane. The pilot throws a switch that changes the angle of the propeller blades. Instead of pushing air back, the blades push air forward, and the air helps to slow down the plane.

Topics: Flight; Forces.

The invention of the jet engine in the late 1930s meant that planes would eventually be able to fly at more than the speed of sound. As the fuel in a jet engine burns, very hot, compressed exhaust gases shoot out the back and push the plane forward. A jet plane works on the same principle that sends a blown-up balloon rushing through the air when you let it go without tying it up.

COPTER

A helicopter's horizontal, spinning propellers (rotors) enable it to hover, as well as move sideways and up and down. What factors affect the flight of a helicopter?

MATERIALS: Strips of paper 6 cm x 28 cm; scissors; paper clips.

DOING IT:

1. Make a "helicopter" by cutting, folding, and bending a slip of paper as follows:

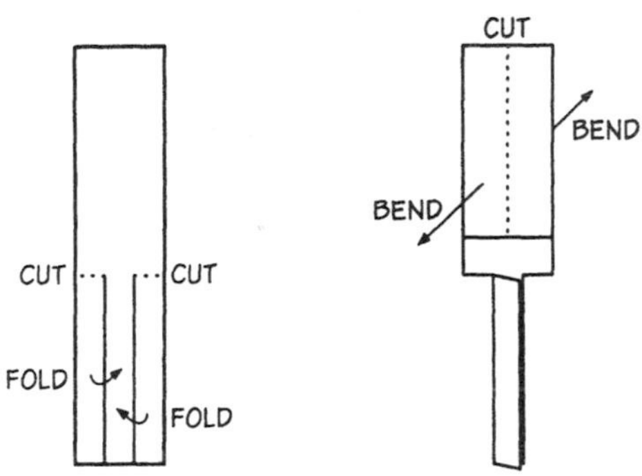

2. Fold up a bit of the helicopter's leg. Hold the fold in place with a paper clip.

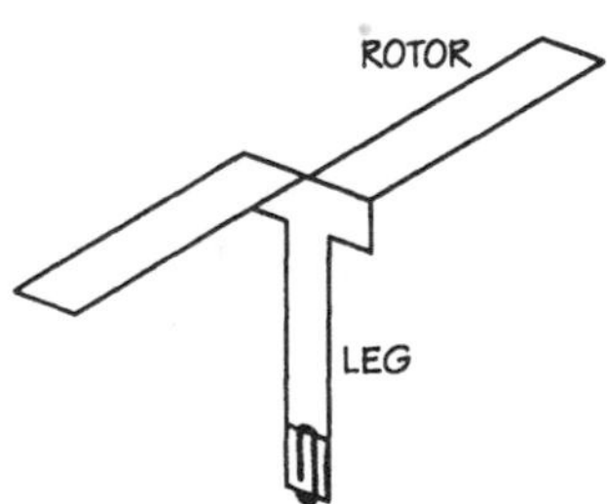

3. Drop the helicopter from a high place (e.g. drop it while standing on a chair) or throw it up into the air and watch it fall. What happens? Does one end always point downward? Does the helicopter right itself if it's dropped upside down?

4. Bend the rotors in the opposite direction. How does this change the helicopter's flight? What happens if the rotors are vertical (not folded out) when you release the helicopter?

5. Add two or three more paper clips to the leg of the helicopter. Does this affect the way it falls?

6. Use the patterns below to make three helicopters with different rotor areas. Which falls the fastest? The slowest?

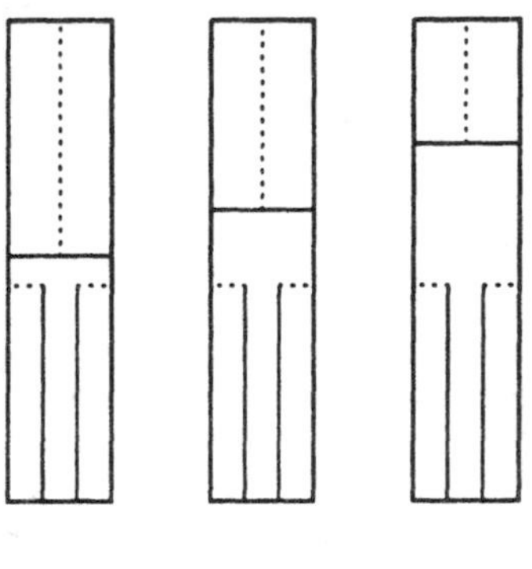

When human beings first began to think about flying, they turned to the natural world for ideas on how to make human flight possible. The most obvious examples of flight in the natural world are birds and insects. But seeds have also provided humans with information about flight. Have you ever watched seeds from maple or sycamore trees fall to the ground? They spin as they fall, like little helicopters. Some of the factors that affect seeds in their journey -- weight, surface area, shape -- also affect real helicopters, and other flying machines.

A helicopter is a flying machine that hovers; that is, it remains up in the air even though it's not moving through the air. Although the great thinker Leonardo da Vinci sketched a kind of helicopter in the late fifteenth century, it took until 1939 before Igor Sikorsky developed the first practical helicopter. The problem was stability and control. If only two or three wing-like shapes rotated (each attached at one end to a shaft), lift was created, but the machine would rise unsteadily and often tip over and fall back to the ground. What was needed was a controllable, stable rotating propeller design that would allow the craft to easily hover or move vertically or horizontally, without unwanted motions.

Topics: Flight.

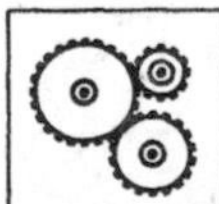

THESE THINGS FLY?!

These flying oddities aren't your typical paper airplane. They may be strange to look at, but they're simple to make and fun to fly.

MATERIALS: Paper; paper or foam cups; tape; straw; elastic bands.

DOING IT:

1. *Straw Flyer:* Cut a paper strip 2 cm x 24 cm and another 1.5 cm x 18 cm. Make the strips into loops by overlapping the ends a couple of centimetres and taping the ends together on the inside and the outside. The overlapping ends should form a sleeve into which you can slip a straw. You may want to keep the straw in place with a bit of tape. What happens when you throw the Straw Flyer like a spear? Is there a difference if the big loop is in front or if the small loop is in front? How does the Straw Flyer's flight compare to that of a plain straw? Try putting the loops in different positions along the straw. Try making the Straw Flyer with two big loops, and then with two small loops. Combine a really big loop with a really small loop. Use more than two loops. Put loops on the top and the bottom of the straw.

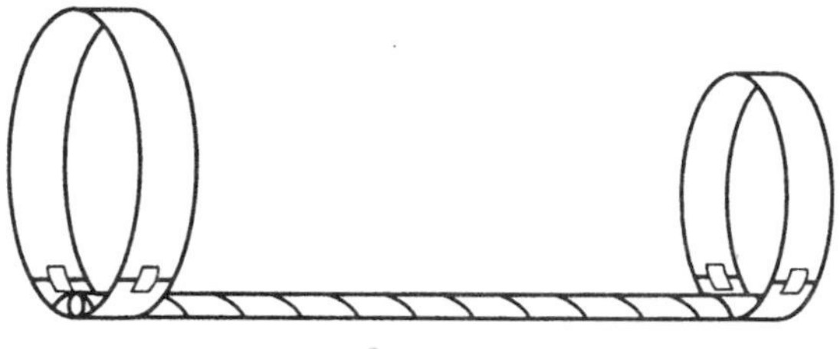

2. *Aero-Cups:* Tape together the bottoms of two paper or foam cups. Loop together the ends of five or six elastic bands to form a long chain. Wrap the elastic-band chain around the centre of the two-cup structure. While making sure that the elastic-band chain comes from the *underside* of the two-cup structure, put your thumb through the end elastic in the chain and stretch out the chain while holding the cups. Release the Aero-Cups and watch them spin through the air. Can you design a similar flying structure using four cups?

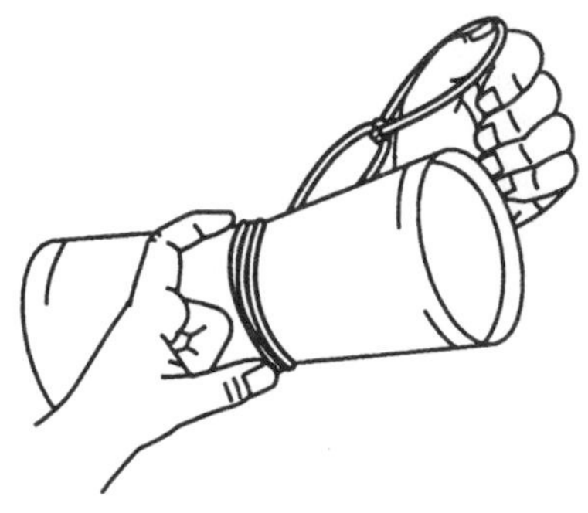

Each loop in the *Straw Flyer* is a circular wing; snip one of the loops at the top, middle and you'll get a basic, flat wing. The Straw Flyer works because air moves more quickly over the top of the wing than under it, and a lift force is created. The *Aero-Cups* work because when they're launched into the air, they spin around as they move forward. As the cups spin, the air underneath them moves more slowly than the air on top. Therefore, there is a pressure difference between the top and bottom air, and a lift force is created.

Topics: Flight.

THE PLANE TRUTH

By making and flying paper airplanes, you can discover some of the basic principles of aerodynamics. Here's one of the simplest paper airplane designs, the Dart.

MATERIALS: Paper (preferably stiff paper); tape. Optional -- scissors.

DOING IT:

1. Fold a sheet of paper lengthwise, exactly down the middle. Unfold it and smooth the paper flat.

2. Fold one of the corners over as far as the centre fold. Then fold the other corner over in the same way.

3. Fold the corners over again so that they meet at the centre fold.

4. Fold the two sides together along the centre fold. Then, to make wings, fold the top portion of each side down toward the centre fold.

5. Use a small piece of tape to fasten the wings together. If you wish, you can snip off about 1 cm of the plane's nose. Tape together the keel (paper under the wings) at both ends.

6. Launch the Dart by holding it at the back of the keel and throwing. How long does the Dart stay in the air? How far can you throw it?

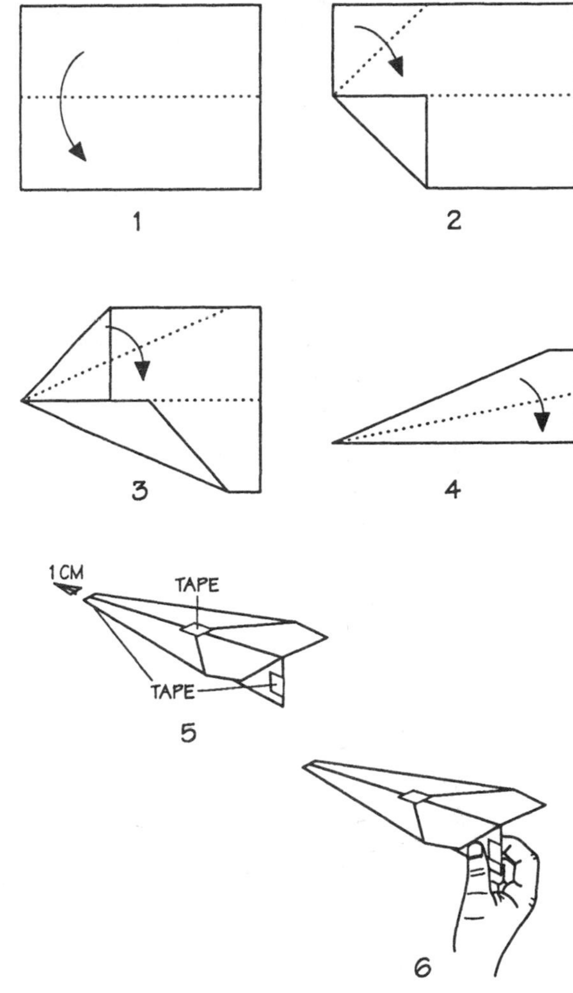

The Anglo-French Concorde airplane, with its streamlined body and pointed nose, made its first flight in 1969. It travels at speeds of around 2000 km/h and can cross the Atlantic Ocean in less than 3 hours (other types of planes take twice that amount of time).

Aerodynamics is the study of the interaction between air and solid bodies moving through it. One of the easiest model paper airplanes to construct is the Dart. The Dart is the old standby. It cuts through air easily and can be used to experiment with factors that affect flight. Aside from learning about aerodynamic principles, airplane models are useful for a number of things. For example, industrial designers make several models of an airplane before beginning the actual -- and very expensive -- production process.

Topics: Flight.

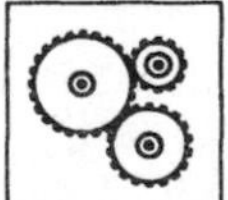

PLANE DESIGN AND FLYING TIPS

These design and flying tips apply to almost any kind of paper airplane. Start with simple planes, and then try more complicated planes.

MATERIALS: Paper airplanes; tape; scissors; paper clips; different weights of paper (e.g. tracing paper, construction paper, writing paper).

DOING IT:

1. *Space:* Paper planes fly best in a large, empty area where there's little or no wind.

2. *Construction:* If a paper plane doesn't fly straight, it may be because it isn't made straight. Every little bend, cut, and dent in the paper changes how a plane flies. All folds should be sharp. Look down along the nose of a paper plane to see if both wings are the same size and bent to the same angle. Check that all the folds and cuts on one side are the same size and shape as those on the other side. If your plane is lopsided, it will never fly straight. If everything looks okay, and the plane still doesn't fly right, experiment with the factors listed below.

3. *Launching Speed:* There's no such thing as the "best" launching speed for paper planes. Different planes need different launching speeds. In general, try to launch a plane so that it glides in a straight path without diving, climbing, or turning. If a plane is launched too quickly, it tends to climb, then stall, and finally dive down. If a plane is launched too slowly, it dives to pick up more speed. Either way, distance and flying time are lost.

4. *Throws:* There are many ways to throw paper planes. Different planes work better with certain throws. For the *keel hold*, hold the back of the plane at the bottom, and then launch the plane with a sharp throw. In the *tail hold*, put your index finger on top of the plane with your thumb and other fingers underneath. Move your hand forward at the speed you think the plane will fly and just let the plane go. Don't jerk or push the plane forward; just let it glide from your hand. The *nose hold* is best for loops and circles. If you want a plane to veer to the left or right, launch it at an angle.

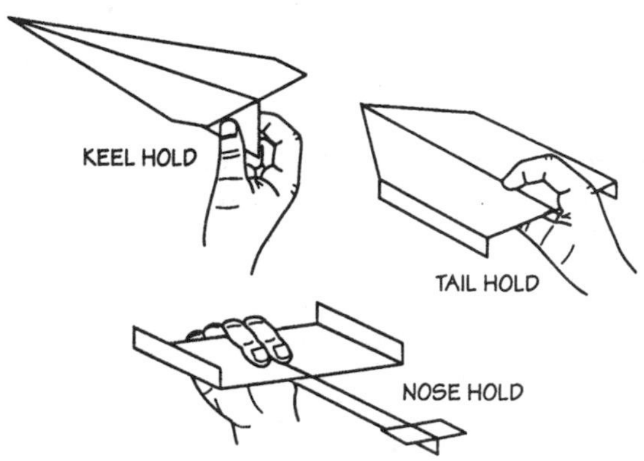

5. *Circles:* A Dart usually won't do circles, but the Barnaby (described later) and other planes with a long wingspan are good at circles. Hold a plane by its nose at your waist. Keep the bottom of the plane toward your body; the wings should be straight up and down. Pull your hand straight across from one side to the other and then let the plane go. The plane should circle and return to you. If a plane won't do circles, be sure it isn't lopsided and try throwing it harder.

6. *Loops:* When you're trying to make a plane loop, curl up the back edge of the tail or wings. For a *downward loop*, start by holding the plane's nose. Aim the nose down and quickly launch the plane with a hard throw. Be careful to launch the plane straight, without twisting your wrist or curving your arm. The plane should make a loop and then fly level. For an *upward loop*, hold the plane by its nose again. Aim the nose up. Pull the plane straight up, and let go when the plane is in front of your face. With practice, the plane should loop away from you and come back so that you can catch it.

As you experiment with paper airplanes, you'll get insights into the problems that airplane pioneers had to overcome and the things that modern flight crews must know about. For example, weight is important in both paper airplanes and full-sized planes. When a real plane is loaded, it can carry only a certain amount of weight. The weight must also be loaded so the plane is balanced (i.e. not too much weight in the nose or tail).

Topics: Flight; Problem-Solving.

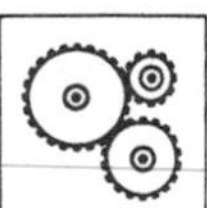

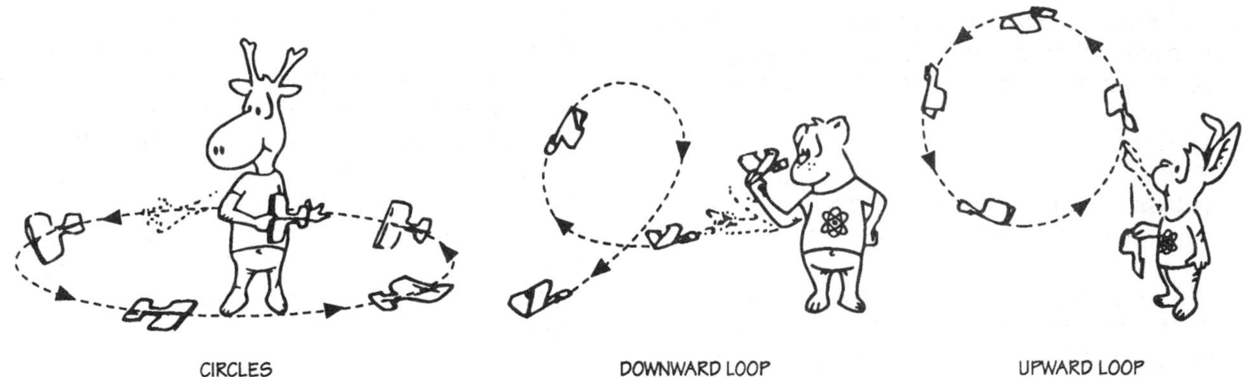

7. *Weight:* Try making several planes using the same design, but different kinds of paper (e.g. tracing paper, construction paper, writing paper). Do the planes fly differently? In what ways? Not only is overall weight important, but so is the way the weight is distributed. Shifting weight can be used to overcome problems like interference from air currents outdoors. Add a paper clip to a plane's nose. How does it fly? What happens if you put a paper clip on the tail instead of the nose? What happens if you add two or more paper clips? How can you tell too much weight has been added?

8. *Ailerons:* Make flaps, or ailerons, for a plane by cutting two 1 cm slits in the back of each wing. Bend the flaps. What happens when both flaps are tilted up? What happens when both flaps are tilted down? What happens if only one of the flaps is bent out? Try tilting one flap up and the other flap down. Try different flap widths.

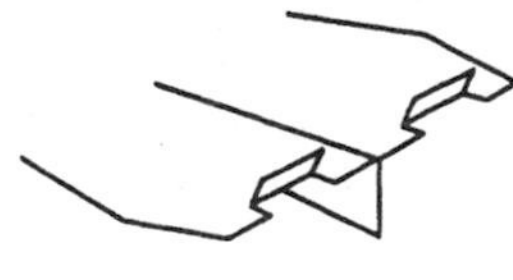

9. *Vertical Stabilizers:* These are used to make a plane fly straight and smooth. Bend the tips of the wings upward. What happens if you have only one stabilizer on a plane instead of two? Try bending the stabilizers down instead of up. Try making small stabilizers, and then try larger stabilizers.

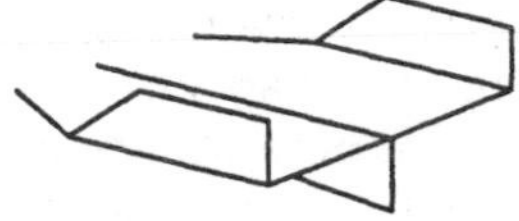

10. *Rudders:* Flaps in vertical stabilizers can be used as rudders which change the direction of a plane's flight. Turn both rudders slightly, the same way, to see one change in flight. Then, turn them the other way. Try bending in just one rudder. Try bending both rudders outward.

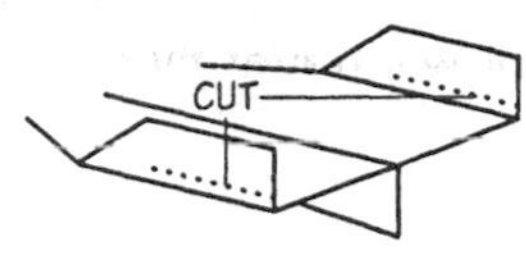

11. *Cambering:* Curve a paper plane's wings downward slightly by running them between your thumbnail and fingers. This will create a slight arch in the wings and the plane may fly better.

12. *Extension:* Come up with your own paper airplane design. Then write instructions, including diagrams, for making the plane. Can someone else follow your instructions and make the plane?

Stunt Flyer

Once you're familiar with making and flying paper airplanes, the Stunt Flyer is an interesting, simple plane to try.

MATERIALS: Paper (preferably stiff paper); tape.

DOING IT:

1. Fold up one corner of a sheet of paper to the opposite side.

2. Fold over point A so that it meets point B.

3. Fold up the bottom tip to the centre.

4. Fold the paper in half.

5. Fold down each wing so that the crease is approximately 2 cm from the bottom of the plane (i.e. keel is 2 cm).

6. Fold up each wing tip by 1 cm.

7. Use a small piece of tape to fasten the wings together. Also, tape together the keel at both ends. You're ready to launch.

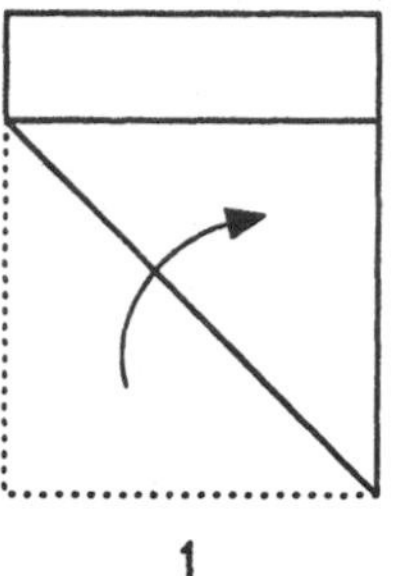

1

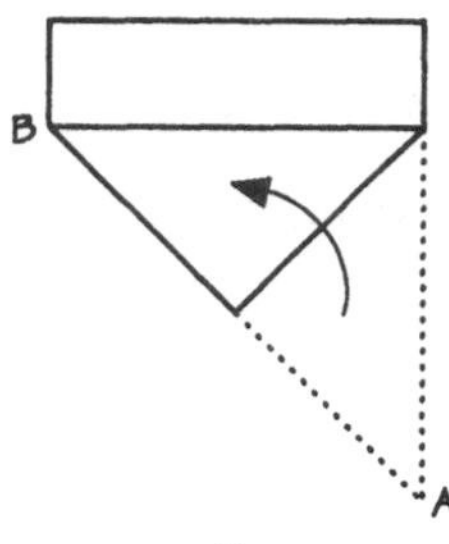

2

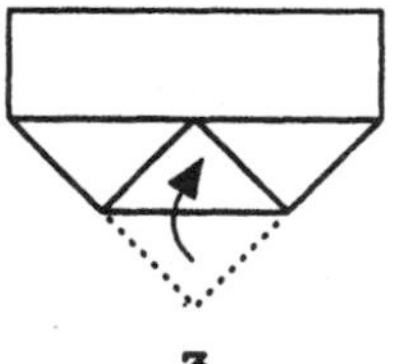

3

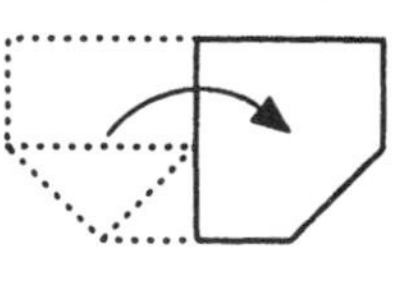

4

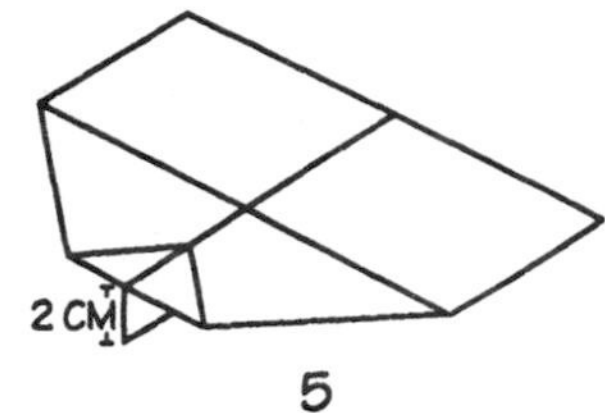

5

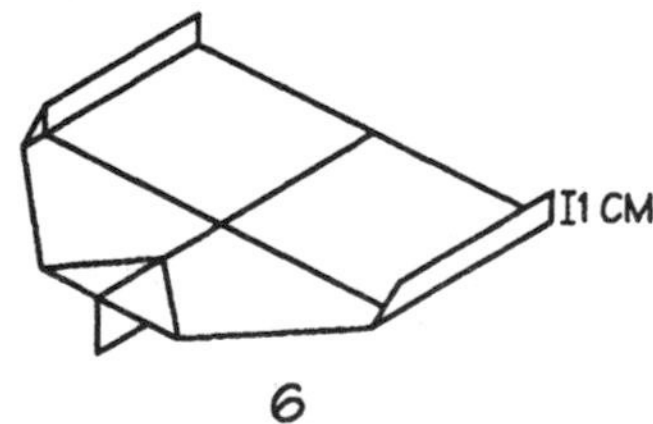

6

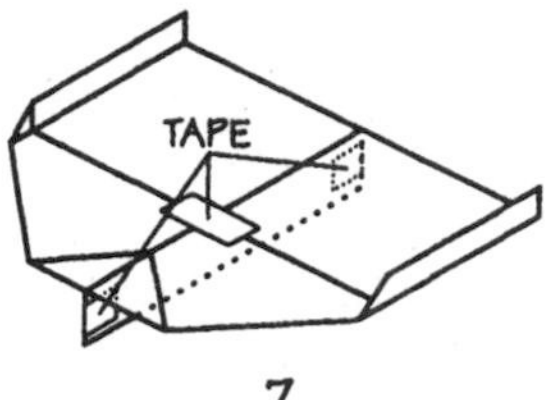

7

A game of aerial golf can be a real test of piloting skills. Set up an obstacle course through buildings, trees, chairs, and so on. Outlined landing areas serve as holes. Keep track of the number of shots people make as they go through the course; the winner is the pilot with the fewest shots. Each shot must be made from the exact point on which a plane lands. Add a shot to a participant's score if his or her plane lands "out of bounds".

The Stunt Flyer is a crazy little plane that will loop-the-loop with the best of them. Use it to try circles and loops (as described on previous page). Adding ailerons can change the plane's flight pattern dramatically.

Topics: Flight.

Blunt Nose

What happens when a plane has a blunt, rather than a pointed, nose? Make this plane and see what it can do.

MATERIALS: Paper (preferably stiff paper).

DOING IT:

1. Fold up one corner of a sheet of paper to the opposite side. Unfold the paper.

2. Fold up the other corner of the paper. Unfold it.

3. Fold up the bottom edge of the paper so that the crease goes through the spot where the first two creases cross. Unfold the paper.

4. Fold the paper along the creases like an accordion.

5. Fold down both corners of the pleat toward the centre tip.

6. Fold up the two bottom points of the first layer of paper.

7. Fold up the bottom tip of the second layer of paper so that it covers the other points.

8. Now comes the tricky part. Look for the two pockets. Underneath these pockets are two, triangular flaps. Tuck these flaps into the pockets to hold them securely in place.

9. Turn the paper over. Fold both wing tips toward the centre.

10. Fold out the edge of each wing.

11. Crease the centre, front of the plane to give it a gentle, upward curve. You're ready to launch.

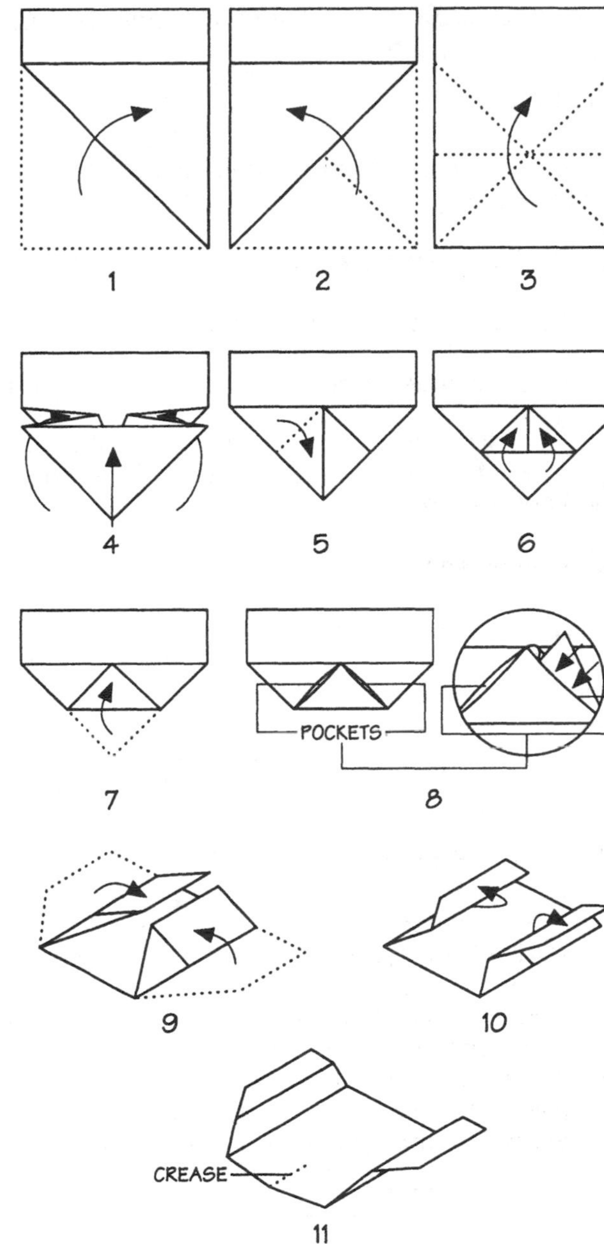

The Blunt Nose stays up in the air for a long time, flies straight, and makes smooth, gentle landings. The plane is a bit complicated to fold, but it's worth it.

Topics: Flight.

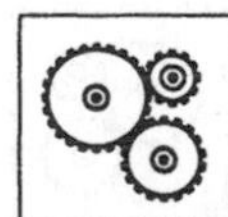

THE BARNABY

The Barnaby was designed by Ralph S. Barnaby, who was a captain in the United States Navy. Make this plane and follow in his footsteps.

MATERIALS: Paper (preferably stiff paper); ruler; pencil; scissors.

DOING IT:

1. Fold a sheet of paper exactly down the middle. Unfold it. Fold the paper exactly down the middle in the other direction. Unfold it. The creases are your guide lines.

2. Make a 1.5 cm fold along the long edge.

3. Fold the folded edge over and over until you meet the middle guide line.

4. The last fold has to be very tight; so press your ruler down hard on the paper and run it along the edge.

5. Fold the paper in half (folded edge on the outside). Draw and cut out the shape shown.

6. Open the plane. Fold up 1 cm of each wing tip. Fold down 1 cm on each side of the tail.

7. Bend up a small portion of the folded-over edge, near the centre. This will stiffen the wings and hold them in place.

8. Bend up the back edges of the wings a bit. You're ready to launch.

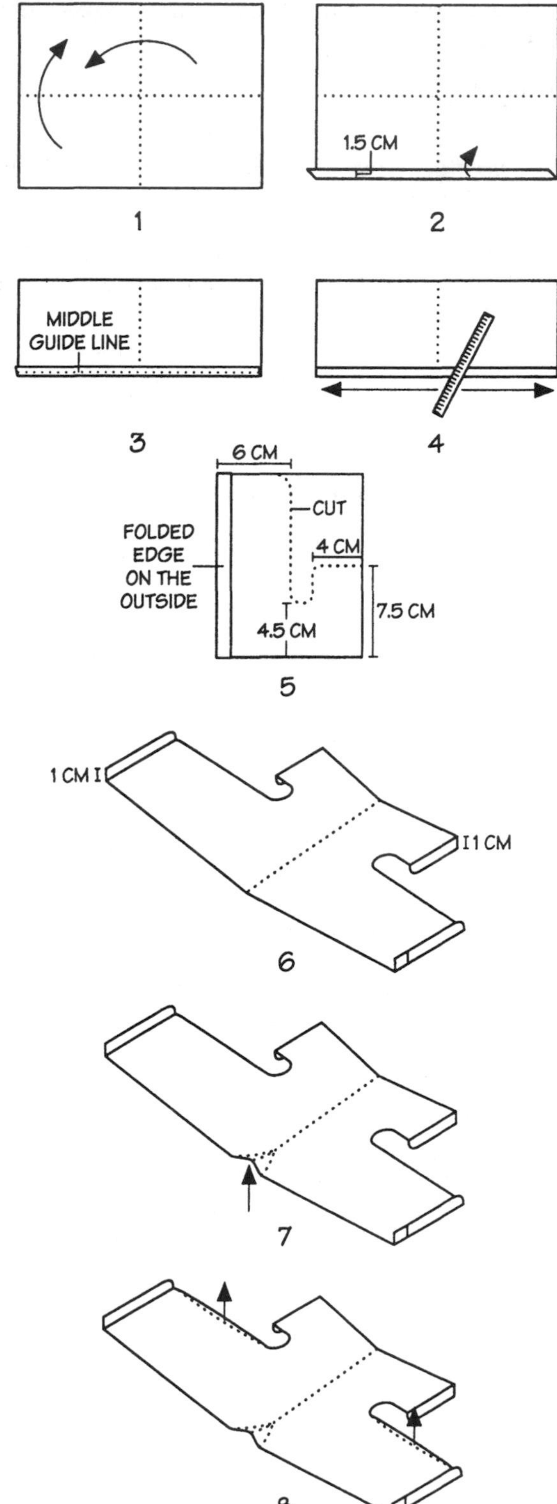

The *Guinness Book of Records* lists Ken Blackburn as holding the record for getting a paper airplane to stay aloft for the longest time -- 16.89 seconds. What's your record?

The Barnaby can really do some fancy flying. It won the aerobatics class in the First International Paper Airplane Competition.

Topics: Flight.

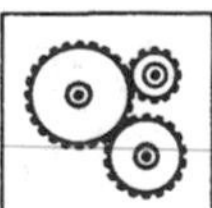

AIR SCORPION

If you like planes that fly fast, this design is for you. After a little folding and cutting, it looks very much like a jet plane.

MATERIALS: Stiff paper; tape; ruler; pencil; scissors.

DOING IT:

1. Fold a sheet of paper lengthwise, exactly down the middle.

2. Mark lines along the top edge of both sides of the folded paper. Mark one line 5 cm from the end and the other line 9 cm from the end.

3. Fold down the far corner to the 9 cm mark. Fold the corner on the other side of the paper in the same way.

4. Fold the overhanging tips up.

5. Open the two halves of the paper. It should look like the illustration.

6. Close the two halves again. Fold the nose back and between the halves.

7. Draw three lines: the first one vertically from the 9 cm mark to the bottom of the fold; another across the bottom of the fold, 1.5 cm up from the fold; and one diagonally from the 5 cm mark.

8. Draw in a tail at the back of the plane. Cut out the shaded area shown.

9. Bend the tail and wings along the line which is 1.5 cm from the fold (i.e. line drawn in step 7).

10. Keep the wings in place with tape. Tape the nose.

11. Draw the tail fin pattern on a folded piece of paper. Cut it out. Tape it to the inside of the back end of the plane. You're ready to launch.

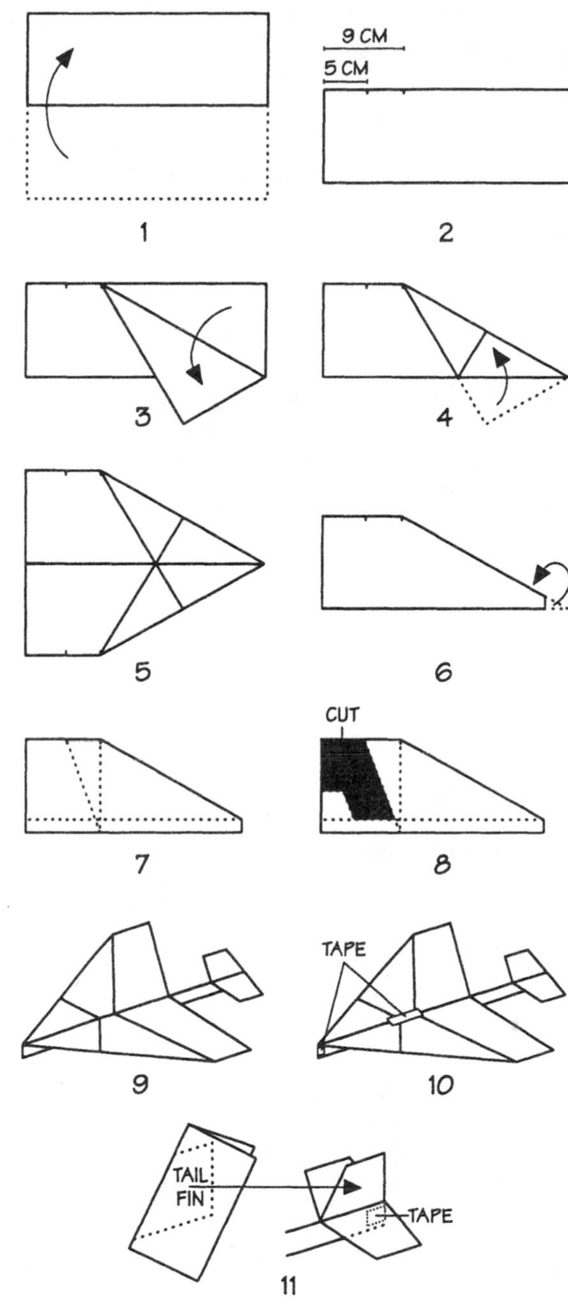

The Air Scorpion is a racing plane. It has swept-back wings and flies fast and straight.

Topics: Flight.

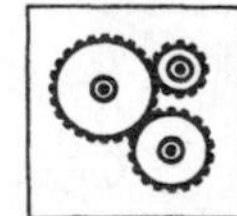

SUPER ZOOMER

This paper airplane involves more construction work than other paper planes, but it's a great flyer and an interesting design.

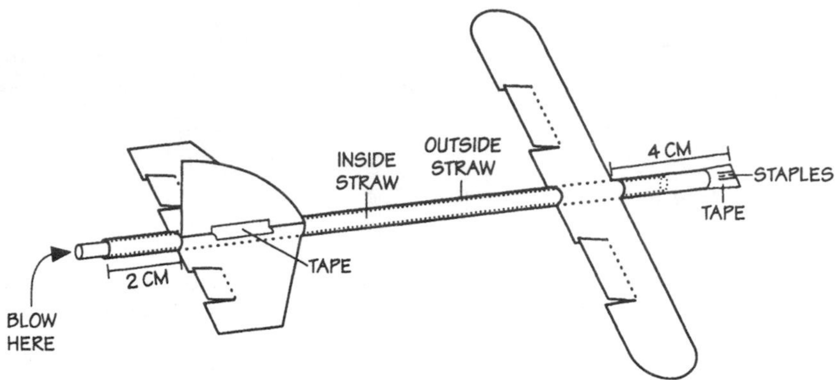

MATERIALS: Thin drinking straw; fat drinking straw (wide enough so that thin straw fits inside); stapler; tape; stiff paper; ruler; pencil; scissors.

DOING IT:

1. Staple one end of a fat straw several times. Seal the end with tape to make it airtight.

2. Fold a sheet of paper in half. Draw the plane parts on the folded paper, as shown.

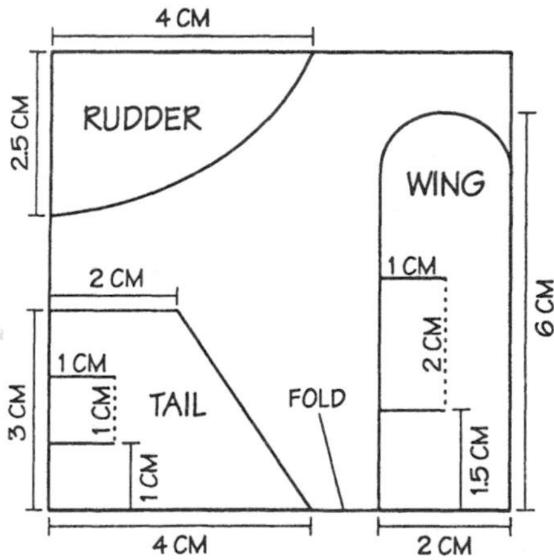

3. Leaving the paper folded, cut out the wing and tail.

4. Make the rudder out of only one thickness of paper.

5. Make the wing and tail flaps by cutting the four solid lines (in illustration). Bend each flap up slightly.

6. Open the wings and tape them to the fat straw, 4 cm from its closed end.

7. Open the tail and tape it to the fat straw, 2 cm from the open end.

8. Tape the rudder to the top of the tail.

9. To fly the plane, put the thin straw inside the fat straw. Bend your head back a little. Holding onto the thin straw, blow into it. The plane should shoot into the air.

10. Experiment with the Super Zoomer, using the design and flying tips discussed earlier.

The Super Zoomer's straw launcher helps to give the plane a good start, and the flaps and rudder work to keep the plane aloft. After trying this plane, your next step might be to build more detailed, realistic model planes using wood and plastic instead of paper.

Topics: Flight.

The era of the jumbo jet began in 1970 when the American Boeing company introduced its wide-bodied 747, which can carry nearly 500 people.

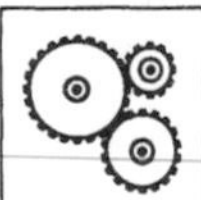

Mini Kite

Many aviation pioneers used kites as they experimented with flight. This small kite can be made quickly and easily.

MATERIALS: Sheet of plastic 30 cm x 30 cm (preferably white, e.g. kitchen trash bag); ruler; felt marker; scissors; tape; thin, plastic straws; ball of kite string. Optional -- coloured markers.

DOING IT:

1. Fold the sheet of plastic in half. Draw the kite's outline and the mouth onto the plastic, following the measurements shown. The pattern shows half the kite; when you unfold the plastic later, you'll have a full kite.

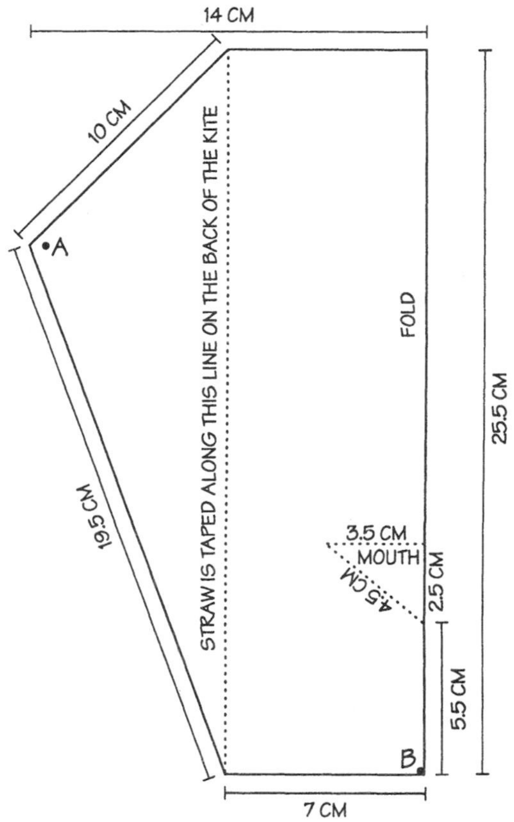

2. Keeping the plastic folded in half, cut out the kite and its mouth.

3. Open the kite up. If you wish, you can use coloured markers to decorate it.

4. Make a long straw by pinching the end of one straw and squishing it into the end of a second straw. Tape the joint. Make another long straw in the same way.

5. Turn the kite over and tape a long straw onto each half of the kite along the dotted line shown on the pattern. Cut off the parts of the straws that go past the plastic.

6. Cut a 50 cm long bridle string. Tie and/or tape the ends of the string to each corner of the kite (where A is on the pattern), after reinforcing the area by placing a piece of tape over the plastic on both sides.

7. Cut a 20 cm long tail string. Tie two plastic scraps (each about 3 cm x 8 cm) 5 cm apart along the tail. Tie and/or tape the tail to point B, after reinforcing the area by placing a piece of tape over the plastic on both sides.

8. Tie a ball of string to the middle of the bridle. The straws should be underneath when the kite is flying. Now you're all set to go fly a kite!

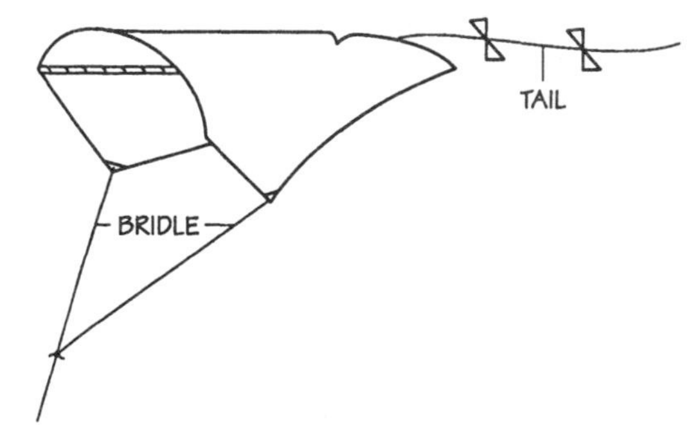

A kite consists of a light frame with a thin material stretched over it, flown in the wind at the end of a long string. Englishman Sir George Cayley, who many consider to be the father of modern airplane flight, attached an arrow-like tail to a kite and made the world's first practical glider. The Wright brothers flew some full-size gliders as kites before climbing into them. Alexander Graham Bell in Canada and Samuel Cody in England both made giant kites capable of carrying a human being.

Topics: Flight.

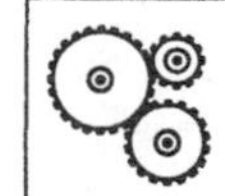

Go Fly A Kite!

Kite construction and flying can be one of the most satisfying challenges around. Here are some guidelines for flying kites.

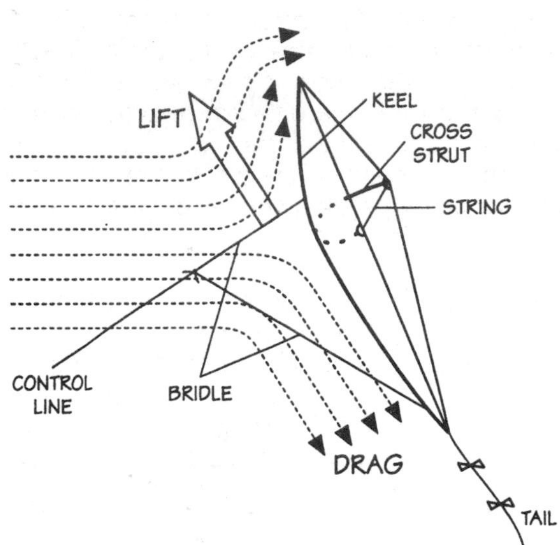

Kites were flown in China more than 2,000 years ago -- a long time before anyone understood how they worked. However, people did notice that a kite wouldn't fly unless there was a wind. While people could "create wind" by running with a kite, the kite would always fall to the ground when they stopped running.

Bernoulli's Principle explains why planes fly, and it also explains why kites fly. If a kite's construction and the angle the kite makes with the wind are correct, the kite meets the air with greater pressure on its front than its back, creating lift. As you tug at the kite so that it flies, instead of being blown away, the kite puts up some resistance to the wind (drag). The shape and size of a kite, as well as the position of the control line and bridle, are related to creating lift and drag. Other factors which influence how well a kite flies are: the amount of wind (certain kite designs fly better in particular wind speeds); the weight of the kite; the strength of the materials and the control line (use a line that won't be broken by the amount of pull exerted by the kite); the length of the tail (the tail balances the kite; also, in strong winds, drag can be increased by adding more tail); and balance (the kite shouldn't be heavier on one side).

Topics: Flight; Air; Forces.

MATERIALS: Kite. Optional -- gloves; lightweight thermometer; tape; lightweight cardboard or heavy paper; scissors.

DOING IT:

1. ***Safety First:*** Fly kites in a large, clear area outdoors, away from buildings, trees, and roads. Stay away from power lines. If your kite contacts a power line, let it go immediately and do not touch it again. Don't fly a kite if it's raining or if there is a thunderstorm nearby; a wet kite string conducts electricity and a thunderstorm contains enough electricity to kill you.

2. *String:* Fishing line is often used for kites. Cotton kite string is also a good choice. It's biodegradable, can be bitten through by birds and used as nesting material if the kite gets caught in a tree, and can be broken by hand in an emergency. Make sure the line is strong, but remember that every decision to increase strength may also mean an increase in weight or in wind resistance. Small kites usually take a control line with 5.5 to 7.0 kg breaking strength.

3. *Storing and Reeling String:* There are many arrangements for storing and reeling the control line (shown below). You can use a stick as a reel if you wind the string on it in a figure eight. The stick arrangement can be too slow, however, when you have to let out line fast at launch time or when you must take in line quickly. For launch, drop the stick on the ground and let the line run out by holding it directly. **The line may move very fast; be careful not to get a line burn. You may want to wear gloves.**

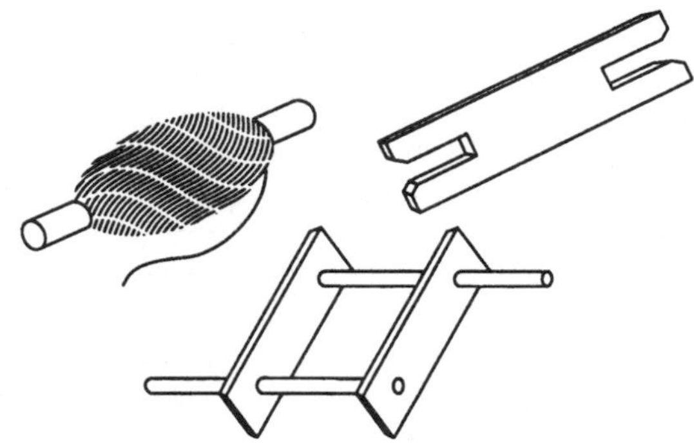

4. *Wind Analysis:* Kite flying is an art. There are a few basic techniques to keep in mind, but the art comes into play when you decide how and when to use the techniques. Always start by examining the wind. If there's no wind, wait. If there is a wind, is it steady or gusty? Strong or gentle? In which direction is the wind blowing? Position your control line and lengthen/shorten your tail (and adjust curvature, if your kite is bowed) as is appropriate.

5. *Control Line and Tail:* Changing where you tie the control line onto the bridle changes the angle at which the kite meets the wind. The more the nose is pulled down (by tying the control line toward the nose), the more the kite tends to fly up and overhead. The more the tail is pulled down (by tying the control line toward the tail), the more the kite hangs back. Experiment to see what works best. Also experiment with different lengths of tail.

6. *Getting It Up:* To fly a kite, face the kite into the wind. Hold the kite up and let out a *little* line. If the kite starts to move out and away, pull in on the line a bit; this will increase the lift. As the kite pops into the vacuum caused by the pressure difference between the front and back of the kite, let out line. Each time the kite starts to come down a bit, pull in some line; then, as soon as there is some lift, you can let the line out slowly. If you let the line out too rapidly, the kite won't present enough resistance to the wind to produce lift; it will lose its best position (called "attitude" or "approach") to the wind and start to fall. A good kite flyer rarely finds it necessary to run in order to get his or her kite into the air. A controlled reeling in and out of the line should do the trick.

7. *Keeping It Up:* If your kite doesn't want to fly well and is jerking back and forth uncontrollably, there may be a problem with the air currents where you're flying the kite. The wind may be blowing around and over trees and buildings, causing gusty air currents that send the kite in different directions. The same problem can happen if the wind is blowing down a hill. An ideal kite flying situation is to stand so that you take advantage of wind blowing steadily up a gentle slope.

8. *Exploring Air Properties:* You can use a kite to explore the properties of the air high above you. As the kite rises, it may encounter winds which are moving in a different direction or much faster than those near the ground. You can guess there's been a change in the wind when your kite changes direction or begins to weave from side to side.

9. *Inversion Layer:* Sometimes, a kite will encounter a heavy layer of colder air called an "inversion layer". The kite acts as though it's bumping up against a ceiling. You need some skillful piloting to punch through into the inversion layer. One technique involves pulling in and out rapidly on the control line. When you pull in, the kite's attitude or angle of flight is changed and the lift increases. Then, when you let the line out a little, you give the kite some movement. This pumping technique may allow your kite to punch through into the layer. Once inside the layer, the kite should continue to rise and fly normally.

10. *Extension:* Measure the approximate air temperature at different altitudes by attaching a *lightweight* thermometer to a kite's keel. Or, send up a thermometer once the kite is in the air. Fasten the thermometer to a piece of light cardboard or heavy paper. To send the thermometer (or anything else) up to your kite, cut a slit into the middle of the cardboard. Slip the cardboard onto the control line and tape the slit closed. The wind will blow the cardboard up the line.

11. *Extension:* In general, the air temperature drops about 5 degrees C for every 500 m of altitude. Attach a thermometer to a kite to measure the change in temperature so that you can estimate how high the kite goes (e.g. if the temperature drops 2.5 degrees C, the kite rose to about 250 m). Note that you have to get the kite down quickly before the temperature reading on the thermometer goes up.

Some kites are so big that it takes teams of as many as 20 people to fly them.

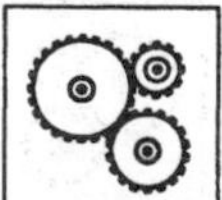

Two-Stick Kite

The Two-Stick Kite is probably one of the most famous kites around. It's relatively easy to make, very strong, and flies well.

MATERIALS: Plastic sheet (e.g. large trash bag), kraft paper, newspaper, or lightweight cloth (which does not let air pass through it, e.g. Mylar, nylon, Dacron); *lightweight*, thin, flexible sticks (e.g. bamboo, white pine, spruce, fibreglass); kite string (strong enough to withstand the wind and pull exerted by the kite); measuring tape; pencil; tape; glue; knife; scissors; old rags or strips of plastic. Optional -- needle and thread; thin paint.

DOING IT:

1. Balance in a kite is very important; the kite *must* be symmetrical in terms of shape and weight. The illustration below provides the overall dimensions for the Two-Stick Kite. Keep symmetry in mind as you measure materials and construct the kite.

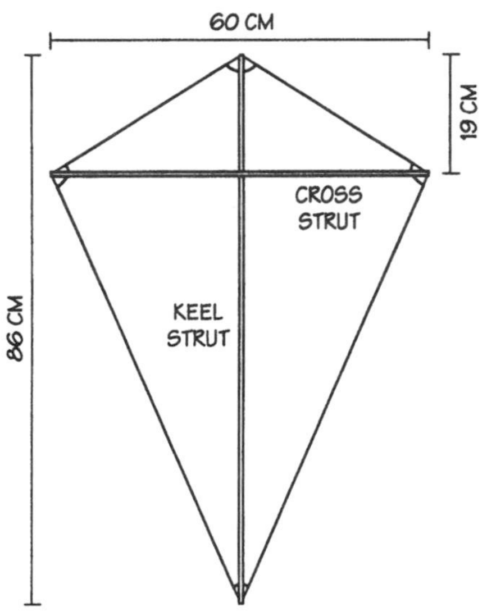

This kite's two-stick construction is recognized by almost everyone. The sticks overlap to form a large cross, and a lightweight material is stretched over this basic frame. Once you master making and flying the Two-Stick Kite, you can move to the many more complicated and elaborate kites that have been designed over the years.

Topics: Flight.

2. Begin kite construction by using a knife to make a notch in each end of both struts so that string can be easily fastened to them.

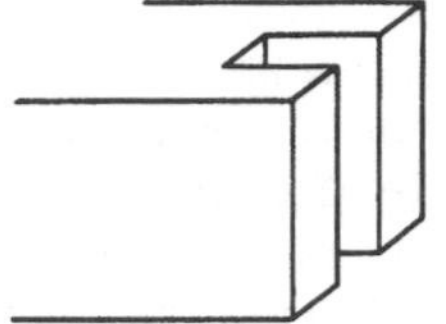

3. Notch the cross strut in the middle and bind it securely to the keel strut. Make sure the struts are at right angles to each other. You may want to put some glue over the string once you've wound it around the struts.

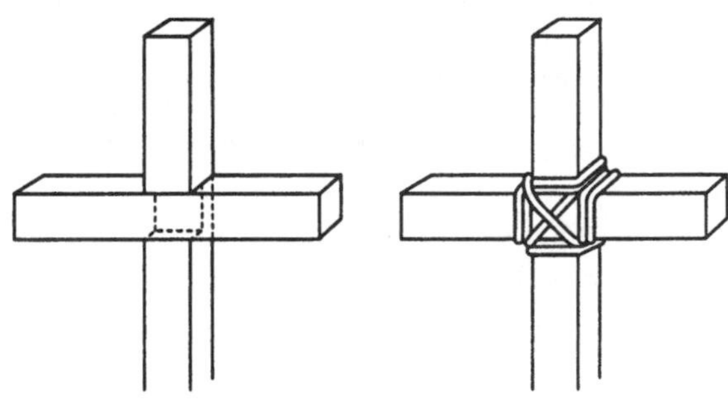

4. Frame the kite with string. Tie one end of a piece of string to the end of a strut. Pull the string along from strut to strut to form the basic diamond shape shown. Firmly attach the string to each strut; make sure that the string won't slip (if it does, the symmetry of the kite will be lost). When you're finished, you should have a taut, flat (struts shouldn't be pulled so tightly that they're starting to bend), diamond-shaped structure that keeps its shape when you handle it.

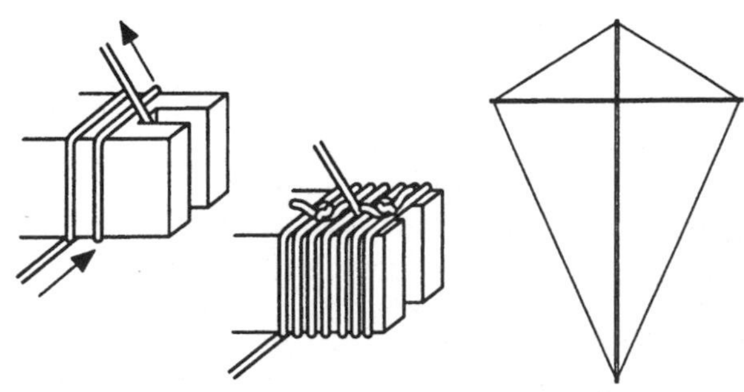

5. Since the struts are notched at the ends, they could split. To prevent this from happening, wrap tape and then string around each notch.

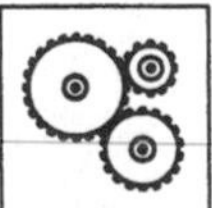

6. Use plastic, kraft paper, newspaper, or lightweight cloth as the kite material. Cut the material about 3 cm larger than the frame so that the material can be folded over the string frame. Cut small half-circles in the material at each point of the diamond so that the ends of the struts stick through. This will allow you to make adjustments to the frame later.

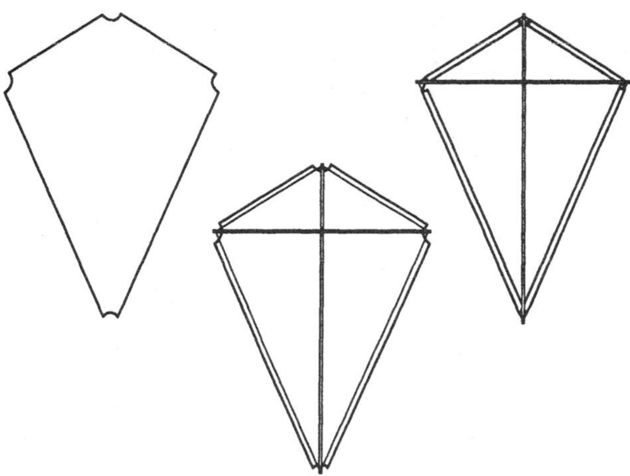

7. Glue the hem together over the string frame (if you're using cloth, you can sew the edges together). The material should be loose enough on the frame to allow slack for adjusting the bend in the struts -- but not so loose that it sags on the frame. Let the glue dry for a day. If you wish, you can then paint the material with thin paint.

8. The bridle should be about 1.5 times the length of the keel. Fasten one end of the bridle to the keel, about 5 cm above the cross strut. To do this, make a small hole in the kite material and reinforce the area with tape. Thread the string through, then fasten it firmly to the keel strut. In the same way, fasten the other end of the bridle about 5 cm up from the bottom of the keel. The best position of the control line on the bridle varies according to the wind's strength. To determine the best point on any particular day, hold the kite up into the wind with one finger hooked onto the bridle. Slide your finger along the bridle until you find the flying angle, or attitude, at which the kite seems to pull the most on your finger. Tie the control line to the bridle at that point.

9. You can fly the kite while it's flat. If you do, you'll need a tail. Cut a length of string 3-5 m long. Tie lightweight pieces of rags or strips of plastic to the string at 0.3 m intervals to make the kite's tail. Fasten the tail to the bottom of the keel, in the same way you attached the bridle to the keel. The tail balances the kite; it helps to keep the kite at the correct flying angle, especially when the wind gusts. Experiment with different lengths of tail. In general, if the wind is light, you'll need less tail on the kite than if the wind is strong. Also, if the kite does fast loops when you don't want it to, try adding more tail (and perhaps adjusting the position of the control line on the bridle).

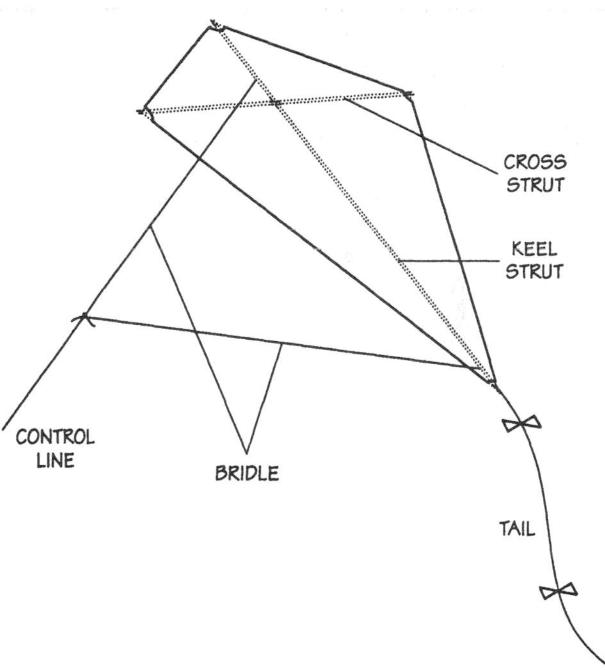

10. You can also fly the kite by giving the struts some curvature. Bowed kites are strong fliers. Change the curvature by loosening or tightening a length of string tied between both ends of the cross strut. Determine the best curvature for the struts by trial and error. When storing the kite, remove this string so that the cross strut is relaxed and doesn't lose its springiness. When the kite has a curvature, can you fly it without a tail? What happens if you add a tail?

OTHER RESOURCES

Science Is . . . is intended as a place to start, a book that encourages exploration and prompts questions. As you become interested in particular areas, you may want more information than is provided in this resource.

In working on the first and second editions of *Science Is . . .*, we have had contact with hundreds of science resources. Many of the resources were quite good; others were disappointing. The following is a list of resources we feel are worth tracking down. As you find and work with these resources, they will lead you to others.

The resources have not been rigorously evaluated based on any formal criteria. However, in our opinion, the resources are strong in one or more of the following areas: interest; understandability; thoroughness; format. Some of the resources have stood the test of time. Others have won awards. Still others are "sleepers" we feel deserve more attention.

The list contains mainly organizations, nonfiction books, and periodicals; we have included a few fiction books, audiocassettes, videotapes, software programs, and kits. We have not focused on formal, core-curriculum materials. Resources have been organized by the ten subject areas in *Science Is . . .*; in addition, there is one section which contains teaching resources and another that lists general activity/information sources. If it seemed that a particular resource might be difficult to track down, we have included a contact address.

The idea behind this resource listing is to point you in a direction for finding other resources that will excite and delight -- resources that will give everyone (young and old alike) more information and insights on a variety of science-related topics; that will encourage children to explore the world around them and ask plenty of questions; and that will help adults guide children in finding answers to questions.

TEACHING / EXPLORING SCIENCE

AIMS (Activities that Integrate Math & Science). The AIMS Education Foundation conducts research, provides workshops and seminars, and publishes elementary & intermediate materials written and tested by teachers. Contact: AIMS Education Foundation, P.O. Box 8120, Fresno, CA 93747, (559) 255-4094.

Appraisal: Science Books for Young People. A quarterly publication that contains reviews, written by librarians and subject specialists, of science trade books. Contact: Appraisal, 5 Holmes Hall, Northeastern University, Boston, MA 02115, (617) 373-7539.

Elementary School Science and How To Teach It. Glenn O. Blough and Julius Schwartz. Holt, Rinehart & Winston, 1984. A book that discusses what needs to be taught and how to teach it. Includes some science activities.

How to Ask the Right Questions. Patricia E. Blosser. National Science Teachers Association, 1991. This booklet helps you analyze your questioning techniques, classify your questions, and improve your questioning behaviour.

How to Teach Elementary School Science. Peter C. Gega. Prentice Hall, 1997. Topic areas covered in this book include how children learn science; how to use close-ended and open-ended activities; how to improve children's thinking; and how to use different resources to teach science.

IDEAAAS: Sourcebook for Science, Mathematics, & Technology Education. A very useful, thorough listing (for parents and teachers) of organizations, associations, agencies, science centres/museums, and resources. Updated annually. Contact: The Learning Team, Suite 256, 10 Long Pond Road, Armonk, NY 10504, (914) 273-2226.

The Learning Cycle and Elementary School Science Teaching. John W. Renner and Edmund A. Marek. Heinemann, 1988. Provides teachers – and parents – with insights into what children think about, how and what children learn, and how this information can be used to teach science. Contact: Heinemann Educational Books, 361 Hanover Street, Portsmouth, NH 03801, (603) 431-7894.

Learning in Science: The Implications of Children's Science. Roger Osborne and Peter Freyberg. Heinemann, 1985. A useful book for teachers and parents that discusses the ways in which children learn science. Contact: Heinemann Educational Books, 361 Hanover Street, Portsmouth, NH 03801, (603) 431-7894.

National Science Teachers Association. Offers publications, news, information, and an online Science Store (which carries some of the resources in the *Science Is...* "Other Resources" listing). Contact: NSTA, 1840 Wilson Blvd, Arlington, VA 22201, (703) 243-7100, www.nsta.org.

The Nature of Science. Frederick Aicken. Heinemann, 1984. A thought-provoking book that looks at the relationship between science and art, history, and the world around us. Contact: Heinemann Educational Books, 361 Hanover Street, Portsmouth, NH 03801, (603) 431-7894.

Resources for Teaching Elementary School Science. National Science Resources Center. National Academy Press, 1996. An excellent resource listing. Useful to teachers and parents. Contact: National Academy Press, 2101 Constitution Avenue NW, Lock Box 285, Washington, DC 20055, (202) 334-3313..

Science and Children. An excellent monthly magazine containing information articles as well as activities. The magazine is aimed at elementary teachers, but has value for parents as well. Contact: National Science Teachers Association, 1840 Wilson Blvd, Arlington, VA 22201, (703) 243-7100.

Science & Stories: Integrating Science and Literature. Hilarie Staton and Tara McCarthy. Goodyear Publishing, 1994. Links grade-level appropriate science to easily available books.

Science Books & Films. This magazine is published nine times a year and contains reviews of trade books, textbooks, films, and videotapes in all areas of science and mathematics. Contact: American Association for the Advancement of Science, 1200 New York Ave NW, Washington, DC 20009, (202) 326-6454.

Science Fare. Wendy Saul and Alan R. Newman. Harper & Row, 1986. A good source book containing ideas and approaches for teaching science. Also included are recommended toys, books, and equipment for enhancing the educational experience.

Science Through Children's Literature: An Integrated Approach. Carol M. Butzow and John W. Butzow. Libraries Unlimited, 2000. An excellent book that covers the life, physical, earth and space sciences.

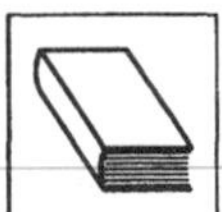

Discussions of each topic area (e.g. trees, rocks, shadows and light) include a recommended fiction book; summary; science topic areas; content-related words; activities; and related books and references.

Teach Your Child Science. Michael Shermer. Lowell House, 1989. A book that encourages parents and their children to explore science together.

Teaching Children About Science. Elaine Levenson. Prentice-Hall, 1985. Ideas and activities for teachers and parents.

Teaching Elementary Science: Who's Afraid of Spiders? Selma Wassermann and J.W. George Ivany. Harper & Row, 1988. A book that presents both the theory and practice of exploring science with children.

Teaching for Thinking: Theory, Strategies and Activities for the Classroom. Louis Raths, Selma Wasserman, Arthur Jonas, and Arnold Rothstein. Teachers College Press, 1986. A solid approach to taking children beyond memorization to higher-order thinking processes such as observation and classification.

Teaching Science Through Discovery. Arthur A. Carin and Robert B. Sund. Merrill, 1989. A guide for helping teachers encourage children's natural curiosity about the world around them. Activity suggestions are included.

Teaching Science To Children: An Integrated Approach. Alfred E. Friedl. Random House, 1986. A book that takes a holistic approach to teaching science. Combines teaching strategies with activities.

TESS (The Educational Software Selector). Educational Products Information Exchange. This is a comprehensive directory of computer software for preschool through college by subject. Separate subject directories are available quarterly. Contact: Educational Products Information Exchange (EPIE) Institute, 103-3 West Montauk Highway, Hampton Bays, NY 11946, (516) 728-9100.

Unesco Sourcebook for Out-of-School Science and Technology Education. Unesco. Paris, France: United Nations Educational, 1986. An international sourcebook listing scientific resources, organizations, museums.

GENERAL ACTIVITIES / INFORMATION

Activities for Teaching About Science and Society. Rodger Bybee, Rita Peterson, Jane Bowyer, and David Butts. Merrill, 1984. Activities that relate to social needs and problems.

Biology for Every Kid: 101 Easy Experiments That Really Work. Janice Vancleave. John Wiley, 1990. Simple, well-illustrated activities in three sections: plants, animals, and humans.

Bubbles, Rainbows and Worms: Science Experiments for Pre-School Children. Sam Ed Brown. Gryphon House, 1981. An excellent primer for children who are too young for *Science Is....*

Concepts and Experiences in Elementary School Science. Peter C. Gega. Macmillan Publishing Co., 1991. A solid, thorough book of information and activities covering light energy and colour, heat energy, sound energy, magnetic interactions, electrical energy, simple machines and how they work, plant life and environment, animal life and environment, and the human body and nutrition.

Creative Sciencing Ideas and Activities for Teachers and Children. Alfred DeVito and Gerald H. Krockover. Little, Brown & Co., 1980. A classic activity book that emphasizes a combination of subject matter and science skills.

Discover: Mysteries of the Past and Present. Katherine Grier. Kids Can Press, 1989. Over 50 activities that help children discover the science behind the scenes in a museum.

DK Science Encyclopedia. DK Publishing, 1998. Fascinating facts and accessible, accurate information make this a valuable reference for all ages, home and school.

Dr. Zed's Brilliant Book of Science Experiments, Dr. Zed's Dazzling Book of Science Activities, Dr. Zed's Science Surprises. Gordon Penrose. Greey de Pencier, 1977, 1982, 1989. Simple, fun activities from "Dr. Zed", presented in his own entertaining style.

An Early Start to Science. Roy Richards, Margaret Collis, and Doug Kincaid. London, England: Macdonald Educational, 1987. An excellent, visually-oriented book for younger children touching on topics from music to gardening to flying things.

OTHER RESOURCES

An Early Start to Technology from Science. Roy Richards. Simon & Schuster, 1990. An excellent, visually-oriented book for younger children touching on topics ranging from bridges to the human skeleton to cooking.

Experiences in Science for Young Children. Donald B. Neuman. Delmar Publishers, 1978. An excellent primer for children who are too young for *Science Is*.... Takes a holistic approach to information and activities related to introducing young children to science.

The Five Biggest Ideas in Science. Charles M. Wynn and Arthur W. Wiggins. John Wiley, 1997. In easy-to-understand terms, this book introduces the basics of current theory by exploring the five major disciplines and the fundamental theory behind each.

Foodworks. Ontario Science Centre. Kids Can Press, 1986. Interesting activities and information about food.

Gee, Wiz! Linda Allison and David Katz. Little, Brown & Company, 1983. Good activities, in a fun format, that introduce a variety of scientific concepts.

The Handy Science Answer Book. Science and Technology Department of Carnegie Library of Pittsburgh. Visible Ink Press, 1996. How many hairs does the average person have on their head? Why do golf balls have dimples? When was the Ice Age? In this perfect school or home reference, find the answers to more than 1,200 frequently asked science and technology questions.

Idea Factory's Super Science Sourcebook I and II. Ellyn Smith, Marilyn Blackmer, and Sandi Schlichting. Idea Factory, 1987, 1989. Filled with activities dealing with the life, physical, and earth sciences. Contact: Idea Factory, P.O. Box 10656, Tampa, FL 33679, (800) 331-6204.

Invitations to Science Inquiry. Tik L. Liem. Science Inquiry Enterprise, 1990. A good science activity book that stresses curiosity prompted by discrepant events.

Janice Vancleave's 201 Awesome, Magical, Bizarre, & Incredible Experiments. John Wiley & Sons, 1994. This book is part of a series by this prolific science author.

The Kids' Question and Answer Book. Editors of OWL Magazine. Greey de Pencier, 1987. A colourfully-illustrated book that covers a wide variety of the everyday questions children ask.

The Leaves are Falling in Rainbows: Science Activities for Early Childhood. Michael E. Knight and Terry L. Graham. Atlanta, GA: Humanics, 1984. A good book for encouraging younger children to explore various science topics.

Life Science Activities for Grades 2-8. Marvin M. Tolman and James O. Morton. West Nyack, NY: Parker Publishing, 1986. Straightforward, hands-on activities involving topics such as plants and seeds, animal adaptation, the five senses, and human body structure.

Magic Mud and Other Great Experiments. Gordon Penrose. Greey de Pencier, 1987. Simple, fun activities from "Dr. Zed", presented in his own entertaining style.

More Science Experiments You Can Eat. Vicki Cobb. Lippincott, 1979. A scientific, tasty look at food.

Mr. Wizard's Supermarket Science. Don Herbert. Random House, 1980. A classic book that contains ideas, tips, and tricks for science activities using readily-available materials.

Odyssey. A science magazine for grades 4-9 published nine times per year. Contact: Cobblestone Publishing, 30 Grove St, Suite C, Peterborough, NH 03458, (800) 821-0115.

OWL. A monthly magazine containing activities and information for children. *Chickadee* magazine, put out by the same publisher, is written for very young children. Contact: Bayard Press, 179 John St, Suite 500, Toronto, ON, M5T 3G5, Canada, (416) 340-2700.

Physical Science Activities for Grades 2-8. Marvin N. Tolman and James O. Morton. West Nyack, NY: Parker Publishing Co., 1986. Discovery activities covering topics such as the nature of matter, energy, sound, and electricity.

Science Around the House. Robert Gardner. Julian Messner, 1985. Your home is a natural place to do science experiments; this book offers plenty of ideas.

The Science Book. Sara Stein. Workman, 1980. A classic science activity book.

The Science Book for Girls and Other Intelligent Beings. Valerie Wyatt. Kids Can Press, 1997. A positive, nonthreatening look at science and science careers.

The Science Discovery Book. Anthony Fredericks, et al. Scott, Foresman & Co., 1987. A resource book of activity-based learning in the life, earth, and physical sciences.

Science Experiences with Everyday Things. Howard R. Munson. Fearon Teacher Aids, 1988. A book that explores scientific principles using common items such as paper and plastic bags, straws, and paper clips.

Science Experiments You Can Eat. Vicki Cobb. Harper & Row, 1972. Look at food in new – and scientific – ways.

Science Magic Tricks. Nathan Shalit. Holt, Rinehart & Winston, 1981. More than 50 tricks based on scientific principles and explained in scientific terms.

Science on a Shoestring. Herb Strongin. Addison-Wesley, 1985. Excellent activities using readily-available materials.

Science Weekly. This magazine is published sixteen times a year and develops current science topics in a way that's exciting for elementary children. Contact: Science Weekly, P.O. Box 70638, Chevy Chase, MD 20813, (301) 680-8804.

Scienceworks. Ontario Science Centre. Kids Can Press, 1984. A well-presented book of science activities.

ScienceWorld. This magazine is published fourteen times a year, is aimed at students in grades 7-10, and contains lively reading, information, and activities. Contact: Scholastic Inc., P.O. Box 3710, Jefferson City, MO 65102, (212) 343-6100.

The Sierra Club Summer Book. Linda Allison. Little, Brown and Co., 1989. A collection of summer activities.

Small Wonders: Hands-on Science Activities for Young Children. Peggy K. Perdue. Scott Foresman & Co., 1989. An excellent primer with simple activities for children who are too young for *Science Is....*

Still More Science Activities. Smithsonian Institution. Galison Books, 1989. Activities that work with information that is accurate and well-presented.

Teaching Science with Everyday Things. Victor E. Schmidt and Verne N. Rockcastle. McGraw-Hill, 1982. A book of activities for teachers and parents who may not be as comfortable with science as they would like to be.

TVOntario Take a Look Series and Look Up Series. TVOntario, 1986, 1989. Two videotape series that look at such topics as energy, waste, fossils, rocks, plants, birds, insects, rain, snow, wind, space, boats, and flight. Contact: TVOntario, 2180 Yonge St, Box 200, Station Q, Toronto, ON, M4T 2T1, Canada, (416) 484-2600.

What Will Happen If...: Young Children and the Scientific Method. Barbara Sprung, et al. Educational Equity Concepts, 1985. A well-organized book containing tested activities for helping children develop basic math and science skills. Contact: Monarch Books, 5000 Dufferin St., Unit K, Downsview, ON, M3H 5T5, Canada, (416) 663-8231.

Who Says You Can't Teach Science: Grades K-6. Alan Ticotsky. Scott, Foresman & Co., 1985. Quick and easy experiments using readily-available materials.

The Whole Cosmos Catalog of Science Activities. Joseph Abruscato and Jack Hassard. Scott, Foresman and Co., 1978. A wonderful source of science activities.

The Wild Inside: Sierra Club's Guide to the Great Indoors. Linda Allison. Little, Brown & Co., 1988. Information and activities for an indoor field trip.

WonderScience. Fun physical sciences activities in a colourful comic book format for students in grades 4-6. Eight issues published per year. Contact: American Chemical Society, 1155 16th St NW, Washington, DC 20036, (202) 872-6165.

Wonderstruck I and II. Bob McDonald and Eric Grace. Toronto, ON: CBC Enterprises, 1988, 1989. Science activities and information presented in a way that makes sense to children. Contact: General Distribution Services, 325 Humber College Blvd, Toronto, ON, M9W 7C3, Canada, (416) 213-1919.

Youth Science Foundation. The YSF is a nonprofit organization that coordinates science fairs across Canada. It has materials with project ideas, as well as information on planning fairs and science olympics. Contact: Youth Science Foundation at (613) 727-8475 or visit www.ysf.ca.

175 Science Experiments to Amuse and Amaze Your Friends. Brenda Walpole. Random House, 1988. Experiments, tricks, and things to make covering topics like water, air, movement, and light.

DISCOVERING SCIENCE

Bet You Can't! Science Impossibilities to Fool You. Vicki Cobb and Kathy Darling. William Morrow, 1980. A classic book of science activities and tricks that use readily-available materials.

The Book of the Unknown. Geraldine Woods and Harold Woods. Random House, 1982. This book poses provocative questions that are bound to prompt children to explore.

The Book of Think. Marilyn Burns. Little, Brown and Company, 1976. A book of fun activities designed to foster thinking and analytical skills.

Bubble-ology. Jacqueline Barber. Lawrence Hall of Science, 1986. Creative activities for exploring the properties of bubbles. Part of the *Great Explorations in Math and Science (GEMS)* curriculum development project. Contact: GEMS, Lawrence Hall of Science, University of California, Berkeley, CA 94720, (510) 642-7771.

Canadian Orienteering Federation. Information on orienteering. Contact: Canadian Orienteering Federation, Box 62052, Convent Glen, Orleans, ON, K1C 2R9, Canada, (613) 830-1147.

Critical Thinking Puzzles and *Challenging Critical Thinking Puzzles*. Michael A. DiSpezio. Sterling Publications, 1996, 1998. These books contain an intriguing array of puzzles, challenges, funky facts, things to build, weird riddles, and other brainteasers.

How to Build a Better Mousetrap Car – and Other Great Experimental Science Fun. Al G. Renner. Dodd, Mead, 1977. Full of science olympic types of challenges.

How to Make Optical Illusion Tricks & Toys. E. Richard Churchill. Sterling Publishing, 1989. More than 60 optical illusion activities.

How to Think Like a Scientist: Answering Questions by the Scientific Method. Stephen P. Kramer. Thomas Y. Crowell, 1987. Short stories that relate everyday experiences to using the scientific method.

I Didn't Know That! Katherine Farris. Greey de Pencier, 1988. A visual book that covers a wide variety of topics and sparks curiosity and discussion.

Loads of Codes and Secret Ciphers. Paul B. Janeczko. Macmillan, 1984. Secret code and message systems are explained and children are challenged to figure out, vary, and create their own messages.

Look! Look! Look! Tana Hoban. Greenwillow Books, 1988. A textless book that uses full-colour photographs, presented in a perspective-challenging way, to sharpen observation skills.

The Magic Detectives. Joe Nickell. Prometheus Books, 1989. Are ghosts real? Is it possible to read minds? Discover the scientific response to "unexplained" events by following in the footsteps of "detectives".

Opt: An Illusionary Tale. Arline Baum and Joseph Baum. Viking Penguin, 1987. A delightful adventure to the kingdom of Opt, a magical world of optical illusions.

The Puzzlers Book. Elizabeth MacLeod (editor). Greey de Pencier Books, 1990. Activities for answering puzzling questions.

Science Brain-Twisters, Paradoxes, and Fallacies. Christopher P. Jargocki. Charles Scribner's Sons, 1976. A book that will get older children thinking.

Science Games & Puzzles. Laurence B. White, Jr. Harper & Row, 1975. A book full of science challenges and experiments.

Science Mind Stretchers. Imogene Forte and Sandra Schurr. Incentive Publications, 1987. A collection of mini-units in the life, earth, and physical sciences that help to extend science concepts and reinforce skill development.

Scientific Eye. Adam Hart-Davis. Sterling Publishing Co., 1989. Encourages children to be clever detectives in solving the scientific mysteries around them.

Think About It! Science Problems of the Day. Anthony D. Fredericks. Creative Publications, 1988. Contains 180 daily problems and 36 weekly challenges focusing on the life, earth, space, and physical sciences.

Topsy-Turvies: More Pictures to Stretch the Imagination. Mitsumasa Anno. Philomel Books, 1989. A textless book that uses full-colour, two-page spreads to challenge the imagination with problems of scale and spatial orientation.

Walter Wick's Optical Tricks. Walter Wick. Scholastic, 1998. A great book that presents a series of optical illusions with explanations.

MATTER & ENERGY

Adventures with Atoms and Molecules: Chemistry Experiments for Young People, Book I and Book II. Robert C. Mebane and Thomas R. Rybolt. Enslow Publishers,

1985, 1987. Chemistry activities that answer challenging questions.

AECL CANDU. Information on CANDU reactors and nuclear energy in Canada. Contact: AECL CANDU, Sheridan Park Research Community, Mississauga, ON, L5K 1B2, Canada, (905) 823-9040.

Awesome Experiments in Electricity & Magnetism and *Awesome Experiments in Light & Sound.* Michael DiSpezio. Sterling Publications, 1998, 1999. Simple, fun experiments that work.

Biography of an Atom. Jacob Bronowski and Millicent Selsam. Harper & Row, 1965. A classic book that describes the cycle of a carbon atom through information from the areas of astronomy, physics, biology, and chemistry.

Chemically Active! Vicki Cobb. Lippincott, 1985. Chemistry activities using household materials.

Colours. Ed Catherall. East Sussex, England: Wayland, 1986. An excellent primer with hands-on activities for children who are too young for *Science Is….*

Explore Matter with Toys: Using and Understanding the Senses. Mickey Sarquis. McGraw-Hill, 1997. Toy-based, tested activities that have children explore the world around them through their five senses.

The Forces With You. Tom Johnston. Gareth Stevens, 1988. An entertaining book with well-written text discussing how forces – such as gravity, friction, elasticity – affect our lives.

Let's Imagine: Electricity. Tom Johnston. London, England: Bodley Head, 1986. A good basic coverage of the topic.

Let's Imagine: Energy. Tom Johnston. London, England: Bodley Head, 1986. A good basic coverage of the topic.

Light! Color! Action! Tom Johnston. Gareth Stevens, 1988. A fun book that explains the phenomena of colour and includes simple activities.

The "Magic" of Electricity. Cary I. Sneider, Alan Gould, and Budd Wentz. Lawrence Hall of Science, 1985. Creative activities for exploring electricity. Part of the *Great Explorations in Math and Science (GEMS)* curriculum development project. Contact: GEMS, Lawrence Hall of Science, University of California, Berkeley, CA 94720, (510) 642-7771.

Messing Around with Baking Chemistry. Bernie Zubrowski. Little, Brown, 1981. Baking a cake becomes a fun – and tasty – scientific experiment, along with some other kitchen investigations.

National Energy Foundation. A nonprofit, educational organization that produces materials on energy (including electricity, nuclear energy, renewable energy) and energy conservation. Contact: National Energy Foundation, 3676 California Ave, Suite A117, Salt Lake City, UT 84104, (801) 908-5800.

Secret Magnets. Herman Schneider and Nina Schneider. Scholastic, 1979. This book describes how to make a "magnetic detector" to help look for hidden magnets at home.

Shadows: Here, There, and Everywhere. Ron Goor and Nancy Goor. Crowell, 1981. A wonderful book that combines art and science to explain why and how shadows come to be.

Soda Science: Designing and Testing Soft Drinks. Bernie Zubrowski. William Morrow, 1997. Simple, fun experiments that explore how to create natural flavours, colours, carbonation, as well as analyze store bought brands of soda.

Teaching the Fun of Physics: 101 Activities to Make Science Education Easy and Enjoyable. Janice Vancleave. Prentice Hall, 1985. Straightforward activities that cover topics such as buoyancy, heat, light refraction, reflection, magnets, electricity, and gravity.

HUMANS

Blood and Guts: A Working Guide to Your Own Insides. Linda Allison. Little, Brown, 1976. A fun book that explores the human body.

The Body Symphony: The Inside Story of Your Whole Body. The Inside Story with Slim Goodbody Series. Agency for Instructional Technology, 1981. A videotape that takes an interesting, fun look inside the human body. Contact: Agency for Instructional Technology, P.O. Box A, Bloomington, IN 47402, (800) 457-4509.

Bodyworks: The Kid's Guide to Food and Physical Fitness. Carol Bershad and Deborah Bernick. Random House, 1979. Activities for and insights into a strong, healthy body.

The Breath of Life: The Inside Story of Respiration. The Inside Story with Slim Goodbody Series. Agency for Instructional Technology, 1981. A videotape that takes an interesting, fun look at how we breathe. Contact: Agency for Instructional Technology, P.O. Box A, Bloomington, IN 47402, (800) 457-4509.

Canadian Dental Association. Materials covering a wide range of dental health issues. Contact: Canadian Dental Association, 1815 Alta Vista Drive, Ottawa, ON, K1G 3Y6, Canada, (613) 523-1770.

Canadian Public Health Association. A variety of publications on health issues. Contact: Canadian Public Health Association, 1565 Carling Avenue, Suite 400, Ottawa, ON, K1Z 8R1, Canada, (613) 725-3769.

Down, Down, Down: The Inside Story of Digestion. The Inside Story with Slim Goodbody Series. Agency for Instructional Technology, 1981. An entertaining videotape with a step-by-step explanation of digestion. Contact: Agency for Instructional Technology, P.O. Box A, Bloomington, IN 47402, (800) 457-4509.

Food Power. Well, Well, Well, with Slim Goodbody Series. Agency for Instructional Technology, 1985. An entertaining videotape about nutritious foods. Contact: Agency for Instructional Technology, P.O. Box A, Bloomington, IN 47402, (800) 457-4509.

For Your Own Protection: Stories Science Photos Tell. Vicki Cobb. Lothrop, Lee and Shepard, 1989. An unusual book about the human body's defense mechanisms.

Go, Grow, Glow. Well, Well, Well, with Slim Goodbody Series. Agency for Instructional Technology, 1985. An entertaining videotape that looks at food and the energy it gives us. Includes a visit with a NASA specialist who talks about food and eating habits in space. Contact: Agency for Instructional Technology, P.O. Box A, Bloomington, IN 47402, (800) 457-4509.

The Human Body: A First Discovery Book. Sylvaine Perols. Cartwheel Books, 1996. A basic but very detailed and straightforward guide to the human body.

Janice Vancleave's Play and Find Out About the Human Body. Janice Vancleave. John Wiley, 1998. 50 simple experiments that explore topics like skin, respiration, the skeleton, and why teeth are different shapes.

Looking at the Body. David Suzuki. Stoddart, 1987. A good publication that contains information and activities related to the human body.

Looking at Senses. David Suzuki. Stoddart, 1986. A good publication that contains detailed information and activities related to the human senses.

Lubba Dubba: The Inside Story of Your Heart and Blood. The Inside Story with Slim Goodbody Series. Agency for Instructional Technology, 1981. An entertaining videotape that tours the system that keeps our blood flowing. Contact: Agency for Instructional Technology, P.O. Box A, Bloomington, IN 47402, (800) 457-4509.

The Magic School Bus Inside the Human Body. Joanna Cole. Scholastic, 1990. This imaginative, fact-based book is part of a popular series about a teacher who takes her class on various field trips.

The Sensational Five: The Inside Story of Your Senses. The Inside Story with Slim Goodbody Series. Agency for Instructional Technology, 1981. An entertaining videotape that looks at the five basic senses, as well as senses like hunger which keep us in touch with our body. Contact: Agency for Instructional Technology, P.O. Box A, Bloomington, IN 47402, (800) 457-4509.

The Senses. Wonders of Learning Kits. National Geographic Society, 1984. A kit that includes audiocassette, booklets, activity guides and worksheets. Introduces the five major senses and explains why they are important to humans and animals. Contact: National Geographic Society, (800) 638-4077.

Stephen Biesty's Incredible Body. Stephen Biesty and Richard Platt. DK Publishing, 1998. Detailed anatomical cross sections of everything from the circulatory system to the human brain.

Using Your Head: The Many Ways of Being Smart. Sara Gilbert. Macmillan, 1984. A discussion of human intelligence.

3D Eyewitness: Human Body. Richard Walker. DK Publishing, 1999. An interactive kit that includes activities and a model nearly twelve inches high with detachable bones and body parts.

THE ENVIRONMENT

Acclimatizing. Steve Van Matre. Martinsville, IN: American Camping Association, 1974. A complete activity program for exploring the natural world.

American Solar Energy Society. Resource material for grades 1-12 on solar energy technology and energy efficiency. Contact: American Solar Energy Society, 2400 Central Ave, Suite G1, Boulder, CO 80301, (303) 443-3130.

Arctic Whales and Whaling. Bobbie Kalman and Ken Faris. Crabtree, 1988. A sensitive look at an important environmental issue: balancing the needs of humans with a respect for animals. Introduces different types of whales and tells the story of the whaling industry, complete with traditional Inuit hunting methods.

Art Lessons That Teach Children About Their Natural Environment. Ruth L. Peck. Parker, 1973. Science can be complemented by art, and this book demonstrates how.

At the Edge of the Pond. Jennifer Owings Dewey. Little, Brown and Co., 1987. A fictional story that explores life in a pond from the shoreline to the surface to the water to the bottom.

Audubon Adventure. A quarterly nature newspaper for elementary children. Contact: National Audubon Society, 700 Broadway, New York, NY 10003, (212) 979-3184.

The Canadian Junior Green Guide. Teri Degler and Pollution Probe. McClelland & Stewart, 1990. An easy-to-read, fun handbook with activities, information, and colourful line drawings.

Canadian Wildlife Federation. Materials on wildlife and endangered species in Canada. Contact: Canadian Wildlife Federation, 350 Michael Cowpland Dr, Kanata, ON, K2M 2W1, Canada, (800) 563-9453.

A Caribou Alphabet. Mary Beth Owens. Brunswick, ME: Dog Ear Press, 1988. A fictional story showing the interdependence of animals and nature, and humans.

City Kids and City Critters! Janet Wier Roberts and Carole Huelbig. McGraw-Hill, 1996. Activities for urban explorers that encourage and teach city kids to preserve wildlife habitats.

The City Kid's Field Guide. Ethan Herberman. Simon and Schuster, 1989. Explore the wide array of animals and plants found in urban neighbourhoods.

City Safaris: A Sierra Club Explorer's Guide to Urban Adventures for Grownups and Kids. Carolyn Shaffer and Erica Fielder. Sierra Club Books, 1987. An ecological perspective on the urban environment.

Come Out, Muskrats. Jim Arnosky. Lothrop, Lee and Shepard, 1989. A beautiful book by a well-respected author that paints a detailed portrait of pond life at sunset.

Conservation: A Thoughtful Way of Explaining Conservation to Children. Robert Ingpen and Margaret Dunkle. Macmillan, 1988. Introduces environmental and conservation basics.

Discovering Nature: Things to Do Inside and Outside with Plants and Animals. Midas Dekkers. Stoddart, 1987. A lively book that covers a wide variety of topics and encourages active exploration.

Discovery. Joseph Brodsky. Farrar Straus Giroux, 1999. An illustrated poem by a Nobel laureate that explores the natural beneath the man-made.

Drawings From Nature. Jim Arnosky. Lothrop, Lee & Shepard Books, 1982. A beautiful book by a well-respected author that fosters an appreciation of the wonders of nature.

Earth Songs. Myra Cohn Livingston and Leonard Everett Fisher. Holiday House, 1986. Poetry and art are combined to inspire respect for our home, Earth.

Education Goes Outdoors. Frank A. Johns, et al. Addison-Wesley Publishing, 1986. Activities for exploring the world outside the classroom, from the schoolyard to a grassy field to the human community.

Endangered Species: Wild & Rare. Ranger Rick's NatureScope. National Wildlife Federation, 1987. Classroom and playground activities that combine science with social studies, mathematics, language arts, drama, music, and art. Contact: McGraw-Hill, (800) 262-4729.

Endangered Wildlife. Martin Banks. Vero Beach, CA: Rourke Enterprises, 1988. A balanced look at endangered animals and natural as well as human causes of extinction.

Energy Probe. Materials on energy management and conservation. Contact: Energy Probe, 225 Brunswick Ave, Toronto, ON, M5S 2M6, Canada, (416) 964-9223.

Environment Canada. Materials on environmental issues in Canada, including publications discussing things individuals can do to protect the environment. Contact: Environment Canada, Enquiry Centre, 351 St. Joseph Blvd, Hull, QC, K1A 0H3, Canada, (819) 997-2800.

A Flower in the Forest. Hugh Lewin and Lisa Kopper. London, England: Hamish Hamilton, 1989. A fictional story about a girl from Latin America whose village is affected by a dam and paper mill.

Friends of the Earth. A network of independent environmental organizations throughout the world. Offers a newsletter for members. Contact: Friends of the Earth, 260 St. Patrick St, Suite 206, Ottawa, ON, K1N 5K5, Canada, (613) 241-0085.

Gaia: An Atlas of Planet Management. Norman Myers (ed.). Doubleday, 1984. An excellent book that looks at the world's resources, how they are being managed, and how management can be improved.

The Girl Who Loved Wild Horses. Paul Gobel. Macmillan Publishing, 1978. A fictional story about a Plains Indian girl that deals with the theme of the interdependence of humans, nature, and the environment.

Greenpeace. Materials on environmental issues. Contact: Greenpeace, 250 Dundas St W, Toronto, ON, M5T 2Z5, Canada, (416) 597-8408.

Hands-On Nature: Information and Activities for Exploring the Environment with Children. Jenepher Lingelbach (editor). Vermont Institute of Natural Science, 1986. Factual information, creative approaches, and hands-on experiences combine to make this book very useful for exploring the natural world. Contact: Vermont Institute of Natural Science, Church Hill, P.O. Box 86, Woodstock, VT 05091, (802) 457-2779.

High in the Mountains. Ruth Yaffe Radin. Macmillan, 1989. A book that encourages an appreciation of the natural world through a fictional story about a child's day of adventure high in the mountains near grandpa's house.

How to Be a Nature Detective. Millicent E. Selsam. Harper & Row, 1966. Ideas for exploring the outdoors.

Humanizing Environmental Education: A Guide for Leading Nature and Human Nature Activities. Clifford E. Knapp and Joel Goodman. Martinsville, IN: American Camping Association, 1981. Useful information on structuring outdoor experiences.

I Was Born in a Tree and Raised by Bees. Jim Arnosky. Bradbury Press, 1988. A delightful book by a well-repected author that follows the forest through the four seasons. Provides information on plant and animal life. Includes activity descriptions.

In the Forest: A Portfolio of Paintings. Jim Arnosky. Lothrop, Lee and Shepard, 1989. A beautiful book of paintings that provides insights into the intricate nature of the ecosystem.

Isn't It a Beautiful Meadow? Wolf Harranth and Winfried Opgenoorth. Oxford University Press, 1985. A fictional story for younger children that follows the inhabitants of a meadow who are forced to move when their home becomes a city.

Keepers of the Earth: Native Stories and Environmental Activities for Children. Michael J. Caduto and Joseph Bruchac. Fulcrum, 1988. A holistic resource that uses a legend, discussions, and questions to introduce each topic. Covers ecology, environment, conservation, and human relations.

A Kid's Guide to How to Save The Planet. Billy Goodman. Avon, 1990. A book that provides background information and suggestions for direct action.

The Kids' Nature Book: 365 Indoor/Outdoor Activities and Experiences. Susan Milord. Williamson Publishing, 1989. A good source of activities.

Looking at the Environment. David Suzuki. Stoddart, 1989. A good publication that contains thorough, interesting information and activities related to the environment.

The Lorax. Theodore Seuss Geisel (Dr. Seuss). Random House, 1971. A fictional story about humanity's need for manufactured items, which produces larger and larger factories, which in turn must be supplied by the natural resources of the area.

The Lost Lake. Allen Say. Houghton Mifflin, 1989. A fictional story about a father and son on a camping trip who come to better appreciate the natural environment.

The Magic School Bus Gets Eaten: A Book About Food Chains. Patricia Relf and Joanna Cole. Scholastic, 1996. Another title in this series of fictional books that incorporate factual information.

Michael Bird-Boy. Tomie DePaola. Prentice-Hall, 1975. A fictional story about pollution that threatens the environment of a small boy. The boy sets out to find the cause of the pollution and offer a solution.

National Energy Foundation. A nonprofit, educational organization that produces materials on energy (including electricity, nuclear energy, renewable

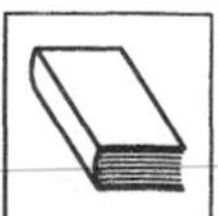

energy) and energy conservation. Contact: National Energy Foundation, 3676 California Ave, Suite A117, Salt Lake City, UT 84104, (801) 908-5800.

National Geographic World. A monthly magazine for children with excellent photography and inviting information. Contact: National Geographic Society, (800) 638-4077.

Nature What's It: Creatures, Plants, Nature's Oddities and More. Lyn Thomas. Greey de Pencier, 1989. Guess the identity of close-up photographs with clues. Photographs are followed by explanations.

Outdoor Education Equipment. Russel E. Bachert and Emerson L. Snooks. Danville, IL: The Interstate Printers & Publishers, Inc., 1974. Instructions for making a variety of equipment for exploring the outdoors.

The Pied Piper of Hamlin. Mercer Mayer. Macmillan Publishing, 1987. This familiar fictional story deals with themes of solid waste disposal, disease, and environmental relationships.

Pollution and Wildlife. Michael Bright. Gloucester Press, 1987. A thought-provoking book that takes a global look at how pollution affects wildlife.

Pollution Probe. Information on environmental issues. Contact: Pollution Probe Foundation, 12 Madison Ave, Toronto, ON, M5R 2S1, Canada, (416) 926-1907.

Project Learning Tree. A workshop offered throughout North America that helps teachers integrate environmental/forestry information into their curriculum. Participants receive resource/activity books. Contact: American Forest & Paper Association, 1111 19th St NW, Suite 800, Washington, DC 20036, (202) 463-2455.

Quiet. Peter Parnall. William Morrow, 1989. Share a young boy's afternoon adventure as he lies immobile in the grass to discover nature from some unusual perspectives.

Ranger Rick. A monthly children's magazine for members that contains indoor and outdoor activities for enjoying and understanding nature. Contact: National Wildlife Federation, 1400 16th Street NW, Washington, DC 20036-2266, (202) 797-6800.

Rediscovery: Ancient Pathways – New Directions. Thom Henley. Lone Pine Publishing, 1996. A guidebook and activity source for outdoor education based on the native perspective. Contact: Lone Pine Publishing, 10145 81st Ave, Edmonton, AB, T6E 1W9, Canada, (800) 661-9017.

Restoring Our Earth. Laurence Pringle. Enslow Publishers, 1987. A clear, well-researched book for older children that explains efforts to restore and protect the natural environment.

Rocky Mountain Institute. Good technical information (geared toward adults) available on a variety of energy and water management issues. Contact: Rocky Mountain Institute, 1739 Snowmass Creek Road, Snowmass, CO 81654-9199, (970) 927-3851.

Sharing Nature with Children. Joseph Bharat Cornell. Ananda Publications, 1983. An excellent book with activities and tips for structuring outdoor experiences.

Sharing Your World. Well, Well, Well, with Slim Goodbody Series. Agency for Instructional Technology, 1985. An entertaining videotape looking at the importance of maintaining our environment. Contact: Agency for Instructional Technology, P.O. Box A, Bloomington, IN 47402, (800) 457-4509.

A Shell on the Beach. Hugh Lewin and Lisa Kopper. London, England: Hamish Hamilton, 1989. A fictional story about a girl who goes to visit the sea and is disappointed to find the beach littered and the sea polluted.

Sierra Club. Information on a variety of environmental issues. Contact: Sierra Club, 85 Second St, 2nd Floor, San Francisco, CA 94105, (415) 977-5500.

Solar Energy Society of Canada. Information on renewable energy. Contact: Solar Energy Society of Canada, 116 Lisgar St, Suite 702, Ottawa, ON, K2P 0C2, Canada, (613) 234-4151.

State of the Ark: An Atlas of Conservation in Action –A Gaia Book. Lee Durrell. Doubleday, 1986. A thorough look at the state of nature with examples from throughout the world.

Sunship Earth. Steve Van Matre. Martinsville, IN: American Camping Association, 1979. Activities for exploring our environment.

Ten-Minute Field Trips. Helen Ross Russell. National Science Teachers Association, 1998. More than 200 explorations of familiar spaces and objects – brick walls, rock outcrops, lawns, broken pavement, weeds, etc.

Where Once There Was a Wood. Denise Fleming. Henry Holt, 1996. A uniquely illustrated fictional story about the variety of wildlife that can be displaced if their environment is destroyed (factual information at the back).

World Wildlife Fund. Offers Schools for Wildlife kit. Contact: World Wildlife Fund Canada, 245 Eglinton Ave East, Suite 410, Toronto, ON, M4P 3J1, Canada, (416) 489-8800.

The Wump World. Bill Peet. Houghton Mifflin, 1970. A fictional story about a simple, grazing environment turned into a polluted, industrial complex.

50 Simple Things Kids Can Do to Save the Earth. The EarthWorks Group. Andrews and McMeel, 1990. A well-written book of activities and action ideas.

ROCKS

The Amazing Dirt Book. Paulette Bourgeois. Kids Can Press, 1990. A well-written, fun book with information and simple activities on "dirt-related" topics such as rocks and fossils, earthquakes, erosion, and farming.

Be A Rockhound. Martin L. Keen. Julian Messner, 1979. A good book for beginning rock collectors.

The Collector's Encyclopedia of Rocks and Minerals. A.F.L. Deeson. Crown Publishers, 1973. A very complete encyclopedia of rocks and minerals. Illustrated with thousands of colour photographs.

Earth Science Activities for Grades 2-8. Marvin N. Tolman and James O. Morton. Parker Publishing, 1986. Over 150 hands-on activities covering a variety of earth sciences topics.

Everybody Needs a Rock. Byrd Baylor. Charles Scribner's Sons, 1974. A story about a child's way to hunt for rocks.

Explore Your World: Rocks & Minerals. Discovery Channel, 1999. Authoritative with great visuals this book combines field identification techniques with background information and practical advice.

Geological Survey of Canada. Information on rock collecting as well as introductory rock and mineral sets. Contact: Geological Survey of Canada, Publication Distribution Office, 601 Booth Street, Ottawa, ON, K1A 0E8, Canada, (613) 995-4342.

How a Rock Came to Be in a Fence on a Road Near a Town. Hy Ruchlis. Walker, 1973. The story of a rock and its travels over millions of years.

The Magic School Bus Inside the Earth. Joanna Cole. Scholastic, 1988. An imaginative fictional story about a teacher who takes her class on an earth science adventure to the centre of the earth. Factual information is conveyed in an entertaining way.

National Air Photo Library. Look at your area in an aerial photograph. The library has over 4 million aerial photographs. Photographs taken from airplanes show surface features such as mountains, canyons, rivers, lakes, forests, vegetation, roads, and buildings. To get an up-to-date price list and detailed information on ordering photographs, contact: National Air Photo Library, 615 Booth Street, Room 180, Ottawa, ON, K1A 0E9, Canada, (613) 995-4560.

Project Earth Science: Geology. Brent A. Ford. National Science Teachers Association, 1996. How do volcanoes form? What causes an earthquake? Why do continents drift? Activities / info to explore geological phenomena.

Prospecting for Gemstones and Minerals. John Sinkankas. Van Nostrand Reinhold Co., 1974. Valuable advice for the beginner. Discusses how to recognize mineral deposits, how to get the minerals out, and how to use the proper tools and equipment.

Rockhounding Clubs. To find a club in your area, look in the yellow pages under Rock and Gem Clubs, Mineral and Lapidary Clubs, or another similar heading. If you can't find any clubs listed, contact the Geological Survey of Canada.

Rocks and Minerals. R.F. Symes. Stoddart, 1988. A beautifully illustrated book that features rocks and minerals from throughout the world.

Sand Creatures and Castles. Bob Reed and Pat Reed. London, England: Hamish Hamilton Children's Books Ltd., 1977. An excellent book with ideas for innovative sand creations.

Stories in Stone. Kevin Cuff. Lawrence Hall of Science, 1999. A look at the formation of igneous, sedimentary, and metamorphic rock, the rock cycle, as well as rock and mineral properties. Part of the *Great Explorations in Math and Science (GEMS)* curriculum development project. Contact: GEMS, Lawrence Hall of Science, University of California, Berkeley, CA 94720, (510) 642-7771.

The Sun, The Wind, and The Rain. Lisa Westberg Peters. Holt, Rinehart & Winston, 1988. A clever story that follows a comparison of a real mountain created by complex natural processes and a mountain of sand built by a young girl on a beach.

PLANTS

ABCedar: An Alphabet of Trees. George Ella Lyon. Orchard Books, 1989. A tree for every letter! A great identification and resource book showing the comparative sizes, formations, berries, leaves, and flowers of trees.

Eat the Fruit, Plant the Seed. Millicent Selsam. William Morrow, 1980. Directions for growing mango, avocado, papaya, citrus, pomegranate, and kiwi.

Field Guide to North American Edible Wild Plants. T.S. Elias and P. Dykeman. Van Nostrand Reinhold, 1982. A good starter resource about wild edibles.

Grow Lab. Guides, posters, and videotapes for growing plants indoors to promote scientific inquiry. Also offer a regular newsletter. Contact: National Gardening Association, 180 Flynn Ave, Burlington, VT 05401, (802) 863-1308.

Kids Gardening: A Kids' Guide to Messing Around in the Dirt. Kim Raftery and Kevin Raftery. Klutz Press, 1989. A good book about growing plants both indoors and out.

Life and Times of the Peanut. Charles Micucci. Houghton Mifflin, 1997. In a lively and engaging combination of words and pictures, this book explores how peanuts grow, how they are farmed, where they are produced, and how they are used.

The Living World: Plants. Colin Walker. Concept Science Series. Scholastic, 1987. A kit (includes activity booklets, guides, and resource package) covering a variety of topics related to plants.

Looking at Plants. David Suzuki. Stoddart, 1985. A good publication that contains activities related to plants.

The Man Who Planted Trees. Jean Giono. Chelsea, VT: Chelsea Green Publishing, 1985. An engaging fictional story about a man who single-handedly reforests foothills in France.

Plant. David Burnie. Stoddart, 1989. A great resource book with well-written text, thorough information, and good photographs and illustrations.

Plants That Never Ever Bloom. Ruth Heller. Paper Star, 1999. Rich, colourful illustrations and informative, rhyming verse unlock a world where mushrooms glow at night and seaweed grows to be gigantic – without a flower in sight!

Project Learning Tree. A workshop offered throughout North America that helps teachers integrate environmental/forestry information into their curriculum. Participants receive resource/activity books. Contact: American Forest & Paper Association, 1111 19th St NW, Suite 800, Washington, DC 20036, (202) 463-2455.

TREEmendous Activities for Young Learners. Mary Rose. Idea Factory, 1987. Filled with activities for studying the outdoors, particularly trees. Contact: Idea Factory, P.O. Box 10656, Tampa, FL 33679, (800) 331-6204.

The Wild, Wild Cookbook. Jean Craighead George. Thomas Y. Crowell, 1982. An excellent guide, arranged by season, for finding, harvesting, and cooking wild plants.

LIVING CREATURES

Adventures with Small Animals. Owen Bishop. John Murray, 1982. Activities for exploring topics such as spiders' webs, aphids, and life in leaves and soil.

All in the Woodland Early. Jane Yolen. William Collins, 1979. Rhythm and rhyme are used to teach the names of North American birds, animals, and insects.

Amazing Mammals, Parts I and II. Ranger Rick's NatureScope. National Wildlife Federation, 1986. Through observations, experiments, games, creative writing, crafts, and physical activities, children explore the general characteristics and behaviour of mammals. Contact: McGraw-Hill, (800) 262-4729.

Amos and Boris. William Steig. Sunburst, 1992. An illustrated fictional book about a mouse and a whale who become friends.

Amphibians and How They Grow. Wonders of Learning Kits. National Geographic Society, 1985. A kit containing audiocassette, learning booklets, resource book, and activity sheets. Contact: National Geographic Society, (800) 638-4077.

Animal Adaptations. Malcolm Penny. The Animal Kingdom Series. East Sussex, England: Wayland, 1988. An interesting book that looks at how animals adapt to different climates, living in the dark, flying, and even to people.

Animal Agriculture. Farm and Food Bytes Series. Agri-Education, 1988. A software package (can be ordered for MAC or MS DOS machines) that comes with resource guide, study manual, fact sheets, and wall chart. Promotes environmental issues and understanding of animals. Contact: Agri-Education, 801 Shakespeare St, P.O. Box 497, Stratford, IA 50249, (515) 838-2785.

The Animal Rights Controversy. Laurence Pringle. Harcourt Brace Jovanovich, 1989. A good book for older children. After presenting the facts and different points of view on this controversial topic, the book encourages readers to make their own decisions.

Animals Should Definitely Not Wear Clothing. Judi Barrett. Atheneum, 1984. A fictional story that deals with the theme of animal adaptation.

The Architecture of Animals: The Equinox Guide to Wildlife Structures. Adrian Forsyth. Camden House, 1989. A beautifully illustrated book that looks at habitat, environment, adaptation, reproduction.

Arctic Animals. Bobbie Kalman. Toronto, ON: Crabtree, 1988. Varied, interesting information and excellent photography make this description of over 30 Arctic animals a real find.

Balega the Elephant. Derek Hall and John Butler. Baby Animals Series. London, England: Walker Books, 1989. A fictional illustrated story for young children that is an accurate portrayal of elephants and their habitats. Each animal featured in this series of books is an endangered species.

Beastly Neighbors: All About Wild Things in the City, or Why Earwigs Make Good Mothers. Mollie Rights. Little, Brown, 1981. Activities in this book include gathering seeds for a windowsill garden, feeding birds, and growing wildflowers.

Before the Sun Dies: The Story of Evolution. Roy A. Gallant. Macmillan, 1989. An excellent, comprehensive introduction to the theory of evolution.

Bird. David Burnie. Stoddart, 1988. Colourful, very detailed, full-size photographs of birds from around the world – and everything associated with them – make this book very interesting.

A Book of Canadian Animals. Charles P. May. Macmillan, 1975. The Canadian orientation in this book is useful.

A Book of Canadian Birds. Charles P. May. Macmillan, 1975. The Canadian orientation in this book is useful.

Bugs to Bunnies. Kenn Goin, Eleanor Ripp, and Kathleen Nastasi Solomon. Chatterbox Press, 1989. Hands-on animal science activities for young children.

Creepy Crawlies and the Scientific Method. Sally Stenhouse Kneidel. Fulcrum Publishing, 1993. Over 100 experiments explore insects and other crawling creatures.

Dinosaur Mountain: Graveyard of the Past. Caroline Arnold. Clarion Books, 1989. An interesting book that follows palaeontologists at work.

Dinosaurs: An A-Z Guide. Michael Benton. Kingfisher Books, 1988. A comprehensive, fully-illustrated guide.

Eric Carle's Animals, Animals. Compiled by Laura Whipple. Philomel Books, 1989. A blend of information and poetic language in an anthology of poems about 74 different animals.

The Fantastic Flying Journey. Gerald Durrell. Stoddart, 1987. A fictional story about a magical hot-air balloon trip during which the travellers meet and talk with many animals.

Feathers Like a Rainbow: An Amazon Indian Tale. Flora Ferreira. Harper & Row, 1989. A fictional story about the birds in the forests surrounding the Amazon River who all have dark feathers until they decide to steal some colours from the hummingbird.

A Field Guide to Animal Tracks. Olaus J. Murie. Houghton Mifflin, 1974. A good beginner's guide to tracking.

Grasshopper on the Road. Arnold Lobel. Harper and Row, 1978. A fictional tale that introduces the world of insects through a grasshopper's journey.

Great Canadian Animal Stories. Muriel Whitaker (editor). Edmonton, AB: Hurtig, 1978. 16 fascinating stories by writers like Farley Mowat, Roderick Haig-Brown, Sheila Burnford, and Ernest Thompson Seton.

Have You Seen Birds? Joanne Oppenheim and Barbara Reid. Scholastic, 1986. A delightful rhyming book – with interesting plasticine relief pictures – that highlights the different characteristics of colourful birds.

In the Beginning: Creation Stories from Around the World. Virginia Hamilton. Harcourt Brace Jovanovich, 1988. A collection of myths from around the world that show how different cultures have different explanations about how life came to be on Earth.

Incredible Insects. Ranger Rick's NatureScope. National Wildlife Federation, 1984. Through games, experiments, and playground activities, children investigate the characteristics of insects. Contact: McGraw-Hill, (800) 262-4729.

Insects and How They Grow. Wonders of Learning Kits. National Geographic Society, 1988. A kit that includes audiocassette, booklets, activity guides and worksheets. Information followed up with an activity program for applying it. Contact: National Geographic Society, (800) 638-4077.

Keep Looking! Millicent Selsam and Joyce Hunt. Macmillan, 1989. A fictional story about a house that looks empty but is really full of all sorts of living creatures.

Lies (People Believe) About Animals. Susan Sussman and Robert James. Whitman, 1987. Simple, direct text that includes interesting stories and bits of information on each animal.

The Lion and the Savannah. Dave Taylor. Crabtree, 1990. A good book that profiles the life of a lion named Simba in the Kenyan savannah. The book's strengths lie in the way it details the savannah ecosystem.

The Living World: Animal Groups. Judith Holloway and Clive Harper. Concept Science Series. Scholastic, 1987. A kit (includes activity booklets, guides, and resource package) covering a variety of animal-related topics.

Looking at Insects. David Suzuki. Stoddart, 1986. A good publication that contains activities related to insects.

The Magic School Bus in the Time of the Dinosaurs. Joanna Cole. Scholastic, 1994. A well-written book in a popular fictional series that incorporates factual information.

Mammal. Steve Parker. Stoddart, 1989. A great resource book with well-written text, thorough information, and good photographs and illustrations.

A Moose for Jessica. Pat A. Wakefield with Larry Carrara. E.P. Dutton, 1987. Based on a real life occurrence, this story about a freckle-faced Hereford cow courted by a wild moose carries with it an environmental message.

The News About Dinosaurs. Patricia Lauber. Bradbury Press, 1989. A concise text contrasts old concepts with new theories based on the latest dinosaur discoveries.

Night Animals. Millicent E. Selsam. Four Winds Press, 1980. A surprising look at what some animals are up to at night.

Pets in a Jar: Collecting and Caring for Small Wild Animals. Seymour Simon. Viking Press, 1975. How to collect animals humanely and explanations on the environment and equipment required to keep an animal out of its habitat.

A Salmon for Simon. Betty Waterton. Douglas & McIntyre, 1980. A fictional story about a boy who is torn between his desire to catch a fish of his own and his sympathy for the fish.

A Second Book of Canadian Animals. Charles P. May. Macmillan, 1977. The Canadian orientation in this book is useful.

Secrets of a Wildlife Watcher. Jim Arnosky. Lothrop, Lee and Shepard, 1983. A beautiful book by a well-respected author that promotes an appreciation of wildlife and explains techniques and equipment for watching wild animals.

Simbi the Gorilla. Derek Hall and John Butler. Baby Animals Series. London, England: Walker Books, 1988. A fictional illustrated story for young children about a young gorilla eating and playing with its family.

Small Rabbit. Miska Miles. Scholastic, 1977. A fictional tale about a rabbit which must learn to avoid its predators.

Step into the Night. Joanne Ryder. Four Winds Press, 1988. A girl listens to, watches, and becomes different animals.

Tracks and Signs. Gwen Allen and Joan Denslow. Oxford University Press, 1975. An interesting look at different animal tracks and signs.

The Very Busy Spider. Eric Carle. Putnam, 1984. A fictional story by a popular author; teaches about spider activities.

The Very Hungry Caterpillar. Eric Carle. Putnam, 1987. A fictional story by a popular author; shows the metamorphosis of a caterpillar.

Watching Foxes. Jim Arnosky. Lothrop, Lee and Shepard, 1985. The story-like format of this dynamic book provides a realistic picture of the life of an animal. Written by a well-respected author.

Why Mosquitoes Buzz in People's Ears. Verna Aardema. Dial Books, 1975. A fictional story about a mosquito brought to trial for bothering both people and animals.

Why the Possum's Tail is Bare: And Other North American Indian Nature Tales. James E. Connolly. Owings Mills, MD: Stemmer House, 1985. A series of fictional tales about animals from nations such as Iroquois, Ojibwa, Micmac, Cree, Blackfoot and Dakota.

WEATHER

Anytime Weather Everywhere. H. Michael Mogil and Barbara G. Levine. How the Weatherworks, 1996. 67 activities – a mix of indoor and outdoor – that explore weather basics.

Atmospheric Environment Service. The "Learning Weather" kit includes an information booklet, a series of weather maps with exercises, and a colourful cloud chart. Contact: Publications Section, Atmospheric Environment Service, Environment Canada, 4905 Dufferin Street, Downsview, ON, M3H 5T4, Canada, (416) 739-4328.

A Book of Weather Clues. Diane Kaiser. Fitzhenry and Whiteside, 1986. Weather prediction clues from sailors, farmers, scientists, and poets.

The Cloud Book. Tomie DePaola. Holiday House, 1975. A creative, accurate look at the ten most common types of clouds.

Cloudy with a Chance of Meatballs. Judi Barrett and Ron Barrett. Macmillan, 1978. A fictional story that educates about weather through a tale about precipitation that falls in the form of food.

Explore Your World: Weather. Discovery Channel, 1999. Authoritative with great visuals, this book combines field identification with fascinating background information and practical advice.

Flash, Crash, Rumble and Roll. Franklyn M. Branley. Harper Row, 1985. An excellent, clearly-written weather information book with colour illustrations.

Looking at Weather. David Suzuki. Stoddart, 1988. An interesting publication that contains activities related to weather.

The Magic School Bus at the Waterworks. Joanna Cole. Scholastic, 1986. The water cycle and the process of providing clean water are detailed in this fictional story about a magical trip through the waterworks.

Raindrops and Rainbows. Rose Wyler. Julian Messner, 1989. A simple book with basic information on weather.

Snow and Ice. J. Kenneth Couchman, John C. MacBean, Adam Stecher, and Daniel F. Wentworth. Holt, Rinehart and Winston, 1971. A good winter science activity book.

Snowflakes. Joan Sugarman. Little, Brown and Co., 1985. Lots of interesting information on snowflakes.

A Walk in the Snow. Phyllis S. Busch. J.B. Lippincott, 1971. An exploration of the winter environment.

Water Dance. Thomas Locker. Harcourt Brace, 1997. An award-winning, beautifully illustrated book that explores the water cycle (factual information included at back).

Weather. Herta S. Breiter. Raintree Publishers, 1988. A good, straightforward book about basic weather concepts.

The Weather Book. Jack Williams. Vintage, 1997. Full-colour graphics and photos explain and illustrate weather concepts, from what makes the sky blue to how a tornado gets its twist. Also includes profiles of top atmospheric scientists.

Weather Watch. Valerie Wyatt. Kids Can Press, 1990. An interesting book that explains what causes weather.

THE HEAVENS

Adventures With Astronomy. Percy Seymour. John Murray Ltd., 1983. A good book for young astronomers.

Ancient Astronomy. Isaac Asimov. Gareth Stevens, 1989. A clear look at the beliefs of astronomers from ancient

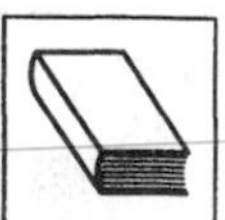

times to 1609 when Galileo's discoveries through the telescope gave birth to modern astronomy.

Astronomy. The largest circulation, English-language astronomy magazine. Aimed at the beginning and intermediate amateur astronomer. Contact: Astronomy, 21027 Crossroads Circle, Waukesha, WI 53187, (262) 796-8776.

Astronomy Today. Isaac Asimov. Gareth Stevens, 1990. Discusses how scientists and amateurs explore the universe, the tools they use, and the discoveries they have made. Excellent photographs and diagrams.

The Church Mice and the Moon. Graham Oakley. Macmillan, 1974. A fictional story about scientists who launch a rocket with mice on board – so they think.

Colonizing the Planets and the Stars. Isaac Asimov. Gareth Stevens, 1990. Explores the possibility of establishing colonies in space, travelling by spacecraft to other galaxies and meeting extraterrestrials. Excellent photographs and illustrations.

Earth, Moon and Stars. Cary I. Sneider. Lawrence Hall of Science, 1999. Activities that explore astronomical subjects including ancient models of the universe and telling time by stars. Part of the *Great Explorations in Math and Science (GEMS)* curriculum development project. Contact: GEMS, Lawrence Hall of Science, University of California, Berkeley, CA 94720, (510) 642-7771.

Earth: Our Planet in Space. Seymour Simon. Four Winds Press, 1984. An accessible book of information for children.

The Earth's Moon. Isaac Asimov. Gareth Stevens, 1988. A thought-provoking book that examines our moon.

Entering Space: An Astronaut's Odyssey. Joseph P. Allen. Workman, 1984. Over 200 colour photographs and a diary-like text make this space traveller's voyage real and exciting.

Explore Your World: Night Sky. Discovery Channel, 1999. Authoritative with wonderful visuals, this book combines field identification techniques with fascinating background information and practical advice.

Exploring the Night Sky: The Equinox Astronomy Guide for Beginners. Terence Dickinson. Firefly, 1989. An award-winning book aimed at young novice stargazers.

Extraterrestrials: A Field Guide for Earthlings. Terence Dickinson. Camden House, 1994. A unique blend of science and imagination, this book explores the views of alien life that have developed in popular culture.

The Grand Tour. Ron Miller and William K. Hartman. Workman, 1981. A space traveller's guide to our solar system complete with colourful illustrations.

How to Be a Space Scientist in Your Own Home. Seymour Simon. J.B. Lippincott, 1982. Experiments to demonstrate gravitational effects, take carbon dioxide out of the air, measure acceleration, and send messages to extraterrestrial life-forms.

Junk in Space. Richard Maurer. Simon & Shuster, 1989. Tons of space litter orbits the earth, because much human-constructed equipment sent into space isn't working or has been abandoned. Interesting text complemented by full-colour photographs.

The Living World: Our Earth. Concept Science Series. Scholastic, 1989. A kit (includes activity booklets, guides, and resource package) which covers a variety of topics related to our planet.

Mythology and the Universe. Isaac Asimov. Gareth Stevens, 1990. Discusses ancient mythological beliefs about the universe. Excellent photos and illustrations.

Nightwatch: A Practical Guide to Viewing the Universe. Terence Dickinson. Firefly, 1998. An excellent beginner's guide to stargazing that includes information on buying telescopes and observing stars throughout the year.

Observer's Handbook. A "must" for any backyard astronomer. Thoroughness and accuracy have made this the most widely-used annual reference for amateur astronomers in Canada. Contact: Royal Astronomical Society of Canada, 136 Dupont Street, Toronto, ON, M5R 1V2, Canada, (416) 924-7973.

The Science in Science Fiction. Peter Nicholls (editor). London, England: Michael Joseph Limited, 1982. An interesting look at the scientific accuracy of science fiction.

Sky News. A quarterly publication that describes the sky each month. Contact: Sky News, 5610 Timberlea Blvd, Mississauga, ON, L4W 4M6, Canada, (800) 267-3999.

Spaceship Earth. Adam Ford. Lothrop, Lee & Shepard, 1981. A book that provides understandable discussions

about meteors, planets, and asteroids, as well as complex ideas like light, gravity, and the Big Bang theory.

Sundials: Their Theory and Construction. Albert Waugh. Dover Publications, 1973. A good book for understanding all the factors that go into constructing a sundial.

They Dance in the Sky: Native American Star Myths. Jean Guard Monroe and Ray A. Williamson. Houghton Mifflin, 1987. An excellent collection of native tribal tales used to explain the wonders of the night sky.

The Universe at Your Fingertips: An Astronomy Activity and Resource Notebook. Andrew Fraknoi. Astronomical Society Pacific, 1995. An 800-page guide that emphasizes hands-on activities.

The Young Oxford Book of Astronomy. Simon and Jacqueline Mitton. Oxford University Press Children's Books, 1998. A great introduction to the planets and stars that explains methods of astronomical investigation and basic astronomy theories.

101 Questions and Answers About the Universe. Roy Gallant. Macmillan, 1984. A book based on actual questions asked by young planetarium visitors.

APPLYING SCIENCE

Accidents May Happen: 50 Inventions Discovered by Mistake. Charlotte Foltz Jones. Delacorte, 1996. Humorous and fascinating insights into a variety of household items, foodstuffs, medicines, and more – from yo-yos to Avon cosmetics to dynamite to typewriter keyboards.

All Around. Robin Kerrod. Science Alive series. Silver Burdett, 1987. A look at how science and technology affect all aspects of our lives. Excellent activities.

Ball Point Pens. Bernie Zubrowski. Little, Brown & Company, 1979. A look at the science behind the ballpoint pen.

Blinkers and Buzzers: Building and Experimenting with Electricity and Magnetism. Bernie Zubrowski. Beech Tree Books, 1991. Turn batteries, bulbs, and wire into traffic lights, telegraphs, burglar alarms, and twelve other electrical devices.

Changing Things. Robin Kerrod. London, England: Macdonald, 1987. A look at change – changing states, how things are made, animal builders, etc. Good activities and discussion about how technology has shaped modern life.

Clocks: Building and Experimenting with Model Timepieces. Bernie Zubrowski. William Morrow, 1988. An activity book with clever designs for various types of timepieces.

Communications. Dan Mackie and Paul Hayes. Hayes Publishing, 1987. Covers telephone, radio, television, walkie talkies, CB radio, fibre optics, microwave, satellites, microchips, electronic mail, networks, and aircraft communications. Contact: Durkin Hayes Publishing Ltd., 3312 Mainway, Burlington, ON, L7M 1A7, Canada, (800) 263-5224.

Energy and Control. Margaret Fennell. London, England: Cassell Publishers, 1989. Experiments and projects on topics such as wind energy, mechanical control, using water for energy and control, and robotic control.

Flight. Dan Mackie. Hayes Publishing, 1986. A well-illustrated book that begins with explaining how birds fly and moves into the various flying machines humans have created. Contact: Durkin Hayes Publishing Ltd., 3312 Mainway, Burlington, ON, L7M 1A7, Canada, (800) 263-5224.

The Great International Paper Airplane Book. Jerry Mander, George Dippel, Howard Gossage. Simon and Schuster, 1967. 128 pages of advanced airplane models.

Have Fun With Magnifying. Ontario Science Centre. Kids Can Press, 1987. Interesting activities on magnification.

How Much is a Million? David M. Schwartz and Steven Kellogg. Lothrop, Lee & Shepard, 1985. Clever text and illustrations show a million, a billion, and a trillion. Factual information provided at the back.

How Things Work: 100 Ways Parents and Kids Can Share the Secrets of Technology. Neil Ardley. Reader's Digest, 1995. 80 experiments from building an escalator to making a simple computer that really works.

How to Teach with Topographic Maps. Dana Van Burgh, Elizabeth N. Lyons, Marcy Boyington. National Science Teachers Association, 1994. Learn the special language of these maps – quadrangles, contour lines, and mapping symbols – and apply it to build basic map-reading skills.

Invention Book. Steven Caney. Workman, 1985. There are two sections in this book: the first, The Inventor's Handbook, guides children through the process of invention, while the second, Great Invention Stories, talks about specific inventors.

Inventors and Inventions. Lorraine Hopping Egan. Scholastic, 1997. Activities that include background information, lesson ideas, and extensions.

Inventors Workshop. Alan J. McCormack. Lake Publishing, 1981. Combines elements of mystery, illusion, humour and fantasy with basic scientific principles.

Kites for All Seasons. Weston W. George. Contemporary Books, 1978. The history, lore, art, and science of kites, together with a practical guide for building and flying kites.

Mapping Small Places. D.F. Wentworth, J.K. Couchman, J.C. MacBean, and A. Stecher. Holt, Rinehart and Winston., 1976. A simple approach to teaching mapping and measurement skills.

Messing Around with Water Pumps and Siphons. Bernie Zubrowski. Little, Brown, [illegible] Starts with simple investigations of pumps ar[illegible]ns and then moves on to the human heart, a[illegible] pumps, and other complex, but familiar, systems.

More Than Magnifiers. Cary I. Sneider. Lawrence Hall of Science, 1988. Creative activities for exploring magnification. Part of the *Great Explorations in Math and Science (GEMS)* curriculum development project. Contact: GEMS, Lawrence Hall of Science, University of California, Berkeley, CA 94720, (510) 642-7771.

The New Way Things Work. David MacAulay. Houghton Mifflin, 1998. An intelligent, fun bestseller that explains how virtually everything works – from zippers and plows to dentist drills and windmills!

The Paper Airplane Book. Seymour Simon. Penguin Books, 1978. A great book for beginners.

Raceways: Having Fun with Balls and Tracks. Bernie Zubrowski. William Morrow, 1985. Games you can construct and play with balls and tracks.

Roller Coaster Science. Jim Wiese. John Wiley, 1994. Experiments that explore everything from the speed of a roller coaster through the physics of toys to the scientific principles behind popcorn.

The Science of Music. Melvin Berger. Crowell, 1989. An excellent book about music, sound, and science.

Simple Machines. Anne Horvatic. E.P. Dutton, 1989. Describes the five simple machines: lever, wheel, inclined plane, screw and wedge. Everyday examples and straightforward text.

Styro-Flyers. Platt Monfort. Random House, 1981. Patterns for 8 planes plus tips for long-lasting flights.

Super Flyers. Neil Francis. Kids Can Press, 1988. Airplane designs that encourage experimentation.

Tops: Building and Experimenting with Spinning Toys. Bernie Zubrowski. William Morrow, 1989. Simple directions, helpful illustrations, and readily-available materials enable children to explore simple tops, strobes, yo-yos, and other spinning toys.

Wheels at Work – Building and Experimenting with Models and Machines. Bernie Zubrowski. William Morrow, 1986. An interesting book that provides instructions for using readily available materials to make simple machines.

INDEX

D

E

F

G

T

U

V

W

X

Y

Z